KU-350-968

DAMAGED

The Life and Letters of

LORD MACAULAY

THOMAS BABINGTON, LORD MACAULAY

Born, Rothley Temple, Leicestershire October 25, 1800
Died, Holly Lodge, Campden Hill December 28, 1859

SIR GEORGE OTTO TREVELYAN, BT.

Born, Rothley Temple, Leicestershire July 20, 1838
Died, Wallington, Cambo, Northumberland August 16, 1928

The Life and Letters of LORD MACAULAY

BY HIS NEPHEW THE RIGHT HON.

Sir George Otto Trevelyan, Bt.

WITH A PREFACE BY

G. M. TREVELYAN

Volumes I and II

OXFORD UNIVERSITY PRESS

1978

Oxford University Press, Walton Street, Oxford OX2 6DP

OXFORD LONDON GLASGOW

NEW YORK TORONTO MELBOURNE WELLINGTON

KUALA LUMPUR SINGAPORE JAKARTA HONG KONG TOKYO

DELHI BOMBAY CALCUTTA MADRAS KARACHI

IBADAN NAIROBI DAR ES SALAAM CAPE TOWN

ISBN 0 19 822487 7

'The Life of Lord Macaulay' was first published in two volumes in 1876. *In 'The World's Classics' it was first published, by arrangement with Messrs. Longmans, Green & Co., Ltd., in two volumes, in* 1932. *It was withdrawn from the series and published in similar format* 1961.
Re-issued in this present form 1978.

Printed in Great Britain by
Lowe & Brydone Printers Limited, Thetford, Norfolk

PREFACE

By G. M. TREVELYAN.

IT is fifty-six years since my father's Life of Macaulay first appeared, in the early spring of 1876. It was at once hailed as a great biography, and is still, I think, so regarded. It takes two to give excellence to any man's *Life and Letters*: the author of the *Life* and the author of the *Letters* must both be up to the mark. These two requirements are here met. Macaulay's letters are excellent reading—some people, like John Morley, have even preferred them to his *History*—and my father's writing is here seen at its very best and most entertaining.

Half a century ago, when there were many alive who remembered Macaulay and his world, the interest taken in the book by most people interested in politics or literature was very great. And even to-day there are people of the older generation who have the contents of the book 'at their fingers' ends' by constant reading. That degree of interest may not come again, but the Life has taken its place, in more senses than one, in the World's Classics. It has helped to fix the idea not only of Macaulay but of his age upon the mind of posterity. Often, in newspapers and elsewhere, I notice references to Macaulay as the 'typical' Victorian, with all the merits and limitations of that downright and optimistic period incarnate in his person. This survival of Macaulay in popular recollection, though mainly due to his own writings, is partly due to the more intimate knowledge of his mind and character obtained through this book.

My father certainly chose the form of biography most suitable to his uncle. He had not Boswell's very rare gift of reproducing the essence of conversation, nor did Macaulay's real strength lie, like Dr. Johnson's, in his tongue, but rather in his pen. His letters would best reveal him and amuse the reader. It would have been equally beside the mark to treat of Macaulay in a subjective, psychological character sketch, such as 'the new biography' prefers, with the documents and letters omitted. Macaulay was not subtle enough for such subtleties, and his letters are much too good to miss. His description of his interview with the clergyman who thought Napoleon was the Beast in Revelation (p. 342 below) both amuses us more and tells us more about Macaulay than a page of psychological analysis. In this book the man lives and speaks for himself.

Nor are there concealments. I say so having read the great mass of intimate Journals from which my father made his excerpts. He has picked and chosen among his uncle's letters and Journals so as to make the book good reading, but he has not picked and chosen to hide Macaulay's failings or to make him a plaster saint. We see him in his habit as he lived. The occasionally uncouth violence of his dislikes of particular men and books, his failure to be just to Croker or pitiful to Robert Montgomery are not hidden. Equally patent is the limitation of his literary sympathies to the literature of the past, more or less exclusive of all that was going on in his own age. But a man who read, probably, more than any other man who ever lived of the literatures of so many different ages and countries from Homer to Jane Austen—including the fathers of the Church!—with such immense relish, may be forgiven for failing properly to appreciate Dickens, Carlyle, and Tennyson.

Indeed I notice that attacks upon Macaulay are very frequently based upon this book. That is as it should be. But from this book also derives the public knowledge of his deep and tender domestic affections, in seeming contrast to his bluff 'cocksureness', but not so really. And it is here that we get the picture of a man devoted to learning and study, not as a task, not even as a profession or for a set purpose, but out of an intellectual eagerness and love of letters and of history, springing up, joyous as a lark, spontaneous and inexhaustible as a well, in quantity at least surpassing the love that any other man is recorded to have borne to literature.

The strong interest of this book derives in part from the double thread of literature and politics, in those days more closely connected than in our own. The discussion as to their relative attractions on pp. 408–10 below is of the essence of the book, for Macaulay's whole life was a comment on that theme. His merits and defects as a historian derive from the fact that his mind was immersed in politics and letters. History was not then a pure science, apart from the political and literary life of the country.

Well, here stands the man, faithfully portrayed by his nephew and by himself. Here he stands fore-square, much loved, much criticized, never likely to be forgotten.

CONTENTS

VOLUME I

Chapter I 1800–1818

Chapter II 1818–1824

Chapter III 1824–1830

Chapter IV 1830–1832

Chapter V 1832–1834

Chapter VI 1834–1838

VOLUME I

CHAPTER I

1800–1818

Plan and scope of the work—History of the Macaulay family—Aulay—Kenneth—Johnson and Boswell—John Macaulay and his children—Zachary Macaulay—His career in the West Indies and in Africa—His character—Visit of the French squadron to Sierra Leone—Zachary Macaulay's marriage—Birth of his eldest son—Lord Macaulay's early years—His childish productions—Mrs. Hannah More—General Macaulay—Choice of a school—Shelford—Dean Milner—Macaulay's early letters—Aspenden Hall—The boy's habits and mental endowments—His home—The Clapham set—The boy's relations with his father—The political ideas amongst which he was brought up, and their influence on the work of his life.

He who undertakes to publish the memoirs of a distinguished man may find a ready apology in the custom of the age. If we measure the effective demand for biography by the supply, the person commemorated need possess but a very moderate reputation, and have played no exceptional part, in order to carry the reader through many hundred pages of anecdote, dissertation, and correspondence. To judge from the advertisements of our circulating libraries, the public curiosity is keen with regard to some who did nothing worthy of special note, and others who acted so continuously in the face of the world that, when their course was run, there was little left for the world to learn about them. It may, therefore, be taken for granted that a desire exists to hear something authentic about the life of a man who has produced works which are universally known, but which bear little or no indication of the private history and the personal qualities of the author.

This was in a marked degree the case with Lord Macaulay. His two famous contemporaries in English literature have, consciously or unconsciously, told their own story in their books. Those who could see between the lines in 'David Copperfield' were aware that they had before them a delightful autobiography; and all who knew how to read Thackeray could trace him in his novels through every stage in his course, on from the day when as a little boy, consigned to the care of English relatives and schoolmasters, he left his mother on the steps of the landing-place at Calcutta. The dates and names were wanting, but the man was there; while the most ardent admirers of Macaulay will admit that a minute study of his literary productions left them, as far as any but an intellectual knowledge of the writer himself was concerned, very much as it found them. A consummate master of his craft, he turned out works which bore the unmistakable marks of the artificer's hand, but which did not reflect his features. It would be almost as hard to compose a picture of the author from the History, the Essays, and the Lays, as to evolve an idea of Shakspeare from Henry the Fifth and Measure for Measure.

But, besides being a man of letters, Lord Macaulay was a statesman, a jurist, and a brilliant ornament of society, at a time when to shine in society was a distinction which a man of eminence and ability might justly value. In these several capacities, it will be said, he was known well, and known widely. But in the first place, as these pages will show, there was one side of his life (to him, at any rate, the most important) of which even the persons with whom he mixed most freely and confidentially in London drawing-rooms, in the Indian Council chamber, and in the lobbies and on the benches of the House of Commons, were only in part aware. And in the next place, those who have seen his features and heard his voice are few already and become yearly fewer; while, by a rare fate in literary annals, the number of those who read his books is still rapidly increasing. For everyone who sat with him in private company or at the transaction of public business,—for every ten who have listened to his oratory in Parliament or from the hustings,—there must be tens of thousands whose interest in history and literature he has awakened and informed by his pen, and who would gladly know what manner of man it was that has done them so great a service.

To gratify that most legitimate wish is the duty of those who have the means at their command. His lifelike image is indelibly impressed upon their minds, (for how could it be otherwise with any who had enjoyed so close relations with such a man?) although the skill which can reproduce that image before the general eye may well be wanting. But his own letters will supply the deficiencies of the biographer. Never did anyone leave behind him more copious materials for enabling others to put together a narrative which might be the history, not indeed of his times, but of the man himself. For in the first place he so soon showed promise of being one who would give those among whom his early years were passed reason to be proud, and still more certain assurance that he would never afford them cause for shame, that what he wrote was preserved with a care very seldom bestowed on childish compositions; and the value set upon his letters by those with whom he corresponded naturally enough increased as years went on. And in the next place he was by nature so incapable of affectation or concealment that he could not write otherwise than as he felt, and, to one person at least, could never refrain from writing all that he felt; so that we may read in his letters, as in a clear mirror, his opinions and inclinations, his hopes and affections, at every succeeding period of his existence. Such letters could never have been submitted to an editor not connected with both correspondents by the strongest ties; and even one who stands in that position must often be sorely puzzled as to what he has the heart to publish and the right to withold.

I am conscious that a near relative has peculiar temptations towards that partiality of the biographer which Lord Macaulay himself so often and so cordially denounced; and the danger is greater in the case of one whose knowledge of him coincided with his later years; for it would not be easy to find a nature which gained more by time than his, and lost less. But believing, as I do, (to use his own words,) that 'if he were now living he would have sufficient judgment and sufficient greatness of mind' to wish to be shown as himself, I will suppress no trait in his disposition, or incident in his career, which might provoke blame or question. Such in all points as he was, the world, which has been so indulgent to him, has a right to know him: and those who best love him do not fear the consequences of freely submitting his character and his actions to the public verdict.

The most devout believers in the doctrine of the transmission of family qualities will be content with tracing back descent through four generations; and all favourable hereditary influences, both intellectual and moral, are assured by a genealogy which derives from a Scotch Manse. In the first decade of the eighteenth century Aulay Macaulay, the great-grandfather of the historian, was minister of Tiree and Coll; where he was 'grievously annoyed by a decreet obtained after instance of the Laird of Ardchattan, taking away his stipend.' The Duchess of Argyll of the day appears to have done her best to see him righted; 'but his health being much impaired, and there being no church or meeting-house, he was exposed to the violence of the weather at all seasons; and having no manse or glebe, and no fund for communion elements, and no mortification for schools or any pious purpose in either of the islands, and the air being unwholesome, he was dissatisfied;' and so, to the great regret of the parishioners whom he was leaving behind, he migrated to Harris, where he discharged the clerical duties for nearly half a century.

Aulay was the father of fourteen children, of whom one, Kenneth, the minister of Ardnamurchan, still occupies a very humble niche in the temple of literature. He wrote a History of St. Kilda which happened to fall into the hands of Dr. Johnson, who spoke of it more than once with favour. His reason for liking the book is characteristic enough. Mr.

Macaulay had recorded the belief prevalent in St. Kilda that, as soon as the factor landed on the island, all the inhabitants had an attack which from the account appears to have partaken of the nature both of influenza and bronchitis. This touched the superstitious vein in Johnson, who praised him for his 'magnanimity' in venturing to chronicle so questionable a phenomenon: the more so because,—said the Doctor,—'Macaulay set out with a prejudice against prejudice, and wanted to be a smart modern thinker.' To a reader of our day the History of St. Kilda appears to be innocent of any trace of such pretension: unless it be that the author speaks slightingly of second-sight, a subject for which Johnson always had a strong hankering. In 1773 Johnson paid a visit to Mr. Macaulay, who by that time had removed to Calder, and began the interview by congratulating him on having produced 'a very pretty piece of topography,'—a compliment which did not seem to the taste of the author. The conversation turned upon rather delicate subjects, and, before many hours had passed, the guest had said to the host one of the very rudest things recorded by Boswell. Later on in the same evening he atoned for his incivility by giving one of the boys of the house a pocket Sallust, and promising to procure him a servitorship at Oxford. Subsequently Johnson pronounced that Mr. Macaulay was not competent to have written the book that went by his name; a decision which, to those who happen to have read the work, will give a very poor notion of my ancestor's abilities.

The eldest son of old Aulay, and the grandfather of Lord Macaulay, was John, born in the year 1720. He was minister successively of Barra, South Uist, Lismore, and Inverary;—the last appointment being a proof of the interest which the family of Argyll continued to take in the fortunes of the Macaulays. He, likewise, during the famous tour in the Hebrides, came across the path of Boswell, who mentions him in an exquisitely absurd paragraph, the first of those in which is described the visit to Inverary Castle.[1] Mr. Macaulay afterwards passed the evening with the travellers at their inn, and provoked Johnson into what Boswell calls warmth, and anyone else would call brutality, by the very proper remark that he had no notion of people being in earnest in good professions if their practice belied them. When we think what well-known ground this was to Lord Macaulay, it is impossible to suppress a wish that the great talker had been at hand to avenge his grandfather and grand-uncle. Next morning 'Mr. Macaulay breakfasted with us, nothing hurt or dismayed by his last night's correction. Being a man of good sense he had a just admiration of Dr. Johnson.' He was rewarded by seeing Johnson at his very best, and hearing him declaim some of the finest lines that ever were written in a manner worthy of his subject.

There is a tradition that, in his younger days, the minister of Inverary proved his Whiggism by giving information to the authorities which almost led to the capture of the young Pretender. It is perhaps a matter of congratulation that this item was not added to the heavy account that the Stuarts have against the Macaulay family. John Macaulay enjoyed a high reputation as a preacher, and was especially renowned for his fluency. In 1774 he removed to Cardross in Dumbartonshire, where, on the bank of the noble estuary of the Clyde, he spent the last fifteen years of a useful and honoured life. He was twice married. His first wife died at the birth of his first child. Eight years afterwards, in 1757, he espoused Margaret,

[1] 'Monday, Oct. 25.—My acquaintance, the Rev. Mr. John M'Aulay, one of the ministers of Inverary, and brother to our good friend at Calder, came to us this morning, and accompanied us to the castle, where I presented Dr. Johnson to the Duke of Argyll. We were shown through the house; and I never shall forget the impression made upon my fancy by some of the ladies' maids tripping about in neat morning dresses. After seeing for a long time little but rusticity, their lively manner, and gay inviting appearance, pleased me so much, that I thought for a moment I could have been a knight-errant for them.'

daughter of Colin Campbell of Inveresragan, who survived him by a single year. By her he had the patriarchal number of twelve children, whom he brought up on the old Scotch system,—common to the households of minister, man of business, farmer, and peasant alike,—on fine air, simple diet, and a solid training in knowledge human and divine. Two generations after, Mr. Carlyle, during a visit to the late Lord Ashburton at the Grange, caught sight of Macaulay's face in unwonted repose, as he was turning over the pages of a book. 'I noticed,' said he, 'the homely Norse features that you find everywhere in the Western Isles, and I thought to myself: "Well! Anyone can see that you are an honest good sort of fellow, made out of oatmeal.' "

Several of John Macaulay's children obtained position in the world. Aulay, the eldest by his second wife, became a clergyman of the Church of England. His reputation as a scholar and antiquary stood high, and in the capacity of a private tutor he became known even in royal circles. He published pamphlets and treatises, the list of which it is not worth while to record, and meditated several large works that perhaps never got much beyond a title. Of all his undertakings the one best deserving commemoration in these pages was a tour that he made into Scotland in company with Mr. Thomas Babington, the owner of Rothley Temple in Leicestershire, in the course of which the travellers paid a visit to the manse at Cardross. Mr. Babington fell in love with one of the daughters of the house, Miss Jean Macaulay, and married her in 1787. Nine years afterwards he had an opportunity of presenting his brother-in-law Aulay Macaulay with the very pleasant living of Rothley.

Alexander, another son of John Macaulay, succeeded his father as minister of Cardross. Colin went into the Indian army, and died a general. He followed the example of the more ambitious among his brother officers, and exchanged military for civil duties. In 1799 he acted as secretary to a political and diplomatic Commission which accompanied the force that marched under General Harris against Seringapatam. The leading Commissioner was Colonel Wellesley, and to the end of General Macaulay's life the great Duke corresponded with him on terms of intimacy, and (so the family flattered themselves) even of friendship. Soon after the commencement of the century Colin Macaulay was appointed Resident at the important native state of Travancore. While on this employment he happened to light upon a valuable collection of books, and rapidly made himself master of the principal European languages, which he spoke and wrote with a facility surprising in one who had acquired them within a few leagues of Cape Comorin.

There was another son of John Macaulay, who in force and elevation of character stood out among his brothers, and who was destined to make for himself no ordinary career. The path which Zachary Macaulay chose to tread did not lead to wealth, or worldly success, or indeed to much worldly happiness. Born in 1768, he was sent out at the age of sixteen by a Scotch house of business as bookkeeper to an estate in Jamaica, of which he soon rose to be sole manager. His position brought him into the closest possible contact with negro slavery. His mind was not prepossessed against the system of society which he found in the West Indies. His personal interests spoke strongly in its favour, while his father, whom he justly respected, could see nothing to condemn in an institution recognised by Scripture. Indeed, the religious world still allowed the maintenance of slavery to continue an open question. John Newton, the real founder of that school in the Church of England of which in after years Zachary Macaulay was a devoted member, contrived to reconcile the business of a slave trader with the duties of a Christian, and to the end of his days gave scandal to some of his disciples, (who by that time were one and all sworn abolitionists,) by his supposed reluctance to see that there could be no fellowship between light and such darkness.

But Zachary Macaulay had eyes of his own to look about him, a clear head for forming a judgment on what he saw, and a conscience which would not permit him to live otherwise than in obedience to its mandates. The young Scotchman's innate respect for his fellows, and his appreciation of all that instruction and religion can do for men, was shocked at the sight of a population deliberately kept ignorant and heathen. His kind heart was wounded by cruelties practised at the will and pleasure of a thousand petty despots. He had read his Bible too literally to acquiesce easily in a state of matters under which human beings were bred and raised like a stock of cattle, while outraged morality was revenged on the governing race by the shameless licentiousness which is the inevitable accompaniment of slavery. He was well aware that these evils, so far from being superficial or remediable, were essential to the very existence of a social fabric constituted like that within which he lived. It was not for nothing that he had been behind the scenes in that tragedy of crime and misery. His philanthropy was not learned by the royal road of tracts, and platform speeches, and monthly magazines. What he knew he had spelt out for himself with no teacher except the aspect of human suffering, and degradation and sin.

He was not one of those to whom conviction comes in a day; and, when convinced, he did nothing sudden. Little more than a boy in age, singularly modest, and constitutionally averse to any course that appeared pretentious or theatrical, he began by a sincere attempt to make the best of his calling. For some years he contented himself with doing what he could, (so he writes to a friend,) 'to alleviate the hardships of a considerable number of my fellow-creatures, and to render the bitter cup of servitude as palatable as possible.' But by the time he was four-and-twenty he became tired of trying to find a compromise between right and wrong, and, refusing really great offers from the people with whom he was connected, he threw up his position, and returned to his native country. This step was taken against the wishes of his father, who was not prepared for the construction which his son put upon the paternal precept that a man should make his practice square with his professions.

But Zachary Macaulay soon had more congenial work to do. The young West Indian overseer was not alone in his scruples. Already for some time past a conviction had been abroad that individual citizens could not divest themselves of their share in the responsibility in which the nation was involved by the existence of slavery in our colonies. Already there had been formed the nucleus of the most disinterested, and perhaps the most successful, popular movement which history records. The question of the slave trade was well before Parliament and the country. Ten years had passed since the freedom of all whose feet touched the soil of our island had been vindicated before the courts at Westminster, and not a few negroes had become their own masters as a consequence of that memorable decision. The patrons of the race were somewhat embarrassed by having these expatriated freedmen on their hands; an opinion prevailed that the traffic in human lives could never be efficiently checked until Africa had obtained the rudiments of civilisation; and, after long discussion, a scheme was matured for the colonisation of Sierra Leone by liberated slaves. A company was organised, with a charter from the Crown, and a board which included the names of Granville Sharpe and Wilberforce. A large capital was speedily subscribed, and the Chair was accepted by Mr. Henry Thornton, a leading City banker and a member of Parliament, whose determined opposition to cruelty and oppression in every form was such as might be expected in one who had inherited from his father the friendship of the poet Cowper. Mr. Thornton heard Macaulay's story from Thomas Babington, with whom he lived on terms of close intimacy and political alliance. The Board, by the advice of its Chairman, passed a resolution appointing the young man Second Member in the Sierra Leone Council, and early in the year 1793 he sailed for Africa, where soon after his arrival he succeeded to the position and duties of Governor.

The Directors had done well to secure a tried man. The colony was at once exposed to the implacable enmity of merchants whose market the agents of the new company spoiled in their capacity of traders, and slave-dealers with whom they interfered in their character of philanthropists. The native tribes in the vicinity, instigated by European hatred and jealousy, began to inflict upon the defenceless authorities of the settlement a series of those monkey-like impertinences which, absurdly as they may read in a narrative, are formidable and ominous when they indicate that savages feel their power. These barbarians, who had hitherto commanded as much rum and gunpowder as they cared to have by selling their neighbours at the nearest barracoon, showed no appreciation for the comforts and advantages of civilisation. Indeed, those advantages were displayed in anything but an attractive shape even within the pale of the company's territory. An aggregation of negroes from Jamaica, London, and Nova Scotia, who possessed no language except an acquired jargon, and shared no associations beyond the recollections of a common servitude, were not very promising apostles for the spread of Western culture and the Christian faith. Things went smoothly enough as long as the business of the colony was mainly confined to eating the provisions that had been brought in the ships; but as soon as the work became real, and the commons short, the whole community smouldered down into chronic mutiny.

Zachary Macaulay was the very man for such a crisis. To a rare fund of patience, and self-command, and perseverance, he united a calm courage that was equal to any trial. These qualities were, no doubt, inherent in his disposition; but no one except those who have turned over his voluminous private journals can understand what constant effort, and what incessant watchfulness, went to maintain throughout a long life a course of conduct, and a temper of mind, which gave every appearance of being the spontaneous fruit of nature. He was not one who dealt in personal experiences; and few among even the friends who loved him like a father or brother, and who would have trusted him with all their fortune on his bare word, knew how entirely his outward behaviour was the express image of his religious belief. The secret of his character and of his actions lay in perfect humility and an absolute faith. Events did not discompose him, because they were sent by One who best knew his own purposes. He was not fretted by the folly of others, or irritated by their hostility, because he regarded the humblest or the worst of mankind as objects, equally with himself, of the divine love and care. On all other points he examined himself so closely that the meditations of a single evening would fill many pages of diary; but so completely in his case had the fear of God cast out all other fear that amidst the gravest perils, and the most bewildering responsibilities, it never occurred to him to question whether he was brave or not. He worked strenuously and unceasingly, never amusing himself from year's end to year's end, and shrinking from any public praise or recognition as from an unlawful gratification, because he was firmly persuaded that, when all had been accomplished and endured, he was yet but an unprofitable servant, who had done that which was his duty to do. Some, perhaps, will consider such motives as old-fashioned, and such convictions as out of date; but self-abnegation, self-control, and self-knowledge that does not give to self the benefit of any doubt, are virtues which are not old-fashioned, and for which, as time goes on, the world is likely to have as much need as ever.[1]

[1] Sir James Stephen writes thus of his friend Macaulay: 'That his understanding was proof against sophistry, and his nerves against fear, were, indeed, conclusions to which a stranger arrived at the first interview with him. But what might be suggesting that expression of countenance, at once

Mr. Macaulay was admirably adapted for the arduous and uninviting task of planting a negro colony. His very deficiencies stood him in good stead; for, in the presence of the elements with which he had to deal, it was well for him that nature had denied him any sense of the ridiculous. Unconscious of what was absurd around him, and incapable of being flurried, frightened, or fatigued, he stood as a centre of order and authority amidst the seething chaos of inexperience and insubordination. The staff was miserably insufficient, and every officer of the Company had to do duty for three in a climate such that a man is fortunate if he can find health for the work of one during a continuous twelvemonth. The Governor had to be in the counting-house, the law-court, the school, and even the chapel. He was his own secretary, his own paymaster, his own envoy. He posted ledgers, he decided causes, he conducted correspondence with the Directors at home, and visited neighbouring potentates on diplomatic missions which made up in danger what they lacked in dignity. In the absence of properly qualified clergymen, with whom he would have been the last to put himself in competition, he preached sermons and performed marriages;—a function which must have given honest satisfaction to one

so earnest and so monotonous—by what manner of feeling those gestures, so uniformly firm and deliberate, were prompted—whence the constant traces of fatigue on those overhanging brows, and on that athletic though ungraceful figure—what might be the charm which excited amongst his chosen circle a faith approaching to superstition, and a love rising to enthusiasm, towards a man whose demeanour was so inanimate, if not austere:—it was a riddle of which neither Gall nor Lavater could have found the key.'

That Sir James himself could read the riddle is proved by the concluding words of a passage marked by a force and tenderness of feeling unusual even in him: 'His earthward affections, active and all-enduring as they were, could yet thrive without the support of human sympathy, because they were sustained by so abiding a sense of the divine presence, and so absolute a submission to the divine will, as raised him habitually to that higher region where the reproach of man could not reach, and the praise of man might not presume to follow him.'

who had been so close a witness of the enforced and systematised immorality of a slave-nursery. Before long something fairly resembling order was established, and the settlement began to enjoy a reasonable measure of prosperity. The town was built, the fields were planted, and the schools filled. The Governor made a point of allotting the lightest work to the negroes who could read and write; and such was the stimulating effect of this system upon education that he confidently looked forward 'to the time when there would be few in the colony unable to read the Bible.' A printing-press was in constant operation, and in the use of a copying-machine the little community was three-quarters of a century ahead of the London public offices.

But a severe ordeal was in store for the nascent civilisation of Sierra Leone. On a Sunday morning in September 1794, eight French sail appeared off the coast. The town was about as defensible as Brighton; and it is not difficult to imagine the feelings which the sans-culottes inspired among Evangelical colonists whose last advices from Europe dated from the very height of the Reign of Terror. There was a party in favour of escaping into the forest with as much property as could be removed at so short a notice: but the Governor insisted that there would be no chance of saving the Company's buildings unless the Company's servants could make up their minds to remain at their posts, and face it out. The squadron moored within musket-shot of the quay, and swept the streets for two hours with grape and bullets; a most gratuitous piece of cruelty that killed a negress and a child, and gave one unlucky English gentleman a fright which ultimately brought him to his grave. The invaders then proceeded to land, and Mr. Macaulay had an opportunity of learning something about the condition of the French marine during the heroic period of the Republic.

A personal enemy of his own, the captain of a Yankee slaver, brought a party of sailors straight to the Governor's house. What followed had best be told in Mr. Macaulay's own words. 'Newell, who was attended by half-a-dozen sans-culottes, almost foaming with rage, presented a pistol to me, and with many oaths demanded instant satisfaction for the slaves who had run away from him to my protection. I made very little reply, but told him he must now *take* such satisfaction as he judged equivalent to his claims, as I was no longer master of my actions. He became so very outrageous that, after bearing with him a little while, I thought it most prudent to repair myself to the French officer, and request his safe-conduct on board the Commodore's ship. As I passed along the wharf the scene was curious enough. The Frenchmen, who had come ashore in filth and rags, were now many of them dressed out with women's shifts, gowns, and petticoats. Others had quantities of cloth wrapped about their bodies, or perhaps six or seven suits of clothes upon them at a time. The scene which presented itself on my getting on board the flag-ship was still more singular. The quarter-deck was crowded by a set of ragamuffins whose appearance beggared every previous description, and among whom I sought in vain for some one who looked like a gentleman. The stench and filth exceeded anything I had ever witnessed in any ship, and the noise and confusion gave me some idea of their famous Mountain. I was ushered into the Commodore's cabin, who at least received me civilly. His name was Citizen Allemand. He did not appear to have the right of excluding any of his fellow-citizens even from this place. Whatever might be their rank, they crowded into it, and conversed familiarly with him.' Such was the discipline of the fleet that had been beaten by Lord Howe on the first of June; and such the raw material of the armies which, under firm hands, and on an element more suited to the military genius of their nation, were destined to triumph at Rivoli and Hohenlinden.

Mr. Macaulay, who spoke French with ease and precision, in his anxiety to save the town used every argument which might prevail on the Commodore, whose Christian name, (if one may use such a phrase with reference to a patriot of the year two of the Republic,) happened oddly enough to be the same as his own. He appealed first to the traditional generosity of Frenchmen towards a fallen enemy, but soon discerned that the quality in question had gone out with the old order of things, if indeed it ever existed. He then represented that a people, who professed to be waging war with the express object of striking off the fetters of mankind, would be guilty of flagrant inconsistency if they destroyed an asylum for liberated slaves; but the Commodore gave him to understand that sentiments which sounded very well in the Hall of the Jacobins, were out of place on the West Coast of Africa. The Governor returned on shore to find the town already completely gutted. It was evident at every turn that, although the Republican battalions might carry liberty and fraternity through Europe on the points of their bayonets, the Republican sailors had found a very different use for the edge of their cutlasses. 'The sight of my own and of the Accountant's offices almost sickened me. Every desk, and every drawer, and every shelf, together with the printing and copying presses, had been completely demolished in the search for money. The floors were strewed with types and papers, and leaves of books; and I had the mortification to see a great part of my own labour, and of the labour of others, for several years totally destroyed. At the other end of the house I found telescopes, hygrometers, barometers, thermometers, and electrical machines lying about in fragments. The view of the town library filled me with lively concern. The volumes were tossed about and defaced with the utmost wantonness; and, if they happened to bear any resemblance to Bibles, they were torn in pieces and trampled on. The collection of natural curiosities next caught my eye. Plants, seeds, dried birds, insects, and drawings were scattered about in great confusion, and some of the sailors were in the act of killing a beautiful musk-cat, which they afterwards ate. Every house was full of Frenchmen, who were hacking, and destroying, and tearing up everything which they could not convert to their own use. The destruction of live stock on this and the following day was immense. In my yard alone they killed fourteen dozen of fowls, and there were not less than twelve hundred hogs shot in town.' It was unsafe to walk in the streets of Freetown during the forty-eight hours that followed its capture, because the French crews, with too much of the Company's port wine in their heads to aim straight, were firing at the pigs of the poor freedmen over whom they had achieved such a questionable victory.

To readers of Erckmann-Chatrian it is unpleasant to be taken thus behind the curtain on which those skilful artists have painted the wars of the early Revolution. It is one thing to be told how the crusaders of '93 and '94 were received with blessings and banquets by the populations to whom they brought freedom and enlightenment, and quite another to read the journal in which a quiet accurate-minded Scotchman tells us how a pack of tipsy ruffians sat abusing Pitt and George to him, over a fricàssee of his own fowls, and among the wreck of his lamps and mirrors which they had smashed as a protest against aristocratic luxury.

'There is not a boy among them who has not learnt to accompany the name of Pitt with an execration. When I went to bed, there was no sleep to be had on account of the sentinels thinking fit to amuse me the whole night through with the revenge they meant to take on him when they got him to Paris. Next morning I went on board the 'Experiment.' The Commodore and all his officers messed together, and I was admitted among them. They are truly the poorest-looking people I ever saw. Even the Commodore has only one suit which can at all distinguish him, not to say from the officers, but from the men. The filth and confusion of their meals was terrible. A chorus of boys usher in the dinner with the Marseilles hymn, and it finishes in the same way. The enthusiasm of all ranks among them is astonishing, but not more so than their blindness. They talk with ecstasy of their revolutionary government, of their bloody executions, of their revolutionary tribunal, of the rapid movement of their revolutionary army with the Corps of Justice and the flying guillotine before it: forgetting that not one of them is not liable to its stroke on the accusation of the greatest vagabond on board. They asked me with triumph if yesterday had not been Sunday. "Oh," said they, "the National Convention have decreed that there is no Sunday, and that the Bible is all a lie."' After such an experience it is not difficult to account for the keen and almost personal interest with which, to the very day of Waterloo, Mr. Macaulay watched through its varying phases the rise and the downfall of the French power. He followed the progress of the British arms with a minute and intelligent attention which from a very early date communicated itself to his son; and the hearty patriotism of Lord Macaulay is perhaps in no small degree the consequence of what his father suffered from the profane and rapacious sans-culottes of the revolutionary squadron.

Towards the middle of October the Republicans took their departure. Even at this distance of time it is provoking to learn that they got back to Brest without meeting an enemy that had teeth to bite. The African climate, however, reduced the squadron to such a plight, that it was well for our frigates that they had not the chance of getting its fever-stricken crews under their hatches. The French never revisited Freetown. Indeed, they had left the place in such a condition that it was not worth their while to return. The houses had been carefully burned to the ground, and the live stock killed. Except the clothes on their backs, and a little brandy and flour, the Europeans had lost everything they had in the world. Till assistance came from the mother country they lived upon such provisions as could be recovered from the reluctant hands of the negro settlers, who providentially had not been able to resist the temptation of helping the Republicans to plunder the Company's stores. Judicious liberality at home, and a year's hard work on the spot, did much to repair the damage; and, when his colony was again upon its feet, Mr. Macaulay sailed to England with the object of recruiting his health, which had broken down under an attack of low fever.

On his arrival he was admitted at once and for ever within the innermost circle of friends and fellow-labourers who were united round Wilberforce and Henry Thornton by indissoluble bonds of mutual personal regard and common public ends. As an indispensable part of his initiation into that very pleasant confederacy, he was sent down to be introduced to Hannah More, who was living at Cowslip Green, near Bristol, in the enjoyment of general respect, mixed with a good deal of what even those who admire her as she deserved must in conscience call flattery. He there met Selina Mills, a former pupil of the school which the Miss Mores kept in the neighbouring city, and a lifelong friend of all the sisters. The young lady is said to have been extremely pretty and attractive, as may well be believed by those who saw her in later years. She was the daughter of a member of the Society of Friends, who at one time was a bookseller in Bristol, and who built there a small street called 'Mills Place,' in which he himself resided. His grandchildren remembered him as an old man of imposing appearance, with long white hair, talking incessantly of Jacob Boehmen. Mr. Mills had sons, one of whom edited a Bristol journal exceedingly well, and is said to have made some figure in light literature. This uncle of Lord Macaulay was a very lively, clever man, full of good stories, of which only one has survived. Young Mills, while resident in London, had looked in at Rowland Hill's chapel, and had there lost a new hat. When he reported the misfortune to his father, the old Quaker replied:

'John, if thee'd gone to the right place of worship, thee'd have kept thy hat upon thy head.' Lord Macaulay was accustomed to say that he got his 'joviality' from his mother's family. If his power of humour was indeed of Quaker origin, he was rather ungrateful in the use to which he sometimes put it.

Mr. Macaulay fell in love with Miss Mills, and obtained her affection in return. He had to encounter the opposition of her relations, who were set upon her making another and a better match, and of Mrs. Patty More, (so well known to all who have studied the somewhat diffuse annals of the More family,) who, in the true spirit of romantic friendship, wished her to promise never to marry at all, but to domesticate herself as a youngest sister in the household at Cowslip Green. Miss Hannah, however, took a more unselfish view of the situation, and advocated Mr. Macaulay's cause with firmness and good feeling. Indeed, he must have been, according to her particular notions, the most irreproachable of lovers, until her own Cœlebs was given to the world. By her help he carried his point in so far that the engagement was made and recognised; but the friends of the young lady would not allow her to accompany him to Africa; and, during his absence from England, which began in the early months of 1796, by an arrangement that under the circumstances was very judicious, she spent much of her time in Leicestershire, with his sister Mrs. Babington.

His first business after arriving at Sierra Leone was to sit in judgment on the ringleaders of a formidable outbreak which had taken place in the colony; and he had an opportunity of proving by example that negro disaffection, from the nature of the race, is peculiarly susceptible to treatment by mild remedies, if only the man in the post of responsibility has got a heart and can contrive to keep his head. He had much more trouble with a batch of missionaries, whom he took with him in the ship, and who were no sooner on board than they began to fall out, ostensibly on controversial topics, but more probably from the same motives that so often set the laity quarrelling during the incessant and involuntary companionship of a sea-voyage. Mr. Macaulay, finding that the warmth of these debates furnished sport to the captain and other irreligious characters, was forced seriously to exert his authority in order to separate and silence the disputants. His report of these occurrences went in due time to the Chairman of the Company, who excused himself for an arrangement which had turned out so ill by telling a story of a servant who, having to carry a number of gamecocks from one place to another, tied them up in the same bag, and found on arriving at his journey's end that they had spent their time in tearing each other to pieces. When his master called him to account for his stupidity he replied: 'Sir, as they were all your cocks, I thought they would be all on one side.'

Things did not go much more smoothly on shore. Mr. Macaulay's official correspondence gives a curious picture of his difficulties in the character of Minister of Public Worship in a black community. 'The Baptists under David George are decent and orderly, but there is observable in them a great neglect of family worship, and sometimes an unfairness in their dealings. To Lady Huntingdon's Methodists, as a body, may with great justice be addressed the first verse of the third chapter of the Revelation. The lives of many of them are very disorderly, and rank antinomianism prevails among them.' But his sense of religion and decency was most sorely tried by Moses Wilkinson, a so-called Wesleyan Methodist, whose congregation, not a very respectable one to begin with, had recently been swollen by a Revival which had been accompanied by circumstances the reverse of edifying.[1] The

[1] Lord Macaulay had in his youth heard too much about negro preachers, and negro administrators, to permit him to entertain any very enthusiastic anticipations with regard to the future of the African race. He writes in his journal for July 8, 1858: 'Motley called. I like him much. We agree wonderfully well about slavery, and it is not often that I meet any person

Governor must have looked back with regret to that period in the history of the colony when he was under-handed in the clerical department.

But his interest in the negro could bear ruder shocks than an occasional outburst of eccentric fanaticism. He liked his work, because he liked those for whom he was working. 'Poor people,' he writes, 'one cannot help loving them. With all their trying humours, they have a warmth of affection which is really irresistible.' For their sake he endured all the risk and worry inseparable from a long engagement kept by the lady among disapproving friends, and by the gentleman at Sierra Leone. He stayed till the settlement had begun to thrive, and the Company had almost begun to pay; and until the Home Government had given marked tokens of favour and protection, which some years later developed into a negotiation under which the colony was transferred to the Crown. It was not till 1799 that he finally gave up his appointment, and left a region which, alone among men, he quitted with unfeigned, and, except in one particular, with unmixed regret. But for the absence of an Eve, he regarded the West Coast of Africa as a veritable Paradise, or, to use his own expression, as a more agreeable Montpelier. With a temper which in the intercourse of society was proof against being ruffled by any possible treatment of any conceivable subject, to the end of his life he showed faint signs of irritation if anyone ventured in his presence to hint that Sierra Leone was unhealthy.

On his return to England he was appointed Secretary to the Company, and was married at Bristol on the 26th of August, 1799. A most close union it was, and, (though in latter years he became fearfully absorbed in the leading object of his existence, and ceased in a measure to be the companion that he had been,) his

with whom I agree on that subject. For I hate slavery from the bottom of my soul; and yet I am made sick by the cant and the silly mock reasons of the Abolitionists. The nigger driver and the negrophile are two odious things to me. I must make Lady Macbeth's reservation: "Had he not resembled—"'

love for his wife, and deep trust and confidence in her, never failed. They took a small house in Lambeth for the first twelve months. When Mrs. Macaulay was near her confinement, Mrs. Babington, who belonged to the school of matrons who hold that the advantage of country air outweighs that of London doctors, invited her sister-in-law to Rothley Temple; and there, in a room panelled from ceiling to floor, like every corner of the ancient mansion, with oak almost black from age,—looking eastward across the park, and southward through an ivy-shaded window into a little garden,—Lord Macaulay was born. It was on the 25th of October 1800, the day of St. Crispin, the anniversary of Agincourt, (as he liked to say,) that he opened his eyes on a world which he was destined so thoroughly to learn and so intensely to enjoy. His father was as pleased as a father could be; but fate seemed determined that Zachary Macaulay should not be indulged in any great share of personal happiness. The next morning the noise of a spinning-jenny, at work in a cottage, startled his horse as he was riding past. He was thrown, and both arms were broken; and he spent in a sick-room the remainder of the only holiday worth the name which, (as far as can be traced in the family records,) he ever took during his married life. Owing to this accident the young couple were detained at Rothley into the winter; and the child was baptised in the private chapel which formed part of the house, on the 26th November, 1800, by the names of Thomas Babington:—the Rev. Aulay Macaulay, and Mr. and Mrs. Babington, acting as sponsors.

The two years which followed were passed in a house in Birchin Lane, where the Sierra Leone Company had its office. The only place where the child could be taken for exercise, and what might be called air, was Drapers' Gardens, which (already under sentence to be covered with bricks and mortar at an early date) lies behind Throgmorton Street, and within a hundred yards of the Stock Exchange. To this dismal yard containing as much gravel as grass, and frowned upon by a board of Rules and Regulations almost as large as itself, his mother used to convoy the nurse and the little boy through the crowds that towards noon swarmed along Cornhill and Threadneedle Street; and thither she would return after a due interval, to escort them back to Birchin Lane. So strong was the power of association upon Macaulay's mind that in after years Drapers' Garden was among his favourite haunts. Indeed, his habit of roaming for hours through and through the heart of the City, (a habit that never left him as long as he could roam at all,) was due in part to the recollections which caused him to regard that region as native ground.

Baby as he was when he quitted it, he retained some impression of his earliest home. He remembered standing up at the nursery window by his father's side, looking at a cloud of black smoke pouring out of a tall chimney. He asked if that was hell; an inquiry that was received with a grave displeasure which at the time he could not understand. The kindly father must have been pained, almost against his own will, at finding what feature of his creed it was that had embodied itself in so very material a shape before his little son's imagination. When in after days Mrs. Macaulay was questioned as to how soon she began to detect in the child a promise of the future, she used to say that his sensibilities and affections were remarkably developed at an age which to her hearers appeared next to incredible. He would cry for joy on seeing her after a few hours' absence, and, (till her husband put a stop to it,) her power of exciting his feelings was often made an exhibition to her friends. She did not regard this precocity as a proof of cleverness; but, like a foolish young mother, only thought that so tender a nature was marked for early death.

The next move which the family made was into as healthy an atmosphere, in every sense, as the most careful parent could wish to select. Mr. Macaulay took a house in the High Street of Clapham, in the part now called the Pavement, on the same side as the Plough inn, but some doors nearer to the Common. It was a roomy comfortable dwelling, with a very small garden behind, and in front a very small one indeed, which has entirely disappeared beneath a large shop thrown out towards the roadway by the present occupier, who bears the name of Heywood. Here the boy passed a quiet and most happy childhood. From the time that he was three years old he read incessantly, for the most part lying on the rug before the fire, with his book on the ground, and a piece of bread and butter in his hand. A very clever woman, who then lived in the house as parlour-maid, told how he used to sit in his nankeen frock, perched on the table by her as she was cleaning the plate, and expounding to her out of a volume as big as himself. He did not care for toys, but was very fond of taking his walk, when he would hold forth to his companion, whether nurse or mother, telling interminable stories out of his own head, or repeating what he had been reading in language far above his years. His memory retained without effort the phraseology of the book which he had been last engaged on, and he talked, as the maid said, 'quite printed words,' which produced an effect that appeared formal, and often, no doubt, exceedingly droll. Mrs. Hannah More was fond of relating how she called at Mr. Macaulay's, and was met by a fair, pretty, slight child, with abundance of light hair, about four years of age, who came to the front door to receive her, and tell her that his parents were out, but that if she would be good enough to come in he would bring her a glass of old spirits: a proposition which greatly startled the good lady, who had never aspired beyond cowslip wine. When questioned as to what he knew about old spirits, he could only say that Robinson Crusoe often had some. About this period his father took him on a visit to Lady Waldegrave at Strawberry Hill, and was much pleased to exhibit to his old friend the fair bright boy, dressed in a green coat with red collar and cuffs, a frill at the throat, and white trousers. After some time had been spent among the wonders of the Orford Collection, of which he ever after carried a catalogue in his head, a servant who was waiting upon the company in the gallery spilt some hot coffee over his legs. The hostess was all kindness and compassion, and when, after a while, she asked how he was feeling, the little fellow looked up in her face and replied: 'Thank you, madam, the agony is abated.'

But it must not be supposed that his quaint manners proceeded from affectation or conceit; for all testimony declares that a more simple and natural child never lived, or a more lively and merry one. He had at his command the resources of the Common; to this day the most unchanged spot within ten miles of St. Paul's, and which to all appearance will ere long hold that pleasant pre-eminence within ten leagues. That delightful wilderness of gorse bushes, and poplar groves, and gravel-pits, and ponds great and small, was to little Tom Macaulay a region of inexhaustible romance and mystery. He explored its recesses; he composed, and almost believed, its legends; he invented for its different features a nomenclature which has been faithfully preserved by two generations of children. A slight ridge, intersected by deep ditches, towards the west of the Common, the very existence of which no one above eight years old would notice, was dignified with the title of the Alps; while the elevated island, covered with shrubs, that gives a name to the Mount pond, was regarded with infinite awe as being the nearest approach within the circuit of his observation to a conception of the majesty of Sinai. Indeed, at this period his infant fancy was much exercised with the threats and terrors of the Law. He had a little plot of ground at the back of the house, marked out as his own by a row of oyster-shells, which a maid one day threw away as rubbish. He went straight to the drawing-room, where his mother was entertaining some visitors, walked into the circle, and said very solemnly: 'Cursed be Sally; for it is written, Cursed is he that removeth his neighbour's land-mark.'

While still the merest child he was sent as a day-scholar to Mr. Greaves, a shrewd Yorkshireman with a turn for science, who had been originally brought to the neighbourhood in order to educate a number of African youths sent over to imbibe Western civilisation at the fountain-head. The poor fellows had found as much difficulty in keeping alive at Clapham as Englishmen experience at Sierra Leone; and, in the end, their tutor set up a school for boys of his own colour, and at one time had charge of almost the entire rising generation of the Common. Mrs. Macaulay explained to Tom that he must learn to study without the solace of bread and butter, to which he replied: 'Yes, mama, industry shall be my bread and attention my butter.' But, as a matter of fact, no one ever crept more unwillingly to school. Each several afternoon he made piteous entreaties to be excused returning after dinner, and was met by the unvarying formula: 'No, Tom, if it rains cats and dogs, you shall go.'

His reluctance to leave home had more than one side to it. Not only did his heart stay behind, but the regular lessons of the class took him away from occupations which in his eyes were infinitely more delightful and important; for these were probably the years of his greatest literary activity. As an author he never again had more facility, or anything like so wide a range. In September 1808, his mother writes: 'My dear Tom continues to show marks of uncommon genius. He gets on wonderfully in all branches of his education, and the extent of his reading, and of the knowledge he has derived from it, are truly astonishing in a boy not yet eight years old. He is at the same time as playful as a kitten. To give you some idea of the activity of his mind I will mention a few circumstances that may interest you and Colin. You will believe that to him we never appear to regard anything he does as anything more than a schoolboy's amusement. He took it into his head to write a compendium of

Universal History about a year ago, and he really contrived to give a tolerably connected view of the leading events from the Creation to the present time, filling about a quire of paper. He told me one day that he had been writing a paper, which Henry Daly was to translate into Malabar, to persuade the people of Travancore to embrace the Christian religion. On reading it I found it to contain a very clear idea of the leading facts and doctrines of that religion, with some strong arguments for its adoption. He was so fired with reading Scott's Lay and Marmion, the former of which he got entirely, and the latter almost entirely, by heart, merely from his delight in reading them, that he determined on writing himself a poem in six cantos which he called the 'Battle of Cheviot.' After he had finished about three of the cantos of about 120 lines each, which he did in a couple of days, he became tired of it. I make no doubt he would have finished his design, but, as he was proceeding with it, the thought struck him of writing an heroic poem to be called 'Olaus the Great, or the Conquest of Mona,' in which, after the manner of Virgil, he might introduce in prophetic song the future fortunes of the family;—among others, those of the hero who aided in the fall of the tyrant of Mysore, after having long suffered from his tyranny;[1] and of another of his race who had exerted himself for the deliverance of the wretched Africans. He has just begun it. He has composed I know not how many hymns. I send you one, as a specimen, in his own handwriting, which he wrote about six months ago on one Monday morning while we were at breakfast.'

The affection of the last generation of his relatives has preserved all these pieces, but the piety of this generation will refrain from submitting them to public criticism. A marginal note, in which Macaulay has expressed his cordial approval of Uncle Toby's[2] remark about the great Lipsius, indicates his own

[1] General Macaulay had been one of Tippoo Sahib's prisoners.
[2] Tristram Shandy, chapter clxiii.

wishes in the matter too clearly to leave any choice for those who come after him. But there still may be read in a boyish scrawl the epitome of Universal History, from 'a new king who knew not Joseph,'—down through Rameses, and Dido, and Tydeus, and Tarquin, and Crassus, and Gallienus, and Edward the Martyr,—to Louis, who 'set off on a crusade against the Albigenses,' and Oliver Cromwell, who 'was an unjust and wicked man.' The hymns remain, which Mrs. Hannah More, surely a consummate judge of the article, pronounced to be 'quite extraordinary for such a baby.' To a somewhat later period probably belongs a vast pile of blank verse, entitled 'Fingal, a poem in XII books;' two of which are in a complete and connected shape, while the rest of the story is lost amidst a labyrinth of many hundred scattered lines, so transcribed as to suggest a conjecture that the boy's demand for foolscap had outrun the paternal generosity.

Of all his performances, that which attracted most attention at the time was undertaken for the purpose of immortalising Olaus Magnus, King of Norway, from whom the clan to which the bard belonged was supposed to derive its name. Two cantos are extant, of which there are several exemplars, in every stage of calligraphy from the largest round hand downwards,—a circumstance which is apparently due to the desire on the part of each of the little Macaulays to possess a copy of the great family epic. The opening stanzas, each of which contains more lines than their author counted years, go swinging along with plenty of animation and no dearth of historical and geographical allusion.

> Day set on Cambria's hills supreme,
> And, Menai, on thy silver stream.
> The star of day had reached the West.
> Now in the main it sunk to rest.
> Shone great Eleindyn's castle tall:
> Shone every battery, every hall:
> Shone all fair Mona's verdant plain;
> But chiefly shone the foaming main.

And again:

> 'Long,' said the Prince, 'shall Olave's name
> Live in the high records of fame.
> Fair Mona now shall trembling stand
> That ne'er before feared mortal hand.
> Mona, that isle where Ceres' flower
> In plenteous autumn's golden hour
> Hides all the fields from man's survey
> As locusts hid old Egypt's day.'

The passage containing a prophetic mention of his father and uncle after the manner of the sixth book of the Æneid, for the sake of which, according to Mrs. Macaulay, the poem was originally designed, can nowhere be discovered. It is possible that in the interval between the conception and the execution the boy happened to light upon a copy of the Rolliad. If such was the case, he already had too fine a sense of humour to have persevered in his original plan after reading that masterpiece of drollery. It is worthy of note that the voluminous writings of his childhood, dashed off at headlong speed in the odds and ends of leisure from school-study and nursery routine, are not only perfectly correct in spelling and grammar, but display the same lucidity of meaning, and scrupulous accuracy in punctuation and the other minor details of the literary art, which characterise his mature works.

Nothing could be more judicious than the treatment that Mr. and Mrs. Macaulay adopted towards their boy. They never handed his productions about, or encouraged him to parade his powers of conversation or memory. They abstained from any word or act which might foster in him a perception of his own genius with as much care as a wise millionaire expends on keeping his son ignorant of the fact that he is destined to be richer than his comrades. 'It was scarcely ever,' writes one who knew him well from the very first, 'that the consciousness was expressed by either of his parents of the superiority of their son over other children. Indeed, with his father I never remember any such expression. What I most observed myself was his extraordinary command of language. When he came to describe to his mother any childish play, I took care to be present, when I could, that I might listen to the way in which he expressed himself, often scarcely exceeded in his later years. Except this trifle, I remember him only as a good-tempered boy, always occupied, playing with his sisters without assumption of any kind.' One effect of this early discipline showed itself in his freedom from vanity and susceptibility,—those qualities which, coupled together in our modern psychological dialect under the head of 'self-consciousness,' are supposed to be the besetting defects of the literary character. Another result was his habitual over-estimate of the average knowledge possessed by mankind. Judging others by himself, he credited the world at large with an amount of information which certainly few have the ability to acquire, or the capacity to retain. If his parents had not been so diligent in concealing from him the difference between his own intellectual stores and those of his neighbours, it is probable that less would have been heard of Lord Macaulay's Schoolboy.

The system pursued at home was continued at Barley Wood, the place where the Misses More resided from 1802 onwards. Mrs. Macaulay gladly sent her boy to a house where he was encouraged without being spoiled, and where he never failed to be a welcome guest. The kind old ladies made a real companion of him, and greatly relished his conversation; while at the same time, with their ideas on education, they would never have allowed him, even if he had been so inclined, to forget that he was a child. Mrs. Hannah More, who had the rare gift of knowing how to live with both young and old, was the most affectionate and the wisest of friends, and readily undertook the superintendence of his studies, his pleasures, and his health. She would keep him with her for weeks, listening to him as he read prose by the ell, declaimed poetry by the hour, and discussed and compared his favourite heroes, ancient, modern, and fictitious, under all points of view and in every possible combination; coaxing him into the garden under pretence of a lecture on botany; sending him from his books to run round the grounds, or play at cooking in the kitchen; giving him Bible lessons which invariably ended in a theological argument, and following him with her advice and sympathy through his multifarious literary enterprises.[1] She writes to his father in 1809: 'I heartily hope that the sea air has been the means of setting you up, and Mrs. Macaulay also, and that the dear little poet has caught his share of bracing. ... Tell Tom I desire to know how "Olaus" goes on. The sea, I suppose, furnished him with some new images.'

The broader and more genial aspect under which life showed itself to the boy at Barley Wood has left its trace in a series of childish squibs and parodies, which may still be read with an interest that his Cambrian and Scandinavian rhapsodies fail to inspire. The most ambitious of these lighter efforts is a pasquinade occasioned by some local scandal, entitled 'Childe Hugh and the labourer, a pathetic ballad.' The 'Childe' of the story was a neighbouring baronet, and the 'Abbot' a neighbouring rector, and the whole performance, intended, as it was, to mimic the spirit of Percy's Reliques, irresistibly suggests a reminiscence of John Gilpin. It is pleasant to know that to Mrs. Hannah More was due the commencement of what eventually became the most readable of libraries, as is shown in a series of letters extending over the entire period of Macaulay's education. When he was six years old she writes: 'Though you are a little boy now, you will one day, if it please God, be a man: but long before you are a man I hope you will be a scholar.

[1] 'The next time,' (my uncle once said to us,) 'that I saw Hannah More was in 1807. The old ladies begged my parents to leave me with them for a week, and this visit was a great event in my life. In parlour and kitchen they could not make enough of me. They taught me to cook; and I was to preach, and they got in people from the fields, and I stood on a chair, and preached sermons. I might have been indicted for holding a conventicle.'

I therefore wish you to purchase such books as will be useful and agreeable to you *then*, and that you employ this very small sum in laying a little tiny corner-stone for your future library.' A year or two afterwards she thanks him for his 'two letters, so neat and free from blots. By this obvious improvement you have entitled yourself to another book. You must go to Hatchard's and choose. I think we have nearly exhausted the Epics. What say you to a little good prose? Johnson's Hebrides, or Walton's Lives, unless you would like a neat edition of Cowper's poems or Paradise Lost for your own eating? In any case choose something which you do not possess. I want you to become a complete Frenchman, that I may give you Racine, the only dramatic poet I know in any modern language that is perfectly pure and good. I think you have hit off the Ode very well, and I am much obliged to you for the Dedication.' The poor little author was already an adept in the traditional modes of requiting a patron.

He had another Mæcenas in the person of General Macaulay, who came back from India in 1810. The boy greeted him with a copy of verses, beginning

> Now safe returned from Asia's parching strand,
> Welcome, thrice welcome to thy native land.

To tell the unvarnished truth, the General's return was not altogether of a triumphant character. After very narrowly escaping with his life from an outbreak at Travancore, incited by a native minister who owed him a grudge, he had given proof of courage and spirit during some military operations which ended in his being brought back to the Residency with flying colours. But, when the fighting was over, he countenanced, and perhaps prompted, measures of retaliation which were ill taken by his superiors at Calcutta. In his congratulatory effusion the nephew presumes to remind the uncle that on European soil there still might be found employment for so redoubtable a sword.

> For many a battle shall be lost and won
> Ere yet thy glorious labours shall be done.

The General did not take the hint, and spent the remainder of his life peacefully enough between London, Bath, and the Continental capitals. He was accustomed to say that his travelling carriage was his only freehold; and, wherever he fixed his temporary residence, he had the talent of making himself popular. At Geneva he was a universal favourite; he always was welcome at Coppet; and he gave the strongest conceivable proof of a cosmopolitan disposition by finding himself equally at home at Rome and at Clapham. When in England he lived much with his relations, to whom he was sincerely attached. He was generous in a high degree, and the young people owed to him books which they otherwise could never have obtained, and treats and excursions which formed the only recreations that broke the uniform current of their lives. They regarded their uncle Colin as the man of the world of the Macaulay family.

Zachary Macaulay's circumstances during these years were good, and constantly improving. For some time he held the post of Secretary to the Sierra Leone Company, with a salary of 500*l.* per annum. He subsequently entered into partnership with a nephew, and the firm did a large business as African merchants under the names of Macaulay and Babington. The position of the father was favourable to the highest interests of his children. A boy has the best chance of being well brought up in a household where there is solid comfort, combined with thrift and simplicity; and the family was increasing too fast to leave any margin for luxurious expenditure. Before the eldest son had completed his thirteenth year he had three brothers and five sisters.[1]

[1] It was in the course of his thirteenth year that the boy wrote his 'Epitaph on Henry Martyn.'

> Here Martyn lies. In manhood's early bloom
> The Christian hero finds a Pagan tomb.
> Religion, sorrowing o'er her favourite son,
> Points to the glorious trophies that he won.
> Eternal trophies! not with carnage red,
> Not stained with tears by hapless captives shed,

In the course of 1812 it began to be evident that Tom had got beyond the educational capabilities of Clapham; and his father seriously contemplated the notion of removing to London in order to place him as a day-scholar at Westminster. Thorough as was the consideration which the parents gave to the matter, their decision was of more importance than they could at the time foresee. If their son had gone to a public school, it is more than probable that he would have turned out a different man, and have done different work. So sensitive and home-loving a boy might for a while have been too depressed to enter fully into the ways of the place; but, as he gained confidence, he could not have withstood the irresistible attractions which the life of a great school exercises over a vivid eager nature, and he would have sacrificed to passing pleasures and emulations a part, at any rate, of those years which, in order to be what he was, it was necessary that he should spend wholly among his books. Westminster or Harrow might have sharpened his faculties for dealing with affairs and with men; but the world at large would have lost more than he could by any possibility have gained. If Macaulay had received the usual education of a young Englishman, he might in all probability have kept his seat for Edinburgh; but he could hardly have written the Essay on Von Ranke, or the description of England in the third chapter of the History.

Mr. Macaulay ultimately fixed upon a private school, kept by the Rev. Mr. Preston, at Little Shelford, a village in the immediate vicinity of Cambridge. The motives which guided this selection were mainly of a religious nature. Mr. Preston held extreme Low Church opinions, and stood in the good books of Mr. Simeon, whose word had long been law in the Cambridge section of the Evangelical circle.

But trophies of the Cross. For that dear name,
Through every form of danger, death, and shame,
Onward he journeyed to a happier shore,
Where danger, death, and shame assault no more.

But whatever had been the inducement to make it, the choice proved singularly fortunate. The tutor, it is true, was narrow in his views, and lacked the taste and judgment to set those views before his pupils in an attractive form. Theological topics dragged into the conversation at unexpected moments, inquiries about their spiritual state, and long sermons which had to be listened to under the dire obligation of reproducing them in an epitome, fostered in the minds of some of the boys a reaction against the outward manifestations of religion:—a reaction which had already begun under the strict system pursued in their respective homes. But, on the other hand, Mr. Preston knew both how to teach his scholars, and when to leave them to teach themselves. The eminent Judge, who divided grown men into two sharply defined and most uncomplimentary categories, was accustomed to say that private schools made poor creatures, and public schools sad dogs; but Mr. Preston succeeded in giving a practical contradiction to Sir William Maule's proposition. His pupils, who were limited to an average of a dozen at a time, got far beyond their share of honours at the university and of distinction in after life. George Stainforth, a grandson of Sir Francis Baring, by his success at Cambridge was the first to win the school an honourable name, which was more than sustained by Henry Malden, now Greek Professor at University College, London, and by Macaulay himself. Shelford was strongly under the influence of the neighbouring university; an influence which Mr. Preston, himself a fellow of Trinity, wisely encouraged. The boys were penetrated with Cambridge ambitions and ways of thought; and frequent visitors brought to the table, where master and pupils dined in common, the freshest Cambridge gossip of the graver sort.

Little Macaulay received much kindness from Dean Milner, the President of Queens' College, then at the very summit of a celebrity which is already of the past. Those who care to search among the embers of that once brilliant reputation can form a fair notion of what Samuel Johnson would have been if he had lived a generation later, and had been absolved from the necessity of earning his bread by the enjoyment of ecclesiastical sinecures, and from any uneasiness as to his worldly standing by the possession of academical dignities and functions. The Dean, who had boundless goodwill for all his fellow-creatures at every period of life, provided that they were not Jacobins or sceptics, recognised the promise of the boy, and entertained him at his college residence on terms of friendliness, and almost of equality. After one of these visits he writes to Mr. Macaulay: 'Your lad is a fine fellow. He shall stand before kings, he shall not stand before mean men.'

Shelford: February 22, 1813.

My dear Papa,—

As this is a whole holiday, I cannot find a better time for answering your letter. With respect to my health, I am very well, and tolerably cheerful, as Blundell, the best and most clever of all the scholars, is very kind, and talks to me, and takes my part. He is quite a friend of Mr. Preston's. The other boys, especially Lyon, a Scotch boy, and Wilberforce, are very good-natured, and we might have gone on very well had not one ——, a Bristol fellow, come here. He is unanimously allowed to be a queer fellow, and is generally characterised as a foolish boy, and by most of us as an ill-natured one. In my learning I do Xenophon every day, and twice a week the Odyssey, in which I am classed with Wilberforce, whom all the boys allow to be very clever, very droll, and very impudent. We do Latin verses twice a week, and I have not yet been laughed at, as Wilberforce is the only one who hears them, being in my class. We are exercised also once a week in English composition, and once in Latin composition, and letters of persons renowned in history to each other. We get by heart Greek grammar or Virgil every evening. As for sermon-writing, I have hitherto got off with credit, and I hope I shall keep up my reputation. We have had the first meeting of our debating society the other day, when a vote of censure was moved for upon Wilberforce, but he getting up said, 'Mr. President, I beg to second the motion.' By this means he escaped. The kindness which Mr. Preston shows me is very great. He always assists me in what I cannot do, and takes me to walk out with him every now and then. My room is a delightful snug little chamber, which nobody can enter, as there is a trick about opening the door. I sit like a king, with my writing-desk before me; for, (would you believe it?) there is a writing-desk in my chest of drawers; my books on one side, my box of papers on the other, with my arm-chair and my candle; for every boy has a candlestick, snuffers, and extinguisher of his own. Being pressed for room, I will conclude what I have to say to-morrow, and ever remain,

Your affectionate son,

THOMAS B. MACAULAY.

The youth who on this occasion gave proof of his parentage by his readiness and humour was Wilberforce's eldest son. A fortnight later on, the subject chosen for discussion was 'whether Lord Wellington or Marlborough was the greatest general. A very warm debate is expected.'

Shelford: April 20, 1813.

My dear Mama,—

Pursuant to my promise I resume my pen to write to you with the greatest pleasure. Since I wrote to you yesterday, I have enjoyed myself more than I have ever done since I came to Shelford. Mr. Hodson called about twelve o'clock yesterday morning with a pony for me and took me with him to Cambridge. How surprised and delighted was I to learn that I was to take a bed at Queens' College in Dean Milner's apartments! Wilberforce arrived soon after, and I spent the day very agreeably, the Dean amusing me with the greatest kindness. I slept there, and came home on horseback to-day just in time for dinner. The Dean has invited me to come again, and Mr. Preston has given his consent. The books which I am at present employed in reading to myself are, in English, Plutarch's Lives, and Milner's Ecclesiastical History; in French, Fénelon's Dialogues of the Dead. I shall send you back the volumes of Madame de Genlis's *petits romans* as soon as possible, and I should be very much obliged for one or two more of them. Everything now seems to feel the influence of spring. The trees are all out. The lilacs are in bloom. The days are long, and I feel that I should be happy were it not that I want home. Even yesterday, when I felt more real satisfaction than I have done for almost three months, I could not help feeling a sort of uneasiness, which indeed I have always felt more or less since I have been here, and which is the only thing that hinders me from being perfectly happy. This day two months will put a period to my uneasiness.

Fly fast the hours, and dawn th' expected morn.

Every night when I lie down I reflect that another day is cut off from the tiresome time of absence.

Your affectionate son,

THOMAS B. MACAULAY.

Shelford: April 26, 1813.

My dear Papa,—

Since I have given you a detail of weekly duties, I hope you will be pleased to be informed of my Sunday's occupations. It is quite a day of rest here, and I really look to it with pleasure through the whole of the week. After breakfast we learn a chapter in the Greek Testament, that is with the aid of our Bibles, and without doing it with a dictionary like other lessons. We then go to church. We dine almost as soon as we come back, and we are left to ourselves till afternoon church. During this time I employ myself in reading, and Mr. Preston lends me any books for which I ask him, so that I am nearly as well off in this respect as at home, except for one thing, which, though I believe it is useful, is not very pleasant. I can only ask for one book at a time, and cannot touch another till I have read it through. We then go to church, and after we come back I read as before till tea-time. After tea we write out the sermon. I cannot help thinking that Mr. Preston uses all imaginable means to make us forget it, for he gives us a glass of wine each on Sunday, and on Sunday only, the very day when we want to have all our faculties awake: and some do literally go to sleep during the sermon, and look rather silly when they wake. I, however, have not fallen into this disaster.

Your affectionate son,

THOMAS B. MACAULAY.

The constant allusions to home politics and to the progress of the Continental struggle, which occur throughout Zachary Macaulay's correspondence with his son, prove how freely, and on what an equal footing, the parent and child already conversed on questions of public interest. The following letter is curious as a specimen of the eagerness with which the boy habitually flung himself into the subjects which occupied his father's thoughts. The renewal of the East India Company's charter was just then under the consideration of Parliament, and the whole energies of the Evangelical party were exerted in order to signalise the occasion by securing our Eastern dominions as a field for the spread of Christianity. Petitions against the continued exclusion of missionaries were in course of circulation throughout the island, the drafts of which had been prepared by Mr. Macaulay.

Shelford: May 8, 1813.

My dear Papa,—

As on Monday it will be out of my power to write, since the examination subjects are to given out then, I write to-day instead to answer your kind and long letter. I am very much pleased that the nation seems to take such interest in the introduction of Christianity into India. My Scotch blood begins to boil at the mention of the 1,750 names that went up from a single country parish. Ask Mama and Selina if they do not now admit my argument with regard to the superior advantages of the Scotch over the English peasantry.

As to my examination preparations, I will if you please give you a sketch of my plan. On Monday, the day on which the examination subjects are given out, I shall begin. My first performance will be my verses and my declamation. I shall then translate the Greek and Latin. The first time of going over I shall mark the passages which puzzle me, and then return to them again. But I shall have also to rub up my Mathematics, (by the bye, I begin the second book of Euclid to-day,) and to study whatever History may be appointed for the examination. I shall not be able to avoid trembling, whether I know my subjects or not. I am however intimidated at nothing but Greek. Mathematics suit my taste, although, before I came, I declaimed against them, and asserted that when I went to College, it should not be to Cambridge. I am occupied with the hope of lecturing Mama and Selina upon Mathematics, as I used to do upon Heraldry, and to change Or, and Argent, and Azure, and Gules, for squares, and points, and circles, and angles, and triangles, and rectangles, and rhomboids, and in a word 'all the pomp and circumstance' of Euclid. When I come home I shall, if my purse is sufficient, bring a couple of rabbits for Selina and Jane.

Your affectionate son,

THOMAS B. MACAULAY.

It will be seen that this passing fondness for mathematics soon changed into bitter disgust.

Clapham: May 28, 1813.

My dear Tom,—

I am very happy to hear that you have so far advanced in your different prize exercises, and with such little fatigue. I know you write with great ease to yourself, and would rather write ten poems than prune one: but remember that excellence is not attained at first. All your pieces are much mended after a little reflection, and therefore take some solitary walks, and think over each separate thing. Spare no time or trouble to render each piece as perfect as you can, and then leave the event without one anxious thought. I have always admired a saying of one of the old heathen philosophers. When a friend was condoling with him that he so well deserved of the gods, and yet that they did not shower their favours on him, as on some others less worthy, he answered, 'I will, however, continue to deserve well of them.' So do you, my dearest. Do your best because it is the will of God you should improve every faculty to the utmost now, and strengthen the powers of your mind by exercise, and then in future you will be better enabled to glorify God with all your powers and talents, be they of a more humble, or higher order, and you shall not fail to be received into everlasting habitations, with the applauding voice of your Saviour, 'Well done, good and faithful servant.' You see how ambitious your mother is. She must have the wisdom of her son acknowledged before Angels, and an assembled world. My wishes can soar no higher, and they can be content with nothing less for any of my children. The first time I saw your face, I repeated those beautiful lines of Watts' cradle hymn,

Mayst thou live to know and fear Him,
Trust and love Him all thy days
Then go dwell for ever near Him,
See His face, and sing His praise:—

and this is the substance of all my prayers for you. In less than a month you and I shall, I trust, be rambling over the Common, which now looks quite beautiful.

I am ever, my dear Tom,
Your affectionate mother,
SELINA MACAULAY.

The commencement of the second half-year at school, perhaps the darkest season of a boy's existence, was marked by an unusually severe and prolonged attack of home-sickness. It would be cruel to insert the first letter written after the return to Shelford from the summer holidays. That which follows it is melancholy enough.

Shelford: August 14, 1813.

My dear Mama,—

I must confess that I have been a little disappointed at not receiving a letter from home to-day. I hope, however, for one to-morrow. My spirits are far more depressed by leaving home than they were last half-year. Everything brings home to my recollection. Everything I read, or see, or hear, brings it to my mind. You told me I should be happy when I once came here, but not an hour passes in which I do not shed tears at thinking of home. Every hope, however unlikely to be realised, affords me some small consolation. The morning on which I went, you told me that possibly I might come home before the holidays. If you can confirm this hope, believe me when I assure you that there is nothing which I would not give for one instant's sight of home. Tell me in your next, expressly, if you can, whether or no there is any likelihood of my coming home before the holidays. If I could gain Papa's leave, I should select my birthday on October 25 as the time which I should wish to spend at that home which absence renders still dearer to me. I think I see you sitting by Papa just after his dinner, reading my letter, and turning to him, with an inquisitive glance, at the end of the paragraph. I think too that I see his expressive shake of the head at it. O, may I be mistaken! You cannot conceive what an alteration a favourable answer would produce in me. If your approbation of my request depends upon my advancing in study, I will work like a cart-horse. If you should refuse it, you will deprive me of the most pleasing illusion which I ever experienced in my life. Pray do not fail to write speedily.

Your dutiful and affectionate son,

T. B. MACAULAY.

His father answered him in a letter of strong religious complexion, full of feeling, and even of beauty, but too long for reproduction in a biography that is not his own.

Mr. Macaulay's deep anxiety for his son's welfare sometimes induced him to lend too ready an ear to busybodies, who informed him of failings in the boy which would have been treated more lightly, and perhaps more wisely, by a less devoted father. In the early months of 1814 he writes as follows, after hearing the tale of some guest of Mr. Preston whom Tom had no doubt contradicted at table in presence of the assembled household.

London: March 4, 1814.

My dear Tom,—

In taking up my pen this morning a passage in Cowper almost involuntarily occurred to me. You will find it at length in his 'Conversation.'

> Ye powers who rule the Tongue, if such there are,
> And make colloquial happiness your care,
> Preserve me from the thing I dread and hate,
> A duel in the form of a debate.
> Vociferated logic kills me quite.
> A noisy man is always in the right.

You know how much such a quotation as this would fall in with my notions, averse as I am to loud and noisy tones, and self-confident, overwhelming, and yet perhaps very unsound arguments. And you will remember how anxiously I dwelt upon this point while you were at home. I have been in hopes that this half-year would witness a great change in you in this respect. My hopes, however, have been a little damped by something which I heard last week through a friend, who seemed to have received an impression that you had gained a high distinction among the young gentlemen at Shelford by the loudness and vehemence of your tones. Now, my dear Tom, you cannot doubt that this gives me pain; and it does so not so much on account of the thing itself, as because I consider it a pretty infallible test of the mind within. I do long and pray most earnestly that the ornament of a meek and quiet spirit may be substituted for vehemence and self-confidence, and that you may be as much distinguished for the former as ever you have been for the latter. It is a school in which I am not ambitious that any child of mine should take a high degree.

If the people of Shelford be as bad as you represent them in your letters, what are they but an epitome of the world at large? Are they ungrateful to you for your kindnesses? Are they foolish, and wicked, and wayward in the use of their faculties? What is all this but what we ourselves are guilty of every day? Consider how much in our case the guilt of such conduct is aggravated by our superior knowledge. We shall not have ignorance to plead in its extenuation, as many of the people of Shelford may have. Now, instead of railing at the people of Shelford, I think the best thing which you and your schoolfellows could do would be to try to reform them. You can buy and distribute useful and striking tracts, as well as Testaments, among such as can read. The cheap Repository and Religious Tract Society will furnish tracts suited to all descriptions of persons: and for those who cannot read—why should you not institute a Sunday school to be taught by yourselves, and in which appropriate rewards being given for good behaviour, not only at school but through the week, great effects of a moral kind might soon be produced? I have exhausted my paper, and must answer the rest of your letter in a few days. In the meantime,

I am ever your most affectionate father,

ZACHARY MACAULAY.

A father's prayers are seldom fulfilled to the letter. Many years were to elapse before the son ceased to talk loudly and with confidence; and the literature that he was destined to distribute through the world was of another order from that which Mr. Macaulay here suggests. The answer, which is addressed to the mother, affords a proof that the boy could already hold his own. The allusions to the Christian Observer, of which his father was editor, and to Dr. Herbert Marsh, with whom the ablest pens of Clapham were at that moment engaged in hot and embittered controversy, are thrown in with an artist's hand.

Shelford: April 11, 1814.

My dear Mama,—

The news is glorious indeed. Peace! Peace with a Bourbon, with a descendant of Henri Quatre, with a prince who is bound to us by all the ties of gratitude. I have some hopes that it will be a lasting peace; that the troubles of the last twenty years may make kings and nations wiser. I cannot conceive a greater punishment to Buonaparte than that which the allies have inflicted on him. How can his ambitious mind support it? All his great projects and schemes, which once made every throne in Europe tremble, are buried in the solitude of an Italian isle. How miraculously everything has been conducted! We almost seem to hear the Almighty saying to the fallen tyrant, 'For this cause have I raised thee up, that I might show in thee My power.'

As I am in very great haste with this letter, I shall have but little time to write. I am sorry to hear that some nameless friend of Papa's denounced my voice as remarkably loud. I have accordingly resolved to speak in a moderate key except on the undermentioned special occasions. *Imprimis*, when I am speaking at the same time with three others. Secondly, when I am praising the Christian Observer. Thirdly, when I am praising Mr. Preston or his sisters I may be allowed to speak in my loudest voice, that they may hear me.

I saw to-day that greatest of churchmen, that pillar of Orthodoxy, that true friend to the Liturgy, that mortal enemy to the Bible Society,—Herbert Marsh, D.D., Professor of Divinity on Lady Margaret's foundation. I stood looking at him for about ten minutes, and shall always continue to maintain that he is a very ill-favoured gentleman as far as outward appearance is concerned. I am going this week to spend a day or two at Dean Milner's, where I hope, nothing unforeseen preventing, to see you in about two months' time.

Ever your affectionate son,

T. B. MACAULAY.

In the course of the year 1814 Mr. Preston removed his establishment to Aspenden Hall near Buntingford, in Hertfordshire: a large old-fashioned mansion, standing amidst extensive shrubberies, and a pleasant undulating domain sprinkled with fine timber. The house has been rebuilt within the last twenty years, and nothing remains of it except the dark oak panelling of the hall in which the scholars made their recitations on the annual speech day. The very pretty church, which stands hard by within the grounds, was undergoing restoration in 1873; and by this time the only existing portion of the former internal fittings is the family pew, in which the boys sat on drowsy summer afternoons, doing what they could to keep their impressions of the second sermon distinct from their reminiscences of the morning. Here Macaulay spent four most industrious years, doing less and less in the class-room as time went on, but enjoying the rare advantage of studying Greek and Latin by the side of such a scholar as Malden. The two companions were equally matched in age and classical attainments, and at the university maintained a rivalry so generous as hardly to deserve the name. Each of the pupils had his own chamber, which the others were forbidden to enter under the penalty of a shilling fine. This prohibition was in general not very strictly observed; but the tutor had taken the precaution of placing Macaulay in a room next his own;—a proximity which rendered the position of an intruder so exceptionally dangerous that even Malden could not remember having once passed his friend's threshold during the whole of their stay at Aspenden.

In this seclusion, removed from the delight of family intercourse, (the only attraction strong enough to draw him from his books,) the boy read widely, unceasingly, more than rapidly. The secret of his immense acquirements lay in two invaluable gifts of nature,—an unerring memory, and the capacity for taking in at a glance the contents of a printed page. During the first part of his life he remembered whatever caught his fancy without going through the process of consciously getting it by heart. As a child, during one of the numerous seasons when the social duties devolved upon Mr. Macaulay, he accompanied his father on an afternoon call, and found on a table the Lay of the Last Minstrel, which he had never before met with. He kept himself quiet with his prize while the elders were talking, and, on his return home, sat down upon his mother's bed, and repeated to her as many cantos as she had the patience or the strength to listen to. At one period of his life he was known to say that, if by some miracle of Vandalism all copies of Paradise Lost and the Pilgrim's Progress were destroyed off the face of the earth, he would undertake to reproduce them both from recollection whenever a revival of learning came. In 1813, while waiting in a Cambridge coffee-room for a postchaise which was to take him to his school, he picked up a county newspaper containing two such specimens of provincial poetical talent as in those days might be read in the corner of any weekly journal. One piece was headed 'Reflections of an Exile;' while the other was a trumpery parody on the Welsh ballad 'Ar hyd y nos,' referring to some local anecdote of an ostler whose nose had been bitten off by a filly. He looked them once through, and never gave them a thought for forty years, at the end of which time he repeated them both without missing,—or, as far as he knew, changing,—a single word.[1]

[1] Sir William Stirling Maxwell says, in a letter with which he has honoured me: 'Of his extraordinary memory I remember Lord Jeffrey telling me an instance. They had had a

As he grew older, this wonderful power became impaired so far that getting by rote the compositions of others was no longer an involuntary process. He has noted in his Lucan the several occasions on which he committed to memory his favourite passages of an author whom he regarded as unrivalled among rhetoricians; and the dates refer to 1836, when he had just turned the middle point of life. During his last years, at his dressing-table in the morning, he would

difference about a quotation from Paradise Lost, and made a wager about it; the wager being a copy of the book, which, on reference to the passage, it was found Jeffrey had won. The bet was made just before, and paid immediately after, the Easter vacation. On putting the volume into Jeffrey's hand, your uncle said, "I don't think you will find me tripping again. I knew it, I thought, pretty well before; but I am sure I know it now." Jeffrey proceeded to examine him, putting him on at a variety of the heaviest passages—the battle of the angels,—the dialogues of Adam and the archangels,—and found him ready to declaim them all, till he begged him to stop. He asked him how he had acquired such a command of the poem, and had for answer: "I had him in the country, and I read it twice over, and I don't think that I shall ever forget it again." At the same time he told Jeffrey that he believed he could repeat everything of his own he had ever printed, and nearly all he had ever written, "except, perhaps, some of my college exercises."

'I myself had an opportunity of seeing and hearing a remarkable proof of your uncle's hold upon the most insignificant verbiage that chance had poured into his ear. I was staying with him at Bowood, in the winter of 1852. Lord Elphinstone,—who had been many years before Governor of Madras,—was telling one morning at breakfast of a certain native barber there, who was famous, in his time, for English doggrel of his own making, with which he was wont to regale his customers. "Of course," said Lord Elphinstone, "I don't remember any of it; but it was very funny, and used to be repeated in society." Macaulay, who was sitting a good way off, immediately said: "I remember being shaved by the fellow, and he recited a quantity of verse to me during the operation, and here is some of it;" and then he went off in a very queer doggrel about the exploits of Bonaparte, of which I recollect the recurring refrain—

But when he saw the British boys,
He up and ran away.

It is hardly conceivable that he had ever had occasion to recall that poem since the day when he escaped from under the poet's razor.'

learn by heart one or another of the little idylls in which Martial expatiates on the enjoyments of a Spanish country-house, or a villa-farm in the environs of Rome;—those delicious morsels of verse which, (considering the sense that modern ideas attach to the name,) it is an injustice to class under the head of epigrams.

Macaulay's extraordinary faculty of assimilating printed matter at first sight remained the same through life. To the end he read books more quickly than other people skimmed them, and skimmed them as fast as anyone else could turn the leaves. 'He seemed to read through the skin,' said one who had often watched the operation. And this speed was not in his case obtained at the expense of accuracy. Anything which had once appeared in type, from the highest effort of genius down to the most detestable trash that ever consumed ink and paper manufactured for better things, had in his eyes an authority which led him to look upon misquotation as a species of minor sacrilege.

With these endowments, sharpened by an insatiable curiosity, from his fourteenth year onward he was permitted to roam almost at will over the whole expanse of literature. He composed little beyond his school exercises, which themselves bear signs of having been written in a perfunctory manner. At this period he had evidently no heart in anything but his reading. Before leaving Shelford for Aspenden he had already invoked the epic muse for the last time.

> Arms and the man I sing, who strove in vain
> To save green Erin from a foreign reign.

The man was Roderic, king of Connaught, whom he got tired of singing before he had well completed two books of the poem. Thenceforward he appears never to have struck his lyre, except in the first enthusiasm aroused by the intelligence of some favourable turn of fortune on the Continent. The flight of Napoleon from Russia was celebrated in a 'Pindaric Ode' duly distributed into strophes and antistrophes; and, when the allies entered Paris, the school put his services into requisition to petition for a holiday in honour of the event. He addressed his tutor in a short poem, which begins with a few sonorous and effective couplets, grows more and more like the parody on Fitzgerald in 'Rejected Addresses,' and ends in a peroration of which the intention is unquestionably mock-heroic:

> Oh, by the glorious posture of affairs,
> By the enormous price that Omnium bears,
> By princely Bourbon's late recovered Crown,
> And by Miss Fanny's safe return from town,
> Oh, do not thou, and thou alone, refuse
> To show thy pleasure at this glorious news!

Touched by the mention of his sister, Mr. Preston yielded: and young Macaulay never turned another verse except at the bidding of his schoolmaster, until, on the eve of his departure for Cambridge, he wrote between three and four hundred lines of a drama, entitled 'Don Fernando,' marked by force and fertility of diction, but somewhat too artificial to be worthy of publication under a name such as his. Much about the same time he communicated to Malden the commencement of a burlesque poem on the story of Anthony Babington; who, by the part that he took in the plots against the life of Queen Elizabeth, had given the family a connection with English history which, however questionable, was in Macaulay's view better than none.

> Each, says the proverb, has his taste. 'Tis true.
> Marsh loves a controversy; Coates a play;
> Bennet a felon; Lewis Way a Jew;
> The Jew the silver spoons of Lewis Way.
> The Gipsy Poetry, to own the truth,
> Has been my love through childhood and in youth.

It is perhaps as well that the project to all appearance stopped with the first stanza, which in its turn was probably written for the sake of a single line. The young man had a better use for his time than to spend it in producing frigid imitations of Beppo.

He was not unpopular among his fellow-pupils, who regarded him with pride and admiration, tempered by the compassion which his utter inability to play at any sort of game would have excited in every school, private or public alike. He troubled himself very little about the opinion of those by whom he was surrounded at Aspenden. It required the crowd and the stir of a university to call forth the social qualities which he possessed in so large a measure. The tone of his correspondence during these years sufficiently indicates that he lived almost exclusively among books. His letters, which had hitherto been very natural and pretty, began to smack of the library, and please less than those written in early boyhood. His pen was overcharged with the metaphors and phrases of other men; and it was not till maturing powers had enabled him to master and arrange the vast masses of literature which filled his memory that his native force could display itself freely through the medium of a style which was all his own. In 1815 he began a formal literary correspondence, after the taste of the previous century, with Mr. Hudson, a gentleman in the Examiner's Office of the East India House.

Aspenden Hall: August 22, 1815.

Dear Sir,—

The Spectator observes, I believe in his first paper, that we can never read an author with much zest unless we are acquainted with his situation. I feel the same in my epistolary correspondence; and, supposing that in this respect we may be alike, I will just tell you my condition. Imagine a house in the middle of pretty large grounds, surrounded by palings. These I never pass. You may therefore suppose that I resemble the Hermit of Parnell.

> As yet by books and swains the world he knew,
> Nor knew if books and swains report it true.

If you substitute newspapers and visitors for books and swains, you may form an idea of what I know of the present state of things. Write to me as one who is ignorant of every event except political occurrences. These I learn regularly: but if Lord Byron were to publish melodies or romances, or Scott metrical tales without number, I should never see them, or perhaps hear of them, till Christmas. Retirement of this kind, though it precludes me from studying the works of the hour, is very favourable for the employment of 'holding high converse with the mighty dead.'

I know not whether 'peeping at the world through the loopholes of retreat' be the best way of forming us for engaging in its busy and active scenes. I am sure it is not a way to my taste. Poets may talk of the beauties of nature, the enjoyments of a country life, and rural innocence: but there is another kind of life which, though unsung by bards, is yet to me infinitely superior to the dull uniformity of country life. London is the place for me. Its smoky atmosphere, and its muddy river, charm me more than the pure air of Hertfordshire, and the crystal currents of the river Rib. Nothing is equal to the splendid varieties of London life, 'the fine flow of London talk,' and the dazzling brilliancy of London spectacles. Such are my sentiments, and, if ever I publish poetry, it shall not be pastoral. Nature is the last goddess to whom my devoirs shall be paid.

Yours most faithfully,
THOMAS B. MACAULAY.

This votary of city life was still two months short of completing his fifteenth year!

Aspenden Hall: August 23, 1815.

My dear Mama,—

You perceive already in so large a sheet, and so small a hand, the promise of a long, a very long, letter; longer, as I intend it, than all the letters which you send in a half-year together. I have again begun my life of sterile monotony, unvarying labour, the dull return of dull exercises in dull uniformity of tediousness. But do not think that I complain.

> My mind to me a kingdom is,
> Such perfect joy therein I find
> As doth exceed all other bliss
> That God or nature hath assigned.

Assure yourself that I am philosopher enough to be happy,—I meant to say not particularly unhappy,—in solitude; but man is an animal made for society. I was gifted with reason, not to speculate in Aspenden Park, but to interchange ideas with some person who can understand me. This is what I miss at Aspenden. There are several here who possess both taste and reading; who can criticize Lord Byron and Southey with much tact and 'savoir du métier.' But here it is not the fashion to think. Hear what I have read since I came here. Hear and wonder! I have in the first place read Boccacio's Decameron, a tale of a hundred cantos. He is a wonderful writer. Whether he tells in humorous or familiar strains the follies of the silly Calandrino, or the witty pranks of Buffalmacco and Bruno, or sings in loftier numbers

> Dames, knights, and arms, and love, the feats that spring
> From courteous minds and generous faith,

or lashes with a noble severity and fearless independence the vices of the monks and the priestcraft of the established religion, he is always elegant, amusing, and, what pleases and surprises most in a writer of so unpolished an age, strikingly delicate and chastised. I prefer him infinitely to Chaucer. If you wish for a good specimen of Boccacio, as soon as you have finished my letter, (which will come, I suppose, by dinner-time,) send Jane up to the library for Dryden's poems, and you will find among them several translations from Boccacio, particularly one entitled 'Theodore and Honoria.'

But, truly admirable as the bard of Florence is, I must not permit myself to give him more than his due share of my letter. I have likewise read Gil Blas, with unbounded admiration of the abilities of Le Sage. Malden and I have read Thalaba together, and are proceeding to the Curse of Kehama. Do not think, however, that I am neglecting more important studies than either Southey or Boccacio. I have read the greater part of the History of James I and Mrs. Montague's essay on Shakespeare, and a great deal of Gibbon. I never devoured so many books in a fortnight. John Smith, Bob Hankinson, and I, went over the Hebrew Melodies together. I certainly think far better of them than we used to do at Clapham. Papa may laugh, and indeed he did laugh me out of my taste at Clapham; but I think that there is a great deal of beauty in the first melody, 'She walks in beauty,' though indeed who it is that walks in beauty is not very exactly defined. My next letter shall contain a production of my muse, entitled 'An Inscription for the Column of Waterloo,' which is to be shown to Mr. Preston to-morrow. What he may think of it I do not know. But I am like my favourite Cicero about my own productions. It is all one to me what others think of them. I never like them a bit less for being disliked by the rest of mankind. Mr. Preston has desired me to bring him up this evening two or three subjects for a Declamation. Those which I have selected are as follows: 1st, a speech in the character of Lord Coningsby, impeaching the Earl of Oxford; 2nd, an essay on the utility of standing armies; 3rd, an essay on the policy of Great Britain with regard to continental possessions. I conclude with sending my love to Papa, Selina, Jane, John, ('but he is not there,' as Fingal pathetically says, when in enumerating his sons who should accompany him to the chase he inadvertently mentions the dead Ryno,) Henry, Fanny, Hannah, Margaret, and Charles. Valete.

T. B. MACAULAY.

This exhaustive enumeration of his brothers and sisters invites attention to that home where he reigned supreme. Lady Trevelyan thus describes their life at Clapham: 'I think that my father's strictness was a good counterpoise to the perfect worship of your uncle by the rest of the family. To us he was an object of passionate love and devotion. To us he could do no wrong. His unruffled sweetness of temper, his unfailing flow of spirits, his amusing talk, all made his presence so delightful that his wishes and his tastes were our law. He hated strangers; and his notion of perfect happiness was to see us all working round him while he read aloud a novel, and then to walk all together on the Common, or, if it rained, to have a frightfully noisy game of hide-and-seek. I have often wondered how our mother could ever have endured our noise in her little house. My earliest recollections speak of the intense happiness of the holidays, beginning with finding him in Papa's room in the morning; the awe at the idea of his having reached home in the dark after we were in bed, and the Saturnalia which at once set in;—no lessons; nothing but fun and merriment for the whole six weeks. In the year 1816 we were at Brighton for the summer holidays, and he read to us Sir Charles Grandison. It was always a habit in our family to read aloud every evening. Among the books selected I can recall Clarendon, Burnet, Shakspeare, (a great treat when my mother took the volume,) Miss Edgeworth, Mackenzie's Lounger, and Mirror, and, as a standing dish, the Quarterly and the Edinburgh Reviews. Poets too, especially Scott and Crabbe, were constantly chosen. Poetry and novels, except during Tom's holidays, were forbidden in the daytime, and stigmatized as "drinking drams in the morning."'

Morning or evening, Mr. Macaulay disapproved of novel-reading; but, too indulgent to insist on having his own way in any but essential matters, he lived to see himself the head of a family in which novels were more read, and better remembered, than in any household of the United Kingdom. The first warning of the troubles that were in store for him was an anonymous letter addressed to him as editor of the Christian Observer, defending works of fiction, and eulogising Fielding and Smollett. This he incautiously inserted in his periodical, and brought down upon himself the most violent objurgations from scandalised contributors, one of whom informed the public that he had committed the obnoxious number to the flames, and should thenceforward cease to take in the Magazine. The editor replied with becoming spirit; although by that time he was aware that the communication, the insertion of which in an unguarded moment had betrayed him into a controversy for which he had so little heart, had proceeded from the pen of his son. Such was young Macaulay's first appearance in print, if we except the index to the thirteenth volume of the Christian Observer, which he drew up during his Christmas holidays of 1814. The place where he performed his earliest literary work can be identified with tolerable certainty. He enjoyed the eldest son's privilege of a separate bedchamber; and there, at the front window on the top story, furthest from the Common and nearest to London, we can fancy him sitting, apart from the crowded play-room, keeping himself warm as best he might, and travelling steadily through the blameless pages the contents of which it was his task to classify for the convenience of posterity.

Lord Macaulay used to remark that Thackeray introduced too much of the Dissenting element into his picture of Clapham in the opening chapters of 'The Newcomes.' The leading people of the place,—with the exception of Mr. William Smith, the Unitarian member of Parliament,—were one and all staunch Churchmen; though they readily worked in concert with those religious communities which held in the main the same views, and pursued the same objects, as themselves. Old John Thornton, the earliest of the Evangelical magnates, when he went on his annual tour to the South Coast or the Scotch mountains, would take with him some Independent or Wesleyan minister who was in need of a holiday; and his followers in the next generation had the most powerful motives for maintaining the alliance which he had inaugurated. They could not neglect such doughty auxiliaries in the memorable war which they waged against cruelty, ignorance, and irreligion, and in their less momentous skirmishes with the votaries of the stage, the racecourse, and the card-table. Without the aid of nonconformist sympathy, and money, and oratory, and organisation, their operations would have been doomed to certain failure. The cordial relations entertained with the members of other denominations by those among whom his youth was passed did much to indoctrinate Macaulay with a lively and genuine interest in sectarian theology. He possessed a minute acquaintance, very rare among men of letters, with the origin and growth of the various forms of faith and practice which have divided the allegiance of his countrymen; not the least important of his qualifications for writing the history of an epoch when the national mind gave itself to religious controversy even more largely than has been its wont.

The method of education in vogue among the Clapham families was simple, without being severe. In the spacious gardens, and the commodious houses of an architecture already dating a century back, which surrounded the Common, there was plenty of freedom, and good fellowship, and reasonable enjoyment for young and old alike. Here again Thackeray has not done justice to a society that united the mental culture, and the intellectual activity, which are developed by the neighbourhood of a great capital, with the wholesome quiet and the homely ways of country life. Hobson and Brian Newcome are not fair specimens of the effect of Clapham influences upon the second generation. There can have been nothing vulgar, and little that was narrow, in a training which produced Samuel Wilberforce, and Sir James Stephen, and Charles and Robert Grant, and Lord Macaulay. The plan on which children were brought up in the chosen home of the Low Church party, during its golden age, will bear comparison with systems about which, in their day, the world was supposed never to tire of hearing, although their ultimate results have been small indeed.

It is easy to trace whence the great bishop and the great writer derived their immense industry. Working came as naturally as walking to sons who could not remember a time when their fathers idled. 'Mr. Wilberforce and Mr. Babington have never appeared downstairs lately, except to take a hasty dinner, and for half an hour after we have supped. The slave-trade now occupies them nine hours daily. Mr. Babington told me last night that he had fourteen hundred folio pages to read, to detect the contradictions, and to collect the answers which corroborate Mr. Wilberforce's assertions in his speeches. These, with more than two thousand pages to be abridged, must be done within a fortnight, and they talk of sitting up one night in every week to accomplish it. The two friends begin to look very ill, but they are in excellent spirits, and at this moment I hear them laughing at some absurd questions in the examination.' Passages such as this are scattered broadcast through the correspondence of Wilberforce and his friends. Fortitude, and diligence, and self-control, and all that makes men good and great, cannot be purchased from professional educators. Charity is not the only quality which begins at home. It is throwing away money to spend a thousand a year on the teaching of three boys, if they are to return from school only to find the older members of their family intent on amusing themselves at any cost of time and trouble, or sacrificing self-respect in ignoble efforts to struggle into a social grade above their own. The child will never place his aims high, and pursue them steadily, unless the parent has taught him what energy, and elevation of purpose, mean not less by example than by precept.

In that company of indefatigable workers none equalled the labours of Zachary Macaulay. Even now when he has been in his grave for more than the third of a century, it seems almost an act of disloyalty to record the public services of a man who thought that he had done less than nothing if his exertions met with praise, or even with recognition. The nature and value of those services may be estimated from the terms in which a very competent judge, who knew how to weigh his words, spoke of the part which Mr. Macaulay played in one only of his numerous enterprises,—the suppression of slavery and the slave-trade. 'That God had called him into being to wage war with this gigantic evil became his immutable conviction. During forty successive years he was ever burdened with this thought. It was the subject of his visions by day and of his dreams by night. To give them reality he laboured as men labour for the honours of a profession or for the subsistence of their children. In that service he sacrificed all that a man may lawfully sacrifice—health, fortune, repose, favour, and celebrity. He died a poor man, though wealth was within his reach. He devoted himself to the severest toil, amidst allurements to luxuriate in the delights of domestic and social intercourse, such as few indeed have encountered. He silently permitted some to usurp his hardly-earned honours, that no selfish controversy might desecrate their common cause. He made no effort to obtain the praises of the world, though he had talents to command, and a temper peculiarly disposed to enjoy them. He drew upon himself the poisoned shafts of calumny, and, while feeling their sting as generous spirits only can feel it, never turned a single step aside from his path to propitiate or to crush the slanderers.'

Zachary Macaulay was no mere man of action. It is difficult to understand when it was that he had time to pick up his knowledge of general literature; or how he made room for it in a mind so crammed with facts and statistics relating to questions of the day that when Wilberforce was at a loss for a piece of information he used to say, 'Let us look it out in Macaulay.' His private papers, which are one long register of unbroken toil, do nothing to clear up the problem. Highly cultivated, however, he certainly was, and his society was in request with many who cared little for the objects which to him were everything. That he should have been esteemed and regarded by Lord Brougham, Francis Horner, and Sir James Mackintosh, seems natural enough; but there is something surprising in finding him in friendly and frequent intercourse with some of his most distinguished French contemporaries. Chateaubriand, Sismondi, the Duc de Broglie, Madame de Staël, and Dumont, the interpreter of Bentham, corresponded with him freely in their own language, which he wrote to admiration. The gratification that his foreign acquaintance felt at the sight of his letters would have been unalloyed but for the pamphlets and blue-books by which they were too often accompanied. It is not difficult to imagine the feelings of a Parisian on receiving two quarto volumes, with the postage only in part prepaid, containing the proceedings of a Committee on Apprenticeship in the West Indies, and including the twelve or fifteen thousand questions and answers on which the Report was founded. It would be hard to meet with a more perfect sample of the national politeness than the passage in which M. Dumont acknowledges one of the less formidable of these unwelcome gifts. 'Mon cher Ami,—Je ne laisserai pas partir Mr. Inglis sans le charger de quelques lignes pour vous, afin de vous remercier du Christian Observer que vous avez eu la bonté de m'envoyer. Vous savez que j'ai *a great taste for it*; mais il faut vous avouer une triste vérité, c'est que je manque absolument de loisir pour le lire. Ne m'en envoyez plus; car je me sens peiné d'avoir sous les yeux de si bonnes choses, dont je n'ai pas le temps de me nourrir.'

'In the year 1817,' Lady Trevelyan writes, 'my parents made a tour in Scotland with your uncle.

Brougham gave them a letter to Jeffrey, who hospitably entertained them; but your uncle said that Jeffrey was not at all at his ease, and was apparently so terrified at my father's religious reputation that he seemed afraid to utter a joke. Your uncle complained grievously that they travelled from manse to manse, and always came in for very long prayers and expositions.[1] I think, with all the love and reverence with which your uncle regarded his father's memory, there mingled a shade of bitterness that he had not met quite the encouragement and appreciation from him which he received from others. But such a son as he was! Never a disrespectful word or look; always anxious to please and amuse; and at last he was the entire stay and support of his father's declining years.

'Your uncle was of opinion that the course pursued by his father towards him during his youth was not judicious. But here I am inclined to disagree with him. There was no want of proof of the estimation in which his father held him, corresponding with him from a very early age as with a man, conversing with him freely, and writing of him most fondly. But, in the desire to keep down any conceit, there was certainly in my father a great outward show of repression and depreciation. Then the faults of your uncle were peculiarly those that my father had no patience with. Himself precise in his arrangements, writing a beautiful hand, particular about neatness, very accurate and calm, detesting strong expressions, and remarkably self-controlled; while his eager impetuous boy, careless of his dress, always forgetting to wash his hands and brush his hair, writing an execrable hand, and folding his letters with a great blotch for a seal, was a constant care and irritation. Many letters to your uncle have I read on these subjects. Sometimes

[1] Macaulay writes in his journal of August 8, 1859: 'We passed my old acquaintance, Dumbarton Castle. I remembered my first visit to Dumbarton, and the old minister, who insisted on our eating a bit of cake with him, and said a grace over it which might have been prologue to a dinner of the Fishmongers' Company, or the Grocers' Company.'

a specimen of the proper way of folding a letter is sent him, (those were the sad days before envelopes were known,) and he is desired to repeat the experiment till he succeeds. General Macaulay's fastidious nature led him to take my father's line regarding your uncle, and my youthful soul was often vexed by the constant reprimands for venial transgressions. But the great sin was the idle reading, which was a thorn in my father's side that never was extracted. In truth, he really acknowledged to the full your uncle's abilities, and felt that if he could only add his own *morale*, his unwearied industry, his power of concentrating his energies on the work in hand, his patient painstaking calmness, to the genius and fervour which his son possessed, then a being might be formed who could regenerate the world. Often in later years I have heard my father, after expressing an earnest desire for some object, exclaim, "If I had only Tom's power of speech!" But he should have remembered that all gifts are not given to one, and that perhaps such a union as he coveted is even impossible. Parents must be content to see their children walk in their own path, too happy if through any road they attain the same end, the living for the glory of God and the good of man.'

From a marvellously early date in Macaulay's life public affairs divided his thoughts with literature, and, as he grew to manhood, began more and more to divide his aspirations. His father's house was much used as a centre of consultation by members of Parliament who lived in the suburbs on the Surrey side of London; and the boy could hardly have heard more incessant, and assuredly not more edifying, political talk if he had been brought up in Downing Street. The future advocate and interpreter of Whig principles was not reared in the Whig faith. Attached friends of Pitt, who in personal conduct, and habits of life, certainly came nearer to their standard than his great rival,—and warmly in favour of a war which, to their imagination, never entirely lost its early character of an internecine contest with atheism,—the

Evangelicals in the House of Commons for the most part acted with the Tories. But it may be doubted whether, in the long run, their party would not have been better without them. By the zeal,[1] the munificence, the laborious activity, with which they pursued their religious and semi-religious enterprises, they did more to teach the world how to get rid of existing institutions than by their votes and speeches at Westminster they contributed to preserve them. With their May meetings, and African Institutions, and Anti-slavery Reporters, and their subscriptions of tens of thousands of pounds, and their petitions bristling with hundreds of thousands of signatures, and all the machinery for informing opinion and bringing it to bear on ministers and legislators which they did so much to perfect and even to invent, they can be regarded as nothing short of the pioneers and

[1] Macaulay, writing to one of his sisters in 1844, says: 'I think Stephen's article on the Clapham Sect the best thing he ever did. I do not think with you that the Claphamites were men too obscure for such delineation. The truth is that from that little knot of men emanated all the Bible Societies, and almost all the Missionary Societies, in the world. The whole organisation of the Evangelical party was their work. The share which they had in providing means for the education of the people was great. They were really the destroyers of the slave-trade, and of slavery. Many of those whom Stephen describes were public men of the greatest weight. Lord Teignmouth governed India at Calcutta. Grant governed India in Leadenhall Street. Stephen's father was Perceval's right-hand man in the House of Commons. It is needless to speak of Wilberforce. As to Simeon, if you knew what his authority and influence were, and how they extended from Cambridge to the most remote corners of England, you would allow that his real sway in the Church was far greater than that of any primate. Thornton, to my surprise, thinks the passage about my father unfriendly. I defended Stephen. The truth is that he asked my permission to draw a portrait of my father for the Edinburgh Review. I told him that I had only to beg that he would not give it the air of a puff: a thing which, for myself and for my friends, I dread far more than any attack. My influence over the Review is so well known that a mere eulogy of my father appearing in that work would only call forth derision. I therefore am really glad that Stephen has introduced into his sketch some little characteristic traits which, in themselves, were not beauties.'

fuglemen of that system of popular agitation which forms a leading feature in our internal history during the past half-century. At an epoch when the Cabinet which they supported was so averse to manifestations of political sentiment that a Reformer who spoke his mind in England was seldom long out of prison, and in Scotland ran a very serious risk of transportation, Toryism sat oddly enough on men who spent their days in the committee-room and their evenings on the platform, and each of whom belonged to more Associations combined for the purpose of influencing Parliament than he could count on the fingers of both his hands.

There was something incongruous in their position; and as time went on they began to perceive the incongruity. They gradually learned that measures dear to philanthropy might be expected to result from the advent to power of their opponents; while their own chief too often failed them at a pinch out of what appeared to them an excessive, and humiliating, deference to interests powerfully represented on the benches behind him. Their eyes were first opened by Pitt's change of attitude with regard to the object that was next all their hearts. There is something almost pathetic in the contrast between two entries in Wilberforce's diary, of which the first has become classical, but the second is not so generally known. In 1787, referring to the movement against the slave-trade, he says: 'Pitt recommended me to undertake its conduct, as a subject suited to my character and talents. At length, I well remember, after a conversation in the open air at the root of an old tree at Holwood, just above the vale of Keston, I resolved to give notice on a fit occasion in the House of Commons of my intention to bring the subject forward.' Twelve years later Mr. Henry Thornton had brought in a Bill for confining the trade within certain limits upon the coast of Africa. 'Upon the second reading of this bill,' writes Wilberforce, 'Pitt coolly put off the debate when I had manifested a design of answering P.'s speech, and so left misrepresentations without a word. William Smith's anger;—Henry Thornton's coolness;—deep impression on me, but conquered, I hope, in a Christian way.'

Besides instructing their successors in the art of carrying on a popular movement, Wilberforce and his followers had a lesson to teach, the value of which not so many perhaps will be disposed to question. In public life, as in private, they habitually had the fear of God before their eyes. A mere handful as to number, and in average talent very much on a level with the mass of their colleagues;—counting in their ranks no orator, or minister, or boroughmonger;—they commanded the ear of the House, and exerted on its proceedings an influence, the secret of which those who have studied the Parliamentary history of the period find it only too easy to understand. To refrain from gambling and ball-giving, to go much to church and never to the theatre, was not more at variance with the social customs of the day than it was the exception in the political world to meet with men who looked to the facts of the case and not to the wishes of the minister, and who before going into the lobby required to be obliged with a reason instead of with a job. Confidence and respect, and (what in the House of Commons is their unvarying accompaniment) power, were gradually, and to a great extent involuntarily, accorded to this group of members. They were not addicted to crotchets, nor to the obtrusive and unseasonable assertion of conscientious scruples. The occasions on which they made proof of independence and impartiality were such as justified, and dignified, their temporary renunciation of party ties. They interfered with decisive effect in the debates on the great scandals of Lord Melville and the Duke of York, and in more than one financial or commercial controversy that deeply concerned the national interests, of which the question of the retaining the Orders in Council was a conspicuous instance. A boy who, like young Macaulay, was admitted to the intimacy of politicians such as these, and was accustomed to hear matters of state discussed exclusively from a public point of view without any afterthought of ambition, or jealousy, or self-seeking, could hardly fail to grow up a patriotic and disinterested man. 'What is far better and more important than all is this, that I believe Macaulay to be incorruptible. You might lay ribbons, stars, garters, wealth, titles before him in vain. He has an honest genuine love of his country, and the world would not bribe him to neglect her interests.' Thus said Sydney Smith, who of all his real friends was the least inclined to over-praise him.

The memory of Thornton and Babington, and the other worthies of their day and set, is growing dim, and their names already mean little in our ears. Part of their work was so thoroughly done that the world, as its wont is, has long ago taken the credit of that work to itself. Others of their undertakings, in weaker hands than theirs, seem out of date among the ideas and beliefs which now are prevalent. At Clapham, as elsewhere, the old order is changing, and not always in a direction which to them would be acceptable or even tolerable. What was once the home of Zachary Macaulay stands almost within the swing of the bell of a stately and elegant Roman Catholic chapel; and the pleasant mansion of Lord Teignmouth, the cradle of the Bible Society, is now a religious house of the Redemptorist Order. But in one shape or another honest performance always lives, and the gains that accrued from the labours of these men are still on the right side of the national ledger. Among the most permanent of those gains is their undoubted share in the improvement of our political integrity by direct, and still more by indirect, example. It would be ungrateful to forget in how large a measure it is due to them that one, whose judgments upon the statesmen of many ages and countries have been delivered to an audience vast beyond all precedent, should have framed his decisions in accordance with the dictates of honour and humanity, of ardent public spirit and lofty public virtue.

CHAPTER II

1818–1824

Macaulay goes to the University—His love for Trinity College—His contemporaries at Cambridge—Charles Austin—The Union Debating Society—University studies, successes, and failures—The Mathematical Tripos—The Trinity Fellowship—William the Third—Letters—Prize poems—Peterloo—Novel-reading—The Queen's Trial—Macaulay's feeling towards his mother—A Reading-party—Hoaxing an editor—Macaulay takes pupils.

In October 1818 Macaulay went into residence at Trinity College, Cambridge. Mr. Henry Sykes Thornton, the eldest son of the member for Southwark, was his companion throughout his university career. The young men lived in the same lodgings, and began by reading with the same tutor: a plan which promised well, because, in addition to what was his own by right, each had the benefit of the period of instruction paid for by the other. But two hours were much the same as one to Macaulay, in whose eyes algebra and geometry were so much additional material for lively and interminable argument. Thornton reluctantly broke through the arrangement, and eventually stood highest among the Trinity wranglers of his year: an elevation which he could hardly have attained if he had pursued his studies in company with one who regarded every successive mathematical proposition as an open question. A Parliamentary election took place while the two friends were still quartered together in Jesus Lane. A tumult in the neighbouring street announced that the citizens were expressing their sentiments by the only channel which was open to them before the days of Reform; and Macaulay, to whom any excitement of a political nature was absolutely irresistible, dragged Thornton to the scene of action, and found the mob breaking the windows of the Hoop hotel, the head-quarters of the successful candidates. His ardour was cooled by receiving a dead cat full in the face. The man who was responsible for the animal came up and apologised very civilly, assuring him that there was no town and gown feeling in the matter, and that the cat had been meant for Mr. Adeane. 'I wish,' replied Macaulay, 'that you had meant it for me, and hit Mr. Adeane.'

After no long while he removed within the walls of Trinity, and resided first in the centre rooms of Bishop's Hostel, and subsequently in the Old Court, between the Gate and the Chapel. The door, which once bore his name, is on the groundfloor, to the left hand as you face the staircase. In more recent years, undergraduates who are accustomed to be out after lawful hours have claimed a right of way through the window which looks towards the town:—to the great annoyance of any occupant who is too good-natured to refuse the accommodation to others, and too steady to need it himself. This power of surreptitious entry had not been discovered in Macaulay's days; and, indeed, he would have cared very little for the privilege of spending his time outside walls which contained within them as many books as even he could read, and more friends than even he could talk to. Wanting nothing beyond what his college had to give, he revelled in the possession of leisure and liberty, in the almost complete command of his own time, in the power of passing at choice from the most perfect solitude to the most agreeable company. He keenly appreciated a society which cherishes all that is genuine, and is only too out-spoken in its abhorrence of pretension and display:—a society in which a man lives with those whom he likes, and with those only; choosing his comrades for their own sake, and so indifferent to the external distinctions of wealth and position that no one who has entered fully into the spirit of college life can ever unlearn its priceless lesson of manliness and simplicity.

Of all his places of sojourn during his joyous and shining pilgrimage through the world, Trinity, and Trinity alone, had any share with his home in Macaulay's affection and loyalty. To the last he regarded it as an ancient Greek, or a mediæval Italian, felt towards his native city. As long as he had place and standing there, he never left it willingly or returned to it without delight. The only step in his course about the wisdom of which he sometimes expressed misgiving was his preference of a London to a Cambridge life. The only dignity that in his later days he was known to covet was an honorary fellowship, which would have allowed him again to look through his window upon the college grass-plots, and to sleep within sound of the splashing of the fountain; again to breakfast on commons, and dine beneath the portraits of Newton and Bacon on the daïs of the hall; again to ramble by moonlight round Neville's cloister, discoursing the picturesque but somewhat exoteric philosophy which it pleased him to call by the name of metaphysics. From the door of his rooms, along the wall of the Chapel, there runs a flagged pathway which affords an acceptable relief from the rugged pebbles that surround it. Here as a Bachelor of Arts he would walk, book in hand, morning after morning throughout the long vacation, reading with the same eagerness and the same rapidity whether the volume was the most abstruse of treatises, the loftiest of poems, or the flimsiest of novels. That was the spot where in his failing years he specially loved to renew the feelings of the past; and some there are who can never revisit it without the fancy that there, if anywhere, his dear shade must linger.

He was fortunate in his contemporaries. Among his intimate friends were the two Coleridges—Derwent, the son, and Henry Nelson, who was destined to be the son-in-law, of the poet: and, how exceptional that destiny was, the readers of Sara Coleridge's letters are now aware. Hyde Villiers, whom an untimely death alone prevented from taking an equal place in a trio of distinguished brothers, was of his year, though not of his college.[1] In the year below were the young men who now bear the titles of Lord Grey, Lord Belper, and Lord Romilly;[2] and after the same interval came

[1] Lord Clarendon, and his brothers, were all Johnians.

[2] This paragraph was written in the summer of 1874. Three

Moultrie, who in his 'Dream of Life,' with a fidelity which he himself pronounced to have been obtained at some sacrifice of grace, has told us how the heroes of his time looked and lived, and Charles Villiers, who still delights our generation by showing us how they talked. Then there was Praed, fresh from editing the Etonian, as a product of collective boyish effort unique in its literary excellence and variety; and Sidney Walker, Praed's gifted schoolfellow, whose promise was blighted by premature decay of powers; and Charles Austin, whose fame would now be more in proportion to his extraordinary abilities, had not his unparalleled success as an advocate tempted him before his day to retire from the toils of a career of whose rewards he already had enough.

With his vigour and fervour, his depth of knowledge and breadth of humour, his close reasoning illustrated by an expansive imagination,—set off, as these gifts were, by the advantage, at that period of life so irresistible, of some experience of the world at home and abroad,—Austin was indeed a king among his fellows.

> Grave, sedate,
> And (if the looks may indicate the age,)
> Our senior some few years: no keener wit,
> No intellect more subtle, none more bold,
> Was found in all our host.

So writes Moultrie, and the testimony of his verse is borne out by John Stuart Mill's prose. 'The impression he gave was that of boundless strength, together with talents which, combined with such apparent force of will and character, seemed capable of dominating the world.' He certainly was the only man who ever succeeded in dominating Macaulay. Brimming over with ideas that were soon to be known by the name of Utilitarian, a panegyrist of American institutions, and an unsparing assailant of ecclesiastical endowments and hereditary privileges, he effectu-

of Macaulay's old college friends, Lord Romilly, Moultrie, and Charles Austin, died, in the hard winter that followed, within a few days of each other.

ally cured the young undergraduate of his Tory opinions, which were never more than skin deep, and brought him nearer to Radicalism than he ever was before or since. The report of this conversion, of which the most was made by ill-natured tale-bearers who met with more encouragement than they deserved, created some consternation in the family circle; while the reading set at Cambridge was duly scandalised at the influence which one, whose classical attainments were rather discursive than exact, had gained over a Craven scholar. To this hour men may be found in remote parsonages who mildly resent the fascination which Austin of Jesus exercised over Macaulay of Trinity.[1]

The day and the night together were too short for one who was entering on the journey of life amidst such a band of travellers. So long as a door was open, or a light burning, in any of the courts, Macaulay was always in the mood for conversation and companionship. Unfailing in his attendance at lecture and chapel, blameless with regard to college laws and college discipline, it was well for his virtue that no curfew was in force within the precincts of Trinity. He never tired of recalling the days when he supped at midnight on milk-punch and roast turkey, drank tea in floods at an hour when older men are intent upon anything rather than on the means of keeping themselves awake, and made little of sitting over the fire till the bell rang for morning chapel in order to see a friend off by the early coach. In the licence of the summer vacation, after some prolonged and festive gathering, the whole party would pour out into the moonlight, and ramble for mile after mile through the country, till the noise of their wide-flowing talk mingled with the twittering of the birds in the hedges which bordered the Coton pathway or the Madingley road. On such occasions it must have

[1] It was at this period of his career that Macaulay said to the late Mr. Hampden Gurney: 'Gurney, I have been a Tory; I am a Radical; *but I never will be a Whig.*'

been well worth the loss of sleep to hear Macaulay plying Austin with sarcasms upon the doctrine of the Greatest Happiness, which then had still some gloss of novelty; putting into an ever-fresh shape the time-honoured jokes against the Johnians for the benefit of the Villierses; and urging an interminable debate on Wordsworth's merits as a poet, in which the Coleridges, as in duty bound, were ever ready to engage. In this particular field he acquired a skill of fence which rendered him the most redoubtable of antagonists. Many years afterwards, at the time when the Prelude was fresh from the press, he was maintaining against the opinion of a large and mixed society that the poem was unreadable. At last, overborne by the united indignation of so many of Wordsworth's admirers, he agreed that the question should be referred to the test of personal experience; and on inquiry it was discovered that the only individual present who had got through the Prelude was Macaulay himself.

It is not only that the witnesses of these scenes unanimously declare that they have never since heard such conversation in the most renowned of social circles. The partiality of a generous young man for trusted and admired companions may well colour his judgment over the space of even half a century. But the estimate of university contemporaries was abundantly confirmed by the outer world. While on a visit to Lord Lansdowne at Bowood, years after they had left Cambridge, Austin and Macaulay happened to get upon college topics one morning at breakfast. When the meal was finished they drew their chairs to either end of the chimney-piece, and talked at each other across the hearth-rug as if they were in a first-floor room in the Old Court of Trinity. The whole company, ladies, artists, politicians, and diners-out, formed a silent circle round the two Cantabs, and, with a short break for lunch, never stirred till the bell warned them that it was time to dress for dinner.

It has all irrevocably perished. With life before

them, and each intent on his own future, none among that troop of friends had the mind to play Boswell to the others. One repartee survives, thrown off in the heat of discussion, but exquisitely perfect in all its parts. Acknowledged without dissent to be the best applied quotation that ever was made within five miles of the Fitzwilliam Museum, it is unfortunately too strictly classical for reproduction in these pages.

We are more easily consoled for the loss of the eloquence which then flowed so full and free in the debates of the Cambridge Union. In 1820 that Society was emerging from a period of tribulation and repression. The authorities of the university, who, as old constituents of Mr. Pitt and warm supporters of Lord Liverpool, had never been very much inclined to countenance the practice of political discussion among the undergraduates, set their faces against it more than ever at an epoch when the temper of the time increased the tendency of young men to run into extremes of partisanship. At length a compromise was extorted from the reluctant hands of the Vice-Chancellor, and the Club was allowed to take into consideration public affairs of a date anterior to the century. It required less ingenuity than the leaders of the Union had at their command to hit upon a method of dealing with the present under the guise of the past. Motions were framed that reflected upon the existing Government under cover of a censure on the Cabinets of the previous generation. Resolutions which called upon the meeting to declare that the boon of Catholic Emancipation should have been granted in the year 1795, or that our Commercial Policy previous to 1800 should have been founded on the basis of Free Trade, were clearly susceptible of great latitude of treatment. And, again, in its character of a reading club, the Society, when assembled for the conduct of private business, was at liberty to review the political creed of the journals of the day in order to decide which of them it should take in, and which it should discontinue. The Examiner newspaper was the flag of many a hard-fought battle; the Morning Chronicle was voted in and out of the rooms half-a-dozen times within a single twelvemonth; while a series of impassioned speeches on the burning question of interference in behalf of Greek Independence were occasioned by a proposition of Malden's 'that *ἡ Ἑλληνικὴ σάλπιγξ* do lie upon the table.'

At the close of the debates, which were held in a large room at the back of the Red Lion in Petty Cury, the most prominent members met for supper in the Hotel, or at Moultrie's lodgings, which were situated close at hand. They acted as a self-appointed Standing Committee, which watched over the general interests of the Union, and selected candidates whom they put in nomination for its offices. The Society did not boast a Hansard:—an omission which, as time went on, some among its orators had no reason to regret. Faint recollections still survive of a discussion upon the august topic of the character of George the Third. 'To whom do we owe it,' asked Macaulay, 'that while Europe was convulsed with anarchy and desolated with war, England alone remained tranquil, prosperous, and secure? To whom but the Good Old King? Why was it that, when neighbouring capitals were perishing in the flames, our own was illuminated only for triumphs?[1] You may find the cause in the same three words: the Good Old King.' Praed, on the other hand, would allow his late monarch neither public merits nor private virtues. 'A good man! If he had been a plain country gentleman with no wider opportunities for mischief, he would at least have bullied his footmen and cheated his steward.'

Macaulay's intense enjoyment of all that was stirring and vivid around him undoubtedly hindered him

[1] This debate evidently made some noise in the university world. There is an allusion to it in a squib of Praed's, very finished and elegant, and beyond all doubt contemporary. The passage relating to Macaulay begins with the lines—

Then the favourite comes with his trumpets and drums,
And his arms and his metaphors crossed.

in the race for university honours; though his success was sufficient to inspirit him at the time, and to give him abiding pleasure in the retrospect. He twice gained the Chancellor's medal for English verse, with poems admirably planned, and containing passages of real beauty, but which may not be republished in the teeth of the panegyric which, within ten years after they were written, he pronounced upon Sir Roger Newdigate. Sir Roger had laid down the rule that no exercise sent in for the prize which he established at Oxford was to exceed fifty lines. This law, says Macaulay, seems to have more foundation in reason than is generally the case with a literary canon, 'for the world, we believe, is pretty well agreed in thinking that the shorter a prize poem is, the better.'

Trinity men find it difficult to understand how it was that he missed getting one of the three silver goblets given for the best English Declamations of the year. If there is one thing which all Macaulay's friends, and all his enemies, admit, it is that he could declaim English. His own version of the affair was that the Senior Dean, a relative of the victorious candidate, sent for him and said: 'Mr. Macaulay, as you have not got the first cup, I do not suppose that you will care for either of the others.' He was consoled, however, by the prize for Latin Declamation; and in 1821 he established his classical repute by winning a Craven University scholarship in company with his friend Malden, and Mr. George Long, who preceded Malden as Professor of Greek at University College, London.

Macaulay detested the labour of manufacturing Greek and Latin verse in cold blood as an exercise; and his Hexameters were never up to the best Etonian mark, nor his Iambics to the highest standard of Shrewsbury. He defined a scholar as one who reads Plato with his feet on the fender. When already well on in his third year he writes: 'I never practised composition a single hour since I have been at Cambridge.' 'Soak your mind with Cicero,' was his constant advice to students at that time of life when writing Latin prose is the most lucrative of accomplishments. The advantage of this precept was proved in the Fellowship examination of the year 1824, when he obtained the honour which in his eyes was the most desirable that Cambridge had to give. The delight of the young man at finding himself one of the sixty masters of an ancient and splendid establishment; the pride with which he signed his first order for the college plate, and dined for the first time at the high table in his own right; the reflection that these privileges were the fruit, not of favour or inheritance, but of personal industry and ability,—were matters on which he loved to dwell long after the world had loaded him with its most envied prizes. Macaulay's feeling on this point is illustrated by the curious reverence which he cherished for those junior members of the college who, some ninety years ago, by a spirited remonstrance addressed to the governing body, brought about a reform in the Trinity Fellowship examination that secured to it the character for fair play, and efficiency, which it has ever since enjoyed. In his copy of the Cambridge Calendar for the year 1859, (the last of his life,) throughout the list of the old mathematical Triposes the words 'one of the eight' appear in his hand-writing opposite the name of each of these gentlemen. And I can never remember the time when it was not diligently impressed upon me that, if I minded my syntax, I might eventually hope to reach a position which would give me three hundred pounds a year, a stable for my horse, six dozen of audit ale every Christmas, a loaf and two pats of butter every morning, and a good dinner for nothing, with as many almonds and raisins as I could eat at dessert.

Macaulay was not chosen a Fellow until his last trial, nominally for the amazing reason that his translations from Greek and Latin, while faithfully representing the originals, were rendered into English that was ungracefully bald and inornate. The real cause was, beyond all doubt, his utter neglect of the special study of the place: a liberty which Cambridge seldom allows to be taken with impunity even by her most favoured sons. He used to profess deep and lasting regret for his early repugnance to scientific subjects; but the fervour of his penitence in after years was far surpassed by the heartiness with which he inveighed against mathematics as long as it was his business to learn them. Everyone who knows the Senate House may anticipate the result. When the Tripos of 1822 made its appearance, his name did not grace the list. In short, to use the expressive vocabulary of the university, Macaulay was gulfed:—a mishap which disabled him from contending for the Chancellor's medals, then the crowning trophies of a classical career. 'I well remember,' says Lady Trevelyan, 'that first trial of my life. We were spending the winter at Brighton when a letter came giving an account of the event. I recollect my mother taking me into her room to tell me, for even then it was known how my whole heart was wrapped up in him, and it was thought necessary to break the news. When your uncle arrived at Brighton, I can recall my mother telling him that he had better go at once to his father, and get it over, and I can see him as he left the room on that errand.'

During the same year he engaged in a less arduous competition. A certain Mr. Greaves of Fulbourn had long since provided a reward of ten pounds for 'the Junior Bachelor of Trinity College who wrote the best essay on the Conduct and Character of William the Third.' As the prize is annual, it is appalling to reflect upon the searching analysis to which the motives of that monarch must by this time have been subjected. The event, however, may be counted as an encouragement to the founders of endowments: for, amidst the succession of juvenile critics whose attention was by his munificence turned in the direction of his favourite hero, Mr. Greaves had at last fallen in with the right man. It is more than probable that to this old Cambridgeshire Whig was due the first idea of that History in whose pages William of Orange stands as the central figure. The essay is still in existence, in a close neat hand, which twenty years of Reviewing never rendered illegible. Originally written as a fair copy, but so disfigured by repeated corrections and additions as to be unfit for the eyes of the college authorities, it bears evident marks of having been held to the flames, and rescued on second, and in this case it will be allowed, on better, thoughts. The exercise, (which is headed by the very appropriate motto,

> Primus qui legibus urbem
> Fundabit, Curibus parvis et paupere terrâ
> Missus in imperium magnum,)

is just such as will very likely be produced in the course of next Easter term by some young man of judgment and spirit, who knows his Macaulay by heart, and will paraphrase him without scruple. The characters of James, of Shaftesbury, of William himself; the Popish plot; the struggle over the Exclusion bill; the reaction from Puritanic rigour into the licence of the Restoration, are drawn on the same lines and painted in the same colours as those with which the world is now familiar. The style only wants condensation, and a little of the humour which he had not yet learned to transfer from his conversation to his writings, in order to be worthy of his mature powers. He thus describes William's lifelong enemy and rival, whose name he already spells after his own fashion:

'Lewis was not a great general. He was not a great legislator. But he was, in one sense of the words, a great king. He was a perfect master of all the mysteries of the science of royalty,—of all the arts which at once extend power and conciliate popularity,—which most advantageously display the merits, or most dexterously conceal the deficiencies, of a sovereign. He was surrounded by great men, by victorious commanders, by sagacious statesmen. Yet, while he availed himself to the utmost of their services, he never incurred any danger from their rivalry. His was a talisman which extorted the obedience of the proudest and mightiest spirits. The haughty and turbulent warriors whose contests had agitated France during his minority yielded to the irresistible spell, and, like the gigantic slaves of the ring and lamp of Aladdin, laboured to decorate and aggrandise a master whom they could have crushed. With incomparable address he appropriated to himself the glory of campaigns which had been planned, and counsels which had been suggested, by others. The arms of Turenne were the terror of Europe. The policy of Colbert was the strength of France. But in their foreign successes, and their internal prosperity, the people saw only the greatness and wisdom of Lewis.'

In the second chapter of the History much of this is compressed into the sentence: 'He had shown, in an eminent degree, two talents invaluable to a prince,—the talent of choosing his servants well, and the talent of appropriating to himself the chief part of the credit of their acts.'

In a passage that occurs towards the close of the essay may be traced something more than an outline of the peroration in which, a quarter of a century later on, he summed up the character and results of the Revolution of 1688.

'To have been a sovereign, yet the champion of liberty; a revolutionary leader, yet the supporter of social order, is the peculiar glory of William. He knew where to pause. He outraged no national prejudice. He abolished no ancient form. He altered no venerable name. He saw that the existing institutions possessed the greatest capabilities of excellence, and that stronger sanctions, and clearer definitions, were alone required to make the practice of the British constitution as admirable as the theory. Thus he imparted to innovation the dignity and stability of antiquity. He transferred to a happier order of things the associations which had attached the people to their former government. As the Roman warrior, before he assaulted Veii, invoked its guardian gods to leave its walls, and to accept the worship and patronise the cause of the besiegers, this great prince, in attacking a system of oppression, summoned to his aid the venerable principles and deeply seated feelings to which that system was indebted for protection.'

A letter, written during the latter years of his life, expresses Macaulay's general views on the subject of University honours. 'If a man brings away from Cambridge self-knowledge, accuracy of mind, and habits of strong intellectual exertion, he has gained more than if he had made a display of showy superficial Etonian scholarship, got three or four Browne's medals, and gone forth into the world a schoolboy and doomed to be a schoolboy to the last. After all, what a man does at Cambridge is, in itself, nothing. If he makes a poor figure in life, his having been Senior Wrangler or University scholar is never mentioned but with derision. If he makes a distinguished figure, his early honours merge in those of a later date. I hope that I do not overrate my own place in the estimation of society. Such as it is, I would not give a halfpenny to add to the consideration which I enjoy, all the consideration that I should derive from having been Senior Wrangler. But I often regret, and even acutely, my want of a Senior Wrangler's knowledge of physics and mathematics; and I regret still more some habits of mind which a Senior Wrangler is pretty certain to possess.' Like all men who know what the world is, he regarded the triumph of a college career as of less value than its disappointments. Those are most to be envied who soonest learn to expect nothing for which they have not worked hard, and who never acquire the habit, (a habit which an unbroken course of University successes too surely breeds,) of pitying themselves overmuch if ever in after life they happen to work in vain.

Cambridge: Wednesday.
(Post-mark, 1818.)

My dear Mother,—

King, I am absolutely certain, would take no more pupils on any account. And, even if he would, he has numerous applicants with prior claims. He has already six, who occupy him six hours in the day, and is likewise lecturer to the college. It would, however, be very easy to obtain an excellent tutor. Lefevre and Malkin are men of first-rate mathematical abilities, and both of our college. I can scarcely bear to write on Mathematics or Mathematicians. Oh for words to express my abomination of that science, if a name sacred to the useful and embellishing arts may be applied to the perception and recollection of certain properties in numbers and figures! Oh that I had to learn astrology, or demonology, or school divinity! Oh that I were to pore over Thomas Aquinas, and to adjust the relation of Entity with the two Predicaments, so that I were exempted from this miserable study! 'Discipline' of the mind! Say rather starvation, confinement, torture, annihilation! But it must be. I feel myself becoming a personification of Algebra, a living trigonometrical canon, a walking table of Logarithms. All my perceptions of elegance and beauty gone, or at least going. By the end of the term my brain will be 'as dry as the remainder biscuit after a voyage.' Oh to change Cam for Isis! But such is my destiny; and, since it is so, be the pursuit contemptible, below contempt, or disgusting beyond abhorrence, I shall aim at no second place. But three years! I cannot endure the thought. I cannot bear to contemplate what I must have to undergo. Farewell then Homer and Sophocles and Cicero.

> Farewell happy fields
> Where joy for ever reigns! Hail, horrors, hail,
> Infernal world!

How does it proceed? Milton's descriptions have been driven out of my head by such elegant expressions as the following

$$\text{Cos}\, x = 1 - \frac{x^2}{1.2} + \frac{x^4}{1.2.3.4} - \frac{x^6}{1.2.3.4.5.6}$$

$$\text{Tan}\, \overline{a+b} = \frac{\text{Tan}\, a + \text{Tan}\, b}{1 - \text{Tan}\, a + \text{Tan}\, b}$$

My classics must be Woodhouse, and my amusements summing an infinite series. Farewell, and tell Selina and Jane to be thankful that it is not a necessary part of female education to get a headache daily without acquiring one practical truth or beautiful image in return. Again, and with affectionate love to my Father, farewell wishes your most miserable and mathematical son

T. B. MACAULAY.

Cambridge: November 9, 1818.

My dear Father,—

Your letter, which I read with the greatest pleasure, is perfectly safe from all persons who could make a bad use of it. The Emperor Alexander's plans as detailed in the conversation between him and Clarkson[1] are almost superhuman; and tower as much above the common hopes and aspirations of philanthropists as the statue which his Macedonian namesake proposed to hew out of Mount Athos excelled the most colossal works of meaner projectors. As Burke said of Henry the Fourth's wish that every peasant in France might have the chicken in his pot comfortably on a Sunday, we may say of these mighty plans, 'The mere wish, the unfulfilled desire, exceeded all that we hear of the splendid professions and exploits of princes.' Yet my satisfaction in the success of that noble cause in which the Emperor seems to be exerting himself with so much zeal is scarcely so great as my regret for the man who would have traced every step of its progress with anxiety, and hailed its success with the most ardent delight. Poor Sir Samuel Romilly! Quando ullum invenient parem? How long may a penal code at once too sanguinary and too lenient, half written in blood like Draco's, and half undefined and loose as the common law of a tribe of savages, be the curse and disgrace of the country? How many years may elapse before a man who knows like him all that law can teach, and possesses at the same time like him a liberality and a discernment of general rights which the technicalities

[1] Thomas Clarkson, the famous assailant of slavery.

of professional learning rather tend to blunt, shall again rise to ornament and reform our jurisprudence? For such a man, if he had fallen in the maturity of years and honours, and been borne from the bed of sickness to a grave by the side of his prototype Hale amidst the tears of nobles and senators, even then, I think, the public sorrow would have been extreme. But that the last moments of an existence of high thoughts and great virtues should have been passed as his were passed! In my feelings the scene at Claremont[1] this time last year was mere dust in the balance in comparison.

Ever your affectionate son,
T. B. M.

Cambridge: Friday, February 5, 1819.

My dear Father,—

I have not of course had time to examine with attention all your criticisms on Pompeii.[2] I certainly am much obliged to you for withdrawing so much time from more important business to correct my effusions. Most of the remarks which I have examined are perfectly just: but as to the more momentous charge, the want of a moral, I think it might be a sufficient defence that, if a subject is given which admits of none, the man who writes without a moral is scarcely censurable. But is it the real fact that no literary employment is estimable or laudable which does not lead to the spread of moral truth or the excitement of virtuous feeling? Books of amusement tend to polish the mind, to improve the style, to give variety to conversation, and to lend a grace to more important accomplishments. He who can effect this has surely done something. Is no useful end served by that writer whose works have soothed weeks of languor and sickness, have relieved the mind exhausted from the pressure of employment by an amusement which delights with-

[1] The death of Princess Charlotte.

[2] The subject of the English poem for the Chancellor's prize of 1819 was the Destruction of Pompeii.

out enervating, which relaxes the tension of the powers without rendering them unfit for future exercise? I should not be surprised to see these observations refuted; and I shall not be sorry if they are so. I feel personally little interest in the question. If my life be a life of literature, it shall certainly be one of literature directed to moral ends.

At all events let us be consistent. I was amused in turning over an old volume of the Christian Observer to find a gentleman signing himself Excubitor, (one of our antagonists in the question of novel-reading,) after a very pious argument on the hostility of novels to a religious frame of mind, proceeding to observe that he was shocked to hear a young lady who had displayed extraordinary knowledge of modern ephemeral literature own herself ignorant of Dryden's fables! Consistency with a vengeance! The reading of modern poetry and novels excites a worldly disposition and prevents ladies from reading Dryden's fables! There is a general disposition among the more literary part of the religious world to cry down the elegant literature of our own times, while they are not in the slightest degree shocked at atrocious profaneness or gross indelicacy when a hundred years have stamped them with the title of classical. I say: 'If you read Dryden you can have no reasonable objection to reading Scott.' The strict antagonist of ephemeral reading exclaims, 'Not so. Scott's poems are very pernicious. They call away the mind from spiritual religion, and from Tancred and Sigismunda.' But I am exceeding all ordinary limits. If these hasty remarks fatigue you, impute it to my desire of justifying myself from a charge which I should be sorry to incur with justice. Love to all at home.

Affectionately yours,

T. B. M.

With or without a moral, the poem carried the day. The subject for the next year was Waterloo. The opening lines of Macaulay's exercise were pretty and simple enough to ruin his chance in an academical competition.

It was the Sabbath morn. How calm and fair
Is the blest dawning of the day of prayer!
Who hath not felt how fancy's mystic power
With holier beauty decks that solemn hour;
A softer lustre in its sunshine sees;
And hears a softer music in its breeze?
Who hath not dreamed that even the skylark's throat
Hails that sweet morning with a gentler note?
Fair morn, how gaily shone thy dawning smile
On the green valleys of my native isle!
How gladly many a spire's resounding height
With peals of transport hailed thy newborn light!
Ah! little thought the peasant then, who blest
The peaceful hour of consecrated rest,
And heard the rustic Temple's arch prolong
The simple cadence of the hallowed song,
That the same sun illumed a gory field,
Where wilder song and sterner music pealed;
Where many a yell unholy rent the air,
And many a hand was raised,—but not in prayer.

The prize fell to a man of another college, and Trinity comforted itself by inventing a story to the effect that the successful candidate had run away from the battle.

In the summer of 1819 there took place a military affair, less attractive than Waterloo as a theme for poets, but which, as far as this country is concerned, has proved even more momentous in its ultimate consequences. On the 16th of August a Reform demonstration was arranged at Manchester resembling those which were common in the Northern districts during the year 1866, except that in 1819 women formed an important element in the procession. A troop of yeomanry, and afterwards two squadrons of hussars, were sent in among the crowd, which was assembled in St. Peter's Fields, the site on which the Free Trade Hall now stands. The men used their swords freely, and the horses their hoofs. The people, who meant anything but fighting, trampled each other down in the attempt to escape. Five or six lives were lost, and fifty or sixty persons were badly hurt; but the painful impression wrought upon the national conscience was well worth the price. British blood has never since been shed by British hands in any civic contest that rose above the level of a lawless riot. The immediate result, however, was to concentrate and embitter party feeling. The grand jury threw out the bills against the yeomen, and found true bills against the popular orators who had called the meeting together. The Common Councilmen of the City of London, who had presented an Address to the Prince Regent reflecting upon the conduct of the Government, were roundly rebuked for their pains. Earl Fitzwilliam was dismissed from the office of Lord Lieutenant, for taking part in a Yorkshire county gathering which had passed resolutions in the same sense as the Address from the City. On the other hand, a Peterloo medal was struck, which is still treasured in such Manchester families as have not learned to be ashamed of the old Manchester politics.

In this heated state of the political atmosphere the expiring Toryism of the Anti-Slavery leaders flamed up once again. 'I declare,' said Wilberforce, 'my greatest cause of difference with the democrats is their laying, and causing people to lay, so great a stress on the concerns of this world as to occupy their whole minds and hearts, and to leave a few scanty and lukewarm thoughts for the heavenly treasure.' Zachary Macaulay, who never canted, and who knew that on the 16th of August the Manchester Magistrates were thinking just as much or as little about religion as the Manchester populace, none the less took the same side as Wilberforce. Having formed for himself, by observations made on the spot, a decided opinion that the authorities ought to be supported, he was much disturbed by reports which came to him from Cambridge.

September, 1819.

My dear Father,—

My mother's letter, which has just arrived, has given me much concern. The letter which has, I am sorry to learn, given you and her uneasiness was written rapidly and thoughtlessly enough, but can scarcely, I think, as far as I remember its tenour, justify some of the extraordinary inferences which it has occasioned. I can only assure you most solemnly that I am not initiated into any democratical societies here, and that I know no people who make politics a common or frequent topic of conversation, except one man who is a determined Tory. It is true that this Manchester business has roused some indignation here, as at other places, and drawn philippics against the powers that be from lips which I never heard opened before but to speak on university contests or university scandal. For myself, I have long made it a rule never to talk on politics except in the most general manner; and I believe that my most intimate associates have no idea of my opinions on the questions of party. I can scarcely be censured, I think, for imparting them to you;—which, however, I should scarcely have thought of doing, (so much is my mind occupied with other concerns,) had not your letter invited me to state my sentiments on the Manchester business.

I hope that this explanation will remove some of your uneasiness. As to my opinions, I have no particular desire to vindicate them. They are merely speculative, and therefore cannot partake of the nature of moral culpability. They are early formed, and I am not solicitous that you should think them superior to those of most people at eighteen. I will, however, say this in their defence. Whatever the affectionate alarm of my dear mother may lead her to apprehend, I am not one of the 'sons of anarchy and confusion' with whom she classes me. My opinions, good or bad, were learnt, not from Hunt and Waithman, but from Cicero, from Tacitus, and from Milton. They are the opinions which have produced men who have ornamented the world, and redeemed human nature from the degradation of ages of superstition and slavery. I may be wrong as to the facts of what occurred at Manchester; but, if they be what I have seen them stated, I can never repent speaking of them with indignation. When I cease to feel the injuries of others warmly, to detest wanton cruelty, and to feel my soul rise against oppression, I shall think myself unworthy to be your son.

I could say a great deal more. Above all I might, I think, ask, with some reason, why a few democratical sentences in a letter, a private letter, of a collegian of eighteen, should be thought so alarming an indication of character, when Brougham and other people, who at an age which ought to have sobered them talk with much more violence, are not thought particularly ill of? But I have so little room left that I abstain, and will only add thus much. Were my opinions as decisive as they are fluctuating, and were the elevation of a Cromwell or the renown of a Hampden the certain reward of my standing forth in the democratic cause, I would rather have my lips sealed on the subject than give my mother or you one hour of uneasiness. There are not so many people in the world who love me that I can afford to pain them for any object of ambition which it contains. If this assurance be not sufficient, clothe it in what language you please, and believe me to express myself in those words which you think the strongest and most solemn. Affectionate love to my mother and sisters. Farewell.

T. B. M.

Cambridge: January 5, 1820.

My dear Father,—

Nothing that gives you disquietude can give me amusement. Otherwise I should have been excessively diverted by the dialogue which you have reported with so much vivacity; the accusation; the predictions; and the elegant agnomen of 'the novel-reader' for which I am indebted to this incognito. I went in some amazement to Malden, Romilly, and Barlow. Their acquaintance comprehends, I will venture to say, almost every man worth knowing in the university in every field of study. They had never heard the appellation applied to me by any man. Their intimacy with me would of course prevent any person from speaking to them on the subject in an insulting manner: for it is not usual here, whatever your unknown informant may do, for a gentleman who does not wish to be kicked downstairs to reply to a man who mentions another as his particular friend, 'Do you mean the blackguard or the novel-reader?' But I am fully convinced that had the charge prevailed to any extent it must have reached the ears of one of those whom I interrogated. At all events I have the consolation of not being thought a novel-reader by three or four who are entitled to judge upon the subject, and whether their opinion be of equal value with that of this John-a-Nokes against whom I have to plead I leave you to decide.

But stronger evidence, it seems, is behind. This gentleman was in company with me. Alas! that I should never have found out how accurate an observer was measuring my sentiments, numbering the novels which I criticised, and speculating on the probability of my being plucked. 'I was familiar with all the novels whose names he had ever heard.' If so frightful an accusation did not stun me at once, I might perhaps hint at the possibility that this was to be attributed almost as much to the narrowness of his reading on this subject as to the extent of mine. There are men here who are mere mathematical blocks; who plod on their eight hours a day to the honours of the Senate House; who leave the groves which witnessed the musings of Milton, of Bacon, and of Gray, without one liberal idea or elegant image, and carry with them into the world minds contracted by unmingled attention to one part of science, and memories stored only with technicalities. How often have I seen such men go forth into society for people to stare at them, and ask each other how it comes that beings so stupid in conversation, so uninformed on every subject of history, of letters, and of taste, could gain such distinction at Cambridge! It is in such circles, which, I am happy to say, I hardly know but by report, that knowledge of modern literature is called novel-reading: a commodious name, invented by ignorance and applied by envy, in the same manner as men without learning call a scholar a pedant, and men without principle call a Christian a Methodist. To me the attacks of such men are valuable as compliments. The man whose friend tells him that he is known to be extensively acquainted with elegant literature may suspect that he is flattering him; but he may feel real and secure satisfaction when some Johnian sneers at him for a novel-reader.[1]

As to the question whether or not I am wasting time, I shall leave that for time to answer. I cannot afford to sacrifice a day every week in defence and explanation as to my habits of reading. I value, most deeply value, that solicitude which arises from your affection for me: but let it not debar me from justice and candour. Believe me ever, my dear Father,

Your most affectionate son,

T. B. M.

The father and son were in sympathy upon what, at this distance of time, appears as the least inviting article of the Whig creed. They were both partisans of the Queen. Zachary Macaulay was inclined in her favour by sentiments alike of friendship, and of the most pardonable resentment. Brougham, her illustrious advocate, had for ten years been the main hope and stay of the movement against Slavery and the Slave Trade; while the John Bull, whose special mission it was to write her down, honoured the Abolitionist party with its declared animosity. However full its columns might be of libels upon the honour of the

[1] My uncle was fond of telling us how he would walk miles out of Cambridge in order to meet the coach which brought the last new Waverley novel.

wives and daughters of Whig statesmen, it could always find room for calumnies against Mr. Macaulay which in ingenuity of fabrication, and in cruelty of intention, were conspicuous even among the contents of the most discreditable publication that ever issued from the London press. When Queen Caroline landed from the Continent in June 1820 the young Trinity undergraduate greeted her Majesty with a complimentary ode, which certainly little resembled those effusions that, in the old courtly days, an University was accustomed to lay at the feet of its Sovereign. The piece has no literary value, and is curious only as reflecting the passion of the hour. The first and last stanzas run as follows:—

Let mirth on every visage shine
And glow in every soul.
Bring forth, bring forth, the oldest wine,
And crown the largest bowl.
Bear to her home, while banners fly
From each resounding steeple,
And rockets sparkle in the sky,
The Daughter of the People.
E'en here, for one triumphant day,
Let want and woe be dumb,
And bonfires blaze, and schoolboys play.
Thank Heaven, our Queen is come!

* * * * *

Though tyrant hatred still denies
Each right that fits thy station,
To thee a people's love supplies
A nobler coronation:
A coronation all unknown
To Europe's royal vermin:
For England's heart shall be thy throne,
And purity thine ermine;
Thy Proclamation our applause,
Applause denied to some;
Thy crown our love; thy shield our laws.
Thank Heaven, our Queen is come!

Early in November, warned by growing excitement outside the House of Lords, and by dwindling majorities within, Lord Liverpool announced that the King's Ministers had come to the determination not to proceed further with the Bill of Pains and Penalties. The joy which this declaration spread through the country has been described as 'beyond the scope of record.'

Cambridge: November 13, 1820.

My dear Father,—

All here is ecstasy. 'Thank God, the country is saved,' were my first words when I caught a glimpse of the papers of Friday night. 'Thank God, the country is saved,' is written on every face and echoed by every voice. Even the symptoms of popular violence, three days ago so terrific, are now displayed with good humour and received with cheerfulness. Instead of curses on the Lords, on every post and every wall is written, 'All is as it should be:' 'Justice done at last:' and similar mottoes expressive of the sudden turn of public feeling. How the case may stand in London I do not know; but here the public danger, like all dangers which depend merely on human opinions and feelings, has disappeared from our sight almost in the twinkling of an eye. I hope that the result of these changes may be the secure re-establishment of our commerce, which I suppose political apprehension must have contributed to depress. I hope, at least, that there is no danger to our own fortunes of the kind at which you seem to hint. Be assured however, my dear Father, that, be our circumstances what they may, I feel firmly prepared to encounter the worst with fortitude, and to do my utmost to retrieve it by exertion. The best inheritance you have already secured to me,—an unblemished name and a good education. And for the rest, whatever calamities befall us, I would not, to speak without affectation, exchange adversity consoled, as with us it must ever be, by mutual affection and domestic happiness, for anything which can be possessed by those who are destitute of the kindness of parents and sisters like mine.

But I think, on referring to your letter, that I insist too much upon the significance of a few words. I hope so, and trust that everything will go well. But it is chapel time, and I must conclude.

Ever most affectionately yours,

T. B. MACAULAY.

Trin. Coll.: March 25, 1821.

My dear Mother,—

I entreat you to entertain no apprehensions about my health. My fever, cough, and sore-throat have all disappeared for the last four days. Many thanks for your intelligence about poor dear John's recovery, which has much exhilarated me. Yet I do not know whether illness to him is not rather a prerogative than an evil. I am sure that it is well worth while being sick to be nursed by a mother. There is nothing which I remember with such pleasure as the time when you nursed me at Aspenden. The other night, when I lay on my sofa very ill and hypochondriac, I was thinking over that time. How sick, and sleepless, and weak I was, lying in bed, when I was told that you were come! How well I remember with what an ecstasy of joy I saw that face approaching me, in the middle of people that did not care if I died that night except for the trouble of burying me! The sound of your voice, the touch of your hand, are present to me now, and will be, I trust in God, to my last hour. The very thought of these things invigorated me the other day; and I almost blessed the sickness and low spirits which brought before me associated images of a tenderness and an affection, which, however imperfectly repaid, are deeply remembered. Such scenes and such recollections are the bright half of human nature and human destiny. All objects of ambition, all rewards of talent, sink into nothing compared with that affection which is independent of good or adverse circumstances, excepting that it is never so ardent, so delicate, or so tender as in the hour of languor or distress. But I must stop. I had no intention of pouring out on paper what

I am much more used to think than to express. Farewell, my dear Mother.

Ever yours affectionately,

T. B. MACAULAY.

Macaulay liked Cambridge too well to spend the long vacation elsewhere except under strong compulsion; but in 1821, with the terrors of the Mathematical Tripos already close at hand, he was persuaded into joining a reading party in Wales with a Mr. Bird as tutor. Eardley Childers, the father of the statesman of that name, has preserved a pleasant little memorial of the expedition.

To Charles Smith Bird, Eardley Childers, Thos. B. Macaulay, William Clayton Walters, Geo. B. Paley, Robert Jarratt, Thos. Jarratt, Edwin Kempson, Ebenezer Ware, Wm. Cornwall, John Greenwood, J. Lloyd, and Jno. Wm. Gleadall, Esquires:

Gentlemen,—We the undersigned, for ourselves and the inhabitants in general of the town of Llanrwst in the county of Denbigh, consider it our duty to express to you the high sense we entertain of your general good conduct and demeanour during your residence here, and we assure you that we view with much regret the period of your separation and departure from amongst us. We are very sensible of the obligation we are under for your uniformly benevolent and charitable exertions upon several public occasions, and we feel peculiar pleasure in thus tendering to you individually our gratitude and thanks.

Wishing you all possible prosperity and happiness in your future avocations, we subscribe ourselves with unfeigned respect, Gentlemen,

Your most obedient servants,

REV. JOHN TILTEY,

&c., &c.

(25 signatures.)

In one respect Macaulay hardly deserved his share of this eulogium. A scheme was on foot in the town to found an auxiliary branch of the Bible Society. A public meeting was called, and Mr. Bird urged upon his eloquent pupil to aid the project with a specimen of Union rhetoric. Macaulay, however, had had enough of the Bible Society at Clapham, and sturdily refused to come forward as its champion at Llanrwst.

Llanrwst: July—, 1821.

My dear Mother,—

You see I know not how to date my letter. My calendar in this sequestered spot is as irregular as Robinson Crusoe's after he had missed one day in his calculation. I have no intelligence to send you, unless a battle between a drunken attorney and an impudent publican which took place here yesterday may deserve the appellation. You may perhaps be more interested to hear that I sprained my foot, and am just recovering from the effects of the accident by means of opodeldoc which I bought at the tinker's. For all trades and professions here lie in a most delightful confusion. The druggist sells hats; the shoemaker is the sole bookseller, if that dignity may be allowed him on the strength of the three Welsh Bibles, and the guide to Caernarvon, which adorn his window; ink is sold by the apothecary; the grocer sells ropes, (a commodity which, I fear, I shall require before my residence here is over,) and tooth-brushes. A clothes-brush is a luxury yet unknown to Llanrwst. As to books, for want of any other English literature, I intend to learn Paradise Lost by heart at odd moments. But I must conclude. Write to me often, my dear Mother, and all of you at home, or you may have to answer for my drowning myself, like Gray's bard, in 'Old Conway's foaming flood,' which is most conveniently near for so poetical an exit.

Ever most affectionately yours,
T. B. M.

Llanrwst: August 31, 1821.

My dear Father,—

I have just received your letter, and cannot but feel concerned at the tone of it. I do not think it quite fair to attack me for filling my letters with remarks on the King's Irish expedition. It has been the great event of this part of the world. I was at Bangor when he sailed. His bows, and the Marquis of Anglesea's fête, were the universal subjects of conversation; and some remarks on the business were as natural from me as accounts of the coronation from you in London. In truth I have little else to say. I see nothing that connects me with the world except the newspapers. I get up, breakfast, read, play at quoits, and go to bed. This is the history of my life. It will do for every day of the last fortnight.

As to the King, I spoke of the business, not at all as a political, but as a moral question,—as a point of correct feeling and of private decency. If Lord —— were to issue tickets for a gala ball immediately after receiving intelligence of the sudden death of his divorced wife, I should say the same. I pretend to no great insight into party politics; but the question whether it is proper for any man to mingle in festivities while his wife's body lies unburied is one, I confess, which I thought myself competent to decide. But I am not anxious about the fate of my remarks, which I have quite forgot, and which, I dare say, were very foolish. To me it is of little importance whether the King's conduct were right or wrong; but it is of great importance that those whom I love should not think me a precipitate, silly, shallow sciolist in politics, and suppose that every frivolous word that falls from my pen is a dogma which I mean to advance as indisputable; and all this only because I write to them without reserve; only because I love them well enough to trust them with every idea which suggests itself to me. In fact, I believe that I am not more precipitate or presumptuous than other people, but only more open. You cannot be more fully convinced than I am how contracted my means are of forming a judgment. If I chose to weigh every word that I uttered or wrote to you, and, whenever I alluded to politics, were to labour and qualify my expressions as if I were drawing up a state paper, my letters might be a great deal wiser, but would not be such letters as I should wish to receive from those whom I loved. Perfect love, we are told, casteth out fear. If I say, as I know I do, a thousand wild and inaccurate things, and employ exaggerated expressions about persons or events in writing to you or to my mother, it is not, I believe, that I want power to systematise my ideas or to measure my expressions, but because I have no objection to letting you see my mind in dishabille. I have a court dress for days of ceremony and people of ceremony, nevertheless. But I would not willingly be frightened into wearing it with you; and I hope you do not wish me to do so.

Ever yours,
T. B. M.

To hoax a newspaper has, time out of mind, been the special ambition of undergraduate wit. In the course of 1821 Macaulay sent to the Morning Post a burlesque copy of verses, entitled 'Tears of Sensibility.' The editor fell an easy victim, but unfortunately did not fall alone.

No pearl of ocean is so sweet
As that in my Zuleika's eye.
No earthly jewel can compete
With tears of sensibility.

Like light phosphoric on the billow,
Or hermit ray of evening sky,
Like ripplings round a weeping willow
Are tears of sensibility.

Like drops of Iris-coloured fountains
By which Endymion loved to lie,
Like dew-gems on untrodden mountains
Are tears of sensibility.

While Zephyr broods o'er moonlight rill
The flowerets droop as if to die,
And from their chaliced cup distil
The tears of sensibility.

The heart obdurate never felt
One link of Nature's magic tie
If ne'er it knew the bliss to melt
In tears of sensibility.

The generous and the gentle heart
Is like that balmy Indian tree
Which scatters from the wounded part
The tears of sensibility.

Then oh! ye Fair, if Pity's ray
E'er taught your snowy breasts to sigh,
Shed o'er my contemplative lay
The tears of sensibility.

November 2, 1821.

My dear Mother,—

I possess some of the irritability of a poet, and it has been a good deal awakened by your criticisms. I could not have imagined that it would have been necessary for me to have said that the execrable trash entitled 'Tears of Sensibility' was merely a burlesque on the style of the magazine verses of the day. I could not suppose that you could have suspected me of *seriously* composing such a farrago of false metaphor and unmeaning epithet. It was meant solely for a caricature on the style of the poetasters of newspapers and journals; and, (though I say it who should not say it,) has excited more attention and received more praise at Cambridge than it deserved. If you have it, read it over again, and do me the justice to believe that such a compound of jargon, nonsense, false images, and exaggerated sentiment, is not the product of my serious labours. I sent it to the Morning Post, because that paper is the ordinary receptacle of trash of the description which I intended to ridicule, and its admission therefore pointed the jest. I see, however, that for the future I must mark more distinctly when I intend to be ironical.

Your affectionate son,

T. B. M.

Cambridge: July 26, 1822.

My dear Father,—

I have been engaged to take two pupils for nine months of the next year. They are brothers, whose father, a Mr. Stoddart, resides at Cambridge. I am to give them an hour a day, each; and am to receive a hundred guineas. It gives me great pleasure to be able even in this degree to relieve you from the burden of my expenses here. I begin my tutorial labours to-morrow. My pupils are young, one being fifteen and the other thirteen years old, but I hear excellent accounts of their proficiency, and I intend to do my utmost for them. Farewell.

T. B. M.

A few days later on he writes: 'I do not dislike teaching; whether it is that I am more patient than I had imagined, or that I have not yet had time to grow tired of my new vocation. I find, also, what at first sight may appear paradoxical, that I read much more in consequence, and that the regularity of habits necessarily produced by a periodical employment which cannot be procrastinated fully compensates for the loss of the time which is consumed in tuition.'

Trinity College, Cambridge: October 1, 1824.

My dear Father,—

I was elected Fellow this morning, shall be sworn in to-morrow, and hope to leave Cambridge on Tuesday for Rothley Temple. The examiners speak highly of the manner in which I acquitted myself, and I have reason to believe that I stood first of the candidates.

I need not say how much I am delighted by my success, and how much I enjoy the thought of the pleasure which it will afford to you, my mother, and our other friends. Till I become a Master of Arts next July the pecuniary emolument which I shall derive will not be great. For seven years from that time it will make me almost an independent man.

Malden is elected. You will take little interest in the rest of our Cambridge successes and disappointments.

Yours most affectionately,

T. B. M.

CHAPTER III

1824–1830

Macaulay is called to the bar—Does not make it a serious profession—Speech before the Anti-Slavery Society—Knight's Quarterly Magazine—The Edinburgh Review and the Essay on Milton—Macaulay's personal appearance and mode of existence—His defects and virtues, likings and antipathies—Croker—Sadler—Zachary Macaulay's circumstances—Description of the family habits of life in Great Ormond Street—Macaulay's sisters—Hannah Macaulay—the Judicious Poet—Macaulay's humour in conversation—His articles in the Review—His attacks on the Utilitarians and on Southey—Blackwood's Magazine—Macaulay is made Commissioner of Bankruptcy—Enters Parliament—Letters from Circuit and Edinburgh.

MACAULAY was called to the bar in 1826, and joined the Northern circuit. On the evening that he first appeared at mess, when the company were retiring for the night, he was observed to be carefully picking out the longest candle. An old King's Counsel, who noticed that he had a volume under his arm, remonstrated with him on the danger of reading in bed, upon which he rejoined with immense rapidity of utterance: 'I always read in bed at home; and, if I am not afraid of committing parricide, and matricide, and fratricide, I can hardly be expected to pay any special regard to the lives of the bagmen of Leeds.' And, so saying, he left his hearers staring at one another, and marched off to his room, little knowing that, before many years were out, he would have occasion to speak much more respectfully of the Leeds bagmen.

Under its social aspect Macaulay heartily enjoyed his legal career. He made an admirable literary use of the Saturnalia which the Northern circuit calls by the name of 'Grand Night,' when personalities of the most pronounced description are welcomed by all except the object of them, and forgiven even by him. His hand may be recognised in a macaronic poem, written in Greek and English, describing the feast at which Alexander murdered Clitus. The death of the victim is treated with an exuberance of fantastic drollery, and a song, put into the mouth of Nearchus, the admiral of Macedonian fleet, and beginning with the lines

When as first I did come back from ploughing the salt water
They paid me off at Salamis, three minæ and a quarter,—

is highly Aristophanic in every sense of the word.

He did not seriously look to the bar as a profession. No persuasion would induce him to return to his chambers in the evening, according to the practice then in vogue. After the first year or two of the period during which he called himself a barrister he gave up even the pretence of reading law, and spent many more hours under the gallery of the House of Commons, than in all the Courts together. The person who knew him best said of him: 'Throughout life he never really applied himself to any pursuit that was against the grain.' Nothing is more characteristic of the man than the contrast between his unconquerable aversion to the science of jurisprudence at the time when he was ostensibly preparing himself to be an advocate, and the zest with which, on his voyage to India, he mastered that science in principle and detail as soon as his imagination was fired by the prospect of the responsibilities of a law-giver.

He got no business worth mention, either in London or on circuit. Zachary Macaulay, who was not a man of the world, did what he could to make interest with the attorneys, and, as a last resource, proposed to his son to take a brief in a suit which he himself had instituted against the journal that had so grossly libelled him. 'I am rather glad,' writes Macaulay from York in March 1827, 'that I was not in London, if your advisers thought it right that I should have appeared as your counsel. Whether it be contrary to professional etiquette I do not know: but I am sure that it would be shocking to public feeling, and particularly imprudent against adversaries whose main strength lies in detecting and exposing indecorum or eccentricity. It would have been difficult to avoid a quarrel with Sugden, with Wetherell, and with old Lord Eldon himself. Then the John Bull would have been upon us with every advantage. The personal part of the consideration it would have been my duty, and my pleasure and pride also, to overlook; but your interests must have suffered.'

Meanwhile he was busy enough in fields better adapted than the law to his talents and his temperament. He took a part in a meeting of the Anti-Slavery Society held at Freemasons' Tavern, on the 25th of June 1824, with the Duke of Gloucester in the chair. The Edinburgh Review described his speech as 'a display of eloquence so signal for rare and matured excellence that the most practised orator may well admire how it should have come from one who then for the first time addressed a public assembly.'

Those who know what the annual meeting of a well-organised and disciplined association is, may imagine the whirlwind of cheers which greeted the declaration that the hour was at hand when 'the peasant of Antilles will no longer crawl in listless and trembling dejection round a plantation from whose fruits he must derive no advantage, and a hut whose door yields him no protection; but, when his cheerful and voluntary labour is performed, he will return with the firm step and erect brow of a British citizen from the field which is his freehold to the cottage which is his castle.'

Surer promise of aptitude for political debate was afforded by the skill with which the young speaker turned to account the recent trial for sedition, and death in prison, of Smith, the Demerara missionary: an event which was fatal to Slavery in the West Indies in the same degree as the execution of John Brown was its deathblow in the United States. 'When this country has been endangered either by arbitrary power or popular delusion, truth has still possessed one irresistible organ, and justice one inviolable tribunal. That organ has been an English press, and that tribunal an English jury. But in those wretched islands we see a press more hostile to truth than any censor, and juries more insensible to justice than any Star Chamber. In those islands alone is exemplified the full meaning of the most tremendous of the curses denounced against the apostate Hebrews, "I will curse your blessings." We can prove this assertion out of the mouth of our adversaries. We remember, and God Almighty forbid that we ever should forget, how, at the trial of Mr. Smith, hatred regulated every proceeding, was substituted for every law, and allowed its victim no sanctuary in the house of mourning, no refuge in the very grave. Against the members of that court-martial the country has pronounced its verdict. But what is the line of defence taken by its advocates? It has been solemnly and repeatedly declared in the House of Commons that a jury composed of planters would have acted with far more injustice than did this court:—this court which has never found a single lawyer to stake his professional character on the legality of its proceedings. The argument is this. Things have doubtless been done which should not have been done. The court-martial sat without a jurisdiction; it convicted without evidence; it condemned to a punishment not warranted by law. But we must make allowances. We must judge by comparison. "Mr. Smith ought to have been very thankful that it was no worse. Only think what would have been his fate if he had been tried by a jury of planters!" Sir, I have always lived under the protection of the British laws, and therefore I am unable to imagine what could be worse: but, though I have small knowledge, I have a large faith: I by no means presume to set any limits to the possible injustice of a West Indian judicature. And since the colonists maintain that a jury composed of their own body not only possibly might, but necessarily must, have acted with more iniquity than this court-martial, I certainly shall not dispute the assertion, though I am utterly unable to conceive the mode.'

That was probably the happiest half-hour of Zachary Macaulay's life. 'My friend,' said Wilberforce, when his turn came to speak, 'would doubtless willingly bear with all the base falsehoods, all the vile calumnies, all the detestable artifices which have been aimed against him, to render him the martyr and victim of our cause, for the gratification he has this day enjoyed in hearing one so dear to him plead such a cause in such a manner.' Keen as his pleasure was, he took it in his own sad way. From the first moment to the last, he never moved a muscle of his countenance, but sat with his eyes fixed on a piece of paper, on which he seemed to be writing with a pencil. While talking with his son that evening, he referred to what had passed only to remark that it was ungraceful in so young a man to speak with folded arms in the presence of royalty.[1]

In 1823 the leading members of the cleverest set of boys who ever were together at a public school found themselves collected once more at Cambridge. Of the former staff of the Etonian, Praed, Moultrie, Nelson Coleridge, and, among others, Mr. Edmond Beales, so well known to our generation as an ardent politician, were now in residence at King's or Trinity. Mr. Charles Knight, too enterprising a publisher to let such a quantity of youthful talent run to waste, started a periodical, which was largely supported by undergraduates and Bachelors of Arts, among whom the veterans of the Eton press formed a brilliant, and, as he vainly hoped, a reliable nucleus of contributors.

Knight's Quarterly Magazine is full of Macaulay, and of Macaulay in the attractive shape which a great author wears while he is still writing to please no one but himself. He unfortunately did not at all please his

[1] See Appendix I at the end of the volume.

father. In the first number, besides a great deal of his that is still worth reading, there were printed under his adopted signature of Tristram Merton two little poems, the nature of which may be guessed from Praed's editorial comments. 'Tristram Merton, I have a strong curiosity to know who Rosamund is. But you will not tell me: and, after all, as far as your verses are concerned, the surname is nowise germane to the matter. As poor Sheridan said, it is too formal to be registered in love's calendar.' And again: 'Tristram, I hope Rosamund and your Fair Girl of France will not pull caps: but I cannot forbear the temptation of introducing your Roxana and Statira to an admiring public.' The verses were such as any man would willingly look back to having written at two and twenty; but their appearance occasioned real misery to Zachary Macaulay, who indeed disapproved of the whole publication from beginning to end, with the exception of an article on West Indian Slavery which his son had inserted with the most filial intention, but which, it must be allowed, was not quite in keeping with the general character of the magazine.

July 9, 1823.

My dear Father,—

I have seen the two last letters which you have sent to my mother. They have given me deep pain; but pain without remorse. I am conscious of no misconduct, and whatever uneasiness I may feel arises solely from sympathy for your distress.

You seem to imagine that the book is edited, or principally written, by friends of mine. I thought that you had been aware that the work is conducted in London, and that my friends and myself are merely contributors, and form a very small proportion of the contributors. The manners of almost all of my acquaintances are so utterly alien from coarseness, and their morals from libertinism, that I feel assured that no objection of that nature can exist to their writings. As to my own contributions I can only say that the Roman Story was read to my mother before it was published, and would have been read to you if you had happened to be at home. Not one syllable of censure was uttered.

The Essay on the Royal Society of Literature was read to you. I made the alterations which I conceived that you desired, and submitted them afterwards to my mother. As to the poetry which you parallel with Little's, if anything vulgar or licentious has been written by myself, I am willing to bear the consequences. If anything of that cast has been written by my friends, I allow that a certain degree of blame attaches to me for having chosen them at least indiscreetly. If, however, a bookseller of whom we knew nothing has coupled improper productions with ours in a work over which we had no control, I cannot plead guilty to anything more than misfortune: a misfortune in which some of the most rigidly moral and religious men of my acquaintance have participated in the present instance.

I am pleading at random for a book which I never saw. I am defending the works of people most of whose names I never heard. I am therefore writing under great disadvantages. I write also in great haste. I am unable even to read over what I have written.

Affectionately yours

T. B. M.

Moved by the father's evident unhappiness, the son promised never to write again for the obnoxious periodical. The second number was so dull and decorous that Zachary Macaulay, who felt that, if the magazine went on through successive quarters reforming its tone in the same proportion, it would soon be on a level of virtue with the Christian Observer, withdrew his objection; and the young man wrote regularly till the short life of the undertaking ended in something very like a quarrel between the publisher and his contributors. It is not the province of biography to dilate upon works which are already before the world; and the results of Macaulay's literary labour during the years 1823 and 1824 have been, perhaps, only too freely reproduced in the volumes which contain his miscellaneous writings. It is, however, worthy of notice that among his earlier efforts in literature his own decided favourite was 'the Conversation between Mr. Abraham Cowley and Mr. John Milton touching the great Civil War.' But an author, who is exempt from vanity, is inclined to rate his own works rather according as they are free from faults than as they abound in beauties; and Macaulay's readers will very generally give the preference to two fragmentary sketches of Roman and Athenian society which sparkle with life, and humour, and a masculine vigorous fancy that had not yet learned to obey the rein. Their crude but genuine merit suggests a regret that he did not in after days enrich the Edinburgh Review with a couple of articles on classical subjects, as a sample of that ripened scholarship which produced the Prophecy of Capys, and the episode relating to the Phalaris controversy in the Essay on Sir William Temple.

Rothley Temple: October 7, 1824.

My dear Father,—

As to Knight's Magazine, I really do not think that, considering the circumstances under which it is conducted, it can be much censured. Every magazine must contain a certain quantity of mere ballast, of no value but as it occupies space. The general tone and spirit of the work will stand a comparison, in a moral point of view, with any periodical publication not professedly religious. I will venture to say that nothing has appeared in it, at least from the first number, from the pen of any of my friends, which can offend the most fastidious. Knight is absolutely in our hands, and most desirous to gratify us all, and me in particular. When I see you in London I will mention to you a piece of secret history which will show you how important our connection with this work may possibly become.

Yours affectionately

T. B. M.

The 'piece of secret history' above referred to was beyond a doubt the commencement of Macaulay's connection with the Edinburgh Review. That famous periodical, which for three and twenty years had shared in and promoted the rising fortune of the Liberal cause, had now attained its height—a height unequalled before or since—of political, social, and literary power. To have the entry of its columns was to command the most direct channel for the spread of opinions, and the shortest road to influence and celebrity. But already the anxious eye of the master seemed to discern symptoms of decline. Jeffrey, in Lord Cockburn's phrase, was 'growing feverish about new writers.' In January 1825 he says in a letter to a friend in London: 'Can you not lay your hands on some clever young man who would write for us? The original supporters of the work are getting old, and either too busy or too stupid, and here the young men are mostly Tories.' Overtures had already been made to Macaulay, and that same year his article on Milton appeared in the August number.

The effect on the author's reputation was instantaneous. Like Lord Byron, he awoke one morning and found himself famous. The beauties of the work were such as all men could recognise, and its very faults pleased. The redundance of youthful enthusiasm which he himself unsparingly condemns in the preface to his collected essays, seemed graceful enough in the eyes of others, if it were only as a relief from the perverted ability of that elaborate libel on our great epic poet which goes by the name of Dr. Johnson's Life of Milton. Murray declared that it would be worth the copyright of Childe Harold to have Macaulay on the staff of the Quarterly. The family breakfast table in Bloomsbury was covered with cards of invitation to dinner from every quarter of London, and his father groaned in spirit over the conviction that thenceforward the law would be less to him than ever. A warm admirer of Robert Hall, Macaulay heard with pride how the great preacher, then well-nigh worn out with that long disease, his life, was discovered lying on the floor, employed in learning by aid of grammar and dictionary enough Italian to enable him to verify the parallel between Milton and Dante. But the compliment that of all others came most nearly home,—the only commendation of his literary talent which even in the innermost domestic circle he was ever known to repeat,—was the sentence with which Jeffrey acknowledged the receipt of his manuscript: 'The more I think, the less I can conceive where you picked up that style.'

Macaulay's outward man was never better described than in two sentences of Praed's Introduction to Knight's Quarterly Magazine. 'There came up a short manly figure, marvellously upright, with a bad neckcloth,[1] and one hand in his waistcoat pocket. Of regular beauty he had little to boast; but in faces where there is an expression of great power, or of great good humour, or both, you do not regret its absence.' This picture, in which every touch is correct, tells all that there is to be told. He had a massive head, and features of a powerful and rugged cast, but so constantly lit up by every joyful and ennobling emotion that it mattered little if, when absolutely quiescent,

[1] 'I well remember,' writes Sir William Stirling Maxwell, 'the first time I met him,—in 1845 or '46, I think,—at dinner at the house of his old friend, Sir John Macleod. I did not know him by sight, and, when he came into the room with two or three other guests, I supposed that he was announced as "General"—I forget what. The party was large, and I was on the other side of the table, and a good way off. But I was very soon struck by the amazing number of subjects on which he seemed at home;—politics, home and foreign,—French literature, and Hebrew poetry;—and I remember thinking, "This is a General with a singularly well-stored mind and badly tied neckcloth." Till, at last, a remark on the prose of Dryden led me to conclude that it could be no one but the Great Essayist.'

his face was rather homely than handsome. While conversing at table no one thought him otherwise than good-looking; but, when he rose, he was seen to be short and stout in figure. 'At Holland House, the other day,' writes his sister Margaret in September 1831, 'Tom met Lady Lyndhurst for the first time. She said to him: "Mr. Macaulay, you are so different to what I expected. I thought you were dark and thin, but you are fair, and really, Mr. Macaulay, you are fat."' He at all times sat and stood straight, full, and square; and in this respect Woolner, in the fine statue at Cambridge, has missed what was undoubtedly the most marked fact in his personal appearance. He dressed badly, but not cheaply. His clothes, though ill put on, were good, and his wardrobe was always enormously overstocked. Later in life he indulged himself in an apparently inexhaustible succession of handsome embroidered waistcoats, which he used to regard with much complacency. He was unhandy to a degree quite unexampled in the experience of all who knew him. When in the open air he wore perfectly new dark kid gloves, into the fingers of which he never succeeded in inserting his own more than half way. After he had sailed for India there were found in his chambers between fifty and sixty strops, hacked into strips and splinters, and razors without beginning or end. About the same period he hurt his hand, and was reduced to send for a barber. After the operation, he asked what was to pay. 'Oh, Sir,' said the man, 'whatever you usually give the person who shaves you.' 'In that case,' said Macaulay, 'I should give you a great gash on each cheek.'

During an epoch when, at our principal seats of education, athletic pursuits are regarded as a leading object of existence rather than as a means of health and recreation, it requires some boldness to confess that Macaulay was utterly destitute of bodily accomplishments, and that he viewed his deficiencies with supreme indifference. He could neither swim, nor row, nor drive, nor skate, nor shoot. He seldom crossed a saddle, and never willingly. When in attendance at Windsor as a cabinet minister he was informed that a horse was at his disposal. 'If her Majesty wishes to see me ride,' he said, 'she must order out an elephant.' The only exercise in which he can be said to have excelled was that of threading crowded streets with his eyes fixed upon a book. He might be seen in such thoroughfares as Oxford Street, and Cheapside, walking as fast as other people walked, and reading a great deal faster than anybody else could read. As a pedestrian he was, indeed, above the average. Till he had passed fifty he thought nothing of going on foot from the Albany to Clapham, and from Clapham on to Greenwich; and, while still in the prime of life, he was for ever on his feet indoors as well as out. 'In those days,' says his cousin, Mrs. Conybeare, 'he walked rapidly up and down a room as he talked. I remember on one occasion, when he was making a call, he stopped short in his walk in the midst of a declamation on some subject, and said, "You have a brick floor here." The hostess confessed that it was true, though she hoped that had been disguised by double matting and a thick carpet. He said that his habit of always walking enabled him to tell accurately the material he was treading on.'

His faults were such as give annoyance to those who dislike a man rather than anxiety to those who love him. Vehemence, over-confidence, the inability to recognise that there are two sides to a question or two people in a dialogue, are defects which during youth are perhaps inseparable from gifts like those with which he was endowed. Moultrie, speaking of his undergraduate days, tells us that

To him
There was no pain like silence—no constraint
So dull as unanimity. He breathed
An atmosphere of argument, nor shrank
From making, where he could not find, excuse
For controversial fight.

At Cambridge he would say of himself that, whenever

anybody enunciated a proposition, all possible answers to it rushed into his mind at once; and it was said of him by others that he had no politics except the opposite of those held by the person with whom he was talking. To that charge, at any rate, he did not long continue liable. He left college a staunch and vehement Whig, eager to maintain against all comers, and at any moment, that none but Whig opinions had a leg to stand upon. His cousin George Babington, a rising surgeon, with whom at one time he lived in the closest intimacy, was always ready to take up the Tory cudgels. The two friends 'would walk up and down the room, crossing each other for hours, shouting one another down with a continuous simultaneous storm of words, until George at length yielded to arguments and lungs combined. Never, so far as I remember, was there any loss of temper. It was a fair, good-humoured, battle in not very mannerly lists.'

Even as a very young man nine people out of ten liked nothing better than to listen to him: which was fortunate; because in his early days he had scanty respect of persons, either as regarded the choice of his topics, or the quantity of his words. But with his excellent temper, and entire absence of conceit, he soon began to learn consideration for others in small things as well as in great. By the time he was fairly launched in London he was agreeable in company, as well as forcible and amusing. Wilberforce speaks of his 'unruffled good-humour.' Sir Robert Inglis, a good observer with ample opportunity of forming a judgment, pronounced that he conversed and did not dictate, and that he was loud but never overbearing. As far back as the year 1826 Crabb Robinson gave a very favourable account of his demeanour in society, which deserves credence as the testimony of one who liked his share of talk, and was not willing to be put in the background for anybody. 'I went to James Stephen, and drove with him to his house at Hendon. A dinner party. I had a most interesting companion in young Macaulay, one of the most promising of the rising generation I have seen for a long time. He has a good face,—not the delicate features of a man of genius and sensibility, but the strong lines and well-knit limbs of a man sturdy in body and mind. Very eloquent and cheerful. Overflowing with words, and not poor in thought. Liberal in opinion, but no radical. He seems a correct as well as a full man. He showed a minute knowledge of subjects not introduced by himself.'

So loyal and sincere was Macaulay's nature that he was unwilling to live upon terms of even apparent intimacy with people whom he did not like, or could not esteem; and, as far as civility allowed, he avoided their advances, and especially their hospitality. He did not choose, he said, to eat salt with a man for whom he could not say a good word in all companies. He was true throughout life to those who had once acquired his regard and respect. Moultrie says of him:

> His heart was pure and simple as a child's
> Unbreathed on by the world: in friendship warm,
> Confiding, generous, constant; and, though now
> He ranks among the great ones of the earth
> And hath achieved such glory as will last
> To future generations, he, I think,
> Would sup on oysters with as right good will
> In this poor home of mine as e'er he did
> On Petty Cury's classical first floor
> Some twenty years ago.

He loved to place his purse, his influence, and his talents at the disposal of a friend; and anyone whom he called by that name he judged with indulgence, and trusted with a faith that would endure almost any strain. If his confidence proved to have been egregiously misplaced, which he was always the last to see, he did not resort to remonstrance or recrimination. His course under such circumstances he described in a couplet from an old French comedy:[1]

> Le bruit est pour le fat, la plainte pour le sot;
> L'honnête homme trompé s'éloigne et ne dit mot.

[1] 'La Coquette corrigée. Comédie par Mr. Delanoue,

He was never known to take part in any family quarrel, or personal broil, of any description whatsoever. His conduct in this respect was the result of self-discipline, and did not proceed from any want of sensibility. 'He is very sensitive,' said his sister Margaret, 'and remembers long, as well as feels deeply, anything in the form of slight.' Indeed, at college his friends used to tell him that his leading qualities were 'generosity and vindictiveness.' Courage he certainly did not lack. During the years when his spirit was high, and his pen cut deep, and when the habits of society were different from what they are at present, more than one adversary displayed symptoms of a desire to meet him elsewhere than on paper. On these occasions, while showing consideration for his opponent, he evinced a quiet but very decided sense of what was due to himself which commanded the respect of all who were implicated, and brought difficulties that might have been grave to an honourable and satisfactory issue.

He reserved his pugnacity for quarrels undertaken on public grounds, and fought out with the world looking on as umpire. In the lists of criticism and of debate it cannot be denied that, as a young man, he sometimes deserved the praise which Dr. Johnson pronounced upon a good hater. He had no mercy for bad writers, and notably for bad poets, unless they were in want of money; in which case he became within his means the most open-handed of patrons. He was too apt to undervalue both the heart and the head of those who desired to maintain the old system of civil and religious exclusion, and who grudged political power to their fellow-countrymen, or at any rate to those of their fellow-countrymen whom he was himself prepared to enfranchise. Independent, frank, and proud almost to a fault, he detested the whole

1756.' In his journal of February 15, 1851, after quoting the couplet, Macaulay adds: 'Odd that two lines of a damned play, and, it should seem, a justly damned play, should have lived near a century and have become proverbial.'

race of jobbers and time-servers, parasites and scandal-mongers, led-captains, led-authors, and led-orators. Some of his antipathies have stamped themselves indelibly upon literary history. He attributed to the Right Honourable John Wilson Croker, Secretary to the Admiralty during the twenty years preceding 1830, qualities which excited his disapprobation beyond control, and possibly beyond measure. His judgment has been confirmed by the public voice, which identifies Croker with the character of Rigby in Mr. Disraeli's Coningsby.

Macaulay was the more formidable as an opponent because he could be angry without losing his command of the situation. His first onset was terrific; but in the fiercest excitement of the mêlée he knew when to call a halt. A certain member of Parliament named Michael Thomas Sadler had fallen foul of Malthus, and very foul indeed of Macaulay, who in two short and telling articles took revenge enough for both.[1] He writes on this subject to Mr. Macvey Napier, who towards the close of 1829 had succeeded Jeffrey in the editorship of the Edinburgh Review: 'The position which we have now taken up is absolutely impregnable, and, if we were to quit it, though we might win a more splendid victory, we should expose ourselves to some risk. My rule in controversy has always been that to which the Lacedæmonians adhered in war: never to break the ranks for the purpose of pursuing a beaten enemy.' He had, indeed, seldom occasion to strike twice. Where he set his mark, there was no need of a second impression. The unduly severe fate of those who crossed his path during the years when his blood was hot teaches a serious lesson on the responsibilities of genius. Croker, and Sadler, and poor Robert Montgomery, and the other less

[1] Macaulay writes to Mr. Napier in February 1831: 'People here think that I have answered Sadler completely. Empson tells me that Malthus is well pleased, which is a good sign. As to Blackwood's trash, I could not get through it. It bore the same relation to Sadler's pamphlet that a bad hash bears to a bad joint.'

eminent objects of his wrath, appear likely to enjoy just so much notoriety, and of such a nature, as he has thought fit to deal out to them in his pages; and it is possible that even Lord Ellenborough may be better known to our grand-children by Macaulay's oration on the gates of Somnauth than by the noise of his own deeds, or the echo of his own eloquence.

When Macaulay went to college he was justified in regarding himself as one who would not have to work for his bread. His father, who believed himself to be already worth a hundred thousand pounds, had statedly declared to the young man his intention of making him, in a modest way, an eldest son; and had informed him that, by doing his duty at the university, he would earn the privilege of shaping his career at choice. In 1818 the family removed to London, and set up an establishment on a scale suited to their improved circumstances in Cadogan Place, which, in everything except proximity to Bond Street, was then hardly less rural than Clapham. But the prosperity of the house of Macaulay and Babington was short-lived. The senior member of the firm gave his whole heart, and five-sixths of his time, to objects unconnected with his business; and he had selected a partner who did not possess the qualities necessary to compensate for his own deficiencies. In 1819 the first indications of possible disaster began to show themselves in the letters to and from Cambridge; while waiting for a fellowship Macaulay was glad to make a hundred guineas by taking pupils; and, as time went on, it became evident that he was to be an eldest son only in the sense that, throughout the coming years of difficulty and distress, his brothers and sisters would depend mainly upon him for comfort, guidance, and support. He acknowledged the claim cheerfully, lovingly, and, indeed, almost unconsciously. It was not in his disposition to murmur over what was inevitable, or to plume himself upon doing what was right. He quietly took up the burden which his father was unable to bear; and, before many years had elapsed, the fortunes of all for whose welfare he considered himself responsible were abundantly assured. In the course of the efforts which he expended on the accomplishment of this result he unlearned the very notion of framing his method of life with a view to his own pleasure; and such was his high and simple nature, that it may well be doubted whether it ever crossed his mind that to live wholly for others was a sacrifice at all.

He resided with his father in Cadogan Place, and accompanied him when, under the pressure of pecuniary circumstances, he removed to a less fashionable quarter of the town. In 1823 the family settled in 50 Great Ormond Street, which runs east and west for some three hundred yards through the region bounded by the British Museum, the Foundling Hospital, and Gray's Inn Road. It was a large rambling house, at the corner of Powis Place, and was said to have been the residence of Lord Chancellor Thurlow at the time when the Great Seal was stolen from his custody. It now forms the east wing of an Homœopathic hospital. Here the Macaulays remained till 1831. 'Those were to me,' says Lady Trevelyan, 'years of intense happiness. There might be money troubles, but they did not touch us. Our lives were passed after a fashion which would seem indeed strange to the present generation. My father, ever more and more engrossed in one object, gradually gave up all society; and my mother never could endure it. We had friends, of course, with whom we stayed out for months together; and we dined with the Wilberforces, the Buxtons, Sir Robert Inglis, and others: but what is now meant by "society" was utterly unknown to us.

'In the morning there was some pretence of work and study. In the afternoon your uncle always took my sister Margaret and myself a long walk. We traversed every part of the City, Islington, Clerkenwell, and the Parks, returning just in time for a six o'clock dinner. What anecdotes he used to pour out about every street, and square, and court, and alley!

There are many places I never pass without "the tender grace of a day that is dead" coming back to me. Then, after dinner, he always walked up and down the drawing-room between us chatting till tea-time. Our noisy mirth, his wretched puns, so many a minute, so many an hour! Then we sang, none of us having any voices, and he, if possible, least of all: but still the old nursery songs were set to music and chanted. My father, sitting at his own table, used to look up occasionally, and push back his spectacles, and, I dare say, wonder in his heart how we could so waste our time. After tea the book then in reading was produced. Your uncle very seldom read aloud himself of an evening, but walked about listening, and commenting, and drinking water.

'The Sundays were in some respects trying days to him. My father's habit was to read a long sermon to us all in the afternoon, and again after evening service another long sermon was read at prayer-time to the servants. Our doors were open to sons of relations or friends; and cousins who were medical students, or clerks in merchants' houses, came in regularly to partake of our Sunday dinner and sermons. Sunday walking, for walking's sake, was never allowed; and even going to a distant church was discouraged. When in Cadogan Place, we always crossed the Five Fields, where Belgrave Square now stands, to hear Dr. Thorpe at the Lock Chapel, and bring him home to dine with us. From Great Ormond Street, we attended St. John's Chapel in Bedford Row, then served by Daniel Wilson, afterwards Bishop of Calcutta. He was succeeded in 1826 by the Rev. Baptist Noel. Your uncle generally went to church with us in the morning, and latterly formed the habit of walking out of town, alone or with a friend, in the after part of the day. I never heard that my father took any notice of this; and, indeed, in the interior of his own family, he never attempted in the smallest degree to check his son in his mode of life, or in the expression of his opinions.

'I believe that breakfast was the pleasantest part of the day to my father. His spirits were then at their best, and he was most disposed to general conversation. He delighted in discussing the newspaper with his son, and lingered over the table long after the meal was finished. On this account he felt it extremely when, in the year 1829, your uncle went to live in chambers, and often said to my mother that the change had taken the brightness out of his day. Though your uncle generally dined with us, yet my father was tired by the evening, so that the breakfast hour was a grievous loss to him, as indeed it was to us all. Truly he was to old and young alike the sunshine of our home; and I believe that no one, who did not know him there, ever knew him in his most brilliant, witty, and fertile vein.'

That home was never more cheerful than during the eight years which followed the close of Macaulay's college life. There had been much quiet happiness at Clapham, and much in Cadogan Place; but it was round the house in Great Ormond Street that the dearest associations gathered. More than forty years afterwards, when Lady Trevelyan was dying, she had herself driven to the spot, as the last drive she ever took, and sat silent in her carriage for many minutes with her eyes fixed upon those well-known walls.[1]

While warmly attached to all his nearest relations, Macaulay lived in the closest and most frequent companionship with his sisters Hannah and Margaret, younger than himself by ten and twelve years respectively. His affection for these two, deep and enduring

[1] In August 1857, Macaulay notes in his diary: 'I sent the carriage home, and walked to the Museum. Passing through Great Ormond Street I saw a bill upon No. 50. I knocked, was let in, and went over the house with a strange mixture of feelings. It is more than twenty-six years since I was in it. The dining-room, and the adjoining room, in which I once slept, are scarcely changed;—the same colouring on the wall, but more dingy. My father's study much the same;—the drawing-rooms too, except the papering. My bedroom just what it was. My mother's bedroom. I had never been in it since her death. I went away sad.'

as it was, had in it no element of blindness or infatuation. Even in the privacy of a diary, or the confidence of the most familiar correspondence, Macaulay, when writing about those whom he loved, was never tempted to indulge in fond exaggeration of their merits. Margaret, as will be seen in the course of this narrative, died young, leaving a memory of outward graces, and sweet and noble mental qualities, which is treasured by all among whom her short existence was passed. As regards the other sister, there are many alive who knew her for what she was; and, for those who did not know her, if this book proves how much of her brother's heart she had, and how well it was worth having, her children will feel that they have repaid their debt even to her.

Education in the Macaulay family was not on system. Of what are ordinarily called accomplishments the daughters had but few, and Hannah fewest of any; but, ever since she could remember anything, she had enjoyed the run of a good standard library, and had been allowed to read at her own time, and according to her own fancy. There were two traits in her nature which are seldom united in the same person: a vivid practical interest in the realities which surrounded her, joined with the power of passing at will into a world of literature and romance in which she found herself entirely at home. The feeling with which Macaulay and his sister regarded books differed from that of other people in kind rather than in degree. When they were discoursing together about a work of history or biography, a bystander would have supposed that they had lived in the times of which the author treated, and had a personal acquaintance with every human being who was mentioned in his pages. Pepys, Addison, Horace Walpole, Dr. Johnson, Madame de Genlis, the Duc de St. Simon, and the several societies in which those worthies moved, excited in their minds precisely the same sort of concern, and gave matter for discussions of exactly the same type, as most people bestow upon the proceedings of their own contemporaries. The past was to them as the present, and the fictitious as the actual. The older novels, which had been the food of their early years, had become part of themselves to such an extent that, in speaking to each other, they frequently employed sentences from dialogues in those novels to express the idea, or even the business, of the moment. On matters of the street or of the household they would use the very language of Mrs. Elton and Mrs. Bennet, Mr. Woodhouse, Mr. Collins, and John Thorpe, and the other inimitable actors on Jane Austen's unpretending stage: while they would debate the love affairs and the social relations of their own circle in a series of quotations from Sir Charles Grandison or Evelina.

The effect was at times nothing less than bewildering. When Lady Trevelyan married, her husband, whose reading had lain anywhere rather than among the circulating libraries, used at first to wonder who the extraordinary people could be with whom his wife and his brother-in-law appeared to have lived. This style of thought and conversation had for young minds a singular and a not unhealthy fascination. Lady Trevelyan's children were brought up among books, (to use the homely simile of an American author), as a stable-boy among horses. The shelves of the library, instead of frowning on us as we played and talked, seemed alive with kindly and familiar faces. But death came, and came again, and then all was changed, and changed as in an instant. There were many favourite volumes out of which the spirit seemed to vanish at once and for ever. We endeavoured unsuccessfully to revive by our own efforts the amusement which we had been taught to find in the faded flatteries and absurdities that passed between Miss Seward and her admirers, or to retrace for ourselves the complications of female jealousy which played round Cowper's tea-table at Olney. We awoke to the discovery that the charm was not in us, nor altogether in the books themselves. The talisman, which endowed with life and meaning all that it touched, had passed away from among us, leaving recollections which are our most cherished, as they must ever be our proudest, possession.

Macaulay thought it probable that he could re-write Sir Charles Grandison from memory, and certainly he might have done so with his sister's help. But his intimate acquaintance with a work was no proof of its merit. 'There was a certain prolific author,' says Lady Trevelyan, 'named Mrs. Meeke, whose romances he all but knew by heart; though he quite agreed in my criticism that they were one just like another, turning on the fortunes of some young man in a very low rank of life who eventually proves to be the son of a Duke. Then there was a set of books by a Mrs. Kitty Cuthbertson, most silly though readable productions, the nature of which may be guessed from their titles:— 'Santo Sebastiano, or the Young Protector,' 'The Forest of Montalbano,' 'The Romance of the Pyrenees,' and 'Adelaide, or the Countercharm.' I remember how, when 'Santo Sebastiano' was sold by auction in India, he and Miss Eden bid against each other till he secured it at a fabulous price; and I possess it still.'

As an indication of the thoroughness with which this literary treasure has been studied, there appears on the last page an elaborate computation of the number of fainting-fits that occur in the course of the five volumes.

Julia de Clifford	11
Lady Delamore	4
Lady Theodosia	4
Lord Glenbrook	2
Lord Delamore	2
Lady Enderfield	1
Lord Ashgrove	1
Lord St. Orville	1
Henry Mildmay	1

A single passage, selected for no other reason than because it is the shortest, will serve as a specimen of these catastrophes: 'One of the sweetest smiles that ever animated the face of mortal now diffused itself over the countenance of Lord St. Orville, as he fell at the feet of Julia in a death-like swoon.'

The fun that went on in Great Ormond Street was of a jovial, and sometimes uproarious, description. Even when the family was by itself, the school-room and the drawing-room were full of young people; and friends and cousins flocked in numbers to a resort where so much merriment was perpetually on foot. There were seasons during the school holidays when the house overflowed with noise and frolic from morning to night; and Macaulay, who at any period of his life could literally spend whole days in playing with children, was master of the innocent revels. Games of hide-and-seek, that lasted for hours, with shouting and the blowing of horns up and down the stairs and through every room, were varied by ballads, which, like the Scalds of old, he composed during the act of recitation, while the others struck in with the chorus. He had no notion whatever of music, but an infallible ear for rhythm. His knack of improvisation he at all times exercised freely. The verses which he thus produced, and which he invariably attributed to an anonymous author whom he styled 'the Judicious Poet,' were exclusively for home consumption. Some of these effusions illustrate a sentiment in his disposition which was among the most decided, and the most frequently and loudly expressed. Macaulay was only too easily bored, and those whom he considered fools he by no means suffered gladly. He once amused his sisters by pouring out whole Iliads of extempore doggrel upon the head of an unfortunate country squire of their acquaintance, who had a habit of detaining people by the button, and who was especially addicted to the society of the higher order of clergy.

> His Grace Archbishop Manners Sutton
> Could not keep on a single button.
> As for Right Reverend John of Chester,
> His waistcoats open at the breast are.

Our friend[1] has filled a mighty trunk
With trophies torn from Doctor Monk,
And he has really tattered foully
The vestments of Archbishop Howley.
No button could I late discern on
The garments of Archbishop Vernon,
And never had his fingers mercy
Upon the garb of Bishop Percy.
The buttons fly from Bishop Ryder
Like corks that spring from bottled cyder,—

and so on, throughout the entire bench, until, after a good half-hour of hearty and spontaneous nonsense, the girls would go laughing back to their Italian and their drawing-boards.

He did not play upon words as a habit, nor did he interlard his talk with far-fetched or overstrained witticisms. His humour, like his rhetoric, was full of force and substance, and arose naturally from the complexion of the conversation or the circumstance of the moment. But when alone with his sisters, and, in after years, with his nieces, he was fond of setting himself deliberately to manufacture conceits resembling those on the heroes of the Trojan War which have been thought worthy of publication in the collected works of Swift. When walking in London he would undertake to give some droll turn to the name of every shopkeeper in the street, and, when travelling, to the name of every station along the line. At home he would run through the countries of Europe, the States of the Union, the chief cities of our Indian Empire, the provinces of France, the Prime Ministers of England, or the chief writers and artists of any given century; striking off puns, admirable, endurable, and execrable, but all irresistibly laughable, which followed each other in showers like sparks from flint. Capping verses was a game of which he never tired. 'In the spring of 1829,' says his cousin Mrs. Conybeare, 'we were staying in Ormond Street. My chief

[1] The name of this gentleman has been concealed, as not being sufficiently known by all to give point, but well enough remembered by some to give pain.

recollection of your uncle during that visit is on the evenings when we capped verses. All the family were quick at it, but his astounding memory made him supereminent. When the time came for him to be off to bed at his chambers, he would rush out of the room uttering some long-sought line, and would be pursued to the top of the stairs by one of the others who had contrived to recall a verse which served the purpose, in order that he might not leave the house victorious: but he, with the hall-door open in his hand, would shriek back a crowning effort, and go off triumphant.'

Nothing of all this can be traced in his letters before the year 1830. Up to that period he corresponded regularly with no one but his father, between whom and himself there existed a strong regard, but scanty sympathy or similarity of pursuits. It was not until he poured out his mind almost daily to those who approached him more nearly in age, and in tastes, that the lighter side of his nature began to display itself on paper. Most of what he addressed to his parents between the time when he left Cambridge, and the time when he entered the House of Commons, may be characterised as belonging to the type of duty-letters, treating of politics, legal gossip, personal adventures, and domestic incidents, with some reticence and little warmth or ease of expression. The periodical insertion on the son's part of anecdotes and observations bearing upon the question of Slavery reminds the reader of those presents of tall recruits with which, at judiciously chosen intervals, Frederic the Great used to conciliate his terrible father. As between the Macaulays, these little filial attentions acquire a certain gracefulness from the fact that, in the circumstances of the family, they could be prompted by no other motive than a dutiful and disinterested affection.

It must not be supposed,—no one who examines the dates of his successive essays will for a moment suppose,—that his attention was distracted, or his energy dissipated, by trifles. Besides the finished study of Machiavelli, and the masterly sketch of our great civil troubles known as the article on Hallam's Constitutional History, he produced much which his mature judgment would willingly have allowed to die, but which had plenty of life in it when it first appeared between the blue and yellow covers. His most formidable enterprise, during the five earliest years of his connection with the great Review, was that passage of arms against the champions of the Utilitarian philosophy in which he touched the mighty shields of James Mill and Jeremy Bentham, and rode slashing to right and left through the ranks of their less distinguished followers. Indeed, while he sincerely admired the chiefs of the school, he had a young man's prejudice against their disciples, many of whom he regarded as 'persons who, having read little or nothing, are delighted to be rescued from the sense of their own inferiority by some teacher who assures them that the studies which they have neglected are of no value, puts five or six phrases into their mouths, lends them an odd number of the Westminster Review, and in a month transforms them into philosophers.' It must be allowed that there was some colour for his opinion. The Benthamite training may have stimulated the finer intellects, (and they were not few,) which came within its influence; but it is impossible to conceive anything more dreary than must have been the condition of a shallow mind, with a native predisposition to sciolism, after its owner had joined a society 'composed of young men agreeing in fundamental principles, acknowledging Utility as their standard in ethics and politics,' 'meeting once a fortnight to read essays and discuss questions conformably to the premises thus agreed on,' and 'expecting the regeneration of mankind, not from any direct action on the sentiments of unselfish benevolence and love of justice, but from the effect of educated intellect enlightening the selfish feelings.' John Stuart Mill, with that candour which is the rarest of his great qualities, gave a generous and authoritative testimony to the merit of these attacks upon his father, and his father's creed, which Macaulay himself lived to wish that he had left unwritten.[1]

He was already famous enough to have incurred the inevitable penalty of success in the shape of the pronounced hostility of Blackwood's Magazine. The feelings which the leading contributors to that periodical habitually entertained towards a young and promising writer were in his case sharpened by political partisanship; and the just and measured severity which he infused into his criticism on Southey's 'Colloquies of Society' brought down upon him the bludgeon to whose strokes poetic tradition has attributed the death of Keats. Macaulay was made of harder stuff, and gave little heed to a string of unsavoury invectives compounded out of such epithets as 'ugly,' 'splay-footed,' and 'shapeless;' such phrases as 'stuff and nonsense,' 'malignant trash,' 'impertinent puppy,' and 'audacity of impudence;' and other samples from the polemical vocabulary of the personage who, by the irony of fate, filled the Chair of Moral Philosophy at Edinburgh. The substance of Professor Wilson's attacks consisted in little more than the reiteration of that charge of intellectual juvenility, which never fails to be employed as the last resource against a man whose abilities are undoubted, and whose character is above detraction.

'*North.* He's a clever lad, James.

'*Shepherd.* Evidently; and a clever lad he'll remain, depend ye upon that, a' the days of his life. A clever lad thirty

[1] 'The author has been strongly urged to insert three papers on the Utilitarian Philosophy, which, when they first appeared, attracted some notice. * * * He has, however, determined to omit these papers, not because he is disposed to retract a single doctrine which they contain, but because he is unwilling to offer what might be regarded as an affront to the memory of one from whose opinions he still widely dissents, but to whose talents and virtues he admits that he formerly did not do justice. * * It ought to be known that Mr. Mill had the generosity, not only to forgive, but to forget the unbecoming acrimony with which he had been assailed, and was, when his valuable life closed, on terms of cordial friendship with his assailant.'—Preface to Macaulay's Collected Essays.

years auld and some odds is to ma mind the maist melancholy sight in nature. Only think of a clever lad o' threescore-and-ten, on his deathbed, wha can look back on nae greater achievement than haeing aince, or aiblins ten times, abused Mr. Southey in the Embro' Review.'

The prophecies of jealousy seldom come true. Southey's book died before its author, with the exception of the passages extracted by Macaulay, which have been reproduced in his essay a hundred times, and more, for once that they were printed in the volumes from which he selected them for his animadversion.

The chambers in which he ought to have been spending his days, and did actually spend his nights between the years 1829 and 1834, were within five minutes' walk of the house in Great Ormond Street. The building of which those chambers formed a part,—8 South Square, Gray's Inn,—has since been pulled down to make room for an extension of the Library; a purpose which, in Macaulay's eyes, would amply compensate for the loss of such associations as might otherwise have attached themselves to the locality. His Trinity fellowship brought him in nearly three hundred pounds annually, and the Edinburgh Review nearly two hundred. In January 1828, during the interregnum that separated the resignation of Lord Goderich and the acceptance of the Premiership by the Duke of Wellington, Lord Lyndhurst made him a Commissioner of Bankruptcy; a rare piece of luck at a time when, as Lord Cockburn tells us, 'a youth of a Tory family, who was discovered to have leaning towards the doctrines of the opposition, was considered as a lost son.' 'The Commission is welcome,' Macaulay writes to his father, 'and I am particularly glad that it has been given at a time when there is no ministry, and when the acceptance of it implies no political obligation. To Lord Lyndhurst I of course feel personal gratitude, and I shall always take care how I speak of him.'

The emoluments of the office made up his income,

for the three or four years during which he held it, to about nine hundred pounds per annum. His means were more than sufficient for his wants, but too small, and far too precarious, for the furtherance of the political aspirations which now were uppermost in his mind. 'Public affairs,' writes Lady Trevelyan, 'were become intensely interesting to him. Canning's accession to power, then his death, the repeal of the Test Act, the Emancipation of the Catholics, all in their turn filled his heart and soul. He himself longed to be taking his part in Parliament, but with a very hopeless longing.

'In February 1830 I was staying at Mr. Wilberforce's at Highwood Hill when I got a letter from your uncle, enclosing one from Lord Lansdowne, who told him that he had been much struck by the articles on Mill, and that he wished to be the means of first introducing their author to public life by proposing to him to stand for the vacant seat at Calne. Lord Lansdowne expressly added that it was your uncle's high moral and private character which had determined him to make the offer, and that he wished in no respect to influence his votes, but to leave him quite at liberty to act according to his conscience. I remember flying into Mr. Wilberforce's study, and, absolutely speechless, putting the letter into his hands. He read it with much emotion, and returned it to me, saying: "Your father has had great trials, obloquy, bad health, many anxieties. One must feel as if Tom were given him for a recompense." He was silent for a moment, and then his mobile face lighted up, and he clapped his hand to his ear, and cried: "Ah! I hear that shout again. Hear! Hear! What a life it was!"'

And so, on the eve of the most momentous conflict that ever was fought out by speech and vote within the walls of a senate-house, the young recruit went gaily to his post in the ranks of that party whose coming fortunes he was prepared loyally to follow, and the history of whose past he was destined eloquently, and perhaps imperishably, to record.

York: April 2, 1826.

My dear Father,—

I am sorry that I have been unable to avail myself of the letters of introduction which you forwarded to me. Since I received them I have been confined to the house with a cold; and, now that I am pretty well recovered, I must take my departure for Pontefract. But, if it had been otherwise, I could not have presented these recommendations. Letters of this sort may be of great service to a barrister: but the barrister himself must not be the bearer of them. On this subject the rule is most strict, at least on our circuit. The hugging of the Bar, like the Simony of the Church, must be altogether carried on by the intervention of third persons. We are sensible of our dependence on the attorneys, and proportioned to that sense of dependence is our affectation of superiority. Even to take a meal with an attorney is a high misdemeanour. One of the most eminent men among us brought himself into a serious scrape by doing so. But to carry a letter of introduction, to wait in the outer room while it is being read, to be then ushered into the presence, to receive courtesies which can only be considered as the condescensions of a patron, to return courtesies which are little else than the blessings of a beggar, would be an infinitely more terrible violation of our professional code. Every barrister to whom I have applied for advice has most earnestly exhorted me on no account whatever to present the letters myself. I should perhaps add that my advisers have been persons who cannot by any possibility feel jealous of me.

In default of anything better I will eke out my paper with some lines which I made in bed last night,—an inscription for a picture of Voltaire.

If thou would'st view one more than man and less,
Made up of mean and great, of foul and fair,
Stop here: and weep and laugh, and curse and bless,
And spurn and worship; for thou seest Voltaire.

That flashing eye blasted the conqueror's spear,
The monarch's sceptre, and the Jesuit's beads;
And every wrinkle in that haggard sneer
Hath been the grave of Dynasties and Creeds.

In very wantonness of childish mirth
He puffed Bastilles, and thrones, and shrines away,
Insulted Heaven, and liberated earth.
Was it for good or evil? Who shall say?

Ever affectionately yours
T. B. M.

York: July 21, 1826.

My dear Father,—

The other day, as I was changing my neck-cloth which my wig had disfigured, my good landlady knocked at the door of my bedroom, and told me that Mr. Smith wished to see me, and was in my room below. Of all names by which men are called there is none which conveys a less determinate idea to the mind than that of Smith. Was he on the circuit? For I do not know half the names of my companions. Was he a special messenger from London? Was he a York attorney coming to be preyed upon, or a beggar coming to prey upon me, a barber to solicit the dressing of my wig, or a collector for the Jews' Society? Down I went, and to my utter amazement beheld the Smith of Smiths, Sydney Smith, alias Peter Plymley. I had forgotten his very existence till I discerned the queer contrast between his black coat and his snow-white head, and the equally curious contrast between the clerical amplitude of his person, and the most unclerical wit, whim, and petulance of his eye. I shook hands with him very heartily; and on the Catholic question we immediately fell, regretted Evans,[1] triumphed over Lord George Beresford, and abused the Bishops. He then very kindly urged me to spend the time between the close of the Assizes and the commencement of the Sessions at his house;

[1] These allusions refer to the general election which had recently taken place.

and was so hospitably pressing that I at last agreed to go thither on Saturday afternoon. He is to drive me over again into York on Monday morning. I am very well pleased at having this opportunity of becoming better acquainted with a man who, in spite of innumerable affectations and oddities, is certainly one of the wittiest and most original writers of our times.

Ever yours affectionately

T. B. M.

Bradford: July 26, 1826.

My dear Father,—

On Saturday I went to Sydney Smith's. His parish lies three or four miles out of any frequented road. He is, however, most pleasantly situated. 'Fifteen years ago,' said he to me, as I alighted at the gate of his shrubbery, 'I was taken up in Piccadilly and set down here. There was no house, and no garden; nothing but a bare field.' One service this eccentric divine has certainly rendered to the Church. He has built the very neatest, most commodious, and most appropriate rectory that I ever saw. All its decorations are in a peculiarly clerical style; grave, simple, and gothic. The bed-chambers are excellent, and excellently fitted up; the sitting-rooms handsome; and the grounds sufficiently pretty. Tindal and Parke, (not the judge of course,) two of the best lawyers, best scholars, and best men in England, were there. We passed an extremely pleasant evening, had a very good dinner, and many amusing anecdotes.

After breakfast the next morning I walked to church with Sydney Smith. The edifice is not at all in keeping with the rectory. It is a miserable little hovel with a wooden belfry. It was, however, well filled, and with decent people, who seemed to take very much to their pastor. I understand that he is a very respectable apothecary; and most liberal of his skill, his medicine, his soup, and his wine, among the sick. He preached a very queer sermon—the former half too familiar and the latter half too florid, but not without some ingenuity of thought and expression.

Sydney Smith brought me to York on Monday morning, in time for the stage-coach which runs to Skipton. We parted with many assurances of good-will. I have really taken a great liking to him. He is full of wit, humour, and shrewdness. He is not one of those show-talkers who reserve all their good things for special occasions. It seems to be his greatest luxury to keep his wife and daughters laughing for two or three hours every day. His notions of law, government, and trade are surprisingly clear and just. His misfortune is to have chosen a profession at once above him and below him. Zeal would have made him a prodigy; formality and bigotry would have made him a bishop; but he could neither rise to the duties of his order, nor stoop to its degradations.

He praised my articles in the Edinburgh Review with a warmth which I am willing to believe sincere, because he qualified his compliments with several very sensible cautions. My great danger, he said, was that of taking a tone of too much asperity and contempt in controversy. I believe that he is right, and I shall try to mend.

Ever affectionately yours

T. B. M.

Lancaster: September 1, 1827.

My dear Father,—

Thank Hannah from me for her pleasant letter. I would answer it if I had anything equally amusing to say in return; but here we have no news, except what comes from London, and is as stale as inland fish before it reaches us. We have circuit anecdotes to be sure; and perhaps you will be pleased to hear that Brougham has been rising through the whole of this struggle. At York Pollock decidedly took the lead. At Durham Brougham overtook him, passed him at Newcastle, and got immensely ahead of him at Carlisle and Appleby, which, to be sure, are the places where his own connections lie. We have not been here quite long enough to determine how he will succeed with the Lancastrians. This has always hitherto been his least favourable place. He appears to improve in industry and prudence. He learns his story more thoroughly, and tells it more clearly, than formerly. If he continues to manage causes as well as he has done of late he must rise to the summit of the profession. I cannot say quite so much for his temper, which this close and constant rivalry does not improve. He squabbles with Pollock more than, in generosity or policy, he ought to do. I have heard several of our younger men wondering that he does not show more magnanimity. He yawns while Pollock is speaking; a sign of weariness which, in their present relation to each other, he would do well to suppress. He has said some very good, but very bitter, things. There was a case of a lead-mine. Pollock was for the proprietors, and complained bitterly of the encroachments which Brougham's clients had made upon this property, which he represented as of immense value. Brougham said that the estimate which his learned friend formed of the property was vastly exaggerated, but that it was no wonder that a person who found it so easy to get gold for his lead should appreciate that heavy metal so highly. The other day Pollock laid down a point of law rather dogmatically. 'Mr. Pollock,' said Brougham, 'perhaps, before you rule the point, you will suffer his Lordship to submit a few observations on it to your consideration.'

I received the Edinburgh paper which you sent me. Silly and spiteful as it is, there is a little truth in it. In such cases I always remember those excellent lines of Boileau:

Moi, qu'une humeur trop libre, un esprit peu soumis,
De bonne heure a pourvu d'utiles ennemis,
Je dois plus à leur haine (il faut que je l'avoue)
Qu'au faible et vain talent dont la France me loue.
Sitôt que sur un vice ils pensent me confondre,
C'est en me guérissant que je sais leur répondre.

This place disagrees so much with me that I shall leave it as soon as the dispersion of the circuit commences,—that is, after the delivery of the last batch of briefs; always supposing, which may be supposed without much risk of mistake, that there are none for me.

Ever yours affectionately

T. B. M.

It was about this period that the Cambridge Senate came to a resolution to petition against the Catholic Claims. The minority demanded a poll, and conveyed a hint to their friends in London. Macaulay, with one or two more to help him, beat up the Inns of Court for recruits, chartered a stage-coach, packed it inside and out with young Whig Masters of Arts, and drove up King's Parade just in time to turn the scale in favour of Emancipation. The whole party dined in triumph at Trinity, and got back to town the same evening; and the Tory journalists were emphatic in their indignation at the deliberate opinion of the University having been overridden by a coachful of 'godless and briefless barristers.'

Court House, Pomfret: April 15, 1828.

My dear Mother,—

I address this epistle to you as the least undeserving of a very undeserving family. You, I think, have sent me one letter since I left London. I have nothing here to do but to write letters: and, what is not very often the case, I have members of Parliament in abundance to frank them, and abundance of matter to fill them with. My Edinburgh expedition has given me so much to say that, unless I write off some of it before I come home, I shall talk you all to death, and be voted a bore in every house which I visit. I will commence with Jeffrey himself. I had almost forgotten his person: and, indeed, I should not wonder if even now I were to forget it again. He has twenty faces almost as unlike each other as my father's to Mr. Wilberforce's, and infinitely more unlike to each other than those of near relatives often are; infinitely more unlike, for example, than those of the two Grants. When absolutely quiescent, reading a paper, or hearing a conversation in which he takes no interest, his countenance shows no indication whatever of intellectual superiority of any kind. But as soon as he is interested, and opens his eyes upon you, the change is like magic. There is a flash in his glance, a violent contortion in his frown, an exquisite humour in his sneer, and a sweetness and brilliancy in his smile, beyond anything that ever I witnessed. A person who had seen him in only one state would not know him if he saw him in another. For he has not, like Brougham, marked features which in all moods of mind remain unaltered. The mere outline of his face is insignificant. The expression is everything; and such power and variety of expression I never saw in any human countenance, not even in that of the most celebrated actors. I can conceive that Garrick may have been like him. I have seen several pictures of Garrick, none resembling another, and I have heard Hannah More speak of the extraordinary variety of countenance by which he was distinguished, and of the unequalled radiance and penetration of his eye. The voice and delivery of Jeffrey resemble his face. He possesses considerable power of mimicry, and rarely tells a story without imitating several different accents. His familiar tone, his declamatory tone, and his pathetic tone are quite different things. Sometimes Scotch predominates in his pronunciation; sometimes it is imperceptible. Sometimes his utterance is snappish and quick to the last degree; sometimes it is remarkable for rotundity and mellowness. I can easily conceive that two people who had seen him on different days might dispute about him as the travellers in the fable disputed about the chameleon.

In one thing, as far as I observed, he is always the same; and that is the warmth of his domestic affections. Neither Mr. Wilberforce, nor my uncle Babington, come up to him in this respect. The flow of his kindness is quite inexhaustible. Not five minutes pass without some fond expression, or caressing gesture, to his wife or his daughter. He has fitted up a study for himself: but he never goes into it. Law papers, reviews, whatever he has to write, he writes in the drawing-room, or in his wife's boudoir. When he goes to other parts of the country on a retainer he takes them in the carriage with him. I do not wonder that he should be a good husband: for his wife is a very amiable woman. But I was surprised to see a man so keen and sarcastic, so much of a scoffer, pouring himself out with such simplicity and tenderness in all sorts of affectionate nonsense. Through our whole journey to Perth he kept up a sort of mock quarrel with his daughter; attacked her about novel-reading, laughed her into a pet, kissed her out of it, and laughed her into it again. She and her mother absolutely idolise him, and I do not wonder at it.

His conversation is very much like his countenance and his voice, of immense variety; sometimes plain and unpretending even to flatness; sometimes whimsically brilliant and rhetorical almost beyond the licence of private discourse. He has many interesting anecdotes, and tells them very well. He is a shrewd observer; and so fastidious that I am not surprised at the awe in which many people seem to stand when in his company. Though not altogether free from affectation himself, he has a peculiar loathing for it in other people, and a great talent for discovering and exposing it. He has a particular contempt, in which I most heartily concur with him, for the *fadaises* of blue-stocking literature, for the mutual flatteries of coteries, the handing about of vers de société, the albums, the conversaziones, and all the other nauseous trickeries of the Sewards, Hayleys, and Sothebys. I am not quite sure that he has escaped the opposite extreme, and that he is not a little too desirous to appear rather a man of the world, an active lawyer, or an easy careless gentleman, than a distinguished writer. I must own that, when Jeffrey and I were by ourselves, he talked much and very well on literary topics. His kindness and hospitality to me were, indeed, beyond description: and his wife was as pleasant and friendly as possible. I liked everything but the hours. We were never up till ten, and never retired till two hours at least after midnight. Jeffrey, indeed, never goes to bed till sleep comes on him overpoweringly, and never rises till forced up by business or hunger. He is extremely well in health; so that I could not help suspecting him of being very hypochondriac; for all his late letters to me have been filled with lamentations about his various maladies. His wife told me, when I congratulated her on his recovery, that I must not absolutely rely on all his accounts of his own diseases. I really think that he is, on the whole, the youngest-looking man of fifty that I know, at least when he is animated.

His house is magnificent. It is in Moray Place, the newest pile of buildings in the town, looking out to the Forth on one side, and to a green garden on the other. It is really equal to the houses in Grosvenor Square. Fine, however, as is the new quarter of Edinburgh, I decidedly prefer the Old Town. There is nothing like it in the island. You have been there: but you have not seen the town: and no lady ever sees a town. It is only by walking on foot through all corners at all hours that cities can be really studied to good purpose. There is a new pillar to the memory of Lord Melville: very elegant, and very much better than the man deserved. His statue is at the top, with a wreath on the head very like a nightcap drawn over the eyes. It is impossible to look at it without being reminded of the fate which the original most richly merited. But my letter will overflow even the ample limits of a frank, if I do not conclude. I hope that you will be properly penitent for neglecting such a correspondent when you receive so long a dispatch, written amidst the bellowing of justices, lawyers, criers, witnesses, prisoners, and prisoners' wives and mothers.

Ever yours affectionately

T. B. M.

Lancaster: March 14, 1829.

My dear Father,—

A single line to say that I am at Lancaster. Where you all are I have not the very slightest notion. Pray let me hear. That dispersion of the Gentiles which our friends the prophets foretell seems to have commenced with our family.

Everything here is going on in the common routine. The only things of peculiar interest are those which we get from the London papers. All minds seem to be perfectly made up as to the certainty of Catholic Emancipation having come at last. The feeling of approbation among the barristers is all but unanimous. The quiet townspeople here, as far as I can see, are very well contented. As soon as I arrived I was asked by my landlady how things had gone. I told her the division, which I had learned from Brougham at Garstang. She seemed surprised at the majority. I asked her if she was against the measure. 'No; she only wished that all Christians would live in peace and charity together.' A very sensible speech, and better than one at least of the members for the county ever made in his life.

I implore you above everything, my dear Father, to keep up your health and spirits. Come what may, the conveniences of life, independence, our personal respectability, and the exercise of the intellect and the affections, we are almost certain of retaining: and everything else is a mere superfluity, to be enjoyed, but not to be missed. But I ought to be ashamed of reading you a lecture on qualities which you are so much more competent to teach than myself.

Ever yours very affectionately

T. B. M.

To Macvey Napier, Esq.

50 Great Ormond Street, London:
January 25, 1830.

My dear Sir,—

I send off by the mail of to-day an article on Southey,—too long, I fear, to meet your wishes, but as short as I could make it.

There were, by the bye, in my last article a few omissions made, of no great consequence in themselves; the longest, I think, a paragraph of twelve or fourteen lines. I should scarcely have thought this worth mentioning, as it certainly by no means exceeds the limits of that editorial prerogative which I most willingly recognise, but that the omissions seemed to me, and to one or two persons who had seen the article in its original state, to be made on a principle which, however sound in itself, does not I think apply to compositions of this description. The passages omitted were the most pointed and ornamented sentences in the review. Now, for high and grave works, a history for example, or a system of political or moral philosophy, Doctor Johnson's rule,—that every sentence which the writer thinks fine ought to be cut out,—is excellent. But periodical works like ours, which unless they strike at the first reading are not likely to strike at all, whose whole life is a month or two, may, I think, be allowed to be sometimes even viciously florid. Probably, in estimating the real value of any tinsel which I may put upon my articles, you and I should not materially differ. But it is not by his own taste, but by the taste of the fish, that the angler is determined in his choice of bait.

Perhaps after all I am ascribing to system what is mere accident. Be assured, at all events, that what I have said is said in perfect good humour, and indicates no mutinous disposition.

The Jews are about to petition Parliament for relief from the absurd restrictions which lie on them,—the last relique of the old system of intolerance. I have been applied to by some of them in the name of the managers of the scheme to write for them in the Edinburgh Review. I would gladly further a cause so good, and you, I think, could have no objection.

Ever yours truly

T. B. MACAULAY.

Bowood: February 10, 1830.

My dear Father,—

I am here in a very nice room, with perfect liberty, and a splendid library at my command. It seems to be thought desirable that I should stay in the neighbourhood, and pay my compliments to my future constituents every other day.

The house is splendid and elegant, yet more remarkable for comfort than for either elegance or splendour. I never saw any great place so thoroughly desirable for a residence. Lord Kerry tells me that his uncle left everything in ruin,—trees cut down, and rooms unfurnished,—and sold the library, which was extremely fine. Every book and picture in Bowood has been bought by the present Lord, and certainly the collection does him great honour.

I am glad that I stayed here. A burgess of some influence, who, at the last election, attempted to get up an opposition to the Lansdowne interest, has just arrived. I called on him this morning, and, though he was a little ungracious at first, succeeded in obtaining his promise. Without him, indeed, my return would have been secure; but both from motives of interest and from a sense of gratitude I think it best to leave nothing undone which may tend to keep Lord Lansdowne's influence here unimpaired against future elections.

Lord Kerry seems to me to be going on well. He has been in very good condition, he says, this week; and hopes to be at the election, and at the subsequent dinner. I do not know when I have taken so much to so young a man. In general my intimacies have been with my seniors: but Lord Kerry is really quite a favourite of mine,—kind, lively, intelligent, modest, with the gentle manners which indicate a long intimacy with the best society, and yet without the least affectation. We have oceans of beer, and mountains of potatoes, for dinner. Indeed, Lady Lansdowne drank beer most heartily on the only day which she passed with us, and, when I told her laughing that she set me at ease on a point which had given me much trouble, she said that she would never suffer any dandy novelist to rob her of her beer or her cheese.

The question between law and politics is a momentous one. As far as I am myself concerned, I should not hesitate: but the interest of my family is also to be considered. We shall see, however, before long what my chance of success as a public man may prove to be. At present it would clearly be wrong in me to show any disposition to quit my profession.

I hope that you will be on your guard as to what you may say to Brougham about this business. He is so angry at it that he cannot keep his anger to himself. I know that he has blamed Lord Lansdowne in the robing-room of the Court of King's Bench. The seat ought, he says, to have been given to another man. If he means Denman, I can forgive, and even respect him, for the feeling which he entertains.

Believe me ever yours most affectionately

T. B. M.

CHAPTER IV

1830–1832

State of public affairs when Macaulay entered Parliament—His maiden speech—The French Revolution of July 1830—Macaulay's letters from Paris—The Palais Royal—Lafayette—Lardner's Cabinet Cyclopædia—The new Parliament meets—Fall of the Duke of Wellington—Scene with Croker—The Reform Bill—Political success—House of Commons life—Macaulay's party spirit—London Society—Mr. Thomas Flower Ellis—Visit to Cambridge—Rothley Temple—Margaret Macaulay's Journal—Lord Brougham—Hopes of Office—Macaulay as a politician—Letters to Hannah Macaulay, Mr. Napier, and Mr. Ellis.

THROUGHOUT the last two centuries of our history there never was a period when a man conscious of power, impatient of public wrongs, and still young enough to love a fight for its own sake, could have entered Parliament with a fairer prospect of leading a life worth living, and doing work that would requite the pains, than at the commencement of the year 1830.

In this volume, which only touches politics in order to show to what extent Macaulay was a politician, and for how long, controversies cannot appropriately be started or revived. This is not the place to enter into a discussion on the vexed question as to whether Mr. Pitt and his successors, in pursuing their system of repression, were justified by the necessities of the long French war. It is enough to assert, what few or none will deny, that, for the space of more than a generation from 1790 onwards, our country had, with a short interval, been governed on declared reactionary principles. We, in whose days Whigs and Tories have often exchanged office, and still more often interchanged policies, find it difficult to imagine what must have been the condition of the kingdom, when one and the same party almost continuously held not only place but power, throughout a period when, to an unexampled degree, 'public life was exasperated by hatred, and the charities of private life soured by political aversion.'[1] Fear, religion, ambition, and self-interest,—everything that could tempt and everything that could deter,—were enlisted on the side of the dominant opinions. To profess Liberal views was to be excluded from all posts of emolument, from all functions of dignity, and from all opportunities of public usefulness. The Whig leaders, while enjoying that security for life and liberty which even in the worst days of our recent history has been the reward of eminence, were powerless in the Commons and isolated in the Lords. No motive but disinterested conviction kept a handful of veterans steadfast round a banner which was never raised except to be swept contemptuously down by the disciplined and overwhelming strength of the ministerial phalanx. Argument and oratory were alike unavailing under a constitution which was indeed a despotism of privilege.

[1] These expressions occur in Lord Cockburn's Memorials of his Time.

The county representation of England was an anomaly, and the borough representation little better than a scandal. The constituencies of Scotland, with so much else that of right belonged to the public, had got into Dundas's pocket. In the year 1820 all the towns north of Tweed together contained fewer voters than are now on the rolls of the single burgh of Hawick, and all the counties together contained fewer voters than are now on the register of Roxburghshire. So small a band of electors was easily manipulated by a party leader who had the patronage of India at his command. The three Presidencies were flooded with the sons and nephews of men who were lucky enough to have a seat in a Town Council, or a superiority in a rural district; and fortunate it was for our empire that the responsibilities of that noblest of all careers soon educated young Indian Civil Servants into something higher than mere adherents of a political party.

While the will of the nation was paralysed within the senate, effectual care was taken that its voice should not be heard without. The press was gagged in England, and throttled in Scotland. Every speech, or sermon, or pamphlet, the substance of which a Crown lawyer could torture into a semblance of sedition, sent its author to the jail, the hulks, or the pillory. In any place of resort where an informer could penetrate, men spoke their minds at imminent hazard of ruinous fines, and protracted imprisonment. It was vain to appeal to Parliament for redress against the tyranny of packed juries, and panic-driven magistrates. Sheridan endeavoured to retain for his countrymen the protection of Habeas Corpus; but he could only muster forty-one supporters. Exactly as many members followed Fox into the lobby when he opposed a bill, which, interpreted in the spirit that then actuated our tribunals, made attendance at an open meeting summoned for the consideration of Parliamentary Reform a service as dangerous as night-poaching, and far more dangerous than smuggling. Only ten more than that number ventured to protest against the introduction of a measure, still more inquisitorial in its provisions and ruthless in its penalties, which rendered every citizen who gave his attention to the removal of public grievances liable at any moment to find himself in the position of a criminal:—that very measure in behalf of which Bishop Horsley had stated in the House of Peers that he did not know what the mass of the people of any country had to do with the laws, except to obey them.

Amidst a population which had once known freedom, and was still fit to be entrusted with it, such a state of matters could not last for ever. Justly proud of the immense success that they had bought by their resolution, their energy, and their perseverance, the Ministers regarded the fall of Napoleon as a party triumph which could only serve to confirm their power. But the last cannon-shot that was fired on the 18th of June, 1815, was in truth the death-knell of the golden age of Toryism. When the passion and ardour of the war gave place to the discontent engendered by a protracted period of commercial distress, the opponents of progress began to perceive that they had to reckon, not with a small and disheartened faction, but with a clear majority of the nation led by the most enlightened, and the most eminent, of its sons. Agitators and incendiaries retired into the background, as will always be the case when the country is in earnest; and statesmen who had much to lose, but were not afraid to risk it, stepped quietly and firmly to the front. The men, and the sons of the men, who had so long endured exclusion from office, embittered by unpopularity, at length reaped their reward. Earl Grey, who forty years before had been hooted through the streets of North Shields with cries of 'No Popery,' lived to bear the most respected name in England; and Brougham, whose opinions differed little from those for expressing which Dr. Priestley in 1791 had his house burned about his ears by the Birmingham mob, was now the popular idol beyond all comparison or competition.

In face of such unanimity of purpose, guided by so much worth and talent, the Ministers lost their nerve, and, like all rulers who do not possess the confidence of the governed, began first to make mistakes, and then to quarrel among themselves. Throughout the years of Macaulay's early manhood the ice was breaking fast. He was still quite young when the concession of Catholic Emancipation gave a moral shock to the Tory party from which it never recovered until the old order of things had finally passed away.[1] It was his fortune to enter into other men's labours after the burden and heat of the day had already been borne, and to be summoned into the field just as the season was at hand for gathering in a ripe and long-expected harvest of beneficent legislation.

On the 5th of April, 1830, he addressed the House of Commons on the second reading of Mr. Robert Grant's bill for the Removal of Jewish Disabilities. Sir James Mackintosh rose with him, but Macaulay got the advantage of the preference that has always been conceded to one who speaks for the first time after gaining his seat during the continuance of a Parliament:—a privilege which, by a stretch of generosity, is now extended to new members who have been returned at a general election. Sir James subsequently took part in the debate; not, as he carefully assured his audience, 'to supply any defects in the speech of his honourable friend, for there were none that he could find, but principally to absolve his own conscience.' Indeed, Macaulay, addressing himself to his task with an absence of pretension such as never fails to conciliate the goodwill of the House towards a maiden speech, put clearly and concisely enough the arguments in favour of the bill:—arguments which,

[1] Macaulay was fond of repeating an answer made to him by Lord Clarendon in the year 1829. The young men were talking over the situation, and Macaulay expressed curiosity as to the terms in which the Duke of Wellington would recommend the Catholic Relief Bill to the Peers. 'Oh,' said the other, 'it will be easy enough. He'll say: "My lords! Attention! Right about face! March!"'

obvious, and almost common-place, as they appear under his straightforward treatment, had yet to be repeated during a space of six and thirty years before they commended themselves to the judgment of our Upper Chamber.

'The power of which you deprive the Jew consists in maces, and gold chains, and skins of parchment with pieces of wax dangling from their edges. The power which you leave the Jew is the power of principal over clerk, of master over servant, of landlord over tenant. As things now stand, a Jew may be the richest man in England. He may possess the means of raising this party and depressing that; of making East Indian directors; of making members of Parliament. The influence of a Jew may be of the first consequence in a war which shakes Europe to the centre. His power may come into play in assisting or thwarting the greatest plans of the greatest princes; and yet, with all this confessed, acknowledged, undenied, you would have him deprived of power! Does not wealth confer power? How are we to permit all the consequences of that wealth but one? I cannot conceive the nature of an argument that is to bear out such a position. If we were to be called on to revert to the day when the warehouses of Jews were torn down and pillaged, the theory would be comprehensible. But we have to do with a persecution so delicate that there is no abstract rule for its guidance. You tell us that the Jews have no legal right to power, and I am bound to admit it: but in the same way, three hundred years ago they had no legal right to be in England, and six hundred years ago they had no legal right to the teeth in their heads. But, if it is the moral right we are to look at, I hold that on every principle of moral obligation the Jew has a right to political power.'

He was on his legs once again, and once only, during his first Session; doing more for future success in Parliament by his silence than he could have effected by half a dozen brilliant perorations. A crisis was rapidly approaching when a man gifted with eloquence, who by previous self-restraint had convinced the House that he did not speak for speaking's sake, might rise almost in a day to the very summit of influence and reputation. The country was under the personal rule of the Duke of Wellington, who had gradually squeezed out of his Cabinet every vestige of Liberalism, and even of independence, and who at last stood so completely alone that he was generally supposed to be in more intimate communication with Prince Polignac than with any of his own colleagues. The Duke had his own way in the Lords; and on the benches of the Commons the Opposition members were unable to carry, or even visibly to improve their prospect of carrying, the measures on which their hearts were set. The Reformers were not doing better in the division lobby than in 1821; and their question showed no signs of having advanced since the day when it had been thrown over by Pitt on the eve of the French Revolution.

But the outward aspect of the situation was very far from answering to the reality. While the leaders of the popular party had been spending themselves in efforts that seemed each more abortive than the last,—dividing only to be enormously outvoted, and vindicating with calmness and moderation the first principles of constitutional government only to be stigmatised as the apostles of anarchy,—a mighty change was surely but imperceptibly effecting itself in the collective mind of their fellow-countrymen.

> For, while the tired waves, vainly breaking,
> Seem here no painful inch to gain,
> Far back, through creeks and inlets making,
> Comes silent, flooding in, the main.

Events were at hand, which unmistakably showed how different was the England of 1830 from the England of 1790. The King died; Parliament was dissolved on the 24th of July; and in the first excitement and bustle of the elections, while the candidates were still on the roads and the writs in the mailbags, came the news that Paris was in arms. The troops fought as well as

Frenchmen ever can be got to fight against the tricolour; but by the evening of the 29th it was all over with the Bourbons. The Minister, whose friendship had reflected such unpopularity on our own Premier, succumbed to the detestation of the victorious people, and his sacrifice did not save the dynasty. What was passing among our neighbours for once created sympathy, and not repulsion, on this side the Channel. One French Revolution had condemned English Liberalism to forty years of subjection, and another was to be the signal which launched it on as long a career of supremacy. Most men said, and all felt, that Wellington must follow Polignac; and the public temper was such as made it well for the stability of our throne that it was filled by a monarch who had attracted to himself the hopes and affection of the nation, and who shared its preferences and antipathies with regard to the leading statesmen of the day.

One result of political disturbance in any quarter of the globe is to fill the scene of action with young members of Parliament, who follow Revolutions about Europe as assiduously as Jew brokers attend upon the movements of an invading army. Macaulay, whose re-election for Calne had been a thing of course, posted off to Paris at the end of August, journeying by Dieppe and Rouen, and eagerly enjoying a first taste of continental travel. His letters during the tour were such as, previously to the age of railroads, brothers who had not been abroad before used to write for the edification of sisters who expected never to go abroad at all. He describes in minute detail manners and institutions that to us are no longer novelties, and monuments which an educated Englishman of our time knows as well as Westminster Abbey, and a great deal better than the Tower. Everything that he saw, heard, ate, drank, paid, and suffered, was noted down in his exuberant diction to be read aloud and commented on over the breakfast table in Great Ormond Street.

'At Rouen,' he says, 'I was struck by the union of venerable antiquity with extreme liveliness and gaiety.

We have nothing of the sort in England. Till the time of James the First, I imagine, our houses were almost all of wood, and have in consequence disappeared. In York there are some very old streets; but they are abandoned to the lowest people, and the gay shops are in the newly-built quarter of the town. In London, what with the fire of 1666, and what with the natural progress of demolition and rebuilding, I doubt whether there are fifty houses that date from the Reformation. But in Rouen you have street after street of lofty stern-looking masses of stone, with Gothic carvings. The buildings are so high, and the ways so narrow, that the sun can scarcely reach the pavements. Yet in these streets, monastic in their aspect, you have all the glitter of Regent Street or the Burlington Arcade. Rugged and dark above, below they are a blaze of ribands, gowns, watches, trinkets, artificial flowers; grapes, melons, and peaches such as Covent Garden does not furnish, filling the windows of the fruiterers; showy women swimming smoothly over the uneasy stones, and stared at by national guards swaggering by in full uniform. It is the Soho Bazaar transplanted into the gloomy cloisters of Oxford.'

He writes to a friend just before he started on his tour: 'There is much that I am impatient to see, but two things specially,—the Palais Royal, and the man who called me the Aristarchus of Edinburgh.' Who this person might be, and whether Macaulay succeeded in meeting him, are questions which his letters leave unsolved; but he must have been a constant visitor at the Palais Royal if the hours that he spent in it bore any relation to the number of pages which it occupies in his correspondence. The place was indeed well worth a careful study; for in 1830 it was not the orderly and decent bazaar of the Second Empire, but was still that compound of Parnassus and Bohemia which is painted in vivid colours in the 'Grand Homme de Province' of Balzac,—still the paradise of such ineffable rascals as Diderot has drawn with terrible fidelity in his 'Neveu de Rameau.'

'If I were to select the spot in all the earth in which the good and evil of civilisation are most strikingly exhibited, in which the arts of life are carried to the highest perfection, and in which all pleasures, high and low, intellectual and sensual, are collected in the smallest space, I should certainly choose the Palais Royal. It is the Covent Garden Piazza, the Paternoster Row, the Vauxhall, the Albion Tavern, the Burlington Arcade, the Crockford's, the Finish, the Athenæum of Paris all in one. Even now, when the first dazzling effect has passed off, I never traverse it without feeling bewildered by its magnificent variety. As a great capital is a country in miniature, so the Palais Royal is a capital in miniature,—an abstract and epitome of a vast community, exhibiting at a glance the politeness which adorns its higher ranks, the coarseness of its populace, and the vices and the misery which lie underneath its brilliant exterior. Everything is there, and everybody. Statesmen, wits, philosophers, beauties, dandies, blacklegs, adventurers, artists, idlers, the king and his court, beggars with matches crying for charity, wretched creatures dying of disease and want in garrets. There is no condition of life which is not to be found in this gorgeous and fantastic Fairyland.'

Macaulay had excellent opportunities for seeing behind the scenes during the closing acts of the great drama that was being played out through those summer months. The Duc de Broglie, then Prime Minister, treated him with marked attention, both as an Englishmen of distinction, and as his father's son. He was much in the Chamber of Deputies, and witnessed that strange and pathetic historical revival when, after an interval of forty such years as mankind had never known before, the aged La Fayette again stood forth, in the character of a disinterested dictator, between the hostile classes of his fellow-countrymen.

'De La Fayette is so overwhelmed with work that I scarcely knew how to deliver even Brougham's letter, which was a letter of business, and should have thought it absurd to send him Mackintosh's, which was a mere letter of introduction. I fell in with an English acquaintance who told me that he had an appointment with La Fayette, and who undertook to deliver them both. I accepted his offer, for, if I had left them with the porter, ten to one they would never have been opened. I hear that hundreds of letters are lying in the lodge of the hotel. Every Wednesday morning, from nine to eleven, La Fayette gives audience to anybody who wishes to speak to him; but about ten thousand people attend on these occasions, and fill, not only the house, but all the courtyard and half the street. La Fayette is Commander in Chief of the National Guard of France. The number of these troops in Paris alone is upwards of forty thousand. The Government find a musket and bayonet; but the uniform, which costs about ten napoleons, the soldiers provide themselves. All the shopkeepers are enrolled, and I cannot sufficiently admire their patriotism. My landlord, Meurice, a man who, I suppose, has realised a million francs or more, is up one night in four with his firelock doing the duty of a common watchman.

'There is, however, something to be said as an explanation of the zeal with which the bourgeoisie give their time and money to the public. The army received so painful a humiliation in the battles of July that it is by no means inclined to serve the new system faithfully. The rabble behaved nobly during the conflict, and have since shown rare humanity and moderation. Yet those who remember the former Revolution feel an extreme dread of the ascendency of mere multitude; and there have been signs, trifling in themselves, but such as may naturally alarm people of property. Workmen have struck. Machinery has been attacked. Inflammatory handbills have appeared upon the walls. At present all is quiet: but the thing may happen, particularly if Polignac and Peyronnet should not be put to death. The Peers wish to save them. The lower orders, who have had five or six thousand of their friends and kinsmen butchered by the frantic wickedness of these men, will hardly submit. 'Eh! eh!' said a fierce old soldier of Napoleon to me the other day. 'L'on dit qu'ils seront déportés: mais ne m'en parle pas. Non! non! Coupez-leur le cou. Sacré! Ça ne passera pas comme ça.'

'This long political digression will explain to you why Monsieur De La Fayette is so busy. He has more to do than all the Ministers together. However, my letters were presented, and he said to my friend that he had a soirée every Tuesday, and should be most happy to see me there. I drove to his house yesterday night. Of the interest which the common Parisians take in politics you may judge by this. I told my driver to wait for me, and asked his number. 'Ah! monsieur, c'est un beau numéro. C'est un brave numéro. C'est 221.' You may remember that the number of deputies who voted the intrepid address to Charles the Tenth, which irritated him into his absurd coup d'état, was 221. I walked into the hotel through a crowd of uniforms, and found the reception-rooms as full as they could hold. I was not able to make my way to La Fayette; but was glad to see him. He looks like the brave, honest, simple, good-natured man that he is.'

Besides what is quoted above, there is very little of general interest in these journal letters; and their publication would serve no purpose except that of informing the present leader of the Monarchists what his father had for breakfast and dinner during a week of 1830, and of enabling him to trace changes in the disposition of the furniture of the De Broglie hotel. 'I believe,' writes Macaulay, 'that I have given the inventory of every article in the Duke's salon. You will think that I have some intention of turning upholsterer.'

His thoughts and observations on weightier matters he kept for an article on the State of Parties in France which he intended to provide for the October number of the Edinburgh Review. While he was still at Paris, this arrangement was rescinded by Mr. Napier in compliance with the wish, or the whim, of Brougham;

and Macaulay's surprise and annoyance vented itself in a burst of indignant rhetoric strong enough to have upset a Government.[1] His wrath,—or that part of it, at least, which was directed against the editor,—did not survive an interchange of letters; and he at once set to work upon turning his material into the shape of a volume for the series of Lardner's Cabinet Cyclopædia, under the title of 'The History of France, from the Restoration of the Bourbons to the Accession of Louis Philippe.' Ten years ago proofs of the first eighty-eight pages were found in Messrs. Spottiswoode's printing office, with a note on the margin to the effect that most of the type was broken up before the sheets had been pulled. The task, as far as it went, was faithfully performed; but the author soon arrived at the conclusion that he might find a more profitable investment for his labour. With his head full of Reform, Macaulay was loth to spend in epitomising history the time and energy that would be better employed in helping to make it.

When the new Parliament met on the 26th of October it was already evident that the Government was doomed. Where the elections were open, Reform had carried the day. Brougham was returned for Yorkshire, a constituency of tried independence, which before 1832 seldom failed to secure the triumph of a cause into whose scale it had thrown its enormous weight. The counties had declared for the Whigs by a majority of eight to five, and the great cities by a majority of eight to one. Of the close boroughs in Tory hands many were held by men who had not forgotten Catholic Emancipation, and who did not mean to pardon their leaders until they had ceased to be Ministers.

In the debate on the Address the Duke of Wellington uttered his famous declaration that the Legislature possessed, and deserved to possess, the full and entire confidence of the country; that its existing constitution was not only practically efficient but theoretically

[1] See on page 183 the letter to Mr. Napier of September 16, 1830.

admirable; and that, if he himself had to frame a system of representation, he should do his best to imitate so excellent a model, though he admitted that the nature of man was incapable at a single effort of attaining to such mature perfection. His bewildered colleagues could only assert in excuse that their chief was deaf, and wish that everybody else had been deaf too. The second ministerial feat was of a piece with the first. Their Majesties had accepted an invitation to dine at Guildhall on the 9th of November. The Lord Mayor elect informed the Home Office that there was danger of riot, and the Premier, (who could not be got to see that London was not Paris because his own political creed happened to be much the same as Prince Polignac's,) advised the King to postpone his visit to the City, and actually talked of putting Lombard Street and Cheapside in military occupation. Such a step taken at such a time by such a man had its inevitable result. Consols, which the Duke's speech on the Address had brought from 84 to 80, fell to 77 in an hour and a half; jewellers and silversmiths sent their goods to the banks; merchants armed their clerks and barricaded their warehouses; and, when the panic subsided, fear only gave place to the shame and annoyance which a loyal people, whose loyalty was at that moment more active than ever, experienced from the reflection that all Europe was discussing the reasons why our King could not venture to dine in public with the Chief Magistrate of his own capital. A strong Minister, who sends the funds down seven per cent. in as many days, is an anomaly that no nation will consent to tolerate; the members of the Cabinet looked forward with consternation to a scheme of Reform which, with the approbation of his party, Brougham had undertaken to introduce on the 15th of November; and when, within twenty-four hours of the dreaded debate, they were defeated on a motion for a committee on the Civil List, their relief at having obtained an excuse for retiring at least equalled that which the country felt at getting rid of them.

Earl Grey, came in, saying (and meaning what he said,) that the principles on which he stood were 'amelioration of abuses, promotion of economy, and the endeavour to preserve peace consistently with the honour of the country.' Brougham, who was very sore at having been forced to postpone his notice on Reform on account of the ministerial crisis, had gratuitously informed the House of Commons on two successive days that he had no intention of taking office. A week later on he accepted the Chancellorship with an inconsistency which his friends readily forgave, for they knew that, when he resolved to join the Cabinet, he was thinking more of his party than of himself: a consideration that naturally enough only sharpened the relish with which his adversaries pounced upon this first of his innumerable scrapes. When the new writ for Yorkshire was moved, Croker commented sharply on the position in which the Chancellor was placed, and remarked that he had often heard Brougham declare that 'the characters of public men formed part of the wealth of England;'—a reminiscence which was delivered with as much gravity and unction as if it had been Mackintosh discoursing on Romilly. Unfortunately for himself, Croker ruined his case by referring to a private conversation, an error which the House of Commons always takes at least an evening to forgive; and Macaulay had his audience with him as he vindicated the absent orator with a generous warmth, which at length carried him so far that he was interrupted by a call to order from the Chair. 'The noble Lord had but a few days for deliberation, and that at a time when great agitation prevailed, and when the country required a strong and efficient Ministry to conduct the government of the State. At such a period a few days are as momentous as months would be at another period. It is not by the clock that we should measure the importance of the changes that might take place during such an interval. I owe no allegiance to the noble Lord who has been transferred to another place; but as a member of this House I cannot banish from my memory the extraordinary eloquence of that noble person within these walls,—an eloquence which has left nothing equal to it behind: and when I behold the departure of the great man from amongst us, and when I see the place in which he sat, and from which he has so often astonished us by the mighty powers of his mind, occupied this evening by the honourable member who has commenced this debate, I cannot express the feelings and emotions to which such circumstances give rise.'

Parliament adjourned over Christmas; and on the 1st of March 1831 Lord John Russell introduced the Reform Bill amidst breathless silence, which was at length broken by peals of contemptuous laughter from the Opposition benches, as he read the list of the hundred and ten boroughs which were condemned to partial or entire disfranchisement. Sir Robert Inglis led the attack upon a measure that he characterised as Revolution in the guise of a statute. Next morning as Sir Robert was walking into town over Westminster Bridge, he told his companion that up to the previous night he had been very anxious, but that his fears were now at an end, inasmuch as the shock caused by the extravagance of the ministerial proposals would infallibly bring the country to its senses. On the evening of that day Macaulay made the first of his Reform speeches. When he sat down the Speaker sent for him, and told him that in all his prolonged experience he had never seen the House in such a state of excitement. Even at this distance of time it is impossible to read aloud the last thirty sentences without an emotion which suggests to the mind what must have been their effect when declaimed by one who felt every word that he spoke, in the midst of an assembly agitated by hopes and apprehensions such as living men have never known, or have long forgotten.[1] Sir Thomas Denman,

[1] 'The question of Parliamentary Reform is still behind. But signs, of which it is impossible to misconceive the import, do most clearly indicate that, unless that question also be speedily settled, property, and order, and all the institutions

who rose later on in the discussion, said, with universal acceptance, that the orator's words remained tingling

of this great monarchy, will be exposed to fearful peril. Is it possible that gentlemen long versed in high political affairs cannot read these signs? Is it possible that they can really believe that the Representative system of England, such as it now is, will last to the year 1860? If not, for what would they have us wait? Would they have us wait, merely that we may show to all the world how little we have profited by our own recent experience? Would they have us wait, that we may once again hit the exact point where we can neither refuse with authority, nor concede with grace? Would they have us wait, that the numbers of the discontented party may become larger, its demands higher, its feelings more acrimonious, its organisation more complete? Would they have us wait till the whole tragicomedy of 1827 has been acted over again? till they have been brought into office by a cry of "No Reform," to be reformers, as they were once before brought into office by a cry of "No Popery," to be emancipators? Have they obliterated from their minds—gladly, perhaps, would some among them obliterate from their minds—the transactions of that year? And have they forgotten all the transactions of the succeeding year? Have they forgotten how the spirit of liberty in Ireland, debarred from its natural outlet, found a vent by forbidden passages? Have they forgotten how we were forced to indulge the Catholics in all the licence of rebels, merely because we chose to withhold from them the liberties of subjects? Do they wait for associations more formidable than that of the Corn Exchange, for contributions larger than the Rent, for agitators more violent than those who, three years ago, divided with the King and the Parliament the sovereignty of Ireland? Do they wait for that last and most dreadful paroxysm of popular rage, for that last and most cruel test of military fidelity? Let them wait, if their past experience shall induce them to think that any high honour or any exquisite pleasure is to be obtained by a policy like this. Let them wait, if this strange and fearful infatuation be indeed upon them, that they should not see with their eyes, or hear with their ears, or understand with their heart. But let us know our interest and our duty better. Turn where we may, within, around, the voice of great events is proclaiming to us, Reform, that you may preserve. Now, therefore, while everything at home and abroad forebodes ruin to those who persist in a hopeless struggle against the spirit of the age, now, while the crash of the proudest throne of the Continent is still resounding in our ears, now, while the roof of a British palace affords an ignominious shelter to the exiled heir of forty kings, now, while we see on every side ancient institutions subverted, and great societies dissolved, now, while the heart of England is still sound, now, while old feelings and old associations retain a power and a charm which may too soon pass

in the ears of all who heard them, and would last in their memories as long as they had memories to employ. That sense of proprietorship in an effort of genius, which the House of Commons is ever ready to entertain, effaced for a while all distinctions of party. 'Portions of the speech,' said Sir Robert Peel, 'were as beautiful as anything I have ever heard or read. It reminded one of the old times.' The names of Fox, Burke, and Canning were during that evening in everybody's mouth; and Macaulay overheard with delight a knot of old members illustrating their criticisms by recollections of Lord Plunket. He had reason to be pleased; for he had been thought worthy of the compliment which the judgment of Parliament reserves for a supreme occasion. In 1866, on the second reading of the Franchise Bill, when the crowning oration of that memorable debate had come to its close amidst a tempest of applause, one or two veterans of the lobby, forgetting Macaulay on Reform,—forgetting, it may be, Mr. Gladstone himself on the Conservative Budget of 1852,—pronounced, amidst the willing assent of a younger generation, that there had been nothing like it since Plunket.

The unequivocal success of the first speech into which he had thrown his full power decided for some

away, now, in this your accepted time, now, in this your day of salvation, take counsel, not of prejudice, not of party spirit, not of the ignominious pride of a fatal consistency, but of history, of reason, of the ages which are past, of the signs of this most portentous time. Pronounce in a manner worthy of the expectation with which this great debate has been anticipated, and of the long remembrance which it will leave behind. Renew the youth of the State. Save property, divided against itself. Save the multitude, endangered by its own ungovernable passions. Save the aristocracy, endangered by its own unpopular power. Save the greatest, the fairest, and most highly civilised community that ever existed, from calamities which may in a few days sweep away all the rich heritage of so many ages of wisdom and glory. The danger is terrible. The time is short. If this bill should be rejected, I pray to God that none of those who concur in rejecting it may ever remember their votes with unavailing remorse, amidst the wreck of laws, the confusion of ranks, the spoliation of property, and the dissolution of social order.'

time to come the tenor of Macaulay's career. During the next three years he devoted himself to Parliament, rivalling Stanley in debate, and Hume in the regularity of his attendance. He entered with zest into the animated and manysided life of the House of Commons, of which so few traces can ordinarily be detected in what goes by the name of political literature. The biographers of a distinguished statesman too often seem to have forgotten that the subject of their labours passed the best part of his waking hours, during the half of every year, in a society of a special and deeply marked character, the leading traits of which are at least as well worth recording as the fashionable or diplomatic gossip that fills so many volumes of memoirs and correspondence. Macaulay's letters sufficiently indicate how thoroughly he enjoyed the ease, the freedom, the hearty good-fellowship, that reign within the precincts of our national senate; and how entirely he recognised that spirit of noble equality, so prevalent among its members, which takes little or no account of wealth, or title, or indeed of reputation won in other fields, but which ranks a man according as the value of his words, and the weight of his influence, bear the test of a standard which is essentially its own.

In February 1831 he writes to Whewell: 'I am impatient for Praed's début. The House of Commons is a place in which I would not promise success to any man. I have great doubts even about Jeffrey. It is the most peculiar audience in the world. I should say that a man's being a good writer, a good orator at the bar, a good mob-orator, or a good orator in debating clubs, was rather a reason for expecting him to fail than for expecting him to succeed in the House of Commons. A place where Walpole succeeded and Addison failed; where Dundas succeeded and Burke failed; where Peel now succeeds and where Mackintosh fails; where Erskine and Scarlett were dinner-bells; where Lawrence and Jekyll, the two wittiest men, or nearly so, of their time, were thought bores, is surely a very strange place. And yet I feel the whole character of the place growing upon me. I begin to like what others about me like, and to disapprove what they disapprove. Canning used to say that the House, as a body, had better taste than the man of best taste in it, and I am very much inclined to think that Canning was right.'

The readers of Macaulay's letters will, from time to time, find reason to wish that the young Whig of 1830 had more frequently practised that studied respect for political opponents, which now does so much to correct the intolerance of party among men who can be adversaries without ceasing to regard each other as colleagues. But this honourable sentiment was the growth of later days; and, at an epoch when the system of the past and the system of the future were night after night in deadly wrestle on the floor of St. Stephen's, the combatants were apt to keep their kindliness, and even their courtesies, for those with whom they stood shoulder to shoulder in the fray. Politicians, Conservative and Liberal alike, who were themselves young during the Sessions of 1866 and 1867, and who can recall the sensations evoked by a contest of which the issues were far less grave and the passions less strong than of yore, will make allowances for one who, with the imagination of a poet and the temperament of an orator, at thirty years old was sent straight into the thickest of the tumult which then raged round the standard of Reform, and will excuse him for having borne himself in that battle of giants as a determined and a fiery partisan.

If to live intensely be to live happily, Macaulay had an enviable lot during those stirring years; and, if the old song-writers had reason on their side when they celebrated the charms of a light purse, he certainly possessed that element of felicity. Among the earliest economical reforms undertaken by the new Government was a searching revision of our Bankruptcy jurisdiction, in the course of which his Commissionership was swept away, without leaving him a penny of compensation. 'I voted for the Bankruptcy Court

Bill,' he said in answer to an inquisitive constituent. 'There were points in that Bill of which I did not approve, and I only refrained from stating those points because an office of my own was at stake.' When this source fell dry he was for a while a poor man; for a member of Parliament, who has others to think of besides himself, is anything but rich on sixty or seventy pounds a quarter as the produce of his pen, and a college income which has only a few more months to run. At a time when his Parliamentary fame stood at its highest he was reduced to sell the gold medals which he had gained at Cambridge; but he was never for a moment in debt; nor did he publish a line prompted by any lower motive than the inspiration of his political faith, or the instinct of his literary genius. He had none but pleasant recollections connected with the period when his fortunes were at their lowest. From the secure prosperity of after life he delighted in recalling the time when, after cheering on the fierce debate for twelve or fifteen hours together, he would walk home by daylight to his chambers, and make his supper on a cheese which was a present from one of his Wiltshire constituents, and a glass of the audit ale which reminded him that he was still a Fellow of Trinity.

With political distinction came social success, more rapid and more substantial, perhaps, than has ever been achieved by one who took so little trouble to win or to retain it. The circumstances of the time were all in his favour. Never did our higher circles present so much that would attract a new-comer, and never was there more readiness to admit within them all who brought the honourable credentials of talent and celebrity. In 1831 the exclusiveness of birth was passing away, and the exclusiveness of fashion had not set in. The Whig party, during its long period of depression, had been drawn together by the bonds of common hopes, and endeavours, and disappointments; and personal reputation, whether literary, political, or forensic, held its own as against the advantages of rank and money to an extent that was never known before, and never since. Macaulay had been well received in the character of an Edinburgh Reviewer, and his first great speech in the House of Commons at once opened to him all the doors in London that were best worth entering. Brought up, as he had been, in a household which was perhaps the strictest and the homeliest among a set of families whose creed it was to live outside the world, it put his strength of mind to the test when he found himself courted and observed by the most distinguished and the most formidable personages of the day. Lady Holland listened to him with unwonted deference, and scolded him with a circumspection that was in itself a compliment. Rogers spoke *of* him with friendliness, and *to* him with positive affection, and gave him the last proof of his esteem and admiration by asking him to name the morning for a breakfast-party. He was treated with almost fatherly kindness by the able and worthy man who is still remembered by the name of Conversation Sharp. Indeed, his deference for the feelings of all whom he liked and respected, which an experienced observer could detect beneath the eagerness of his manner and the volubility of his talk, made him a favourite among those of a generation above his own. He bore his honours quietly, and enjoyed them with the natural and hearty pleasure of a man who has a taste for society, but whose ambitions lie elsewhere. For the space of three seasons he dined out almost nightly, and spent many of his Sundays in those suburban residences which, as regards the company and the way of living, are little else than sections of London removed into a purer air.

Before very long his habits and tastes began to incline in the direction of domesticity, and even of seclusion; and, indeed, at every period of his life he would gladly desert the haunts of those whom Pope and his contemporaries used to term 'the great,' to seek the cheerful and cultured simplicity of his home, or the conversation of that one friend who had a share in the familiar confidence which Macaulay otherwise reserved for his nearest relatives. This was Mr. Thomas Flower Ellis, whose reports of the proceedings in King's Bench, extending over a whole generation, have established and perpetuated his name as that of an acute and industrious lawyer. He was older than Macaulay by four years. Though both Fellows of the same college, they missed each other at the university, and it was not until 1827, on the Northern circuit, that their acquaintance began. 'Macaulay has joined,' writes Mr. Ellis: 'an amusing person; somewhat boyish in his manner, but very original.' The young barristers had in common an insatiable love of the classics; and similarity of character, not very perceptible on the surface, soon brought about an intimacy which ripened into an attachment as important to the happiness of both concerned as ever united two men through every stage of life and vicissitude of fortune. Mr. Ellis had married early; but in 1839 he lost his wife, and Macaulay's helpful and heartfelt participation in his great sorrow riveted the links of a chain that was already indissoluble. The letters contained in this volume will tell, better than the words of any third person, what were the points of sympathy between the two companions, and in what manner they lived together till the end came. Mr. Ellis survived his friend little more than a year; not complaining or lamenting, but going about his work like a man from whose day the light has departed.

Brief and rare were the vacations of the most hard-worked Parliament that had sat since the times of Pym and Hampden. In the late autumn of 1831, the defeat of the Reform Bill in the House of Lords delivered over the country to agitation, resentment, and alarm; and gave a short holiday to public men who were not Ministers, magistrates, or officers in the yeomanry. Hannah and Margaret Macaulay accompanied their brother on a visit to Cambridge, where they met with the welcome which young Masters of

Arts delight in providing for the sisters of a comrade of whom they are fond and proud.

'On the evening that we arrived,' says Lady Trevelyan, 'we met at dinner Whewell, Sedgwick, Airy, and Thirlwall: and how pleasant they were, and how much they made of us, two happy girls, who were never tired of seeing, and hearing, and admiring! We breakfasted, lunched, and dined with one or the other of the set during our stay, and walked about the colleges all day with the whole train.[1] Whewell was then tutor: rougher, but less pompous, and much more agreeable, than in after years; though I do not think that he ever cordially liked your uncle. We then went on to Oxford, which from knowing no one there seemed terribly dull to us by comparison with Cambridge, and we rejoiced our brother's heart by sighing after Trinity.'

During the first half of his life Macaulay spent some months of every year at the seat of his uncle, Mr. Babington, who kept open house for his nephews and nieces throughout the summer and autumn. Rothley Temple, which lies in a valley beyond the first ridge that separates the flat unattractive country immediately round Leicester from the wild and beautiful scenery of Charnwood Forest, is well worth visiting as a singularly unaltered specimen of an old English home. The stately trees; the grounds, half park and half meadow; the cattle grazing up to the very windows; the hall, with its stone pavement rather below than above the level of the soil, hung with armour rude and rusty enough to dispel the suspicion of its having passed through a collector's hands; the low ceilings; the dark oak wainscot, carved after primitive designs, that covered every inch of wall in bedroom and corridor; the general air which the whole interior presented of having been put to rights at the date of

[1] A reminiscence from that week of refined and genial hospitality survives in the Essay on Madame d'Arblay. The reception which Miss Burney would have enjoyed at Oxford, if she had visited it otherwise than as an attendant on Royalty, is sketched off with all the writer's wonted spirit, and more than his wonted grace.

the Armada and left alone ever since;—all this antiquity contrasted quaintly, but prettily enough, with the youth and gaiety that lit up every corner of the ever-crowded though comfortable mansion. In wet weather there was always a merry group sitting on the staircase, or marching up and down the gallery; and, wherever the noise and fun were most abundant, wherever there was to be heard the loudest laughter and the most vehement expostulation, Macaulay was the centre of a circle which was exclaiming at the levity of his remarks about the Blessed Martyr; disputing with him on the comparative merits of Pascal, Racine, Corneille, Molière, and Boileau; or checking him as he attempted to justify his godparents by running off a list of all the famous Thomases in history. The place is full of his memories. His favourite walk was a mile of field-road and lane which leads from the house to a lodge on the highway; and his favourite point of view in that walk was a slight acclivity, whence the traveller from Leicester catches his first sight of Rothley Temple, with its background of hill and greenwood. He is remembered as sitting at the window in the hall, reading Dante to himself, or translating it aloud as long as any listener cared to remain within ear-shot. He occupied, by choice, a very small chamber on the ground floor, through the window of which he could escape unobserved while afternoon callers were on their way between the front door and the drawing-room. On such occasions he would take refuge in a boat moored under the shade of some fine oaks which still exist, though the ornamental water on whose bank they stood has since been converted into dry land.

A journal kept at intervals by Margaret Macaulay, some extracts from which have here been arranged in the form of a continuous narrative, affords a pleasant and faithful picture of her brother's home-life during the years 1831 and 1832. With an artless candour, from which his reputation will not suffer, she relates the alternations of hope and disappointment through which the young people passed when it began to be a question whether or not he would be asked to join the Administration.

'I think I was about twelve when I first became very fond of my brother, and from that time my affection for him has gone on increasing during a period of seven years. I shall never forget my delight and enchantment when I first found that he seemed to like talking to me. His manner was very flattering to such a child, for he always took as much pains to amuse me, and to inform me on anything I wished to know, as he could have done to the greatest person in the land. I have heard him express great disgust towards those people who, lively and agreeable abroad, are a dead weight in the family circle. I think the remarkable clearness of his style proceeds in some measure from the habit of conversing with very young people, to whom he has a great deal to explain and impart.

'He reads his works to us in the manuscript, and, when we find fault, as I very often do with his being too severe upon people, he takes it with the greatest kindness, and often alters what we do not like. I hardly ever, indeed, met with a sweeter temper than his. He is rather hasty, and when he has not time for an instant's thought, he will sometimes return a quick answer, for which he will be sorry the moment he has said it. But in a conversation of any length, though it may be on subjects that touch him very nearly, and though the person with whom he converses may be very provoking and extremely out of temper, I never saw him lose his. He never uses this superiority, as some do, for the purpose of irritating another still more by coolness; but speaks in a kind, good-natured manner, as if he wished to bring the other back to temper without appearing to notice that he had lost it.

'He at one time took a very punning turn, and we laid a wager in books, my Mysteries of Udolpho against his German Theatre, that he could not make two hundred puns in one evening. He did it, however, in two hours, and, although they were of course most of them miserably bad, yet it was a proof of great quickness.

'*Saturday, February* 26, 1831.—At dinner we talked of the Grants. Tom said he had found Mr. Robert Grant walking about in the lobbies of the House of Commons, and saying that he wanted somebody to defend his place in the Government, which he heard was going to be attacked.

"What did you say to him?" we asked. "Oh, I said nothing; but, if they'll give me the place, I'll defend it. When I am Judge Advocate, I promise you that I will not go about asking anyone to defend me."

'After dinner we played at capping verses, and after that at a game in which one of the party thinks of something for the others to guess at. Tom gave the slug that killed Perceval, the lemon that Wilkes squeezed for Doctor Johnson, the pork-chop which Thurtell ate after he had murdered Weare, and Sir Charles Macarthy's jaw which was sent by the Ashantees as a present to George the Fourth.

'Some one mentioned an acquaintance who had gone to the West Indies, hoping to make money, but had only ruined the complexions of his daughters. Tom said:—

> Mr. Walker was sent to Berbice
> By the greatest of statesmen and earls.
> He went to bring back yellow boys,
> But he only brought back yellow girls.

'I never saw anything like the fun and humour that kindles in his eye when a repartee or verse is working in his brain.

'*March* 3, 1831.—Yesterday morning Hannah and I walked part of the way to his chambers with Tom, and, as we separated, I remember wishing him good luck and success that night. He went through it most triumphantly, and called down upon himself admiration enough to satisfy even his sister. I like so much the manner in which he receives compliments. He does not pretend to be indifferent, but smiles in his kind and animated way, with "I am sure it is very kind of you to say so," or something of that nature. His voice from cold and over-excitement got quite into a scream towards the last part. A person told him that he had not heard such speaking since Fox. "You have not heard such screaming since Fox," he said.

'*March* 24, 1831.—By Tom's account, there never was such a scene of agitation as the House of Commons presented at the passing of the second reading of the Reform Bill the day before yesterday, or rather yesterday, for they did not divide till three or four in the morning. When dear Tom came the next day he was still very much excited, which I found to my cost, for when I went out to walk with him he walked so very fast that I could scarcely keep up with him at all. With sparkling eyes he described the whole scene of the preceding evening in the most graphic manner.

' "I suppose the Ministers are all in high spirits," said Mamma. "In spirits, Ma'am? I'm sure I don't know. In bed, I'll answer for it." Mamma asked him for franks, that she might send his speech to a lady[1] who, though of high Tory principles, is very fond of Tom, and has left him in her will her valuable library. "Oh, no," he said, "don't send it. If you do, she'll cut me off with a prayer-book."

'Tom is very much improved in his appearance during the last two or three years. His figure is not so bad for a man of thirty as for a man of twenty-two. He dresses better, and his manners, from seeing a great deal of society, are very much improved. When silent and occupied in thought, walking up and down the room as he always does, his hands clenched and muscles working with the intense exertion of his mind, strangers would think his countenance stern; but I remember a writing-master of ours, when Tom had come into the room and left it again, saying, "Ladies, your brother looks like a lump of good-humour!"

'*March* 30, 1831.—Tom has just left me, after a very interesting conversation. He spoke of his extreme idleness. He said: "I never knew such an idle man as I am. When I go in to Empson or Ellis their tables are always covered with books and papers. I cannot stick at anything for above a day or two. I mustered industry enough to teach myself Italian. I wish to speak Spanish. I know I could master the difficulties in a week, and read any book in the language at the end of a month, but I have not the courage to attempt it. If there had not been really something in me, idleness would have ruined me."

'I said that I was surprised at the great accuracy of his information, considering how desultory his reading had been. "My accuracy as to facts," he said, "I owe to a cause which many men would not confess. It is due to my love of castle-building. The past is in my mind soon constructed into a romance." He then went on to describe the way in which from his childhood his imagination had been filled by the study of history. "With a person of my turn," he said, "the minute touches are of as great interest, and perhaps greater, than the most important events. Spending so much time as I do in solitude, my mind would have rusted by gazing vacantly at the shop windows. As it is, I am no sooner in

[1] This lady was Mrs. Hannah More.

the streets than I am in Greece, in Rome, in the midst of the French Revolution. Precision in dates, the day or hour in which a man was born or died, become absolutely necessary. A slight fact, a sentence, a word, are of importance in my romance. Pepys's Diary formed almost inexhaustible food for my fancy. I seem to know every inch of Whitehall. I go in at Hans Holbein's gate, and come out through the matted gallery. The conversations which I compose between great people of the time are long, and sufficiently animated: in the style, if not with the merits, of Sir Walter Scott's. The old parts of London, which you are sometimes surprised at my knowing so well, those old gates and houses down by the river, have all played their part in my stories." He spoke, too, of the manner in which he used to wander about Paris, weaving tales of the Revolution, and he thought that he owed his command of language greatly to this habit.

'I am very sorry that the want both of ability and memory should prevent my preserving with greater truth a conversation which interested me very much.

'*May* 21, 1831.—Tom was from London at the time my mother's death occurred, and things fell out in such a manner that the first information he received of it was from the newspapers. He came home directly. He was in an agony of distress, and gave way at first to violent bursts of feeling. During the whole of the week he was with us all day, and was the greatest comfort to us imaginable. He talked a great deal of our sorrow, and led the conversation by degrees to other subjects, bearing the whole burden of it himself, and interesting us without jarring with the predominant feeling of the time. I never saw him appear to greater advantage—never loved him more dearly.

'*September* 1831.—Of late we have walked a good deal. I remember pacing up and down Brunswick Square and Lansdowne Place for two hours one day, deep in the mazes of the most subtle metaphysics;—up and down Cork Street, engaged over Dryden's poetry and the great men of that time;—making jokes all the way along Bond Street, and talking politics everywhere.

'Walking in the streets with Tom and Hannah, and talking about the hard work the heads of his party had got now, I said: "How idle they must think you, when they meet you here in the busy part of the day!" "Yes, here I am," said he, "walking with two unidea'd girls.[1] However, if one of the Ministry says to me, "Why walk you here all the day idle?" I shall say, "Because no man has hired me."

'We talked of eloquence, which he has often compared to fresco-painting: the result of long study and meditation, but at the moment of execution thrown off with the greatest rapidity: what has apparently been the work of a few hours being destined to last for ages.

'Mr. Tierney said he was sure Sir Philip Francis had written Junius, for he was the proudest man he ever knew, and no one ever heard of anything he had done to be proud of.

'*November* 14, 1831, *half-past-ten.*—On Friday last Lord Grey sent for Tom. His note was received too late to be acted on that day. On Saturday came another, asking him to East Sheen on that day, or Sunday. Yesterday, accordingly, he went, and stayed the night, promising to be here as early as possible to-day. So much depends upon the result of this visit! That he will be offered a place I have not the least doubt. He will refuse a Lordship of the Treasury, a Lordship of the Admiralty, or the Mastership of the Ordnance. He will accept the Secretaryship of the Board of Control, but will not thank them for it; and would not accept that, but that he thinks it will be a place of importance during the approaching discussions on the East Indian monopoly.

'If he gets a sufficient salary, Hannah and I shall most likely live with him. Can I possibly look forward to anything happier? I cannot imagine a course of life that would suit him better than thus to enjoy the pleasures of domestic life without its restraints; with sufficient business, but not, I hope, too much.

'At one o'clock he came. I went out to meet him. "I have nothing to tell you. Nothing. Lord Grey sent for me to speak about a matter of importance, which must be strictly private."

'*November* 27.—I am just returned from a long walk, during which the conversation turned entirely on one subject. After a little previous talk about a certain great personage,[2] I asked Tom when the present coolness be-

[1] Boswell relates in his tenth chapter how Johnson scolded Langton for leaving 'his social friends, to go and sit with a set of wretched unidea'd girls.'

[2] The personage was Lord Brougham, who at this time was

tween them began. He said: "Nothing could exceed my respect and admiration for him in early days. I saw at that time private letters in which he spoke highly of my articles, and of me as the most rising man of the time. After a while, however, I began to remark that he became extremely cold to me, hardly ever spoke to me on circuit, and treated me with marked slight. If I were talking to a man, if he wished to speak to him on politics or anything else that was not in any sense a private matter, he always drew him away from me instead of addressing us both. When my article on Hallam came out, he complained to Jeffrey that I took up too much of the Review; and, when my first article on Mill appeared, he foamed with rage, and was very angry with Jeffrey for having printed it."

'"But," said I, "the Mills are friends of his, and he naturally did not like them to be attacked."

'"On the contrary," said Tom, "he had attacked them fiercely himself: but he thought I had made a hit, and was angry accordingly. When a friend of mine defended my articles to him, he said: 'I know nothing of the articles. I have not read Macaulay's articles.' What can be imagined more absurd that his keeping up an angry correspondence with Jeffrey about articles he has never read? Well, the next thing was that Jeffrey, who was about to give up the editorship, asked me if I would take it. I said that I would gladly do so, if they would remove the headquarters of the Review to London. Jeffrey wrote to him about it. He disapproved of it so strongly that the plan was given up. The truth was that he felt that his power over the Review diminished as mine increased, and he saw that he would have little indeed if I were editor.

'"I then came into Parliament. I do not complain that he should have preferred Denman's claims to mine, and that he should have blamed Lord Lansdowne for not considering him. I went to take my seat. As I turned from the table at which I had been taking the oaths, he stood as near to me as you do now, and he cut me dead. We never spoke in the House, excepting once, that I can remember, when a few words passed between us in the lobby. I have sat close to him when many men of whom I knew nothing have introduced themselves to me to shake hands, and congratulate me after making a speech, and he has never said a single word. I know that it is jealousy, because I am not

too formidable for the poor girl to venture to write his name at length even in a private journal.

the first man whom he has used in this way. During the debate on the Catholic claims he was so enraged because Lord Plunket had made a very splendid display, and because the Catholics had chosen Sir Francis Burdett instead of him to bring the Bill forward, that he threw every difficulty in its way. Sir Francis once said to him: 'Really, Mr. ——, you are so jealous that it is impossible to act with you.' I never will serve in an Administration of which he is the head. On that I have most firmly made up my mind. I do not believe that it is in his nature to be a month in office without caballing against his colleagues.[1]

' "He is, next to the King, the most popular man in England. There is no other man whose entrance into any town in the kingdom would be so certain to be with huzzaing and taking off of horses. At the same time he is in a very ticklish situation, for he has no real friends. Jeffrey, Sydney Smith, Mackintosh, all speak of him as I now speak to you. I was talking to Sydney Smith of him the other day, and said that, great as I felt his faults to be, I must allow him a real desire to raise the lower orders, and do good by education, and those methods upon which his heart has been always set. Sydney would not allow this, or any other, merit. Now, if those who are called his friends feel towards him, as they all do, angry and sore at his overbearing, arrogant, and neglectful conduct, when those reactions in public feeling, which must come, arrive, he will have nothing to return upon, no place of refuge, no band of such tried friends as Fox and Canning had to support him. You will see that he will soon place himself in a false position before the public. His popularity will go down, and he will find himself alone. Mr. Pitt, it is true, did not study to strengthen himself by friendships; but this was not from jealousy. I do not love the man, but I believe he was quite superior to that. It was from a solitary pride he had. I heard at Holland House the other day that Sir Philip Francis said that, though he hated Pitt, he must confess there was something fine in seeing how he maintained his post by himself. 'The lion walks alone,' he said. 'The jackals herd together.' " '

This conversation, to those who have heard Macau-

[1] 'There never was a direct personal rival, or one who was in a position which, however reluctantly, implied rivalry, to whom he has been just; and on the fact of this ungenerous jealousy I do not understand that there is any difference of opinion.'—Lord Cockburn's Journal.

lay talk, bears unmistakable signs of having been committed to paper while the words,—or, at any rate, the outlines,—of some of the most important sentences were fresh in his sister's mind. Nature had predestined the two men to mutual antipathy. Macaulay, who knew his own range and kept within it, and who gave the world nothing except his best and most finished work, was fretted by the slovenly omniscience of Brougham, who affected to be a walking encyclopædia, 'a kind of semi-Solomon, half knowing everything from the cedar to the hyssop.'[1] The student, who, in his later years, never left his library for the House of Commons without regret, had little in common with one who, like Napoleon, held that a great reputation was a great noise; who could not change horses without making a speech, see the Tories come in without offering to take a judgeship, or allow the French to make a Revolution without proposing to naturalise himself as a citizen of the new Republic. The statesman who never deserted an ally, or distrusted a friend, could have no fellowship with a freelance, ignorant of the very meaning of loyalty; who, if the surfeited pen of the reporter had not declined its task, would have enriched our collections of British oratory by at least one Philippic against every colleague with whom he had ever acted. The many who read this conversation by the light of the public history of Lord Melbourne's Administration, and still more the few who have access to the secret history of Lord Grey's Cabinet, will acknowledge that seldom was a prediction so entirely fulfilled, or a character so accurately read. And that it was not a prophecy composed after the event is proved by the circumstance that it stands recorded in the handwriting of one who died before it was accomplished.

'*January* 3, 1832.—Yesterday Tom dined at Holland House, and heard Lord Holland tell this story. Some paper was to be published by Mr. Fox, in which mention was

[1] These words are extracted from a letter written by Macaulay.

made of Mr. Pitt having been employed at a club in a manner that would have created scandal. Mr. Wilberforce went to Mr. Fox, and asked him to omit the passage. "Oh, to be sure," said Mr. Fox; "if there are any good people who would be scandalised, I will certainly put it out!" Mr. Wilberforce then preparing to take his leave, he said: "Now, Mr. Wilberforce, if, instead of being about Mr. Pitt, this had been an account of my being seen gaming at White's on a Sunday, would you have taken so much pains to prevent it being known?" "I asked this," said Mr. Fox, "because I wanted to see what he would say, for I knew he would not tell a lie about it. He threw himself back, as his way was, and only answered: 'Oh, Mr. Fox, you are always so pleasant!' "

'*January* 8, 1832.—Yesterday Tom dined with us, and stayed late. He talked almost uninterruptedly for six hours. In the evening he made a great many impromptu charades in verse. I remember he mentioned a piece of impertinence of Sir Philip Francis. Sir Philip was writing a history of his own time, with characters of its eminent men, and one day asked Mr. Tierney if he should like to hear his own character. Of course he said "Yes," and it was read to him. It was very flattering, and he expressed his gratification for so favourable a description of himself. "Subject to revision, you must remember, Mr. Tierney," said Sir Philip, as he laid the manuscript by: "subject to revision according to what may happen in the future."

'I am glad Tom has reviewed old John Bunyan. Many are reading it who never read it before. Yesterday, as he was sitting in the Athenæum, a gentlemen called out: "Waiter, is there a copy of the Pilgrim's Progress in the library? As might be expected, there was not.

'*February* 12, 1832.—This evening Tom came in, Hannah and I being alone. He was in high boyish spirits. He had seen Lord Lansdowne in the morning, who had requested to speak with him. His Lordship said that he wished to have a talk about his taking office, not with any particular thing in view, as there was no vacancy at present, and none expected, but that he should be glad to know his wishes in order that he might be more able to serve him in them.

'Tom, in answer, took rather a high tone. He said he was a poor man, but that he had as much as he wanted, and, as far as he was personally concerned, had no desire for office. At the same time he thought that, after the

Reform Bill had passed, it would be absolutely necessary that the Government should be strengthened; that he was of opinion that he could do it good service; that he approved of its general principles, and should not be unwilling to join it. Lord Lansdowne said that they all,—and he particularly mentioned Lord Grey,—felt of what importance to them his help was, and that he now perfectly understood his views.

'*February* 13, 1832.—It has been much reported, and has even appeared in the newspapers, that the Ministers were doing what they could to get Mr. Robert Grant out of the way to make room for Tom. Last Sunday week it was stated in the John Bull that Madras had been offered to the Judge Advocate for this purpose, but that he had refused it. Two or three nights since, Tom, in endeavouring to get to a high bench in the House, stumbled over Mr. Robert Grant's legs, as he was stretched out half asleep. Being roused he apologised in the usual manner, and then added, oddly enough: "I am very sorry, indeed, to stand in the way of your mounting."

'*March* 15, 1832.—Yesterday Hannah and I spent a very agreeable afternoon with Tom.

'He began to talk of his idleness. "He really came and dawdled with us all day long; he had not written a line of his review of Burleigh's Life, and he shrank from beginning on such a great work." I asked him to put it by for the present, and write a light article on novels. This he seemed to think he should like, and said he could get up an article on Richardson in a very short time, but he knew of no book that he could hang it on. Hannah advised that he should place at the head of this article a fictitious title in Italian of a critique on Clarissa Harlowe, published at Venice. He seemed taken with this idea, but said that, if he did such a thing, he must never let his dearest friend know.

'I was amused with a parody of Tom's on the nursery song 'Twenty pounds shall marry me," as applied to the creation of Peers.

> What though now opposed I be?
> Twenty Peers shall carry me.
> If twenty won't, thirty will,
> For I'm his Majesty's bouncing Bill.

Sir Robert Peel has been extremely complimentary to him. One sentence he repeated to us: "My only feeling towards that gentleman is a not ungenerous envy, as I listened to that wonderful flow of natural and beautiful language, and to that utterance which, rapid as it is, seems scarcely able to convey its rich freight of thought and fancy!" People say that these words were evidently carefully prepared.

'I have just been looking round our little drawing-room, as if trying to impress every inch of it on my memory, and thinking how in future years it will rise before my mind as the scene of many hours of light-hearted mirth: how I shall again see him, lolling indolently on the old blue sofa, or strolling round the narrow confines of our room. With such a scene will come the remembrance of his beaming countenance, happy affectionate smile, and joyous laugh; while, with everyone at ease around him, he poured out the stores of his full mind in his own peculiarly beautiful and expressive language, more delightful here than anywhere else, because more perfectly unconstrained. The name which passes through this little room in the quiet, gentle tones of sisterly affection is a name which will be repeated through distant generations, and go down to posterity linked with eventful times and great deeds."

The last words here quoted will be very generally regarded as the tribute of a sister's fondness. Many, who readily admit that Macaulay's name will go down to posterity linked with eventful times and great deeds, make that admission with reference to times not his own, and deeds in which he had no part except to commemorate them with his pen. To him, as to others, a great reputation of a special order brought with it the consequence that the credit, which he deserved for what he had done well, was overshadowed by the renown of what he did best. The world, which has forgotten that Newton excelled as an administrator, and Voltaire as a man of business, remembers somewhat faintly that Macaulay was an eminent orator and, for a time at least, a strenuous politician. The universal voice of his contemporaries, during the first three years of his parliamentary career, testifies to the leading part which he played in the House of Commons, so long as with all his heart he cared, and with all his might he tried, to play it. Jeffrey, (for it is well to adduce none but first-rate evidence,) says in his account of an evening's discussion on the second reading of the Reform Bill: 'Not a very striking debate. There was but one exception, and it was a brilliant one. I mean Macaulay, who surpassed his former appearance in closeness, fire, and vigour, and very much improved the effect of it by a more steady and graceful delivery. It was prodigiously cheered, as it deserved, and I think puts him clearly at the head of the great speakers, if not the debaters, of the House.' And again, on the 17th of December: 'Macaulay made, I think, the best speech he has yet delivered; the most condensed, at least, and with the greatest weight of matter. It contained, indeed, the only argument to which any of the speakers who followed him applied themselves.' Lord Cockburn, who sat under the gallery for twenty-seven hours during the last three nights of the Bill, pronounced Macaulay's speech to have been 'by far the best;' though, like a good Scotchman, he asserts that he heard nothing at Westminster which could compare with Dr. Chalmers in the General Assembly. Sir James Mackintosh writes from the Library of the House of Commons: 'Macaulay and Stanley have made two of the finest speeches ever spoken in Parliament;' and a little further on he classes together the two young orators as 'the chiefs of the next, or rather of this, generation.'

To gain and keep the position that Mackintosh assigned him Macaulay possessed the power, and in early days did not lack the will. He was prominent on the Parliamentary stage, and active behind the scenes; —the soul of every honourable project which might promote the triumph of his principles, and the ascendency of his party. One among many passages in his correspondence may be quoted without a very serious breach of ancient and time-worn confidences. On the 17th of September, 1831, he writes to his sister Hannah: 'I have been very busy since I wrote last, moving heaven and earth to render it certain that, if our ministers are so foolish as to resign in the event of a defeat in the Lords, the Commons may be firm and united; and I think that I have arranged a plan which will secure a bold and instant declaration on our part, if necessary. Lord Ebrington is the man whom I have in my eye as our leader. I have had much conversation with him, and with several of our leading county members. They are all staunch; and I will answer for this,—that, if the ministers should throw us over, we will be ready to defend ourselves.'

The combination of public spirit, political instinct, and legitimate self-assertion, which was conspicuous in Macaulay's character, pointed him out to some whose judgment had been trained by long experience of affairs as a more than possible leader in no remote future; and it is not for his biographer to deny that they had grounds for their conclusion. The prudence, the energy, the self-reliance, which he displayed in another field, might have been successfully directed to the conduct of an executive policy, and the management of a popular assembly. Macaulay never showed himself deficient in the qualities which enable a man to trust his own sense; to feel responsibility, but not to fear it; to venture where others shrink; to decide while others waver; with all else that belongs to the vocation of a ruler in a free country. But it was not his fate: it was not his work: and the rank which he might have claimed among the statesmen of Britain was not ill exchanged for the place which he occupies in the literature of the world.

To Macvey Napier, Esq.

York: March 22, 1830.

My dear Sir,—

I was in some doubt as to what I should be able to do for Number 101, and I deferred writing till I could make up my mind. If my friend Ellis's article on Greek History, of which I have formed high expectations, could have been ready, I should have taken a holiday. But, as there is no chance of that for the next number, I ought, I think, to consider myself as his bail, and to surrender myself to your disposal in his stead.

I have been thinking of a subject, light and trifling

enough, but perhaps not the worse for our purpose on that account. We seldom want a sufficient quantity of heavy matter. There is a wretched poetaster of the name of Robert Montgomery who has written some volumes of detestable verses on religious subjects, which by mere puffing in magazines and newspapers have had an immense sale, and some of which are now in their tenth or twelfth editions. I have for some time past thought that the trick of puffing, as it is now practised both by authors and publishers, is likely to degrade the literary character, and to deprave the public taste, in a frightful degree. I really think that we ought to try what effect satire will have upon this nuisance, and I doubt whether we can ever find a better opportunity.

Yours very faithfully
T. B. MACAULAY.

To Macvey Napier, Esq.

London: August 19, 1830.

My dear Sir,—

The new number appeared this morning in the shop windows. The article on Niebuhr contains much that is very sensible; but it is not such an article as so noble a subject required. I am not like Ellis, Niebuhr-mad; and I agree with many of the remarks which the reviewer has made both on this work, and on the school of German critics and historians. But surely the reviewer ought to have given an account of the system of exposition which Niebuhr has adopted, and of the theory which he advances respecting the Institutions of Rome. The appearance of the book is really an era in the intellectual history of Europe, and I think that the Edinburgh Review ought at least to have given a luminous abstract of it. The very circumstance that Niebuhr's own arrangement and style are obscure, and that his translators have need of translators to make them intelligible to the multitude, rendered it more desirable that a clear and neat statement of the points in controversy should be laid before the public. But it is useless to talk of what cannot be mended. The best editors cannot always have good writers, and the best writers cannot always write their best.

I have no notion on what ground Brougham imagines that I am going to review his speech. He never said a word to me on the subject. Nor did I ever say either to him, or to anyone else, a single syllable to that effect. At all events I shall not make Brougham's speech my text. We have had quite enough of puffing and flattering each other in the Review. It is a vile taste for men united in one literary undertaking to exchange their favours.

I have a plan of which I wish to know your opinion. In ten days, or thereabouts, I set off for France, where I hope to pass six weeks. I shall be in the best society, that of the Duc de Broglie, Guizot, and so on. I think of writing an article on the Politics of France since the Restoration, with characters of the principal public men, and a parallel between the present state of France and that of England. I think that this might be made an article of extraordinary interest. I do not say that I could make it so. It must, you will perceive, be a long paper, however concise I may try to be: but as the subject is important, and I am not generally diffuse, you must not stint me. If you like this scheme, let me know as soon as possible.

Ever yours truly

T. B. MACAULAY.

It cannot be denied that there was some ground for the imputation of systematic puffing which Macaulay urges with a freedom that a modern editor would hardly permit to the most valued contributor. Brougham had made a speech on Slavery in the House of Commons; but time was wanting to get the Corrected Report published soon enough for him to obtain his tribute of praise in the body of the Review. The unhappy Mr. Napier was actually reduced to append a notice to the July number regretting that 'this powerful speech, which, as we are well informed, produced an impression on those who heard it not likely to be forgotten, or to remain barren of effects, should have reached us at a moment when it was no longer possible for us to notice its contents at any length. . . . On the eve of a general election to the first Parliament of a new reign, we could have wished to be able to contribute our aid towards the diffusion of the facts and arguments here so strikingly and commandingly stated and enforced, among those who are about to exercise the elective franchise. . . . We trust that means will be taken to give the widest possible circulation to the Corrected Report. Unfortunately, we can, at present, do nothing more than lay before our readers its glowing peroration—so worthy of this great orator, this unwearied friend of liberty and humanity.'

To Macvey Napier, Esq.

Paris: September 16, 1830.

My dear Sir,—

I have just received your letter, and I cannot deny that I am much vexed at what has happened. It is not very agreeable to find that I have thrown away the labour, the not unsuccessful labour as I thought, of a month; particularly as I have not many months of perfect leisure. This would not have happened if Brougham had notified his intentions to you earlier, as he ought in courtesy to you, and to everybody connected with the Review, to have done. He must have known that this French question was one on which many people would be desirous to write.

I ought to tell you that I had scarcely reached Paris when I received a letter containing a very urgent application from a very respectable quarter. I was desired to write a sketch, in one volume, of the late Revolution here. Now, I really hesitated whether I should not make my excuses to you, and accept this proposal,—not on account of the pecuniary terms, for about these I have never much troubled myself,—but because I should have had ampler space for this noble subject than the Review would have afforded. I thought, however, that this would not be a fair or friendly course towards you. I accordingly told the applicants that I had promised you an article, and that I could not well write twice in one month on the same subject without repeating myself. I therefore declined; and recommended a person whom I thought quite capable of producing an attractive book on these events. To that person my correspondent has probably applied. At all events I cannot revive the negotiation. I cannot hawk my rejected articles up and down Paternoster Row.

I am, therefore, a good deal vexed at this affair; but I am not at all surprised at it. I see all the difficulties of your situation. Indeed, I have long foreseen them. I always knew that in every association, literary or political, Brougham would wish to domineer. I knew also that no Editor of the Edinburgh Review could, without risking the ruin of the publication, resolutely oppose the demands of a man so able and powerful. It was because I was certain that he would exact submissions which I am not disposed to make that I wished last year to give up writing for the Review. I had long been meditating a retreat. I thought Jeffrey's abdication a favourable time for effecting it; not, as I hope you are well assured, from any unkind feeling towards you; but because I knew that, under any Editor, mishaps such as that which has now occurred would be constantly taking place. I remember that I predicted to Jeffrey what has now come to pass almost to the letter.

My expectations have been exactly realised. The present constitution of the Edinburgh Review is this, that, at whatever time Brougham may be pleased to notify his intention of writing on any subject, all previous engagements are to be considered as annulled by that notification. His language translated into plain English is this: 'I must write about this French Revolution, and I will write about it. If you have told Macaulay to do it, you may tell him to let it alone.

If he has written an article, he may throw it behind the grate. He would not himself have the assurance to compare his own claims with mine. I am a man who act a prominent part in the world: he is nobody. If he must be reviewing, there is my speech about the West Indies. Set him to write a puff on that. What have people like him to do, except to eulogise people like me?' No man likes to be reminded of his inferiority in such a way, and there are some particular circumstances in this case which render the admonition more unpleasant than it would otherwise be. I know that Brougham dislikes me; and I have not the slightest doubt that he feels great pleasure in taking this subject out of my hands, and at having made me understand, as I do most clearly understand, how far my services are rated below his. I do not blame you in the least. I do not see how you could have acted otherwise. But, on the other hand, I do not see why I should make any efforts or sacrifices for a Review which lies under an intolerable dictation. Whatever my writings may be worth, it is not for want of strong solicitations, and tempting offers, from other quarters that I have continued to send them to the Edinburgh Review. I adhered to the connection solely because I took pride and pleasure in it. It has now become a source of humiliation and mortification.

I again repeat, my dear Sir, that I do not blame you in the least. This, however, only makes matters worse. If you had used me ill, I might complain, and might hope to be better treated another time. Unhappily you are in a situation in which it is proper for you to do what it would be improper in me to endure. What has happened now may happen next quarter, and must happen before long, unless I altogether refrain from writing for the Review. I hope you will forgive me if I say that I feel what has passed too strongly to be inclined to expose myself to a recurrence of the same vexations.

Yours most truly

T. B. MACAULAY.

A few soft words induced Macaulay to reconsider his threat of withdrawing from the Review; but, even before Mr. Napier's answer reached him, the feeling of personal annoyance had already been effaced by a greater sorrow. A letter arrived, announcing that his sister Jane had died suddenly and most unexpectedly. She was found in the morning lying as though still asleep, having passed away so peacefully as not to disturb a sister who had spent the night in the next room, with a door open between them. Mrs. Macaulay never recovered from this shock. Her health gave way, and she lived into the coming year only so long as to enable her to rejoice in the first of her son's Parliamentary successes.

Paris: September 26.

My dear Father,—

This news has broken my heart. I am fit neither to go nor to stay. I can do nothing but sit down in my room, and think of poor dear Jane's kindness and affection. When I am calmer, I will let you know my intentions. There will be neither use nor pleasure in remaining here. My present purpose, as far as I can form one, is to set off in two or three days for England; and in the meantime to see nobody, if I can help it, but Dumont, who has been very kind to me. Love to all,—to all who are left me to love. We must love each other better.

T. B. M.

London: March 30, 1831.

Dear Ellis,—

I have little news for you, except what you will learn from the papers as well as from me. It is clear that the Reform Bill must pass, either in this or in another Parliament. The majority of one does not appear to me, as it does to you, by any means inauspicious. We should perhaps have had a better plea for a dissolution if the majority had been the other way. But surely a dissolution under such circumstances would have been a most alarming thing. If there should be a dissolution now, there will not be that ferocity in the public mind which there would have been if the House of Commons had refused to entertain the Bill at all. I confess that, till we had a majority, I was half inclined to tremble at the storm which we had raised. At present I think that we are absolutely certain of victory, and of victory without commotion.

Such a scene as the division of last Tuesday I never saw, and never expect to see again. If I should live fifty years, the impression of it will be as fresh and sharp in my mind as if it had just taken place. It was like seeing Cæsar stabbed in the Senate House, or seeing Oliver taking the mace from the table; a sight to be seen only once, and never to be forgotten. The crowd overflowed the House in every part. When the strangers were cleared out, and the doors locked, we had six hundred and eight members present,—more by fifty-five than ever were in a division before. The Ayes and Noes were like two volleys of cannon from opposite sides of a field of battle. When the opposition went out into the lobby, an operation which took up twenty minutes or more, we spread ourselves over the benches on both sides of the House: for there were many of us who had not been able to find a seat during the evening.[1] When the doors were shut we began to speculate on our numbers. Everybody was desponding. 'We have lost it. We are only two hundred and eighty at most. I do not think we are two hundred and fifty. They are three hundred. Alderman Thompson has counted them. He says they are two hundred and ninety-nine.' This was the talk on our benches. I wonder that men who have been long in Parliament do not acquire a better coup d'œil for numbers. The House, when only the Ayes were in it, looked to me a very fair House,—much fuller than it generally is even on debates of considerable interest. I had no hope, however, of three hundred. As the tellers passed along

[1] 'The practice in the Commons, until 1836, was to send one party forth into the lobby, the other remaining in the House.'—Sir T. Erskine May's 'Parliamentary Practice.'

our lowest row on the left hand side the interest was insupportable,—two hundred and ninety-one,—two hundred and ninety-two,—we were all standing up and stretching forward, telling with the tellers. At three hundred there was a short cry of joy,—at three hundred and two another,—suppressed however in a moment: for we did not yet know what the hostile force might be. We knew, however, that we could not be severely beaten. The doors were thrown open, and in they came. Each of them, as he entered, brought some different report of their numbers. It must have been impossible, as you may conceive, in the lobby, crowded as they were, to form any exact estimate. First we heard that they were three hundred and three; then that number rose to three hundred and ten; then went down to three hundred and seven. Alexander Baring told me that he had counted, and that they were three hundred and four. We were all breathless with anxiety, when Charles Wood, who stood near the door, jumped up on a bench and cried out, 'They are only three hundred and one.' We set up a shout that you might have heard to Charing Cross, waving our hats, stamping against the floor, and clapping our hands. The tellers scarcely got through the crowd: for the House was thronged up to the table, and all the floor was fluctuating with heads like the pit of a theatre. But you might have heard a pin drop as Duncannon read the numbers. Then again the shouts broke out, and many of us shed tears. I could scarcely refrain. And the jaw of Peel fell; and the face of Twiss was as the face of a damned soul; and Herries looked like Judas taking his necktie off for the last operation. We shook hands, and clapped each other on the back, and went out laughing, crying, and huzzaing into the lobby. And no sooner were the outer doors opened than another shout answered that within the House. All the passages, and the stairs into the waiting-rooms, were thronged by people who had waited till four in the morning to know the issue. We passed through a narrow lane between two thick masses of them; and all the way down they were shouting and waving their hats, till we got into the open air. I called a cabriolet, and the first thing the driver asked was, 'Is the Bill carried?' 'Yes, by one.' 'Thank God for it, Sir.' And away I rode to Gray's Inn,—and so ended a scene which will probably never be equalled till the reformed Parliament wants reforming; and that I hope will not be till the days of our grandchildren, till that truly orthodox and apostolical person Dr. Francis Ellis is an archbishop of eighty.

As for me, I am for the present a sort of lion. My speech has set me in the front rank, if I can keep there; and it has not been my luck hitherto to lose ground when I have once got it. Sheil and I are on very civil terms. He talks largely concerning Demosthenes and Burke. He made, I must say, an excellent speech; too florid and queer, but decidedly successful.

Why did not Price speak? If he was afraid, it was not without reason: for a more terrible audience there is not in the world. I wish that Praed had known to whom he was speaking. But, with all his talent, he has no tact, and he has fared accordingly. Tierney used to say that he never rose in the House without feeling his knees tremble under him: and I am sure that no man who has not some of that feeling will ever succeed there.

Ever yours

T. B. MACAULAY.

London: May 27, 1831.

My dear Hannah,—

Let me see if I can write a letter à la Richardson:—a little less prolix it must be, or it will exceed my ounce. By the bye, I wonder that Uncle Selby never grudged the postage of Miss Byron's letters. According to the nearest calculation that I can make, her correspondence must have enriched the post office of Ashby Canons by something more than the whole annual interest of her fifteen thousand pounds.

I reached Lansdowne House by a quarter to eleven,

and passed through the large suite of rooms to the great Sculpture Gallery. There were seated and standing perhaps three hundred people, listening to the performers, or talking to each other. The room is the handsomest and largest, I am told, in any private house in London. I enclose our musical bill of fare. Fanny, I suppose, will be able to expound it better than I. The singers were more showily dressed than the auditors, and seemed quite at home. As to the company, there was just everybody in London (except that little million and a half that you wot of,)—the Chancellor, and the First Lord of the Admiralty, and Sydney Smith, and Lord Mansfield, and all the Barings and the Fitzclarences, and a hideous Russian spy, whose face I see everywhere, with a star on his coat. During the interval between the delights of 'I tuoi frequenti,' and the ecstasies of 'Se tu m'ami,' I contrived to squeeze up to Lord Lansdowne. I was shaking hands with Sir James Macdonald, when I heard a command behind us: 'Sir James, introduce me to Mr. Macaulay:' and we turned, and there sate a large bold-looking woman, with the remains of a fine person, and the air of Queen Elizabeth. 'Macaulay,' said Sir James, 'let me present you to Lady Holland.' Then was her ladyship gracious beyond description, and asked me to dine and take a bed at Holland House next Tuesday. I accepted the dinner, but declined the bed, and I have since repented that I so declined it. But I probably shall have an opportunity of retracting on Tuesday.

To-night I go to another musical party at Marshall's, the late M.P. for Yorkshire. Everybody is talking of Paganini and his violin. The man seems to be a miracle. The newspapers say that long streamy flakes of music fall from his string, interspersed with luminous points of sound which ascend the air and appear like stars. This eloquence is quite beyond me.

Ever yours

T. B. M.

London: May 28, 1831.

My dear Hannah,—

More gaieties and music-parties; not so fertile of adventures as that memorable masquerade whence Harriet Byron was carried away; but still I hope that the narrative of what passed there will gratify 'the venerable circle.' Yesterday I dressed, called a cab, and was whisked away to Hill Street. I found old Marshall's house a very fine one. He ought indeed to have a fine one; for he has, I believe, at least thirty thousand a year. The carpet was taken up, and chairs were set out in rows, as if we had been at a religious meeting. Then we had flute-playing by the first flute-player in England, and pianoforte-strumming by the first pianoforte-strummer in England, and singing by all the first singers in England, and Signor Rubini's incomparable tenor, and Signor Curioni's incomparable counter-tenor, and Pasta's incomparable expression. You who know how airs much inferior to these take my soul, and lap it in Elysium, will form some faint conception of my transport. Sharp beckoned me to sit by him in the back row. These old fellows are so selfish. 'Always,' said he, 'establish yourself in the middle of the row against the wall: for, if you sit in the front or next the edges, you will be forced to give up your seat to the ladies who are standing.' I had the gallantry to surrender mine to a damsel who had stood for a quarter of an hour; and I lounged into the ante-rooms, where I found Samuel Rogers. Rogers and I sate together on a bench in one of the passages, and had a good deal of very pleasant conversation. He was,—as indeed he has always been to me,—extremely kind, and told me that, if it were in his power, he would contrive to be at Holland House with me, to give me an insight into its ways. He is the great oracle of that circle.

He has seen the King's letter to Lord Grey, respecting the Garter; or at least has authentic information about it. It is a happy stroke of policy, and will, they say, decide many wavering votes in the House of

Lords. The King, it seems, requests Lord Grey to take the order, as a mark of royal confidence in him 'at so critical a time:'—significant words, I think.

Ever yours

T. B. MACAULAY.

To Hannah More Macaulay.

London: May 30, 1831.

Well, my dear, I have been to Holland House. I took a glass coach, and arrived, through a fine avenue of elms, at the great entrance towards seven o'clock. The house is delightful;—the very perfection of the old Elizabethan style;—a considerable number of very large and very comfortable rooms, rich with antique carving and gilding, but carpeted and furnished with all the skill of the best modern upholsterers. The library is a very long room,—as long, I should think, as the gallery at Rothley Temple,—with little cabinets for study branching out of it, warmly and snugly fitted up and looking out on very beautiful grounds. The collection of books is not, like Lord Spencer's, curious; but it contains almost everything that one ever wished to read. I found nobody there when I arrived but Lord Russell, the son of the Marquess of Tavistock. We are old House of Commons friends: so we had some very pleasant talk, and in a little while in came Allen, who is warden of Dulwich College, and who lives almost entirely at Holland House. He is certainly a man of vast information and great conversational powers Some other gentlemen dropped in, and we chatted till Lady Holland made her appearance. Lord Holland dined by himself on account of his gout. We sat down to dinner in a fine long room, the wainscot of which is rich with gilded coronets, roses, and portcullises. There were Lord Albemarle, Lord Alvanley, Lord Russell, Lord Mahon,—a violent Tory, but a very agreeable companion, and a very good scholar. There was Cradock, a fine fellow who was the Duke of Wellington's aide-de-camp in 1815, and some other people whose names I did not catch. What however is more to the purpose, there was a most excellent dinner. I have always heard that Holland House is famous for its good cheer, and certainly the reputation is not unmerited. After dinner Lord Holland was wheeled in, and placed very near me. He was extremely amusing and good-natured.

In the drawing-room I had a long talk with Lady Holland about the antiquities of the house, and about the purity of the English language, wherein she thinks herself a critic. I happened, in speaking about the Reform Bill, to say that I wished that it had been possible to form a few commercial constituencies, if the word constituency were admissible. 'I am glad you put that in,' said her ladyship. 'I was just going to give it you. It is an odious word. Then there is *talented*, and *influential*, and *gentlemanly*. I never could break Sheridan of *gentlemanly*, though he allowed it to be wrong.' We talked about the word *talents* and its history. I said that it had first appeared in theological writing, that it was a metaphor taken from the parable in the New Testament, and that it had gradually passed from the vocabulary of divinity into common use. I challenged her to find it in any classical writer on general subjects before the Restoration, or even before the year 1700. I believe that I might safely have gone down later. She seemed surprised by this theory, never having, so far as I could judge, heard of the parable of the talents. I did not tell her, though I might have done so, that a person who professes to be a critic in the delicacies of the English language ought to have the Bible at his fingers' ends.

She is certainly a woman of considerable talents and great literary acquirements. To me she was excessively gracious; yet there is a haughtiness in her courtesy which, even after all that I had heard of her, surprised me. The centurion did not keep his soldiers in better order than she keeps her guests. It is to one 'Go,' and he goeth; and to another 'Do this,' and it is done. 'Ring the bell, Mr. Macaulay.' 'Lay down that screen, Lord Russell; you will spoil it.' 'Mr. Allen, take a candle and show Mr. Cradock the picture of Buonaparte.' Lord Holland is, on the other hand, all kindness, simplicity, and vivacity. He talked very well both on politics and on literature. He asked me in a very friendly manner about my father's health, and begged to be remembered to him.

When my coach came, Lady Holland made me promise that I would on the first fine morning walk out to breakfast with them, and see the grounds;—and, after drinking a glass of very good iced lemonade, I took my leave, much amused and pleased. The house certainly deserves its reputation for pleasantness, and her ladyship used me, I believe, as well as it is her way to use anybody.

Ever yours
T. B. M.

To Hannah M. Macaulay.

Court of Commissioners,
Basinghall Street: May 31, 1831.

My dear Sister,—

How delighted I am that you like my letters, and how obliged by yours! But I have little more than my thanks to give for your last. I have nothing to tell about great people to-day. I heard no fine music yesterday, saw nobody above the rank of a baronet, and was shut up in my own room reading and writing all the morning. This day seems likely to pass in much the same way, except that I have some bankruptcy business to do, and a couple of sovereigns to receive. So here I am, with three of the ugliest attorneys that ever deserved to be transported sitting opposite to me; a disconsolate-looking bankrupt, his hands in his empty pockets, standing behind; a lady scolding for her money, and refusing to be comforted because it is not; and a surly butcher-like looking creditor, growling like a house-dog, and saying, as plain as looks can say: 'If I sign your certificate, blow me, that's all.' Among these fair and interesting forms, on a piece of official paper, with a pen and ink found at the expense of the public, am I writing to Nancy.

These dirty courts, filled with Jew money-lenders, sheriffs' officers, attorneys' runners, and a crowd of people who live by giving sham bail and taking false oaths, are not by any means such good subjects for a lady's correspondent as the Sculpture Gallery at Lansdowne House, or the conversatory at Holland House, or the notes of Pasta, or the talk of Rogers. But we cannot be always fine. When my Richardsonian epistles are published, there must be dull as well as amusing letters among them; and this letter is, I think, as good as those sermons of Sir Charles to Geronymo which Miss Byron hypocritically asked for, or as the greater part of that stupid last volume.

We shall soon have more attractive matter. I shall walk out to breakfast at Holland House; and I am to dine with Sir George Philips, and with his son the member for Steyning, who have the best of company; and I am going to the fancy ball of —— the Jew. He met me in the street, and implored me to come. 'You need not dress more than for an evening party. You had better come. You will be delighted. It will be so very pretty.' I thought of Dr. Johnson and the herdsman with his 'See, such pretty goats.'[1] However, I told my honest Hebrew that I would come. I may perhaps, like the Benjamites, steal away some Israelite damsel in the middle of her dancing.

But the noise all round me is becoming louder, and a baker in a white coat is bellowing for the book to prove a debt of nine pounds fourteen shillings and fourpence. So I must finish my letter and fall to business.

Ever yours
T. B. M.

[1] See Boswell's Tour to the Hebrides, Sept. 1, 1773. 'The Doctor was prevailed with to mount one of Vass's grays. As he rode upon it downhill, it did not go well, and he grumbled. I walked on a little before, but was excessively entertained with the method taken to keep him in good humour. Hay led the horse's head, talking to Dr. Johnson as

To Hannah M. Macaulay.

London: June 1, 1831.

My dear Sister,—

My last letter was a dull one. I mean this to be very amusing. My last was about Basinghall Street, attorneys, and bankrupts. But for this,—take it dramatically in the German style.

Fine morning. Scene, the great entrance of Holland House.

Enter MACAULAY *and* TWO FOOTMEN *in livery.*

First Footman.—Sir, may I venture to demand your name?
Macaulay.—Macaulay, and thereto I add M.P.
And that addition, even in these proud halls,
May well ensure the bearer some respect.
Second Footman.—And art thou come to breakfast with our Lord?
Macaulay.—I am: for so his hospitable will,
And hers—the peerless dame ye serve—hath bade.
First Footman.—Ascend the stair, and thou above shalt find,
On snow-white linen spread, the luscious meal.

(*Exit* MACAULAY *upstairs.*)

In plain English prose, I went this morning to breakfast at Holland House. The day was fine, and I arrived at twenty minutes after ten. After I had lounged a short time in the dining-room, I heard a gruff good-natured voice asking, 'Where is Mr. Macaulay? Where have you put him?' and in his armchair Lord Holland was wheeled in. He took me round the apartments, he riding and I walking. He gave me the history of the most remarkable portraits in the library, where there is, by the bye, one of the few bad pieces of Lawrence that I have seen—a head of Charles James Fox, an ignominious failure. Lord Holland said that it was the worst ever painted of so eminent a

much as he could: and, (having heard him, in the forenoon, express a pastoral pleasure on seeing the goats browsing,) just when the Doctor was uttering his displeasure, the fellow cried, with a very Highland accent, "See, such pretty goats!" Then he whistled *whu!* and made them jump.'

man by so eminent an artist. There is a very fine head of Machiavelli, and another of Earl Grey, a very different sort of man. I observed a portrait of Lady Holland painted some thirty years ago. I could have cried to see the change. She must have been a most beautiful woman. She still looks, however, as if she had been handsome, and shows in one respect great taste and sense. She does not rouge at all; and her costume is not youthful, so that she looks as well in the morning as in the evening. We came back to the dining-room. Our breakfast party consisted of my Lord and Lady, myself, Lord Russell, and Luttrell. You must have heard of Luttrell. I met him once at Rogers's; and I have seen him, I think, in other places. He is a famous wit,—the most popular, I think, of all the professed wits,—a man who has lived in the highest circles, a scholar, and no contemptible poet. He wrote a little volume of verse entitled 'Advice to Julia,'—not first rate, but neat, lively, piquant, and showing the most consummate knowledge of fashionable life.

We breakfasted on very good coffee, and very good tea, and very good eggs, butter kept in the midst of ice, and hot rolls. Lady Holland told us her dreams; how she had dreamed that a mad dog bit her foot, and how she set off to Brodie, and lost her way in St. Martin's Lane, and could not find him. She hoped, she said, the dream would not come true. I said that I had had a dream which admitted of no such hope; for I had dreamed that I heard Pollock speak in the House of Commons, that the speech was very long, and that he was coughed down. This dream of mine diverted them much.

After breakfast Lady Holland offered to conduct me to her own drawing-room, or, rather, commanded my attendance. A very beautiful room it is, opening on a terrace, and wainscoted with miniature paintings interesting from their merit, and interesting from their history. Among them I remarked a great many,—thirty, I should think,—which even I, who am no great connoisseur, saw at once could come from no hand but Stothard's. They were all on subjects from Lord Byron's poems. 'Yes,' said she; 'poor Lord Byron sent them to me a short time before the separation. I sent them back, and told him that, if he gave them away, he ought to give them to Lady Byron. But he said that he would not, and that if I did not take them, the bailiffs would, and that they would be lost in the wreck.' Her ladyship then honoured me so far as to conduct me through her dressing-room into the great family bedchamber to show me a very fine picture by Reynolds of Fox, when a boy, birdsnesting. She then consigned me to Luttrell, asking him to show me the grounds.

Through the grounds we went, and very pretty I thought them. In the Dutch garden is a fine bronze bust of Napoleon, which Lord Holland put up in 1817, while Napoleon was a prisoner at St. Helena. The inscription was selected by his lordship, and is remarkably happy. It is from Homer's Odyssey. I will translate it, as well as I can extempore, into a measure which gives a better idea of Homer's manner than Pope's sing-song couplet.

For not, be sure, within the grave
Is hid that prince, the wise, the brave;
But in an islet's narrow bound,
With the great Ocean roaring round,
The captive of a foeman base
He pines to view his native place.

There is a seat near the spot which is called Rogers's seat. The poet loves, it seems, to sit there. A very elegant inscription by Lord Holland is placed over it.

Here Rogers sate; and here for ever dwell
With me those pleasures which he sang so well.

Very neat and condensed, I think. Another inscription by Luttrell hangs there. Luttrell adjured me with mock pathos to spare his blushes; but I am author enough to know what the blushes of authors mean. So I read the lines, and very pretty and polished they were, but too many to be remembered from one reading.

Having gone round the grounds I took my leave,

very much pleased with the place. Lord Holland is extremely kind. But that is of course; for he is kindness itself. Her ladyship too, which is by no means of course, is all graciousness and civility. But, for all this, I would much rather be quietly walking with you: and the great use of going to these fine places is to learn how happy it is possible to be without them. Indeed, I care so little for them that I certainly should not have gone to-day, but that I thought that I should be able to find materials for a letter which you might like.

Farewell.

T. B. MACAULAY.

To Hannah M. Macaulay.

London: June 3, 1831.

My dear Sister,—

I cannot tell you how delighted I am to find that my letters amuse you. But sometimes I must be dull like my neighbours. I paid no visits yesterday, and have no news to relate to-day. I am sitting again in Basinghall Street; and Basil Montagu is haranguing about Lord Verulam, and the way of inoculating one's mind with truth; and all this à propos of a lying bankrupt's balance-sheet.[1]

Send me some gossip, my love. Tell me how you go on with German. What novel have you commenced? Or, rather, how many dozen have you finished? Recommend me one. What say you to 'Destiny'? Is the 'Young Duke' worth reading? and what do you think of 'Laurie Todd'?

I am writing about Lord Byron so pathetically that I make Margaret cry, but so slowly that I am afraid I shall make Napier wait. Rogers, like a civil gentleman, told me last week to write no more reviews, and to publish separate works; adding, what for him is a

[1] 'Those who are acquainted with the Courts in which Mr. Montagu practises with so much ability and success, will know how often he enlivens the discussion of a point of law by citing some weighty aphorism, or some brilliant illustration, from the De Augmentis or the Novum Organum.'—Macaulay's Review of Basil Montagu's Edition of Bacon.

very rare thing, a compliment: 'You may do anything, Mr. Macaulay.' See how vain and insincere human nature is! I have been put into so good a temper with Rogers that I have paid him, what is as rare with me as with him, a very handsome compliment in my review.[1] It is not undeserved; but I confess that I cannot understand the popularity of his poetry. It is pleasant and flowing enough; less monotonous than most of the imitations of Pope and Goldsmith; and calls up many agreeable images and recollections. But that such men as Lord Grenville, Lord Holland, Hobhouse, Lord Byron, and others of high rank in intellect, should place Rogers, as they do, above Southey, Moore, and even Scott himself, is what I cannot conceive. But this comes of being in the highest society of London. What Lady Jane Granville called the Patronage of Fashion can do as much for a middling poet as for a plain girl like Miss Arabella Falconer.[2]

But I must stop. This rambling talk has been scrawled in the middle of haranguing, squabbling, swearing, and crying. Since I began it I have taxed four bills, taken forty depositions, and rated several perjured witnesses.

Ever yours
T. B. M.

[1] 'Well do we remember to have heard a most correct judge of poetry revile Mr. Rogers for the incorrectness of that most sweet and graceful passage:—

Such grief was ours,—it seems but yesterday,—
When in thy prime, wishing so much to stay,
'Twas thine, Maria, thine without a sigh
At midnight in a sister's arms to die.
Oh! thou wast lovely; lovely was thy frame,
And pure thy spirit as from heaven it came:
And, when recalled to join the blest above,
Thou diedst a victim to exceeding love
Nursing the young to health. In happier hours,
When idle Fancy wove luxuriant flowers,
Once in thy mirth thou badst me write on thee;
And now I write what thou shalt never see.'

Macaulay's Essay on Byron.

[2] Lady Jane, and Miss Arabella, appear in Miss Edgeworth's 'Patronage.'

To Hannah and Margaret Macaulay.

London: June 7, 1831.

Yesterday I dined at Marshall's, and was almost consoled for not meeting Ramohun Roy by a very pleasant party. The great sight was the two wits, Rogers and Sydney Smith. Singly I have often seen them: but to see them both together was a novelty, and a novelty not the less curious because their mutual hostility is well known, and the hard hits which they have given to each other are in everybody's mouth. They were very civil, however. But I was struck by the truth of what Matthew Bramble, a person of whom you probably never heard, says in Smollett's Humphrey Clinker: that one wit in a company, like a knuckle of ham in soup, gives a flavour: but two are too many. Rogers and Sydney Smith would not come into conflict. If one had possession of the company, the other was silent; and, as you may conceive, the one who had possession of the company was always Sydney Smith, and the one who was silent was always Rogers. Sometimes, however, the company divided, and each of them had a small congregation. I had a good deal of talk with both of them; for, in whatever they may disagree, they agree in always treating me with very marked kindness.

I had a good deal of pleasant conversation with Rogers. He was telling me of the curiosity and interest which attached to the persons of Sir Walter Scott and Lord Byron. When Sir Walter Scott dined at a gentleman's in London some time ago, all the servant-maids in the house asked leave to stand in the passage and see him pass. He was, as you may conceive, greatly flattered. About Lord Byron, whom he knew well, he told me some curious anecdotes. When Lord Byron passed through Florence, Rogers was there. They had a good deal of conversation, and Rogers accompanied him to his carriage. The inn had fifty windows in front. All the windows were crowded with women, mostly English women, to catch a glance at their favourite poet. Among them were some at whose houses he had often been in England, and with whom he had lived on friendly terms. He would not notice them, or return their salutations. Rogers was the only person that he spoke to.

The worst thing that I know about Lord Byron is the very unfavourable impression which he made on men, who certainly were not inclined to judge him harshly, and who, as far as I know, were never personally ill-used by him. Sharp and Rogers both speak of him as an unpleasant, affected, splenetic person. I have heard hundreds and thousands of people who never saw him rant about him: but I never heard a single expression of fondness for him fall from the lips of any of those who knew him well. Yet, even now, after the lapse of five-and-twenty years, there are those who cannot talk for a quarter of an hour about Charles Fox without tears.

Sydney Smith leaves London on the 20th, the day before Parliament meets for business. I advised him to stay, and see something of his friends who would be crowding to London. 'My flock!' said this good shepherd. 'My dear Sir, remember my flock!

The hungry sheep look up and are not fed.'

I could say nothing to such an argument; but I could not help thinking that, if Mr. Daniel Wilson had said such a thing, it would infallibly have appeared in his funeral sermon, and in his Life by Baptist Noel. But in poor Sydney's mouth it sounded like a joke. He begged me to come and see him at Combe Florey. 'There I am, Sir, the priest of the Flowery Valley, in a delightful parsonage, about which I care a good deal, and a delightful country, about which I do not care a straw.' I told him that my meeting him was some compensation for missing Ramohun Roy. Sydney broke forth: 'Compensation! Do you mean to insult me? A beneficed clergyman, an orthodox clergyman, a nobleman's chaplain, to be no more than compensation for a Brahmin; and a heretic Brahmin too, a fellow who has lost his own religion and can't find another; a vile heterodox dog, who, as I am credibly informed, eats beef-steaks in private! A man who has lost his caste! who ought to have melted lead poured down his nostrils, if the good old Vedas were in force as they ought to be.'

These are some Boswelliana of Sydney; not very clerical, you will say, but indescribably amusing to the hearers, whatever the readers may think of them. Nothing can present a more striking contrast to his rapid, loud, laughing utterance, and his rector-like amplitude and rubicundity, than the low, slow, emphatic tone, and the corpse-like face of Rogers. There is as great a difference in what they say as in the voice and look with which they say it. The conversation of Rogers is remarkably polished and artificial. What he says seems to have been long meditated, and might be published with little correction. Sydney talks from the impulse of the moment, and his fun is quite inexhaustible.

Ever yours
T. B. M.

To Hannah M. Macaulay.

London: June 8, 1831.

My dear Sister,—

Yesterday night I went to the Jew's. I had indeed no excuse for forgetting the invitation: for, about a week after I had received the green varnished billet, and answered it, came another in the self-same words and addressed to Mr. Macaulay, Junr. I thought that my answer had miscarried; so down I sate, and composed a second epistle to the Hebrews. I afterwards found that the second invitation was meant for Charles.

I set off a little after ten, having attired myself simply as for a dinner-party. The house is a very fine one. The door was guarded by peace-officers, and besieged by starers. My host met me in a superb court-dress, with his sword at his side. There was a most sumptuous-looking Persian, covered with gold lace. Then there was an Italian bravo with a long beard. Two old gentlemen, who ought to have been wiser, were fools enough to come in splendid Turkish costumes at which everybody laughed. The fancy-dresses were worn almost exclusively by the young people. The ladies for the most part contented themselves with a few flowers and ribands oddly disposed. There was, however, a beautiful Mary Queen of Scots, who looked as well as dressed the character perfectly; an angel of a Jewess in a Highland plaid; and an old woman, or rather a woman,—for through her disguise it was impossible to ascertain her age,—in the absurdest costume of the last century. These good people soon began their quadrilles and galopades, and were enlivened by all the noise that twelve fiddlers could make for their lives.

You must not suppose the company was made up of these mummers. There was Dr. Lardner, and Long, the Greek Professor in the London University, and Sheil, and Strutt, and Romilly, and Owen the philanthropist. Owen laid hold on Sheil, and gave him a lecture on Co-operation which lasted for half an hour. At last Sheil made his escape. Then Owen seized Mrs. Sheil,—a good Catholic, and a very agreeable woman,—and began to prove to her that there could be no such thing as moral responsibility. I had fled at the first sound of his discourse, and was talking with Strutt and Romilly, when behold! I saw Owen leave Mrs. Sheil and come towards us. So I cried out 'Sauve qui peut!' and we ran off. But before we had got five feet from where we were standing, who should meet us face to face but Old Basil Montagu? 'Nay, then,' said I, 'the game is up. The Prussians are on our rear. If we are to be bored to death there is no help for it.' Basil seized Romilly; Owen took possession of Strutt; and I was blessing myself on my escape, when the only human being worthy to make a third with such a pair, J——, caught me by the arm, and begged to have a quarter of an hour's conversation with me. While I was suffering under J——, a smart impudent-looking young dog, dressed like a sailor in a blue jacket and check shirt, marched up, and asked a Jewish-looking damsel near me to dance with him. I thought that I had seen the fellow before; and, after a little looking, I perceived that it was Charles; and most knowingly, I assure you, did he perform a quadrille with Miss Hilpah Manasess.

If I were to tell you all that I saw I should exceed my ounce. There was Martin the painter, and Procter, alias Barry Cornwall, the poet or poetaster. I did not see one Peer, or one star, except a foreign order or two, which I generally consider as an intimation to look to my pockets. A German knight is a dangerous neighbour in a crowd.[1] After seeing a galopade very prettily danced by the Israelitish women, I went downstairs, reclaimed my hat, and walked into the dining-room. There, with some difficulty, I squeezed myself between a Turk and a Bernese peasant, and obtained an ice, a macaroon, and a glass of wine. Charles was there, very active in his attendance on his fair Hilpah. I bade him good night. 'What!' said young Hopeful, 'are you going yet?' It was near one o'clock; but this joyous tar seemed to think it impossible that anybody could dream of leaving such delightful enjoyments till daybreak. I left him staying Hilpah with flagons, and walked quietly home. But it was some time before I could get to sleep. The sound of fiddles was in mine ears; and gaudy dresses, and black hair, and Jewish noses, were fluctuating up and down before mine eyes.

There is a fancy ball for you. If Charles writes a history of it, tell me which of us does it best.

Ever yours
T. B. M.

To Hannah M. Macaulay.

London: June 10, 1831.

My dear Sister,—

I am at Basinghall Street, and I snatch this quarter of an hour, the only quarter of an hour which I am

[1] Macaulay ended by being a German knight himself.

likely to secure during the day, to write to you. I will not omit writing two days running, because, if my letters give you half the pleasure which your letters give me, you will, I am sure, miss them. I have not, however, much to tell. I have been very busy with my article on Moore's Life of Byron. I never wrote anything with less heart. I do not like the book: I do not like the hero; I have said the most I could for him, and yet I shall be abused for speaking as coldly of him as I have done.

I dined the day before yesterday at Sir George Philips's with Sotheby, Morier the author of 'Hadji Baba,' and Sir James Mackintosh. Morier began to quote Latin before the ladies had left the room, and quoted it by no means to the purpose. After their departure he fell to repeating Virgil, choosing passages which everybody else knows and does not repeat. He, though he tried to repeat them, did not know them, and could not get on without my prompting. Sotheby was full of his translation of Homer's Iliad, some specimens of which he has already published. It is a complete failure; more literal than that of Pope, but still tainted with the deep radical vice of Pope's version, a thoroughly modern and artificial manner. It bears the same kind of relation to the Iliad that Robertson's narrative bears to the story of Joseph in the book of Genesis.

There is a pretty allegory in Homer—I think in the last book, but I forget precisely where—about two vessels, the one filled with blessings and the other with sorrow, which stand, says the poet, on the right and left hand of Jupiter's throne, and from which he dispenses good and evil at his pleasure among men. What word to use for these vessels has long posed the translators of Homer. Pope, who loves to be fine, calls them *urns*. Cowper, who loves to be coarse, calls them *casks*;—a translation more improper than Pope's; for a cask is, in our general understanding, a wooden vessel; and the Greek word means an earthen vessel. There is a curious letter of Cowper's to one of his female correspondents about this unfortunate word. She begged that Jupiter might be allowed a more elegant piece of furniture for his throne than a cask. But Cowper was peremptory. I mentioned this incidentally when we were talking about translations. This set Sotheby off. 'I,' said he, 'have translated it *vase*. I hope that meets your ideas. Don't you think vase will do? Does it satisfy you?' I told him, sincerely enough, that it satisfied me; for I must be most unreasonable to be dissatisfied at anything that he chooses to put in a book which I never shall read. Mackintosh was very agreeable; and, as usually happens when I meet him, I learned something from him.[1]

The great topic now in London is not, as you perhaps fancy, Reform, but Cholera. There is a great panic; as great a panic as I remember, particularly in the City. Rice shakes his head, and says that this is the most serious thing that has happened in his time; and assuredly, if the disease were to rage in London as it has lately raged in Riga, it would be difficult to imagine anything more horrible. I, however, feel no uneasiness. In the first place I have a strong leaning towards the doctrines of the anti-contagionists. In the next place I repose a great confidence in the excellent food and the cleanliness of the English.

I have this instant received your letter of yesterday with the enclosed proof-sheets. Your criticism is to a certain extent just: but you have not considered the whole sentence together. *Depressed* is in itself better than *weighed down*: but 'the oppressive privileges which had depressed industry' would be a horrible cacophony. I hope that word convinces you. I have often observed that a fine Greek compound is an excellent substitute for a reason.

I met Rogers at the Athenæum. He begged me to breakfast with him, and name my day, and promised

[1] Macaulay wrote to one of his nieces in September 1859: 'I am glad that Mackintosh's Life interests you. I knew him well; and a kind friend he was to me when I was a young fellow, fighting my way uphill.'

that he would procure me as agreeable a party as he could find in London. Very kind of the old man, is it not? and, if you knew how Rogers is thought of, you would think it as great a compliment as could be paid to a Duke. Have you seen what the author of the 'Young Duke' says about me: how rabid I am, and how certain I am to rat?

Ever yours
T. B. M.

Macaulay's account of the allusion to himself in the 'Young Duke' is perfectly accurate; and yet, when read as a whole, the passage in question does not appear to have been ill-naturedly meant.[1] It is much what any young literary man outside the House of Commons might write of another who had only been inside that House for a few weeks; and it was probably forgotten by the author within twenty-four hours after the ink was dry. It is to be hoped that the commentators of the future will not treat it as an authoritative record of Mr. Disraeli's estimate of Lord Macaulay's political character.

To Hannah M. Macaulay.

London: June 25, 1831.

My dear Sister,—

There was, as you will see, no debate on Lord John Russell's motion. The Reform Bill is to be brought in, read once, and printed, without discussion. The contest will be on the second reading, and will be protracted, I should think, through the whole of the week after next:—next week it will be, when you read this letter.

I breakfasted with Rogers yesterday. There was

[1] 'I hear that Mr. Babington Macaulay is to be returned. If he speaks half as well as he writes, the House will be in fashion again. I fear that he is one of those who, like the individual whom he has most studied, will give up to a party what was meant for mankind. At any rate, he must get rid of his rabidity. He writes now on all subjects as if he certainly intended to be a renegade, and was determined to make the contrast complete.' —The Young Duke, book v. chap. vi.

nobody there but Moore. We were all on the most friendly and familiar terms possible; and Moore, who is, Rogers tells me, excessively pleased with my review of his book, showed me very marked attention. I was forced to go away early on account of bankrupt business; but Rogers said that we must have the talk out; so we are to meet at his house again to breakfast. What a delightful house it is! It looks out on the Green Park just at the most pleasant point. The furniture has been selected with a delicacy of taste quite unique. Its value does not depend on fashion, but must be the same while the fine arts are held in any esteem. In the drawing-room, for example, the chimney-pieces are carved by Flaxman into the most beautiful Grecian forms. The book-case is painted by Stothard, in his very best manner, with groups from Chaucer, Shakespeare, and Boccaccio. The pictures are not numerous; but every one is excellent. In the dining-room there are also some beautiful paintings. But the three most remarkable objects in that room are, I think, a cast of Pope taken after death by Roubiliac; a noble model in terra-cotta by Michael Angelo, from which he afterwards made one of his finest statues, that of Lorenzo de' Medici; and, lastly, a mahogany table on which stands an antique vase.

When Chantrey dined with Rogers some time ago he took particular notice of the vase, and the table on which it stands, and asked Rogers who made the table. 'A common carpenter,' said Rogers. 'Do you remember the making of it?' said Chantrey. 'Certainly,' said Rogers, in some surprise. 'I was in the room while it was finished with the chisel, and gave the workman directions about placing it. 'Yes,' said Chantrey, 'I was the carpenter. I remember the room well, and all the circumstances.' A curious story, I think, and honourable both to the talent which raised Chantrey, and to the magnanimity which kept him from being ashamed of what he had been.

Ever yours affectionately

T. B. M.

To Hannah M. Macaulay.

London: June 29, 1831.

My dear Sister,—

We are not yet in the full tide of Parliamentary business. Next week the debates will be warm and long. I should not wonder if we had a discussion of five nights. I shall probably take a part in it.

I have breakfasted again with Rogers. The party was a remarkable one,—Lord John Russell, Tom Moore, Tom Campbell, and Luttrell. We were all very lively. An odd incident took place after breakfast, while we were standing at the window and looking into the Green Park. Somebody was talking about diners-out. 'Ay,' said Campbell—

'Ye diners-out from whom we guard our spoons.'

Tom Moore asked where the line was. 'Don't you know?' said Campbell. 'Not I,' said Moore. 'Surely,' said Campbell, 'it is your own.' 'I never saw it in my life,' said Moore. 'It is in one of your best things in the Times,' said Campbell. Moore denied it. Hereupon I put in my claim, and told them that it was mine. Do you remember it? It is in some lines called the Political Georgics, which I sent to the Times about three years ago. They made me repeat the lines, and were vociferous in praise of them. Tom Moore then said, oddly enough: 'There is another poem in the Times that I should like to know the author of;—A Parson's Account of his Journey to the Cambridge Election.' I laid claim to that also. 'That is curious,' said Moore. 'I begged Barnes to tell me who wrote it. He said that he had received it from Cambridge, and touched it up himself, and pretended that all the best strokes were his. I believed that he was lying, because I never knew him to make a good joke in his life. And now the murder is out.' They asked me whether I had put anything else in the Times. Nothing, I said, except the Sortes Virgilianæ, which Lord John remembered well. I never mentioned the Cambridge

Journey, or the Georgics, to any but my own family: and I was therefore, as you may conceive, not a little flattered to hear in one day Moore praising one of them, and Campbell praising the other.

I find that my article on Byron is very popular; one among a thousand proofs of the bad taste of the public. I am to review Croker's edition of Bozzy. It is wretchedly ill done. The notes are poorly written, and shamefully inaccurate. There is, however, much curious information in it. The whole of the Tour to the Hebrides is incorporated with the Life. So are most of Mrs. Thrale's anecdotes, and much of Sir John Hawkins's lumbering book. The whole makes five large volumes. There is a most laughable sketch of Bozzy, taken by Sir T. Lawrence when young. I never saw a character so thoroughly hit off. I intend the book for you, when I have finished my criticism on it. You are, next to myself, the best read Boswellite that I know. The lady whom Johnson abused for flattering him[1] was certainly, according to Croker, Hannah More. Another ill-natured sentence about a Bath lady [2] whom Johnson called 'empty-headed' is also applied to your god-mother.

Ever yours
T. B. M.

To Hannah M. Macaulay.

London: July 6, 1831.

My dear Sister,—

I have been so busy during the last two or three days that I have found no time to write to you. I have now good news for you. I spoke yesterday night with a success beyond my utmost expectations. I am half ashamed to tell you the compliments which I have received: but you well know that it is not from vanity, but to give you pleasure, that I tell you what is said

[1] See Boswell's Life of Johnson, April 15, 1778.

[2] 'He would not allow me to praise a lady then at Bath; observing, "She does not gain upon me, sir; I think her empty-headed."'

about me. Lord Althorp told me twice that it was the best speech he had ever heard; Graham, and Stanley, and Lord John Russell spoke of it in the same way; and O'Connell followed me out of the house to pay me the most enthusiastic compliments. I delivered my speech much more slowly than any that I have before made, and it is in consequence better reported than its predecessors, though not well. I send you several papers. You will see some civil things in the leading articles of some of them. My greatest pleasure, in the midst of all this praise, is to think of the pleasure which my success will give to my father and my sisters. It is happy for me that ambition has in my mind been softened into a kind of domestic feeling, and that affection has at least as much to do as vanity with my wish to distinguish myself. This I owe to my dear mother, and to the interest which she always took in my childish successes. From my earliest years, the gratification of those whom I love has been associated with the gratification of my own thirst for fame, until the two have become inseparably joined in my mind.

Ever yours

T. B. M.

To Hannah M. Macaulay.

London: July 8, 1831.

My dear Sister,—

Do you want to hear all the compliments that are paid to me? I shall never end, if I stuff my letters with them: for I meet nobody who does not give me joy. Baring tells me that I ought never to speak again. Howick sent a note to me yesterday to say that his father wished very much to be introduced to me, and asked me to dine with them yesterday, as, by great good luck, there was nothing to do in the House of Commons. At seven I went to Downing Street, where Earl Grey's official residence stands. It is a noble house. There are two splendid drawing-rooms, which overlook St. James's Park. Into these I was shown. The servant told me that Lord Grey was still at the House of Lords, and that her Ladyship had just gone to dress. Howick had not mentioned the hour in his note. I sate down, and turned over two large portfolios of political caricatures. Earl Grey's own face was in every print. I was very much diverted. I had seen some of them before; but many were new to me, and their merit is extraordinary. They were the caricatures of that remarkably able artist who calls himself H. B. In about half an hour Lady Georgiana Grey, and the Countess, made their appearance. We had some pleasant talk, and they made many apologies. The Earl, they said, was unexpectedly delayed by a question which had arisen in the Lords. Lady Holland arrived soon after, and gave me a most gracious reception; shook my hand very warmly, and told me, in her imperial decisive manner, that she had talked with all the principal men on our side about my speech, that they all agreed that it was the best that had been made since the death of Fox, and that it was more like Fox's speaking than anybody's else. Then she told me that I was too much worked, that I must go out of town, and absolutely insisted on my going to Holland House to dine, and take a bed, on the next day on which there is no Parliamentary business. At eight we went to dinner. Lord Howick took his father's place, and we feasted very luxuriously. At nine Lord Grey came from the House with Lord Durham, Lord Holland, and the Duke of Richmond. They dined on the remains of our dinner with great expedition, as they had to go to a Cabinet Council at ten. Of course I had scarcely any talk with Lord Grey. He was, however, extremely polite to me, and so were his colleagues. I liked the ways of the family.

I picked up some news from these Cabinet Ministers. There is to be a Coronation on quite a new plan: no banquet in Westminster Hall, no feudal services, no champion, no procession from the Abbey to the Hall, and back again. But there is to be a service in the Abbey. All the Peers are to come in state and in their robes, and the King is to take the oaths, and be crowned and anointed in their presence. The spectacle will be finer than usual to the multitude out of doors. The few hundreds who could obtain admittance to the Hall will be the only losers.

Ever yours
T. B. M.

To Hannah M. Macaulay.

London: July 11, 1831.

My dear Sister,—

Since I wrote to you I have been out to dine and sleep at Holland House. We had a very agreeable and splendid party; among others the Duke and Duchess of Richmond, and the Marchioness of Clanricarde, who, you know, is the daughter of Canning. She is very beautiful, and very like her father, with eyes full of fire, and great expression in all her features. She and I had a great deal of talk. She showed much cleverness and information, but, I thought, a little more of political animosity than is quite becoming in a pretty woman. However, she has been placed in peculiar circumstances. The daughter of a statesman who was a martyr to the rage of faction may be pardoned for speaking sharply of the enemies of her parent: and she did speak sharply. With knitted brows, and flashing eyes, and a look of feminine vengeance about her beautiful mouth, she gave me such a character of Peel as he would certainly have had no pleasure in hearing.

In the evening Lord John Russell came; and, soon after, old Talleyrand. I had seen Talleyrand in very large parties, but had never been near enough to hear a word that he said. I now had the pleasure of listening for an hour and a half to his conversation. He is certainly the greatest curiosity that I ever fell in with. His head is sunk down between two high shoulders. One of his feet is hideously distorted. His face is as pale as that of a corpse, and wrinkled to a frightful degree. His eyes have an odd glassy stare quite peculiar to them. His hair, thickly powdered and pomatumed, hangs down his shoulders on each side as straight as a pound of tallow candles. His conversation, however, soon makes you forget his ugliness and infirmities. There is a poignancy without effort in all that he says, which reminded me a little of the character which the wits of Johnson's circle give of Beauclerk. For example, we talked about Metternich and Cardinal Mazarin. 'J'y trouve beaucoup à redire. Le Cardinal trompait; mais il ne mentait pas. Or, M. de Metternich ment toujours, et ne trompe jamais.' He mentioned M. de St. Aulaire,—now one of the most distinguished public men of France. I said: 'M. de Saint-Aulaire est beau-père de M. le duc de Cazes, n'est-ce pas?' 'Non, monsieur,' said Talleyrand; 'l'on disait, il y a douze ans, que M. de Saint-Aulaire étoit beau-père de M. de Cazes; l'on dit maintenant que M. de Cazes est gendre de M. de Saint-Aulaire.'[1] It was not easy to describe the change in the relative positions of two men more tersely and more sharply; and these remarks were made in the lowest tone, and without the slightest change of muscle, just as if he had been remarking that the day was fine. He added: 'M. de Saint-Aulaire a beaucoup d'esprit. Mais il est dévot, et, ce qui pis est, dévot honteux. Il va se cacher dans quelque hameau pour faire ses Pâques.' This was a curious remark from a Bishop. He told several stories about the political men of France: not of any great value in themselves; but his way of telling them was beyond all praise,—concise, pointed, and delicately satirical. When he had departed, I could not help breaking out into admiration of his talent for relating anecdotes. Lady Holland said that he had been considered for nearly forty years as the best teller of a story in Europe, and that there was certainly nobody like him in that respect.

When the Prince was gone, we went to bed. In the

[1] This saying remained in Macaulay's mind. He quotes it on the margin of his Aulus Gellius, as an illustration of the passage in the nineteenth book in which Julius Cæsar is described, absurdly enough, as 'perpetuus ille dictator, Cneii Pompeii socer.'

morning Lord John Russell drove me back to London in his cabriolet, much amused with what I had seen and heard. But I must stop.

Ever yours
T. B. M.

To Hannah M. Macaulay.

Basinghall Street: July 15, 1831.

My dear Sister,—

The rage of faction at the present moment exceeds anything that has been known in our day. Indeed I doubt whether, at the time of Mr. Pitt's first becoming Premier, at the time of Sir Robert Walpole's fall, or even during the desperate struggles between the Whigs and Tories at the close of Anne's reign, the fury of party was so fearfully violent. Lord Mahon said to me yesterday that friendships of long standing were everywhere giving way, and that the schism between the reformers and the anti-reformers was spreading from the House of Commons into every private circle. Lord Mahon himself is an exception. He and I are on excellent terms. But Praed and I become colder every day.

The scene of Tuesday night beggars description. I left the House at about three, in consequence of some expressions of Lord Althorp's which indicated that the Ministry was inclined to yield on the question of going into Committee on the Bill. I afterwards much regretted that I had gone away; not that my presence was necessary; but because I should have liked to have sate through so tremendous a storm. Towards eight in the morning the Speaker was almost fainting. The Ministerial members, however, were as true as steel. They furnished the Ministry with the resolution which it wanted. 'If the noble Lord yields,' said one of our men, 'all is lost.' Old Sir Thomas Baring sent for his razor, and Benett, the member for Wiltshire, for his night-cap; and they were both resolved to spend the whole day in the House rather than give way. If the Opposition had not yielded, in two hours half London would have been in Old Palace Yard.

Since Tuesday the Tories have been rather cowed. But their demeanour, though less outrageous than at the beginning of the week, indicates what would in any other time be called extreme violence. I have not been once in bed till three in the morning since last Sunday. To-morrow we have a holiday. I dine at Lansdowne House. Next week I dine with Littleton, the member of Staffordshire, and his handsome wife. He told me that I should meet two men whom I am curious to see, Lord Plunket and the Marquess Wellesley: let alone the Chancellor, who is not a novelty to me.

Ever yours
T. B. M.

To Hannah M. Macaulay.

London: July 25, 1831

My dear Sister,—

On Saturday evening I went to Holland House. There I found the Dutch Ambassador, M. de Weissembourg, Mr. and Mrs. Vernon Smith, and Admiral Adam, a son of old Adam, who fought the duel with Fox. We dined like Emperors, and jabbered in several languages. Her Ladyship, for an esprit fort, is the greatest coward that I ever saw. The last time that I was there she was frightened out of her wits by the thunder. She closed all the shutters, drew all the curtains, and ordered candles in broad day to keep out the lightning, or rather the appearance of the lightning. On Saturday she was in a terrible taking about the cholera; talked of nothing else; refused to eat any ice because somebody said that ice was bad for the cholera; was sure that the cholera was at Glasgow; and asked me why a cordon of troops was not instantly placed around that town to prevent all intercourse between the infected and the healthy spots. Lord Holland made light of her fears. He is a thoroughly good-natured, open, sensible man; very lively; very intellectual; well read in politics, and in the lighter literature both of ancient and modern times. He sets me more at ease than almost any person that I know, by a certain good-humoured way of contradicting that he has. He always begins by drawing down his shaggy eyebrows, making a face extremely like his uncle, wagging his head and saying: 'Now do you know, Mr. Macaulay, I do not quite see that. How do you make it out?' He tells a story delightfully; and bears the pain of his gout, and the confinement and privations to which it subjects him, with admirable fortitude and cheerfulness. Her Ladyship is all courtesy and kindness to me; but her demeanour to some others, particularly to poor Allen, is such as it quite pains me to witness. He is really treated like a negro slave. 'Mr. Allen, go into my drawing-room and bring my reticule.' 'Mr. Allen, go and see what can be the matter that they do not bring up dinner.' 'Mr. Allen, there is not enough turtle-soup for you. You must take gravy-soup or none.' Yet I can scarcely pity the man. He has an independent income; and, if he can stoop to be ordered about like a footman, I cannot so much blame her for the contempt with which she treats him.

Perhaps I may write again to-morrow.

Ever yours

T. B. M.

To Hannah M. Macaulay.

Library of the House of Commons
July 26, 1831.

My dear Sister,—

Here I am seated, waiting for the debate on the borough of St. Germains with a very quiet party,—Lord Milton, Lord Tavistock, and George Lamb. But, instead of telling you in dramatic form [1] my conversa-

[1] This refers to a passage in a former letter, likewise written from the Library of the House.

' "Macaulay!" Who calls Macaulay? Sir James Graham. What can he have to say to me? Take it dramatically:

Sir J. G. Macaulay!

Macaulay. What?

Sir J. G. Whom are you writing to, that you laugh so much over your letter?

tions with Cabinet Ministers, I shall, I think, go back two or three days, and complete the narrative which I left imperfect in my epistle of yesterday.

At half after seven on Sunday I was set down at Littleton's palace, for such it is, in Grosvenor Place. It really is a noble house: four superb drawing-rooms on the first floor, hung round with some excellent pictures—a Hobbema, (the finest by that artist in the world, it is said,) and Lawrence's charming portrait of Mrs. Littleton. The beautiful original, by the bye, did not make her appearance. We were a party of gentlemen. But such gentlemen! Listen, and be proud of your connection with one who is admitted to eat and drink in the same room with beings so exalted. There were two Chancellors, Lord Brougham and Lord Plunket. There was Earl Gower; Lord St. Vincent; Lord Seaford; Lord Duncannon; Lord Ebrington; Sir James Graham; Sir John Newport; the two Secretaries of the Treasury, Rice and Ellice; George Lamb; Denison; and half a dozen more Lords and distinguished Commoners, not to mention Littleton himself. Till last year he lived in Portman Square. When he changed his residence his servants gave him warning. They could not, they said, consent to go into such an unheard-of part of the world as Grosvenor Place. I can only say that I have never been in a finer house than Littleton's, Lansdowne House excepted,—and perhaps Lord Milton's, which is also in Grosvenor Place. He gave me a dinner of dinners. I talked with Denison, and with nobody else. I have found out that the real use of conversational powers is to put them forth in tête-à-tête. A man is flattered by your talking

Macaulay. To my constituents at Calne, to be sure. They expect news of the Reform Bill every day.

Sir J. G. Well, writing to constituents is less of a plague to you than to most people, to judge by your face.

Macaulay. How do you know that I am not writing a billet doux to a lady?

Sir J. G. You look more like it, by Jove!

Cutlar Ferguson, M.P. for Kirkcudbright. Let ladies and constituents alone, and come into the House. We are going on to the case of the borough of Great Bedwin immediately.'

your best to him alone. Ten to one he is piqued by your overpowering him before a company. Denison was agreeable enough. I heard only one word from Lord Plunket, who was remarkably silent. He spoke of Doctor Thorpe, and said that, having heard the Doctor in Dublin, he should like to hear him again in London. 'Nothing easier,' quoth Littleton; 'his chapel is only two doors off; and he will be just mounting the pulpit.' 'No,' said Lord Plunket; 'I can't lose my dinner.' An excellent saying, though one which a less able man than Lord Plunket might have uttered.

At midnight I walked away with George Lamb, and went—where for a ducat? 'To bed,' says Miss Hannah. Nay, my sister, not so; but to Brooks's. There I found Sir James Macdonald; Lord Duncannon, who had left Littleton's just before us; and many other Whigs and ornaments of human nature. As Macdonald and I were rising to depart we saw Rogers, and I went to shake hands with him. You cannot think how kind the old man was to me. He shook my hand over and over, and told me that Lord Plunket longed to see me in a quiet way, and that he would arrange a breakfast party in a day or two for that purpose.

Away I went from Brooks's—but whither? 'To bed now, I am sure,' says little Anne. No, but on a walk with Sir James Macdonald to the end of Sloane Street, talking about the Ministry, the Reform Bill, and the East India question.

Ever yours

T. B. M.

To Hannah M. Macaulay.

House of Commons Smoking Room: Saturday.

My dear Sister,—

The newspapers will have explained the reason of our sitting to-day. At three this morning I left the House. At two this afternoon I have returned to it, with the thermometer at boiling heat, and four hundred and fifty people stowed together like negroes in the pious John Newton's slave-ship. I have accordingly left Sir Francis Burdett on his legs, and repaired to the smoking-room; a large, wainscoted, uncarpeted place, with tables covered with green baize and writing materials. On a full night it is generally thronged towards twelve o'clock with smokers. It is then a perfect cloud of fume. There have I seen, (tell it not to the West Indians,) Buxton blowing fire out of his mouth. My father will not believe it. At present, however, all the doors and windows are open, and the room is pure enough from tobacco to suit my father himself.

Get Blackwood's new number. There is a description of me in it. What do you think he says that I am? 'A little, splay-footed, ugly, dumpling of a fellow, with a mouth from ear to ear.' Conceive how such a charge must affect a man so enamoured of his own beauty as I am.

I said a few words the other night. They were merely in reply, and quite unpremeditated, and were not ill received. I feel that much practice will be necessary to make me a good debater on points of detail; but my friends tell me that I have raised my reputation by showing that I was quite equal to the work of extemporaneous reply. My manner, they say, is cold and wants care. I feel this myself. Nothing but strong excitement, and a great occasion, overcomes a certain reserve and mauvaise honte which I have in public speaking; not a mauvaise honte which in the least confuses me, or makes me hesitate for a word, but which keeps me from putting any fervour into my tone or my action. This is perhaps in some respects an advantage; for, when I *do* warm, I am the most vehement speaker in the House, and nothing strikes an audience so much as the animation of an orator who is generally cold.

I ought to tell you that Peel was very civil, and cheered me loudly; and that impudent leering Croker congratulated the House on the proof which I had given of my readiness. He was afraid, he said, that I had been silent so long on account of the many allusions which had been made to Calne. Now that I had risen again he hoped that they should hear me often.

See whether I do not dust that varlet's jacket for him in the next number of the Blue and Yellow. I detest him more than cold boiled veal.[1]

After the debate I walked about the streets with Bulwer till near three o'clock. I spoke to him about his novels with perfect sincerity, praising warmly, and criticising freely. He took the praise as a greedy boy takes apple-pie, and the criticism as a good dutiful boy takes senna-tea. He has one eminent merit, that of being a most enthusiastic admirer of mine; so that I may be the hero of a novel yet, under the name of Delamere or Mortimer. Only think what an honour!

Bulwer is to be editor of the New Monthly Magazine. He begged me very earnestly to give him something for it. I would make no promises; for I am already over head and ears in literary engagements. But I may possibly now and then send him some trifle or other. At all events I shall expect him to puff me well. I do not see why I should not have my puffers as well as my neighbours.

I am glad that you have read Madame de Staël's Allemagne. The book is a foolish one in some respects; but it abounds with information, and shows great mental power. She was certainly the first woman of her age; Miss Edgeworth, I think, the second; and Miss Austen the third.

Ever yours
T. B. M.

To Hannah M. Macaulay.

London: August 29, 1831.

My dear Sister,—

Here I am again settled, sitting up in the House of

[1] 'By the bye,' Macaulay writes elsewhere, 'you never saw such a scene as Croker's oration on Friday night. He abused Lord John Russell; he abused Lord Althorp; he abused the Lord Advocate, and we took no notice;—never once groaned or cried "No!" But he began to praise Lord Fitzwilliam;—"a venerable nobleman, an excellent and amiable nobleman," and so forth; and we all broke out together with "Question!" "No, no!" "This is too bad!" "Don't, don't!" He then called Canning his right honourable friend. "Your friend! damn your impudent face!" said the member who sate next me.'

Commons till three o'clock five days in the week, and getting an indigestion at great dinners the remaining two. I dined on Saturday with Lord Althorp, and yesterday with Sir James Graham. Both of them gave me exactly the same dinner; and, though I am not generally copious on the repasts which my hosts provide for me, I must tell you, for the honour of official hospitality, how our Ministers regale their supporters. Turtle, turbot, venison, and grouse, formed part of both entertainments.

Lord Althorp was extremely pleasant at the head of his own table. We were a small party; Lord Ebrington, Hawkins, Captain Spencer, Stanley, and two or three more. We all of us congratulated Lord Althorp on his good health and spirits. He told us that he never took exercise now; that from his getting up, till four o'clock, he was engaged in the business of his office; that at four he dined, went down to the House at five, and never stirred till the House rose, which is always after midnight; that he then went home, took a basin of arrow-root with a glass of sherry in it, and went to bed, where he always dropped asleep in three minutes. 'During the week,' said he, 'which followed my taking office, I did not close my eyes for anxiety. Since that time I have never been awake a quarter of an hour after taking off my clothes.' Stanley laughed at Lord Althorp's arrow-root, and recommended his own supper, cold meat and warm negus; a supper which I will certainly begin to take when I feel a desire to pass the night with a sensation as if I was swallowing a nutmeg-grater every third minute.

We talked about timidity in speaking. Lord Althorp said that he had only just got over his apprehensions. 'I was as much afraid,' he said, 'last year as when first I came into Parliament. But now I am forced to speak so often that I am quite hardened. Last Thursday I was up forty times.' I was not much surprised at this in Lord Althorp, as he is certainly one of the most modest men in existence. But I was surprised to hear Stanley say that he never rose without great uneasiness. 'My throat and lips,' he said, 'when I am going to speak, are as dry as those of a man who is going to be hanged.' Nothing can be more composed and cool than Stanley's manner. His fault is on that side. A little hesitation at the beginning of a speech is graceful; and many eminent speakers have practised it, merely in order to give the appearance of unpremeditated reply to prepared speeches; but Stanley speaks like a man who never knew what fear, or even modesty, was. Tierney, it is remarkable, who was the most ready and fluent debater almost ever known, made a confession similar to Stanley's. He never spoke, he said, without feeling his knees knock together when he rose.

My opinion of Lord Althorp is extremely high. In fact, his character is the only stay of the Ministry. I doubt whether any person has ever lived in England who, with no eloquence, no brilliant talents, no profound information, with nothing in short but plain good sense and an excellent heart, possessed so much influence both in and out of Parliament. His temper is an absolute miracle. He has been worse used than any Minister ever was in debate; and he has never said one thing inconsistent, I do not say with gentlemanlike courtesy, but with real benevolence. Lord North, perhaps, was his equal in suavity and good-nature; but Lord North was not a man of strict principles. His administration was not only an administration hostile to liberty, but it was supported by vile and corrupt means,—by direct bribery, I fear, in many cases. Lord Althorp has the temper of Lord North with the principles of Romilly. If he had the oratorical powers of either of those men, he might do anything. But his understanding, though just, is slow, and his elocution painfully defective. It is, however, only justice to him to say that he has done more service to the Reform Bill even as a debater than all the other Ministers together, Stanley excepted.

We are going,—by *we* I mean the Members of Parliament who are for reform,—as soon as the Bill is through the Commons, to give a grand dinner to

Lord Althorp and Lord John Russell, as a mark of our respect. Some people wished to have the other Cabinet Ministers included: but Grant and Palmerston are not in sufficiently high esteem among the Whigs to be honoured with such a compliment.

Ever yours
T. B. M.

To Hannah M. Macaulay.

London: September 9, 1831.

My dear Sister,—

I scarcely know where to begin, or where to end, my story of the magnificence of yesterday. No pageant can be conceived more splendid. The newspapers will happily save me the trouble of relating minute particulars. I will therefore give you an account of my own proceedings, and mention what struck me most. I rose at six. The cannon awaked me; and, as soon as I got up, I heard the bells pealing on every side from all the steeples in London. I put on my court-dress, and looked a perfect Lovelace in it. At seven the glass coach, which I had ordered for myself and some of my friends, came to the door. I called in Hill Street for William Marshall, M.P. for Beverley, and in Cork Street for Strutt the Member for Derby, and Hawkins the Member for Tavistock. Our party being complete, we drove through crowds of people, and ranks of horseguards in cuirasses and helmets, to Westminster Hall, which we reached as the clock struck eight.

The House of Commons was crowded, and the whole assembly was in uniform. After prayers we went out in order by lot, the Speaker going last. My county, Wiltshire, was among the first drawn; so I got an excellent place in the Abbey, next to Lord Mahon, who is a very great favourite of mine, and a very amusing companion, though a bitter Tory.

Our gallery was immediately over the great altar. The whole vast avenue of lofty pillars was directly in front of us. At eleven the guns fired, the organ struck up, and the procession entered. I never saw so magnificent a scene. All down that immense vista of gloomy arches there was one blaze of scarlet and gold. First came heralds in coats stiff with embroidered lions, unicorns, and harps; then nobles bearing the regalia, with pages in rich dresses carrying their coronets on cushions; then the Dean and Prebendaries of Westminster in copes of cloth of gold; then a crowd of beautiful girls and women, or at least of girls and women who at a distance looked altogether beautiful, attending on the Queen. Her train of purple velvet and ermine was borne by six of these fair creatures. All the great officers of state in full robes, the Duke of Wellington with his Marshal's staff, the Duke of Devonshire with his white rod, Lord Grey with the Sword of State, and the Chancellor with his seals, came in procession. Then all the Royal Dukes with their trains borne behind them, and last the King leaning on two Bishops. I do not, I dare say, give you the precise order. In fact, it was impossible to discern any order. The whole abbey was one blaze of gorgeous dresses, mingled with lovely faces.

The Queen behaved admirably, with wonderful grace and dignity. The King very awkwardly. The Duke of Devonshire looked as if he came to be crowned instead of his master. I never saw so princely a manner and air. The Chancellor looked like Mephistopheles behind Margaret in the church. The ceremony was much too long, and some parts of it were carelessly performed. The Archbishop mumbled. The Bishop of London preached, well enough indeed, but not so effectively as the occasion required; and, above all, the bearing of the King made the foolish parts of the ritual appear monstrously ridiculous, and deprived many of the better parts of their proper effect. Persons who were at a distance perhaps did not feel this; but I was near enough to see every turn of his finger, and every glance of his eye. The moment of the crowning was extremely fine. When the Archbishop placed the crown on the head of the King, the trumpets sounded, and the whole audience cried out 'God save the King.'

All the Peers and Peeresses put on their coronets, and the blaze of splendour through the Abbey seemed to be doubled. The King was then conducted to the raised throne, where the Peers successively did him homage, each of them kissing his cheek, and touching the crown. Some of them were cheered, which I thought indecorous in such a place, and on such an occasion. The Tories cheered the Duke of Wellington; and our people, in revenge, cheered Lord Grey and Brougham.

You will think this a very dull letter for so great a subject: but I have only had time to scrawl these lines in order to catch the post. I have not a minute to read them over. I lost yesterday, and have been forced to work to-day. Half my article on Boswell went to Edinburgh the day before yesterday. I have, though I say it who should not say it, beaten Croker black and blue.[1] Impudent as he is, I think he must be ashamed of the pickle in which I leave him.

Ever yours
T. B. M.

To Hannah M. Macaulay.

London: September 13, 1831.

My dear Sister,—

I am in high spirits at the thought of soon seeing you all in London, and being again one of a family, and of

[1] Mr. Carlyle reviewed Croker's book in 'Fraser's Magazine,' a few months after the appearance of Macaulay's article in the 'Edinburgh.' The two critics seem to have arrived at much the same conclusion as to the merits of the work. 'In fine,' writes Mr. Carlyle, 'what ideas Mr. Croker entertains of a literary *whole*, and the thing called *Book*, and how the very Printer's Devils did not rise in mutiny against such a conglomeration as this, and refuse to print it, may remain a problem. . . . It is our painful duty to declare, aloud, if that be necessary, that his gift, as weighed against the hard money which the booksellers demand for giving it you, is (in our judgment) very much the lighter. No portion, accordingly, of our small floating capital has been embarked in the business, or ever shall be. Indeed, were we in the market for such a thing, there is simply *no* edition of Boswell to which this last would seem preferable.'

a family which I love so much. It is well that one has something to love in private life; for the aspect of public affairs is very menacing;—fearful, I think, beyond what people in general imagine. Three weeks, however, will probably settle the whole, and bring to an issue the question, Reform or Revolution. One or the other I am certain that we must and shall have. I assure you that the violence of the people, the bigotry of the Lords, and the stupidity and weakness of the Ministers, alarm me so much that even my rest is disturbed by vexation and uneasy forebodings; not for myself; for I may gain, and cannot lose; but for this noble country which seems likely to be ruined without the miserable consolation of being ruined by great men. All seems fair as yet, and will seem fair for a fortnight longer. But I know the danger from information more accurate and certain than, I believe, anybody not in power possesses; and I perceive, what our men in power do not perceive, how terrible the danger is.

I called on Lord Lansdowne on Sunday. He told me distinctly that he expected the Bill to be lost in the Lords, and that, if it were lost, the Ministers must go out. I told him, with as much strength of expression as was suited to the nature of our connection, and to his age and rank, that, if the Ministers receded before the Lords, and hesitated to make Peers, they and the Whig party were lost; that nothing remained but an insolent oligarchy on the one side, and an infuriated people on the other; and that Lord Grey and his colleagues would become as odious and more contemptible than Peel and the Duke of Wellington. Why did they not think of all this earlier? Why put their hand to the plough, and look back? Why begin to build without counting the cost of finishing? Why raise the public appetite, and then baulk it? I told him that the House of Commons would address the King against a Tory Ministry. I feel assured that it would do so. I feel assured that, if those who are bidden will not come, the highways and hedges will be ransacked to get together a reforming Cabinet. To one thing my mind is made up. If nobody else will move an address to the Crown against a Tory Ministry, I will.

Ever yours
T. B. M.

London: October 17, 1831.

My dear Ellis,—

I should have written to you before, but that I mislaid your letter and forgot your direction. When shall you be in London? Of course you do not mean to sacrifice your professional business to the work of numbering the gates, and telling the towers, of boroughs in Wales.[1] You will come back, I suppose, with your head full of ten pound householders instead of ἥρωες, and of Caermarthen and Denbigh instead of Carians and Pelasgians. Is it true, by the bye, that the Commissioners are whipped on the boundaries of the boroughs by the beadles, in order that they may not forget the precise line which they have drawn? I deny it wherever I go, and assure people that some of my friends who are in the Commission would not submit to such degradation.

You must have been hard-worked indeed, and soundly whipped too, if you have suffered as much for the Reform Bill as we who debated it. I believe that there are fifty members of the House of Commons who have done irreparable injury to their health by attendance on the discussions of this session. I have got through pretty well, but I look forward, I confess, with great dismay to the thought of recommencing; particularly as Wetherell's cursed lungs seem to be in as good condition as ever.

I have every reason to be gratified by the manner in which my speeches have been received. To say the truth, the station which I now hold in the House is such that I should not be inclined to quit it for any place which was not of considerable importance.

[1] Mr. Ellis was one of the Commissioners appointed to arrange the boundaries of Parliamentary boroughs in connection with the Reform Bill.

What you saw about my having a place was a blunder of a stupid reporter's. Croker was taunting the Government with leaving me to fight their battle, and to rally their followers; and said that the honourable and learned member for Calne, though only a practising barrister in title, seemed to be in reality the most efficient member of the Government. By the bye, my article on Croker has not only smashed his book, but has hit the Westminster Review incidentally. The Utilitarians took on themselves to praise the accuracy of the most inaccurate writer that ever lived, and gave as an instance of it a note in which, as I have shown, he makes a mistake of twenty years and more. John Mill is in a rage, and says that they are in a worse scrape than Croker; John Murray says that it is a damned nuisance: and Croker looks across the House of Commons at me with a leer of hatred, which I repay with a gracious smile of pity.

I am ashamed to have said so much about myself. But you asked for news about me. No request is so certain to be granted, or so certain to be a curse to him who makes it as that which you have made to me.

Ever yours

T. B. MACAULAY.

London: January 9, 1832.

Dear Napier,—

I have been so much engaged by bankrupt business, as we are winding up the affairs of many estates, that I shall not be able to send off my article about Hampden till Thursday the 12th. It will be, I fear, more than forty pages long. As Pascal said of his eighteenth letter, I would have made it shorter if I could have kept it longer. You must indulge me, however; for I seldom offend in that way.

It is in part a narrative. This is a sort of composition which I have never yet attempted. You will tell me, I am sure with sincerity, how you think that I succeed in it. I have said as little about Lord Nugent's book as I decently could.

Ever yours
T. B. M.

London: January 19, 1832.

Dear Napier,—

I will try the Life of Lord Burleigh, if you will tell Longman to send me the book. However bad the work may be, it will serve as a heading for an article on the times of Elizabeth. On the whole, I thought it best not to answer Croker. Almost all the little pamphlet which he published, (or rather printed, for I believe it is not for sale,) is made up of extracts from Blackwood: and I thought that a contest with your grog-drinking, cock-fighting, cudgel-playing Professor of Moral Philosophy would be too degrading. I could have demolished every paragraph of the defence. Croker defended his *θνητοὶ φίλοι*[1] by quoting a passage

[1] 'Mr. Croker has favoured us with some Greek of his own. "At the altar," says Dr. Johnson, "I recommended my *θ φ*." "These letters," says the editor, "(which Dr. Strahan seems not to have understood,) probably mean *θνητοὶ φίλοι*, *departed friends*." Johnson was not a first-rate Greek scholar; but he knew more Greek than most boys when they leave school; and no schoolboy could venture to use the word *θνητοί* in the sense which Mr. Croker ascribes to it without imminent danger of a flogging.'—Macaulay's Review of Croker's Boswell.

Macaulay's opinion of Doctor Johnson, as a man and an author, may best be studied in the Life which he contributed to the Encyclopædia Britannica a short while before he died. Matthew Arnold paid it as sincere a compliment as ever was paid by a great critic, for he asked leave to reprint it at length as an introduction to his own 'Six Chief Lives from Johnson's Lives of the Poets,' in front of which it now stands. 'That Life,' (so Mr. Arnold says in the Preface to his book,) 'is a work which shows Macaulay at his very best; a work written when his style was matured, and when his resources were in all their fulness. The subject, too, was one which he knew thoroughly, and for which he felt cordial sympathy.' When Mr. Arnold applied for permission to use Macaulay's article,—a permission which, as far as in me lay, was gladly given,—he told me that he esteemed the piece to be the most admirable example of literary biography in our language.

of Euripides which, as every scholar knows, is corrupt; which is nonsense and false metre if read as he reads it; and which Markland and Matthiæ have set right by a most obvious correction. But, as nobody seems to have read his vindication, we can gain nothing by refuting it.

Ever yours

T. B. MACAULAY.

CHAPTER V

1832–1834

Macaulay is invited to stand for Leeds—The Reform Bill passes—Macaulay appointed Commissioner of the Board of Control—His life in office—Letters to his sisters—Contested election at Leeds—Macaulay's bearing as a candidate—Canvassing—Pledges—Intrusion of religion into politics—Placemen in Parliament—Liverpool—Margaret Macaulay's marriage—How it affected her brother—He is returned for Leeds—Becomes Secretary of the Board of Control—Letters to Hannah Macaulay—Session of 1832—Macaulay's Speech on the India Bill—His regard for Lord Glenelg—Letters to Hannah Macaulay—The West Indian question—Macaulay resigns Office—He gains his point, and resumes his place—Emancipation of the Slaves—Death of Wilberforce—Macaulay is appointed Member of the Supreme Council of India—Letters to Hannah Macaulay, Lord Lansdowne, and Mr. Napier—Altercation between Lord Althorp and Mr. Shiel—Macaulay's appearance before the Committee of Investigation—He sails for India.

DURING the earlier half of the year 1832 the vessel of Reform was still labouring heavily; but, long before she was through the breakers, men had begun to discount the treasures which she was bringing into port. The time was fast approaching when the country would be called upon to choose its first Reformed Parliament. As if the spectacle of what was doing at Westminster did not satisfy their appetite for political excitement, the Constituencies of the future could not refrain from anticipating the fancied pleasures of an electoral struggle. Impatient to exercise their privileges, and to show that they had as good an eye for a man as those patrons of nomination seats whose discernment was being vaunted nightly in a dozen speeches from the Opposition benches of the House of Commons, the great cities were vying with each other to seek representatives worthy of the occasion and of themselves. The Whigs of Leeds, already provided with one candidate in a member of the great local firm of the Marshalls, resolved to seek for another among the distinguished politicians of their party. As early as October 1831 Macaulay had received a requisition from that town, and had pledged himself to stand as soon as it had been elevated into a Parliamentary borough. The Tories, on their side, brought forward Mr. Michael Sadler, the very man on whose behalf the Duke of Newcastle had done 'what he liked with his own' in Newark,—and, at the last general election, had done it in vain. Sadler, smarting from the lash of the Edinburgh Review, infused into the contest an amount of personal bitterness that for his own sake might better have been spared; and, during more than a twelve-month to come, Macaulay lived the life of a candidate whose own hands are full of public work at a time when his opponent has nothing to do except to make himself disagreeable. But, having once undertaken to fight the battle of the Leeds Liberals, he fought it stoutly and cheerily; and he would have been the last to claim it as a merit, that, with numerous opportunities of a safe and easy election at his disposal, he remained faithful to the supporters who had been so forward to honour him with their choice.

The old system died hard; but in May 1832 came its final agony. The Reform Bill had passed the Commons, and had been read a second time in the Upper House; but the facilities which Committee affords for maiming and delaying a measure of great magnitude and intricacy proved too much for the self-control of the Lords. The King could not bring himself to adopt that wonderful expedient by which the unanimity of the three branches of our legislature may, in the last resort, be secured. Deceived by an utterly fallacious analogy, his Majesty began to be persuaded that the path of concession would lead him whither it had led Louis the Sixteenth; and he resolved to halt on that path at the point where his Ministers advised him to force the hands of their lordships by creating peers. The supposed warnings of the French Revolution, which had been dinned into the ears of the country by every Tory orator from Peel to Sibthorpe, at last had produced their effect on the royal imagination. Earl Grey resigned, and the Duke of Wellington, with a loyalty which certainly did not stand in need of such an unlucky proof, came forward to meet the storm. But its violence was too much even for his courage and constancy. He could not get colleagues to assist him in the Cabinet, or supporters to vote with him in Parliament, or soldiers to fight for him in the streets; and it was evident that in a few days his position would be such as could only be kept by fighting.

The revolution had in truth commenced. At a meeting of the political unions on the slope of Newhall Hill at Birmingham a hundred thousand voices had sung the words:

> God is our guide. No swords we draw.
> We kindle not war's battle fires.
> By union, justice, reason, law,
> We claim the birthright of our sires.

But those very men were now binding themselves by a declaration that, unless the Bill passed, they would pay no taxes, nor purchase property distrained by the tax-gatherer. In thus renouncing the first obligation of a citizen they did in effect draw the sword, and they would have been cravens if they had left it in the scabbard. Lord Milton did something to enhance the claim of his historic house upon the national gratitude by giving practical effect to this audacious resolve; and, after the lapse of two centuries, another Great Rebellion, more effectual than its predecessor, but so brief and bloodless that history does not recognise it as a rebellion at all, was inaugurated by the essentially English proceeding of a quiet country gentleman telling the Collector to call again. The crisis lasted just a week. The Duke had no mind for a succession of Peterloos, on a vaster scale, and with a different issue. He advised the King to recall his Ministers; and his Majesty, in his turn, honoured the refractory lords with a most significant circular letter, respectful in form, but unmistakable in tenor. A hundred peers of the Opposition took the hint, and contrived to be absent whenever Reform was before the House. The Bill was read for a third time by a majority of five to one on the 4th of June; a strange, and not very complimentary, method of celebrating old George the Third's birthday. On the 5th it received the last touches in the Commons; and on the 7th it became an Act, in very much the same shape, after such and so many vicissitudes, as it wore when Lord John Russell first presented it to Parliament.

Macaulay, whose eloquence had signalised every stage of the conflict, and whose printed speeches are, of all its authentic records, the most familiar to readers of our own day, was not left without his reward. He was appointed one of the Commissioners of the Board of Control, which, for three quarters of a century from 1784 onwards, represented the Crown in its relations to the East India directors. His duties, like those of every individual member of a Commission, were light or heavy as he chose to make them; but his own feeling with regard to those duties must not be deduced from the playful allusions contained in letters dashed off, during the momentary leisure of an over-busy day, for the amusement of two girls who barely numbered forty years between them. His speeches and essays teem with expressions of a far deeper than official interest in India and her people; and his minutes remain on record, to prove that he did not affect the sentiment for a literary or oratorical purpose. The attitude of his own mind with regard to our Eastern empire is depicted in the passage on

Burke, in the essay on Warren Hastings, which commences with the words, 'His knowledge of India—,' and concludes with the sentence, 'Oppression in Bengal was to him the same thing as oppression in the streets of London.' That passage, unsurpassed as it is in force of language, and splendid fidelity of detail, by anything that Macaulay ever wrote or uttered, was inspired, as all who knew him could testify, by sincere and entire sympathy with that great statesman of whose humanity and breadth of view it is the merited, and not inadequate, panegyric.

In Margaret Macaulay's journal there occurs more than one mention of her brother's occasional fits of contrition on the subject of his own idleness; but these regrets and confessions must be taken for what they are worth, and for no more. He worked much harder than he gave himself credit for. His nature was such that whatever he did was done with all his heart, and all his power; and he was constitutionally incapable of doing it otherwise. He always underestimated the tension and concentration of mind which he brought to bear upon his labours, as compared with that which men in general bestow on whatever business they may have in hand; and, towards the close of life, this honourable self-deception no doubt led him to draw far too largely upon his failing strength, under the impression that there was nothing unduly severe in the efforts to which he continued to brace himself with ever increasing difficulty.

During the eighteen months that he passed at the Board of Control he had no time for relaxation, and very little for the industry which he loved the best. Giving his days to India, and his nights to the inexorable demands of the Treasury Whip, he could devote a few hours to the Edinburgh Review only by rising at five when the rules of the House of Commons had allowed him to get to bed betimes on the previous evening. Yet, under these conditions, he contrived to provide Mr. Napier with the highly finished articles on Horace Walpole and Lord Chatham, and to gratify a political opponent, who was destined to be a life-long friend, by his kindly criticism and spirited summary of Lord Mahon's 'History of the War of the Succession in Spain.' And, in the 'Friendship's Offering' of 1833, one of those mawkish annual publications of the album species which were then in fashion, appeared his poem of the Armada; whose swinging couplets read as if somewhat out of place in the company of such productions as 'The Mysterious Stranger, or the Bravo of Banff;' 'Away to the Greenwood, a song;' and 'Lines on a Window that had been frozen,' beginning with,

> Pellucid pane, this morn on thee
> My fancy shaped both tower and tree.

To Hannah and Margaret Macaulay.

Bath: June 10, 1832.

My dear Sisters,—

Everything has gone wrong with me. The people at Calne fixed Wednesday for my re-election on taking office; the very day on which I was to have been at a public dinner at Leeds. I shall therefore remain here till Wednesday morning, and read Indian politics in quiet. I am already deep in Zemindars, Ryots, Polygars, Courts of Phoujdary, and Courts of Nizamut Adawlut. I can tell you which of the native Powers are subsidiary, and which independent, and read you lectures of an hour on our diplomatic transactions at the courts of Lucknow, Nagpore, Hydrabad, and Poonah. At Poonah, indeed, I need not tell you that there is no court; for the Paishwa, as you are doubtless aware, was deposed by Lord Hastings in the Pindarree War. Am I not in fair training to be as great a bore as if I had myself been in India?—that is to say, as great a bore as the greatest.

I am leading my watering-place life here; reading, writing, and walking all day; speaking to nobody but the waiter and the chambermaid; solitary in a great crowd, and content with solitude. I shall be in London again on Thursday, and shall also be an M.P. From that day you may send your letters as freely as ever; and pray do not be sparing of them. Do you read any novels at Liverpool? I should fear that the good Quakers would twitch them out of your hands, and appoint their portion in the fire. Yet probably you have some safe place, some box, some drawer with a key, wherein a marble-covered book may lie for Nancy's Sunday reading. And, if you do not read novels, what do you read? How does Schiller go on? I have sadly neglected Calderon: but, whenever I have a month to spare, I shall carry my conquests far and deep into Spanish literature.

Ever yours
T. B. M.

To Hannah and Margaret Macaulay.

London: July 2, 1832.

My dear Sisters,—

I am, I think, a better correspondent than you two put together. I will venture to say that I have written more letters, by a good many, than I have received, and this with India and the Edinburgh Review on my hands; the Life of Mirabeau to be criticised; the Rajah of Travancore to be kept in order; and the bad money, which the Emperor of the Burmese has had the impudence to send us by way of tribute, to be exchanged for better. You have nothing to do but to be good, and write. Make no excuses, for your excuses are contradictory. If you see sights, describe them: for then you have subjects. If you stay at home, write: for then you have time. Remember that I never saw the cemetery or the railroad. Be particular, above all, in your accounts of the Quakers. I enjoin this especially on Nancy; for from Meg I have no hope of extracting a word of truth.

I dined yesterday at Holland House: all Lords except myself. Lord Radnor, Lord Poltimore, Lord

King, Lord Russell, and his uncle Lord John. Lady Holland was very gracious, praised my article on Burleigh to the skies, and told me, among other things, that she had talked on the preceding day for two hours with Charles Grant upon religion, and had found him very liberal and tolerant. It was, I suppose, the cholera which sent her Ladyship to the only saint in the Ministry for ghostly counsel. Poor Macdonald's case was most undoubtedly cholera. It is said that Lord Amesbury also died of cholera, though no very strange explanation seems necessary to account for the death of a man of eighty-four. Yesterday it was rumoured that the three Miss Molyneuxes, of whom by the way there are only two, were all dead in the same way; that the Bishop of Worcester and Lord Barham were no more; and many other foolish stories. I do not believe there is the slightest ground for uneasiness; though Lady Holland apparently considers the case so serious that she has taken her conscience out of Allen's keeping, and put it into the hands of Charles Grant.

Here I end my letter; a great deal too long already for so busy a man to write, and for such careless correspondents to receive.

T. B. M.

To Hannah and Margaret Macaulay.

London: July 6, 1832.

Be you Foxes, be you Pitts,
You must write to silly chits.
Be you Tories, be you Whigs,
You must write to sad young gigs.
On whatever board you are—
Treasury, Admiralty, War,
Customs, Stamps, Excise, Control,—
Write you must, upon my soul.

So sings the judicious poet: and here I sit in my parlour, looking out on the Thames, and divided, like Garrick in Sir Joshua's picture, between Tragedy and Comedy;—a letter to you, and a bundle of papers about Hydrabad, and the firm of Palmer and Co., late bankers to the Nizam.

Poor Sir Walter Scott is going back to Scotland by sea to-morrow. All hope is over; and he has a restless wish to die at home. He is many thousand pounds worse than nothing. Last week he was thought to be so near his end that some people went, I understand, to sound Lord Althorp about a public funeral. Lord Althorp said, very like himself, that if public money was to be laid out, it would be better to give it to the family than to spend it in one day's show. The family, however, are said to be not ill off.

I am delighted to hear of your proposed tour, but not so well pleased to be told that you expect to be bad correspondents during your stay at Welsh inns. Take pens and ink with you, if you think that you shall find none at the Bard's Head, or the Glendower Arms. But it will be too bad if you send me no letters during a tour which will furnish so many subjects. Why not keep a journal, and minute down in it all that you see and hear? and remember that I charge you, as the venerable circle charged Miss Byron, to tell me of every person who 'regards you with an eye of partiality.'

What can I say more? as the Indians end their letters. Did not Lady Holland tell me of some good novels? I remember:—Henry Masterton, three volumes, an amusing story and a happy termination. Smuggle it in, next time that you go to Liverpool, from some circulating library; and deposit it in a lock-up place out of the reach of them that are clothed in drab; and read it together at the curling hour.

My article on Mirabeau will be out in the forthcoming number. I am not a good judge of my own compositions, I fear; but I think that it will be popular. A Yankee has written to me to say that an edition of my works is about to be published in America with my life prefixed, and that he shall be obliged to me to tell him when I was born, whom I married, and so forth. I guess I must answer him slick right away. For, as the judicious poet observes,

> Though a New England man lolls back in his chair,
> With a pipe in his mouth, and his legs in the air,
> Yet surely an Old England man such as I
> To a kinsman by blood should be civil and spry.

How I run on in quotation! But, when I begin to cite the verses of our great writers, I never can stop. Stop I must, however.

Yours
T. B. M.

To Hannah and Margaret Macaulay.

London: July 18, 1832.

My dear Sisters,—

I have heard from Napier. He speaks rapturously of my article on Dumont,[1] but sends me no money. Allah blacken his face! as the Persians say. He has not yet paid me for Burleigh.

We are worked to death in the House of Commons, and we are henceforth to sit on Saturdays. This, indeed, is the only way to get through our business. On Saturday next we shall, I hope, rise before seven, as I am engaged to dine on that day with pretty, witty Mrs. ——. I fell in with her at Lady Grey's great crush, and found her very agreeable. Her husband is nothing in society. Rogers has some very good stories about their domestic happiness,—stories confirming a theory of mine which, as I remember, made you very angry. When they first married, Mrs. —— treated her husband with great respect. But, when his novel came out and failed completely, she changed her conduct, and has, ever since that unfortunate publication, henpecked the poor author unmercifully. And the case, says Rogers, is the harder, because it is suspected that she wrote part of the book herself. It is like the scene in Milton where Eve, after tempting

[1] Dumont's 'Life of Mirabeau.' See the Miscellaneous Writings of Lord Macaulay.

Adam, abuses him for yielding to temptation. But do you not remember how I told you that much of the love of women depended on the eminence of men? And do you not remember how, or behalf of your sex, you resented the imputation?

As to the present state of affairs, abroad and at home, I cannot sum it up better than in these beautiful lines of the poet:

Peel is preaching, and Croker is lying.
The cholera's raging, the people are dying.
When the House is the coolest, as I am alive,
The thermometer stands at a hundred and five.
We debate in a heat that seems likely to burn us,
Much like the three children who sang in the furnace.
The disorders at Paris have not ceased to plague us:
Don Pedro, I hope, is ere this on the Tagus:
In Ireland no tithe can be raised by a parson:
Mr. Smithers is just hanged for murder and arson:
Dr. Thorpe has retired from the Lock, and 'tis said
That poor little Wilks will succeed in his stead.

Ever yours
T. B. M.

To Hannah and Margaret Macaulay.

London: July 21, 1832.

My dear Sisters,—

I am glad to find that there is no chance of Nancy's turning Quaker. She would, indeed, make a queer kind of female Friend.

What the Yankees will say about me I neither know nor care. I told them the dates of my birth, and of my coming into Parliament. I told them also that I was educated at Cambridge. As to my early bon-mots, my crying for holidays, my walks to school through showers of cats and dogs, I have left all those for the 'Life of the late Right Honourable Thomas Babington Macaulay, with large extracts from his correspondence, in two volumes, by the Very Rev. J. Macaulay, Dean of Durham, and Rector of Bishopsgate, with a superb portrait from the picture by Pickersgill in the possession of the Marquis of Lansdowne.'

As you like my verses, I will some day or other write you a whole rhyming letter. I wonder whether any man ever wrote doggrel so easily. I run it off just as fast as my pen can move, and that is faster by about three words in a minute than any other pen that I know. This comes of a schoolboy habit of writing verses all day long. Shall I tell you the news in rhyme? I think I will send you a regular sing-song gazette.

We gained a victory last night as great as e'er was known.
We beat the Opposition upon the Russian loan.
They hoped for a majority, and also for our places.
We won the day by seventy-nine. You should have seen their faces.
Old Croker, when the shout went down our rank, looked blue with rage.
You'd have said he had the cholera in the spasmodic stage.
Dawson was red with ire as if his face was smeared with berries;
But of all human visages the worst was that of Herries.
Though not his friend, my tender heart I own could not but feel
A little for the misery of poor Sir Robert Peel.
But hang the dirty Tories! and let them starve and pine!
Huzza for the majority of glorious seventy-nine!

Ever yours
T. B. M.

To Hannah and Margaret Macaulay.

House of Commons Smoking-Room:
July 23, 1832.

My dear Sisters,—

I am writing here, at eleven at night, in this filthiest of all filthy atmospheres, and in the vilest of all vile company; with the smell of tobacco in my nostrils, and the ugly, hypocritical face of Lieutenant —— before my eyes. There he sits writing opposite to me. To whom, for a ducat? To some secretary of an Hibernian Bible Society; or to some old woman who gives cheap tracts, instead of blankets, to the starving peasantry of Connemara; or to some good Protestant Lord who bullies his Popish tenants. Reject not my letter, though it is redolent of cigars and genuine pigtail; for this is the room—

The room,—but I think I'll describe it in rhyme,
That smells of tobacco and chloride of lime.
The smell of tobacco was always the same:
But the chloride was brought since the cholera came.

But I must return to prose, and tell you all that has fallen out since I wrote last. I have been dining with the Listers at Knightsbridge. They are in a very nice house, next, or almost next, to that which the Wilberforces had. We had quite a family party. There were George Villiers, and Hyde Villiers, and Edward Villiers. Charles was not there. George and Hyde rank very high in my opinion. I liked their behaviour to their sister much. She seems to be the pet of the whole family: and it is natural that she should be so. Their manners are softened by her presence; and any roughness and sharpness which they have in intercourse with men vanishes at once. They seem to love the very ground that she treads on; and she is undoubtedly a charming woman, pretty, clever, lively, and polite.

I was asked yesterday evening to go to Sir John Burke's, to meet another heroine who was very curious to see me. Whom do you think? Lady Morgan. I thought, however, that, if I went, I might not improbably figure in her next novel; and, as I am not ambitious of such an honour, I kept away. If I could fall in with her at a great party, where I could see unseen and hear unheard, I should very much like to make observations on her: but I certainly will not, if I can help it, meet her face to face, lion to lioness.

That confounded, chattering ——, has just got into an argument about the Church with an Irish papist who has seated himself at my elbow: and they keep such a din that I cannot tell what I am writing. There they go. The Lord Lieutenant—the Bishop of Derry—Magee—O'Connell—your Bible meetings—your

Agitation meetings—the propagation of the Gospel—Maynooth College—the Seed of the Woman shall bruise the Serpent's head. My dear Lieutenant, you will not only bruise, but break, my head with your clatter. Mercy! Mercy! However, here I am at the end of my letter, and I shall leave the two demoniacs to tear each other to pieces.

Ever yours
T. B. M.

To Hannah and Margaret Macaulay.

Library of the H. of C.
July 30, 1832, 11 o'clock at night.

My dear Sisters,—

Here I am. Daniel Whittle Harvey is speaking: the House is thin: the subject is dull: and I have stolen away to write to you. Lushington is scribbling at my side. No sound is heard but the scratching of our pens, and the ticking of the clock. We are in a far better atmosphere than in the smoking-room, whence I wrote to you last week; and the company is more decent, inasmuch as that naval officer, whom Nancy blames me for describing in just terms, is not present.

By the bye, you know doubtless the lines which are in the mouth of every member of Parliament, depicting the comparative merits of the two rooms. They are, I think, very happy.

If thou goest into the Smoking-room
Three plagues will thee befall,—
The chloride of lime, the tobacco smoke,
And the Captain who 's worst of all,—
The canting Sea-captain,
The prating Sea-captain,
The Captain who 's worst of all.

If thou goest into the Library
Three good things will thee befall,—
Very good books, and very good air,
And M*c**l*y, who 's best of all,—
The virtuous M*c**l*y,
The prudent M*c**l*y,
M*c**l*y who 's best of all.

Oh, how I am worked! I never see Fanny from Sunday to Sunday. All my civilities wait for that blessed day; and I have so many scores of visits to pay that I can scarcely find time for any of that Sunday reading in which, like Nancy, I am in the habit of indulging. Yesterday, as soon as I was fixed in my best and had breakfasted, I paid a round of calls to all my friends who had the cholera. Then I walked to all the clubs of which I am a member, to see the newspapers. The first of these two works you will admit to be a work of mercy; the second, in a political man, one of necessity. Then, like a good brother, I walked under a burning sun to Kensington to ask Fanny how she did, and stayed there two hours. Then I went to Knightsbridge to call on Mrs. Lister, and chatted with her till it was time to go and dine at the Athenæum. Then I dined, and after dinner, like a good young man, I sate and read Bishop Heber's journal till bedtime. There is a Sunday for you! I think that I excel in the diary line. I will keep a journal like the Bishop, that my memory may

Smell sweet, and blossom in the dust.

Next Sunday I am to go to Lord Lansdowne's at Richmond, so that I hope to have something to tell you. But on second thoughts I will tell you nothing, nor ever will write to you again, nor ever speak to you again. I have no pleasure in writing to undutiful sisters. Why do you not send me longer letters? But I am at the end of my paper, so that I have no more room to scold.

Ever yours
T. B. M.

To Hannah and Margaret Macaulay.

London: August 14, 1832.

My dear Sisters,—

Our work is over at last; not, however, till it has half killed us all.[1] On Saturday we met,—for the last

[1] On the 8th August, 1832, Macaulay writes to Lord Mahon: 'We are now strictly on duty. No furloughs even for

time, I hope, on business. When the House rose, I set off for Holland House. We had a small party, but a very distinguished one. Lord Grey, the Chancellor, Lord Palmerston, Luttrell, and myself were the only guests. Allen was of course at the end of the table, carving the dinner and sparring with my Lady. The dinner was not so good as usual; for the French cook was ill; and her Ladyship kept up a continued lamentation during the whole repast. I should never have found out that everything was not as it should be but for her criticisms. The soup was too salt; the cutlets were not exactly comme il faut; and the pudding was hardly enough boiled. I was amused to hear from the splendid mistress of such a house the same sort of apologies which —— made when her cook forgot the joint, and sent up too small a dinner to table. I told Luttrell that it was a comfort to me to find that no rank was exempted from these afflictions.

They talked about ——'s marriage. Lady Holland vehemently defended the match; and, when Allen said that —— had caught a Tartar, she quite went off into one of her tantrums: 'She a Tartar! Such a charming girl a Tartar! He is a very happy man, and your language is insufferable: insufferable, Mr. Allen.' Lord Grey had all the trouble in the world to appease her. His influence, however, is very great. He prevailed on her to receive Allen again into favour, and to let Lord Holland have a slice of melon, for which he had been petitioning most piteously, but which she had steadily refused on account of his gout. Lord Holland thanked Lord Grey for his intercession.

a dinner engagement, or a sight of Taglioni's legs, can be obtained. It is very hard to keep forty members in the House. Sibthorpe and Leader are on the watch to count us out; and from six till two we never venture further than the smoking-room without apprehension. In spite of all our exertions, the end of the Session seems further and further off every day. If you would do me the favour of inviting Sibthorpe to Chevening Park you might be the means of saving my life, and that of thirty or forty more of us, who are forced to swallow the last dregs of the oratory of this Parliament; and nauseous dregs they are.'

'Ah, Lord Grey, I wish you were always here. It is a fine thing to be Prime Minister.' This tattle is worth nothing, except to show how much the people whose names will fill the history of our times resemble, in all essential matters, the quiet folks who live in Mecklenburg Square and Brunswick Square.

I slept in the room which was poor Mackintosh's. The next day, Sunday, —— came to dinner. He scarcely ever speaks in the society of Holland House. Rogers, who is the bitterest and most cynical observer of little traits of character that ever I knew, once said to me of him: 'Observe that man. He never talks to men; he never talks to girls; but, when he can get into a circle of old tabbies, he is just in his element. He will sit clacking with an old woman for hours together. That always settles my opinion of a young fellow.'

I am delighted to find that you like my review on Mirabeau, though I am angry with Margaret for grumbling at my Scriptural allusions, and still more angry with Nancy for denying my insight into character. It is one of my strong points. If she knew how far I see into hers, she would be ready to hang herself.

Ever yours

T. B. M.

To Hannah and Margaret Macaulay.

London: August 16, 1832.

My dear Sisters,—

We begin to see a hope of liberation. To-morrow, or on Saturday at furthest, we hope to finish our business. I did not reach home till four this morning, after a most fatiguing and yet rather amusing night. What passed will not find its way into the papers, as the gallery was locked during most of the time. So I will tell you the story.

There is a bill before the House prohibiting those processions of Orangemen which have excited a good deal of irritation in Ireland. This bill was committed yesterday night. Shaw, the Recorder of Dublin, an honest man enough, but a bitter Protestant fanatic, complained that it should be brought forward so late in the Session. Several of his friends, he said, had left London believing that the measure had been abandoned. It appeared, however, that Stanley and Lord Althorp had given fair notice of their intention; so that, if the absent members had been mistaken, the fault was their own; and the House was for going on. Shaw said warmly that he would resort to all the means of delay in his power, and moved that the chairman should leave the chair. The motion was negatived by forty votes to two. Then the first clause was read. Shaw divided the House again on that clause. He was beaten by the same majority. He moved again that the chairman should leave the chair. He was beaten again. He divided on the second clause. He was beaten again. He then said that he was sensible that he was doing very wrong; that his conduct was unhandsome and vexatious; that he heartily begged our pardons; but that he had said that he would delay the bill as far as the forms of the House would permit; and that he must keep his word. Now came a discussion by which Nancy, if she had been in the ventilator,[1] might have been greatly edified, touching the nature of vows; whether a man's promise given to himself,—a promise from which nobody could reap any advantage, and which everybody wished him to violate,—constituted an obligation. Jephtha's daughter was a case in point, and was cited by somebody sitting near me. Peregrine Courtenay on one side of the House, and Lord Palmerston on the other, attempted to enlighten the poor Orangeman on the question of casuistry. They might as well have preached to any madman out of St. Luke's. 'I feel,' said the silly creature, 'that I am doing wrong, and acting very unjustifiably. If gentlemen will forgive me, I will never do so again. But I must keep my word.' We roared with laughter every time he repeated his apologies. The orders of the

[1] A circular ventilator, in the roof of the House of Commons, was the only Ladies' Gallery that existed in the year 1832.

House do not enable any person absolutely to stop the progress of a bill in Committee, but they enable him to delay it grievously. We divided seventeen times, and between every division this vexatious Irishman made us a speech of apologies and self-condemnation. Of the two who had supported him at the beginning of his freak one soon sneaked away. The other, Sibthorpe, stayed to the last, not expressing remorse like Shaw, but glorying in the unaccommodating temper he showed and in the delay which he produced. At last the bill went through. Then Shaw rose; congratulated himself that his vow was accomplished; said that the only atonement he could make for conduct so unjustifiable was to vow that he would never make such a vow again; promised to let the bill go through its future stages without any more divisions; and contented himself with suggesting one or two alterations in the details. 'I hint at these amendments,' he said. 'If the Secretary for Ireland approves of them, I hope he will not refrain from introducing them because they are brought forward by me. I am sensible that I have forfeited all claim to the favour of the House. I will not divide on any future stage of the bill.' We were all heartily pleased with these events: for the truth was that the seventeen divisions occupied less time than a real hard debate would have done, and were infinitely more amusing. The oddest part of the business is that Shaw's frank good-natured way of proceeding, absurd as it was, has made him popular. He was never so great a favourite with the House as after harassing it for two or three hours with the most frivolous opposition. This is a curious trait of the House of Commons. Perhaps you will find this long story, which I have not time to read over again, very stupid and unintelligible. But I have thought it my duty to set before you the evil consequences of making vows rashly, and adhering to them superstitiously; for in truth, my Christian brethren, or rather my Christian sisters, let us consider &c. &c. &c.

But I reserve the sermon on promises, which I had intended to preach, for another occasion.

Ever yours

T. B. M.

To Hannah and Margaret Macaulay.

London: August 17, 1832.

My dear Sisters,—

I brought down my story of Holland House to dinner-time on Saturday evening. To resume my narrative, I slept there on Sunday night. On Monday morning, after breakfast, I walked to town with Luttrell, whom I found a delightful companion. Before we went, we sate and chatted with Lord Holland in the library for a quarter of an hour. He was very entertaining. He gave us an account of a visit which he paid long ago to the Court of Denmark; and of King Christian, the madman, who was at last deprived of all real share in the government on account of his infirmity. 'Such a Tom of Bedlam I never saw,' said Lord Holland. 'One day the Neapolitan Ambassador came to the levée, and made a profound bow to his Majesty. His Majesty bowed still lower. The Neapolitan bowed down his head almost to the ground; when, behold! the King clapped his hands on his Excellency's shoulders, and jumped over him like a boy playing at leap-frog. Another day the English Ambassador was sitting opposite the King at dinner. His Majesty asked him to take wine. The glasses were filled. The Ambassador bowed, and put the wine to his lips. The King grinned hideously and threw his wine into the face of one of the footmen. The other guests kept the most profound gravity: but the Englishman, who had but lately come to Copenhagen, though a practised diplomatist, could not help giving some signs of astonishment. The King immediately addressed him in French: "Eh, mais, Monsieur l'Envoyé d'Angleterre, qu'avez-vous donc? Pourquoi riez-vous? Est-ce qu'il y ait quelque chose qui vous ait diverti? Faites-moi le plaisir de me l'indiquer. J'aime beaucoup les ridicules."'

Parliament is up at last. We official men are now left alone at the West End of London, and are making up for our long confinement in the mornings by feasting together at night. On Wednesday I dined with Labouchere at his official residence in Somerset House. It is well that he is a bachelor: for he tells me that the ladies his neighbours make bitter complaints of the unfashionable situation in which they are cruelly obliged to reside gratis. Yesterday I dined with Will Brougham, and an official party, in Mount Street. We are going to establish a Club to be confined to members of the House of Commons in place under the present Government, who are to dine together weekly at Grillon's Hotel, and to settle the affairs of the State better, I hope, than our masters at their Cabinet dinners.

Ever yours
T. B. M.

To Hannah M. Macaulay.

London: September 20, 1832.

My dear Sister,—

I am home again from Leeds, where everything is going on as well as possible. I, and most of my friends, feel sanguine as to the result. About half my day was spent in speaking, and hearing other people speak; in squeezing and being squeezed; in shaking hands with people whom I never saw before, and whose faces and names I forget within a minute after being introduced to them. The rest was passed in conversation with my leading friends, who are very honest substantial manufacturers. They feed me on roast beef and Yorkshire pudding; at night they put me into capital bedrooms: and the only plague which they give me is that they are always begging me to mention some food or wine for which I have a fancy, or some article of comfort and convenience which I may wish them to procure.

I travelled to town with a family of children who ate without intermission from Market Harborough, where they got into the coach, to the Peacock at

Islington, where they got out of it. They breakfasted as if they had fasted all the preceding day. They dined as if they had never breakfasted. They ate on the road one large basket of sandwiches, another of fruit, and a boiled fowl: besides which there was not an orange-girl, an old man with cakes, or a boy with filberts, who came to the coach-side when we stopped to change horses, of whom they did not buy something.

I am living here by myself with no society, or scarcely any, except my books. I read a play of Calderon before I breakfast; then look over the newspaper; frank letters; scrawl a line or two to a foolish girl in Leicestershire; and walk to my Office. There I stay till near five, examining claims of money-lenders on the native sovereigns of India, and reading Parliamentary papers. I am beginning to understand something about the Bank, and hope, when next I go to Rothley Temple, to be a match for the whole firm of Mansfield and Babington on questions relating to their own business. When I leave the Board, I walk for two hours; then I dine; and I end the day quietly over a basin of tea and a novel.

On Saturday I go to Holland House, and stay there till Monday. Her Ladyship wants me to take up my quarters almost entirely there; but I love my own chambers and independence, and am neither qualified nor inclined to succeed Allen in his post. On Friday week, that is to-morrow week, I shall go for three days to Sir George Philips's, at Weston, in Warwickshire. He has written again in terms half complaining; and, though I can ill spare time for the visit, yet, as he was very kind to me when his kindness was of some consequence to me, I cannot, and will not, refuse.

Ever yours

T. B. M.

To Hannah M. Macaulay.

My dear Sister,— London: September 25, 1832.

I went on Saturday to Holland House, and stayed there Sunday. It was legitimate Sabbath employment,—visiting the sick,—which, as you well know, always stands first among the works of mercy enumerated in good books. My Lord was ill, and my Lady thought herself so. He was, during the greater part of the day, in bed. For a few hours he lay on his sofa, wrapped in flannels. I sate by him about twenty minutes, and was then ordered away. He was very weak and languid; and, though the torture of the gout was over, was still in pain: but he retained all his courage, and all his sweetness of temper. I told his sister that I did not think that he was suffering much. 'I hope not,' said she; 'but it is impossible to judge by what he says; for through the sharpest pain of the attack he never complained.' I admire him more, I think, than any man whom I know. He is only fifty-seven, or fifty-eight. He is precisely the man to whom health would be particularly valuable: for he has the keenest zest for those pleasures which health would enable him to enjoy. He is, however, an invalid, and a cripple. He passes some weeks of every year in extreme torment. When he is in his best health he can only limp a hundred yards in a day. Yet he never says a cross word. The sight of him spreads good humour over the face of every one who comes near him. His sister, an excellent old maid as ever lived, and the favourite of all the young people of her acquaintance, says that it is quite a pleasure to nurse him. She was reading the 'Inheritance' to him as he lay in bed, and he enjoyed it amazingly. She is a famous reader; more quiet and less theatrical than most famous readers, and therefore the fitter for the bed-side of a sick man. Her Ladyship had fretted herself into being ill, could eat nothing but the breast of a partridge, and was frightened out of her wits by hearing a dog howl. She was sure that this noise portended her death, or my Lord's. Towards the evening, however, she brightened up, and was in very good spirits. My visit was not very lively. They dined at four, and the company was, as you may suppose at this season, but scanty. Charles Greville, commonly called, heaven knows why, Punch Greville, came on the Saturday. Byng, named from his hair Poodle Byng, came on the Sunday. Allen, like the poor, we had with us always. I was grateful, however, for many pleasant evenings passed there when London was full, and Lord Holland out of bed. I therefore did my best to keep the house alive. I had the library and the delightful gardens to myself during most of the day, and I got through my visit very well.

News you have in the papers. Poor Scott is gone, and I cannot be sorry for it. A powerful mind in ruins is the most heart-breaking thing which it is possible to conceive. Ferdinand of Spain is gone too; and, I fear, old Mr. Stephen is going fast. I am safe at Leeds. Poor Hyde Villiers is very ill. I am seriously alarmed about him. Kindest love to all.

Ever yours
T. B. M.

To Hannah M. Macaulay.

Weston House: September 29, 1832.

My dear Sister,—

I came hither yesterday, and found a handsome house, pretty grounds, and a very kind host and hostess. The house is really very well planned. I do not know that I have ever seen so happy an imitation of the domestic architecture of Elizabeth's reign. The oriels, towers, terraces, and battlements are in the most perfect keeping; and the building is as convenient within as it is picturesque without. A few weather-stains, or a few American creepers, and a little ivy, would make it perfect: and all that will come, I suppose, with time. The terrace is my favourite spot. I always liked 'the trim gardens' of which Milton speaks, and thought that Brown and his imitators went too far in bringing forests and sheep-walks up to the very windows of drawing-rooms.

I came through Oxford. It was as beautiful a day as the second day of our visit, and the High Street was in all its glory. But it made me quite sad to find myself there without you and Margaret. All my old Oxford associations are gone. Oxford, instead of being, as it used to be, the magnificent old city of the seventeenth century,—still preserving its antique character among the improvements of modern times, and exhibiting in the midst of upstart Birminghams and Manchesters the same aspect which it wore when Charles held his court at Christchurch, and Rupert led his cavalry over Magdalene Bridge,—is now to me only the place where I was so happy with my little sisters. But I was restored to mirth, and even to indecorous mirth, by what happened after we had left the fine old place behind us. There was a young fellow of about five-and-twenty, mustachioed and smartly dressed, in the coach with me. He was not absolutely uneducated: for he was reading a novel, the Hungarian Brothers, the whole way. We rode, as I told you, through the High Street. The coach stopped to dine; and this youth passed half an hour in the midst of that city of palaces. He looked about him with his mouth open, as he re-entered the coach, and all the while that we were driving away past the Ratcliffe Library, the Great Court of All Souls, Exeter, Lincoln, Trinity, Balliol, and St. John's. When we were about a mile on the road he spoke the first words that I had heard him utter. 'That was a pretty town enough. Pray, sir, what is it called?' I could not answer him for laughing; but he seemed quite unconscious of his own absurdity.

Ever yours
T. B. M.

During all the period covered by this correspondence the town of Leeds was alive with the agitation of a turbulent, but not very dubious, contest. Macaulay's relations with the electors whose votes he was courting are too characteristic to be omitted altogether from the story of his life; though the style of his speeches and manifestoes is more likely to excite the admiring envy of modern members of Parliament, than to be taken as a model for their communications to their own constituents. This young politician, who depended on office for his bread, and on a seat in the House of Commons for office, adopted from the first an attitude of high and almost peremptory independence which would have sat well on a Prime Minister in his grand climacteric. The following letter, (some passages of which have been here omitted, and others slightly condensed,) is strongly marked in every line with the personal qualities of the writer.

London: August 3, 1832.

'My dear Sir,—I am truly happy to find that the opinion of my friends at Leeds on the subject of canvassing agrees with that which I have long entertained. The practice of begging for votes is, as it seems to me, absurd, pernicious, and altogether at variance with the true principles of representative government. The suffrage of an elector ought not to be asked, or to be given as a personal favour. It is as much for the interest of constituents to choose well, as it can be for the interest of a candidate to be chosen. To request an honest man to vote according to his conscience is superfluous. To request him to vote against his conscience is an insult. The practice of canvassing is quite reasonable under a system in which men are sent to Parliament to serve themselves. It is the height of absurdity under a system under which men are sent to Parliament to serve the public. While we had only a mock representation, it was natural enough that this practice should be carried to a great extent. I trust it will soon perish with the abuses from which it sprung. I trust that the great and intelligent body of people who have obtained the elective franchise will see that seats in the House of Commons ought not to be given, like rooms in an almshouse, to urgency of solicitation; and that a man who surrenders his vote to caresses and supplications forgets his duty as much as if he sold it for a bank-note. I hope to see the day when an Englishman will think it as great an affront to be courted and fawned upon in his capacity of elector as in his capacity of juryman. He would be shocked at the thought of finding an unjust verdict because the plaintiff or the defendant had been very civil and pressing; and, if he would reflect, he would, I think, be equally shocked at the thought of voting for a candidate for whose public character he felt no esteem, merely because that candidate had called upon him, and begged very hard, and had shaken his hand very warmly. My conduct is before the electors of Leeds. My opinions shall on all occasions be stated to them with perfect frankness. If they approve that conduct, if they concur in those opinions, they ought, not for my sake, but for their own, to choose me as their member. To be so chosen I should indeed consider as a high and enviable honour; but I should think it no honour to be returned to Parliament by persons who, thinking me destitute of the requisite qualifications, had yet been wrought upon by cajolery and importunity to poll for me in despite of their better judgment.

'I wish to add a few words touching a question which has lately been much canvassed; I mean the question of pledges. In this letter, and in every letter which I have written to my friends at Leeds, I have plainly declared my *opinions*. But I think it, at this conjuncture, my duty to declare that I will give *no pledges*. I will not bind myself to make or to support any particular motion. I will state as shortly as I can some of the reasons which have induced me to form this determination. The great beauty of the representative system is, that it unites the advantages of popular control with the advantages arising from a division of labour. Just as a physician understands medicine better than an ordinary man, just as a shoemaker makes shoes better than an ordinary man, so a person whose life is passed in transacting affairs of State becomes a better statesman than an ordinary man. In politics, as well as every other department of life, the public ought to have the means of checking those who serve it. If a man finds that he derives no benefit from the prescription of his physician, he calls in another. If his shoes do not fit him, he changes his shoemaker. But when he has called in a physician of whom he hears a good report, and whose general practice he believes to be judicious, it would be absurd in him to tie down that physician to order particular pills and particular draughts. While he continues to be the customer of a shoemaker, it would be absurd in him to sit by and mete every motion of that shoemaker's hand. And in the same manner, it would, I think, be absurd in him to require positive pledges, and to exact daily and hourly obedience, from his representative. My opinion is, that electors ought at first to choose cautiously; then to confide liberally; and, when the term for which they have selected their member has expired, to review his conduct equitably, and to pronounce on the whole taken together.

'If the people of Leeds think proper to repose in me that confidence which is necessary to the proper discharge of the duties of a representative, I hope that I shall not abuse it. If it be their pleasure to fetter their members by positive promises, it is in their power to do so. I can only say that on such terms I cannot conscientiously serve them.

'I hope, and feel assured, that the sincerity with which I make this explicit declaration, will, if it deprive me of the votes of my friends at Leeds, secure to me what I value far more highly, their esteem.

'Believe me ever, my dear Sir,
'Your most faithful Servant,
'T. B. MACAULAY.'

This frank announcement, taken by many as a slight, and by some as a downright challenge, produced remonstrances which, after the interval of a week, were answered by Macaulay in a second letter; worth reprinting if it were only for the sake of his fine parody upon the popular cry which for two years past had been the watchword of Reformers.

'I was perfectly aware that the avowal of my feelings on the subject of pledges was not likely to advance my interest at Leeds. I was perfectly aware that many of my most respectable friends were likely to differ from me: and therefore I thought it the more necessary to make, uninvited, an explicit declaration of my feelings. If ever there was a time when public men were in an especial measure bound to speak *the truth, the whole truth, and nothing but the truth*, to the people, this is that time. Nothing is easier than for a candidate to avoid unpopular topics as long as possible, and, when they are forced on him, to take refuge in evasive and unmeaning phrases. Nothing is easier than for him to give extravagant promises while an election is depending, and to forget them as soon as the return is made. I will take no such course. I do not wish to obtain a single vote on false pretences. Under the old system I have never been the flatterer of the great. Under the new system I will not be the flatterer of the people. The truth, or what appears to me to be such, may sometimes be distasteful to those whose good opinion I most value. I shall nevertheless always abide by it, and trust to their good sense, to their second thoughts, to the force of reason, and the progress of time. If, after all, their decision should be unfavourable to me, I shall submit to that decision with fortitude and good humour. It is not necessary to my happiness that I should sit in Parliament; but it is necessary to my happiness that I should possess, in Parliament or out of Parliament, the consciousness of having done what is right.'

Macaulay had his own ideas as to the limits within which constituents are justified in exerting their privilege of questioning a candidate; and, on the first occasion when those limits were exceeded, he made a notable example of the transgressor. During one of his public meetings, a voice was heard to exclaim from the crowd in the body of the hall: 'An elector wishes to know the religious creed of Mr. Marshall and Mr. Macaulay.' The last-named gentleman was on his legs in a moment. 'Let that man stand up!' he cried. 'Let him stand on a form, where I can see him!' The offender, who proved to be a Methodist preacher, was hoisted on to a bench by his indignant neighbours; nerving himself even in that terrible moment by a lingering hope that he might yet be able to hold his own. But the unhappy man had not a chance against Macaulay, who harangued him as if he were the living embodiment of religious intolerance and illegitimate curiosity. 'I have heard with the greatest shame and sorrow the question which has been proposed to me; and with peculiar pain do I learn that this question was proposed by a minister of religion. I do most deeply regret that any person should think it necessary to make a meeting like this an arena for theological discussion. I will not be a party to turning this assembly to such a purpose. My answer is short, and in one word. Gentlemen, I am a Christian.' At this declaration the delighted audience began to cheer; but Macaulay would have none of their applause. 'This is no subject,' he said, 'for acclamation. I will say no more. No man shall speak of me as the person who, when this disgraceful inquisition was entered upon in an assembly of Englishmen, brought forward the most sacred subjects to be canvassed here, and be turned into a matter for hissing or for cheering. If on any future occasion it should happen that Mr. Carlile should favour any large meeting with his infidel attacks upon the Gospel, he shall not have it to say that I set the example. Gentlemen, I have done; I tell you, I will say no more; and if the person who has thought fit to ask this question has the feelings worthy of a teacher of religion, he will not, I think, rejoice that he has called me forth.'

This ill-fated question had been prompted by a report, diligently spread through the town, that the Whig candidates were Unitarians; a report which, even if correct, would probably have done little to damage their electioneering prospects. There are few general remarks which so uniformly hold good as the observation that men are not willing to attend the religious worship of people who believe less than themselves, or to vote at elections for people who believe more than themselves. While the congregations at a high Anglican service are in part composed of Low churchmen and Broad churchmen; while Presbyterians and Wesleyans have no objection to a sound discourse from a divine of the Establishment; it is seldom the case that any but Unitarians are seen inside a Unitarian chapel. On the other hand, at the general election of 1874, when not a solitary Roman Catholic was returned throughout the length and breadth of the island of Great Britain, the Unitarians retained their long acknowledged pre-eminence as the most over-represented sect in the kingdom.

While Macaulay was stern in his refusal to gratify his electors with the customary blandishments, he gave them plenty of excellent political instruction;

which he conveyed to them in rhetoric, not premeditated with the care that alone makes speeches readable after a lapse of years, but for this very reason all the more effective when the passion of the moment was pouring itself from his lips in a stream of faultless, but unstudied, sentences. A course of mobs, which turned Cobden into an orator, made of Macaulay a Parliamentary debater; and the ear and eye of the House of Commons soon detected, in his replies from the Treasury bench, welcome signs of the invaluable training that can be got nowhere except on the hustings and the platform. There is no better sample of Macaulay's extempore speaking than the first words which he addressed to his committee at Leeds after the Reform Bill had received the Royal assent. 'I find it difficult to express my gratification at seeing such an assembly convened at such a time. All the history of our own country, all the history of other countries, furnishes nothing parallel to it. Look at the great events in our own former history, and in every one of them, which, for importance, we can venture to compare with the Reform Bill, we shall find something to disgrace and tarnish the achievement. It was by the assistance of French arms and of Roman bulls that King John was harassed into giving the Great Charter. In the times of Charles I, how much injustice, how much crime, how much bloodshed and misery, did it cost to assert the liberties of England! But in this event, great and important as it is in substance, I confess I think it still more important from the manner in which it has been achieved. Other countries have obtained deliverances equally signal and complete, but in no country has that deliverance been obtained with such perfect peace; so entirely within the bounds of the Constitution; with all the forms of law observed; the government of the country proceeding in its regular course; every man going forth unto his labour until the evening. France boasts of her three days of July, when her people rose, when barricades fenced the streets, and the entire population of the capital in arms successfully vindicated their liberties. They boast, and justly, of those three days of July; but I will boast of our ten days of May. We, too, fought a battle, but it was with moral arms. We, too, placed an impassable barrier between ourselves and military tyranny; but we fenced ourselves only with moral barricades. Not one crime committed, not one acre confiscated, not one life lost, not one instance of outrage or attack on the authorities or the laws. Our victory has not left a single family in mourning. Not a tear, not a drop of blood, has sullied the pacific and blameless triumph of a great people.'

The Tories of Leeds, as a last resource, fell to denouncing Macaulay as a placeman: a stroke of superlative audacity in a party which, during eight-and-forty years, had been out of office for only fourteen months. It may well be imagined that he found plenty to say in his own defence. 'The only charge which malice can prefer against me is that I am a placeman. Gentlemen, is it your wish that those persons who are thought worthy of the public confidence should never possess the confidence of the King? Is it your wish that no men should be Ministers but those whom no populous places will take as their representatives? By whom, I ask, has the Reform Bill been carried? By Ministers. Who have raised Leeds into the situation to return members to Parliament? It is by the strenuous efforts of a patriotic Ministry that that great result has been produced. I should think that the Reform Bill had done little for the people, if under it the service of the people was not consistent with the service of the Crown.'

Just before the general election Hyde Villiers died, and the Secretaryship to the Board of Control became vacant. Macaulay succeeded his old college friend in an office that gave him weighty responsibility, defined duties, and, as it chanced, exceptional opportunities for distinction. About the same time, an event occurred which touched him more nearly than could any possible turn of fortune in the world of politics. His sisters Hannah and Margaret had for some months been almost domesticated among a pleasant nest of villas which lie in the southern suburb of Liverpool, on Dingle Bank: a spot whose natural beauty nothing can spoil, until in the fulness of time its inevitable destiny shall convert it into docks. The young ladies were the guests of Mr. John Cropper, who belonged to the Society of Friends, a circumstance which readers who have got thus far into the Macaulay correspondence will doubtless have discovered for themselves. Before the visit was over, Margaret became engaged to the brother of her host, Mr. Edward Cropper, a man in every respect worthy of the personal esteem and the commercial prosperity which have fallen to his lot.

There are many who will be surprised at finding in Macaulay's letters, both now and hereafter, indications of certain traits in his disposition with which the world, knowing him only through his political actions and his published works, may perhaps be slow to credit him; but which, taking his life as a whole, were predominant in their power to affect his happiness and give matter for his thoughts. Those who are least partial to him will allow that his was essentially a virile intellect. He wrote, he thought, he spoke, he acted, like a man. The public regarded him as an impersonation of vigour, vivacity, and self-reliance; but his own family, together with one, and probably only one, of his friends, knew that his affections were only too tender, and his sensibilities only too acute. Others may well be loth to parade what he concealed; but a portrait of Macaulay, from which these features were omitted, would be imperfect to the extent of misrepresentation: and it must be acknowledged that, where he loved, he loved more entirely, and more exclusively, than was well for himself. It was improvident in him to concentrate such intensity of feeling upon relations who, however deeply they were attached to him, could not always be in a position to requite him with the whole of their time, and the whole of their heart. He suffered much for that improvidence; but he was too just and too kind to permit that others should suffer with him; and it is not for one who obtained by inheritance a share of his inestimable affection to regret a weakness to which he considers himself by duty bound to refer.

How keenly Macaulay felt the separation from his sister it is impossible to do more than indicate. He never again recovered that tone of thorough boyishness, which had been produced by a long unbroken habit of gay and affectionate intimacy with those younger than himself; indulged in without a suspicion on the part of any concerned that it was in its very nature transitory and precarious. For the first time he was led to doubt whether his scheme of life was indeed a wise one; or, rather, he began to be aware that he had never laid out any scheme of life at all. But with that unselfishness which was the key to his character and to much of his career, (resembling in its quality what we sometimes admire in a woman, rather than what we ever detect in a man,) he took successful pains to conceal his distress from those over whose happiness it otherwise could not have failed to cast a shadow.

'The attachment between brothers and sisters,' he writes in November 1832, 'blameless, amiable, and delightful as it is, is so liable to be superseded by other attachments that no wise man ought to suffer it to become indispensable to him. That women shall leave the home of their birth, and contract ties dearer than those of consanguinity, is a law as ancient as the first records of the history of our race, and as unchangeable as the constitution of the human body and mind. To repine against the nature of things, and against the great fundamental law of all society, because, in consequence of my own want of foresight, it happens to bear heavily on me, would be the basest and most absurd selfishness.

'I have still one more stake to lose. There remains

one event for which, when it arrives, I shall, I hope, be prepared. From that moment, with a heart formed, if ever any man's heart was formed, for domestic happiness, I shall have nothing left in this world but ambition. There is no wound, however, which time and necessity will not render endurable: and, after all, what am I more than my fathers,—than the millions and tens of millions who have been weak enough to pay double price for some favourite number in the lottery of life, and who have suffered double disappointment when their ticket came up a blank?'

To Hannah M. Macaulay.

Leeds: December 12, 1832.

My dear Sister,—

The election here is going on as well as possible. To-day the poll stands thus:

Marshall	Macaulay	Sadler
1,804	1,792	1,353

The probability is that Sadler will give up the contest. If he persists, he will be completely beaten. The voters are under 4,000 in number; those who have already polled are 3,100; and about five hundred will not poll at all. Even if we were not to bring up another man, the probability is that we should win. On Sunday morning early I hope to be in London; and I shall see you in the course of the day.

I had written thus far when your letter was delivered to me. I am sitting in the midst of two hundred friends, all mad with exultation and party spirit, all glorying over the Tories, and thinking me the happiest man in the world. And it is all that I can do to hide my tears, and to command my voice, when it is necessary for me to reply to their congratulations. Dearest, dearest sister, you alone are now left to me. Whom have I on earth but thee? But for you, in the midst of all these successes, I should wish that I were lying by poor Hyde Villiers. But I cannot go on. I am wanted to write an address to the electors: and I shall lay it on Sadler pretty heavily. By what strange fascination is it that ambition and resentment exercise such power over minds which ought to be superior to them? I despise myself for feeling so bitterly towards this fellow as I do. But the separation from dear Margaret has jarred my whole temper. I am cried up here to the skies as the most affable and kind-hearted of men, while I feel a fierceness and restlessness within me, quite new, and almost inexplicable.

Ever yours
T. B. M.

To Hannah M. Macaulay.

London: December 24, 1832.

My dear Sister,—

I am much obliged to you for your letter, and am gratified by all its contents, except what you say about your own cough. As soon as you come back, you shall see Dr. Chambers, if you are not quite well. Do not oppose me in this: for I have set my heart on it. I dined on Saturday at Lord Essex's in Belgrave Square. But never was there such a take-in. I had been given to understand that his Lordship's cuisine was superintended by the first French artists, and that I should find there all the luxuries of the Almanach des Gourmands. What a mistake! His lordship is luxurious, indeed, but in quite a different way. He is a true Englishman. Not a dish on his table but what Sir Roger de Coverley, or Sir Hugh Tyrold,[1] might have set before his guests. A huge haunch of venison on the sideboard; a magnificent piece of beef at the bottom of the table; and before my Lord himself smoked, not a dindon aux truffes, but a fat roasted goose stuffed with sage and onions. I was disappointed, but very agreeably; for my tastes are, I fear, incurably vulgar, as you may perceive by my fondness for Mrs. Meeke's novels.

[1] The uncle of Miss Burney's Camilla.

Our party consisted of Sharp; Lubbock; Watson, M.P. for Canterbury; and Rich, the author of 'What will the Lords do?' who wishes to be M.P. for Knaresborough. Rogers was to have been of the party; but his brother chose that very day to die upon, so that poor Sam had to absent himself. The Chancellor was also invited, but he had scampered off to pass his Christmas with his old mother in Westmoreland. We had some good talk, particularly about Junius's Letters. I learned some new facts which I will tell you when we meet. I am more and more inclined to believe that Francis was one of the people principally concerned.

Ever yours
T. B. M.

On the 29th of January, 1833, commenced the first Session of the Reformed Parliament. The main incidents of that Session, so fruitful in great measures of public utility, belong to general history; if indeed Clio herself is not fated to succumb beneath the stupendous undertaking of turning Hansard into a narrative imbued with human interest. O'Connell,—criticising the King's speech at vast length, and passing in turns through every mood from the most exquisite pathos to downright and undisguised ferocity,—at once plunged the House into a discussion on Ireland, which alternately blazed and smouldered through four livelong nights. Sheil and Grattan spoke finely; Peel and Stanley admirably; Bulwer made the first of his successes, and Cobbett the second of his failures; but the longest and the loudest cheers were those which greeted each of the glowing periods in which Macaulay, as the champion of the Whig party, met the great agitator face to face with high, but not intemperate, defiance.[1] In spite of this flattering reception, he

[1] 'We are called base, and brutal, and bloody. Such are the epithets which the honourable and learned member for Dublin thinks it becoming to pour forth against the party to which he owes every political privilege that he enjoys. The time will come when history will do justice to the Whigs of England,

seldom addressed the House. A subordinate member of a Government, with plenty to do in his own department, finds little temptation, and less encouragement, to play the debater. The difference of opinion between the two Houses concerning the Irish Church Temporalities Bill, which constituted the crisis of the year, was the one circumstance that excited in Macaulay's mind any very lively emotions; but those emotions, being denied their full and free expression in the oratory of a partisan, found vent in the doleful prognostications of a despairing patriot which fill his letters throughout the months of June and July. His abstinence from the passing topics of Parliamentary controversy obtained for him a friendly, as well as an attentive, hearing from both sides of the House whenever he spoke on his own subjects; and did much to smooth the progress of those immense and salutary reforms with which the Cabinet had resolved to accompany the renewal of the India Company's Charter.

So rapid had been the march of events under that strange imperial system established in the East by the

and will faithfully relate how much they did and suffered for Ireland. I see on the benches near me men who might, by uttering one word against Catholic Emancipation,—nay, by merely abstaining from uttering a word in favour of Catholic Emancipation,—have been returned to this House without difficulty or expense, and who, rather than wrong their Irish fellow-subjects, were content to relinquish all the objects of their honourable ambition, and to retire into private life with conscience and fame untarnished. As to one eminent person, who seems to be regarded with especial malevolence by those who ought never to mention his name without respect and gratitude, I will only say this, that the loudest clamour which the honourable and learned gentleman can excite against Lord Grey will be trifling when compared with the clamour which Lord Grey withstood in order to place the honourable and learned gentleman where he now sits. Though a young member of the Whig party, I will venture to speak in the name of the whole body. I tell the honourable and learned gentleman, that the same spirit which sustained us in a just contest for him will sustain us in an equally just contest against him. Calumny, abuse, royal displeasure, popular fury, exclusion from office, exclusion from Parliament, we were ready to endure them all, rather than that he should be less than a British subject. We never will suffer him to be more.'

enterprise and valour of three generations of our countrymen, that each of the periodical revisions of that system was, in effect, a revolution. The legislation of 1813 destroyed the monopoly of the Indian trade. In 1833 the time had arrived when it was impossible any longer to maintain the monopoly of the China trade; and the extinction of this remaining commercial privilege could not fail to bring upon the Company commercial ruin. Skill, and energy, and caution, however happily combined, would not enable rulers who were governing a population larger than that governed by Augustus, and making every decade conquests more extensive than the conquests of Trajan, to compete with private merchants in an open market. England, mindful of the inestimable debt which she owed to the great Company, did not intend to requite her benefactors by imposing on them a hopeless task. Justice and expediency could be reconciled by one course, and one only:—that of buying up the assets and liabilities of the Company on terms the favourable character of which should represent the sincerity of the national gratitude. Interest was to be paid from the Indian exchequer at the rate of ten guineas a year on every hundred pounds of stock; the Company was relieved of its commercial attributes, and became a corporation charged with the function of ruling Hindoostan; and its directors, as has been well observed, remained princes, but merchant princes no longer.

The machinery required for carrying into effect this gigantic metamorphosis was embodied in a bill every one of whose provisions breathed the broad, the fearless, and the tolerant spirit with which Reform had inspired our counsels. The earlier Sections placed the whole property of the Company in trust for the Crown, and enacted that 'from and after the 22nd day of April 1834 the exclusive right of trading with the dominions of the Emperor of China, and of trading in tea, shall cease.' Then came Clauses which threw open the whole continent of India as a place of residence for all subjects of his Majesty; which pronounced the doom of Slavery; and which ordained that no native of the British territories in the East should 'by reason only of his religion, place of birth, descent, or colour, be disabled from holding any place, office, or employment.' The measure was introduced by Mr. Charles Grant, the President of the Board of Control, and was read a second time on Wednesday the 10th July. On that occasion Macaulay defended the bill in a thin House: a circumstance which may surprise those who are not aware that on a Wednesday, and with an Indian question on the paper, Cicero replying to Hortensius would hardly draw a quorum. Small as it was, the audience contained Lord John Russell, Peel, O'Connell, and other masters in the Parliamentary craft. Their unanimous judgment was summed up by Charles Grant, in words which everyone who knows the House of Commons will recognise as being very different from the conventional verbiage of mutual senatorial flattery. 'I must embrace the opportunity of expressing, not what I felt, (for language could not express it,) but of making an attempt to convey to the House my sympathy with it in its admiration of the speech of my honourable and learned friend: a speech which, I will venture to assert, has never been exceeded within these walls for the development of statesmanlike policy and practical good sense. It exhibited all that is noble in oratory; all that is sublime, I had almost said, in poetry; all that is truly great, exalted, and virtuous in human nature. If the House at large felt a deep interest in this magnificent display, it may judge of what were my emotions when I perceived in the hands of my honourable friend the great principles which he expounded glowing with fresh colours, and arrayed in all the beauty of truth.'

There is no praise more gratefully treasured than that which is bestowed by a generous chief upon a subordinate with whom he is on the best of terms. Macaulay to the end entertained for Lord Glenelg that sentiment of loyalty which a man of honour and feeling will always cherish with regard to the statesman under whom he began his career as a servant of the Crown.[1] The Secretary repaid the President for his unvarying kindness and confidence by helping him to get the bill through committee with that absence of friction which is the pride and delight of official men. The vexed questions of Establishment and Endowment, (raised by the clauses appointing bishops to Madras and Bombay, and balancing them with as many salaried Presbyterian chaplains,) increased the length of the debates and the number of the divisions; but the Government carried every point by large majorities, and, with slight modifications in detail, and none in principle, the measure became law with the almost universal approbation both of Parliament and the country.

To Hannah M. Macaulay.

House of Commons.
Monday night, half-past 12.

My dear Sister,—

The papers will scarcely contain any account of what passed yesterday in the House of Commons in the middle of the day. Grant and I fought a battle with Briscoe and O'Connell in defence of the Indian people, and won it by 38 to 6. It was a rascally claim of a dishonest agent of the Company against the employers whom he had cheated, and sold to their own tributaries.[2] The nephew of the original claimant has

[1] The affinity between this sentiment, and that of the Quæstor towards his first Proconsul, so well described in the Orations against Verres, is one among the innumerable points of resemblance between the public life of ancient Rome and modern England.

[2] In his great Indian speech Macaulay referred to this affair, in a passage, the first sentence of which has, by frequent quotation, been elevated into an apophthegm: 'A broken head in Cold Bath Fields produces a greater sensation than three pitched battles in India. A few weeks ago we had to decide on a claim brought by an individual against the revenues of India. If it had been an English question the walls would scarcely

been pressing his case on the Board most vehemently. He is an attorney living in Russell Square, and very likely hears the word at St. John's Chapel. He hears it however to very little purpose: for he lies as much as if he went to hear a 'cauld clatter of morality' at the parish church.

I remember that, when you were at Leamington two years ago, I used to fill my letters with accounts of the people with whom I dined. High life was new to me then; and now it has grown so familiar that I should not, I fear, be able, as I formerly was, to select the striking circumstances. I have dined with sundry great folks since you left London, and I have attended a very splendid rout at Lord Grey's. I stole thither, at about eleven, from the House of Commons with Stewart Mackenzie. I do not mean to describe the beauty of the ladies, nor the brilliancy of stars and uniforms. I mean only to tell you one circumstance which struck, and even affected me. I was talking to Lady Charlotte Lindsay, the daughter of Lord North, a great favourite of mine, about the apartments and the furniture, when she said with a good deal of emotion: 'This is an interesting visit to me. I have never been in this house for fifty years. It was here that I was born; I left it a child when my father fell from power in 1782; and I have never crossed the threshold since.' Then she told me how the rooms seemed dwindled to her; how the staircase, which appeared to her in recollection to be the most spacious and magnificent that she had ever seen, had disappointed her. She longed, she said, to go over the garrets and rummage her old nursery. She told me how, in the No-Popery riots of 1780, she was taken out of bed at two o'clock in the morning. The mob threatened Lord North's house. There were soldiers at the windows, and an immense and furious crowd in Downing Street. She saw, she said, from her nursery

have held the members who would have flocked to the division. It was an Indian question; and we could scarcely, by dint of supplication, make a House.'

the fires in different parts of London; but she did not understand the danger; and only exulted in being up at midnight. Then she was conveyed through the Park to the Horse Guards as the safest place; and was laid, wrapped up in blankets, on the table in the guard-room in the midst of the officers. 'And it was such fun,' she said, 'that I have ever after had rather a liking for insurrections.'

I write in the midst of a crowd. A debate on Slavery is going on in the Commons; a debate on Portugal in the Lords. The door is slamming behind me every moment, and people are constantly going out and in. Here comes Vernon Smith. 'Well, Vernon, what are they doing?' 'Gladstone has just made a very good speech, and Howick is answering him.' 'Aye, but in the House of Lords?' 'They will beat us by twenty, they say.' 'Well, I do not think it matters much.' 'No; nobody out of the House of Lords cares either for Don Pedro, or for Don Miguel.'

There is a conversation between two official men in the Library of the House of Commons on the night of the 3rd June 1833, reported word for word. To the historian three centuries hence this letter will be invaluable. To you, ungrateful as you are, it will seem worthless.

Ever yours
T. B. M.

To Hannah M. Macaulay.

Smoking-Room of the House of Commons:
June 6, 1833.

My Darling,—

Why am I such a fool as to write to a gypsey at Liverpool, who fancies that none is so good as she if she sends one letter for my three? A lazy chit whose fingers tire with penning a page in reply to a quire! There, Miss, you read all the first sentence of my epistle, and never knew that you were reading verse. I have some gossip for you about the Edinburgh Review. Napier is in London, and has called on me several times. He has been with the publishers, who tell him that the sale is falling off; and in many private parties, where he hears sad complaints. The universal cry is that the long dull articles are the ruin of the Review. As to myself, he assures me that my articles are the only things which keep the work up at all. Longman and his partners correspond with about five hundred booksellers in different parts of the kingdom. All these booksellers, I find, tell them that the Review sells, or does not sell, according as there are, or are not, articles by Mr. Macaulay. So, you see, I, like Mr. Darcy,[1] shall not care how proud I am. At all events, I cannot but be pleased to learn that, if I should be forced to depend on my pen for subsistence, I can command what price I choose.

The House is sitting; Peel is just down; Lord Palmerston is speaking; the heat is tremendous; the crowd stifling; and so here I am in the smoking-room, with three Repealers making chimneys of their mouths under my very nose.

> To think that this letter will bear to my Anna
> The exquisite scent of O'Connor's Havannah!

You know that the Lords have been foolish enough to pass a vote implying censure on the Ministers.[2] The Ministers do not seem inclined to take it of them. The King has snubbed their Lordships properly; and in about an hour, as I guess, (for it is near eleven,) we shall have come to a Resolution in direct opposition to that agreed to by the Upper House. Nobody seems to care one straw for what the Peers say about any public matter. A Resolution of the Court of Common Council, or of a meeting at Freemasons' Hall, has often made a greater sensation than this declaration of a branch of the Legislature against the

[1] The central male figure in 'Pride and Prejudice.'

[2] On June 3rd, 1833, a vote of censure on the Portuguese policy of the Ministry was moved by the Duke of Wellington, and carried in the Lords by 79 votes to 69. On June 6th a counter-resolution was carried in the Commons by 361 votes to 98.

Executive Government. The institution of the Peerage is evidently dying a natural death.

I dined yesterday—where, and on what, and at what price I am ashamed to tell you. Such scandalous extravagance and gluttony I will not commit to writing. I blush when I think of it. You, however, are not wholly guiltless in this matter. My nameless offence was partly occasioned by Napier; and I have a very strong reason for wishing to keep Napier in good humour. He has promised to be at Edinburgh when I take a certain damsel thither; to look out for very nice lodgings for us in Queen Street; to show us everything and everybody; and to see us as far as Dunkeld on our way northward, if we do go northward. In general I abhor visiting; but at Edinburgh we must see the people as well as the walls and windows; and Napier will be a capital guide.

Ever yours
T. B. M.

To Hannah M. Macaulay.

London: June 14, 1833.

My dear Sister,—

I do not know what you may have been told. I may have grumbled, for aught I know, at not having more letters from you; but, as to being angry, you ought to know by this time what sort of anger mine is when you are its object.

You have seen the papers, I dare say, and you will perceive that I did not speak yesterday night.[1] The House was thin. The debate was languid. Grant's speech had done our work sufficiently for one night; and both he and Lord Althorp advised me to reserve myself for the Second Reading.

What have I to tell you? I will look at my engagement book, to see where I am to dine.

Friday June 14 – Lord Grey.
Saturday June 15 – Mr. Boddington.
Sunday June 16 – Mr. S. Rice.

[1] The night of the First Reading of the India Bill.

Saturday June 22 – Sir R. Inglis.
Thursday June 27 – The Earl of Ripon.
Saturday June 29 – Lord Morpeth.

Read, and envy, and pine, and die. And yet I would give a large slice of my quarter's salary, which is now nearly due, to be at the Dingle. I am sick of Lords with no brains in their heads, and Ladies with paint on their cheeks, and politics, and politicians, and that reeking furnace of a House. As the poet says,

Oh! rather would I see this day
My little Nancy well and merry
Than the blue riband of Earl Grey,
Or the blue stockings of Miss Berry.

Margaret tells us that you are better, and better, and better. I want to hear that you are well. At all events our Scotch tour will set you up. I hope, for the sake of the tour, that we shall keep our places; but I firmly believe that, before many days have passed, a desperate attempt will be made in the House of Lords to turn us out. If we stand the shock, we shall be firmer than ever. I am not without anxiety as to the result: yet I believe that Lord Grey understands the position in which he is placed, and, as for the King, he will not forget his last blunder, I will answer for it, even if he should live to the age of his father.[1]

But why plague ourselves about politics when we have so much pleasanter things to talk of? The Parson's Daughter: don't you like the Parson's Daughter? What a wretch Harbottle was! And Lady Frances, what a sad worldly woman! But Mrs. Harbottle, dear suffering angel! and Emma Lovel, all excellence! Dr. Mac Gopus you doubtless like; but you probably do not admire the Duchess and Lady Catherine. There is a regular coze over a novel for you! But, if you will have my opinion, I think it

[1] This 'last blunder' was the refusal of the King to stand by his Ministers in May 1832. Macaulay proved a bad prophet; for, after an interval of only three years, William the Fourth repeated his blunder in an aggravated form.

Theodore Hook's worst performance; far inferior to the Surgeon's Daughter; a set of fools making themselves miserable by their own nonsensical fancies and suspicions. Let me hear your opinion; for I will be sworn that,

> In spite of all the serious world,
> Of all the thumbs that ever twirled,
> Of every broadbrim-shaded brow,
> Of every tongue that e'er said 'thou,'
> You still read books in marble covers
> About smart girls and dapper lovers.

But what folly I have been scrawling! I must go to work.

> I cannot all day
> Be neglecting Madras
> And slighting Bombay
> For the sake of a lass.

Kindest love to Edward, and to the woman who owns him.

Ever yours
T. B. M.

London: June 17, 1833.

Dear Hannah,—

All is still anxiety here. Whether the House of Lords will throw out the Irish Church Bill, whether the King will consent to create new Peers, whether the Tories will venture to form a Ministry, are matters about which we are all in complete doubt. If the Ministry should really be changed, Parliament will, I feel quite sure, be dissolved. Whether I shall have a seat in the next Parliament I neither know nor care. I shall regret nothing for myself but our Scotch tour. For the public I shall, if this Parliament is dissolved, entertain scarcely any hopes. I see nothing before us but a frantic conflict between extreme opinions; a short period of oppression; then a convulsive reaction; and then a tremendous crash of the Funds, the Church, the Peerage, and the Throne. It is enough to make the most strenuous royalist lean a little to republicanism to think that the whole question between safety and general destruction may probably, at this most fearful conjuncture, depend on a single man whom the accident of his birth has placed in a situation to which certainly his own virtues or abilities would never have raised him.

The question must come to a decision, I think, within the fortnight. In the meantime the funds are going down, the newspapers are storming, and the faces of men on both sides are growing day by day more gloomy and anxious. Even during the most violent part of the contest for the Reform Bill I do not remember to have seen so much agitation in the political circles. I have some odd anecdotes for you, which I will tell you when we meet. If the Parliament should be dissolved, the West Indian and East Indian Bills are of course dropped. What is to become of the slaves? What is to become of the tea-trade? Will the negroes, after receiving the Resolutions of the House of Commons promising them liberty, submit to the cart-whip? Will our merchants consent to have the trade with China, which has just been offered to them, snatched away? The Bank Charter, too, is suspended. But that is comparatively a trifle. After all, what is it to me who is in or out, or whether those fools of Lords are resolved to perish, and drag the King to perish with them in the ruin which they have themselves made? I begin to wonder what the fascination is which attracts men, who could sit over their tea and their books in their own cool quiet room, to breathe bad air, hear bad speeches, lounge up and down the long gallery, and doze uneasily on the green benches till three in the morning. Thank God, these luxuries are not necessary to me. My pen is sufficient for my support, and my sister's company is sufficient for my happiness. Only let me see her well and cheerful and let offices in Government, and seats in Parliament, go to those who care for them. If I were to leave public life to-morrow, I declare that, except for the vexation which it might give you and one or two others, the event would not be in the slightest degree painful to me. As you boast of having a greater insight into character than I allow to you, let me know how you explain this philosophical disposition of mine, and how you reconcile it with my ambitious inclinations. That is a problem for a young lady who professes knowledge of human nature.

Did I tell you that I dined at the Duchess of Kent's, and sate next that loveliest of women, Mrs. Littleton? Her husband, our new Secretary for Ireland, told me this evening that Lord Wellesley, who sate near us at the Duchess's, asked Mrs. Littleton afterwards who it was that was talking to her. 'Mr. Macaulay.' 'Oh!' said the Marquess, 'I am very sorry I did not know it. I have a most particular desire to be acquainted with that man.' Accordingly Littleton has engaged me to dine with him, in order to introduce me to the Marquess. I am particularly curious, and always was, to know him. He has made a great and splendid figure in history, and his weaknesses, though they make his character less worthy of respect, make it more interesting as a study. Such a blooming old swain I never saw; hair combed with exquisite nicety, a waistcoat of driven snow, and a star and garter put on with rare skill.

To-day we took up our Resolutions about India to the House of Lords. The two Houses had a conference on the subject in an old Gothic room called the Painted Chamber. The painting consists in a mildewed daub of a woman in the niche of one of the windows. The Lords sate in little cocked hats along a table; and we stood uncovered on the other side, and delivered in our Resolutions. I thought that before long it may be our turn to sit, and theirs to stand.

Ever yours
T. B. M.

London: June 21, 1833.

Dear Hannah,—

I cannot tell you how delighted I was to learn from Fanny this morning that Margaret pronounces you to be as well as she could wish you to be. Only continue so, and all the changes of public life will be as indifferent to me as to Horatio. If I am only spared the misery of seeing you suffer, I shall be found

> A man that fortune's buffets and rewards
> Has ta'en with equal thanks.

Whether we are to have buffets or rewards is known only to Heaven and to the Peers. I think that their Lordships are rather cowed. Indeed, if they venture on the course on which they lately seemed bent, I would not give sixpence for a coronet or a penny for a mitre.

I shall not read the Repealers; and I think it very impudent in you to make such a request. Have I nothing to do but to be your novel-taster? It is rather your duty to be mine. What else have you to do? I have read only one novel within the last week, and a most precious one it was: the Invisible Gentleman. Have you ever read it? But I need not ask. No doubt it has formed part of your Sunday studies. A wretched, trumpery, imitation of Godwin's worst manner. What a number of stories I shall have to tell you when we meet!—which will be, as nearly as I can guess, about the 10th or 12th of August. I shall be as rich as a Jew by that time.

> Next Wednesday will be quarter-day;
> And then, if I'm alive,
> Of sterling pounds I shall receive
> Three hundred seventy-five.
> Already I possess in cash
> Two hundred twenty-four,
> Besides what I have lent to John
> Which makes up twenty more.
> Also the man who editeth
> The Yellow and the Blue
> Doth owe me ninety pounds at least,
> All for my last review.
> So, if my debtors pay their debts,
> You'll find, dear sister mine,
> That all my wealth together makes
> Seven hundred pounds and nine.

Ever yours
T. B. M.

The rhymes in which Macaulay unfolds his little budget derive a certain dignity and meaning from the events of the ensuing weeks. The unparalleled labours of the Anti-Slavery leaders were at length approaching a successful issue, and Lord Grey's Cabinet had declared itself responsible for the emancipation of the West Indian negroes. But it was already beginning to be known that the Ministerial scheme, in its original shape, was not such as would satisfy even the more moderate Abolitionists. Its most objectionable feature was shadowed forth in the third of the Resolutions with which Mr. Stanley, who had the question in charge, prefaced the introduction of his bill: 'That all persons, now slaves, be entitled to be registered as apprenticed labourers, and to acquire thereby all the rights and privileges of freemen, subject to the restriction of labouring, for a time to be fixed by Parliament, for their present owners.' It was understood that twelve years would be proposed as the period of apprenticeship; although no trace of this intention could be detected in the wording of the Resolution. Macaulay, who thought twelve years far too long, felt himself justified in supporting the Government during the preliminary stages; but he took occasion to make some remarks indicating that circumstances might occur which would oblige him to resign office, and adopt a line of his own.

As time went on it became evident that his firmness would be put to the test; and a severe test it was. A rising statesman, whose prospects would be irremediably injured by abruptly quitting a Government that seemed likely to be in power for the next quarter of a century; a zealous Whig, who shrank from the very appearance of disaffection to his party; a man of sense, with no ambition to be called Quixotic; a member for a large constituency, possessed of only seven hundred pounds in the world when his purse was at its fullest; above all, an affectionate son and brother, now, more than ever, the main hope and reliance of those whom he held most dear;—it may well be believed that he was not in a hurry to act the martyr. His father's affairs were worse than bad. The African firm, without having been reduced to declare itself bankrupt, had ceased to exist as a house of business; or existed only so far that for some years to come every penny that Macaulay earned, beyond what the necessities of life demanded, was scrupulously devoted to paying, and at length to paying off, his father's creditors: a dutiful enterprise in which he was assisted by his brother Henry,[1] a young man of high spirit and excellent abilities, who had recently been appointed one of the Commissioners of Arbitration in the Prize Courts at Sierra Leone.

The pressure of pecuniary trouble was now beginning to make itself felt even by the younger members of the family. About this time, or perhaps a little earlier, Hannah Macaulay writes thus to one of her cousins: 'You say nothing about coming to us. You must come in good health and spirits. Our trials ought not greatly to depress us; for, after all, all we want is money, the easiest want to bear; and, when we have so many mercies—friends who love us and whom we love; no bereavements; and, above all, (if it be not our own fault,) a hope full of immortality—let us not be so ungrateful as to repine because we are without what in itself cannot make our happiness.'

Macaulay's colleagues, who, without knowing his whole story, knew enough to be aware that he could ill afford to give up office, were earnest in their remonstrances; but he answered shortly, and almost roughly: 'I cannot go counter to my father. He has devoted his whole life to the question, and I cannot grieve him by giving way when he wishes me to stand firm.' During the crisis of the West India Bill, Zachary Macaulay and his son were in constant correspondence. There is something touching in the picture which these letters present of the older man,

[1] Henry married in 1841 a daughter of his brother's old political ally, Lord Denman. He died at Boa Vista, in 1846, leaving two sons, Henry, and Joseph Macaulay.

(whose years were coming to a close in poverty which was the consequence of his having always lived too much for others,) discussing quietly and gravely how, and when, the younger was to take a step that in the opinion of them both would be fatal to his career: and this with so little consciousness that there was anything heroic in the course which they were pursuing, that it appears never to have occurred to either of them that any other line of conduct could possibly be adopted.

Having made up his mind as to what he should do, Macaulay set about it with as good a grace as is compatible with the most trying position in which a man, and especially a young man, can find himself. Carefully avoiding the attitude of one who bargains or threatens, he had given timely notice in the proper quarter of his intentions and his views. At length the conjuncture arrived when decisive action could no longer be postponed. On the 24th of July Mr. Thomas Fowell Buxton moved an amendment in Committee, limiting the apprenticeship to the shortest period necessary for establishing the system of free labour. Macaulay, whose resignation was already in Lord Althorp's hands, made a speech which produced all the more effect as being inornate, and, at times, almost awkward. Even if deeper feelings had not restrained the range of his fancy and the flow of his rhetoric, his judgment would have told him that it was not the moment for an oratorical display. He began by entreating the House to extend to him that indulgence which it had accorded on occasions when he had addressed it 'with more confidence and with less harassed feelings.' He then, at some length, exposed the effects of the Government proposal. 'In free countries the master has a choice of labourers, and the labourer has a choice of masters; but in slavery it is always necessary to give despotic power to the master. This bill leaves it to the magistrate to keep peace between master and slave. Every time that the slave takes twenty minutes to do that which the master thinks he should do in fifteen, recourse must be had to the magistrate. Society would day and night be in a constant state of litigation, and all differences and difficulties must be solved by judicial interference.'

He did not share in Mr. Buxton's apprehension of gross cruelty as a result of the apprenticeship. 'The magistrate would be accountable to the Colonial Office, and the Colonial Office to the House of Commons, in which every lash which was inflicted under magisterial authority would be told and counted. My apprehension is that the result of continuing for twelve years this dead slavery,—this state of society destitute of any vital principle,—will be that the whole negro population will sink into weak and drawling inefficacy, and will be much less fit for liberty at the end of the period than at the commencement. My hope is that the system will die a natural death; that the experience of a few months will so establish its utter inefficiency as to induce the planters to abandon it, and to substitute for it a state of freedom. I have voted,' he said, 'for the Second Reading, and I shall vote for the Third Reading; but, while the bill is in Committee, I shall join with other honourable gentlemen in doing all that is possible to amend it.'

Such a declaration, coming from the mouth of a member of the Government, gave life to the debate, and secured to Mr. Buxton an excellent division, which under the circumstances was equivalent to a victory. The next day Mr. Stanley rose; adverted shortly to the position in which the Ministers stood; and announced that the term of apprenticeship would be reduced from twelve years to seven. Mr. Buxton, who, with equal energy and wisdom, had throughout the proceedings acted as leader of the Anti-slavery party in the House of Commons, advised his friends to make the best of the concession; and his counsel was followed by all those Abolitionists who were thinking more of their cause than of themselves. It is worthy of remark that Macaulay's prophecy came true, though not at so early a date as he ventured to anticipate. Four years of the provisional system brought all parties to acquiesce in the premature termination of a state of things which denied to the negro the blessings of freedom, and to the planter the profits of slavery.

'The papers,' Macaulay writes to his father, 'will have told you all that has happened, as far as it is known to the public. The secret history you will have heard from Buxton. As to myself, Lord Althorp told me yesterday night that the Cabinet had determined not to accept my resignation. I have therefore the singular good luck of having saved both my honour and my place, and of having given no just ground of offence either to the Abolitionists or to my party-friends. I have more reason than ever to say that honesty is the best policy.'

This letter is dated the 27th of July. On that day week, Wilberforce was carried to his grave in Westminster Abbey. 'We laid him,' writes Macaulay, 'side by side with Canning, at the feet of Pitt, and within two steps of Fox and Grattan.' He died with the promised land full in view. Before the end of August Parliament abolished slavery, and the last touch was put to the work that had consumed so many pure and noble lives. In a letter of congratulation to Zachary Macaulay, Mr. Buxton says: 'Surely you have reason to rejoice. My sober and deliberate opinion is that you have done more towards this consumation than any other man. For myself, I take pleasure in acknowledging that you have been my tutor all the way through, and that I could have done nothing without you.' Such was the spirit of these men, who, while the struggle lasted, were prodigal of health and ease; but who, in the day of triumph, disclaimed, each for himself, even that part of the merit which their religion allowed them to ascribe to human effort and self-sacrifice.

Dear Hannah,— London: July 11, 1833

I have been so completely overwhelmed with business for some days that I have not been able to find time for writing a line. Yesterday night we read the

India Bill a second time. It was a Wednesday, and the reporters gave hardly any account of what passed. They always resent being forced to attend on that day, which is their holiday. I made the best speech, by general agreement, and in my own opinion, that I ever made in my life. I was an hour and three-quarters up; and such compliments as I had from Lord Althorp, Lord Palmerston, Lord John Russell, Wynne, O'Connell, Grant, the Speaker, and twenty other people, you never heard. As there is no report of the speech, I have been persuaded, rather against my will, to correct it for publication. I will tell you one compliment that was paid me, and which delighted me more than any other. An old member said to me: 'Sir, having heard that speech may console the young people for never having heard Mr. Burke.'[1]

The Slavery Bill is miserably bad. I am fully resolved not to be dragged through the mire, but to oppose, by speaking and voting, the clauses which I think objectionable. I have told Lord Althorp this, and have again tendered my resignation. He hinted that he thought that the Government would leave me at liberty to take my own line, but that he must consult his colleagues. I told him that I asked for no favour; that I knew what inconvenience would result if official men were allowed to dissent from Ministerial measures, and yet to keep their places; and that I should not think myself in the smallest degree ill-used if the Cabinet accepted my resignation. This is the present posture of affairs. In the meantime the two Houses are at daggers drawn. Whether the Government will last to the end of the Session I neither know nor care. I am sick of Boards, and of the House of Commons; and pine for a few quiet days, a cool country breeze, and a little chatting with my dear sister.

Ever yours
T. B. M.

[1] A Tory member said that Macaulay resembled both the Burkes: that he was like the first from his eloquence, and like the second from his stopping other people's mouths.

To Hannah M. Macaulay.

My dear Sister,— London: July 19, 1833.

I snatch a few minutes to write a single line to you. We went into Committee on the India Bill at twelve this morning, sate till three, and are just set at liberty for two hours. At five we recommence, and shall be at work till midnight. In the interval between three and five I have to despatch the current business of the office, which, at present, is fortunately not heavy; to eat my dinner, which I shall do at Grant's; and to write a short scrawl to my little sister.

My work, though laborious, has been highly satisfactory. No Bill, I believe, of such importance,—certainly no important Bill in my time,—has been received with such general approbation. The very cause of the negligence of the reporters, and of the thinness of the House, is that we have framed our measure so carefully as to give little occasion for debate. Littleton, Denison, and many other members, assure me that they never remember to have seen a Bill better drawn or better conducted.

On Monday night, I hope, my work will be over. Our Bill will have been discussed, I trust, for the last time in the House of Commons; and, in all probability, I shall within forty-eight hours after that time be out of office. I am fully determined not to give way about the West India Bill; and I can hardly expect,—I am sure I do not wish,—that the Ministers should suffer me to keep my place and oppose their measure. Whatever may befall me or my party, I am much more desirous to come to an end of this interminable Session than to stay either in office or in Parliament. The Tories are quite welcome to take everything, if they will only leave me my pen and my books, a warm fireside, and you chattering beside it. This sort of philosophy, an odd kind of cross between Stoicism and Epicureanism, I have learned, where most people unlearn all their philosophy, in crowded senates and fine drawing-rooms.

But time flies, and Grant's dinner will be waiting. He keeps open house for us during this fight.

Ever yours

T. B. M.

London: July 22, 1833.

My dear Father,—

We are still very anxious here. The Lords, though they have passed the Irish Church Bill through its first stage, will very probably mutilate it in Committee. It will then be for the Ministers to decide whether they can with honour keep their places. I believe that they will resign if any material alteration should be made; and then everything is confusion.

These circumstances render it very difficult for me to shape my course right with respect to the West India Bill, the Second Reading of which stands for this evening. I am fully resolved to oppose several of the clauses. But to declare my intention publicly, at a moment when the Government is in danger, would have the appearance of ratting. I must be guided by circumstances; but my present intention is to say nothing on the Second Reading. By the time that we get into Committee the political crisis will, I hope, be over; the fate of the Church Bill will be decided one way or the other; and I shall be able to take my own course on the Slavery question without exposing myself to the charge of deserting my friends in a moment of peril.

Ever yours affectionately

T. B. MACAULAY.

To Hannah M. Macaulay.

London: July 24, 1833.

My dear Sister,—

You will have seen by the papers that the West India debate on Monday night went off very quietly in little more than an hour. To-night we expect the great struggle, and I fear that, much against my inclination, I must bear a part in it. My resignation is in Lord Althorp's hands. He assures me that he will do his utmost to obtain for me liberty to act as I like on this question: but Lord Grey and Stanley are to be consulted, and I think it very improbable that they will consent to allow me so extraordinary a privilege. I know that, if I were Minister, I would not allow such latitude to any man in office; and so I told Lord Althorp. He answered in the kindest and most flattering manner; told me that in office I had surpassed their expectations, and that, much as they wished to bring me in last year, they wished much more to keep me in now. I told him in reply that the matter was one for the Ministers to settle, purely with a view to their own interest; that I asked for no indulgence; that I could make no terms; and that, what I would not do to serve them, I certainly would not do to keep my place. Thus the matter stands. It will probably be finally settled within a few hours.

This detestable Session goes on lengthening, and lengthening, like a human hair in one's mouth. (Do you know that delicious sensation?) Last month we expected to have been up before the middle of August. Now we should be glad to be quite certain of being in the country by the first of September. One comfort I shall have in being turned out: I will not stay a day in London after the West India Bill is through Committee; which I hope it will be before the end of next week.

The new Edinburgh Review is not much amiss; but I quite agree with the publishers, the editor, and the reading public generally, that the number would have been much the better for an article of thirty or forty pages from the pen of a gentleman who shall be nameless.

Ever yours

T. B. M.

To Hannah M. Macaulay.

My dear Sister,— London: July 25, 1833.

The plot is thickening. Yesterday Buxton moved an instruction to the Committee on the Slavery Bill, which the Government opposed, and which I supported. It was extremely painful to me to speak against all my political friends;—so painful that at times I could hardly go on. I treated them as mildly as I could; and they all tell me that I performed my difficult task not ungracefully. We divided at two this morning, and were 151 to 158. The Ministers found that, if they persisted, they would infallibly be beaten. Accordingly they came down to the House at twelve this day, and agreed to reduce the apprenticeship to seven years for the agricultural labourers, and to five years for the skilled labourers. What other people may do I cannot tell; but I am inclined to be satisfied with this concession; particularly as I believe that if we press the thing further, they will resign, and we shall have no Bill at all, but instead of it a Tory Ministry and a dissolution. Some people flatter me with the assurance that our large minority, and the consequent change in the Bill, have been owing to me. If this be so, I have done one useful act at least in my life.

I shall now certainly remain in office; and if, as I expect, the Irish Church Bill passes the Lords, I may consider myself as safe till the next Session; when Heaven knows what may happen. It is still quite uncertain when we may rise. I pine for rest, air, and a taste of family life, more than I can express. I see nothing but politicians, and talk about nothing but politics.

I have not read Village Belles. Tell me, as soon as you can get it, whether it is worth reading. As John Thorpe[1] says: 'Novels! Oh Lord! I never read novels. I have something else to do.'

Farewell
T. B. M.

To Hannah M. Macaulay.

London: July 27, 1833.

My dear Sister,—

Here I am, safe and well, at the end of one of the most stormy weeks that the oldest man remembers in

[1] The young Oxford man in 'Northanger Abbey.'

Parliamentary affairs. I have resigned my office, and my resignation has been refused. I have spoken and voted against the Ministry under which I hold my place. The Ministry has been so hard run in the Commons as to be forced to modify its plan; and has received a defeat in the Lords,[1]—a slight one, to be sure, and on a slight matter,—yet such that I, and many others, fully believed twenty-four hours ago that they would have resigned. In fact, some of the Cabinet,—Grant among the rest, to my certain knowledge,—were for resigning. At last Saturday has arrived. The Ministry is as strong as ever. I am as good friends with the Ministers as ever. The East India Bill is carried through our House. The West India Bill is so far modified that, I believe, it will be carried. The Irish Church Bill has got through the Committee in the Lords; and we are all beginning to look forward to a Prorogation in about three weeks.

To-day I went to Haydon's to be painted into his great picture of the Reform Banquet. Ellis was with me, and declares that Haydon has touched me off to a nicety. I am sick of pictures of my own face. I have seen within the last few days one drawing of it, one engraving, and three paintings. They all make me a very handsome fellow. Haydon pronounces my profile a gem of art, perfectly antique; and, what is worth the praise of ten Haydons, I was told yesterday that Mrs. Littleton, the handsomest woman in London, had paid me exactly the same compliment. She pronounced Mr. Macaulay's profile to be a study for an artist. I have bought a new looking-glass and razor-case on the strength of these compliments, and am meditating on the expediency of having my hair cut in the Burlington Arcade, rather than in Lamb's Conduit Street. As Richard says,

> Since I am crept in favour with myself,
> I will maintain it with some little cost.

[1] On the 25th of July the Archbishop of Canterbury carried an amendment on the Irish Church Bill, against the Government, by 84 votes to 82.

I begin, like Sir Walter Elliot,[1] to rate all my acquaintance according to their beauty. But what nonsense I write, and in times that make many merry men look grave!

Ever yours
T. B. M.

To Hannah M. Macaulay.

London: July 29, 1833.

My dear Sister,—

I dined last night at Holland House. There was a very pleasant party. My Lady was courteous, and my Lord extravagantly entertaining: telling some capital stories about old Bishop Horsley, which were set off with some of the drollest mimicry that I ever saw. Among many others there were Sir James Graham; and Dr. Holland, who is a good scholar as well as a good physician; and Wilkie, who is a modest pleasing companion as well as an excellent artist. For ladies, we had her Grace of——; and her daughter Lady ——, a fine, buxom, sonsy lass, with more colour than, I am sorry to say, is often seen among fine ladies. So our dinner and our soirée were very agreeable.

We narrowly escaped a scene at one time. Lord —— is in the navy, and is now on duty in the fleet at the Tagus. We got into a conversation about Portuguese politics. His name was mentioned, and Graham, who is First Lord of the Admiralty, complimented the Duchess on her son's merit, to which, he said, every despatch bore witness. The Duchess forthwith began to entreat that he might be recalled. He was very ill, she said. If he stayed longer on that station she was sure that he would die: and then she began to cry. I cannot bear to see women cry, and the matter became serious, for her pretty daughter began to bear her company. That hard-hearted Lord —— seemed to be diverted by the scene. He, by all accounts, has been doing little else than making women cry during the last five-and-twenty years. However, we all were as still as death while the wiping of eyes and the blowing of noses proceeded. At last Lord Holland contrived to

[1] The Baronet in 'Persuasion.'

restore our spirits; but, before the Duchess went away, she managed to have a tête-à-tête with Graham, and, I have no doubt, begged and blubbered to some purpose. I could not help thinking how many honest stout-hearted fellows are left to die on the most unhealthy stations for want of being related to some Duchess who has been handsome, or to some Duchess's daughter who still is so.

The Duchess said one thing that amused us. We were talking about Lady Morgan. 'When she first came to London,' said Lord Holland, 'I remember that she carried a little Irish harp about with her wherever she went.' Others denied this. I mentioned what she says in her Book of the Boudoir. There she relates how she went one evening to Lady ——'s with her little Irish harp, and how strange everybody thought it. 'I see nothing very strange,' said her Grace, 'in her taking her harp to Lady ——'s. If she brought it safe away with her, that would have been strange indeed.' On this, as a friend of yours says, we la-a-a-a-a-a-ft.

I am glad to find that you approve of my conduct about the Niggers. I expect, and indeed wish, to be abused by the Agency Society. My father is quite satisfied, and so are the best part of my Leeds friends.

I amuse myself, as I walk back from the House at two in the morning, with translating Virgil. I am at work on one of the most beautiful episodes, and am succeeding pretty well. You shall have what I have done when I come to Liverpool, which will be, I hope, in three weeks or thereanent.

Ever yours
T. B. M.

To Hannah M. Macaulay.

My dear Sister,— London: July 31, 1833.

Political affairs look cheeringly. The Lords passed the Irish Church Bill yesterday, and mean, we understand, to give us little or no trouble about the India Bill. There is still a hitch in the Commons about the West India Bill, particularly about the twenty millions for compensation to the planters; but we expect to carry our point by a great majority. By the end of next week we shall be very near the termination of our labours. Heavy labours they have been.

So Wilberforce is gone! We talk of burying him in Westminster Abbey; and many eminent men, both Whigs and Tories, are desirous to join in paying him this honour. There is, however, a story about a promise given to old Stephen that they should both lie in the same grave. Wilberforce kept his faculties, and, (except when he was actually in fits,) his spirits, to the very last. He was cheerful and full of anecdote only last Saturday. He owned that he enjoyed life much, and that he had a great desire to live longer. Strange in a man who had, I should have said, so little to attach him to this world, and so firm a belief in another: in a man with an impaired fortune, a weak spine, and a worn-out stomach! What is this fascination which makes us cling to existence in spite of present sufferings and of religious hopes? Yesterday evening I called at the house in Cadogan Place, where the body is lying. I was truly fond of him: that is, 'je l'aimais comme l'on aime.' And how is that? How very little one human being generally cares for another! How very little the world misses anybody! How soon the chasm left by the best and wisest men closes! I thought, as I walked back from Cadogan Place, that our own selfishness when others are taken away ought to teach us how little others will suffer at losing us. I thought that, if I were to die to-morrow, not one of the fine people, whom I dine with every week, will take a côtelette aux petits pois the less on Saturday at the table to which I was invited to meet them, or will smile less gaily at the ladies over the champagne. And I am quite even with them. What are those pretty lines of Shelley?

> Oh, world, farewell!
> Listen to the passing bell.
> It tells that thou and I must part
> With a light and heavy heart.

There are not ten people in the world whose deaths would spoil my dinner; but there are one or two whose deaths would break my heart. The more I see of the world, and the more numerous my acquaintance becomes, the narrower and more exclusive my affection grows, and the more I cling to my sisters, and to one or two old tried friends of my quiet days. But why should I go on preaching to you out of Ecclesiastes? And here comes, fortunately, to break the train of my melancholy reflections, the proof of my East India Speech from Hansard: so I must put my letter aside, and correct the press.

Ever yours
T. B. M.

To Hannah M. Macaulay.

London: August 2, 1833

My dear Sister,—

I agree with your judgment on Chesterfield's Letters. They are for the most part trash; though they contain some clever passages, and the style is not bad. Their celebrity must be attributed to causes quite distinct from their literary merit, and particularly to the position which the author held in society. We see in our own time that the books written by public men of note are generally rated at more than their real value: Lord Grenville's little compositions, for example; Canning's verses; Fox's history; Brougham's treatises. The writings of people of high fashion, also, have a value set on them far higher than that which intrinsically belongs to them. The verses of the late Duchess of Devonshire, or an occasional prologue by Lord Alvanley, attract a most undue share of attention. If the present Duke of Devonshire, who is the very 'glass of fashion and mould of form,' were to publish a book with two good pages, it would be extolled as a masterpiece in half the drawing-rooms of London. Now Chesterfield was, what no person in our time has been or can be, a great political leader, and at the same time the acknowledged chief of the fashionable world; at the head of the House of Lords, and at the head of *ton*; Mr. Canning and the Duke of Devonshire in one. In our time the division of labour is carried so far that such a man could not exist. Politics require the whole of energy, bodily and mental, during half the year; and leave very little time for the bow window at White's in the day, or for the crush-room of the Opera at night. A century ago the case was different. Chesterfield was at once the most distinguished orator in the Upper House, and the undisputed sovereign of wit and fashion. He held this eminence for about forty years. At last it became the regular custom of the higher circles to laugh whenever he opened his mouth, without waiting for his *bon mot*. He used to sit at White's with a circle of young men of rank round him, applauding every syllable that he uttered. If you wish for a proof of the kind of position which Chesterfield held among his contemporaries, look at the prospectus of Johnson's Dictionary. Look even at Johnson's angry letter. It contains the strongest admission of the boundless influence which Chesterfield exercised over society. When the letters of such a man were published, of course they were received more favourably by far than they deserved.

So much for criticism. As to politics, everything seems tending to repose; and I should think that by this day fortnight we shall probably be prorogued. The Jew Bill was thrown out yesterday night by the Lords. No matter. Our turn will come one of these days.

If you want to see me puffed and abused by somebody who evidently knows nothing about me, look at the New Monthly for this month. Bulwer, I see, has given up editing it. I suppose he is making money in some other way; for his dress must cost as much as that of any five other members of Parliament.

To-morrow Wilberforce is to be buried. His sons acceded, with great eagerness, to the application made to them by a considerable number of the members of both Houses that the funeral should be public. We meet to-morrow at twelve at the House of Commons, and we shall attend the coffin into the Abbey. The Duke of Wellington, Lord Eldon, and Sir R. Peel have put down their names, as well as the Ministers and the Abolitionists.

My father urges me to pay some tribute to Wilberforce in the House of Commons. If any debate should take place on the third reading of the West India Bill in which I might take part, I should certainly embrace the opportunity of doing honour to his memory. But I do not expect that such an occasion will arise. The House seems inclined to pass the Bill without more contest; and my father must be aware that anything like theatrical display,—anything like a set funeral oration not springing naturally out of the discussion of a question,—is extremely distasteful to the House of Commons.

I have been clearing off a great mass of business, which had accumulated at our office while we were conducting our Bill through Parliament. To-day I had the satisfaction of seeing the green boxes, which a week ago were piled up with papers three or four feet high, perfectly empty. Admire my superhuman industry. This I will say for myself, that, when I do sit down to work, I work harder and faster than any person that I ever knew.

Ever yours
T. B. M.

The next letter, in terms too clear to require comment, introduces the mention of what proved to be the most important circumstance in Macaulay's life.

To Hannah M. Macaulay.

London: August 17, 1833.

My dear Sister,—

I am about to write to you on a subject which to you and Margaret will be one of the most agitating interest; and which, on that account chiefly, is so to me.

By the new India Bill it is provided that one of the members of the Supreme Council, which is to govern our Eastern Empire, is to be chosen from among persons who are not servants of the Company. It is probable, indeed nearly certain, that the situation will be offered to me.

The advantages are very great. It is a post of the highest dignity and consideration. The salary is ten thousand pounds a year. I am assured by persons who know Calcutta intimately, and who have themselves mixed in the highest circles and held the highest offices at that Presidency, that I may live in splendour there for five thousand a year, and may save the rest of the salary with the accruing interest. I may therefore hope to return to England at only thirty-nine, in the full vigour of life, with a fortune of thirty thousand pounds. A larger fortune I never desired.

I am not fond of money, or anxious about it. But, though every day makes me less and less eager for wealth, every day shows me more and more strongly how necessary a competence is to a man who desires to be either great or useful. At present the plain fact is that I can continue to be a public man only while I can continue in office. If I left my place in the Government, I must leave my seat in Parliament too. For I must live: I can live only by my pen: and it is absolutely impossible for any man to write enough to procure him a decent subsistence, and at the same time to take an active part in politics. I have not during this Session been able to send a single line to the Edinburgh Review: and, if I had been out of office, I should have been able to do very little. Edward Bulwer has just given up the New Monthly Magazine on the ground that he cannot conduct it, and attend to his Parliamentary duties. Cobbett has been compelled to neglect his Register so much that its sale has fallen almost to nothing. Now, in order to live like a gentleman, it would be necessary for me to write, not as I have done hitherto, but regularly, and even daily. I have never made more than two hundred a year by my pen. I could not support myself in comfort on less than five hundred: and I shall in all probability have many others to support. The prospects of our family are, if possible, darker than ever.

In the meantime my political outlook is very gloomy. A schism in the Ministry is approaching. It requires only that common knowledge of public affairs, which any reader of the newspapers may possess, to see this; and I have more, much more, than common knowledge on the subject. They cannot hold together. I tell you in perfect seriousness that my chance of keeping my present situation for six months is so small, that I would willingly sell it for fifty pounds down. If I remain in office, I shall, I fear, lose my political character. If I go out, and engage in opposition, I shall break most of the private ties which I have formed during the last three years. In England I see nothing before me, for some time to come, but poverty, unpopularity, and the breaking up of old connections.

If there were no way out of these difficulties, I would encounter them with courage. A man can always act honourably and uprightly; and, if I were in the Fleet Prison or the rules of the King's Bench, I believe that I could find in my own mind resources which would preserve me from being positively unhappy. But, if I could escape from these impending disasters, I should wish to do so. By accepting the post which is likely to be offered to me, I withdraw myself for a short time from the contests of faction here. When I return, I shall find things settled, parties formed into new combinations, and new questions under discussion. I shall then be able, without the scandal of a violent separation, and without exposing myself to the charge of inconsistency, to take my own line. In the meantime I shall save my family from distress; and shall return with a competence honestly earned, as rich as if I were Duke of Northumberland or Marquess of Westminster, and able to act on all public questions without even a temptation to deviate from the strict line of duty. While in India, I shall have to discharge duties not painfully laborious, and of the highest and most honourable kind. I shall have whatever that country affords of comfort or splendour; nor will my absence be so long that my friends, or the public here, will be likely to lose sight of me.

The only persons who know what I have written to you are Lord Grey, the Grants, Stewart Mackenzie, and George Babington. Charles Grant and Stewart Mackenzie, who know better than most men the state of the political world, think that I should act unwisely in refusing this post: and this though they assure me,—and, I really believe, sincerely,—that they shall feel the loss of my society very acutely. But what shall I feel? And with what emotions, loving as I do my country and my family, can I look forward to such a separation, enjoined, as I think it is, by prudence and by duty? Whether the period of my exile shall be one of comfort,—and, after the first shock, even of happiness,—depends on you. If, as I expect, this offer shall be made to me, will you go with me? I know what a sacrifice I ask of you. I know how many dear and precious ties you must, for a time, sunder. I know that the splendour of the Indian Court, and the gaieties of that brilliant society of which you would be one of the leading personages, have no temptation for you. I can bribe you only by telling you that, if you will go with me, I will love you better than I love you now, if I can.

I have asked George Babington about your health and mine. He says that he has very little apprehension for me, and none at all for you. Indeed, he seemed to think that the climate would be quite as likely to do you good as harm.

All this is most strictly secret. You may, of course, show the letter to Margaret; and Margaret may tell Edward: for I never cabal against the lawful authority of husbands. But further the thing must not go. It would hurt my father, and very justly, to hear of it from anybody before he hears of it from myself; and, if the least hint of it were to get abroad, I should be placed in a very awkward position with regard to the people at Leeds. It is possible, though not probable, that difficulties may arise at the India House; and I do not mean to say anything to any person, who is not already in the secret, till the Directors have made their choice, and till the King's pleasure has been taken.

And now think calmly over what I have written. I would not have written on the subject even to you, till the matter was quite settled, if I had not thought that you ought to have full time to make up your mind. If you feel an insurmountable aversion to India, I will do all in my power to make your residence in England comfortable during my absence, and to enable you to confer instead of receiving benefits. But if my dear sister would consent to give me, at this great crisis of my life, that proof, that painful and arduous proof, of her affection, which I beg of her, I think that she will not repent of it. She shall not, if the unbounded confidence and attachment of one to whom she is dearer than life can compensate her for a few years' absence from much that she loves.

Dear Margaret! She will feel this. Consult her, my love, and let us both have the advantage of such advice as her excellent understanding, and her warm affection for us, may furnish. On Monday next, at the latest, I expect to be with you. Our Scotch tour, under these circumstances, must be short. By Christmas it will be fit that the new Councillor should leave England. His functions in India commence next April. We shall leave our dear Margaret, I hope, a happy mother.

Farewell, my dear sister. You cannot tell how impatiently I shall wait for your answer.

T. B. M.

This letter, written under the influence of deep and

varied emotions, was read with feelings of painful agitation and surprise. India was not then the familiar name that it has become to a generation which regards a visit to Cashmere as a trip to be undertaken between two London seasons, and which discusses over its breakfast table at home the decisions arrived at on the previous afternoon in the Council-room of Simla or Calcutta. In those rural parsonages and middle-class households where service in our Eastern territories now presents itself in the light of a probable and desirable destiny for a promising son, those same territories were forty years ago regarded as an obscure and distant region of disease and death. A girl who had seen no country more foreign than Wales, and crossed no water broader and more tempestuous than the Mersey, looked forward to a voyage which (as she subsequently learned by melancholy experience) might extend over six weary months, with an anxiety that can hardly be imagined by us who spend only half as many weeks on the journey between Dover and Bombay. A separation from beloved relations under such conditions was a separation indeed; and, if Macaulay and his sister could have foreseen how much of what they left at their departure they would fail to find on their return, it is a question whether any earthly consideration could have induced them to quit their native shore. But Hannah's sense of duty was too strong for these doubts and tremors; and, happily, (for on the whole her resolution was a fortunate one,) she resolved to accompany her brother in an expatriation which he never would have faced without her. With a mind set at ease by a knowledge of her intention, he came down to Liverpool as soon as the Session was at an end; and carried her off on a jaunt to Edinburgh, in a post-chaise furnished with Horace Walpole's letters for their common reading, and Smollett's collected works for his own. Before October he was back at the Board of Control; and his letters recommenced, as frequent and rather more serious and business-like than of old.

London: October 5, 1833.

Dear Hannah,—

Life goes on so quietly here, or rather stands so still, that I have nothing, or next to nothing, to say. At the Athenæum I now and then fall in with some person passing through town on his way to the Continent or to Brighton. The other day I met Sharp, and had a long talk with him about everything and everybody,—metaphysics, poetry, politics, scenery, and painting. One thing I have observed in Sharp, which is quite peculiar to him among town-wits and diners-ou He never talks scandal. If he can say nothing good of a man, he holds his tongue. I do not, of course, mean that in confidential communication about politics he does not speak freely of public men; but about the foibles of private individuals I do not believe that, much as I have talked with him, I ever heard him utter one word. I passed three or four hours very agreeably in his company at the club.

I have also seen Kenny for an hour or two. I do not know that I ever mentioned Kenny to you. When London is overflowing, I meet such numbers of people that I cannot remember half their names. This is the time at which every acquaintance, however slight, attracts some degree of attention. In the desert island, even poor Poll was something of a companion to Robinson Crusoe. Kenny is a writer of a class which, in our time, is at the very bottom of the literary scale. He is a dramatist. Most of the farces, and three-act plays, which have succeeded during the last eight or ten years, are, I am told, from his pen. Heaven knows that, if they are the farces and plays which I have seen, they do him but little honour. However, this man is one of our great comic writers. He has the merit, such as it is, of hitting the very bad taste of our modern audiences better than any other person who has stooped to that degrading work. We had a good deal of literary chat; and I thought him a clever shrewd fellow.

My father is poorly: not that anything very serious

is the matter with him: but he has a cold, and is in low spirits.

Ever yours
T. B. M.

London: October 14, 1833.

Dear Hannah,—

I have just finished my article on Horace Walpole. This is one of the happy moments of my life: a stupid task performed; a weight taken off my mind. I should be quite joyous if I had only you to read it to. But to Napier it must go forthwith; and, as soon as I have finished this letter, I shall put it into the general post with my own fair hands. I was up at four this morning to put the last touch to it. I often differ with the majority about other people's writings, and still oftener about my own; and therefore I may very likely be mistaken; but I think that this article will be a hit. We shall see. Nothing ever cost me more pains than the first half; I never wrote anything so flowingly as the latter half; and I like the latter half the best. I have laid it on Walpole so unsparingly that I shall not be surprised if Miss Berry should cut me. You know she was Walpole's favourite in her youth. Neither am I sure that Lord and Lady Holland will be well pleased. But they ought to be obliged to me: for I refrained for their sake from laying a hand, which has been thought to be not a light one, on that old rogue the first Lord Holland.[1]

Charles Grant is still at Paris; ill, he says. I never knew a man who wanted setting to rights so often. He goes as badly as your watch.

My father is at me again to provide for P—. What on earth have I to do with P—? The relationship is one which none but Scotchmen would recognise. The lad is such a fool that he would utterly disgrace

[1] Lord Holland, once upon a time, speaking to Macaulay of his grandfather, said: 'He had that temper which kind folks had been pleased to say belongs to my family; but he shared the fault that belonged to that school of statesmen, an utter disbelief in public virtue.'

my recommendation. And, as if to make the thing more provoking, his sisters say that he must be provided for in England, for that they cannot think of parting with him. This, to be sure, matters little: for there is at present just as little chance of getting anything in India as in England.

But what strange folly this is which meets me in every quarter; people wanting posts in the army, the navy, the public offices, and saying that, if they cannot find such posts, they must starve! How do all the rest of mankind live? If I had not happened to be engaged in politics, and if my father had not been connected, by very extraordinary circumstances, with public men, we should never have dreamed of having places. Why cannot P— be apprenticed to some hatter or tailor? He may do well in such a business: he will do detestably ill as a clerk in my office. He may come to make good coats: he will never, I am sure, write good despatches. There is nothing truer than Poor Richard's saw: 'We are taxed twice as heavily by our pride as by the state.' The curse of England is the obstinate determination of the middle classes to make their sons what they call gentlemen. So we are overrun by clergymen without livings; lawyers without briefs; physicians without patients; authors without readers; clerks soliciting employment, who might have thriven, and been above the world, as bakers, watchmakers, or innkeepers. The next time my father speaks to me about P—, I will offer to subscribe twenty guineas towards making a pastry-cook of him. He had a sweet tooth when he was a child.

So you are reading Burnet! Did you begin from the beginning? What do you think of the old fellow? He was always a great favourite of mine;—honest, though careless; a strong party man on the right side, yet with much kind feeling towards his opponents, and even towards his personal enemies. He is to me a most entertaining writer; far superior to Clarendon in the art of amusing, though of course far Clarendon's inferior in discernment, and in dignity and correctness of style. Do you know, by the bye, Clarendon's life of himself? I like it, the part after the Restoration at least, better than his great History.

I am very quiet; rise at seven or half-past; read Spanish till ten; breakfast; walk to my office; stay there till four; take a long walk; dine towards seven; and am in bed before eleven. I am going through Don Quixote again, and admire it more than ever. It is certainly the best novel in the world, beyond all comparison.

Ever yours
T. B. M.

To Hannah M. Macaulay.

London: October 21, 1833.

My dear Sister,—

Grant is here at last, and we have had a very long talk about matters both public and private. The Government would support my appointment; but he expects violent opposition from the Company. He mentioned my name to the Chairs, and they were furious. They know that I have been against them through the whole course of the negotiations which resulted in the India Bill. They put their opposition on the ground of my youth,—a very flattering objection to a man who this week completes his thirty-third year. They spoke very highly of me in other respects; but they seemed quite obstinate.

The question now is whether their opposition will be supported by the other Directors. If it should be so, I have advised Grant most strongly to withdraw my name, to put up some other man, and then to fight the battle to the utmost. We shall be suspected of jobbing if we proceed to extremities on behalf of one of ourselves; but we can do what we like, if it is in favour of some person whom we cannot be suspected of supporting from interested motives. From the extreme unreasonableness and pertinacity which are discernible in every communication that we receive from the India House at present, I am inclined to think that I have no chance of being chosen by them, without a dispute in which I should not wish the Government to engage for such a purpose. Lord Grey says that I have a right to their support if I ask for it; but that, for the sake of his administration generally, he is very adverse to my going. I do not think that I shall go. However, a few days will decide the matter.

I have heard from Napier. He praises my article on Walpole in terms absolutely extravagant. He says that it is the best that I ever wrote; and, *entre nous*, I am not very far from agreeing with him. I am impatient to have your opinion. No flattery pleases me so much as domestic flattery. You will have the Number within the week.

Ever yours
T. B. M.

To Macvey Napier, Esq.

London: October 21, 1833.

Dear Napier,—

I am glad to learn that you like my article. I like it myself; which is not much my habit. Very likely the public, which has often been kinder to my performances than I was, may on this, as on other occasions, differ from me in opinion. If the paper has any merit, it owes it to the delay of which you must, I am sure, have complained very bitterly in your heart. I was so thoroughly dissatisfied with the article, as it stood at first, that I completely re-wrote it; altered the whole arrangement; left out ten or twelve pages in one part; and added twice as many in another. I never wrote anything so slowly as the first half, or so rapidly as the last half.

You are in an error about Akenside, which I must clear up for his credit, and for mine. You are confounding the Ode to Curio and the Epistle to Curio. The latter is generally printed at the end of Akenside's works, and is, I think, the best thing that he ever wrote. The Ode is worthless. It is merely an abridgment of the Epistle executed in the most unskilful way. Johnson says, in his Life of Akenside, that no poet ever so much mistook his powers as Akenside when he took to lyric composition. 'Having,' I think the words are, 'written with great force and poignancy his Epistle to Curio, he afterwards transformed it into an Ode only disgraceful to its author.'[1]

When I said that Chesterfield had lost by the publication of his letters, I of course considered that he had much to lose; that he has left an immense reputation, founded on the testimony of all his contemporaries of all parties, for wit, taste, and eloquence; that what remains of his Parliamentary oratory is superior to anything of that time that has come down to us, except a little of Pitt's. The utmost that can be said of the letters is that they are the letters of a cleverish man; and there are not many which are entitled even to that praise. I think he would have stood higher if we had been left to judge of his powers,—as we judge of those of Chatham, Mansfield, Charles Townshend, and many others,—only by tradition, and by fragments of speeches preserved in Parliamentary reports.

I said nothing about Lord Byron's criticism on Walpole, because I thought it, like most of his Lordship's criticism, below refutation. On the drama Lord Byron wrote more nonsense than on any subject. He wanted to have restored the unities. His practice proved as unsuccessful as his theory was

[1] 'Akenside was one of the fiercest and the most uncompromising of the young patriots out of Parliament. When he found that the change of administration had produced no change of system, he gave vent to his indignation in the "Epistle to Curio," the best poem that he ever wrote; a poem, indeed, which seems to indicate that, if he had left lyrical composition to Gray and Collins, and had employed his powers in grave and elevated satire, he might have disputed the pre-eminence of Dryden.' This passage occurs in Macaulay's Essay on Horace Walpole. In the course of the same Essay, Macaulay remarks that 'Lord Chesterfield stands much lower in the estimation of posterity than he would have done if his letters had never been published.'

absurd. His admiration of the 'Mysterious Mother' was of a piece with his thinking Gifford, and Rogers, greater poets than Wordsworth, and Coleridge.

Ever yours truly

T. B. MACAULAY.

London: October 28, 1833.

Dear Hannah,—

I wish to have Malkin as head of the Commission at Canton, and Grant seems now to be strongly bent on the same plan.[1] Malkin is a man of singular temper, judgment, and firmness of nerve. Danger and responsibility, instead of agitating and confusing him, always bring out whatever there is in him. This was the reason of his great success at Cambridge. He made a figure there far beyond his learning or his talents, though both his learning and his talents are highly respectable. But the moment that he sate down to be examined, which is just the situation in which all other people, from natural flurry, do worse than at other times, he began to do his very best. His intellect became clearer, and his manner more quiet, than usual. He is the very man to make up his mind in three minutes if the Viceroy of Canton were in a rage, the mob bellowing round the doors of the factory, and an English ship of war making preparations to bombard the town.

À propos of places, my father has been at me again about P—. Would you think it? This lad has a hundred and twenty pounds a year for life! I could not believe my ears, but so it is; and I, who have not a penny, with half a dozen brothers and sisters as poor as myself, am to move heaven and earth to push this boy who, as he is the silliest, is also, I think, the richest relation that I have in the world.

I am to dine on Thursday with the Fishmongers' Company, the first company for gourmandise in the world. Their magnificent Hall near London Bridge

[1] Sir Benjamin Malkin, a college friend of Macaulay, was afterwards a Judge in the Supreme Court at Calcutta.

is not yet built, but, as respects eating and drinking, I shall be no loser; for we are to be entertained at the Albion Tavern. This is the first dinner-party that I shall have been to for a long time. There is nobody in town that I know except official men and they have left their wives and households in the country. I met Poodle Byng, it is true, the day before yesterday in the street; and he begged me to make haste to Brooks's; for Lord Essex was there, he said, whipping up for a dinner-party; cursing and swearing at all his friends for being out of town; and wishing—what an honour! —that Macaulay was in London. I preserved all the dignity of a young lady in an *affaire du cœur*. 'I shall not run after my Lord, I assure you. If he wants me, he knows where he may hear of me.' This nibble is the nearest approach to a dinner-party that I have had.

Ever yours
T. B. M.

London: November 1, 1833.

Dear Hannah,—

I have not much to add to what I told you yesterday; but everything that I have to add looks one way. We have a new Chairman and Deputy Chairman, both very strongly in my favour. Sharp, by whom I sate yesterday at the Fishmongers' dinner, told me that my old enemy James Mill had spoken to him on the subject. Mill is, as you have heard, at the head of one of the principal departments of the India House. The late Chairman consulted him about me; hoping, I suppose, to have his support against me. Mill said, very handsomely, that he would advise the Company to take me; for, as public men went, I was much above the average, and, if they rejected me, he thought it very unlikely that they would get anybody so fit. This is all the news that I have to give you. It is not much. But I wish to keep you as fully informed of what is going on as I am myself.

Old Sharp told me that I was acting quite wisely, but that he should never see me again; and he cried as he said it.[1] I encouraged him: and told him that I hoped to be in England again before the end of 1839, and that there was nothing impossible in our meeting again. He cheered up after a time; told me that he should correspond with me, and give me all the secret history both of politics and of society; and promised to select the best books, and send them regularly to me.

The Fishmongers' dinner was very good, but not so profusely splendid as I had expected. There has been a change, I find, and not before it was wanted. They had got at one time to dining at ten guineas a head. They drank my health, and I harangued them with immense applause. I talked all the evening to Sharp. I told him what a dear sister I had, and how readily she had agreed to go with me. I had told Grant the same in the morning. Both of them extolled my good fortune in having such a companion.

Ever yours
T. B. M.

London: November —, 1833.

Dear Hannah,—

Things stand as they stood; except that the report of my appointment is every day spreading more widely; and that I am beset by advertising dealers begging leave to make up a hundred cotton shirts for me, and fifty muslin gowns for you, and by clerks out of place begging to be my secretaries. I am not in very high spirits to-day, as I have just received a letter from poor Ellis, to whom I had not communicated my intentions till yesterday. He writes so affectionately and so plaintively that he quite cuts me to the heart. There are few indeed from whom I shall part with so much pain; and he, poor fellow, says that, next to his wife, I am the person for whom he feels the most thorough attachment, and in whom he places the most unlimited confidence.

[1] Mr. Sharp died in 1837, before Macaulay's return from India.

On the 11th of this month there is to be a dinner given to Lushington by the electors of the Tower Hamlets. He has persecuted me with importunities to attend, and make a speech for him; and my father has joined in the request. It is enough, in these times, Heaven knows, for a man who represents, as I do, a town of a hundred and twenty thousand people to keep his own constituents in good humour; and the Spitalfields weavers, and Whitechapel butchers, are nothing to me. But, ever since I succeeded in what everybody allows to have been the most hazardous attempt of the kind ever made,—I mean in persuading an audience of manufacturers, all Whigs or Radicals, that the immediate alteration of the corn-laws was impossible,—I have been considered as a capital physician for desperate cases in politics. However,—to return from that delightful theme, my own praises,—Lushington, who is not very popular with the rabble of the Tower Hamlets, thinks that an oration from me would give him a lift. I could not refuse him directly, backed as he was by my father. I only said that I would attend if I were in London on the 11th; but I added that, situated as I was, I thought it very probable that I should be out of town.

I shall go to-night to Miss Berry's soirée. I do not know whether I told you that she resented my article on Horace Walpole so much that Sir Stratford Canning advised me not to go near her. She was Walpole's greatest favourite. His Reminiscences are addressed to her in terms of the most gallant eulogy. When he was dying at past eighty, he asked her to marry him, merely that he might make her a Countess and leave her his fortune. You know that in Vivian Grey she is called Miss Otranto. I always expected that my article would put her into a passion, and I was not mistaken; but she has come round again, and sent me a most pressing and kind invitation the other day.

I have been racketing lately, having dined twice with Rogers, and once with Grant. Lady Holland is in a most extraordinary state. She came to Rogers's, with Allen, in so bad a humour that we were all forced to rally, and make common cause against her. There was not a person at table to whom she was not rude; and none of us were inclined to submit. Rogers sneered; Sydney made merciless sport of her, Tom Moore looked excessively impertinent; Bobus put her down with simple straightforward rudeness; and I treated her with what I meant to be the coldest civility. Allen flew into a rage with us all, and especially with Sydney, whose guffaws, as the Scotch say, were indeed tremendous. When she and all the rest were gone, Rogers made Tom Moore and me sit down with him for half an hour, and we coshered over the events of the evening. Rogers said that he thought Allen's firing up in defence of his patroness the best thing that he had seen in him. No sooner had Tom and I got into the street than he broke forth: 'That such an old stager as Rogers should talk such nonsense, and give Allen credit for attachment to anything but his dinner! Allen was bursting with envy to see us so free, while he was conscious of his own slavery.'

Her Ladyship has been the better for this discipline. She has overwhelmed me ever since with attentions and invitations. I have at last found out the cause of her ill-humour, or at least of that portion of it of which I was the object. She is in a rage at my article on Walpole, but at what part of it I cannot tell. I know that she is very intimate with the Waldegraves, to whom the manuscripts belong, and for whose benefit the letters were published. But my review was surely not calculated to injure the sale of the book. Lord Holland told me, in an aside, that he quite agreed with me, but that we had better not discuss the subject.

A note; and, by my life, from my Lady Holland: 'Dear Mr. Macaulay, pray wrap yourself very warm, and come to us on Wednesday.' No, my good Lady. I am engaged on Wednesday to dine at the Albion

Tavern with the Directors of the East India Company; now my servants; next week, I hope, to be my masters.

Ever yours
T. B. M.

To Hannah M. Macaulay.

London: November 22, 1833.

My dear Sister,—

The decision is postponed for a week; but there is no chance of an unfavourable result. The Chairs have collected the opinions of their brethren; and the result is, that, of the twenty-four Directors, only six or seven at the most will vote against me.

I dined with the Directors on Wednesday at the Albion Tavern. We had a company of about sixty persons, and many eminent military men amongst them. The very courteous manner in which several of the Directors begged to be introduced to me, and drank my health at dinner, led me to think that the Chairs have not overstated the feeling of the Court. One of them, an old Indian and a great friend of our uncle the General, told me in plain words that he was glad to hear that I was to be in their service. Another, whom I do not even know by sight, pressed the Chairman to propose my health. The Chairman with great judgment refused. It would have been very awkward to have had to make a speech to them in the present circumstances.

Of course, my love, all your expenses, from the day of my appointment, are my affair. My present plan, formed after conversation with experienced East Indians, is not to burden myself with an extravagant outfit. I shall take only what will be necessary for the voyage. Plate, wine, coaches, furniture, glass, china, can be bought in Calcutta as well as in London. I shall not have money enough to fit myself out handsomely with such things here; and to fit myself out shabbily would be folly. I reckon that we can bring our whole expense for the passage within the twelve hundred pounds allowed by the Company. My calculation is that our cabins and board will cost

250*l.* apiece. The passage of our servants 50*l.* apiece. That makes up 600*l.* My clothes and etceteras, as Mrs. Meeke observes,[1] will, I am quite sure, come within 200*l.* Yours will, of course, be more. I will send you 300*l.* to lay out as you like; not meaning to confine you to it, by any means; but you would probably prefer having a sum down to sending in your milliner's bills to me. I reckon my servant's outfit at 50*l.*; your maid's at as much more. The whole will be 1200*l.*

One word about your maid. You really must choose with great caution. Hitherto the Company has required that all ladies, who take maidservants with them from this country to India, should give security to send them back within two years. The reason was, that no class of people misconducted themselves so much in the East as female servants from this country. They generally treat the natives with gross insolence; an insolence natural enough to people accustomed to stand in a subordinate relation to others when, for the first time, they find a great population placed in a servile relation towards them. Then, too, the state of society is such that they are very likely to become mistresses of the wealthy Europeans, and to flaunt about in magnificent palanquins, bringing discredit on their country by the immorality of their lives and the vulgarity of their manners. On these grounds the Company has hitherto insisted upon their being sent back at the expense of those who take them out. The late Act will enable your servant to stay in India, if she chooses to stay. I hope, therefore, that you will be careful in your selection. You see how much depends upon it. The happiness and concord of our native household, which will probably consist of sixty or seventy people, may be destroyed by her, if she should be ill-tempered and arrogant. If she should be weak and vain, she will probably form connections that will ruin her

[1] Mrs. Meeke was his favourite among bad novel-writers. See page 123.

morals and her reputation. I am no preacher, as you very well know; but I have a strong sense of the responsibility under which we shall both lie with respect to a poor girl, brought by us into the midst of temptations of which she cannot be aware, and which have turned many heads that might have been steady enough in a quiet nursery or kitchen in England.

To find a man and wife, both of whom would suit us, would be very difficult; and I think it right, also, to offer to my clerk to keep him in my service. He is honest, intelligent, and respectful; and, as he is rather inclined to consumption, the change of climate would probably be useful to him. I cannot bear the thought of throwing any person who has been about me for five years, and with whom I have no fault to find, out of bread, while it is in my power to retain his services.

Ever yours

T. B. M.

London: December 5, 1833.

Dear Lord Lansdowne,—

I delayed returning an answer to your kind letter till this day, in order that I might be able to send you definite intelligence. Yesterday evening the Directors appointed me to a seat in the Council of India. The votes were nineteen for me, and three against me.

I feel that the sacrifice which I am about to make is great. But the motives which urge me to make it are irresistible. Every day that I live I become less and less desirous of great wealth. But every day makes me more sensible of the importance of a competence. Without a competence it is not very easy for a public man to be honest: it is almost impossible for him to be thought so. I am so situated that I can subsist only in two ways: by being in office, and by my pen. Hitherto, literature has been merely my relaxation,—the amusement of perhaps a month in the year. I have never considered it as the means of support. I have chosen my own topics, taken my own time, and dictated my own terms. The thought of becoming a bookseller's hack; of writing to relieve, not the fulness of the mind, but the emptiness of the pocket; of spurring a jaded fancy to reluctant exertion; of filling sheets with trash merely that the sheets may be filled; of bearing from publishers and editors what Dryden bore from Tonson, and what, to my own knowledge, Mackintosh bore from Lardner, is horrible to me. Yet thus it must be, if I should quit office. Yet to hold office merely for the sake of emolument would be more horrible still. The situation, in which I have been placed for some time back, would have broken the spirit of many men. It has rather tended to make me the most mutinous and unmanageable of the followers of the Government. I tendered my resignation twice during the course of the last Session. I certainly should not have done so if I had been a man of fortune. You, whom malevolence itself could never accuse of coveting office for the sake of pecuniary gain, and whom your salary very poorly compensates for the sacrifice of ease, and of your tastes, to the public service, cannot estimate rightly the feelings of a man who knows that his circumstances lay him open to the suspicion of being actuated in his public conduct by the lowest motives. Once or twice, when I have been defending unpopular measures in the House of Commons, that thought has disordered my ideas, and deprived me of my presence of mind.

If this were all, I should feel that, for the sake of my own happiness and of my public utility, a few years would be well spent in obtaining an independence. But this is not all. I am not alone in the world. A family which I love most fondly is dependent on me. Unless I would see my father left in his old age to the charity of less near relations; my youngest brother unable to obtain a good professional education; my sisters, who are more to me than any sisters ever were to a brother, forced to turn governesses or humble companions,—I must do something, I must make some effort. An opportunity has offered itself. It is in my power to make the last days of my father comfortable, to educate my brother, to provide for my sisters, to procure a competence for myself. I may hope, by the time I am thirty-nine or forty, to return to England with a fortune of thirty thousand pounds. To me that would be affluence. I never wished for more.

As far as English politics are concerned, I lose, it is true, a few years. But, if your kindness had not introduced me very early to Parliament,—if I had been left to climb up the regular path of my profession, and to rise by my own efforts,—I should have had very little chance of being in the House of Commons at forty. If I have gained any distinction in the eyes of my countrymen,—if I have acquired any knowledge of Parliamentary and official business, and any habitude for the management of great affairs,—I ought to consider these things as clear gain.

Then, too, the years of my absence, though lost, as far as English politics are concerned, will not, I hope, be wholly lost, as respects either my own mind or the happiness of my fellow-creatures. I can scarcely conceive a nobler field than that which our Indian Empire now presents to a statesman. While some of my partial friends are blaming me for stooping to accept a share in the government of that Empire, I am afraid that I am aspiring too high for my qualifications. I sometimes feel, I most unaffectedly declare, depressed and appalled by the immense responsibility which I have undertaken. You are one of the very few public men of our time who have bestowed on Indian affairs the attention which they deserve; and you will therefore, I am sure, fully enter into my feelings.

And now, dear Lord Lansdowne, let me thank you most warmly for the kind feeling which has dictated your letter. That letter is, indeed, but a very small part of what I ought to thank you for. That at an early age I have gained some credit in public life; that I have done some little service to more than one good cause; that I now have it in my power to repair the ruined fortunes of my family, and to save those who are dearest to me from the misery and humiliation of dependence; that I am almost certain, if I live, of obtaining a competence by honourable means before I am past the full vigour of manhood,—all this I owe to your kindness. I will say no more. I will only entreat you to believe that neither now, nor on any former occasion, have I ever said one thousandth part of what I feel.

If it will not be inconvenient to you, I propose to go to Bowood on Wednesday next. Labouchere will be my fellow-traveller. On Saturday we must both return to town. Short as my visit must be, I look forward to it with great pleasure.

Believe me, ever,
Yours most faithfully and affectionately
T. B. MACAULAY.

To Hannah M. Macaulay.

London: December 5, 1833.

My dear Sister,—

I am overwhelmed with business, clearing off my work here, and preparing for my new functions. Plans of ships, and letters from captains, pour in without intermission. I really am mobbed with gentlemen begging to have the honour of taking me to India at my own time. The fact is that a Member of Council is a great catch, not merely on account of the high price which he directly pays for accommodation, but because other people are attracted by him. Every father of a young writer, or a young cadet, likes to have his son on board the same vessel with the great man, to dine at the same table, and to have a chance of attracting his notice. Everything in India is given by the Governor in Council; and, though I have no direct voice in the disposal of patronage, my indirect influence may be great.

Grant's kindness through all these negotiations has been such as I really cannot describe. He told me yesterday, with tears in his eyes, that he did not know what the Board would do without me. I attribute his feeling partly to Robert Grant's absence;—not that Robert ever did me ill offices with him; far from it; but Grant's is a mind that cannot stand alone. It is,—begging your pardon for my want of gallantry,—a feminine mind. It turns, like ivy, to some support. When Robert is near him, he clings to Robert. Robert being away, he clings to me. This may be a weakness in a public man; but I love him the better for it.

I have lately met Sir James Graham at dinner. He took me aside, and talked to me on my appointment with a warmth of kindness which, though we have been always on good terms, surprised me. But the approach of a long separation, like the approach of death, brings out all friendly feelings with unusual strength. The Cabinet, he said, felt the loss strongly. It was great at the India Board, but in the House of Commons, (he used the word over and over,) 'irreparable.' They all, however, he said, agreed that a man of honour could not make politics a profession unless he had a competence of his own, without exposing himself to privation of the severest kind. They felt that they had never had it in their power to do all they wished to do for me. They had no means of giving me a provision in England; and they could not refuse me what I asked in India. He said very strongly that they all thought that I judged quite wisely; and added that, if God heard his prayers, and spared my health, I should make a far greater figure in public life than if I had remained during the next five or six years in England.

I picked up in a print-shop the other day some superb views of the suburbs of Chowringhee, and the villas of the Garden Reach. Selina professes that she is ready to die with envy of the fine houses and verandahs. I heartily wish we were back again in a nice plain brick house, three windows in front, in Cadogan Place or Russell Square, with twelve or fifteen hundred a year, and a spare bedroom,—(we,

like Mrs. Norris,[1] must always have a spare bedroom,)
—for Edward and Margaret. Love to them both.

Ever yours
T. B. M.

To Macvey Napier, Esq.

London: December 5, 1833.

Dear Napier,—

You are probably not unprepared for what I am about to tell you. Yesterday evening the Directors of the East India Company elected me one of the members of the Supreme Council. It will, therefore, be necessary that in a few weeks,—ten weeks, at furthest,—I should leave this country for a few years.

It would be mere affectation in me to pretend not to know that my support is of some importance to the Edinburgh Review. In the situation in which I shall now be placed, a connection with the Review will be of some importance to me. I know well how dangerous it is for a public man wholly to withdraw himself from the public eye. During an absence of six years, I run some risk of losing most of the distinction, literary and political, which I have acquired. As a means of keeping myself in the recollection of my countrymen during my sojourn abroad the Review will be invaluable to me: nor do I foresee that there will be the slightest difficulty in my continuing to write for you at least as much as ever. I have thought over my late articles, and I really can scarcely call to mind a single sentence in any one of them which might not have been written at Calcutta as easily as in London. Perhaps in India I might not have the means of detecting two or three of the false dates in Croker's Boswell. But that would have been all. Very little, if any, of the effect of my most popular articles is produced either by minute research into rare books, or by allusions to mere topics of the day.

[1] A leading personage in Miss Austen's 'Mansfield Park.'

I think therefore that we might establish a commerce mutually beneficial. I shall wish to be supplied with all the good books which come out in this part of the world. Indeed, many books which in themselves are of little value, and which, if I were in England, I should not think it worth while to read, will be interesting to me in India; just as the commonest daubs, and the rudest vessels, at Pompeii attract the minute attention of people who would not move their eyes to see a modern signpost, or a modern kettle. Distance of place, like distance of time, makes trifles valuable.

What I propose, then, is that you should pay me for the articles which I may send you from India, not in money, but in books. As to the amount I make no stipulations. You know that I have never haggled about such matters. As to the choice of books, the mode of transmission, and other matters, we shall have ample time to discuss them before my departure. Let me know whether you are willing to make an arrangement on this basis.

I have not forgotten Chatham in the midst of my avocations. I hope to send you an article on him early next week.

Ever yours sincerely

T. B. MACAULAY.

From the Right Hon. Francis Jeffrey to Macvey Napier, Esq.

24, Moray Place:
Saturday evening, December 7.

My dear Napier,—

I am very much obliged to you for the permission to read this. It is to me, I will confess, a solemn and melancholy announcement. I ought not, perhaps, so to consider it. But I cannot help it. I was not prepared for six years, and I must still hope that it will not be so much. At my age, and with that climate for him, the chances of our ever meeting again are terribly endangered by such a term. He does not know the extent of the damage which his secession may be to the great cause of Liberal government. His anticipations and offers about the Review are generous and pleasing, and must be peculiarly gratifying to you. I think, if you can, you should try to see him before he goes, and I envy you the meeting.

Ever very faithfully yours

F. JEFFREY.

To Hannah M. Macaulay.

London: December 21, 1833.

My dear Sister,—

Yesterday I dined at Boddington's. We had a very agreeable party: Duncannon, Charles Grant, Sharp, Chantrey the sculptor, Bobus Smith, and James Mill. Mill and I were extremely friendly, and I found him a very pleasant companion, and a man of more general information than I had imagined.

Bobus was very amusing. He is a great authority on Indian matters. He was during several years Advocate-General in Bengal, and made all his large fortune there. I asked him about the climate. Nothing, he said, could be pleasanter, except in August and September. He never ate or drank so much in his life. Indeed, his looks do credit to Bengal; for a healthier man of his age I never saw. We talked about expenses. 'I cannot conceive,' he said, 'how anybody at Calcutta can live on less than 3,000*l.* a year, or can contrive to spend more than 4,000*l.*' We talked of the insects and snakes, and he said a thing which reminded me of his brother Sydney: 'Always, Sir, manage to have at your table some fleshy, blooming, young writer or cadet, just come out; that the musquitoes may stick to him, and leave the rest of the company alone.'

I have been with George Babington to the Asia. We saw her to every disadvantage, all litter and confusion: but she is a fine ship, and our cabins will be very good. The captain I like much. He is an agreeable, intelligent, polished man of forty; and very good-looking, considering what storms and changes of climate he has gone through. He advised me strongly to put little furniture into our cabins. I told him to have yours made as neat as possible, without regard to expense. He has promised to have it furnished simply, but prettily; and when you see it, if any addition occurs to you, it shall be made. I shall spare nothing to make a pretty little boudoir for you. You cannot think how my friends here praise you. You are quite Sir James Graham's heroine.

To-day I breakfasted with Sharp, whose kindness is as warm as possible. Indeed, all my friends seem to be in the most amiable mood. I have twice as many invitations as I can accept; and I have been frequently begged to name my own party. Empty as London is, I never was so much beset with invitations. Sharp asked me about you. I told him how much I regretted my never having had any opportunity of showing you the best part of London society. He said that he would take care that you should see what was best worth seeing before your departure. He promises to give us a few breakfast-parties and dinner-parties, where you will meet as many as he can muster of the best set in town,—Rogers, Luttrell, Rice, Tom Moore, Sydney Smith, Grant, and other great wits and politicians. I am quite delighted at this; both because you will, I am sure, be amused, and pleased, at a time when you ought to have your mind occupied, and because even to have mixed a little in a circle so brilliant will be of advantage to you in India. You have neglected and very rightly and sensibly, frivolous accomplishments: you have not been at places of fashionable diversion: and it is, therefore, the more desirable that you should appear among the dancing, pianoforte-playing, opera-going, damsels at Calcutta as one who has seen society better than any that they ever approached. I hope that you will not disapprove of what I have done. I accepted Sharp's offer for you eagerly.

Ever yours
T. B. M.

To Hannah M. Macaulay.

London: January 2, 1834.

My dear Sister,—

I am busy with an article[1] for Napier. I cannot in the least tell at present whether I shall like it or not. I proceed with great ease; and in general I have found that the success of my writings has been in proportion to the ease with which they have been written.

I had a most extraordinary scene with Lady Holland. If she had been as young and handsome as she was thirty years ago, she would have turned my head. She was quite hysterical about my going; paid me such compliments as I cannot repeat; cried; raved; called me dear, dear Macaulay. 'You are sacrificed to your family. I see it all. You are too good to them. They are always making a tool of you; last Session about the slaves; and now sending you to India!' I always do my best to keep my temper with Lady Holland for three reasons: because she is a woman; because she is very unhappy in her health, and in the circumstances of her position; and because she has a real kindness for me. But at last she said something about you. This was too much, and I was beginning to answer her in a voice trembling with anger, when she broke out again: 'I beg your pardon. Pray forgive me, dear Macaulay. I was very impertinent. I know you will forgive me. Nobody has such a temper as you. I have said so a hundred times. I said so to Allen only this morning. I am sure you will bear with my weakness. I shall never see you again:' and she cried, and I cooled: for it would have been to very little purpose to be angry with her. I hear that it is not to me alone that she runs on in this way. She storms at the Ministers for letting me go. I was told that at one dinner she became so violent that even Lord Holland, whose temper, whatever his wife may say, is much cooler than mine, could not command himself, and broke out: 'Don't talk such non-

[1] The first article on Lord Chatham.

sense, my Lady! What, the devil! Can we tell a gentleman who has a claim upon us that he must lose his only chance of getting an independence in order that he may come and talk to you in an evening?'

Good-bye, and take care not to become so fond of your own will as my Lady. It is now my duty to omit no opportunity of giving you wholesome advice. I am henceforward your sole guardian. I have bought Gisborne's Duties of Women, Moore's Fables for the Female Sex, Mrs. King's Female Scripture Characters, and Fordyce's Sermons. With the help of these books I hope to keep my responsibility in order on our voyage, and in India.

Ever yours
T. B. M.

To Hannah M. Macaulay.

London: January 4, 1834.

My dear Sister,—

I am now buying books; not trashy books which will only bear one reading; but good books for a library. I have my eye on all the bookstalls; and I shall no longer suffer you, when we walk together in London, to drag me past them as you used to do. Pray make out a list of any which you would like to have. The provision which I design for the voyage is Richardson, Voltaire's works, Gibbon, Sismondi's History of the French, Davila, the Orlando in Italian, Don Quixote in Spanish, Homer in Greek, Horace in Latin. I must also have some books of jurisprudence, and some to initiate me in Persian and Hindostanee. Shall I buy 'Dunallan' for you? I believe that in your eyes it would stand in the place of all the rest together. But, seriously, let me know what you would like me to procure.

Ellis is making a little collection of Greek classics for me, Sharp has given me one or two very rare and pretty books, which I much wanted. All the Edinburgh Reviews are being bound, so that we shall have a complete set, up to the forthcoming number, which will contain an article of mine on Chatham. And this reminds me that I must give over writing to you, and fall to my article. I rather think that it will be a good one.

Ever yours
T. B. M.

London: February 13, 1834.

Dear Napier,—

It is true that I have been severely tried by ill-health during the last few weeks; but I am now rapidly recovering, and am assured by all my medical advisers that a week of the sea will make me better than ever I was in my life.

I have several subjects in my head. One is Mackintosh's History; I mean the fragment of the large work. Another plan which I have is a very fine one, if it could be well executed. I think that the time is come when a fair estimate may be formed of the intellectual and moral character of Voltaire. The extreme veneration, with which he was regarded during his lifetime, has passed away; the violent reaction, which followed, has spent itself; and the world can now, I think, bear to hear the truth, and to see the man exhibited as he was,—a strange mixture of greatness and littleness, virtues and vices. I have all his works, and shall take them in my cabin on the voyage. But my library is not particularly rich in those books which illustrate the literary history of his times. I have Rousseau, and Marmontel's Memoirs, and Madame du Deffand's Letters, and perhaps a few other works which would be of use. But Grimm's Correspondence, and several other volumes of memoirs and letters, would be necessary. If you would make a small collection of the works which would be most useful in this point of view, and send it after me as soon as possible, I will do my best to draw a good Voltaire. I fear that the article must be enormously long,—seventy pages perhaps; but you know that I do not run into unnecessary lengths.

I may perhaps try my hand on Miss Austen's novels. That is a subject on which I shall require no assistance from books.

Whatever volumes you may send me ought to be half-bound; or the white ants will devour them before they have been three days on shore. Besides the books which may be necessary for the Review, I should like to have any work of very striking merit which may appear during my absence. The particular department of literature which interests me most is history; above all, English history. Any valuable book on that subject I should wish to possess. Sharp, Miss Berry, and some of my other friends, will perhaps, now and then, suggest a book to you. But it is principally on your own judgment that I must rely to keep me well supplied.

Yours most truly

T. B. MACAULAY.

On the 4th of February Macaulay bade farewell to his electors, in an address which the Leeds Tories probably thought too high-flown for the occasion.[1] But he had not yet done with the House of Commons.

[1] 'If, now that I have ceased to be your servant, and am only your sincere and grateful friend, I may presume to offer you advice which must, at least, be allowed to be disinterested, I would say to you: Act towards your future representatives as you have acted towards me. Choose them, as you chose me, without canvassing and without expense. Encourage them, as you encouraged me, always to speak to you fearlessly and plainly. Reject, as you have hitherto rejected, the wages of dishonour. Defy, as you have hitherto defied, the threats of petty tyrants. Never forget that the worst and most degrading species of corruption is the corruption which operates, not by hopes, but by fears. Cherish those noble and virtuous principles for which we have struggled and triumphed together—the principles of liberty and toleration, of justice and order. Support, as you have steadily supported, the cause of good government; and may all the blessings which are the natural fruits of good government descend upon you and be multiplied to you an hundredfold! May your manufactures flourish; may your trade be extended; may your riches increase! May the works of your skill, and the signs of your prosperity, meet me in the furthest regions of the East, and give me fresh cause to be proud of the intelligence, the industry, and the spirit of my constituents!'

Parliament met on the first Tuesday in the month; and, on the Wednesday, O'Connell, who had already contrived to make two speeches since the Session began, rose for a third time to call attention to words uttered during the recess by Mr. Hill, the Member for Hull. That gentleman, for want of something better to say to his constituents, had told them that he happened to know 'that an Irish Member, who spoke with great violence against every part of the Coercion Bill, and voted against every clause of it, went to Ministers and said: "Don't bate a single atom of that Bill, or it will impossible for any man to live in Ireland."' O'Connell called upon Lord Althorp, as the representative of the Government, to say what truth there was in this statement. Lord Althorp, taken by surprise, acted upon the impulse of the moment, which in his case was a feeling of reluctance to throw over poor Mr. Hill to be bullied by O'Connell and his redoubtable tail. After explaining that no set and deliberate communication of the nature mentioned had been made to the Ministers, his Lordship went on to say that he 'should not act properly if he did not declare that he had good reason to believe that some Irish Members did, in private conversation, use very different language' from what they had employed in public.

It was chivalrously, but most unwisely, spoken. O'Connell at once gave the cue by inquiring whether he himself was among the Members referred to, and Lord Althorp assured him that such was not the case. The Speaker tried to interfere; but the matter had gone too far. One Irish representative after another jumped up to repeat the same question with regard to his own case, and received the same answer. At length Sheil rose, and asked whether he was one of the Members to whom the Noble Lord had alluded. Lord Althorp replied: 'Yes. The honourable and learned gentleman is one.' Sheil, 'in the face of his country, and the presence of his God,' asserted that the individual who had given any such information to the Noble Lord was guilty of a 'gross and scandalous calumny,' and added that he understood the Noble Lord to have made himself responsible for the imputation. Then ensued one of those scenes in which the House of Commons appears at its very worst. All the busybodies, as their manner is, rushed to the front; and hour after hour slipped away in an unseemly, intricate, and apparently interminable wrangle. Sheil was duly called upon to give an assurance that the affair should not be carried beyond the walls of the House. He refused to comply, and was committed to the charge of the Sergeant at Arms. The Speaker then turned to Lord Althorp, who promised in Parliamentary language not to send a challenge. Upon this, as is graphically enough described in the conventional terms of Hansard, 'Mr. O'Connell made some observation to the honourable Member sitting next him which was not heard in the body of the House. Lord Althorp immediately rose, and amid loud cheers, and with considerable warmth, demanded to know what the honourable and learned gentleman meant by his gesticulation;' and then, after an explanation from O'Connell, his Lordship went on to use phrases which very clearly signified that, though he had no cause for sending a challenge, he had just as little intention of declining one; upon which he likewise was made over to the Sergeant. Before, however, honourable Members went to their dinners, they had the relief of learning that their refractory colleagues had submitted to the Speaker's authority, and had been discharged from custody.

There was only one way out of the difficulty. On the 10th of February a Committee of Investigation was appointed, composed of Members who enjoyed a special reputation for discretion. Mr. Hill called his witnesses. The first had nothing relevant to tell. Macaulay was the second; and he forthwith cut the matter short by declaring that, on principle, he refused to disclose what had passed in private conversation: a sentiment which was actually cheered by the Committee. One sentence of common sense brought the absurd embroilment to a rational conclusion. Mr. Hill saw his mistake; begged that no further evidence might be taken; and, at the next sitting of the House, withdrew his charge in unqualified terms of self-abasement and remorse. Lord Althorp readily admitted that he had acted 'imprudently as a man, and still more imprudently as a Minister,' and stated that he considered himself bound to accept Sheil's denial: but he could not manage so to frame his remarks as to convey to his hearers the idea that his opinion of that honourable gentleman had been raised by the transaction. Sheil acknowledged the two apologies with effusion proportioned to their respective value; and so ended an affair which, at the worst, had evoked a fresh proof of that ingrained sincerity of character for the sake of which his party would have followed Lord Althorp to the death.[1]

Gravesend: February 15, 1834.

Dear Lord Lansdowne,—

I had hoped that it would have been in my power to shake hands with you once more before my departure; but this deplorably absurd affair in the House of Commons has prevented me from calling on you. I lost a whole day while the Committee were deciding whether I should, or should not, be forced to repeat all the foolish, shabby, things that I had heard Sheil say at Brooks's.

I cannot leave England without sending a few lines to you,—and yet they are needless. It is unnecessary for me to say with what feelings I shall always remember our connection, and with what interest I shall always learn tidings of you and of your family.

Yours most sincerely

T. B. MACAULAY.

[1] In Macaulay's journal for June 3, 1851, we read: 'I went to breakfast with the Bishop of Oxford, and there learned that Sheil was dead. Poor fellow! We talked about Sheil, and I related my adventure of February 1834. Odd that it should have been so little known, or so completely forgotten! Everybody thought me right, as I certainly was.'

CHAPTER VI

1834–1838

The outward voyage—Arrival at Madras—Macaulay is summoned to join Lord William Bentinck in the Neilgherries—His journey up-country—His native servant—Arcot—Bangalore—Seringapatam—Ascent of the Neilgherries—First sight of the Governor-General—Letters to Mr. Ellis, and the Miss Macaulays—A summer on the Neilgherries—Native Christians—Clarissa—A tragi-comedy—Macaulay leaves the Neilgherries, travels to Calcutta, and there sets up house—Letters to Mr. Napier, and Mrs. Cropper—Mr. Trevelyan—Marriage of Hannah Macaulay—Death of Mrs. Cropper—Macaulay's work in India—His Minutes for Council—Freedom of the Press—Literary gratitude—Second Minute on the Freedom of the Press—The Black Act—A Calcutta public meeting—Macaulay's defence of the policy of the Indian Government—His Minute on Education—He becomes President of the Committee of Public Instruction—His industry in discharging the functions of that post—Specimens of his official writing—Results of his labours—He is appointed President of the Law Commission, and recommends the framing of a Criminal Code—Appearance of the Code—Comments of Mr. Fitzjames Stephen—Macaulay's private life in India—Oriental delicacies—Breakfast parties—Macaulay's longing for England—Calcutta and Dublin—Departure from India—Letters to Mr. Ellis, Mr. Sharp, Mr. Napier, and Mr. Z. Macaulay.

FROM the moment that a deputation of Falmouth Whigs, headed by their Mayor, came on board to wish Macaulay his health in India and a happy return to England, nothing occurred that broke the monotony of an easy and rapid voyage. 'The catching of a shark; the shooting of an albatross; a sailor tumbling down the hatchway and breaking his head; a cadet getting drunk and swearing at the captain,' are incidents to which not even the highest literary power can impart the charm of novelty in the eyes of the readers of a seafaring nation. The company on the quarter-deck was much on a level with the average society of an East Indiaman. 'Hannah will give you the histories of all these good people at length, I dare say, for she was extremely social;

danced with the gentlemen in the evenings, and read novels and sermons with the ladies in the mornings. I contented myself with being very civil whenever I was with the other passengers, and took care to be with them as little as I could. Except at meals, I hardly exchanged a word with any human being. I never was left for so long a time so completely to my own resources; and I am glad to say that I found them quite sufficient to keep me cheerful and employed. During the whole voyage I read with keen and increasing enjoyment. I devoured Greek, Latin, Spanish, Italian, French, and English; folios, quartos, octavos, and duodecimos.'

On the 10th of June the vessel lay to off Madras; and Macaulay had his first introduction to the people for whom he was appointed to legislate in the person of a boatman who pulled through the surf on his raft. 'He came on board with nothing on him but a pointed yellow cap, and walked among us with a self-possession and civility which, coupled with his colour and his nakedness, nearly made me die of laughing.' This gentleman was soon followed by more responsible messengers who brought tidings the reverse of welcome. Lord William Bentinck, who was then Governor-General, was detained by ill-health at Ootacamund in the Neilgherry Hills; a place which, by name at least, is now as familiar to Englishmen as Malvern; but which in 1834 was known to Macaulay, by vague report, as situated somewhere 'in the mountains of Malabar, beyond Mysore.' The state of public business rendered it necessary that the Council should meet; and, as the Governor-General had left one member of that body in Bengal as his deputy, he was not able to make a quorum until his new colleague arrived from England. A pressing summons to attend his Lordship in the Hills placed Macaulay in some embarrassment on account of his sister, who could not with safety commence her Eastern experiences by a journey of four hundred miles up the country in the middle of June. Happily the second letter which he opened proved to be from Bishop Wilson, who insisted that the son and daughter of so eminent an Evangelical as the Editor of the Christian Observer, themselves part of his old congregation in Bedford Row, should begin their Indian life nowhere except under his roof. Hannah, accordingly, continued her voyage, and made her appearance in Calcutta circles with the Bishop's Palace as a home, and Lady William Bentinck as a kind, and soon an affectionate, chaperon; while her brother remained on shore at Madras, somewhat consoled for the separation by finding himself in a country where so much was to be seen and where, as far as the English residents were concerned, he was regarded with a curiosity at least equal to his own.

During the first few weeks nothing came amiss to him. 'To be on land after three months at sea is of itself a great change. But to be in such a land! The dark faces, with white turbans, and flowing robes: the trees not our trees: the very smell of the atmosphere that of a hothouse, and the architecture as strange as the vegetation.' Every feature in that marvellous scene delighted him both in itself, and for the sake of the innumerable associations and images which it conjured up in his active and well-stored mind. The salute of fifteen guns that greeted him, as he set his foot on the beach, reminded him that he was in a region where his countrymen could exist only on the condition of their being warriors and rulers. When on a visit of ceremony to a dispossessed Rajah or Nabob, he pleased himself with the reflection that he was face to face with a prince who in old days governed a province as large as a first-class European kingdom, conceding to his Suzerain, the Mogul, no tribute beyond 'a little outward respect such as the great Dukes of Burgundy used to pay to the Kings of France; and who now enjoyed the splendid and luxurious insignificance of an abdicated prince which fell to the lot of Charles the Fifth or Queen Christina of Sweden,' with a court that preserved the forms of royalty, the right of keeping as many badly armed and worse paid ragamuffins as he could retain under his tawdry standard, and the privilege of 'occasionally sending letters of condolence and congratulation to the King of England, in which he calls himself his Majesty's good brother and ally.'

Macaulay set forth on his journey within a week from his landing, travelling by night, and resting while the sun was at its hottest. He has recorded his first impressions of Hindostan in a series of journal letters addressed to his sister Margaret. The fresh and vivid character of those impressions—the genuine and multiform interest excited in him by all that met his ear or eye—explain the secret of the charm which enabled him in after days to overcome the distaste for Indian literature entertained by that personage who, for want of a better, goes by the name of the general reader. Macaulay reversed in his own case, the experience of those countless writers on Indian themes who have successively blunted their pens against the passive indifference of the British public; for his faithful but brilliant studies of the history of our Eastern Empire are to this day incomparably the most popular[1] of his works. It may be possible, without injury to the fame of the author, to present a few extracts from a correspondence, which is in some sort the raw material of productions that have

[1] When published in a separate form the articles on Lord Clive and Warren Hastings have sold nearly twice as well as the articles on Lord Chatham, nearly thrice as well as the article on Addison, and nearly five times as well as the article on Byron. The great Sepoy mutiny, while it something more than doubled the sale of the essay on Warren Hastings, all but trebled the sale of the essay on Lord Clive; but, taking the last twenty years together, there has been little to choose between the pair. The steadiness and permanence of the favour with which they are regarded may be estimated by the fact that, during the five years between 1870 and 1874, as compared with the five years between 1865 and 1869, the demand for them has been in the proportion of seven to three; and, as compared with the five years between 1860 and 1864, in the proportion of three to one.

already secured their place among our national classics:

'In the afternoon of the 17th June I left Madras. My train consisted of thirty-eight persons. I was in one palanquin, and my servant followed in another. He is a half-caste. On the day on which we set out he told me he was a Catholic; and added, crossing himself and turning up the whites of his eyes, that he had recommended himself to the protection of his patron saint, and that he was quite confident that we should perform our journey in safety. I thought of Ambrose Llamela, Gil Blas's devout valet, who arranges a scheme for robbing his master of his portmanteau, and, when he comes back from meeting his accomplices, pretends that he has been to the cathedral to implore a blessing on their voyage. I did him, however, a great injustice; for I have found him a very honest man, who knows the native languages; and who can dispute a charge, bully a negligent bearer, arrange a bed, and make a curry. But he is so fond of giving advice that I fear he will some day or other, as the Scotch say, raise my corruption, and provoke me to send him about his business. His name, which I never hear without laughing, is Peter Prim.

'Half my journey was by daylight, and all that I saw during that time disappointed me grievously. It is amazing how small a part of the country is under cultivation. Two-thirds at least, as it seemed to me, was in the state of Wandsworth Common, or, to use an illustration which you will understand better, of Chatmoss. The people whom we met were as few as in the Highlands of Scotland. But I have been told that in India the villages generally lie at a distance from the roads, and that much of the land, which when I passed through it looked like parched moor that had never been cultivated, would after the rains be covered with rice.'

After traversing this landscape for fifteen hours he reached the town of Arcot, which, under his handling, was to be celebrated far and wide as the cradle of our greatness in the East.

'I was most hospitably received by Captain Smith, who commanded the garrison. After dinner the palanquins went forward with my servant, and the Captain and I took a ride to see the lions of the neighbourhood. He mounted me on a very quiet Arab, and I had a pleasant excursion. We passed through a garden which was attached to the residence of the Nabob of the Carnatic, who anciently held his court at Arcot. The garden has been suffered to run to waste, and is only the more beautiful for having been neglected. Garden, indeed, is hardly a proper word. In England it would rank as one of our noblest parks, from which it differs principally in this, that most of the fine trees are fruit trees. From this we came to a mountain pass which reminded me strongly of Borradaile, near Derwentwater, and through this defile we struck into the road, and rejoined the bearers.'

And so he went forward on his way, recalling at every step the reminiscence of some place, or event, or person; and, thereby, doubling for himself, and perhaps for his correspondent, the pleasure which the reality was capable of affording. If he put up at a collector's bungalow, he liked to think that his host ruled more absolutely and over a larger population than 'a Duke of Saxe-Weimar or a Duke of Lucca;' and, when he came across a military man with a turn for reading, he pronounced him 'as Dominie Sampson said of another Indian Colonel, "a man of great erudition, considering his imperfect opportunities."'

On the 19th of June he crossed the frontier of Mysore; reached Bangalore on the morning of the 20th, and rested there for three days in the house of the Commandant.

'On Monday, the 23rd, I took leave of Colonel Cubbon, who told me, with a warmth which I was vain enough to think sincere, that he had not passed three such pleasant days for thirty years. I went on all night, sleeping soundly in my palanquin. At five I was waked, and found that a carriage was waiting for me. I had told Colonel Cubbon that I very much wished to see Seringapatam. He had written to the British authorities at the town of Mysore, and an officer had come from the Residency to show me all that was to be seen. I must now digress into Indian politics; and let me tell you that, if you read the little that I shall say about them, you will know more on the subject than half the members of the Cabinet.'

After a few pages occupied by a sketch of the history of Mysore during the preceding century, Macaulay proceeds:

'Seringapatam has always been a place of peculiar interest to me. It was the scene of the greatest events of Indian history. It was the residence of the greatest of Indian princes. From a child, I used to hear it talked of every day. Our uncle Colin was imprisoned there for four years, and he was afterwards distinguished at the siege. I remember that there was, in a shop-window at Clapham, a daub of the taking of Seringapatam, which, as a boy, I often used to stare at with the greatest interest. I was delighted to have an opportunity of seeing the place; and, though my expectations were high, they were not disappointed.

'The town is depopulated; but the fortress, which was one of the strongest in India, remains entire. A river almost as broad as the Thames at Chelsea breaks into two branches, and surrounds the walls, above which are seen the white minarets of a mosque. We entered, and found everything silent and desolate. The mosque, indeed, is still kept up, and deserves to be so: but the palace of Tippoo has fallen into utter ruin. I saw, however, with no small interest, the airholes of the dungeon in which the English prisoners were confined, and the water-gate leading down to the river where the body of Tippoo was found still warm by the Duke of Wellington, then Colonel Wellesley. The exact spot through which the English soldiers fought their way against desperate disadvantages into the fort is still perfectly discernible. But, though only thirty-five years have elapsed since the fall of the city, the palace is in the condition of Tintern Abbey and Melrose Abbey. The courts, which bear a great resemblance to those of the Oxford Colleges, are completely overrun with weeds and flowers. The Hall of Audience, once considered the finest in India, still retains some very faint traces of its old magnificence. It is supported on a great number of light and lofty wooden pillars, resting on pedestals of black granite. These pillars were formerly covered with gilding, and here and there the glitter may still be perceived. In a few more years not the smallest trace of this superb chamber will remain. I am surprised that more care was not taken by the English to preserve so splendid a memorial of the greatness of him whom they had conquered. It was not like Lord Wellesley's general mode of proceeding; and I soon saw a proof of his taste and liberality. Tippoo raised a most sumptuous mausoleum to his father, and attached to it a mosque which he endowed. The buildings are carefully maintained at the expense of our Government. You walk up from the fort through a narrow path, bordered by flower beds and cypresses, to the front of the mausoleum, which is very beautiful, and in general character closely resembles the most richly carved of our small Gothic chapels. Within are three tombs, all covered with magnificent palls embroidered in gold with verses from the Koran. In the centre lies Hyder; on his right the mother of Tippoo; and Tippoo himself on the left.'

During his stay at Mysore, Macaulay had an interview with the deposed Rajah; whose appearance, conversation, palace, furniture, jewels, soldiers, elephants, courtiers, and idols, he depicts in a letter, intended for family perusal, with a minuteness that would qualify him for an Anglo-Indian Richardson. By the evening of the 24th June he was once more on the road; and, about noon on the following day, he began to ascend the Neilgherries, through scenery which, for the benefit of readers who had never seen the Pyrenees or the Italian slopes of an Alpine pass, he likened to 'the vegetation of Windsor Forest, or Blenheim, spread over the mountains of Cumberland.' After reaching the summit of the table-land, he passed through a wilderness where for eighteen miles together he met nothing more human than a monkey, until a turn of the road disclosed the pleasant surprise of an amphitheatre of green hills encircling a small lake, whose banks were dotted with red-tiled cottages surrounding a pretty Gothic church. The whole station presented 'very much the look of a rising English watering-place. The largest house is occupied by the Governor-General. It is a spacious and handsome building of stone. To this I was carried, and immediately ushered into his Lordship's presence. I found him sitting by a fire in a carpeted library. He received me with the greatest kindness, frankness, and hospitality. He is, as far as I can yet judge, all that I have heard; that is to say, rectitude, openness, and good-nature, personified.' Many months of close friendship and common labours did but confirm Macaulay in this first view of Lord William Bentinck. His estimate of that singularly noble character survives in the closing sentence of the essay on Lord Clive; and is inscribed on the base of the statue which, standing in front of the Town Hall, may be seen far and wide over the great expanse of grass that serves as the park, the parade-ground, and the race-course of Calcutta.

To Thomas Flower Ellis.

Ootacamund: July 1, 1834.

Dear Ellis,—

You need not get your map to see where Ootacamund is: for it has not found its way into the maps. It is a new discovery; a place to which Europeans resort for their health, or, as it is called by the Company's servants,—blessings on their learning,—a *sanaterion*. It lies at the height of 7,000 feet above the sea.

While London is a perfect gridiron, here am I, at 13° North from the equator, by a blazing wood fire, with my windows closed. My bed is heaped with blankets, and my black servants are coughing round me in all directions. One poor fellow in particular looks so miserably cold that, unless the sun comes out, I am likely soon to see under my own roof the spectacle which, according to Shakspeare, is so interesting to the English,—a dead Indian.[1]

I travelled the whole four hundred miles between this and Madras on men's shoulders. I had an agreeable journey on the whole. I was honoured by an interview with the Rajah of Mysore, who insisted on showing me all his wardrobe, and his picture gallery. He has six or seven coloured English prints. not much inferior to those which I have seen in the sanded parlour of a country inn; 'Going to Cover,' 'The Death of the Fox,' and so forth. But the bijou

[1] The Tempest, act ii. scene 2.

of his gallery, of which he is as vain as the Grand Duke can be of the Venus, or Lord Carlisle of the Three Maries, is a head of the Duke of Wellington, which has, most certainly, been on a sign-post in England.

Yet after all, the Rajah was by no means the greatest fool whom I found at Mysore. I alighted at a bungalow appertaining to the British Residency. There I found an Englishman who, without any preface, accosted me thus: 'Pray, Mr. Macaulay, do not you think that Buonaparte was the Beast?' 'No, Sir, I cannot say that I do.' 'Sir, he was the Beast. I can prove it. I have found the number 666 in his name. Why, Sir, if he was not the Beast, who was?' This was a puzzling question, and I am not a little vain of my answer. 'Sir,' said I, 'the House of Commons is the Beast. There are 658 members of the House; and these, with their chief officers,—the three clerks, the Sergeant and his deputy, the Chaplain, the doorkeeper, and the librarian,—make 666.' 'Well, Sir, that is strange. But I can assure you that, if you write Napoleon Buonaparte in Arabic, leaving out only two letters, it will give 666.' 'And pray, Sir, what right have you to leave out two letters? And, as St. John was writing Greek, and to Greeks, is it not likely that he would use the Greek rather than the Arabic notation?' 'But, Sir,' said this learned divine, 'everybody knows that the Greek letters were never used to mark numbers.' I answered with the meekest look and voice possible: 'I do not think that everybody knows that. Indeed I have reason to believe that a different opinion,—erroneous no doubt,—is universally embraced by all the small minority who happen to know any Greek.' So ended the controversy. The man looked at me as if he thought me a very wicked fellow; and, I dare say, has by this time discovered that, if you write my name in Tamul, leaving out T in Thomas, B in Babington, and M in Macaulay, it will give the number of this unfortunate Beast.

I am very comfortable here. The Governor-

General is the frankest and best-natured of men. The chief functionaries, who have attended him hither, are clever people, but not exactly on a par as to general attainments with the society to which I belonged in London. I thought, however, even at Madras, that I could have formed a very agreeable circle of acquaintance; and I am assured that at Calcutta I shall find things far better. After all, the best rule in all parts of the world, as in London itself, is to be independent of other men's minds. My power of finding amusement without companions was pretty well tried on my voyage. I read insatiably; the Iliad and Odyssey, Virgil, Horace, Cæsar's Commentaries, Bacon de Augmentis, Dante, Petrarch, Ariosto, Tasso, Don Quixote, Gibbon's Rome, Mill's India, all the seventy volumes of Voltaire, Sismondi's History of France, and the seven thick folios of the Biographia Britannica. I found my Greek and Latin in good condition enough. I liked the Iliad a little less, and the Odyssey a great deal more than formerly. Horace charmed me more than ever; Virgil not quite so much as he used to do. The want of human character, the poverty of his supernatural machinery, struck me very strongly. Can anything be so bad as the living bush which bleeds and talks, or the Harpies who befoul Æneas's dinner? It is as extravagant as Ariosto, and as dull as Wilkie's Epigoniad. The last six books, which Virgil had not fully corrected, pleased me better than the first six. I like him best on Italian ground. I like his localities; his national enthusiasm; his frequent allusions to his country, its history, its antiquities, and its greatness. In this respect he often reminded me of Sir Walter Scott, with whom, in the general character of his mind, he had very little affinity. The Georgics pleased me better; the Eclogues best,—the second and tenth above all. But I think the finest lines in the Latin language are those five which begin,

Sepibus in nostris parvam te roscida mala—[1]

[1] Eclogue viii. 37.

I cannot tell you how they struck me. I was amused to find that Voltaire pronounces that passage to be the finest in Virgil.

I liked the Jerusalem better than I used to do. I was enraptured with Ariosto; and I still think of Dante, as I thought when I first read him, that he is a superior poet to Milton, that he runs neck and neck with Homer, and that none but Shakspeare has gone decidedly beyond him.

As soon as I reach Calcutta I intend to read Herodotus again. By the bye, why do not you translate him? You would do it excellently; and a translation of Herodotus, well executed, would rank with original compositions. A quarter of an hour a day would finish the work in five years. The notes might be made the most amusing in the world. I wish you would think of it. At all events, I hope you will do something which may interest more than seven or eight people. Your talents are too great, and your leisure time too small, to be wasted in inquiries so frivolous, (I must call them,) as those in which you have of late been too much engaged; whether the Cherokees are of the same race with the Chickasaws; whether Van Diemen's Land was peopled from New Holland, or New Holland from Van Diemen's Land; what is the precise mode of appointing a headman in a village in Timbuctoo. I would not give the worst page in Clarendon or Fra Paolo for all that ever was, or ever will be, written about the migrations of the Leleges and the laws of the Oscans.

I have already entered on my public functions, and I hope to do some good. The very wigs of the Judges in the Court of King's Bench would stand on end if they knew how short a chapter my Law of Evidence will form. I am not without many advisers. A native of some fortune in Madras has sent me a paper on legislation. 'Your honour must know,' says this judicious person, 'that the great evil is that men swear falsely in this country. No judge knows what to believe. Surely if your honour can make men to swear truly, your honour's fame will be great, and the Company will flourish. Now, I know how men may be made to swear truly; and I will tell your honour for your fame, and for the profit of the Company. Let your honour cut off the great toe of the right foot of every man who swears falsely, whereby your honour's fame will be extended.' Is not this an exquisite specimen of legislative wisdom?

I must stop. When I begin to write to England, my pen runs as if it would run on for ever.

Ever yours affectionately

T. B. M.

To Miss Fanny and Miss Selina Macaulay.

Ootacamund: August 10, 1834.

My dear Sisters,—

I sent last month a full account of my journey hither, and of the place, to Margaret, as the most stationary of our family; desiring her to let you all see what I had written to her. I think that I shall continue to take the same course. It is better to write one full and connected narrative than a good many imperfect fragments.

Money matters seem likely to go on capitally. My expenses, I find, will be smaller than I anticipated. The Rate of Exchange, if you know what that means, is very favourable indeed; and, if I live, I shall get rich fast. I quite enjoy the thought of appearing in the light of an old hunks who knows on which side his bread is buttered; a warm man; a fellow who will cut up well. This is not a character which the Macaulays have been much in the habit of sustaining; but I can assure you that, after next Christmas, I expect to lay up, on an average, about seven thousand pounds a year, while I remain in India.

At Christmas I shall send home a thousand, or twelve hundred, pounds for my father, and you all. I cannot tell you what a comfort it is to me to find that I shall be able to do this. It reconciles me to all the pains—acute enough, sometimes, God knows,—

of banishment. In a few years, if I live—probably in less than five years from the time at which you will be reading this letter—we shall be again together in a comfortable, though a modest, home; certain of a good fire, a good joint of meat, and a good glass of wine; without owing obligations to anybody; and perfectly indifferent, at least as far as our pecuniary interest is concerned, to the changes of the political world. Rely on it, my dear girls, that there is no chance of my going back with my heart cooled towards you. I came hither principally to save my family, and I am not likely while here to forget them.

Ever yours
T. B. M.

The months of July and August Macaulay spent on the Neilgherries, in a climate equable as Madeira and invigorating as Braemar; where thickets of rhododendron fill the glades and clothe the ridges; and where the air is heavy with the scent of rose-trees of a size more fitted for an orchard than a flower-bed, and bushes of heliotrope thirty paces round. The glories of the forests and of the gardens touched him in spite of his profound botanical ignorance, and he dilates more than once upon his 'cottage buried in laburnums, or something very like them, and geraniums which grow in the open air.' He had the more leisure for the natural beauties of the place, as there was not much else to interest even a traveller fresh from England.

'I have as yet seen little of the idolatry of India; and that little, though excessively absurd, is not characterised by atrocity or indecency. There is nothing of the sort at Ootacamund. I have not, during the last six weeks, witnessed a single circumstance from which you would have inferred that this was a heathen country. The bulk of the natives here are a colony from the plains below, who have come up hither to wait on the European visitors, and who seem to trouble themselves very little about caste or religion. The Todas, the aboriginal population of these hills, are a very curious race. They had a grand funeral a little while ago. I should have gone if it had not been a Council day; but I found afterwards that I had lost nothing. The whole ceremony consisted in sacrificing bullocks to the manes of the defunct. The roaring of the poor victims was horrible. The people stood talking and laughing till a particular signal was made, and immediately all the ladies lifted up their voices and wept. I have not lived three and thirty years in this world without learning that a bullock roars when he is knocked down, and that a woman can cry whenever she chooses.

'By all that I can learn, the Catholics are the most respectable portion of the native Christians. As to Swartz's people in the Tanjore, they are a perfect scandal to the religion which they profess. It would have been thought something little short of blasphemy to say this a year ago; but now it is considered impious to say otherwise, for they have got into a violent quarrel with the missionaries and the Bishop. The missionaries refused to recognise the distinctions of caste in the administration of the Sacrament of the Lord's Supper, and the Bishop supported them in the refusal. I do not pretend to judge whether this was right or wrong. Swartz and Bishop Heber conceived that the distinction of caste, however objectionable politically, was still only a distinction of rank; and that, as in English churches the gentlefolks generally take the Sacrament apart from the poor of the parish, so the high-caste natives might be allowed to communicate apart from the Pariahs.

'But, whoever was first in the wrong, the Christians of Tanjore took care to be most so. They called in the interposition of Government, and sent up such petitions and memorials as I never saw before or since; made up of lies, invectives, bragging, cant, bad grammar of the most ludicrous kind, and texts of Scripture quoted without the smallest application. I remember one passage by heart, which is really only a fair specimen of the whole: "These missionaries, my Lord, loving only filthy lucre, bid us to eat Lord-supper with Pariahs as lives ugly, handling dead men, drinking rack and toddy, sweeping the streets, mean fellows altogether, base persons, contrary to that which Saint Paul saith: I determined to know nothing among you save Jesus Christ and Him crucified."

'Was there ever a more appropriate quotation? I believe that nobody on either side of the controversy found out a text so much to the purpose as one which I cited to the Council of India, when we were discussing this business: "If this be a question of words, and names, and of your law, look ye to it: for I will be no judge of such matters." But though, like Gallio, I drove them and their petitions from my judgment seat, I could not help saying to one of the missionaries, who is here on the Hills, that I thought it a pity to break up the Church of Tanjore on account of a matter which such men as Swartz and Heber had not been inclined to regard as essential. "Sir," said the reverend gentleman, "the sooner the Church of Tanjore is broken up the better. You can form no notion of the worthlessness of the native Christians there." I could not dispute this point with him; but neither could I help thinking, though I was too polite to say so, that it was hardly worth the while of so many good men to come fifteen thousand miles over sea and land in order to make proselytes, who, their very instructors being judges, were more children of hell than before.'

Unfortunately Macaulay's stay on the Neilgherries coincided with the monsoon. 'The rain streamed down in floods. It was very seldom that I could see a hundred yards in front of me. During a month together I did not get two hours' walking.' He began to be bored, for the first and last time in his life; while his companions, who had not his resources, were ready to hang themselves for very dulness. The ordinary amusements with which, in the more settled parts of India, our countrymen beguile the rainy season, were wanting in a settlement that had only lately been reclaimed from the desert; in the immediate vicinity of which you still ran the chance of being 'trod into the shape of half a crown by a wild elephant, or eaten by the tigers, which prefer this situation to the plains below for the same reason that takes so many Europeans to India: they encounter an uncongenial climate for the sake of what they can get.' There were no books in the place except those that Macaulay had brought with him, among which, most luckily, was Clarissa Harlowe. Aided by the rain outside, he soon talked his favourite romance into general favour. The reader will consent to put up with one or two slight inaccuracies in order to have the story told by Thackeray.

'I spoke to him once about Clarissa. "Not read Clarissa!" he cried out. "If you have once read Clarissa, and are infected by it, you can't leave it. When I was in India I passed one hot season in the Hills; and there were the Governor-General, and the Secretary of Government, and the Commander-in-Chief, and their wives. I had Clarissa with me; and, as soon as they began to read, the whole station was in a passion of excitement about Miss Harlowe, and her misfortunes, and her scoundrelly Lovelace. The Governor's wife seized the book; the Secretary waited for it; the Chief Justice could not read it for tears." He acted the whole scene: he paced up and down the Athenæum library. I dare say he could have spoken pages of the book; of that book, and of what countless piles of others!'

An old Scotch doctor, a Jacobin and a free-thinker, who could only be got to attend church by the positive orders of the Governor-General, cried over the last volume until he was too ill to appear at dinner.[1] The Chief Secretary,—afterwards, as Sir William Macnaghten, the hero and the victim of the darkest episode in our Indian history,—declared that reading this copy of Clarissa, under the inspiration of its owner's enthusiasm, was nothing less than an epoch in his life. After the lapse of thirty years, when Ootacamund had long enjoyed the advantage of a book-club and a circulating library, the tradition of Macaulay and his novel still lingered on with a tenacity most unusual in the ever-shifting society of an Indian station.

'At length Lord William gave me leave of absence. My bearers were posted along the road; my palanquins were packed; and I was to start next day; when an event took

[1] Degenerate readers of our own day have actually been provided with an abridgment of Clarissa, itself as long as an ordinary novel. A wiser course than buying the abridgment would be to commence the original at the Third Volume. In the same way, if anyone, after obtaining the outline of Lady Clementina's story from a more adventurous friend, will read Sir Charles Grandison, skipping all letters from Italians, to Italians, and about Italians, he will find that he has got hold of a delightful, and not unmanageable, book.

place which may give you some insight into the state of the laws, morals, and manners among the natives.

'My new servant, a Christian, but such a Christian as the missionaries make in this part of the world, had been persecuted most unmercifully for his religion by the servants of some other gentlemen on the Hills. At last they contrived to excite against him (whether justly or unjustly I am quite unable to say) the jealousy of one of Lord William's under-cooks. We had accordingly a most glorious tragi-comedy; the part of Othello by the cook aforesaid; Desdemona by an ugly, impudent Pariah girl, his wife; Iago by Colonel Casement's servant; and Michael Cassio by my rascal. The place of the handkerchief was supplied by a small piece of sugar-candy which Desdemona was detected in the act of sucking, and which had found its way from my canisters to her fingers. If I had any part in the piece, it was, I am afraid, that of Roderigo, whom Shakspeare describes as a "foolish gentleman," and who also appears to have had "money in his purse."

'On the evening before my departure my bungalow was besieged by a mob of blackguards. The Native Judge came with them. After a most prodigious quantity of jabbering, of which I could not understand one word, I called the Judge, who spoke tolerable English, into my room, and learned from him the nature of the case. I was, and still am, in doubt as to the truth of the charge. I have a very poor opinion of my man's morals, and a very poor opinion also of the veracity of his accusers. It was, however, so very inconvenient for me to be just then deprived of my servant that I offered to settle the business at my own expense. Under ordinary circumstances this would have been easy enough, for the Hindoos of the lower castes have no delicacy on these subjects. The husband would gladly have taken a few rupees, and walked away; but the persecutors of my servant interfered, and insisted that he should be brought to trial in order that they might have the pleasure of smearing him with filth, giving him a flogging, beating kettles before him, and carrying him round on an ass with his face to the tail.

'As the matter could not be accommodated, I begged the Judge to try the case instantly; but the rabble insisted that the trial should not take place for some days. I argued the matter with them very mildly, and told them that I must go next day, and that, if my servant were detained, guilty or innocent, he must lose his situation. The gentle and reasoning tone of my expostulations only made them impudent. They are, in truth, a race so accustomed to be trampled on by the strong that they always consider humanity as a sign of weakness. The Judge told me that he never heard a gentleman speak such sweet words to the people. But I was now at an end of my sweet words. My blood was beginning to boil at the undisguised display of rancorous hatred and shameless injustice. I sate down, and wrote a line to the Commandant of the station, begging him to give orders that the case might be tried that very evening. The Court assembled, and continued all night in violent contention. At last the Judge pronounced my servant not guilty. I did not then know, what I learned some days after, that this respectable magistrate had received twenty rupees on the occasion.

'The husband would now gladly have taken the money which he refused the day before; but I would not give him a farthing. The rascals who had raised the disturbance were furious. My servant was to set out at eleven in the morning, and I was to follow at two. He had scarcely left the door when I heard a noise. I looked forth, and saw that the gang had pulled him out of his palanquin, torn off his turban, stripped him almost naked, and were, as it seemed, about to pull him to pieces. I snatched up a sword-stick, and ran into the middle of them. It was all I could do to force my way to him, and, for a moment, I thought my own person was in danger as well as his. I supported the poor wretch in my arms; for, like most of his countrymen, he is a chicken-hearted fellow, and was almost fainting away. My honest barber, a fine old soldier in the Company's service, ran off for assistance, and soon returned with some police officers. I ordered the bearers to turn round, and proceeded instantly to the house of the Commandant. I was not long detained here. Nothing can be well imagined more expeditious than the administration of justice in this country, when the judge is a Colonel, and the plaintiff a Councillor. I told my story in three words. In three minutes the rioters were marched off to prison, and my servant, with a sepoy to guard him, was fairly on his road and out of danger.'

Early next morning Macaulay began to descend the pass.

'After going down for about an hour we emerged from the clouds and moisture, and the plain of Mysore lay before us

—a vast ocean of foliage on which the sun was shining gloriously. I am very little given to cant about the beauties of nature, but I was moved almost to tears. I jumped off the palanquin, and walked in front of it down the immense declivity. In two hours we descended about three thousand feet. Every turning in the road showed the boundless forest below in some new point of view. I was greatly struck with the resemblance which this prodigious jungle, as old as the world and planted by nature, bears to the fine works of the great English landscape gardeners. It was exactly a Wentworth Park as large as Devonshire. After reaching the foot of the hills, we travelled through a succession of scenes which might have been part of the garden of Eden. Such gigantic trees I never saw. In a quarter of an hour I passed hundreds the smallest of which would bear a comparison with any of those oaks which are shown as prodigious in England. The grass, the weeds, and the wild flowers grew as high as my head. The sun, almost a stranger to me, was now shining brightly; and, when late in the afternoon I again got out of my palanquin and looked back, I saw the large mountain ridge from which I had descended twenty miles behind me, still buried in the same mass of fog and rain in which I had been living for weeks.

'On Tuesday, the 16th' (of September), 'I went on board at Madras. I amused myself on the voyage to Calcutta with learning Portuguese, and made myself almost as well acquainted with it as I care to be. I read the Lusiad, and am now reading it a second time. I own that I am disappointed in Camoens; but I have so often found my first impressions wrong on such subjects that I still hope to be able to join my voice to that of the great body of critics. I never read any famous foreign book, which did not, in the first perusal, fall short of my expectations; except Dante's poem, and Don Quixote, which were prodigiously superior to what I had imagined. Yet in these cases I had not pitched my expectations low.'

He had not much time for his Portuguese studies. The run was unusually fast, and the ship only spent a week in the Bay of Bengal, and forty-eight hours in the Hooghly He found his sister comfortably installed in Government House, where he himself took up his quarters during the next six weeks; Lady

William Bentinck having been prepared to welcome him as her guest by her husband's letters, more than one of which ended with the words 'e un miracolo.' Towards the middle of November, Macaulay began housekeeping for himself; living, as he always loved to live, rather more generously than the strict necessities of his position demanded. His residence, then the best in Calcutta, has long since been converted into the Bengal Club.

To Macvey Napier, Esq.

Calcutta: December 10, 1834.

Dear Napier,—

First to business. At length I send you the article on Mackintosh; an article which has the merit of of length, whatever it may be deficient in. As I wished to transmit it to England in duplicate, if not in triplicate, I thought it best to have two or three copies coarsely printed here under the seal of strict secrecy. The printers at Edinburgh will, therefore, have no trouble in deciphering my manuscript, and the corrector of the press will find his work done to his hands.

The disgraceful imbecility, and the still more disgraceful malevolence, of the editor have, as you will see, moved my indignation not a little. I hope that Longman's connection with the Review will not prevent you from inserting what I have said on this subject. Murray's copy writers are unsparingly abused by Southey and Lockhart in the Quarterly; and it would be hard indeed if we might not in the Edinburgh strike hard at an assailant of Mackintosh.

I shall now begin another article. The subject I have not yet fixed upon; perhaps the romantic poetry of Italy, for which there is an excellent opportunity; Panizzi's reprint of Boiardo; perhaps the little volume of Burnet's Characters edited by Bishop Jebb. This reminds me that I have to acknowledge the receipt of a box from Longman, containing this little book; and other books of much greater value, Grimm's

Correspondence, Jacquemont's Letters, and several foreign works on jurisprudence. All that you have yet sent have been excellently chosen. I will mention, while I am on this subject, a few books which I want, and which I am not likely to pick up here—Daru's Histoire de Venise; St. Real's Conjuration de Venise; Fra Paolo's works; Monstrelet's Chronicle; and Coxe's book on the Pelhams. I should also like to have a really good edition of Lucian.

My sister desires me to send you her kind regards. She remembers her visit to Edinburgh, and your hospitality, with the greatest pleasure. Calcutta is called, and not without some reason, the city of palaces: but I have seen nothing in the East like the view from the Castle Rock, nor expect to see anything like it till we stand there together again.

Kindest regards to Lord Jeffrey.

Yours most truly

T. B. MACAULAY.

To Mrs. Cropper.

Calcutta: December 7, 1834.

Dearest Margaret,—

I rather suppose that some late letters from Nancy may have prepared you to learn what I am now about to communicate. She is going to be married, and with my fullest and warmest approbation. I can truly say that, if I had to search India for a husband for her, I could have found no man to whom I could with equal confidence have entrusted her happiness. Trevelyan is about eight and twenty. He was educated at the Charter-house, and then went to Haileybury, and came out hither. In this country he has distinguished himself beyond any man of his standing by his great talent for business; by his liberal and enlarged views of policy; and by literary merit, which, for his opportunities, is considerable. He was at first placed at Delhi under ——, a very powerful and a very popular man, but extremely corrupt. This man tried to initiate Trevelyan in his own infamous practices. But the young fellow's spirit was too noble for such things. When only twenty-one years of age he publicly accused ——, then almost at the head of the service, of receiving bribes from the natives. A perfect storm was raised against the accuser. He was almost everywhere abused and very generally cut. But with a firmness and ability scarcely ever seen in any man so young, he brought his proofs forward, and, after an inquiry of some weeks, fully made out his case. —— was dismissed in disgrace, and is now living obscurely in England. The Government here and the Directors at home applauded Trevelyan in the highest terms; and from that time he has been considered as a man likely to rise to the very top of the service. Lord William told him to ask for anything that he wished for. Trevelyan begged that something might be done for his elder brother, who is in the Company's army. Lord William told him that he richly earned that or anything else, and gave Lieutenant Trevelyan a very good diplomatic employment. Indeed Lord William, a man who makes no favourites, has always given to Trevelyan the strongest marks, not of a blind partiality, but of a thoroughly well-grounded and discriminating esteem.

Not long ago Trevelyan was appointed by him to the Under Secretaryship for foreign affairs, an office of a very important and confidential nature. While holding the place he was commissioned to report to Government on the operation of the Internal Transit duties of India. About a year ago his Report was completed. I shall send to England a copy or two of it by the first safe conveyance: for nothing that I can say of his abilities, or of his public spirit, will be half so satisfactory. I have no hesitation in affirming that it is a perfect masterpiece in its kind. Accustomed as I have been to public affairs, I never read an abler State paper; and I do not believe that there is, I will not say in India, but in England, another man of twenty-seven who could have written it. Trevelyan is a most stormy reformer. Lord William said to me, before anyone had observed Trevelyan's attentions to Nancy: 'That man is almost always on the right side in every question; and it is well that he is so, for he gives a most confounded deal of trouble when he happens to take the wrong one.'[1] He is quite at the head of that active party among the younger servants of the Company who take the side of improvement. In particular, he is the soul of every scheme for diffusing education among the natives of this country. His reading has been very confined; but to the little that he has read he has brought a mind as active and restless as Lord Brougham's, and much more judicious and honest.

As to his person, he always looks like a gentleman, particularly on horseback. He is very active and athletic, and is renowned as a great master in the most exciting and perilous of field sports, the spearing of wild boars. His face has a most characteristic expression of ardour and impetuosity, which makes his countenance very interesting to me. Birth is a thing that I care nothing about; but his family is one of the oldest and best in England.

During the important years of his life, from twenty to twenty-five, or thereabouts, Trevelyan was in a remote province of India, where his whole time was divided between public business and field sports, and where he seldom saw a European gentleman and never a European lady. He has no small talk. His mind is full of schemes of moral and political improvement, and his zeal boils over in his talk. His topics, even in courtship, are steam navigation, the education of the natives, the equalisation of the sugar duties, the substitution of the Roman for the Arabic alphabet in the Oriental languages.

I saw the feeling growing from the first: for, though I generally pay not the smallest attention to

[1] Macaulay used to apply to his future brother-on-law the remark which Julius Cæsar made with regard to his young friend Brutus: 'Magni refert hic quid velit; sed quidquid volet, valdè volet.'

those matters, I had far too deep an interest in Nancy's happiness not to watch her behaviour to everybody who saw much of her. I knew it, I believe, before she knew it herself; and I could most easily have prevented it by merely treating Trevelyan with a little coldness, for he is a man whom the smallest rebuff would completely discourage. But you will believe, my dearest Margaret, that no thought of such base selfishness ever passed through my mind. I would as soon have locked my dear Nancy up in a nunnery as have put the smallest obstacle in the way of her having a good husband. I therefore gave every facility and encouragement to both of them. What I have myself felt it is unnecessary to say. My parting from you almost broke my heart. But when I parted from you I had Nancy: I had all my other relations: I had my friends: I had my country. Now I have nothing except the resources of my own mind, and the consciousness of having acted not ungenerously. But I do not repine. Whatever I suffer I have brought on myself. I have neglected the plainest lessons of reason and experience. I have staked my happiness without calculating the chances of the dice. I have hewn out broken cisterns; I have leant on a reed; I have built on the sand; and I have fared accordingly. I must bear my punishment as I can; and, above all, I must take care that the punishment does not extend beyond myself.

Nothing can be kinder than Nancy's conduct has been. She proposes that we should form one family; and Trevelyan, (though, like most lovers, he would, I imagine, prefer having his goddess to himself,) consented with strong expressions of pleasure. The arrangement is not so strange as it might seem at home. The thing is often done here; and those quarrels between servants, which would inevitably mar any such plan in England, are not to be apprehended in an Indian establishment. One advantage there will be in our living together of a most incontestable sort: we shall both be able to save more money. Trevelyan will soon be entitled to his furlough; but he proposes not to take it till I go home.

I shall write in a very different style from this to my father. To him I shall represent the marriage as what it is, in every respect except its effect on my own dreams of happiness—a most honourable and happy event; prudent in a worldly point of view; and promising all the felicity which strong mutual affection, excellent principles on both sides, good temper, youth, health, and the general approbation of friends can afford. As for myself, it is a tragical dénouement of an absurd plot. I remember quoting some nursery rhymes, years ago, when you left me in London to join Nancy at Rothley Temple or Leamington, I forget which. Those foolish lines contain the history of my life.

> There were two birds that sat on a stone;
> One flew away, and there was but one.
> The other flew away, and then there was none;
> And the poor stone was left all alone.

Ever, my dearest Margaret, yours

T. B. MACAULAY.

A passage from a second letter to the same person deserves to be quoted, as an instance of how a good man may be unable to read aright his own nature, and a wise man to forecast his own future. 'I feel a growing tendency to cynicism and suspicion. My intellect remains; and is likely, I sometimes think, to absorb the whole man. I still retain, (not only undiminished, but strengthened by the very events which have deprived me of everything else,) my thirst for knowledge; my passion for holding converse with the greatest minds of all ages and nations; my power of forgetting what surrounds me, and of living with the past, the future, the distant, and the unreal. Books are becoming everything to me. If I had at this moment my choice of life, I would bury myself in one of those immense libraries that we saw together at the universities, and never pass a waking hour without a book before me.' So little was Macaulay aware that, during the years which were to come, his thoughts and cares would be less than ever for himself, and more for others, and that his existence would be passed amidst a bright atmosphere of affectionate domestic happiness, which, until his own death came, no accident was thenceforward destined to overcloud.

But, before his life assumed the equable and prosperous tenor in which it continued to the end, one more trouble was in store for him. Long before the last letters to his sister Margaret had been written, the eyes which were to have read them had been closed for ever. The fate of so young a wife and mother touched deeply all who had known her, and some who knew her only by name.[1] When the melancholy news arrived in India, the young couple were spending their honeymoon in a lodge in the Governor-General's park at Barrackpore. They immediately returned to Calcutta, and, under the shadow of a great sorrow,[2] began their sojourn in their brother's house, who, for his part, did what he might to drown his grief in floods of official work.

[1] Moultrie made Mrs. Cropper's death the subject of some verses on which her relatives set a high value. He acknowledges his little poem to be the tribute of one who had been a stranger to her whom it was written to commemorate:

> And yet methinks we are not strange: so many claims there be
> Which seem to weave a viewless band between my soul and thee.
> Sweet sister of my early friend, the kind, the single-hearted,
> Than whose remembrance none more bright still gilds the days departed!
> Beloved, with more than sister's love, by some whose love to me
> Is now almost my brightest gem in this world's treasury.

[2] 'April 8. Lichfield. Easter Sunday. After the service was ended we went over the Cathedral. When I stood before the famous children by Chantrey, I could think only of one thing; that, when last I was there, in 1832, my dear sister Margaret was with me, and that she was greatly affected. I could not command my tears, and was forced to leave our party, and walk about by myself.'—Macaulay's Journal for the year 1849.

The narrative of that work may well be the despair of Macaulay's biographer. It would be inexcusable to slur over what in many important respects was the most honourable chapter of his life; while, on the other hand, the task of interesting Englishmen in the details of Indian administration is an undertaking which has baffled every pen except his own. In such a dilemma the safest course is to allow that pen to tell the story for itself; or rather so much of the story as, by concentrating the attention of the reader upon matters akin to those which are in frequent debate at home, may enable him to judge whether Macaulay, at the council-board and the bureau, was the equal of Macaulay in the senate and the library.

Examples of his Minute-writing may with some confidence be submitted to the criticism of those whose experience of public business has taught them in what a Minute should differ from a Despatch, a Memorial, a Report, and a Decision. His method of applying general principles to the circumstances of a special case, and of illustrating those principles with just as much literary ornament as would place his views in a pictorial form before the minds of those whom it was his business to convince, is strikingly exhibited in the series of papers by means of which he reconciled his colleagues in the Council, and his masters in Leadenhall Street, to the removal of the modified Censorship which existed in India previously to the year 1835.

'It is difficult,' he writes, 'to conceive that any measures can be more indefensible than those which I propose to repeal. It has always been the practice of politic rulers to disguise their arbitrary measures under popular forms and names. The conduct of the Indian Government with respect to the Press has been altogether at variance with this trite and obvious maxim. The newspapers have for years been allowed as ample a measure of practical liberty as that which they enjoy in England. If any inconveniences arise from the liberty of political discussion, to those inconveniences we are already subject. Yet while our policy is thus liberal and indulgent, we are daily reproached and taunted with the bondage in which we keep the Press. A strong feeling on this subject appears to exist throughout the European community here; and the loud complaints which have lately been uttered are likely to produce a considerable effect on the English people, who will see at a glance that the law is oppressive, and who will not know how completely it is inoperative.

'To impose strong restraints on political discussion is an intelligible policy, and may possibly—though I greatly doubt it—be in some countries a wise policy. But this is not the point at issue. The question before us is not whether the Press shall be free, but whether, being free, it shall be called free. It is surely mere madness in a Government to make itself unpopular for nothing; to be indulgent, and yet to disguise its indulgence under such outward forms as bring on it the reproach of tyranny. Yet this is now our policy. We are exposed to all the dangers—dangers, I conceive, greatly over-rated—of a free Press; and at the same time we contrive to incur all the opprobrium of a censorship. It is universally allowed that the licensing system, as at present administered, does not keep any man who can buy a press from publishing the bitterest and most sarcastic reflections on any public measure, or any public functionary. Yet the very words "license to print" have a sound hateful to the ears of Englishmen in every part of the globe. It is unnecessary to inquire whether this feeling be reasonable; whether the petitioners who have so strongly pressed this matter on our consideration would not have shown a better judgment if they had been content with their practical liberty, and had reserved their murmurs for practical grievances. The question for us is not what they ought to do, but what we ought to do; not whether it be wise in them to complain when they suffer no injury, but whether it be wise in us to incur odium unaccompanied by the smallest accession of security or of power.

'One argument only has been urged in defence of the present system. It is admitted that the Press of Bengal has long been suffered to enjoy practical liberty, and that nothing but an extreme emergency could justify the Government in curtailing that liberty. But, it is said, such an emergency may arise, and the Government ought to retain in its hands the power of adopting, in that event, the sharp, prompt, and decisive measures which may be necessary for the preservation of the Empire. But when we consider with what vast powers, extending over all classes of people, Parliament has armed the Governor-General in Council, and, in extreme cases, the Governor-General alone, we shall probably be inclined to allow little weight to this argument. No Government in the world is better provided with the means of meeting extraordinary dangers by extraordinary precautions. Five persons, who may be brought together in half an hour, whose deliberations are secret, who are not shackled by any of those forms which elsewhere delay legislative measures, can, in a single sitting, make a law for stopping every press in India. Possessing as we do the unquestionable power to interfere, whenever the safety of the State may require it, with overwhelming rapidity and energy, we surely ought not, in quiet times, to be constantly keeping the offensive form and ceremonial of despotism before the eyes of those whom, nevertheless, we permit to enjoy the substance of freedom.'

Eighteen months elapsed; during which the Calcutta Press found occasion to attack Macaulay with a breadth and ferocity of calumny such as few public men, in any age or country, have ever endured, and none, perhaps, have ever forgiven. There were many mornings when it was impossible for him to allow the newspapers to lie about his sister's drawing-room. The Editor of the Periodical which called itself, and had a right to call itself, the '*Friend of India*,' undertook to shame his brethren by publishing a collection of their invectives; but it was very soon evident that no decent journal could venture to foul its pages by reprinting the epithets, and the anecdotes, which constituted the daily greeting of the literary men of Calcutta to their fellow-craftsman of the Edinburgh Review. But Macaulay's cheery and robust common sense carried him safe and sound through an ordeal which has broken down sterner natures than his, and embittered as stainless lives. The allusions in his correspondence, all the more surely because they are brief and rare, indicate that the torrent of obloquy to which he was exposed interfered neither with his temper nor with his happiness; and how little he allowed it to disturb his judgment or distort his public spirit is proved by the tone of a State paper, addressed to the Court of Directors in September 1836, in which he eagerly vindicates the freedom of the Calcutta Press, at a time when the writers of that Press, on the days when they were pleased to be decent, could find for him no milder appellations than those of cheat, swindler, and charlatan.

'I regret that on this, or on any subject, my opinion should differ from that of the Honourable Court. But I still conscientiously think that we acted wisely when we passed the law on the subject of the Press; and I am quite certain that we should act most unwisely if we were now to repeal that law.

'I must, in the first place, venture to express an opinion that the importance of that question is greatly over-rated by persons, even the best informed and the most discerning, who are not actually on the spot. It is most justly observed by the Honourable Court that many of the arguments which may be urged in favour of a free Press at home do not apply to this country. But it is, I conceive, no less true that scarcely any of those arguments which have been employed in Europe to defend restriction on the Press apply to a Press such as that of India.

'In Europe, and especially in England, the Press is an engine of tremendous power, both for good and for evil. The most enlightened men, after long experience both of its salutary and of its pernicious operation, have come to the conclusion that the good on the whole preponderates. But that there is no inconsiderable amount of evil to be set off against the good has never been disputed by the warmest friend to freedom of discussion.

'In India the Press is comparatively a very feeble engine. It does far less good and far less harm than in Europe. It sometimes renders useful services to the public. It sometimes brings to the notice of the Government evils the existence of which would otherwise have been unknown. It operates, to some extent, as a salutary check on public functionaries. It does something towards keeping the administration pure. On the other hand, by misrepresenting public measures, and by flattering the prejudices of those who support it, it sometimes produces a slight degree of excitement in a very small portion of the community.

'How slight that excitement is, even when it reaches its

greatest height, and how little the Government has to fear from it, no person whose observation has been confined to European societies will readily believe. In this country the number of English residents is very small, and, of that small number, a great proportion are engaged in the service of the State, and are most deeply interested in the maintenance of existing institutions. Even those English settlers who are not in the service of the Government have a strong interest in its stability. They are few; they are thinly scattered among a vast population, with whom they have neither language, nor religion, nor morals, nor manners, nor colour in common; they feel that any convulsion which should overthrow the existing order of things would be ruinous to themselves. Particular acts of the Government —especially acts which are mortifying to the pride of caste naturally felt by an Englishman in India—are often angrily condemned by these persons. But every indigo-planter in Tirhoot, and every shopkeeper in Calcutta, is perfectly aware that the downfall of the Government would be attended with the destruction of his fortune, and with imminent hazard to his life.

'Thus, among the English inhabitants of India, there are no fit subjects for that species of excitement which the Press sometimes produces at home. There is no class among them analogous to that vast body of English labourers and artisans whose minds are rendered irritable by frequent distress and privation, and on whom, therefore, the sophistry and rhetoric of bad men often produce a tremendous effect. The English papers here might be infinitely more seditious than the most seditious that were ever printed in London without doing harm to anything but their own circulation. The fire goes out for want of some combustible material on which to seize. How little reason would there be to apprehend danger to order and property in England from the most inflammatory writings, if those writings were read only by Ministers of State, Commissioners of the Customs and Excise, Judges and Masters in Chancery, upper clerks in Government offices, officers in the army, bankers, landed proprietors, barristers, and master manufacturers! The most timid politician would not anticipate the smallest evil from the most seditious libels, if the circulation of those libels were confined to such a class of readers; and it is to such a class of readers that the circulation of the English newspapers in India is almost entirely confined.'

The motive for the scurrility with which Macaulay was assailed by a handful of sorry scribblers was his advocacy of the Act familiarly known as the Black Act, which withdrew from British subjects resident in the provinces their so-called privilege of bringing civil appeals before the Supreme Court at Calcutta. Such appeals were thenceforward to be tried by the Sudder Court, which was manned by the Company's Judges, 'all of them English gentlemen of liberal education: as free as even the Judges of the Supreme Court from any imputation of personal corruption, and selected by the Government from a body which abounds in men as honourable and as intelligent as ever were employed in the service of any state.' The change embodied in the Act was one of little practical moment; but it excited an opposition based upon arguments and assertions of such a nature that the success or failure of the proposed measure became a question of high and undeniable importance.

'In my opinion,' writes Macaulay, 'the chief reason for preferring the Sudder Court is this—that it is the court which we have provided to administer justice, in the last resort, to the great body of the people. If it is not fit for that purpose, it ought to be made so. If it is fit to administer justice to the great body of the people, why should we exempt a mere handful of settlers from its jurisdiction? There certainly is, I will not say the reality, but the semblance of partiality and tyranny in the distinction made by the Charter Act of 1813. That distinction seems to indicate a notion that the natives of India may well put up with something less than justice, or that Englishmen in India have a title to something more than justice. If we give our own countrymen an appeal to the King's Courts, in cases in which all others are forced to be contented with the Company's Courts, we do in fact cry down the Company's Courts. We proclaim to the Indian people that there are two sorts of justice—a coarse one, which we think good enough for them, and another of superior quality, which we keep for ourselves. If we take pains to show that we distrust our highest courts, how can we expect that the natives of the country will place confidence in them?

'The draft of the Act was published, and was, as I fully

expected, not unfavourably received by the British in the Mofussil.[1] Seven weeks have elapsed since the notification took place. Time has been allowed for petitions from the furthest corners of the territories subject to this Presidency. But I have heard of only one attempt in the Mofussil to get up a remonstrance; and the Mofussil newspapers which I have seen, though generally disposed to cavil at all the acts of the Government, have spoken favourably of this measure.

'In Calcutta the case has been somewhat different; and this is a remarkable fact. The British inhabitants of Calcutta are the only British-born subjects in Bengal who will not be affected by the proposed Act; and they are the only British subjects in Bengal who have expressed the smallest objection to it. The clamour, indeed, has proceeded from a very small portion of the society of Calcutta. The objectors have not ventured to call a public meeting, and their memorial has obtained very few signatures. But they have attempted to make up by noise and virulence for what has been wanting in strength. It may at first sight appear strange that a law, which is not unwelcome to those who are to live under it, should excite such acrimonious feelings among people who are wholly exempted from its operation. But the explanation is simple. Though nobody who resides at Calcutta will be sued in the Mofussil courts, many people who reside at Calcutta have, or wish to have, practice in the Supreme Court. Great exertions have accordingly been made, though with little success, to excite a feeling against this measure among the English inhabitants of Calcutta.

'The political phraseology of the English in India is the same with the political phraseology of our countrymen at home; but it is never to be forgotten that the same words stand for very different things at London and at Calcutta. We hear much about public opinion, the love of liberty, the influence of the Press. But we must remember that public opinion means the opinion of five hundred persons who have no interest, feeling, or taste in common with the fifty millions among whom they live; that the love of liberty means the strong objection which the five hundred feel to every measure which can prevent them from acting as they choose towards the fifty millions, that the Press is altogether supported by the five hundred, and has no motive to plead the cause of the fifty millions.

[1] The term 'Mofussil' is used to denote the provinces of the Bengal Presidency, as opposed to the Capital.

'We know that India cannot have a free Government. But she may have the next best thing—a firm and impartial despotism. The worst state in which she can possibly be placed is that in which the memorialists would place her. They call on us to recognise them as a privileged order of freemen in the midst of slaves. It was for the purpose of averting this great evil that Parliament, at the same time at which it suffered Englishmen to settle in India, armed us with those large powers which, in my opinion, we ill deserve to possess, if we have not the spirit to use them now.'

Macaulay had made two mistakes. He had yielded to the temptation of imputing motives, a habit which the Spectator newspaper has pronounced to be his one intellectual vice, finely adding that it is 'the vice of rectitude;' and he had done worse still, for he had challenged his opponents to a course of agitation. They responded to the call. After preparing the way by a string of communications to the public journals, in which their objections to the Act were set forth at enormous length, and with as much point and dignity as can be obtained by a copious use of italics and capital letters, they called a public meeting, the proceedings at which were almost too ludicrous for description. 'I have seen,' said one of the speakers, 'at a Hindoo festival, a naked dishevelled figure, his face painted with grotesque colours, and his long hair besmeared with dirt and ashes. His tongue was pierced with an iron bar, and his breast was scorched by the fire from the burning altar which rested on his stomach. This revolting figure, covered with ashes, dirt, and bleeding voluntary wounds, may the next moment ascend the Sudder bench, and in a suit between a Hindoo and an Englishman think it an act of sanctity to decide against law in favour of the professor of the true faith.' Another gentleman, Mr. Longueville Clarke, reminded 'the tyrant' that

> There yawns the sack, and yonder rolls the sea.

'Mr. Macaulay may treat this as an idle threat; but his knowledge of history will supply him with many examples of what has occurred when resistance has been provoked by milder instances of despotism than the decimation of a people.' This pretty explicit recommendation to lynch a Member of Council was received with rapturous applause.

At length arose a Captain Biden, who spoke as follows: 'Gentlemen, I come before you in the character of a British seaman, and on that ground claim your attention for a few moments. Gentlemen, there has been much talk during the evening of laws, and regulations, and rights, and liberties: but you all seem to have forgotten that this is the anniversary of the glorious Battle of Waterloo. I beg to propose, and I call on the statue of Lord Cornwallis and yourselves to join me in three cheers for the Duke of Wellington and the Battle of Waterloo.' The audience, who by this time were pretty well convinced that no grievance which could possibly result under the Black Act could equal the horrors of a crowd in the Town Hall of Calcutta during the latter half of June, gladly caught at the diversion, and made noise enough to satisfy even the gallant orator. The business was brought to a hurried close, and the meeting was adjourned till the following week.

But the luck of Macaulay's adversaries pursued them still. One of the leading speakers at the adjourned meeting, himself a barrister, gave another barrister the lie, and a tumult ensued which Captain Biden in vain endeavoured to calm by his favourite remedy. 'The opinion at Madras, Bombay, and Canton,' said he,—and in so saying he uttered the only sentence of wisdom which either evening had produced,—'is that there is no public opinion at Calcutta but the lawyers. And now,—who has the presumption to call it a burlesque?—let's give three cheers for the Battle of Waterloo, and then I'll propose an amendment which shall go into the whole question.' The Chairman, who certainly had earned the vote of thanks for 'his very extraordinary patience,' which Captain Biden was appropriately selected to move, contrived to get resolutions passed in favour of petitioning Parliament and the Home Government against the obnoxious Act.

The next few weeks were spent by the leaders of the movement in squabbling over the preliminaries of duels that never came off, and applying for criminal informations for libel against each other, which their beloved Supreme Court very judiciously refused to grant; but in the course of time the petitions were signed, and an agent was selected, who undertook to convey them to England. On the 22nd of March, 1838, a Committee of Inquiry into the operation of the Act was moved for in the House of Commons; but there was nothing in the question which tempted Honourable Members to lay aside their customary indifference with regard to Indian controversies, and the motion fell through without a division. The House allowed the Government to have its own way in the matter; and any possible hesitation on the part of the Ministers was borne down by the emphasis with which Macaulay claimed their support. 'I conceive,' he wrote, 'that the Act is good in itself, and that the time for passing it has been well chosen. The strongest reason, however, for passing it is the nature of the opposition which it has experienced. The organs of that opposition repeated every day that the English were the conquerors, and the lords, of the country; the dominant race; the electors of the House of Commons, whose power extends both over the Company at home, and over the Governor-General in Council here. The constituents of the British legislature, they told us, were not to be bound by laws made by any inferior authority. The firmness with which the Government withstood the idle outcry of two or three hundred people, about a matter with which they had nothing to do, was designated as insolent defiance of public opinion. We were enemies of freedom, because we would not suffer a small white aristocracy to domineer over millions. How utterly at variance these principles are with reason, with justice, with the honour of the British Government, and with the dearest interests of the Indian people, it is unnecessary for me to point out. For myself, I can only say that, if the Government is to be conducted on such principles, I am utterly disqualified, by all my feelings and opinions, from bearing any part in it, and cannot too soon resign my place to some person better fitted to hold it.'

It is fortunate for India that a man with the tastes, and the training, of Macaulay came to her shores as one vested with authority, and that he came at the moment when he did; for that moment was the very turning-point of her intellectual progress. All educational action had been at a stand for some time back, on account of an irreconcilable difference of opinion in the Committee of Public Instruction; which was divided, five against five, on either side of a controversy,—vital, inevitable, admitting of neither postponement nor compromise, and conducted by both parties with a pertinacity and a warmth that was nothing but honourable to those concerned. Half of the members were for maintaining and extending the old scheme of encouraging Oriental learning by stipends paid to students in Sanscrit, Persian, and Arabic; and by liberal grants for the publication of works in those languages. The other half were in favour of teaching the elements of knowledge in the vernacular tongues, and the higher branches in English. On his arrival, Macaulay was appointed President of the Committee; but he declined to take any active part in its proceedings until the Government had finally pronounced on the question at issue. Later in January 1835 the advocates of the two systems, than whom ten abler men could not be found in the service, laid their opinions before the Supreme Council; and, on the 2nd of February, Macaulay, as a member of that Council, produced a minute in which he adopted and defended the views of the English section in the Committee.

'How stands the case? We have to educate a people who

cannot at present be educated by means of their mother-tongue. We must teach them some foreign language. The claims of our own language it is hardly necessary to recapitulate. It stands pre-eminent even among the languages of the West. It abounds with works of imagination not inferior to the noblest which Greece has bequeathed to us; with models of every species of eloquence; with historical compositions, which, considered merely as narratives, have seldom been surpassed, and which, considered as vehicles of ethical and political instruction, have never been equalled; with just and lively representations of human life and human nature; with the most profound speculations on metaphysics, morals, government, jurisprudence, and trade; with full and correct information respecting every experimental science which tends to preserve the health, to increase the comfort, or to expand the intellect of man. Whoever knows that language has ready access to all the vast intellectual wealth which all the wisest nations of the earth have created and hoarded in the course of ninety generations. It may safely be said that the literature now extant in that language is of far greater value than all the literature which three hundred years ago was extant in all the languages of the world together. Nor is this all. In India, English is the language spoken by the ruling class. It is spoken by the higher class of natives at the seats of government. It is likely to become the language of commerce throughout the seas of the East. It is the language of two great European communities which are rising, the one in the south of Africa, the other in Australasia; communities which are every year becoming more important, and more closely connected with our Indian Empire. Whether we look at the intrinsic value of our literature or at the particular situation of this country, we shall see the strongest reason to think that, of all foreign tongues, the English tongue is that which would be the most useful to our native subjects.

'The question now before us is simply whether, when it is in our power to teach this language, we shall teach languages in which, by universal confession, there are no books on any subject which deserve to be compared to our own; whether, when we can teach European science, we shall teach systems which, by universal confession, whenever they differ from those of Europe, differ for the worse; and whether, when we can patronise sound philosophy and true history, we shall countenance, at the public expense, medical doctrines, which would disgrace an English farrier —astronomy, which would move laughter in the girls at an English boarding-school—history, abounding with kings thirty feet high, and reigns thirty thousand years long—and geography made up of seas of treacle and seas of butter.

'We are not without experience to guide us. History furnishes several analogous cases, and they all teach the same lesson. There are in modern times, to go no further, two memorable instances of a great impulse given to the mind of a whole society—of prejudice overthrown—of knowledge diffused—of taste purified—of arts and sciences planted in countries which had recently been ignorant and barbarous.

'The first instance to which I refer is the great revival of letters among the western nations at the close of the fifteenth and the beginning of the sixteenth century. At that time almost everything that was worth reading was contained in the writings of the ancient Greeks and Romans. Had our ancestors acted as the Committee of Public Instruction has hitherto acted; had they neglected the language of Cicero and Tacitus; had they confined their attention to the old dialects of our own island; had they printed nothing, and taught nothing at the universities but chronicles in Anglo-Saxon, and romances in Norman French, would England have been what she now is? What the Greek and Latin were to the contemporaries of More and Ascham, our tongue is to the people of India. The literature of England is now more valuable than that of classical antiquity. I doubt whether the Sanscrit literature be as valuable as that of our Saxon and Norman progenitors. In some departments—in history, for example—I am certain that it is much less so.

'Another instance may be said to be still before our eyes. Within the last hundred and twenty years a nation which had previously been in a state as barbarous as that in which our ancestors were before the Crusades has gradually emerged from the ignorance in which it was sunk, and has taken its place among civilised communities. I speak of Russia. There is now in that country a large educated class, abounding with persons fit to serve the state in the highest functions, and in no wise inferior to the most accomplished men who adorn the best circles of Paris and London. There is reason to hope that this vast Empire, which in the time of our grandfathers was probably behind the Punjab, may, in the time of our grandchildren, be pressing close on France and Britain in the career of improvement. And how was this change effected? Not by flattering national prejudices; not by feeding the mind of the young Muscovite with the old woman's stories which his rude fathers had believed; not by filling his head with lying legends about St. Nicholas; not by encouraging him to study the great question, whether the world was or was not created on the 13th of September; not by calling him "a learned native," when he has mastered all these points of knowledge; but by teaching him those foreign languages in which the greatest mass of information had been laid up, and thus putting all that information within his reach. The languages of western Europe civilised Russia. I cannot doubt that they will do for the Hindoo what they have done for the Tartar.'

This Minute, which in its original shape is long enough for an article in a quarterly review, and as businesslike as a Report of a Royal Commission, set the question at rest at once and for ever. On the 7th of March, 1835, Lord William Bentinck decided that 'the great object of the British Government ought to be the promotion of European literature and science among the natives of India;' two of the Orientalists retired from the Committee of Public Instruction; several new members, both English and native, were appointed; and Macaulay entered upon the functions of President with an energy and assiduity which in his case was an infallible proof that his work was to his mind.

The post was no sinecure. It was an arduous task to plan, found, and construct, in all its grades, the education of such a country as India. The means at Macaulay's disposal were utterly inadequate for the undertaking on which he was engaged. Nothing resembling an organised staff was as yet in existence. There were no Inspectors of Schools. There were no training colleges for masters. There were no boards of experienced managers. The machinery consisted of voluntary committees acting on the spot, and corresponding directly with the superintending body at Calcutta. Macaulay rose to the occasion, and threw himself into the routine of administration and control with zeal sustained by diligence and tempered by tact. 'We were hardly prepared,' said a competent critic, 'for the amount of conciliation which he evinces in dealing with irritable colleagues and subordinates, and for the strong, sterling, practical common sense with which he sweeps away rubbish, or cuts the knots of local and departmental problems.' The mastery which a man exercises over himself, and the patience and forbearance displayed in his dealings with others, are generally in proportion to the value which he sets upon the objects of his pursuit. If we judge Macaulay by this standard, it is plain that he cared a great deal more for providing our Eastern Empire with an educational outfit that would work and wear than he ever cared for keeping his own seat in Parliament or pushing his own fortunes in Downing Street. Throughout his innumerable Minutes, on all subjects from the broadest principle to the narrowest detail, he is everywhere free from crochets and susceptibilities; and everywhere ready to humour any person who will make himself useful, and to adopt any appliance which can be turned to account.

'I think it highly probable that Mr. Nicholls may be to blame, because I have seldom known a quarrel in which both parties were not to blame. But I see no evidence that he is so. Nor do I see any evidence which tends to prove that Mr. Nicholls leads the Local Committee by the nose. The Local Committee appear to have acted with perfect propriety, and I cannot consent to treat them in the manner recommended by Mr. Sutherland. If we appoint the Colonel to be a member of their body, we shall in effect pass a most severe censure on their proceedings. I dislike the suggestion of putting military men on the Committee as a check on the civilians. Hitherto we have never, to the best of my belief, been troubled by any such idle jealousies. I would appoint the fittest men without caring to what branch of the service they belonged, or whether they belonged to the service at all.'[1]

[1] This, and the following extracts, are taken from a volume of Macaulay's Minutes, 'now first collected from Records in

Exception had been taken to an applicant for a mastership, on the ground that he had been a preacher with a strong turn for proselytising.

'Mr. —— seems to be so little concerned about proselytising, that he does not even know how to spell the word; a circumstance which, if I did not suppose it to be a slip of the pen, I should think a more serious objection than the "Reverend" which formerly stood before his name. I am quite content with his assurances.'

In default of better, Macaulay was always for employing the tools which came to hand. A warm and consistent advocate of appointment by competitive examination, wherever a field for competition existed, he was no pedantic slave to a theory. In the dearth of schoolmasters, which is a feature in every infant educational system, he refused to reject a candidate who 'mistook Argos for Corinth,' and backed the claims of any aspirant of respectable character who could 'read, write, and work a sum.'

'By all means accept the King of Oude's present; though, to be sure, more detestable maps were never seen. One would think that the revenues of Oude, and the treasure of Saadut Ali, might have borne the expense of producing something better than a map in which Sicily is joined on to the toe of Italy, and in which so important an eastern island as Java does not appear at all.'

'As to the corrupting influence of the zenana, of which Mr. Trevelyan speaks, I may regret it; but I own that I cannot help thinking that the dissolution of the tie between parent and child is as great a moral evil as can be found in any zenana. In whatever degree infant schools relax that tie they do mischief. For my own part, I would rather hear a boy of three years old lisp all the bad words in the language than that he should have no feelings of family affection—that his character should be that which must be expected in one who has had the misfortune of having a schoolmaster in place of a mother.'

the Department of Public Instruction, by H. Woodrow, Esq., M.A., Inspector of Schools at Calcutta, and formerly Fellow of Caius College, Cambridge.' The collection was published in India.

'I do not see the reason for establishing any limit as to the age of scholars. The phenomena are exactly the same which have always been found to exist when a new mode of education has been rising into fashion. No man of fifty now learns Greek with boys; but in the sixteenth century it was not at all unusual to see old Doctors of Divinity attending lectures side by side with young students.'

'With respect to making our College libraries circulating libraries, there is much to be said on both sides. If a proper subscription is demanded from those who have access to them, and if all that is raised by this subscription is laid out in adding to the libraries, the students will be no losers by the plan. Our libraries, the best of them at least, would be better than any which would be readily accessible at an up-country station; and I do not know why we should grudge a young officer the pleasure of reading our copy of Boswell's Life of Johnson or Marmontel's Memoirs, if he is willing to pay a few rupees for the privilege.'

These utterances of cultured wisdom or homely mother-wit are sometimes expressed in phrases almost as amusing, though not so characteristic, as those which Frederick the Great used to scrawl on the margin of reports and despatches for the information of his secretaries.

'We are a little too indulgent to the whims of the people in our employ. We pay a large sum to send a master to a distant station. He dislikes the place. The collector is uncivil; the surgeon quarrels with him; and he must be moved. The expenses of the journey have to be defrayed. Another man is to be transferred from a place where he is comfortable and useful. Our masters run from station to station at our cost, as vapourish ladies at home run about from spa to spa. All situations have their discomforts; and there are times when we all wish that our lot had been cast in some other line of life, or in some other place.'

With regard to a proposed coat of arms for Hooghly College, he says

'I do not see why the mummeries of European heraldry should be introduced into any part of our Indian system. Heraldry is not a science which has any eternal rules. It is a system of arbitrary canons, originating in pure caprice.

Nothing can be more absurd and grotesque than armorial bearings, considered in themselves. Certain recollections, certain associations, make them interesting in many cases to an Englishman; but in those recollections and associations the natives of India do not participate. A lion, rampant, with a folio in his paw, with a man standing on each side of him, with a telescope over his head, and with a Persian motto under his feet, must seem to them either very mysterious, or very absurd.'

In a discussion on the propriety of printing some books of Oriental science, Macaulay writes:

'I should be sorry to say anything disrespectful of that liberal and generous enthusiasm for Oriental literature which appears in Mr. Sutherland's minute: but I own that I cannot think that we ought to be guided in the distribution of the small sum, which the Government has allotted for the purpose of education, by considerations which seem a little romantic. That the Saracens a thousand years ago cultivated mathematical science is hardly, I think, a reason for our spending any money in translating English treatises on mathematics into Arabic. Mr. Sutherland would probably think it very strange if we were to urge the destruction of the Alexandrian Library as a reason against patronising Arabic literature in the nineteenth century. The undertaking may be, as Mr. Sutherland conceives, a great national work. So is the breakwater at Madras. But under the orders which we have received from the Government, we have just as little to do with one as with the other.'

Now and then a stroke, aimed at Hooghly College, hits nearer home. That men of thirty should be bribed to continue their education into mature life 'seems very absurd. Moghal Jan has been paid to learn something during twelve years. We are told that he is lazy and stupid: but there are hopes that in four years more he will have completed his course of study. We have had quite enough of these lazy, stupid schoolboys of thirty.'

'I must frankly own that I do not like the list of books. Grammars of rhetoric and grammars of logic are among the most useless furniture of a shelf. Give a boy a Robinson

Crusoe. That is worth all the grammars of rhetoric and logic in the world. We ought to procure such books as are likely to give the children a taste for the literature of the West; not books filled with idle distinctions and definitions, which every man who has learned them makes haste to forget. Who ever reasoned better for having been taught the difference between a syllogism and an enthymeme? Who ever composed with greater spirit and elegance because he could define an oxymoron or an aposiopesis? I am not joking, but writing quite seriously, when I say that I would much rather order a hundred copies of Jack the Giant-killer for our schools than a hundred copies of any grammar of rhetoric or logic that ever was written.'

'Goldsmith's Histories of Greece and Rome are miserable performances, and I do not at all like to lay out 50*l.* on them, even after they have received all Mr. Pinnock's improvements. I must own too, that I think the order for globes and other instruments unnecessarily large. To lay out 324*l.* at once on globes alone, useful as I acknowledge those articles to be, seems exceedingly profuse, when we have only about 3,000*l.* a year for all purposes of English education. One 12-inch or 18-inch globe for each school is quite enough; and we ought not, I think, to order sixteen such globes when we are about to establish only seven schools. Useful as the telescopes, the theodolites, and the other scientific instruments mentioned in the indent undoubtedly are, we must consider that four or five such instruments run away with a year's salary of a schoolmaster, and that, if we purchase them, it will be necessary to defer the establishment of schools.'

At one of the colleges at Calcutta the distribution of prizes was accompanied by some histrionic performances on the part of the pupils.

'I have no partiality,' writes Macaulay, 'for such ceremonies. I think it a very questionable thing whether, even at home, public spouting and acting ought to form part of the system of a place of education. But in this country such exhibitions are peculiarly out of place. I can conceive nothing more grotesque than the scene from the Merchant of Venice, with Portia represented by a little black boy. Then, too, the subjects of recitation were ill chosen. We are attempting to introduce a great nation to a knowledge of the richest and noblest literature in the world. The society of Calcutta assemble to see what progress we are making; and we produce as a sample a boy who repeats some blackguard doggerel of George Colman's, about a fat gentleman who was put to bed over an oven, and about a man-midwife who was called out of his bed by a drunken man at night. Our disciple tries to hiccup, and tumbles and staggers about in imitation of the tipsy English sailors whom he has seen at the punch houses. Really, if we can find nothing better worth reciting than this trash, we had better give up English instruction altogether.'

'As to the list of prize books, I am not much better satisfied. It is absolutely unintelligible to me why Pope's Works and my old friend Moore's Lalla Rookh should be selected from the whole mass of English poetry to be prize books. I will engage to frame, *currente calamo*, a better list. Bacon's Essays, Hume's England, Gibbon's Rome, Robertson's Charles V., Robertson's Scotland, Robertson's America, Swift's Gulliver, Robinson Crusoe, Shakspeare's Works, Paradise Lost, Milton's smaller poems, Arabian Nights, Park's Travels, Anson's Voyage, the Vicar of Wakefield, Johnson's Lives, Gil Blas, Voltaire's Charles XII, Southey's Nelson, Middleton's Life of Cicero.

'This may serve as a specimen. These are books which will amuse and interest those who obtain them. To give a boy Abercrombie on the Intellectual Powers, Dick's Moral Improvement, Young's Intellectual Philosophy, Chalmers's Poetical Economy!!! (in passing I may be allowed to ask what that means?) is quite absurd. I would not give orders at random for books about which we know nothing. We are under no necessity of ordering at haphazard. We know Robinson Crusoe, and Gulliver, and the Arabian Nights, and Anson's Voyage, and many other delightful works which interest even the very young, and which do not lose their interest to the end of our lives. Why should we order blindfold such books as Markham's New Children's Friend, the Juvenile Scrap Book, the Child's Own Book, Niggens's Earth, Mudie's Sea, and somebody else's Fire and Air?—books which, I will be bound for it, none of us ever opened.

'The list ought in all its parts to be thoroughly recast. If Sir Benjamin Malkin will furnish the names of ten or twelve works of a scientific kind, which he thinks suited for prizes, the task will not be difficult; and, with his help, I will gladly undertake it. There is a marked distinction between a prize book and a school book. A prize book ought to be a book which a boy receives with pleasure, and turns over and over, not as a task, but spontaneously. I have not forgotten my own school-boy feelings on this subject. My pleasure at obtaining a prize was greatly enhanced by the knowledge that my little library would receive a very agreeable addition. I never was better pleased than when at fourteen I was master of Boswell's Life of Johnson, which I had long been wishing to read. If my master had given me, instead of Boswell, a Critical Pronouncing Dictionary, or a Geographical Class book, I should have been much less gratified by my success.'

The idea had been started of paying authors to write books in the languages of the country. On this Macaulay remarks:

'To hire four or five people to make a literature is a course which never answered and never will answer in any part of the world. Languages grow. They cannot be built. We are now following the slow but sure course on which alone we can depend for a supply of good books in the vernacular languages of India. We are attempting to raise up a large class of enlightened natives. I hope that, twenty years hence, there will be hundreds, nay thousands, of natives familiar with the best models of composition, and well acquainted with Western science. Among them some persons will be found who will have the inclination and the ability to exhibit European knowledge in the vernacular dialects. This I believe to be the only way in which we can raise up a good vernacular literature in this country.'

These hopeful anticipations have been more than fulfilled. Twice twenty years have brought into existence, not hundreds or thousands, but hundreds of thousands, of natives who can appreciate European knowledge when laid before them in the English language, and can reproduce it in their own. Taking one year with another, upwards of a thousand works of literature and science are published annually in Bengal alone, and at least four times that number throughout the entire continent. Our colleges have more than six thousand students on their books, and two hundred thousand boys are receiving a liberal education in schools of the higher order. For the improvement of the mass of the people, nearly seven thousand young men are in training as Certificated Masters. The amount allotted in the budget to the item of Public Instruction has increased more than seventy-fold since 1835; and is largely supplemented by the fees which parents of all classes willingly contribute when once they have been taught the value of a commodity the demand for which is created by the supply. During many years past the generosity of wealthy natives has to a great extent been diverted from the idle extravagance of pageants and festivals, to promote the intellectual advancement of their fellow-countrymen. On several different occasions, at a single stroke of the pen, our Indian universities have been endowed with twice, three times, four times the amount of the slender sum which Macaulay had at his command. But none the less was he the master-engineer, whose skill and foresight determined the direction of the channels, along which this stream of public and private munificence was to flow for the regeneration of our Eastern Empire.

It may add something to the merit of Macaulay's labours in the cause of Education that those labours were voluntary and unpaid; and voluntary and unpaid likewise was another service which he rendered to India, not less durable than the first, and hardly less important. A clause in the Act of 1833 gave rise to the appointment of a Commission to inquire into the Jurisprudence and Jurisdiction of our Eastern Empire. Macaulay, at his own instigation, was appointed President of that Commission. He had not been many months engaged in his new duties before he submitted a proposal, by the adoption of which his own industry and the high talents of his colleagues, Mr. Cameron and Sir John Macleod, might be turned to the best account by being employed in framing a Criminal Code for the whole Indian Empire. 'This Code,' writes Macaulay, 'should not be a mere digest of existing usages and regulations, but should comprise all the reforms which the Commission may think desirable. It should be framed on two great principles,—the principle of suppressing crime with the smallest possible amount of suffering, and the principle of ascertaining truth at the smallest possible cost of time and money. The Commissioners should be particularly charged to study conciseness, as far as it is consistent with perspicuity. In general, I believe, it will be found that perspicuous and concise expressions are not only compatible, but identical.'

The offer was eagerly accepted, and the Commission fell to work. The results of that work did not show themselves quickly enough to satisfy the most practical, and, (to its credit be it spoken,) the most exacting of Governments; and Macaulay was under the necessity of explaining and excusing a procrastination, which was celerity itself as compared with any codifying that had been done since the days of Justinian.

'During the last rainy season,—a season, I believe, peculiarly unhealthy,—every member of the Commission, except myself, was wholly incapacitated for exertion. Mr. Anderson has been twice under the necessity of leaving Calcutta, and has not, till very lately, been able to labour with his accustomed activity. Mr. Macleod has been, till within the last week or ten days, in so feeble a state that the smallest effort seriously disordered him; and his health is so delicate that, admirably qualified as he is, by very rare talents, for the discharge of his functions, it would be imprudent, in forming any prospective calculation, to reckon on much service from him. Mr. Cameron, of the importance of whose assistance I need not speak, has been, during more than four months, utterly unable to do any work, and has at length been compelled to ask leave of absence, in order to visit the Cape, for the recovery of his health. Thus, as the Governor-General has stated, Mr. Millett and myself have, during a considerable time, constituted the whole effective strength of the Commission. Nor has Mr. Millett been able to devote to the business of the Commission his whole undivided attention.

'I must say that, even if no allowance be made for the untoward occurrences which have retarded our progress, that progress cannot be called slow. People who have never considered the importance and difficulty of the task in which we are employed are surprised to find that a Code cannot be spoken off extempore, or written like an article in a magazine. I am not ashamed to acknowledge that there are several chapters in the Code on which I have been employed for months; of which I have changed the whole plan ten or twelve times; which contain not a single word as it originally stood; and with which I am still very far indeed from being satisfied. I certainly shall not hurry on my share of the work to gratify the childish impatience of the ignorant. Their censure ought to be a matter of perfect indifference to men engaged in a task, on the right performance of which the welfare of millions may, during a long series of years, depend. The cost of the Commission is as nothing when compared with the importance of such a work. The time during which the Commission has sat is as nothing compared with the time during which that work will produce good, or evil, to India.

'Indeed, if we compare the progress of the Indian Code with the progress of Codes under circumstances far more favourable, we shall find little reason to accuse the Law Commission of tardiness. Buonaparte had at his command the service of experienced jurists to any extent to which he chose to call for them; yet his legislation proceeded at a far slower rate than ours. The French Criminal Code was begun, under the Consulate, in March 1801; and yet the Code of Criminal Procedure was not completed till 1808, and the Penal Code not till 1810. The Criminal Code of Louisiana was commenced in February 1821. After it had been in preparation during three years and a half, an accident happened to the papers which compelled Mr. Livingstone to request indulgence for another year. Indeed, when I remember the slow progress of law reforms at home, and when I consider that our Code decides hundreds of questions, every one of which, if stirred in England, would give occasion to voluminous controversy and to many animated debates, I must acknowledge that I am inclined to fear that we have been guilty rather of precipitation than of delay.'

This Minute was dated the 2nd of January, 1837; and in the course of the same year the Code appeared, headed by an Introductory Report in the shape of a letter to the Governor-General, and followed by an Appendix containing eighteen notes, each in itself an essay. The most readable of all Digests, its pages are alive with illustrations drawn from history, from literature, and from the habits and occurrences of everyday life. The offence of fabricating evidence is exemplified by a case which may easily be recognised as that of Lady Macbeth and the grooms;[1] and the offence of voluntary culpable homicide by an imaginary incident of a pit covered with sticks and turf, which irresistibly recalls a reminiscence of Jack the Giant-killer. The chapters on theft and trespass establish the rights of book owners as against book stealers, book borrowers, and book defacers,[2] with an affectionate precision which would have gladdened the heart of Charles Lamb or Sir Walter Scott. In the chapter on manslaughter, the judge is enjoined to treat with lenity an act done in the first anger of a husband or father, provoked by the intolerable outrage of a certain kind of criminal assault. 'Such an assault produced the Sicilian Vespers. Such an assault called forth the memorable blow of Wat Tyler.' And, on the question whether the severity of a hurt should be considered in apportioning the

[1] 'A, after wounding a person with a knife, goes into the room where Z is sleeping, smears Z's clothes with blood, and lays the knife under Z's pillow; intending not only that suspicion may thereby be turned away from himself, but also that Z may be convicted of voluntarily causing grievous hurt. A is liable to punishment as a fabricator of false evidence.'

[2] 'A, being on friendly terms with Z, goes into Z's library, in Z's absence, and takes a book without Z's express consent. Here, it is probable that A may have conceived that he had Z's implied consent to use Z's books. If this was A's impression, A has not committed theft.

'A takes up a book belonging to Z, and reads it, not having any right over the book, and not having the consent of any person entitled to authorise A so to do. A trespasses.

'A, being exasperated at a passage in a book which is lying on the counter of Z, snatches it up, and tears it to pieces. A has not committed theft, as he has not acted fraudulently, though he may have committed criminal trespass and mischief.'

punishment, we are reminded of 'examples which are universally known. Harley was laid up more than twenty days by the wound which he received from Guiscard;' while 'the scratch which Damien gave to Louis the Fifteenth was so slight that it was followed by no feverish symptoms.' Such a sanguine estimate of the diffusion of knowledge with regard to the details of ancient crimes could proceed from no pen but that of the writer who endowed schoolboys with the erudition of professors, and the talker who, when he poured forth the stores of his memory, began each of his disquisitions with the phrase, 'don't you remember?'

If it be asked whether or not the Penal Code fulfils the ends for which it was framed, the answer may safely be left to the gratitude of Indian civilians, the younger of whom carry it about in their saddle-bags, and the older in their heads. The value which it possesses in the eyes of a trained English lawyer may be gathered from the testimony of Macaulay's eminent successor, Mr. Fitzjames Stephen, who writes of it thus:

'In order to appreciate the importance of the Penal Code, it must be borne in mind what crime in India is. Here, in England, order is so thoroughly well established that the crime of the country is hardly more than an annoyance. In India, if crime is allowed to get to a head, it is capable of destroying the peace and prosperity of whole tracts of country. The mass of the people in their common moods are gentle, submissive, and disposed to be innocent; but, for that very reason, bold and successful criminals are dangerous in the extreme. In old days, when they joined in gangs or organised bodies, they soon acquired political importance. Now, in many parts of India, crime is quite as uncommon as in the least criminal parts of England; and the old high-handed systematised crime has almost entirely disappeared. This great revolution (for it is nothing less) in the state of society of a whole continent has been brought about by the regular administration of a rational body of criminal law.

'The administration of criminal justice is entrusted to a very small number of English magistrates, organised according to a carefully-devised system of appeal and supervision which represents the experience of a century. This system is not unattended by evils; but it is absolutely necessary to enable a few hundred civilians to govern a continent. Persons in such a position must be provided with the plainest instructions as to the nature of their duties. These instructions, in so far as the administration of criminal justice is concerned, are contained in the Indian Penal Code and the Code of Criminal Procedure. The Code of Criminal Procedure contains 541 sections, and forms a pamphlet of 210 widely printed octavo pages. The Penal Code consists of 510 sections. Pocket editions of these Codes are published, which may be carried about as easily as a pocket Bible; and I doubt whether, even in Scotland, you would find many people who know their Bibles as Indian civilians know their Codes.

After describing the confusion and complication of the criminal law of our Indian Empire before it was taken in hand by the Commission of 1834, Mr. Stephen proceeds to say:

'Lord Macaulay's great work was far too daring and original to be accepted at once. It was a draft when he left India in 1838. His successors made remarks on it for twenty-two years. Those years were filled with wars and rumours of wars. The Afghan disasters and triumphs, the war in Central India, the wars with the Sikhs, Lord Dalhousie's annexations, threw law reform into the background, and produced a state of mind not very favourable to it. Then came the Mutiny, which in its essence was the breakdown of an old system; the renunciation of an attempt to effect an impossible compromise between the Asiatic and the European view of things, legal, military, and administrative. The effect of the Mutiny on the Statute-Book was unmistakable. The Code of Civil Procedure was enacted in 1859. The Penal Code was enacted in 1860, and came into operation on the 1st of January, 1862. The credit of passing the Penal Code into law, and of giving to every part of it the improvements which practical skill and technical knowledge could bestow, is due to Sir Barnes Peacock, who held Lord Macaulay's place during the most anxious years through which the Indian Empire has passed. The Draft and Revision are both eminently creditable to their authors; and the result of their successive efforts has been to reproduce in a concise, and even beautiful, form the spirit of the law of England; the most technical, the most clumsy, and the most bewildering of all systems of criminal law; though I think, if its principles are fully understood, it is the most rational. If anyone doubts this assertion, let him compare the Indian Penal Code with such a book as Mr. Greaves's edition of Russell on Crimes. The one subject of homicide, as treated by Mr. Greaves and Russell, is, I should think, twice as long as the whole Penal Code; and it does not contain a tenth part of the matter.

'The point which always has surprised me most in connection with the Penal Code is, that it proves that Lord Macaulay must have had a knowledge of English criminal law which, considering how little he had practised it, may fairly be called extraordinary.[1] He must have possessed the gift of going at once to the very root of the matter, and of sifting the corn from the chaff to a most unusual degree; for his draft gives the substance of the criminal law of England, down to its minute working details, in a compass which, by comparison with the original, may be regarded as almost absurdly small. The Indian Penal Code is to the English criminal law what a manufactured article ready for use is to the materials out of which it is made. It is to the French "Code Pénal," and, I may add, to the North German Code of 1871, what a finished picture is to a sketch. It is far simpler, and much better expressed, than Livingstone's Code for Louisiana; and its practical success has been complete. The clearest proof of this is that hardly any questions have arisen upon it which have had to be determined by the courts; and that few and slight amendments have had to be made in it by the Legislature.'

Without troubling himself unduly about the matter, Macaulay was conscious that the world's estimate of his public services would be injuriously affected by the popular notion, which he has described as 'so flattering to mediocrity,' that a great writer cannot be a great administrator; and it is possible that this consciousness had something to do with the heartiness and fervour which he threw into his defence of the

[1] Macaulay's practice at the bar had been less than little, according to an account which he gave of it at a public dinner: 'My own forensic experience, gentlemen, has been extremely small; for my only recollection of an achievement that way is that at quarter sessions I once convicted a boy of stealing a parcel of cocks and hens.'

author of 'Cato' against the charge of having been an inefficient Secretary of State. There was much in common between his own lot and that of the other famous essayist who had been likewise a Whig statesman; and this similarity in their fortunes may account in part for the indulgence, and almost tenderness, with which he reviewed the career and character of Addison. Addison himself, at his villa in Chelsea, and still more amidst the gilded slavery of Holland House, might have envied the literary seclusion, ample for so rapid a reader, which the usages of Indian life permitted Macaulay to enjoy. 'I have a very pretty garden,' he writes, 'not unlike our little grass-plot at Clapham but larger. It consists of a fine sheet of turf, with a gravel walk round it, and flower-beds scattered over it. It looks beautiful just now after the rains, and I hear that it keeps its verdure during a great part of the year. A flight of steps leads down from my library into the garden, and it is so well shaded that you may walk there till ten o'clock in the morning.'

Here, book in hand, and in dressing-gown and slippers, he would spend those two hours after sun-rise which Anglo-Indian gentlemen devote to riding, and Anglo-Indian ladies to sleeping off the arrears of the sultry night. Regularly, every morning, his studies were broken in upon by the arrival of his baby niece, who came to feed the crows with the toast which accompanied his early cup of tea; a ceremony during which he had much ado to protect the child from the advances of a multitude of birds, each almost as big as herself, which hopped and fluttered round her as she stood on the steps of the verandah. When the sun drove him indoors, (which happened sooner than he had promised himself, before he had learned by experience what the hot season was,) he went to his bath and toilette, and then to breakfast; 'at which we support nature under the exhausting effects of the climate by means of plenty of eggs, mango-fish, snipe-pies, and frequently a hot beefsteak. My cook is renowned through Calcutta for his skill. He brought me attestations of a long succession of gourmands, and among them one from Lord Dalhousie, who pronounced him decidedly the first artist in Bengal.[1] This great man, and his two assistants, I am to have for thirty rupees a month. While I am on the subject of the cuisine, I may as well say all that I have to say about it at once. The tropical fruits are wretched. The best of them is inferior to our apricot or gooseberry. When I was a child, I had a notion of its being the most exquisite of treats to eat plantains and yams, and to drink palm-wine. How I envied my father for having enjoyed these luxuries! I have now enjoyed them all, and I have found, like much greater men on much more important occasions, that all is vanity. A plantain is very like a rotten pear,—so like that I would lay twenty to one that a person blindfolded would not discover the difference. A yam is better. It is like an indifferent potato. I tried palm-wine at a pretty village near Madras, where I slept one night. I told Captain Barron that I had been curious to taste that liquor ever since I first saw, eight or nine and twenty years ago, the picture of the negro climbing the tree in Sierra Leone. The next morning I was roused by a servant, with a large bowl of juice fresh from the tree. I drank it, and found it very like ginger-beer in which the ginger has been sparingly used.'

Macaulay necessarily spent away from home the days on which the Supreme Council, or the Law Commission, held their meetings; but the rest of his work, legal, literary, and educational, he carried on in the quiet of his library. Now and again, a morning was consumed in returning calls; an expenditure of time which it is needless to say that he sorely grudged. 'Happily, the good people here are too busy to be at home. Except the parsons, they are all usefully occupied somewhere or other, so that I have only to

[1] Lord Dalhousie, the father of the Governor-General, was Commander-in-Chief in India during the years 1830 and 1831.

leave cards; but the reverend gentlemen are always within doors in the heat of the day, lying on their backs, regretting breakfast, longing for tiffin, and crying out for lemonade.' After lunch he sate with Mrs. Trevelyan, translating Greek or reading French for her benefit; and Scribe's comedies and Saint Simon's Memoirs beguiled the long languid leisure of the Calcutta afternoon, while the punkah swung overhead, and the air came heavy and scented through the moistened grass-matting which shrouded the windows. At the approach of sunset, with its attendant breeze, he joined his sister in her drive along the banks of the Hooghly; and they returned by star-light,—too often to take part in a vast banquet of forty guests, dressed as fashionably as people can dress at ninety degrees East from Paris; who, one and all, had far rather have been eating their curry, and drinking their bitter beer, at home, in all the comfort of muslin and nankeen. Macaulay is vehement in his dislike of 'those great formal dinners, which unite all the stiffness of a levée to all the disorder and discomfort of a two-shilling ordinary. Nothing can be duller. Nobody speaks except to the person next him. The conversation is the most deplorable twaddle! and, as I always sit next to the lady of the highest rank, or, in other words, to the oldest, ugliest, and proudest woman in the company, I am worse off than my neighbours.'

Nevertheless he was far too acute a judge of men to undervalue the special type of mind which is produced and fostered by the influences of an Indian career. He was always ready to admit that there is no better company in the world than a young and rising civilian; no one who has more to say that is worth hearing, and who can say it in a manner better adapted to interest those who know good talk from bad. He delighted in that freedom from pedantry, affectation, and pretension which is one of the most agreeable characteristics of a service, to belong to which is in itself so effectual an education, that a bore is a phenomenon notorious everywhere within a hundred miles of the station which has the honour to possess him, and a fool is quoted by name throughout all the three Presidencies. Macaulay writes to his sisters at home: 'The best way of seeing society here is to have very small parties. There is a little circle of people whose friendship I value, and in whose conversation I take pleasure: the Chief Justice, Sir Edward Ryan; my old friend, Malkin;[1] Cameron and Macleod, the Law Commissioners; Macnaghten, among the older servants of the Company, and Mangles, Colvin, and John Peter Grant among the younger. These, in my opinion, are the flower of Calcutta society, and I often ask some of them to a quiet dinner.' On the Friday of every week, these chosen few met round Macaulay's breakfast table to discuss the progress which the Law Commission had made in its labours; and each successive point which was started opened the way to such a flood of talk,—legal, historical, political, and personal,—that the company would sit far on towards noon over the empty tea-cups, until an uneasy sense of accumulating despatch-boxes drove them, one by one, to their respective offices.

There are scattered passages in these letters which prove that Macaulay's feelings, during his protracted absence from his native country, were at times almost as keen as those which racked the breast of Cicero, when he was forced to exchange the triumphs of the Forum, and the cozy suppers with his brother augurs, for his hateful place of banishment at Thessalonica, or his hardly less hateful seat of government at Tarsus. The complaints of the English statesman do not,

[1] It cannot be said that all the claims made upon Macaulay's friendship were acknowledged as readily as those of Sir Benjamin Malkin. 'I am dunned unmercifully by place-hunters. The oddest application that I have received is from that rascal ——, who is somewhere in the interior. He tells me he is sure that prosperity has not changed me; that I am still the same John Macaulay who was his dearest friend, his more than brother: and that he means to come up, and live with me at Calcutta. If he fulfils his intention, I will have him taken before the police-magistrates.'

however, amount in volume to a fiftieth part of those reiterated out-pourings of lachrymose eloquence with which the Roman philosopher bewailed an expatriation that was hardly one-third as long. 'I have no words,' writes Macaulay, very much under-estimating the wealth of his own vocabulary, 'to tell you how I pine for England, or how intensely bitter exile has been to me, though I hope that I have borne it well. I feel as if I had no other wish than to see my country again and die. Let me assure you that banishment is no light matter. No person can judge of it who has not experienced it. A complete revolution in all the habits of life; an estrangement from almost every old friend and acquaintance; fifteen thousand miles of ocean between the exile and everything that he cares for: all this is, to me at least, very trying. There is no temptation of wealth, or power, which would induce me to go through it again. But many people do not feel as I do. Indeed, the servants of the Company rarely have such a feeling; and it is natural that they should not have it, for they are sent out while still schoolboys, and when they know little of the world. The moment of emigration is to them also the moment of emancipation; and the pleasures of liberty and affluence to a great degree compensate them for the loss of their home. In a few years they become Orientalised, and, by the time that they are of my age, they would generally prefer India, as a residence, to England. But it is a very different matter when a man is transplanted at thirty-three.'

Making, as always, the best of everything, he was quite ready to allow that he might have been placed in a still less agreeable situation. In the following extract from a letter to his friend, Mrs. Drummond, there is much which will come home to those who are old enough to remember how vastly the Dublin of 1837 differed, for the worse, from the Dublin of 1875. 'It now seems likely that you may remain in Ireland for years. I cannot conceive what has induced you to submit to such an exile. I declare, for my own part, that, little as I love Calcutta, I would rather stay here than be settled in the Phœnix Park. The last residence which I would choose would be a place with all the plagues, and none of the attractions, of a capital; a provincial city on fire with factions political and religious, peopled by raving Orangemen and raving Repealers, and distracted by a contest between Protestantism as fanatical as that of Knox and Catholicism as fanatical as that of Bonner. We have our share of the miseries of life in this country. We are annually baked four months, boiled four more, and allowed the remaining four to become cool if we can. At this moment the sun is blazing like a furnace. The earth, soaked with oceans of rain, is steaming like a wet blanket. Vegetation is rotting all round us. Insects and undertakers are the only living creatures which seem to enjoy the climate. But, though our atmosphere is hot, our factions are lukewarm. A bad epigram in a newspaper, or a public meeting attended by a tailor, a pastry-cook, a reporter, two or three barristers, and eight or ten attorneys, are our most formidable annoyances. We have agitators in our own small way, Tritons of the minnows, bearing the same sort of resemblance to O'Connell that a lizard bears to an alligator. Therefore Calcutta for me, in preference to Dublin.'

He had good reason for being grateful to Calcutta, and still better for not showing his gratitude by prolonging his stay there over a fourth summer and autumn. 'That tremendous crash of the great commercial houses which took place a few years ago has produced a revolution in fashions. It ruined one half of the English society in Bengal, and seriously injured the other half. A large proportion of the most important functionaries here are deeply in debt, and accordingly, the mode of living is now exceedingly quiet and modest. Those immense subscriptions, those public tables, those costly equipages and entertainments of which Heber, and others who saw Calcutta a few years back, say so much, are never heard of. Speaking for myself, it was a great piece of good fortune that I came hither just at the time when the general distress had forced everybody to adopt a moderate way of living. Owing very much to that circumstance, (while keeping house, I think, more handsomely than any other member of Council,) I have saved what will enable me to do my part towards making my family comfortable; and I shall have a competency for myself, small indeed, but quite sufficient to render me as perfectly independent as if I were the possessor of Burleigh or Chatsworth.'[1]

'The rainy season of 1837 has been exceedingly unhealthy. Our house has escaped as well as any; yet Hannah is the only one of us who has come off untouched. The baby has been repeatedly unwell. Trevelyan has suffered a good deal, and is kept right only by occasional trips in a steamer down to the mouth of the Hooghly. I had a smart touch of fever, which happily stayed but an hour or two, and I took such vigorous measures that it never came again; but I remained unnerved and exhausted for nearly a fortnight. This was my first, and I hope my last, taste of Indian maladies. It is a happy thing for us all that we are not to pass another year in the reek of this deadly marsh.' Macaulay wisely declined to set the hope of making another lac of rupees against the risk, to himself and others, of such a fate as subsequently befell Lord Canning and Mr. James Wilson. He put the finishing stroke to his various labours; resigned his seat in the Council, and his Presidentships of the Law Commission and the Committee of Public Instruction; and, in company with the Trevelyans, sailed for England in the first fortnight of the year 1838.

[1] Macaulay writes to Lord Mahon on the last day of December 1836: 'In another year I hope to leave this country, with a fortune which you would think ridiculously small, but which will make me as independent as if I had all that Lord Westminster has above the ground, and Lord Durham below it. I have no intention of again taking part in politics; but I cannot tell what effect the sight of the old Hall and Abbey may produce on me.'

To Mr. Thomas Flower Ellis.

Calcutta: December 15, 1834.

Dear Ellis,—

Many thanks for your letter. It is delightful in this strange land to see the handwriting of such a friend. We must keep up our spirits. We shall meet, I trust, in little more than four years, with feelings of regard only strengthened by our separation. My spirits are not bad; and they ought not to be bad. I have health; affluence; consideration; great power to do good; functions which, while they are honourable and useful, are not painfully burdensome; leisure for study; good books; an unclouded and active mind; warm affections; and a very dear sister. There will soon be a change in my domestic arrangements. My sister is to be married next week. Her lover, who is lover enough to be a knight of the Round Table, is one of the most distinguished of our young Civilians. I have the very highest opinion of his talents both for action and for discussion. Indeed, I should call him a man of real genius. He is also, what is even more important, a man of the utmost purity of honour, of a sweet temper, and of strong principle. His public virtue has gone through very severe trials, and has come out resplendent. Lord William, in congratulating me the other day, said that he thought my destined brother-in-law the ablest young man in the service. His name is Trevelyan. He is a nephew of Sir John Trevelyan, a baronet; in Cornwall I suppose, by the name; for I never took the trouble to ask.

He and my sister will live with me during my stay here. I have a house about as large as Lord Dudley's in Park Lane, or rather larger, so that I shall accommodate them without the smallest difficulty. This arrangement is acceptable to me, because it saves me from the misery of parting with my sister in this strange land; and is, I believe, equally gratifying to Trevelyan, whose education, like that of other Indian servants, was huddled up hastily at home; who has an insatiable thirst for knowledge of every sort; and who looks on me as little less than an oracle of wisdom. He came to me the other morning to know whether I would advise him to give up his Greek, which he feared he had nearly lost. I gave him Homer, and asked him to read a page; and I found that, like most boys of any talent who had been at the Charterhouse, he was very well grounded in that language. He read with perfect rapture, and has marched off with the book, declaring that he shall never be content till he has finished the whole. This, you will think, is not a bad brother-in-law for a man to pick up in 22 degrees of North latitude, and 100 degrees of East longitude.

I read much, and particularly Greek; and I find that I am, in all essentials, still not a bad scholar. I could, I think, with a year's hard study, qualify myself to fight a good battle for a Craven's scholarship. I read, however, not as I read at College, but like a man of the world. If I do not know a word, I pass it by unless it is important to the sense. If I find, as I have of late often found, a passage which refuses to give up its meaning at the second reading, I let it alone. I have read during the last fortnight, before breakfast, three books of Herodotus, and four plays of Æschylus. My admiration of Æschylus has been prodigiously increased by this re-perusal. I cannot conceive how any person of the smallest pretension to taste should doubt about his immeasurable superiority to every poet of antiquity, Homer only excepted. Even Milton, I think, must yield to him. It is quite unintelligible to me that the ancient critics should have placed him so low. Horace's notice of him in the Ars Poetica is quite ridiculous. There is, to be sure, the 'magnum loqui;' but the great topic insisted on is the skill of Æschylus as a manager, as a property-man; the judicious way in which he boarded the stage; the masks, the buskins, and the dresses.[1] And, after all, the 'magnum loqui,'

[1] Post hunc personæ pallæque repertor honestæ
Æschylus et modicis instravit pulpita tignis,
Et docuit magnumque loqui, nitique cothurno.

though the most obvious characteristic of Æschylus, is by no means his highest or his best. Nor can I explain this by saying that Horace had too tame and unimaginative a mind to appreciate Æschylus. Horace knew what he could himself do, and, with admirable wisdom, he confined himself to that; but he seems to have had a perfectly clear comprehension of the merit of those great masters whom he never attempted to rival. He praised Pindar most enthusiastically. It seems incomprehensible to me that a critic, who admired Pindar, should not admire Æschylus far more.

Greek reminds me of Cambridge and of Thirlwall. When you see Thirlwall, tell him that I congratulate him from the bottom of my soul on having suffered in so good a cause; and that I would rather have been treated as he has been treated, on such an account, than have the Mastership of Trinity.[1] There would be some chance for the Church, if we had more Churchmen of the same breed, worthy successors of Leighton and Tillotson.

From one Trinity Fellow I pass to another. (This letter is quite a study to a metaphysician who wishes to illustrate the Law of Association.) We have no official tidings yet of Malkin's appointment to the vacant seat on the Bench at Calcutta. I cannot tell you how delighted I am at the prospect of having him here. An honest enlightened Judge, without professional narrowness, is the very man whom we want on public grounds. And, as to my private feelings, nothing could be more agreeable to me than to have an old friend, and so estimable a friend, brought so near to me in this distant country.

Ever, dear Ellis,

Yours very affectionately

T. B. MACAULAY.

[1] The subjoined extract from the letter of a leading member of Trinity College explains Macaulay's indignation. 'Thirlwall published a pamphlet in 1834, on the admission of Dissenters to the University. The result was that he was either deprived of his Assistant Tutorship or had to give it up. Thirlwall left Cambridge soon afterwards. I suppose that, if he had remained, he would have been very possibly Wordsworth's successor in the Mastership.'

Calcutta: February 8, 1835.

Dear Ellis,—

The last month has been the most painful that I ever went through. Indeed, I never knew before what it was to be miserable. Early in January, letters from England brought me news of the death of my youngest sister. What she was to me no words can express. I will not say that she was dearer to me than anything in the world; for my sister who was with me was equally dear; but she was as dear to me as one human being can be to another. Even now, when time has begun to do its healing office, I cannot write about her without being altogether unmanned. That I have not utterly sunk under this blow I owe chiefly to literature. What a blessing it is to love books as I love them;—to be able to converse with the dead, and to live amidst the unreal! Many times during the last few weeks I have repeated to myself those fine lines of old Hesiod:

> *εἰ γάρ τις καὶ πένθος ἔχων νεοκηδέϊ θυμῷ*
> *ἄζηται κραδίην ἀκαχήμενος, αὐτὰρ ἀοιδὸς*
> *μουσάων θεράπων κλεῖα προτέρων ἀνθρώπων*
> *ὑμνήσῃ, μάκαράς τε θεοὺς οἳ Ὄλυμπον ἔχουσι,*
> *αἶψ' ὅγε δυσφρονέων ἐπιλήθεται, οὐδέ τι κηδέων*
> *μέμνηται· ταχέως δὲ παρέτραπε δῶρα θεάων.*[1]

I have gone back to Greek literature with a passion quite astonishing to myself. I have never felt anything like it. I was enraptured with Italian during the six months which I gave up to it; and I was little less pleased with Spanish. But, when I went back to Greek, I felt as if I had never known before what intellectual enjoyment was. Oh that wonderful people! There is not one art, not one science, about which we may not use the same expression which Lucretius has

[1] 'For if to one whose grief is fresh, as he sits silent with sorrow-stricken heart, a minstrel, the henchman of the Muses, celebrates the men of old and the gods who possess Olympus; straightway he forgets his melancholy, and remembers not at all his grief, beguiled by the blessed gift of the goddesses of song.' In Macaulay's Hesiod this passage is scored with three lines in pencil.

employed about the victory over superstition, 'Primum Graius homo—.'

I think myself very fortunate in having been able to return to these great masters while still in the full vigour of life, and when my taste and judgment are mature. Most people read all the Greek that they ever read before they are five and twenty. They never find time for such studies afterwards till they are in the decline of life; and then their knowledge of the language is in a great measure lost, and cannot easily be recovered. Accordingly, almost all the ideas that people have of Greek literature, are ideas formed while they were still very young. A young man, whatever his genius may be, is no judge of such a writer as Thucydides. I had no high opinion of him ten years ago. I have now been reading him with a mind accustomed to historical researches, and to political affairs; and I am astonished at my own former blindness, and at his greatness. I could not bear Euripides at college. I now read my recantation. He has faults undoubtedly. But what a poet! The Medea, the Alcestis, the Troades, the Bacchæ, are alone sufficient to place him in the very first rank. Instead of depreciating him, as I have done, I may, for aught I know, end by editing him.

I have read Pindar,—with less pleasure than I feel in reading the great Attic poets, but still with admiration. An idea occurred to me which may very likely have been noticed by a hundred people before. I was always puzzled to understand the reason for the extremely abrupt transitions in those Odes of Horace which are meant to be particularly fine. The 'justum et tenacem' is an instance. All at once you find yourself in heaven, Heaven knows how. What the firmness of just men in times of tyranny, or of tumult, has to do with Juno's oration about Troy it is hardly possible to conceive. Then, again, how strangely the fight between the Gods and the Giants is tacked on to the fine hymn to the Muses in that noble ode, 'Descende cœlo et dic age tibiâ'! This always struck me as a great fault, and an inexplicable one; for it is peculiarly alien from the calm good sense, and good taste, which distinguish Horace.

My explanation of it is this. The Odes of Pindar were the acknowledged models of lyric poetry. Lyric poets imitated his manner as closely as they could; and nothing was more remarkable in his compositions than the extreme violence and abruptness of the transitions. This in Pindar was quite natural and defensible. He had to write an immense number of poems on subjects extremely barren, and extremely monotonous. There could be little difference between one boxing-match and another. Accordingly, he made all possible haste to escape from the immediate subject, and to bring in, by hook or by crook, some local description; some old legend; something or other, in short, which might be more susceptible of poetical embellishment, and less utterly threadbare, than the circumstances of a race or a wrestling-match. This was not the practice of Pindar alone. There is an old story which proves that Simonides did the same, and that sometimes the hero of the day was nettled at finding how little was said about him in the Ode for which he was to pay. This abruptness of transition was, therefore, in the Greek lyric poets, a fault rendered inevitable by the peculiarly barren and uniform nature of the subjects which they had to treat. But, like many other faults of great masters, it appeared to their imitators a beauty; and a beauty almost essential to the grander Ode. Horace was perfectly at liberty to choose his own subjects, and to treat them after his own fashion. But he confounded what was merely accidental in Pindar's manner with what was essential; and because Pindar, when he had to celebrate a foolish lad from Ægina who had tripped up another's heels at the Isthmus, made all possible haste to get away from so paltry a topic to the ancient heroes of the race of Æacus, Horace took it into his head that he ought always to begin as far from the subject as possible, and then arrive at it by some strange and sudden bound. This is my solution. At least I can find no better. The most obscure passage,—at least the strangest passage,—in all Horace may be explained by supposing that he was misled by Pindar's example: I mean that odd parenthesis in the 'Qualem Ministrum:'

quibus
Mos unde deductus per omne—.

This passage, taken by itself, always struck me as the harshest, queerest, and most preposterous digression in the world. But there are several things in Pindar very like it.[1]

You must excuse all this, for I labour at present under a suppression of Greek, and am likely to do so for at least three years to come. Malkin may be some relief; but I am quite unable to guess whether he means to come to Calcutta. I am in excellent bodily health, and I am recovering my mental health; but I have been sorely tried. Money matters look well. My new brother-in-law and I are brothers in more than law. I am more comfortable than I expected to be in this country; and, as to the climate, I think it, beyond all comparison, better than that of the House of Commons.

Yours affectionately
T. B. MACAULAY.

Writing three days after the date of the foregoing letter, Macaulay says to his old friend Mr. Sharp: 'You see that my mind is not in great danger of rusting. The danger is that I may become a mere pedant. I feel a habit of quotation growing on me: but I resist that devil, for such it is, and it flees from me. It is all that I can do to keep Greek and Latin out of all my letters. Wise sayings of Euripides are even now at my fingers' ends. If I did not maintain a constant struggle against this propensity, my correspondence would resemble the notes to the 'Pursuits of Literature.' It is a dangerous thing for a man with a very strong memory to read very much. I could give you three or four

[1] Orelli makes an observation, much to the same effect, in his note on this passage in his edition of 1850.

quotations this moment in support of that proposition; but I will bring the vicious propensity under subjection, if I can.'[1]

Calcutta, May 29, 1835.

Dear Ellis,—

I am in great want of news. We know that the Tories dissolved at the end of December, and we also know that they were beaten towards the end of February.[2] As to what passed in the interval, we are quite in the dark. I will not plague you with comments on events which will have been driven out of your mind by other events before this reaches you, or with prophecies which may be falsified before you receive them. About the final issue I am certain. The language of the first great reformer is that which I should use in reply to the exultation of our Tories here, if there were any of them who could understand it:

> *σέβου, προσεύχου, θῶπτε τὸν κρατοῦντ' ἀεί·*
> *ἐμοὶ δ' ἔλασσον Ζηνὸς, ἢ μηδὲν, μέλει.*
> *δράτω· κρατείτω τόνδε τὸν βραχὺν χρόνον*
> *ὅπως θέλει· δαρὸν γὰρ οὐκ ἄρξει θεοῖς.*[3]

As for myself, I rejoice that I am out of the present

[1] Many years later Macaulay wrote to my mother: 'Dr. —— came, and I found him a very clever man; a little of a coxcomb, but, I dare say, not the worse physician for that. He must have quoted Horace and Virgil six times at least à propos of his medical inquiries. Horace says, in a poem in which he jeers the Stoics, that even a wise man is out of sorts when "pituita molesta est;" which is, being interpreted, "when his phlegm is troublesome." The Doctor thought it necessary to quote this passage in order to prove that phlegm is troublesome;—a proposition, of the truth of which, I will venture to say, no man on earth is better convinced than myself.'

[2] In November 1834 the King called Sir Robert Peel to power: after having, of his own accord, dismissed the Whig Ministry. Parliament was dissolved, but the Tories did not succeed in obtaining a majority. After three months of constant and angry fighting, Peel was driven from office in April 1835.

[3] 'Worship thou, adore, and flatter the monarch of the hour. To me Jove is of less account than nothing. Let him have his will, and his sceptre, for this brief season; for he will not long be the ruler of the Gods.' It is needless to say that poor William the Fourth was the Jove of the Whig Prometheus.

storm. 'Suave mari magno;' or, as your new Premier, if he be still Premier, construes, 'It is a source of melancholy satisfaction.' I may, indeed, feel the effects of the changes here, but more on public than private grounds. A Tory Governor-General is not very likely to agree with me about the very important law reforms which I am about to bring before the Council. But he is not likely to treat me ill personally; or, if he does,

ἀλλ' οὔ τι χαίρων, ἢν τόδ' ὀρθωθῇ βέλος,[1]

as Philoctetes says. In a few months I shall have enough to enable me to live, after my very moderate fashion, in perfect independence at home; and whatever debts any Governor-General may choose to lay on me at Calcutta shall be paid off, he may rely on it, with compound interest, at Westminster.

My time is divided between public business and books. I mix with society as little as I can. My spirits have not yet recovered,—I sometimes think that they will never wholly recover,—the shock which they received five months ago. I find that nothing soothes them so much as the contemplation of those miracles of art which Athens has bequeathed to us. I am really becoming, I hope not a pedant, but certainly an enthusiast about classical literature. I have just finished a second reading of Sophocles. I am now deep in Plato, and intend to go right through all his works. His genius is above praise. Even where he is most absurd,—as, for example, in the Cratylus,—he shows an acuteness, and an expanse of intellect, which is quite a phenomenon by itself. The character of Socrates does not rise upon me. The more I read about him, the less I wonder that they poisoned him. If he had treated me as he is said to have treated Protagoras, Hippias, and Gorgias, I could never have forgiven him.

Nothing has struck me so much in Plato's dialogues as the raillery. At college, somehow or other, I did not understand or appreciate it. I cannot describe to you the way in which it now tickles me. I often sink

[1] 'It shall be to his cost, so long as this bow carries true.'

forward on my huge old Marsilius Ficinus in a fit of laughter. I should say that there never was a vein of ridicule so rich, at the same time so delicate. It is superior to Voltaire's; nay, to Pascal's. Perhaps there are one or two passages in Cervantes, and one or two in Fielding, that might give a modern reader a notion of it.

I have very nearly finished Livy. I never read him through before. I admire him greatly, and would give a quarter's salary to recover the lost Decades. While I was reading the earlier books I went again through Niebuhr. And I am sorry to say that, having always been a little sceptical about his merits, I am now a confirmed unbeliever. I do not of course mean that he has no merit. He was a man of immense learning, and of great ingenuity. But his mind was utterly wanting in the faculty by which a demonstrated truth is distinguished from a plausible supposition. He is not content with suggesting that an event may have happened. He is certain that it happened, and calls on the reader to be certain too, (though not a trace of it exists in any record whatever,) because it would solve the phenomena so neatly. Just read over again, if you have forgotten it, the conjectural restoration of the Inscription in page 126 of the second volume; and then, on your honour as a scholar and a man of sense, tell me whether in Bentley's edition of Milton there is anything which approaches to the audacity of that emendation. Niebuhr requires you to believe that some of the greatest men in Rome were burned alive in the Circus; that this event was commemorated by an inscription on a monument, one half of which is still in existence; but that no Roman historian knew anything about it; and that all tradition of the event was lost, though the memory of anterior events much less important has reached our time. When you ask for a reason, he tells you plainly that such a thing cannot be established by reason; that he is sure of it; and that you must take his word. This sort of intellectual despotism always moves me to mutiny, and generates a disposition to pull down the reputation of the dogmatist. Niebuhr's learning was immeasurably superior to mine; but I think myself quite as good a judge of evidence as he was. I might easily believe him if he told me that there were proofs which I had never seen; but, when he produces all his proofs, I conceive that I am perfectly competent to pronounce on their value.

As I turned over his leaves just now, I lighted on another instance of what I cannot but call ridiculous presumption. He says that Martial committed a blunder in making the penultimate of Porsena short. Strange that so great a scholar should not know that Horace had done so too!

Minacis aut Etrusca Porsenæ manus.

There is something extremely nauseous to me in a German Professor telling the world, on his own authority, and without giving the smallest reason, that two of the best Latin poets were ignorant of the quantity of a word which they must have used in their exercises at school a hundred times.

As to the general capacity of Niebuhr for political speculations, let him be judged by the Preface to the Second Volume. He there says, referring to the French Revolution of July 1830, that 'unless God send us some miraculous help, we have to look forward to a period of destruction similar to that which the Roman world experienced about the middle of the third century.' Now, when I see a man scribble such abject nonsense about events which are passing under our eyes, what confidence can I put in his judgment as to the connection of causes and effects in times very imperfectly known to us?

But I must bring my letter, or review, to a close. Remember me most kindly to your wife. Tell Frank that I mean to be a better scholar than he when I come back, and that he must work hard if he means to overtake me.

Ever, dear Ellis,
Your affectionate friend
T. B. MACAULAY.

Calcutta: August 25, 1835.

Dear Ellis,—

Cameron arrived here about a fortnight ago, and we are most actively engaged in preparing a complete Criminal Code for India. He and I agree excellently. Ryan, the most liberal of Judges, lends us his best assistance. I heartily hope, and fully believe, that we shall put the whole Penal law, and the whole law of Criminal Procedure, into a moderately sized volume. I begin to take a very warm interest in this work. It is, indeed, one of the finest employments of the intellect that it is easy to conceive. I ought, however, to tell you that, the more progress I make as a legislator, the more intense my contempt for the mere technical study of law becomes.

I am deep in the examination of the political theories of the old philosophers. I have read Plato's Republic, and his Laws; and I am now reading Aristotle's Politics; after which I shall go through Plato's two treatises again. I every now and then read one of Plutarch's Lives on an idle afternoon; and in this way I have got through a dozen of them. I like him prodigiously. He is inaccurate, to be sure, and a romancer: but he tells a story delightfully, and his illustrations and sketches of character are as good as anything in ancient eloquence. I have never, till now, rated him fairly.

As to Latin, I am just finishing Lucan, who remains pretty much where he was in my opinion; and I am busily engaged with Cicero, whose character, moral and intellectual, interests me prodigiously. I think that I see the whole man through and through. But this is too vast a subject for a letter. I have gone through all Ovid's poems. I admire him; but I was tired to death before I got to the end. I amused myself one evening with turning over the Metamorphoses, to see if I could find any passage of ten lines which could, by possibility, have been written by Virgil. Whether I was in ill luck or no I cannot tell; but I hunted for half an hour without the smallest success.

At last I chanced to light on a little passage more Virgilian, to my thinking, than Virgil himself. Tell me what you say to my criticism. It is part of Apollo's speech to the laurel

Semper habebunt
Te coma, te citharæ, te nostræ, laure, pharetræ
Tu ducibus Latiis aderis, cum læta triumphum
Vox canet, et longas visent Capitolia pompas.
Portibus Augustis eadem fidissima custos
Ante fores stabis, mediamque tuebere quercum.

As to other Latin writers, Sallust has gone sadly down in my opinion. Cæsar has risen wonderfully. I think him fully entitled to Cicero's praise.[1] He has won the honour of an excellent historian while attempting merely to give hints for history. But what are they all to the great Athenian? I do assure you that there is no prose composition in the world, not even the De Coronâ, which I place so high as the seventh book of Thucydides. It is the ne plus ultra of human art. I was delighted to find in Gray's letters the other day this query to Wharton: 'The retreat from Syracuse—Is it or is it not the finest thing you ever read in your life?'

Did you ever read Athenæus through? I never did; but I am meditating an attack on him. The multitude of quotations looks very tempting; and I never open him for a minute without being paid for my trouble.

Yours very affectionately

T. B. MACAULAY.

[1] In the dialogue 'De Claris Oratoribus' Cicero makes Atticus say that a consummate judge of style, (who is evidently intended for Cicero himself,) pronounces Cæsar's Latin to be the most elegant, with one implied exception, that had ever been heard in the Senate or the Forum. Atticus then goes on to detail at full length a compliment which Cæsar had paid to Cicero's powers of expression; and Brutus declares with enthusiasm that such praise, coming from such a quarter, is worth more than a Triumph, as Triumph's were then given; and inferior in value only to the honours which were voted to the statesman who had baffled Catiline. The whole passage is a model of self-glorification, exquisite in skill and finish.

Calcutta: December 30, 1835.

Dear Ellis,—

What the end of the Municipal Reform Bill is to be I cannot conjecture. Our latest English intelligence is of the 15th of August. The Lords were then busy in rendering the only great service that I expect them ever to render to the nation; that is to say, in hastening the day of reckoning.[1] But I will not fill my paper with English politics.

I am in excellent health. So are my sister and brother-in-law, and their little girl, whom I am always nursing; and of whom I am becoming fonder than a wise man, with half my experience, would choose to be of anything except himself. I have but very lately begun to recover my spirits. The tremendous blow which fell on me at the beginning of this year has left marks behind it which I shall carry to my grave. Literature has saved my life and my reason. Even now, I dare not, in the intervals of business, remain alone for a minute without a book in my hand. What my course of life will be, when I return to England, is very doubtful. But I am more than half determined to abandon politics, and to give myself wholly to letters; to undertake some great historical work which may be at once the business and the amusement of my life; and to leave the pleasure of pestiferous rooms, sleepless nights, aching heads, and diseased stomachs to Roebuck and to Praed.

In England I might probably be of a very different opinion. But, in the quiet of my own little grass-plot, —when the moon, at its rising, finds me with the Philoctetes or the De Finibus in my hand,—I often wonder what strange infatuation leads men who can do something better to squander their intellect, their health, their energy, on such subjects as those which most statesmen are engaged in pursuing. I comprehend perfectly how a man who can debate, but who

[1] In the middle of August the Irish Tithe Bill went up to the House of Lords, where it was destined to undergo a mutilation which was fatal to its existence.

would make a very indifferent figure as a contributor to an annual or a magazine,—such a man as Stanley, for example,—should take the only line by which he can attain distinction. But that a man before whom the two paths of literature and politics lie open, and who might hope for eminence in either, should choose politics, and quit literature, seems to me madness. On the one side is health, leisure, peace of mind, the search after truth, and all the enjoyments of friendship and conversation. On the other side is almost certain ruin to the constitution, constant labour, constant anxiety. Every friendship which a man may have, becomes precarious as soon as he engages in politics. As to abuse, men soon become callous to it, but the discipline which makes them callous is very severe. And for what is it that a man who might, if he chose, rise and lie down at his own hour, engage in any study, enjoy any amusement, and visit any place, consents to make himself as much a prisoner as if he were within the rules of the Fleet; to be tethered during eleven months of the year within the circle of half a mile round Charing Cross; to sit, or stand, night after night for ten or twelve hours, inhaling a noisome atmosphere, and listening to harangues of which nine-tenths are far below the level of a leading article in a newspaper? For what is it that he submits, day after day, to see the morning break over the Thames, and then totters home, with bursting temples, to his bed? Is it for fame? Who would compare the fame of Charles Townshend to that of Hume, that of Lord North to that of Gibbon, that of Lord Chatham to that of Johnson? Who can look back on the life of Burke and not regret that the years which he passed in ruining his health and temper by political exertions were not passed in the composition of some great and durable work? Who can read the letters to Atticus, and not feel that Cicero would have been an infinitely happier and better man, and a not less celebrated man, if he had left us fewer speeches, and more Academic Questions and Tusculan Disputations; if he had passed the time which he spent in brawling with Vatinius and Clodius in producing a history of Rome superior even to that of Livy? But these, as I said, are meditations in a quiet garden, situated far beyond the contagious influence of English faction. What I might feel if I again saw Downing Street and Palace Yard is another question. I tell you sincerely my present feelings.

I have cast up my reading account, and brought it to the end of the year 1835. It includes December 1834; for I came into my house and unpacked my books at the end of November 1834. During the last thirteen months I have read Æschylus twice; Sophocles twice; Euripides once; Pindar twice; Callimachus; Apollonius Rhodius; Quintus Calaber; Theocritus twice; Herodotus; Thucydides; almost all Xenophon's works; almost all Plato; Aristotle's Politics, and a good deal of his Organon, besides dipping elsewhere in him; the whole of Plutarch's Lives; about half of Lucian; two or three books of Athenæus; Plautus twice; Terence twice; Lucretius twice; Catullus; Tibullus; Propertius; Lucan; Statius; Silius Italicus; Livy; Velleius Paterculus; Sallust; Cæsar; and, lastly, Cicero. I have, indeed, still a little of Cicero left; but I shall finish him in a few days. I am now deep in Aristophanes and Lucian. Of Aristophanes I think as I always thought; but Lucian has agreeably surprised me. At school I read some of his Dialogues of the Dead when I was thirteen; and, to my shame, I never, to the best of my belief, read of line of him since. I am charmed with him. His style seems to me to be superior to that of any extant writer who lived later than the age of Demosthenes and Theophrastus. He has a most peculiar and delicious vein of humour. It is not the humour of Aristophanes; it is not that of Plato: and yet is akin to both;—not quite equal, I admit, to either, but still exceedingly charming. I hardly know where to find an instance of a writer, in the decline of a literature, who has shown an invention so rich, and a taste so pure. But, if I get on these matters, I shall fill sheet after sheet. They must wait till we take another long walk, or another tavern dinner, together; that is, till the summer of 1838.

I had a long story to tell you about a classical examination here; but I have not time. I can only say that some of the competitors tried to read the Greek with the papers upside down; and that the great man of the examination, the Thirlwall of Calcutta, a graduate of Trinity College, Dublin, translated the words of Theophrastus, ὅσας λειτουργίας λελειτούργηκε, 'how many times he has performed divine service.'[1]

Ever yours affectionately

T. B. MACAULAY.

That the enormous list of classical works recorded in the foregoing letter was not only read through, but read with care, is proved by the pencil marks, single, double, and treble, which meander down the margin of such passages as excited the admiration of the student; and by the remarks, literary, historical, and grammatical, with which the critic has interspersed every volume, and sometimes every page. In the case of a favourite writer, Macaulay frequently corrects the errors of the press, and even the punctuation, as minutely as if he were preparing the book for another edition. He read Plautus, Terence, and Aristophanes four times through at Calcutta; and Euripides thrice.[2] In his copy of Quintus Calaber, (a versifier who is less unknown by the title of Quintus Smyrnæus,) appear the entries,

'September 22, 1835.'
'Turned over, July 13, 1837.'

It may be doubted whether the Pandects would have attained the celebrity which they enjoy, if, in the course of the three years during which Justinian's Law

[1] 'How many public services he had discharged at his own expense.' Macaulay used to say that a lady who dips into Mr. Grote's history, and learns that Alcibiades won the heart of his fellow-citizens by the novelty of his theories and the splendour of his liturgies, may get a very false notion of that statesman's relations with the Athenian public.

[2] See Appendix II at the end of the second volume.

Commission was at work, the president Tribonian had read Quintus Smyrnæus twice.

Calcutta: May 30, 1836.

Dear Ellis,—

I have just received your letter dated December 28. How time flies! Another hot season has almost passed away, and we are daily expecting the beginning of the rains. Cold season, hot season, and rainy season are all much the same to me. I shall have been two years on Indian ground in less than a fortnight, and I have not taken ten grains of solid, or a pint of liquid, medicine during the whole of that time. If I judged only from my own sensations, I should say that this climate is absurdly maligned; but the yellow, spectral, figures which surround me serve to correct the conclusions which I should be inclined to draw from the state of my own health.

One execrable effect the climate produces. It destroys all the works of man with scarcely one exception. Steel rusts; razors lose their edge; thread decays; clothes fall to pieces; books moulder away, and drop out of their bindings; plaster cracks; timber rots; matting is in shreds. The sun, the steam of this vast alluvial tract, and the infinite armies of white ants, make such havoc with buildings that a house requires a complete repair every three years. Ours was in this situation about three months ago; and, if we had determined to brave the rains without any precautions, we should, in all probability, have had the roof down on our heads. Accordingly we were forced to migrate for six weeks from our stately apartments and our flower-beds, to a dungeon where we were stifled with the stench of native cookery, and deafened by the noise of native music. At last we have returned to our house. We found it all snow-white and pea-green; and we rejoice to think that we shall not again be under the necessity of quitting it, till we quit it for a ship bound on a voyage to London.

We have been for some months in the middle of

what the people here think a political storm. To a person accustomed to the hurricanes of English faction this sort of tempest in a horsepond is merely ridiculous. We have put the English settlers up the country under the exclusive jurisdiction of the Company's Courts in civil actions in which they are concerned with natives. The English settlers are perfectly contented; but the lawyers of the Supreme Court have set up a yelp which they think terrible, and which has infinitely diverted me. They have selected me as the object of their invectives, and I am generally the theme of five or six columns of prose and verse daily. I have not patience to read a tenth part of what they put forth. The last ode in my praise which I perused began,

Soon we hope they will recall ye,
Tom Macaulay, Tom Macaulay.

The last prose which I read was a parallel between me and Lord Strafford.

My mornings, from five to nine, are quite my own. I still give them to ancient literature. I have read Aristophanes twice through since Christmas; and have also read Herodotus, and Thucydides again. I got into a way last year of reading a Greek play every Sunday. I began on Sunday the 18th of October with the Prometheus, and next Sunday I shall finish with the Cyclops of Euripides. Euripides has made a complete conquest of me. It has been unfortunate for him that we have so many of his pieces. It has, on the other hand, I suspect, been fortunate for Sophocles that so few of his have come down to us. Almost every play of Sophocles, which is now extant, was one of his masterpieces. There is hardly one of them which is not mentioned with high praise by some ancient writer. Yet one of them, the Trachiniæ, is, to my thinking, very poor and insipid. Now, if we had nineteen plays of Sophocles, of which twelve or thirteen should be no better than the Trachiniæ,—and if, on the other hand, only seven pieces of Euripides had come down to us, and if those seven had been the Medea, the Bacchæ, the Iphigenia in Aulis, the Orestes, the Phœnissæ, the Hippolytus, and the Alcestis,—I am not sure that the relative position which the two poets now hold in our estimation would not be greatly altered.

I have not done much in Latin. I have been employed in turning over several third-rate and fourth-rate writers. After finishing Cicero, I read through the works of both the Senecas, father and son. There is a great deal in the Controversiæ both of curious information, and of judicious criticism. As to the son, I cannot bear him. His style affects me in something the same way with that of Gibbon. But Lucius Seneca's affectation is even more rank than Gibbon's. His works are made up of mottoes. There is hardly a sentence which might not be quoted; but to read him straightforward is like dining on nothing but anchovy sauce. I have read, as one does read such stuff, Valerius Maximus, Annæus Florus, Lucius Ampelius, and Aurelius Victor. I have also gone through Phædrus. I am now better employed. I am deep in the Annals of Tacitus, and I am at the same time reading Suetonius.

You are so rich in domestic comforts that I am inclined to envy you. I am not, however, without my share. I am as fond of my little niece as her father. I pass an hour or more every day nursing her, and teaching her to talk. She has got as far as Ba, Pa, and Ma; which, as she is not eight months old, we consider as proofs of a genius little inferior to that of Shakspeare or Sir Isaac Newton.

The municipal elections have put me in good spirits as to English politics. I was rather inclined to despondency.

Ever yours affectionately

T. B. MACAULAY.

Calcutta: July 25, 1836.

My dear Ellis,—

I have heard from you again, and glad I always am to hear from you. There are few things to which I look forward with more pleasure than to our meeting.

It is really worth while to go into banishment for a few years for the pleasure of going home again. Yet that home will in some things be a different home—oh how different a home!—from that to which I expected to return. But I will not stir up the bitterness of sorrow which has at last subsided.

You take interest, I see, in my Greek and Latin studies. I continue to pursue them steadily and actively. I am now reading Demosthenes with interest and admiration indescribable. I am slowly, at odd minutes, getting through the stupid trash of Diodorus. I have read through Seneca, and an affected empty scribbler he is. I have read Tacitus again, and, by the bye, I will tell you a curious circumstance relating to that matter. In my younger days I always thought the Annals a prodigiously superior work to the History. I was surprised to find that the Annals seemed cold and poor to me on the last reading. I began to think that I had overrated Tacitus. But, when I began the History, I was enchanted, and thought more highly of him than ever. I went back to the Annals, and liked them even better than the History. All at once the explanation of this occurred to me. While I was reading the Annals I was reading Thucydides. When I began the History, I began the Hellenics. What made the Annals appear cold and poor to me was the intense interest which Thucydides inspired. Indeed, what colouring is there which would not look tame when placed side by side with the magnificent light, and the terrible shade, of Thucydides? Tacitus was a great man, but he was not up to the Sicilian expedition. When I finished Thucydides, and took up Xenophon, the case was reversed. Tacitus had been a foil to Thucydides. Xenophon was a foil to Tacitus.

I have read Pliny the Younger. Some of the Epistles are interesting. Nothing more stupid than the Panegyric was ever preached in the University church. I am reading the Augustan History, and Aulus Gellius. Aulus is a favourite of mine. I think him one of the best writers of his class.

I read in the evenings a great deal of English, French, and Italian; and a little Spanish. I have picked up Portuguese enough to read Camoens with care; and I want no more. I have adopted an opinion about the Italian historians quite different from that which I formerly held, and which, I believe, is generally considered as orthodox. I place Fra Paolo decidedly at the head of them, and next to him Davila, whom I take to be the best modern military historian except Colonel Napier. Davila's battle of Ivry is worthy of Thucydides himself. Next to Davila I put Guicciardini, and last of all Machiavelli. But I do not think that you ever read much Italian.

The English poetry of the day has very few attractions for me. Van Artevelde is far the best specimen that I have lately seen. I do not much like Talfourd's Ion; but I mean to read it again. It contains pretty lines; but, to my thinking, it is neither fish nor flesh. There is too much, and too little, of the antique about it. Nothing but the most strictly classical costume can reconcile me to a mythological plot; and Ion is a modern philanthropist, whose politics and morals have been learned from the publications of the Society for the Diffusion of Useful Knowledge.

I do not know whether the noise which the lawyers of the Supreme Court have been raising against our legislative authority has reached, or will reach, England. They held a public meeting, which ended,—or rather began, continued, and ended,—in a riot; and ever since then the leading agitators have been challenging each other, refusing each other's challenges, libelling each other, swearing the peace against each other, and blackballing each other. Mr. Longueville Clarke, who aspires to be the O'Connell of Calcutta, called another lawyer a liar. The last-mentioned lawyer challenged Mr. Longueville Clarke. Mr. Longueville Clarke refused to fight, on the ground that his opponent had been guilty of hugging attorneys. The Bengal Club accordingly blackballed Longueville. This, and some other similar occurrences, have made the opposition here thoroughly ridiculous and contemptible. They will probably send a petition home; but, unless the House of Commons has undergone a great change since 1833, they have no chance there.

I have almost brought my letter to a close without mentioning the most important matter about which I had to write. I dare say you have heard that my uncle General Macaulay, who died last February, has left me 10,000*l.* This legacy, together with what I shall have saved by the end of 1837, will make me quite a rich man; richer than I even wish to be as a single man; and every day renders it more unlikely that I should marry.

We have had a very unhealthy season; but sickness has not come near our house. My sister, my brother-in-law, and their little child, are as well as possible. As to me, I think that, as Buonaparte said of himself after the Russian campaign, J'ai le diable au corps.

Ever yours affectionately

T. B. MACAULAY.

To Macvey Napier, Esq.

Calcutta: November 26, 1836.

Dear Napier,—

At last I send you an article of interminable length about Lord Bacon. I hardly know whether it is not too long for an article in a Review; but the subject is of such vast extent that I could easily have made the paper twice as long as it is.

About the historical and political part there is no great probability that we shall differ in opinion; but what I have said about Bacon's philosophy is widely at variance with what Dugald Stewart, and Mackintosh, have said on the same subject. I have not your essay; nor have I read it since I read it at Cambridge, with very great pleasure, but without any knowledge of the subject. I have at present only a very faint and general recollection of its contents, and have in vain tried to procure a copy of it here. I fear, however, that, differing widely as I do from Stewart and Mackintosh, I shall hardly agree with you. My opinion is formed, not at second hand, like those of nine-tenths of the people who talk about Bacon; but after several very attentive perusals of his greatest works, and after a good deal of thought. If I am in the wrong, my errors may set the minds of others at work, and may be the means of bringing both them, and me, to a knowledge of the truth. I never bestowed so much care on anything that I have written. There is not a sentence in the latter half of the article which has not been repeatedly recast. I have no expectation that the popularity of the article will bear any proportion to the trouble which I have expended on it. But the trouble has been so great a pleasure to me that I have already been greatly overpaid. Pray look carefully to the printing.

In little more than a year I shall be embarking for England, and I have determined to employ the four months of my voyage in mastering the German language. I should be much obliged to you to send me out, as early as you can, so that they may be certain to arrive in time, the best grammar, and the best dictionary, that can be procured; a German Bible; Schiller's works; Goethe's works; and Niebuhr's History, both in the original, and in the translation. My way of learning a language is always to begin with the Bible, which I can read without a dictionary. After a few days passed in this way, I am master of all the common particles, the common rules of syntax, and a pretty large vocabulary. Then I fall on some good classical work. It was in this way that I learned both Spanish and Portuguese, and I shall try the same course with German.

I have little or nothing to tell you about myself. My life has flowed away here with strange rapidity. It seems but yesterday that I left my country; and I am writing to beg you to hasten preparations for my return. I continue to enjoy perfect health, and the little political squalls which I have had to weather here are mere capfuls of wind to a man who has gone through the great hurricanes of English faction.

I shall send another copy of the article on Bacon by another ship.

Yours very truly
T. B. MACAULAY.

Calcutta: November 28, 1836.

Dear Napier,—

There is an oversight in the article on Bacon which I shall be much obliged to you to correct. I have said that Bacon did not deal at all in idle rants 'like those in which Cicero and Mr. Shandy sought consolation for the loss of Tullia and of Bobby.' Nothing can, as a general remark, be more true, but it escaped my recollection that two or three of Mr. Shandy's consolatory sentences are quoted from Bacon's Essays. The illustration, therefore, is singularly unfortunate. Pray alter it thus; 'in which Cicero vainly sought consolation for the loss of Tullia.' To be sure, it is idle to correct such trifles at a distance of fifteen thousand miles.

Yours ever
T. B. MACAULAY.

From Lord Jeffrey to Macvey Napier, Esq.

May 2, 1837.

My dear N.,—

What mortal could ever dream of cutting out the least particle of this precious work, to make it fit better into your Review? It would be worse than paring down the Pitt Diamond to fit the old setting of a Dowager's ring. Since Bacon himself, I do not know that there has been anything so fine. The first five or six pages are in a lower tone, but still magnificent, and not to be deprived of a word.

Still, I do not object to consider whether it might not be best to serve up the rich repast in two courses; and on the whole I incline to that partition. 120 pages might cloy even epicures, and would be sure to surfeit the vulgar; and the biography and philosophy are so entirely distinct, and of not very unequal length, that the division would not look like a fracture.

FRANCIS JEFFREY.

In the end, the article appeared entire; occupying 104 pages of the Review; and accompanied by an apology for its length in the shape of one of those editorial appeals to 'the intelligent scholar,' and 'the best class of our readers,' which never fail of success.

The letters addressed to Zachary Macaulay are half filled with anecdotes of the nursery; pretty enough, but such as only a grandfather could be expected to read. In other respects, the correspondence is chiefly remarkable for the affectionate ingenuity with which the son selects such topics as would interest the father.

Calcutta: October 12, 1836.

My dear Father,—

We were extremely gratified by receiving, a few days ago, a letter from you which, on the whole, gave a good account of your health and spirits. The day after to-morrow is the first anniversary of your little granddaughter's birthday. The occasion is to be celebrated with a sort of droll puppet-show, much in fashion among the natives; an exhibition much in the style of Punch in England, but more dramatic and more showy. All the little boys and girls from the houses of our friends are invited, and the party will, I have no doubt, be a great deal more amusing than the stupid dinners and routs with which the grown-up people here kill the time.

In a few months,—I hope, indeed, in a few weeks,—we shall send up the Penal Code to Government. We have got rid of the punishment of death, except in the case of aggravated treason and wilful murder. We shall also get rid indirectly of everything that can properly be called slavery in India. There will remain civil claims on particular people for particular services,

English envoy. Nothing so detestable ever came from the Minerva Press. I have read Theocritus again, and like him better than ever.

As to Latin, I made a heroic attempt on Pliny's Natural History; but I stuck after getting through about a quarter of it. I have read Ammianus Marcellinus, the worst written book in ancient Latin. The style would disgrace a monk of the tenth century; but Marcellinus has many of the substantial qualities of a good historian. I have gone through the Augustan history, and much other trash relating to the lower empire; curious as illustrating the state of society, but utterly worthless as composition. I have read Statius again and thought him as bad as ever. I really found only two lines worthy of a great poet in all the Thebaïs. They are these. What do you think of my taste?

> Clamorem, bello qualis supremus apertis
> Urbibus, aut pelago jam descendente carinâ.

I am now busy with Quintilian and Lucan, both excellent writers. The dream of Pompey in the seventh book of the Pharsalia is a very noble piece of writing. I hardly know an instance in poetry of so great an effect produced by means so simple. There is something irresistibly pathetic in the lines:

> Qualis erat populi facies, clamorque faventum
> Olim cum juvenis—

and something unspeakably solemn in the sudden turn which follows:

> Crastina dira quies—

There are two passages in Lucan which surpass in eloquence anything that I know in the Latin language. One is the enumeration of Pompey's exploits:

> Quod si tam sacro dignaris nomine saxum—

The other is the character which Cato gives of Pompey,

> Civis obit, inquit—

a pure gem of rhetoric, without one flaw, and, in my

opinion, not very far from historical truth.[1] When I consider that Lucan died at twenty-six, I cannot help ranking him among the most extraordinary men that ever lived.

I am glad that you have so much business, and sorry that you have so little leisure. In a few years you will be a Baron of the Exchequer; and then we shall have ample time to talk over our favourite classics. Then I will show you a most superb emendation of Bentley's in Ampelius, and I will give you unanswerable reasons for pronouncing that Gibbon was mistaken in supposing that Quintus Curtius wrote under Gordian.

Remember me most kindly to Mrs. Ellis. I hope that I shall find Frank writing as good Alcaics as his father.

Ever yours affectionately

T. B. MACAULAY.

Dear Ellis,— Calcutta: March 8, 1837.

I am at present very much worked, and have been so for a long time past. Cameron, after being laid up for some months, sailed at Christmas for the Cape, where

[1] The following remarks occur at the end of Macaulay's copy of the Pharsalia:

August 30, 1835.

'When Lucan's age is considered, it is impossible not to allow that the poem is a very extraordinary one: more extraordinary, perhaps, than if it had been of a higher kind; for it is more common for the imagination to be in full vigour at an early time of life than for a young man to obtain a complete mastery of political and philosophical rhetoric. I know no declamation in the world, not even Cicero's best, which equals some passages in the Pharsalia. As to what were meant for bold poetical flights,—the sea-fight at Marseilles, the Centurion who is covered with wounds, the snakes in the Libyan desert,—it is all as detestable as Cibber's Birthday Odes. The furious partiality of Lucan takes away much of the pleasure which his talents would otherwise afford. A poet who is, as has often been said, less a poet than a historian, should to a certain degree conform to the laws of history. The manner in which he represents the two parties is not to be reconciled with the laws even of fiction. The senators are demigods; Pompey, a pure lover of his country; Cato, the abstract idea of virtue; while Cæsar, the finest gentleman, the most humane conqueror, and the most popular politician that Rome ever produced, is a bloodthirsty ogre. If Lucan had lived, he would probably have improved greatly.' 'Again, December 9, 1836.'

I hope his health will be repaired; for this country can very ill spare him. However, we have almost brought our great work to a conclusion. In about a month we shall lay before the Government a complete Penal Code for a hundred millions of people, with a commentary explaining and defending the provisions of the text. Whether it is well, or ill, done heaven knows. I only know that it seems to me to be very ill done when I look at it by itself; and well done when I compare it with Livingstone's Code, with the French Code, or with the English statutes which have been passed for the purpose of consolidating and amending the Criminal Law. In health I am as well as ever I was in my life. Time glides fast. One day is so like another that, but for a habit which I acquired soon after I reached India of pencilling in my books the date of my reading them, I should have hardly any way of estimating the lapse of time. If I want to know when an event took place, I call to mind which of Calderon's plays, or of Plutarch's Lives, I was reading on that day. I turn to the book; find the date; and am generally astonished to see that, what seems removed from me by only two or three months, really happened nearly a year ago.

I intend to learn German on my voyage home, and I have indented largely, (to use our Indian official term), for the requisite books. People tell me that it is a hard language; but I cannot easily believe that there is a language which I cannot master in four months, by working ten hours a day. I promise myself very great delight and information from German literature; and, over and above, I feel a sort of presentiment, a kind of admonition of the Deity, which assures me that the final cause of my existence,—the end for which I was sent into this vale of tears,—was to make game of certain Germans. The first thing to be done in obedience to this heavenly call is to learn German; and then I may perhaps try, as Milton says,

Frangere Saxonicas Britonum sub Marte phalanges.

Ever yours affectionately

T. B. MACAULAY.

The years which Macaulay spent in India formed a transition period between the time when he kept no journal at all, and the time when the daily portion of his journal was completed as regularly as the daily portion of his History. Between 1834 and 1838, he contented himself with jotting down any circumstance that struck his fancy in the book which he happened to have in hand. The records of his Calcutta life, written in half a dozen different languages, are scattered throughout the whole range of classical literature from Hesiod to Macrobius. At the end of the eighty-ninth Epistle of Seneca we read: 'April 14, 1836. Hodie præmia distribui *τοις ἐν τῳ μουσειῳ Σανσκριτικῳ νεανισκοις*.'[1]

On the last page of the Birds of Aristophanes: 'Jan. 16, 1836. *οἱ πρεσβεῖς οἱ παρὰ τοῡ βασιλέως τῶν Νηπαυλιτων εἰσήγοντο χθες ἐς Καλκουτταν*.'[2]

On the first page of Theocritus: 'March 20, 1835. Lord W. Bentinck sailed this morning.'

On the last page of the 'De Amicitiâ:' 'March 5, 1836. Yesterday Lord Auckland arrived at Government House, and was sworn in.'

Beneath an idyl of Moschus, of all places in the world, Macaulay notes the fact of Peel being First Lord of the Treasury; and he finds space, between two quotations in Athenæus, to commemorate a Ministerial majority of 29 on the Second Reading of the Irish Church Bill.

A somewhat nearer approach to a formal diary may be found in his Catullus, which contains a catalogue of the English books that he read in the cold season of 1835–36; as for instance:

Gibbons' Answer to Davis .	November 6 and 7
Gibbon on Virgil's VI Æneid .	November 7

[1] 'To-day I distributed the prizes to the students of the Sanscrit College.'

[2] 'The ambassadors from the King of Nepaul entered Calcutta yesterday.' It may be observed that Macaulay wrote Greek with or without accents, according to the humour, or hurry, of the moment.

Whately's Logic . . . November 15
Thirlwall's Greece . . . November 22
Edinburgh Review . . . November 29

And all this was in addition to his Greek and Latin studies, to his official work, to the French that he read with his sister, and the unrecorded novels that he read to himself; which last would alone have afforded occupation for two ordinary men, unless this month of November was different from every other month of his existence since the day that he left Mr. Preston's schoolroom. There is something refreshing, amidst the long list of graver treatises, to light upon a periodical entry of '*Πικυικινα*'; the immortal work of a Classic who has had more readers in a single year than Statius and Seneca in all their eighteen centuries together. Macaulay turned over with indifference, and something of distaste, the earlier chapters of that modern Odyssey. The first touch which came home to him was Jingle's 'Handsome Englishman!' In that phrase he recognised a master; and, by the time that he landed in England, he knew his Pickwick almost as intimately as his Grandison.

Calcutta: June 15, 1837.

Dear Napier,—

Your letter about my review of Mackintosh miscarried, vexatiously enough. I should have been glad to know what was thought of my performance among friends and foes; for here we have no information on such subjects. The literary correspondents of the Calcutta newspapers seem to be penny-a-line men, whose whole stock of literature comes from the conversations in the Green Room.

My long article on Bacon has, no doubt, been in your hands some time. I never, to the best of my recollection, proposed to review Hannah More's Life or Works. If I did, it must have been in jest. She was exactly the very last person in the world about whom I should choose to write a critique. She was a very kind friend to me from childhood. Her notice first called out my literary tastes. Her presents laid the foundation of my library. She was to me what Ninon was to Voltaire,—begging her pardon for comparing her to a bad woman, and yours for comparing myself to a great man. She really was a second mother to me. I have a real affection for her memory. I therefore could not possibly write about her unless I wrote in her praise; and all the praise which I could give to her writings, even after straining my conscience in her favour, would be far indeed from satisfying any of her admirers.

I will try my hand on Temple, and on Lord Clive. Shaftesbury I shall let alone. Indeed, his political life is so much connected with Temple's that, without endless repetition, it would be impossible for me to furnish a separate article on each. Temple's Life and Works; the part which he took in the controversy about the ancients and moderns; the Oxford confederacy against Bentley; and the memorable victory which Bentley obtained, will be good subjects. I am in training for this part of the subject, as I have twice read through the Phalaris controversy since I arrived in India.

I have been almost incessantly engaged in public business since I sent off the paper on Bacon; but I expect to have comparative leisure during the short remainder of my stay here. The Penal Code of India is finished, and is in the press. The illness of two of my colleagues threw the work almost entirely on me. It is done, however; and I am not likely to be called upon for vigorous exertion during the rest of my Indian career.

Yours ever

T. B. MACAULAY.

If you should have assigned Temple, or Clive, to anybody else, pray do not be uneasy on that account. The pleasure of writing pays itself.

Calcutta: December 18, 1837.

Dear Ellis,—

My last letter was on a deeply melancholy subject, the death of our poor friend Malkin. I have felt very much for his widow. The intensity of her affliction, and the fortitude and good feeling which she showed as soon as the first agony was over, have interested me greatly in her. Six or seven of Malkin's most intimate friends here have joined with Ryan and me, in subscribing to put up a plain marble tablet in the cathedral, for which I have written an inscription.[1]

My departure is now near at hand. This is the last letter which I shall write to you from India. Our passage is taken in the Lord Hungerford; the most celebrated of the huge floating hotels which run between London and Calcutta. She is more renowned for the comfort and luxury of her internal arrangements than for her speed. As we are to stop at the Cape for a short time, I hardly expect to be with you till the end of May, or the beginning of June. I intend to make myself a good German scholar by the time of my arrival in England. I have already, at leisure moments, broken the ice. I have read about half of the New Testament in Luther's translation, and am now getting rapidly, for a beginner, through Schiller's History of the Thirty Years' War. My German library consists of all Goethe's works, all Schiller's works, Muller's History of Switzerland, some of Tieck, some of Lessing, and other works of less fame. I hope to despatch them all on my way home. I like Schiller's style exceedingly. His history contains a great deal of very just and deep thought, conveyed in language so popular and agreeable that dunces would think him superficial.

I lately took it into my head to obtain some knowledge of the Fathers, and I read therefore a good deal of Athanasius, which by no means raised him in my opinion. I procured the magnificent edition of Chrysostom, by Montfaucon, from a public library here, and turned over the eleven huge folios, reading wherever the subject was of peculiar interest. As to reading him through, the thing is impossible. These volumes

[1] This inscription appears in Lord Macaulay's Miscellaneous Works.

contain matter at least equal to the whole extant literature of the best times of Greece, from Homer to Aristotle inclusive. There are certainly some very brilliant passages in his homilies. It seems curious that, though the Greek literature began to flourish so much earlier than the Latin, it continued to flourish so much later. Indeed, if you except the century which elapsed between Cicero's first public appearance and Livy's death, I am not sure that there was any time at which Greece had not writers equal or superior to their Roman contemporaries. I am sure that no Latin writer of the age of Lucian is to be named with Lucian; that no Latin writer of the age of Longinus is to be named with Longinus; that no Latin prose of the age of Chrysostom can be named with Chrysostom's compositions. I have read Augustin's Confessions. The book is not without interest; but he expresses himself in the style of a field-preacher.

Our Penal Code is to be published next week. It has cost me very intense labour; and, whatever its faults may be, it is certainly not a slovenly performance. Whether the work proves useful to India or not, it has been of great use, I feel and know, to my own mind.[1]

Ever yours affectionately

T. B. MACAULAY.

[1] In October 1854, Macaulay writes to my mother: 'I cannot but be pleased to find that, at last, the Code on which I bestowed the labour of two of the best years of my life has had justice done to it. Had this justice been done sixteen years ago, I should probably have given much more attention to legislation, and much less to literature than I have done. I do not know that I should have been either happier or more useful than I have been.'

CHAPTER VII

1838–1839

Death of Zachary Macaulay—Mr. Wallace and Mackintosh—Letters to Mr. Napier, and Mr. Ellis—Sir Walter Scott—Lord Brougham—First mention of the History—Macaulay goes abroad—His way of regarding scenery—Châlons-sur-Marne — Lyons — Marseilles — Genoa — Pisa — Florence—Macaulay refuses the Judge Advocateship—Florence to Rome—Thrasymene—St. Peter's—The New Zealander—The Vatican—The Temporal Power—The doctrine of the Immaculate Conception—Letter to Lord Lansdowne—The Canadian Insurrection—Gibbon—Rome to Naples—Bulwer's novels—Impressions of Naples—Virgil's tomb—Macaulay sets out homewards—Mr. Goulburn—Versailles.

THE Lord Hungerford justified her reputation of a bad sailer, and the homeward voyage was protracted into the sixth month. This unusual delay, combined with the knowledge that the ship had met with very rough weather after leaving the Cape, gave rise to a report that she had been lost with all on board, and brought a succession of Whig politicians into the City to inquire at Lloyd's about the safety of her precious freight. But it was in the character of a son and brother, and not of a party orator, that Macaulay was most eagerly and anxiously expected. He had, indeed, been sorely missed. 'You can have no conception,' wrote one of his sisters, in the year 1834, 'of the change which has come over this household. It is as if the sun had deserted the earth. The chasm Tom's departure has made can never be supplied. He was so unlike any other being one ever sees, and his visits amongst us were a sort of refreshment which served not a little to enliven and cheer our monotonous way of life; but now day after day rises and sets without object or interest, so that sometimes I almost feel aweary of this world.'

Things did not mend as time went on. With Zachary Macaulay, as has been the case with so many like him, the years which intervened between the time when his work was done, and the time when he went to receive his wages, were years of trouble, of sorrow, and even of gloom. Failing health; failing eyesight; the sense of being helpless, and useless after an active and beneficent career; the consciousness of dependence upon others at an age when the moral disadvantages of poverty are felt even more keenly than youth feels its material discomforts;—such were the clouds that darkened the close of a life which had never been without its trials. During the months that his children were on their homeward voyage his health was breaking fast; and before the middle of May he died, without having again seen their faces. Sir James Stephen, writing to Fanny Macaulay, says: 'I know not how to grieve for the loss of your father, though it removes from this world one of the oldest, and, assuredly, one of the most excellent friends I have ever had. What rational man would not leap for joy at the offer of bearing all his burdens, severe as they were, if he could be assured of the same approving conscience and of the same blessed reward? He was almost the last survivor of a noble brotherhood now reunited in affection, and in employment. Mr. Wilberforce, Henry Thornton, Babington, my father, and other not less dear, though less conspicuous, companions of his many labours, have ere now greeted him as their associate in the world of spirits; and, above all, he has been welcomed by his Redeemer with "Well done, good and faithful servant."'

Zachary Macaulay's bust in Westminster Abbey bears on its pedestal a beautiful inscription, (which is, and probably will remain, his only biography,) in which much more is told, than he himself would wish to have been told, about a man

WHO DURING FORTY SUCCESSIVE YEARS,
PARTAKING IN THE COUNSELS AND THE LABOURS
WHICH, GUIDED BY FAVOURING PROVIDENCE,
RESCUED AFRICA FROM THE WOES,
AND THE BRITISH EMPIRE FROM THE GUILT,
OF SLAVERY AND THE SLAVE-TRADE,
MEEKLY ENDURED THE TOIL, THE PRIVATION, AND THE REPROACH,
RESIGNING TO OTHERS THE PRAISE AND THE REWARD.

His tomb has for many years past been cut off from the body of the nave by an iron railing equally meaningless and unsightly; which withdraws from the eyes of his fellow-countrymen an epitaph at least as provocative to patriotism as those of the innumerable military and naval heroes of the Seventeenth and Eighteenth centuries, who fell in wars the very objects of which are for the most part forgotten, or remembered only to be regretted.[1]

The first piece of business which Macaulay found waiting to be settled on his return to England was sufficiently disagreeable. As far back as July 1835, he had reviewed Sir James Mackintosh's History of the Revolution of 1688. This valuable fragment was edited by a Mr. Wallace, who accompanied it with a biographical sketch of his author, whom he treated throughout with an impertinence which had an air of inexcusable disloyalty; but which in truth was due to nothing worse than self-sufficiency, thrown into unpleasant relief by the most glaring bad taste. Macaulay, who from a boy had felt for Mackintosh that reverence which is

Dearer to true young hearts than their own praise,

fell upon the editor with a contemptuous vigour, of which some pretty distinct traces remain in the essay as it at present appears in the collected editions, where the following sentence may still be read: 'It is plain that Thomas Burnet and his writings were never heard of by the gentleman who has been employed to edit this volume, and who, not content with deforming Sir James Mackintosh's text by such blunders, has prefixed to it a bad memoir, has appended to it a bad continuation, and has thus succeeded in expanding the volume into one of the thickest, and debasing it into

[1] Since these lines were printed, the railing has been taken down by the orders of Dean Stanley, who is always ready to remove ecclesiastical barriers.

A complete and excellent biography of Zachary Macaulay was published in 1900 by his grand-daughter, Viscountess Knutsford.

one of the worst, that we ever saw.' What the first vehemence of Macaulay's indignation was, may be estimated by the fact that this passage, as it now stands, has been deprived of half its sting.

One extract from the article, in its original form, merits to be reproduced here, because it explains, and in some degree justifies, Macaulay's wrath, and in itself is well worth reading.

'He' (the editor) 'affects, and for aught we know, feels, something like contempt for the celebrated man whose life he has undertaken to write, and whom he was incompetent to serve in the capacity even of a corrector of the press. Our readers may form a notion of the spirit in which the whole narrative is composed from expressions which occur at the beginning. This biographer tells us that Mackintosh, on occasion of taking his medical degree at Edinburgh, "not only put off the writing of his Thesis to the last moment, but was an hour behind his time on the day of examination, and kept the Academic Senate waiting for him in full conclave." This irregularity, which no sensible professor would have thought deserving of more than a slight reprimand, is described by the biographer, after a lapse of nearly half a century, as an incredible instance "not so much of indolence, as of gross negligence and bad taste." But this is not all. Our biographer has contrived to procure a copy of the Thesis, and has sate down, with his As in præsenti and his Propria quæ maribus at his side, to pick out blunders in a composition written by a youth of twenty-one on the occasion alluded to. He finds one mistake—such a mistake as the greatest scholar might commit when in haste, and as the veriest schoolboy would detect when at leisure. He glories over this precious discovery with all the exultation of a pedagogue. "Deceived by the passive termination of the verb *defungor*, Mackintosh misuses it in a passive sense." He is not equally fortunate in his other discovery. "*Laude conspurcare*," whatever he may think, is not an improper phrase. Mackintosh meant to say that there are men whose praise is a disgrace. No person, we are sure, who has read this memoir, will doubt that there are men whose abuse is an honour.'

Mr. Wallace did not choose to rest quietly under a castigation which even Macaulay subsequently admitted to have been in excess of his deserts.

3 Clarges Street, London: June 14, 1838.

Dear Napier,—

I did not need your letter to satisfy me of your kindness, and of the pleasure which my arrival would give you. I have returned with a small independence, but still an independence. All my tastes and wishes lead me to prefer literature to politics. When I say this to my friends here, some of them seem to think that I am out of my wits, and others that I am coquetting to raise my price. I, on the other hand, believe that I am wise, and know that I am sincere.

I shall be curious, when we meet, to see your correspondence with Wallace. Empson seemed to be a little uneasy lest the foolish man should give me trouble. I thought it impossible that he could be so absurd; and, as I have now been in London ten days without hearing of him, I am confirmed in my opinion. In any event you need not be anxious. If it be absolutely necessary to meet him, I will. But I foresee no such necessity; and, as Junius says, I never will give a proof of my spirit at the expense of my understanding.

Ever yours most truly

T. B. MACAULAY.

London: August 14, 1838.

Dear Napier,—

Your old friend Wallace and I have been pretty near exchanging shots. However, all is accommodated, and, I think, quite unexceptionably. The man behaved much better to me than he did to you. Perhaps time has composed his feelings. He had, at all events, the advantage of being in good hands. He sent me by Tom Steele,—a furious O'Connellite, but a gentleman, a man of honour, and, on this occasion at least, a man of temper,—a challenge very properly worded. He accounted, handsomely enough, for the delay by saying that my long absence, and the recent loss in my family, prevented him from applying to me immediately on my return. I put the matter into Lord Strafford's hands. I had, to tell you the truth, no notion that a meeting could be avoided; for the man behaved so obstinately well that there was no possibility of taking Empson's advice, and sending for the police; and, though I was quite ready to disclaim all intention of giving personal offence, and to declare that, when I wrote the review, I was ignorant of Mr. Wallace's existence, I could not make any apology, or express the least regret, for having used strong language in defence of Mackintosh. Lord Strafford quite approved of my resolution. But he proposed a course which had never occurred to me; which at once removed all scruples on my side; and which, to my great surprise, Steele and Wallace adopted without a moment's hesitation. This was that Wallace should make a preliminary declaration that he meant, by his memoir, nothing disrespectful or unkind to Mackintosh, but the direct contrary; and that then I should declare that, in consequence of Mr. Wallace's declaration, I was ready to express my regret if I had used any language that could be deemed personally offensive. This way of settling the business appeared to both Lord Strafford and Rice perfectly honourable; and I was of the same mind: for certainly the language which I used could be justified only on the ground that Wallace had used Mackintosh ill; and, when Wallace made a preliminary declaration that he intended nothing but kindness and honour to Mackintosh, I could not properly refuse to make some concession. I was much surprised that neither Steele nor Wallace objected to Lord Strafford's proposition; but, as they did not object, it was impossible for me to do so. In this way the matter was settled,—much better settled than by refusing to admit Wallace to the privileges of a gentleman. I hope that you will be satisfied with the result. The kind anxiety which you have felt about me renders me very desirous to know that you approve of my conduct.

Yours ever

T. B. MACAULAY.

3 Clarges Street: June 26, 1838.

Dear Napier,—

I assure you that I would willingly, and even eagerly, undertake the subject which you propose, if I thought that I should serve you by doing so. But, depend upon it, you do not know what you are asking for. I have done my best to ascertain what I can and what I cannot do. There are extensive classes of subjects which I think myself able to treat as few people can treat them. After this, you cannot suspect me of any affectation of modesty; and you will therefore believe that I tell you what I sincerely think, when I say that I am not successful in analysing the effect of works of genius. I have written several things on historical, political, and moral questions, of which, on the fullest re-consideration, I am not ashamed, and by which I should be willing to be estimated; but I have never written a page of criticism on poetry, or the fine arts, which I would not burn if I had the power. Hazlitt used to say of himself, 'I am nothing if not critical.' The case with me is directly the reverse. I have a strong and acute enjoyment of works of the imagination; but I have never habituated myself to dissect them. Perhaps I enjoy them the more keenly, for that very reason. Such books as Lessing's Laocoön,[1] such passages as the criticism on Hamlet in Wilhelm Meister, fill me with wonder and despair. Now, a review of Lockhart's book ought to be a review of Sir Walter's literary performances. I enjoy many of them; —nobody, I believe, more keenly,—but I am sure that there are hundreds who will criticise them far better. Trust to my knowledge of myself. I never in my life was more certain of anything than of what I tell you, and I am sure that Lord Jeffrey will tell you exactly the same.

There are other objections of less weight, but not quite unimportant. Surely it would be desirable that

[1] 'I began Lessing's Laocoön, and read forty or fifty pages: sometimes dissenting, but always admiring and learning.'—Macaulay's Journal for September 21, 1851.

some person who knew Sir Walter, who had at least seen him and spoken with him, should be charged with this article. Many people are living who had a most intimate acquaintance with him. I know no more of him than I know of Dryden or Addison, and not a tenth part so much as I know of Swift, Cowper, or Johnson. Then again, I have not, from the little that I do know of him, formed so high an opinion of his character as most people seem to entertain, and as it would be expedient for the Edinburgh Review to express. He seems to me to have been most carefully, and successfully, on his guard against the sins which most easily beset literary men. On that side he multiplied his precautions, and set double watch. Hardly any writer of note has been so free from the petty jealousies, and morbid irritabilities, of our caste. But I do not think that he kept himself equally pure from faults of a very different kind, from the faults of a man of the world. In politics, a bitter and unscrupulous partisan; profuse and ostentatious in expense; agitated by the hopes and fears of a gambler; perpetually sacrificing the perfection of his compositions, and the durability of his fame, to his eagerness for money; writing with the slovenly haste of Dryden, in order to satisfy wants which were not, like those of Dryden, caused by circumstances beyond his control, but which were produced by his extravagant waste or rapacious speculation; this is the way in which he appears to me. I am sorry for it, for I sincerely admire the greater part of his works: but I cannot think him a high-minded man, or a man of very strict principle. Now these are opinions which, however softened, it would be highly unpopular to publish, particularly in a Scotch Review.

But why cannot you prevail on Lord Jeffrey to furnish you with this article? No man could do it half so well. He knew and loved Scott; and would perform the critical part of the work, which is much the most important, incomparably. I have said a good deal in the hope of convincing you that it is not without reason that I decline a task which I see that you wish me to undertake.

I am quite unsettled. Breakfasts every morning, dinners every evening, and calls all day, prevent me from making any regular exertion. My books are at the baggage warehouse. My book-cases are in the hands of the cabinet-maker. Whatever I write at present I must, as Bacon somewhere says, spin like a spider out of my own entrails, and I have hardly a minute in the week for such spinning. London is in a strange state of excitement. The western streets are in a constant ferment. The influx of foreigners and rustics has been prodigious, and the regular inhabitants are almost as idle and curious as the sojourners. Crowds assemble perpetually, nobody knows why, with a sort of vague expectation that there will be something to see; and, after staring at each other, disperse without seeing anything. This will last till the Coronation is over. The only quiet haunts are the streets of the City. For my part I am sick to death of the turmoil, and almost wish myself at Calcutta again, or becalmed on the equator.

Ever yours most truly

T. B. MACAULAY.

3 Clarges Street, London: July 20, 1838.

Dear Napier,—

As to Brougham, I understand and feel for your embarrassments. I may perhaps refine too much; but I should say that this strange man, finding himself almost alone in the world, absolutely unconnected with either Whigs or Conservatives, and not having a single vote in either House of Parliament at his command except his own, is desirous to make the Review his organ. With this intention, unless I am greatly deceived, after having during several years contributed little or nothing of value, he has determined to exert himself as if he were a young writer struggling into note, and to make himself important to the work by his literary services. And he certainly has succeeded.

His late articles, particularly the long one in the April number,[1] have very high merit. They are, indeed, models of magazine writing as distinguished from other sorts of writing. They are not, I think, made for duration. Everything about them is exaggerated, incorrect, sketchy. All the characters are either too black, or too fair. The passions of the writer do not suffer him even to maintain the decent appearance of impartiality. And the style, though striking and animated, will not bear examination through a single paragraph. But the effect of the first perusal is great; and few people read an article in a review twice. A bold, dashing, scene-painting manner is that which always succeeds best in periodical writing; and I have no doubt that these lively and vigorous papers of Lord Brougham will be of more use to you than more highly finished compositions. His wish, I imagine, is to establish in this way such an ascendency as may enable him to drag the Review along with him to any party to which his furious passions may lead him; to the Radicals; to the Tories; to any set of men by whose help he may be able to revenge himself on old friends, whose only crime is that they could not help finding him to be an habitual and incurable traitor. Hitherto your caution and firmness have done wonders. Yet already he has begun to use the word 'Whig' as an epithet of reproach, exactly as it is used in the lowest writings of the Tories, and of the extreme Radicals; exactly as it is used in Blackwood, in Fraser, in the Age, in Tait's Magazine. There are several instances in the article on Lady Charlotte Bury. 'The Whig notions of female propriety.' 'The Whig secret tribunal.' I have no doubt that the tone of his papers will become more and more hostile to the Government; and that, in a short time, it will be necessary for you to take one of three courses, to every one of which there are strong objections;—to

[1] This is the article on the 'Diary illustrative of the times of George the Fourth, interspersed with original letters from the late Queen Caroline, and from various other distinguished persons.'

break with him; to admit his papers into the Review, while the rest of the Review continues to be written in quite a different tone; or to yield to his dictation, and to let him make the Review a mere tool of his ambition and revenge.

As to Brougham's feelings towards myself, I know, and have known for a long time, that he hates me. If during the last ten years I have gained any reputation either in politics or in letters,—if I have had any success in life,—it has been without his help or countenance, and often in spite of his utmost exertions to keep me down. It is strange that he should be surprised at my not calling on him since my return. I did not call on him when I went away. When he was Chancellor, and I was in office, I never once attended his levée. It would be strange indeed if now, when he is squandering the remains of his public character in an attempt to ruin the party of which he was a member then, and of which I am a member still, I should begin to pay court to him. For the sake of the long intimacy which subsisted between him and my father, and of the mutual good offices which passed between them, I will not, unless I am compelled, make any public attack on him. But this is really the only tie which restrains me: for I neither love him, nor fear him.

With regard to the Indian Penal Code, if you are satisfied that Empson really wishes to review it on its own account, and not merely out of kindness to me, I should not at all object to his doing so. The subject is one of immense importance. The work is of a kind too abstruse for common readers, and can be made known to them only through the medium of some popular exposition. There is another consideration which weighs much with me. The Press in India has fallen into the hands of the lower legal practitioners, who detest all law-reform; and their scurrility, though mere matter of derision to a person accustomed to the virulence of English factions, is more formidable than you can well conceive to the members of the Civil Service, who are quite unaccustomed to be dragged rudely before the public. It is, therefore, highly important that the members of the Indian Legislature, and of the Law Commission, should be supported against the clamorous abuse of the scribblers who surround them by seeing that their performances attract notice at home, and are judged with candour and discernment by writers of a far higher rank in literature than the Calcutta editors. For these reasons I should be glad to see an article on the Penal Code in the Edinburgh Review. But I must stipulate that my name may not be mentioned, and that everything may be attributed to the Law Commission as a body. I am quite confident that Empson's own good taste, and regard for me, will lead him, if he should review the Code, to abstain most carefully from everything that resembles puffing. His regard to truth and the public interest will, of course, lead him to combat our opinions freely wherever he thinks us wrong.

There is little chance that I shall see Scotland this year. In the autumn I shall probably set out for Rome, and return to London in the spring. As soon as I return, I shall seriously commence my History. The first part, (which, I think, will take up five octavo volumes,) will extend from the Revolution to the commencement of Sir Robert Walpole's long administration; a period of three or four and thirty very eventful years. From the commencement of Walpole's administration to the commencement of the American war, events may be despatched more concisely. From the commencement of the American war it will again become necessary to be copious. These, at least, are my present notions. How far I shall bring the narrative down I have not determined. The death of George the Fourth would be the best halting-place. The History would then be an entire view of all the transactions which took place, between the Revolution which brought the Crown into harmony with the Parliament, and the Revolution which brought the Parliament into harmony with the nation. But there are great and obvious objections to contemporary history. To be sure, if I live to be seventy, the events of George the Fourth's reign will be to me then what the American war and the Coalition are to me now.

Whether I shall continue to reside in London seems to me very uncertain. I used to think that I liked London; but, in truth, I liked things which were in London, and which are gone. My family is scattered. I have no Parliamentary or official business to bind me to the capital. The business to which I propose to devote myself is almost incompatible with the distractions of a town life. I am sick of the monotonous succession of parties, and long for quiet and retirement. To quit politics for letters is, I believe, a wise choice. To cease to be a member of Parliament only to become a diner-out would be contemptible; and it is not easy for me to avoid becoming a mere diner-out if I reside here.

Ever yours

T. B. M.

London: September 15, 1838.

Dear Ellis,—

On Monday I shall set off for Liverpool by the railroad, which will then be opened for the whole way. I shall remain there about a week. The chief object of my visit is to see my little nephew, the son of my sister Margaret. It is no visit of pleasure, though I hear everything most hopeful and pleasing about the boy's talents and temper.[1] Indeed, it is not without a great effort that I force myself to go. But I will say no more on this subject, for I cannot command myself when I approach it.

Empson came to London yesterday night, with his lady in high beauty and good humour. It is, you know, quite a proverbial truth that wives never tolerate an intimacy between their husbands and any old friends, except in two cases: the one, when the old friend was,

[1] The boy died in 1847, having already shown as fair promise of remarkable ability, and fine character, as can be given at the age of thirteen. 'I feel the calamity much,' Macaulay wrote. 'I had left the dear boy my library, little expecting that I should ever wear mourning for him.'

before the marriage, a friend of both wife and husband; the other, when the friendship is of later date than the marriage. I may hope to keep Empson's friendship under the former exception, as I have kept yours under the latter.

Empson brings a sad account of poor Napier: all sorts of disquiet and trouble, with dreadful, wearing, complaints which give his friends the gravest cause for alarm. And, as if this were not enough, Brougham is persecuting him with the utmost malignity. I did not think it possible for human nature, in an educated civilised man,—a man, too, of great intellect,—to have become so depraved. He writes to Napier in language of the most savage hatred, and of the most extravagant vaunting. The Ministers, he says, have felt only his little finger. He will now put forth his red right hand. They shall have no rest. As to me, he says that I shall rue my baseness in not calling on him. But it is against Empson that he is most furious. He says that, in consequence of this new marriage,[1] he will make it the chief object of his life to prevent Jeffrey from ever being Lord President of the Court of Session. He thinks that there is some notion of making Empson editor of the Review. If that be done, he says, he will relinquish every other object in order to ruin the Review. He will lay out his last sixpence in that enterprise. He will make revenge on Empson the one business of the remaining years of his life. Empson says that nothing so demoniacal was ever written in the world. For my part, since he takes it into his head to be angry, I am pleased that he goes on in such a way; for he is much less formidable in such a state than he would be if he kept his temper. I sent to Napier on Thursday a long article on Temple. It is superficial; but on that account, among others, I shall be surprised if it does not take.

Hayter has painted me for his picture of the House of Commons. I cannot judge of his performance. I can only say, as Charles the Second did on a similar

[1] Mr. Empson had married the daughter of Lord Jeffrey.

occasion, 'Odds fish, if I am like this, I am an ugly fellow.'

Yours ever
T. B. M.

In the middle of October Macaulay started for a tour in Italy. Just past middle life, with his mind already full, and his imagination still fresh and his health unbroken,—it may be doubted whether any traveller had carried thither a keener expectation of enjoyment since Winckelmann for the first time crossed the Alps. A diary, from which extracts will be given in the course of this chapter, curiously illustrates the feelings with which he regarded the scenes around him. He viewed the works, both of man and of nature, with the eyes of an historian, and not of an artist. The leading features of a tract of country impressed themselves rapidly and indelibly on his observation; all its associations and traditions swept at once across his memory; and every line of good poetry, which its fame, or its beauty, had inspired, rose almost involuntarily to his lips. But, compared with the wealth of phrases on which he could draw at will when engaged on the description of human passions, catastrophes, and intrigues, his stock of epithets applicable to mountains, seas, and clouds was singularly scanty; and he had no ambition to enlarge it. When he had recorded the fact that the leaves were green, the sky blue, the plain rich, and the hills clothed with wood, he had said all he had to say, and there was an end of it. He had neither the taste, nor the power, for rivalling those novelists who have more colours in their vocabulary than ever Turner had on his palette; and who spend over the lingering phases of a single sunset as much ink as Richardson consumed in depicting the death of his villain, or the ruin of his heroine. 'I have always thought,' said Lady Trevelyan, 'that your uncle was incomparable in showing a town, or the place where any famous event occurred; but that he did not care for scenery merely as scenery. He enjoyed the country in his way. He liked sitting out on a lawn, and seeing grass and flowers around him. Occasionally a view made a great impression on him, such as the view down upon Susa, going over Mont Cenis; but I doubt whether any scene pleased his eye more than his own beloved Holly Lodge, or Mr. Thornton's garden at Battersea Rise. When we were recalling the delights of an excursion among the Surrey hills, or in the byways at the English lakes, he would be inclined to ask "What went ye out for to see?" Yet he readily took in the points of a landscape; and I remember being much struck by his description of the country before you reach Rome, which he gives in Horatius. When I followed him over that ground many years after, I am sure that I marked the very turn in the road where the lines struck him:

> From where Cortona lifts to heaven
> Her diadem of towers;—

and so on through "reedy Thrasymene," and all the other localities of the poem.'

'*Chalons-sur-Saône. Tuesday, October* 23, 1838.—The road from Autun is for some way more beautiful than anything I had yet seen in France; or indeed, in that style, anywhere else, except, perhaps, the ascent to the tableland of the Neilgherries. I traversed a winding pass, near two miles in length, running by the side of a murmuring brook, and between hills covered with forest. The landscape appeared in the richest colouring of October, under a sun like that of an English June. The earth was the earth of autumn, but the sky was the sky of summer. The foliage,—dark green, light green, purple, red, and yellow,—seen by the evening sun, produced the effect of the plumage of the finest eastern birds. I walked up the pass exceedingly pleased. To enjoy scenery you should ramble amidst it; let the feelings to which it gives rise mingle with other thoughts; look around upon it in intervals of reading; and not go to it as one goes to see the lions fed at a fair. The beautiful is not to be stared at, but to be lived with. I have no pleasure from books which equals that of reading over for the hundredth time great productions which I almost know by heart; and it is just the same with scenery.'

'*Lyons. Thursday, October* 25.—My birthday. Thirty-eight years old. Thought of Job, Swift, and Antony.[1] Dressed and went down to the steamer. I was delighted by my first sight of the blue, rushing, healthful-looking Rhone. I thought, as I wandered along the quay, of the singular love and veneration which rivers excite in those who live on their banks; of the feeling of the Hindoos about the Ganges; of the Hebrews about the Jordan; of the Egyptians about the Nile; of the Romans,

"Cuique fuit rerum promissa potentia Tibrin;—"

of the Germans about the Rhine. Is it that rivers have, in a greater degree than almost any other inanimate object, the appearance of animation, and something resembling character? They are sometimes slow and dark-looking; sometimes fierce and impetuous; sometimes bright, dancing, and almost flippant. The attachment of the French for the Rhone may be explained into a very natural sympathy. It is a vehement, rapid stream. It seems cheerful and full of animal spirits, even to petulance. But this is all fanciful.'[2]

'*October* 26.—On board the steamer for Avignon. Saw the famous junction of the two rivers, and thought of Lord

[1] 'Swift early adopted,' says Sir Walter Scott, 'the custom of observing his birthday as a term, not of joy, but of sorrow, and of reading, when it annually recurred, the striking passage of Scripture in which Job laments and execrates the day upon which it was said in his father's house "that a man child was born." '

'Antony' may possibly be an allusion to the 11th scene of the 3rd act of 'Antony and Cleopatra:'

It is my birthday,
I had thought to have held it poor.

It is more than possible that the reference was to the fine passage commencing,

They tell me 'tis my birthday, and I'll keep it
With double pomp of sadness:

in the 1st act of 'All for Love, or the World well lost.' The lines occur in one of Macaulay's three favourite dialogues of Dryden. See vol. vii, p. 157, of the Albany edn. of Macaulay's Works, and the footnote on p. 537 of this book. (1909.)

[2] On September 9, 1853, Macaulay writes at Geneva: 'We walked to the junction of the Rhone and the Arve. My old friend the Rhone is what he is down at Pont St. Esprit,—the bluest, brightest, swiftest, most joyous of rivers.'

Chatham's simile.[1] But his expression "languid, though of no depth," is hardly just to the Saône, however just it may be to the Duke of Newcastle. We went down at a noble rate. The day, which had been dank and foggy, became exceedingly beautiful. After we had left Valence the scenery grew wilder; the hills bare and rocky like the sides of Lethe water in Cumberland; the mountains of Dauphiné in the distance reminded me of the outline of Ceylon as I saw it from the sea; and, here and there, I could catch a glimpse of white peaks which I fancied to be the summits of the Alps. I chatted with the French gentlemen on board, and found them intelligent and polite. We talked of their roads and public works, and they complimented me on my knowledge of French history and geography. "Ah, monsieur, vous avez beaucoup approfondi ces choses-là." The evening was falling when we came to the Pont St. Esprit, a famous work of the monks, which pretends to no ornament and needs none.'

'*October* 28.—The day began to break as we descended into Marseilles. It was Sunday; but the town seemed only so much the gayer. I looked hard for churches, but for a long time I saw none. At last I heard bells, and the noise guided me to a chapel, mean inside, and mean outside, but crowded as Simeon's church used to be crowded at Cambridge. The Mass was nearly over. A fine steamer sails to-morrow for Leghorn. I am going to lock this hulking volume up, and I shall next open it in Tuscany.'

'*Wednesday, October* 31.—This was one of the most remarkable days of my life. After being detained, by the idle precautions which are habitual with these small absolute Governments, for an hour on deck, that the passengers might be counted; for another hour in a dirty room, that the agent of police might write down all our names; and for a third hour in another smoky den, while a custom-house officer opened razor-cases to see that they concealed no muslin, and turned over dictionaries to be sure that they contained no treason or blasphemy, I hurried on

[1] 'One fragment of this celebrated oration remains in a state of tolerable preservation. It is the comparison between the coalition of Fox and Newcastle, and the junction of the Rhone and the Saône. "At Lyons," said Pitt, "I was taken to see the place where the two rivers meet; the one gentle, feeble, languid, and, though languid, yet of no depth; the other a boisterous and impetuous torrent. But different as they are, they meet at last." '—Macaulay's Essay on Chatham.

shore, and by seven in the morning I was in the streets of Genoa. Never have I been more struck and enchanted. There was nothing mean or small to break the charm, as one huge, massy, towering palace succeeded to another. True it is that none of these magnificent piles is a strikingly good architectural composition; but the general effect is majestic beyond description. When the King of Sardinia became sovereign of Genoa, he bought the house of the Durazzo family, and found himself at once lodged as nobly as a great prince need wish to be. What a city, where a king has only to go into the market to buy a Luxembourg or a St. James's! Next to the palaces, or rather quite as much, I admired the churches. Outside they are poor and bad, but within they dazzled and pleased me more than I can express. It was the awakening of a new sense, the discovery of an unsuspected pleasure. I had drawn all my notions of classical interiors from the cold, white, and naked walls of such buildings as St. Paul's or St. Geneviève's; but the first church door that I opened at Genoa let me into another world. One harmonious glow pervaded the whole of the long Corinthian arcade from the entrance to the altar. In this way I passed the day, greatly excited and delighted.'

With this, perhaps the only jingling sentence which he ever left unblotted, Macaulay closes the account of his first, but far from his last, visit to the queen of the Tyrrhenian sea. To the end of his days, when comparing, as he loved to compare, the claims of European cities to the prize of beauty, he would place at the head of the list the august names of Oxford, Edinburgh, and Genoa.

'*November* 2.—I shall always have an interesting recollection of Pisa. There is something pleasing in the way in which all the monuments of Pisan greatness lie together, in a place not unlike the close of an English cathedral, surrounded with green turf, still kept in the most perfect preservation, and evidently matters of admiration and of pride to the whole population. Pisa has always had a great hold on my mind: partly from its misfortunes, and partly, I believe, because my first notions about the Italian Republics were derived from Sismondi, whom I read while at school; and Sismondi, who is, or fancies that he is, of Pisan descent, does all in his power to make the country of his ancestors an object of interest. I like Pisa, too, for having been Ghibelline. After the time of Frederick Barbarossa my preference, as far as one can have preferences in so wretched a question, are all Ghibelline.

'As I approached Florence, the day became brighter; and the country looked, not indeed strikingly beautiful, but very pleasing. The sight of the olive-trees interested me much. I had, indeed, seen what I was told were olive-trees, as I was whirled down the Rhone from Lyons to Avignon; but they might, for anything I saw, have been willows or ash-trees. Now they stood, covered with berries, along the road for miles. I looked at them with the same sort of feeling with which Washington Irving says that he heard the nightingale for the first time when he came to England, after having read descriptions of her in poets from his childhood. I thought of the Hebrews, and their numerous images drawn from the olive; of the veneration in which the tree was held by the Athenians; of Lysias's speech; of the fine ode in the Œdipus at Colonus; of Virgil and Lorenzo de' Medici. Surely it is better to travel in mature years, with all these things in one's head, than to rush over the Continent while still a boy!'

'*Florence, November* 3.—Up before eight, and read Boiardo, at breakfast. My rooms look into a court adorned with orange trees and marble statues. I never look at the statues without thinking of poor Mignon.

> Und Marmorbilder stehn und sehn mich an:
> Was hat man dir, du armes Kind, gethan?

I know no two lines in the world which I would sooner have written than those. I went to a Gabinetto Litterario hard by, subscribed, and read the last English newspapers. I crossed the river, and walked through some of the rooms in the Palazzo Pitti; greatly admiring a little painting by Raphael from Ezekiel, which was so fine that it almost reconciled me to seeing God the Father on canvas.

'Then to the Church of Santa Croce: an ugly mean outside; and not much to admire in the architecture within, but consecrated by the dust of some of the greatest men that ever lived. It was to me what a first visit to Westminster Abbey would be to an American. The first tomb which caught my eye, as I entered, was that of Michael Angelo. I was much moved, and still more so when going forward, I saw the stately monument lately erected to Dante. The figure of the poet seemed to me fine and finely

placed; and the inscription very happy; his own words, the proclamation which resounds through the shades when Virgil returns—

Onorate l'altissimo poeta.

The two allegorical figures were not much to my taste. It is particularly absurd to represent Poetry weeping for Dante. These weeping figures are all very well, when a tomb is erected to a person lately dead; but, when a group of sculpture is set up over a man who has been dead more than five hundred years, such lamentation is nonsensical. Who can help laughing at the thought of tears of regret shed because a man who was born in the time of our Henry the Third is not still alive? Yet I was very near shedding tears of a different kind as I looked at this magnificent monument, and thought of the sufferings of the great poet, and of his incomparable genius, and of all the pleasure which I have derived from him, and of his death in exile, and of the late justice of posterity. I believe that very few people have ever had their minds more thoroughly penetrated with the spirit of any great work than mine is with that of the Divine Comedy. His execution I take to be far beyond that of any other artist who has operated on the imagination by means of words

O degli altri poeti onore e lume,
Vagliami il lungo studio e 'l grande amore
Che m' han fatto cercar lo tuo volume.[1]

I was proud to think that I had a right to apostrophise him thus. I went on, and next I came to the tomb of Alfieri, set up by his mistress, the Countess of Albany. I passed forward, and in another minute my foot was on the grave of Machiavel.'

'*November* 7.—While walking about the town, I picked up a little Mass-book, and read for the first time in my life—strange, and almost disgraceful, that it should be so—the service of the Mass from beginning to end. It seemed to me inferior to our Communion service in one most important point. The phraseology of Christianity has in Latin a barbarous air, being altogether later than the age of pure Latinity. But the English language has grown up in

[1] Glory and light of all the tuneful train,
May it avail me that I long with zeal
Have sought thy volume, and with love immense
Have conn'd it o'er!

Christian times; and the whole vocabulary of Christianity is incorporated with it. The fine passage in the Communion Service: "Therefore with Angels, and Archangels, and all the company of heaven," is English of the best and most genuine description. But the answering passage in the Mass: "Laudant Angeli, adorant dominationes, tremunt potestates, cœli Cœlorumque virtutes ac beati Seraphim," would not merely have appeared barbarous, but would have been utterly unintelligible,—a mere gibberish,—to every one of the great masters of the Latin tongue, Plautus, Cicero, Cæsar, and Catullus. I doubt whether even Claudian would have understood it. I intend to frequent the Romish worship till I come thoroughly to understand this ceremonial.'

Florence: November 4, 1838.

Dear Napier,—

I arrived here the day before yesterday in very good health, after a journey of three weeks from London. I find that it will be absolutely impossible for me to execute the plan of reviewing Panizzi's edition of Boiardo in time for your next Number. I have not been able to read one half of Boiardo's poem, and, in order to do what I propose, I must read Berni's rifacimento too, as well as Pulci's Morgante; and this, I fear, will be quite out of the question. The day is not long enough for what I want to do in it: and if I find this to be the case at Florence, I may be sure that at Rome I shall have still less leisure. However, it is my full intention to be in England in February, and, on the day on which I reach London, I will begin to work for you on Lord Clive.

I know little English news. I steal a quarter of an hour in the day from marbles and altar-pieces to read the Times, and the Morning Chronicle. Lord Brougham, I have a notion, will often wish that he had left Lord Durham alone. Lord Durham will be in the House of Lords, with his pugnacious spirit, and with his high reputation among the Radicals. In oratorical abilities there is, of course, no comparison between the men; but Lord Durham has quite talents enough to expose Lord Brougham, and has quite as

much acrimony and a great deal more nerve than Lord Brougham himself. I should very much like to know what the general opinion about this matter is. My own suspicion is that the Tories in the House of Lords will lose reputation, though I do not imagine that the Government will gain any. As to Brougham, he has reached that happy point at which it is equally impossible for him to gain character and lose it.

Ever, dear Napier,

Yours most truly

T. B. MACAULAY.

There was, indeed, very little reputation to be gained out of the business. No episode in our political history is more replete with warning to honest and public-spirited men, who, in seeking to serve their country, forget what is due to their own interests and their own security, than the story of Lord Durham. He accepted the Governorship of Canada during a supreme crisis in the affairs of that colony. He carried with him thither the confidence of the great body of his fellow-countrymen—a confidence which he had conciliated by his earnest and courageous demeanour in the warfare of Parliament; by the knowledge that, when he undertook his present mission, he had stipulated for the largest responsibility, and refused the smallest emolument; and, above all, by the appeal which, before leaving England, he made in the House of Lords to friends and foes alike. 'I feel,' he said, 'that I can accomplish my task only by the cordial and energetic support,—a support which I am sure I shall obtain,—of my noble friends the members of her Majesty's Cabinet; by the co-operation of the Imperial Parliament; and, permit me to say, by the generous forbearance of the noble lords opposite, to whom I have always been politically opposed.' From his political opponents, in the place of generous forbearance, he met with unremitting persecution; and as for the character of the support which he obtained from those Ministers who had themselves placed him in the forefront of the battle, it is more becoming to leave it for Tory historians to recount the tale. To Lord Brougham's treatment of his former colleague justice is done in the last sentence of Macaulay's letter. But on one point Macaulay was mistaken. Lord Durham never called his enemies to account, and still less his friends. His heart was broken, but not estranged. His tongue, which had too seldom, perhaps, refrained from speaking out what was brave and true, could keep silence when silence was demanded by the claims of past alliances and the memory of old friendships. During the remnant of his life, Lord Durham continued to support the Whig Cabinet with all the loyalty and modesty of a young Peer hopeful of an Under Secretaryship, or grateful for having been selected to second the Address. But none the less had the blow gone home; and the Administration, which had so long been trembling and dying, was destined to survive by many months the most single-minded and high-natured among that company of statesmen who had wrought for our people the great deliverance of 1832.

'*Friday, November* 9.—Went to Dante's "bel San Giovanni," and heard Mass there. Then to another church, and heard another Mass. I begin to follow the service as well as the body of the hearers, which is not saying much. I paid a third visit to Santa Croce, and noticed in the cloister a monument to a little baby, "Il più bel bambino che mai fosse;" not a very wise inscription for parents to put up; but it brought tears into my eyes. I thought of the little thing who lies in the cemetery at Calcutta.[1] I meditated some verses for my ballad of Romulus,[2] but made only one stanza to my satisfaction. I finished Casti's Giuli Tre, and have liked it less than I expected. The humour of the work consists in endless repetition. It is a very hazardous experiment to attempt to make fun out of that which is the great cause of yawning, perpetual harping on the same topic. Sir Walter Scott was very fond of this device for exciting laughter: as witness Lady Margaret, and "his

[1] A little niece, who died in 1837, three months old.

[2] The poem which was published as 'The Prophecy of Capys.'

Sacred Majesty's disjune;" Claude Halcro, and Glorious John; Sir Dugald Dalgetty, and the Marischal College of Aberdeen; the Baillie, and his father, the deacon; old Trapbois, and "for a consideration." It answered, perhaps, once, for ten times that it failed.'

'*Saturday, November* 10, 1838.—A letter from Mr. Aubin, our Chargé d'Affaires here, to say that he has a confidential message for me, and asking when he might call. I sent word that I would call on him as soon as I had breakfasted. I had little doubt that the Ministers wanted my help in Parliament. I went to him, and he delivered to me two letters—one from Lord Melbourne, and the other from Rice. They press me to become Judge Advocate and assure me that a seat in Parliament may be procured for me with little expense. Rice dwells much on the salary, which he says is 2,500*l.* a year. I thought it had been cut down; but he must know. He also talks of the other advantages connected with the place. The offer did not strike me as even tempting. The money I do not want. I have little; but I have enough. The Right Honourable before my name is a bauble which it would be far, very far indeed, beneath me to care about. The power is nothing. As an independent Member of Parliament I should have infinitely greater power. Nay, as I am, I have far greater power. I can now write what I choose; and what I write may produce considerable effect on the public mind. In office I must necessarily be under restraint. If, indeed, I had a Cabinet Office I should be able to do something in support of my own views of government; but a man in office, and out of the Cabinet, is a mere slave. I have left the bitterness of that slavery once. Though I hardly knew where to turn for a morsel of bread, my spirit rose against the intolerable thraldom. I was mutinous, and once actually resigned. I then went to India to get independence, and I have got it, and I will keep it. So I wrote to Lord Melbourne and Rice. I told them that I would cheerfully do anything to serve them in Parliament; but that office, except indeed office of the highest rank, to which I have no pretensions, had not the smallest allurements for me; that the situation of a subordinate was unsuited to my temper; that I had tried it, that I had found it insupportable, and that I would never make the experiment again. I begged them not to imagine that I thought a place which Mackintosh had been anxious to obtain beneath me. Very far from it. I admitted it to be above the market price of my services; but it was below the fancy price which a peculiar turn of mind led me to put on my liberty and my studies. The only thing that would ever tempt me to give up my liberty and my studies was the power to effect great things; and of that power, as they well knew, no man had so little as a man in office out of the Cabinet.

'I never in my life took an important step with greater confidence in my own judgment, or with a firmer conviction that I was doing the best for my own happiness, honour, and usefulness. I have no relentings. If they take me at my word, and contrive to bring me into Parliament without office, I shall be, I think, in the most eligible of situations: but this I do not much expect.'

On the 12th of November Macaulay set out from Florence, by way of Cortona and Perugia.

'*Tuesday, November* 13.—My journey lay over the field of Thrasymenus, and, as soon as the sun rose, I read Livy's description of the scene, and wished that I had brought Polybius too. However, it mattered little, for I could see absolutely nothing. I was exactly in the situation of the consul Flaminius; completely hid in the morning fog. I did not discern the lake till the road came quite close to it, and then my view extended only over a few yards of reedy mud and shallow water, so that I can truly say that I have seen precisely what the Roman army saw on that day. After some time we began to ascend, and came at last, with the help of oxen, to an eminence on which the sun shone bright. All the hill tops round were perfectly clear, and the fog lay in the valley below like a lake winding among the mountains. I then understood the immense advantage which Hannibal derived from keeping his divisions on the heights, where he could see them all, and where they could all see each other, while the Romans were stumbling and groping, without the possibility of concert, through the thick haze below. Towards evening I began to notice the white oxen of Clitumnus.'

'*November* 14.—Up and off by half-past four. The sun triumphed over the mist just as I reached Narni. The scenery was really glorious: far finer than that of Matlock or the Wye, in something of the same style. The pale line of the river which brawled below, though in itself not agreeable, was interesting from classical recollections. I thought how happily Virgil had touched the most striking and characteristic features of Italian landscape. As the day wore on, I saw the Tiber for the first time. I saw Mount Soracte, and, unlike Lord Byron, I loved the sight for Horace's sake.[1] And so I came to Civita Castellana, where I determined to stop, though it was not much after two. I did not wish to enter Rôme by night. I wanted to see the dome of St. Peter's from a distance, and to observe the city disclosing itself by degrees.'

'*November* 15.—On arriving this morning, I walked straight from the hotel door to St. Peter's. I was so much excited by the expectation of what I was to see that I could notice nothing else. I was quite nervous. The colonnade in front is noble—very, very noble: yet it disappointed me; and would have done so had it been the portico of Paradise. In I went, and I was for a minute fairly stunned by the magnificence and harmony of the interior. I never in my life saw, and never, I suppose, shall again see, anything so astonishingly beautiful. I really could have cried with pleasure. I rambled about for half an hour or more, paying little or no attention to details, but enjoying the effect of the sublime whole.

'In rambling back to the Piazza di Spagna I found myself before the portico of the Pantheon. I was as much struck and affected as if I had not known that there was such a building in Rome. There it was, the work of the age of Augustus; the work of men who lived with Cicero, and Cæsar, and Horace, and Virgil. What would they have said if they had seen it stuck all over with "Invito Sacro," and "Indulgenza perpetua"?'

'*November* 16.—As soon as it cleared up I hastened to St. Peter's again. There was one spot near which an Englishman could not help lingering for a few minutes. In one of the side aisles, a monument by Canova marks the burial-place of the latest princes of the House of Stuart; James the Third; Charles Edward; and Cardinal York, whom the last of the Jacobites affected to call Henry the Ninth. I then went towards the river, to the spot where the old Pons Sublicius stood and looked about to see how my Horatius agreed with the topography. Pretty well: but his house must be on Mount Palatine; for he would never see Mount Cœlius from the spot where he fought.[2] Thence to the

[1] See Canto IV of 'Childe Harold,' stanzas 74 to 77.

[2] But he saw on Palatinus
The white porch of his home,
And he spake to the noble river
That rolls by the walls of Rome.

Capitol, and wandered through the gallery of paintings placed there by Benedict the Fourteenth, my favourite Pope.'

'*November* 22.—I went to see a famous relic of antiquity lately discovered; the baker's tomb. This baker and his wife, and the date of his baking performances, and the meaning of that mysterious word "apparet," are now the great subjects of discussion amongst the best circles of Rome. Strange city; once sovereign of the world, whose news now consists in the discovery of the buried tomb of a tradesman who has been dead at least fifteen hundred years! The question whether "apparet" is the short for "apparitoris" is to them what the Licinian Rogations and the Agrarian Laws were to their fathers; what the Catholic Bill and the Reform Bill have been to us. Yet, to indulge in a sort of reflection which I often fall into here, the day may come when London, then dwindled to the dimensions of the parish of St. Martin's, and supported in its decay by the expenditure of wealthy Patagonians and New Zealanders,[1] may have no more important questions to decide than the arrangement of "Afflictions sore long time I bore" on the grave-stone of the wife of some baker in Houndsditch.'

'*November* 26.—At ten Colyar came, and we set out.[2] The day would furnish matter for a volume. We went to the English College, and walked about the cloisters; interesting cloisters to an Englishman. There lie several of our native dignitaries who died at Rome before the Reformation. There lie, too, the bones of many Jacobites, honest martyrs to a worthless cause. We looked into the refectory, much like the halls of the small colleges at Cambridge in my time,—that of Peterhouse, for example,—and smelling strongly of yesterday's supper, which strengthened the resemblance. We found the principal, Dr. Wiseman, a young ecclesiastic full of health and vigour,—much such a ruddy, strapping divine as I remember Whewell eighteen

[1] It may be worth mention that the celebrated New Zealander appears at the end of the third paragraph of the essay on Von Ranke's History of the Popes.

[2] Mr. Colyar was an English Catholic gentleman, residing in Rome, who was particularly well-informed with regard to everything concerning the city, ancient and modern. He was in high favour with priests and prelates, and was therefore an invaluable acquaintance for English travellers; at whose disposal he was very ready to place both his knowledge and his influence.

years ago,—in purple vestments standing in the cloister. With him was Lord Clifford, in the uniform of a Deputy Lieutenant of Devonshire, great from paying his court to Pope Gregory. He was extremely civil, and talked with gratitude of General Macaulay's kindness to him in Italy. Wiseman chimed in. Indeed, I hear my uncle's praises wherever I go. Lord Clifford is not at all like my notion of a great Catholic Peer of old family. I always imagine such an one proud and stately, with the air of a man of rank, but not of fashion; such a personage as Mrs. Inchbald's Catholic Lord in the Simple Story, or as Sir Walter's Lord Glenallan without the remorse. But Lord Clifford is all quicksilver. He talked about the Pope's reception of him and Lord Shrewsbury. His Holiness is in high health and spirits, and is a little more merry than strict formalists approve. Lord Shrewsbury says that he seems one moment to be a boy eager for play, and the next to be another Leo arresting the march of Attila. The poor King of Prussia, it seems, is Attila. We went into Dr. Wiseman's apartments, which are snugly furnished in the English style, and altogether are very like the rooms of a senior Fellow of Trinity. After visiting the library, where I had a sight of the identical copy of Fox's Book of Martyrs in which Parsons made notes for his answer, I took leave of my countrymen with great good-will.

'We then crossed the river, and turned into the Vatican. I had walked a hundred feet through the library without the faintest notion that I was in it. No books, no shelves were visible. All was light and brilliant; nothing but white, and red, and gold; blazing arabesques, and paintings on ceiling and wall. And this was the Vatican Library; a place which I used to think of with awe as a far sterner and darker Bodleian! The books and manuscripts are all in low wooden cases ranged round the walls; and, as these cases are painted in light colours, they harmonise with the gay aspect of everything around them, and might be supposed to contain musical instruments, masquerade dresses, or china for the dances and suppers for which the apartments seem to be meant. They bore inscriptions, however, more suited to my notions of the place.

'Thence I went through the Museum, quite distracted by the multitude and magnificence of the objects which it contained. The splendour of the ancient marbles, the alabaster, the huge masses of porphyry, the granites of various colours, made the whole seem like a fairy region.

I wonder that nobody in this moneyed and luxurious age attempts to open quarries like those which supplied the ancients. The wealth of modern Europe is far greater than that of the Roman Empire; and these things are highly valued, and bought at enormous prices. And yet we content ourselves with digging for them in the ruins of this old city and its suburbs, and never think of seeking them in the rocks from which the Romans extracted them. Africa and Greece were the parts of the world which afforded the most costly marbles; and, perhaps, now that the French have settled in Africa, and that a Bavarian prince reigns in Greece, some researches may be made.

'I looked into the apartments where the works in mosaic are carried on. A noble figure of Isaiah by Raphael had just been completed. We ought to have a similar workshop connected with the National Gallery. What a glorious vestibule to a palace might be made with the Cartoons in mosaic covering the walls! The best portraits of the great men of England, reproduced in the same material, beginning with Holbein's Wolsey and More, and coming down to Lawrence's Wellington and Canning, would be worthy decorations to the new Houses of Parliament. I should like to see the walls of St. Paul's encrusted with porphyry and verde antique, and the ceiling and dome glittering with mosaics and gold.

'The Demosthenes is very noble. There can be no doubt about the face of Demosthenes. There are two busts of him in the Vatican, besides this statue. They are all exactly alike, being distinguished by the strong projection of the upper lip. The face is lean, wrinkled, and haggard; the expression singularly stern and intense. You see that he was no trifler, no jester, no voluptuary; but a man whose soul was devoured by ambition, and constantly on the stretch. The soft, sleek, plump, almost sleepy, though handsome, face of Æschines presents a remarkable contrast. I was much interested by the bust of Julius, with the head veiled. It is a most striking countenance, indeed. He looks like a man meant to be master of the world. The endless succession of these noble works bewildered me, and I went home almost exhausted with pleasurable excitement.'

In a letter written during the latter half of December, Macaulay gives his impressions of the Papal Government at greater length than in his diary. 'Rome was full enough of English when I arrived, but now the crowd is insupportable. I avoid society, as much as I can without being churlish: for it is boyish to come to Italy for the purpose of mixing with the set, and hearing the tattle, to which one is accustomed in Mayfair. The Government treats us very well. The Pope winks at a Protestant chapel, and indulges us in a reading-room, where the Times and Morning Chronicle make their appearance twelve days after they are published in London. It is a pleasant city for an English traveller. He is not harassed or restrained. He lives as he likes, and reads what he likes, and suffers little from the vices of the administration; but I can conceive nothing more insupportable than the situation of a layman who should be a subject of the Pope. In this government there is no avenue to distinction for any but priests. Every office of importance, diplomatic, financial, and judicial, is held by the clergy. A prelate, armed with most formidable powers, superintends the police of the streets. The military department is directed by a Commission, over which a Cardinal presides. Some petty magistracy is the highest promotion to which a lawyer can look forward; and the greatest nobles of this singular State can expect nothing better than some place in the Pope's household, which may entitle them to walk in procession on the great festivals. Imagine what England would be if all the members of Parliament, the Ministers, the Judges, the Ambassadors, the Governors of Colonies, the very Commanders-in-Chief and Lords of the Admiralty, were, without one exception, bishops or priests; and if the highest post open to the noblest, wealthiest, ablest, and most ambitious layman were a Lordship of the Bedchamber! And yet this would not come up to the truth, for our clergy can marry; but here every man who takes a wife cuts himself off for ever from all dignity and power, and puts himself into the same position as a Catholic in England before the Emancipation Bill. The Church is therefore filled with men who are led into it merely by ambition, and who, though they might have been useful and respectable as laymen, are hypocritical and immoral as churchmen; while on the other hand the State suffers greatly, for you may guess what sort of Secretaries at War and Chancellors of the Exchequer are likely to be found among bishops and canons. Corruption infects all the public offices. Old women above, liars and cheats below—that is the Papal administration. The States of the Pope are, I suppose, the worst governed in the civilised world; and the imbecility of the police, the venality of the public servants, the desolation of the country, and the wretchedness of the people, force themselves on the observation of the most heedless traveller. It is hardly an exaggeration to say that the population seems to consist chiefly of foreigners, priests, and paupers. Indeed, whenever you meet a man who is neither in canonicals nor rags, you may bet two to one that he is an Englishman.'

'*Tuesday, December* 4.—I climbed the Janiculan Hill to the Convent of St. Onofrio, and went into the church. It contains only one object of interest; a stone in the pavement, with the words "Hic jacet Torquatus Tassus." He died in this convent, just before the day fixed for his coronation at the Capitol. I was not quite in such raptures as I have heard other people profess. Tasso is not one of my favourites, either as a man or a poet. There is too little of the fine frenzy in his verses, and too much in his life.

'I called on the American Consul. He was very civil, and, à la mode d'Amérique, talked to me about my writings.[1] I turned the conversation instantly. No topic,

[1] An injury of this nature was still fresh in Macaulay's mind. Writing from Florence he says: 'I do not scamper about with a note-book in my hand, and a cicerone gabbling in my ear; but I go often and stay long at the places which interest me. I sit quietly an hour or two every morning in the finest churches, watching the ceremonial, and the demeanour of the congregation. I seldom pass less than an hour daily in the Tribune, where the Venus de Medici stands, surrounded by other master-pieces in sculpture and painting. Yesterday, as I was looking at some superb portraits by Raphael and Titian, a Yankee clergyman introduced himself to me; told me that he had heard who I was; that he begged to thank me for my writings in the name of his countrymen; that he had himself

I am glad to say, is less to my taste. I dined by myself, and read an execrably stupid novel called Tylney Hall. Why do I read such stuff?'

'*Saturday, December* 8.—No letters at the post-office; the reading-room shut; and the churches full. It is the feast of the Immaculate Conception of the Virgin Mary; a day held in prodigious honour by the Franciscans, who first, I believe, introduced this absurd notion, which even within the Catholic Church the Dominicans have always combated, and which the Council of Trent, if I remember Fra Paolo right, refused to pronounce orthodox. I spent much of the day over Smollett's History. It is exceedingly bad: detestably so.[1] I cannot think what had happened to him. His carelessness, partiality, passion, idle invective, gross ignorance of facts, and crude general theories, do not surprise me much. But the style wherever he tries to be elevated, and wherever he attempts to draw a character, is perfectly nauseous; which I cannot understand. He says of old Horace Walpole that he was an ambassador without dignity, and a plenipotentiary without address. I declare I would rather have a hand cut off than publish such a precious antithesis.'

'*Tuesday, December* 18.—I stayed at home till late, reading and meditating. I have altered some parts of Horatius to my mind; and I have thought a good deal during the last few days about my History. The great difficulty of a work of this kind is the beginning. How is it to be joined on to the preceding events! Where am I to commence it?

reprinted my paper on Bacon; that it had a great run in the States; and that my name was greatly respected there. I bowed, thanked him, and stole away; leaving the Grand Duke's pictures a great deal sooner than I had intended.'

The same scene, with the same actors, was repeated on the next day beneath the frown of the awful Duke who sits aloft in the Chapel of the Medici, adjoining the Church of San Lorenzo; whither Macaulay had repaired 'to snatch a Mass, as one of Sir Walter's heroes says.'

[1] Even Charles Lamb, who was far too chivalrous to leave a favourite author in the lurch, can find nothing to say in defence of Smollett's History except a delightful, but perfectly gratuitous, piece of impertinence to Hume. 'Smollett they' (the Scotch) 'have neither forgotten nor forgiven for his delineation of Rory and his companion upon their first introduction to our metropolis. Speak of Smollett as a great genius, and they will retort upon you Hume's History compared with *his* Continuation of it. What if the historian had continued Humphrey Clinker?'

I cannot plunge, slap dash, into the middle of events and characters. I cannot, on the other hand, write a history of the whole reign of James the Second as a preface to the history of William the Third; and, if I did, a history of Charles the Second would still be equally necessary as a preface to that of the reign of James the Second. I sympathise with the poor man who began the war of Troy "gemino ab ovo." But, after much consideration, I think that I can manage, by the help of an introductory chapter or two, to glide imperceptibly into the full current of my narrative. I am more and more in love with the subject. I really think that posterity will not willingly let my book die.

'To St. Peter's again. This is becoming a daily visit.'

Rome: December 19, 1838.

Dear Lord Lansdowne,—

I have received your kind letter, and thank you for it. I have now had ample time to reflect on the determination which I expressed to Lord Melbourne and Rice; and I am every day more and more satisfied that the course which I have taken is the best for myself, and the best also for the Government. If I thought it right to follow altogether my own inclinations, I should entirely avoid public life. But I feel that these are not times for flinching from the Whig banner. I feel that at this juncture no friend of toleration and of temperate liberty is justified in withholding his support from the Ministers; and I think that, in the present unprecedented and inexplicable scarcity of Parliamentary talent among the young men of England, a little of that talent may be of as much service as far greater powers in times more fertile of eloquence. I would therefore make some sacrifice of ease, leisure, and money, in order to serve the Government in the House of Commons. But I do not think that public duty at all requires me to overcome the dislike which I feel for official life. On the contrary, my duty and inclination are here on one side. For I am certain that, as an independent Member of Parliament, I should have far more weight than as Judge Advocate. It is impossible for me to be ignorant of my position in the world, and of the misconstructions to which it exposes me. Entering Parliament as Judge Advocate, I should be considered as a mere political adventurer. My speeches might be complimented as creditable rhetorical performances; but they would never produce the sort of effect which I have seen produced by very rude sentences stammered by such men as Lord Spencer and Lord Ebrington. If I enter Parliament as a placeman, nobody will believe, what nevertheless is the truth, that I am quite as independent, quite as indifferent to salary, as the Duke of Northumberland can be. As I have none of that authority which belongs to large fortune and high rank, it is absolutely necessary to my comfort, and will be greatly conducive to my usefulness, that I should have the authority which belongs to proved disinterestedness. I should also, as a Member of Parliament not in office, have leisure for other pursuits, which I cannot bear to think of quitting, and which you kindly say you do not wish me to quit. A life of literary repose would be most to my own taste. Of my literary repose I am, however, willing to sacrifice exactly as much as public duty requires me to sacrifice; but I will sacrifice no more; and by going into Parliament without office I both make a smaller personal sacrifice, and do more service to the public, than by taking office. I hope that you will think these reasons satisfactory; for you well know that, next to my own approbation, it would be my first wish to have yours.

I have been more delighted than I can express by Italy, and above all by Rome. I had no notion that an excitement so powerful and so agreeable, still untried by me, was to be found in the world. I quite agree with you in thinking that the first impression is the weakest; and that time, familiarity, and reflection, which destroy the charm of so many objects, heighten the attractions of this wonderful place. I hardly know whether I am more interested by the old Rome or by the new Rome—by the monuments of the extraordinary empire which has perished, or by the institutions of the still more extraordinary empire which, after all the shocks which it has sustained, is still full of life and of perverted energy. If there were not a single ruin, fine building, picture, or statue in Rome, I should think myself repaid for my journey by having seen the head-quarters of Catholicism, and learned something of the nature and effect of the strange Brahminical government established in the Ecclesiastical State. Have you read Von Ranke's History of the Papacy since the Reformation? I have owed much of my pleasure here to what I learned from him.

Rome is full of English. We could furnish exceedingly respectable Houses of Lords and Commons. There are at present twice as many coroneted carriages in the Piazza di Spagna as in St. James's parish.

Ever, my dear Lord,

Yours most faithfully

T. B. MACAULAY.

'*Saturday, December* 22.—The Canadian insurrection seems to be entirely crushed. I fear that the victorious caste will not be satisfied without punishments so rigorous as would dishonour the English Government in the eyes of all Europe, and in our own eyes ten years hence. I wish that Ministers would remember that the very people who bawl for wholesale executions now will be the first to abuse them for cruelty when this excitement is gone by. The Duke of Cumberland in Scotland did only what all England was clamouring for; but all England changed its mind, and the Duke became unpopular for yielding to the cry which was set up in a moment of fear and resentment. As to hanging men by the hundred, it really is not to be thought of with patience. Ten or twelve examples well selected would be quite sufficient, together with the slaughter and burning which have already taken place. If the American prisoners are transported, or kept on the roads at hard labour, their punishment will do more good than a great wholesale execution. The savage language of some of the newspapers, both in Canada and London, makes me doubt whether we are so far beyond the detestable Carlists and Christinos of Spain as I had hoped.

'I read a good deal of Gibbon. He is grossly partial to the pagan persecutors; quite offensively so. His opinion of the Christian fathers is very little removed from mine; but his excuses for the tyranny of their oppressors give to his book the character which Porson describes.[1] He writes like a man who had received some personal injury from Christianity, and wished to be revenged on it, and all its professors. I dined at home, and read some more of Pelham in the evening. I know few things of the kind so good as the character of Lord Vincent.'

Macaulay, who had not yet lost his taste for a show, took full advantage of his presence at Rome during the Christmas festivals. He pronounced the procession in St. Peter's to be the finest thing of the kind that he had ever seen: but it would be unfair on him to expose to general criticism his off-hand description of a pageant which no written sentences, however carefully arranged and polished, could depict one-tenth as vividly as the colours in which Roberts loved to paint the swarming aisles of a stately cathedral. And yet, perhaps, not even Titian himself (although in a picture at the Louvre, according to Mr. Ruskin, he has put a whole scheme of dogmatic theology into the backs of a row of bishops) could find means to represent on canvas the sentiments which suggest themselves to the spectators of this the most impressive of earthly ceremonies. 'I was deeply moved,' says Macaulay, 'by reflecting on the immense antiquity of the Papal dignity, which can certainly boast of a far longer, clear, known, and uninterrupted succession than any dignity in the world; linking together, as it does, the two great ages of human civilisation. Our modern

[1] The passage alluded to occurs in the Preface to the Letters to Archdeacon Travis, which Macaulay regarded as a work of scholarship second only to Bentley's Phalaris. 'His' (Gibbon's) 'reflections are often just and profound. He pleads eloquently for the rights of mankind, and the duty of toleration; nor does his humanity ever slumber unless when women are ravished or the Christians persecuted. . . . He often makes, when he cannot readily find, an occasion to insult our religion; which he hates so cordially that he might seem to revenge some personal insult. Such is his eagerness in the cause, that he stoops to the most despicable pun, or to the most awkward perversion of language, for the pleasure of turning the Scriptures into ribaldry, or of calling Jesus an imposter.

feudal kings are mere upstarts compared with the successors in regular order, not, to be sure, of Peter, but of Silvester and Leo the Great.'

There was one person among the bystanders, through whose brain thoughts of this nature were doubtless coursing even more rapidly than through Macaulay's own. 'On Christmas eve I found Gladstone in the throng; and I accosted him; as we had met, though we had never been introduced to each other. He received my advances with very great *empressement* indeed, and we had a good deal of pleasant talk.'

'*December* 29.—I went to Torlonia's to get money for my journey. What a curious effect it has to see a bank in a palace, among orange trees, colonnades, marble statues, and all the signs of the most refined luxury! It carries me back to the days of the merchant princes of Florence; when philosophers, poets, and painters crowded to the house of Cosmo de' Medici. I drew one hundred pounds worth of scudi, and had to lug it through the streets in a huge canvas bag, muttering with strong feeling Pope's "Blest paper credit." I strolled through the whole of the vast collection of the Vatican with increasing pleasure. The Communion of St. Jerome seems to me finer and finer every time that I look at it; and the Transfiguration has at last made a complete conquest of me. In spite of all the faults of the plan, I feel it to be the first picture in the world. Then to St. Peter's for the last time, and rambled about it quite sadly. I could not have believed that it would have pained me so much to part from stone and mortar.'

'*January* 1, 1839.—I shall not soon forget the three days which I passed between Rome and Naples. As I descended the hill of Velletri, the huge Pontine Marsh was spread out below like a sea. I soon got into it; and, thank God, soon got out of it. If the Government has not succeeded in making this swamp salubrious, at any rate measures have been taken for enabling people to stay in it as short a time as possible. The road is raised, dry, and well paved; as hard as a rock, and as straight as an arrow. It reminded me of the road in the Pilgrim's Progress, running through the Slough of Despond, the quagmire in the Valley of the Shadow of Death, and the Enchanted Land. At the frontier the custom-house officer begged me to give him a place in my carriage to Mola. I refused, civilly, but firmly. I gave him three crowns not to plague me by searching my baggage, which indeed was protected by a *lascia passare*. He pocketed the three crowns, but looked very dark and sullen at my refusal to accept his company. Precious fellow; to think that a public functionary to whom a little silver is a bribe is fit society for an English gentleman!

'I had a beautiful view of the Bay of Gaeta, with Vesuvius at an immense distance. The whole country is most interesting historically. They pretend to point out on the road the exact spot where Cicero was murdered. I place little more faith in these localities than in the head of St. Andrew or the spear of Longinus; but it is certain that hereabouts the event took place. The inn at Mola, in which I slept, is called the Villa di Cicerone. The chances are infinite that none of the ruins now extant belonged to Cicero; but it pleased me to think how many great Romans, when Rome was what England is now, loved to pass their occasional holidays on this beautiful coast. I travelled across the low country through which Horace's Liris flows; by the marshes of Minturnæ, where Marius hid himself from the vengeance of Sulla: over the field where Gonsalvo de Cordova gained the great victory of Garigliano. The plain of Capua seemed to retain all its old richness. Since I have been in Italy, I have often thought it very strange that the English have never introduced the olive into any of those vast regions which they have colonised. I do not believe that there is an olive tree in all the United States, or in South Africa, or in Australasia.

'On my journey through the Pontine Marshes I finished Bulwer's Alice. It affected me much, and in a way in which I have not been affected by novels these many years. Indeed, I generally avoid all novels which are said to have much pathos. The suffering which they produce is to me a very real suffering, and of that I have quite enough without them. I think of Bulwer, still, as I have always thought. He has considerable talent and eloquence; but he is fond of writing about what he only half understands, or understands not at all. His taste is bad; and bad from a cause which lies deep and is not to be removed: from want of soundness, manliness, and simplicity of mind. This work, though better than any thing of his that I have read, is far too long.'[1]

[1] ' "My Novel" again,' Macaulay says elsewhere; 'but was not tempted to go on with it. Why is it that I can read twenty

'*Thursday*, *January* 3.—I must say that the accounts which I had heard of Naples are very incorrect. There is far less beggary than at Rome, and far more industry. Rome is a city of priests. It reminded me of the towns in Palestine which were set apart to be inhabited by the Levites. Trade and agriculture seem only to be tolerated as subsidiary to devotion. Men are allowed to work; because, unless somebody works, nobody can live; and, if nobody lives, nobody can pray. But, as soon as you enter Naples, you notice a striking contrast. It is the difference between Sunday and Monday. Here the business of civil life is evidently the great thing, and religion is the accessory. A poet might introduce Naples as Martha, and Rome as Mary. A Catholic may think Mary's the better employment; but even a Catholic, much more a Protestant, would prefer the table of Martha. I must ask many questions about these matters. At present, my impressions are very favourable to Naples. It is the only place in Italy that has seemed to me to have the same sort of vitality which you find in all the great English ports and cities. Rome and Pisa are dead and gone; Florence is not dead, but sleepeth; while Naples overflows with life.

'I have a letter from Empson, who tells me that everybody speaks handsomely about my refusal of the Judge Advocateship. Holt Mackenzie praised the Code highly at Rogers's the other day. I am glad of it. It is, however, a sort of work which must wait long for justice, as I well knew when I laboured at it.'

'*Naples*, *Sunday*, *January* 6.—I climbed to the top of the hill to see Virgil's tomb. The tomb has no interest but what it derives from its name. I do not know the history of this ruin; but, if the tradition be an immemorial tradition—if nobody can fix any time when it originated—I should be inclined to think it authentic. Virgil was just the man whose burial-place was likely to be known to every generation which has lived since his death. There has been no period, from the Augustan age downward, when there were not readers of the Æneid in Italy. The

times over the trash of ——, and that I cannot read Bulwer's books, though I see him to be a man of very considerable parts? It is odd; but of all writers of fiction who possess any talent at all, Bulwer, with very distinguished talent, amuses me the least. "Pelham," perhaps, is an exception. Where lies the secret of being amusing? And how is it that art, eloquence, diligence, may all be employed in making a book dull?'

suspicious time with the religion of the Catholic Church is the early time. I suppose nobody doubts that the sepulchre now shown as that of Christ is the same with the sepulchre of Helena, or that the place now pointed out as the tomb of St. Paul is the same which was so considered in the days of Chrysostom. The local traditions of Christianity are clear enough during the last 1,300 or 1,400 years. It is during the first two or three centuries that the chain fails. Now, as to Virgil, there can be no doubt that his burial-place would have been as well known till the dissolution of the Western Empire as that of Shakespeare is now; and, even in the dark ages, there would always have been a certain number of people interested about his remains. I returned to my hotel exceedingly tired with walking and climbing. I dined; had a pint of bottled porter, worth all the Falernian of these days; and finished the evening by my fireside over Theodore Hook's "Jack Brag." He is a clever, coarse, vulgar writer.'

'*Friday, January* 11.—When I woke it was snowing; so that I determined to give up Pæstum, for which I was rather sorry when, at about eleven, it became fine and clear. But I was not quite well, and it is bitterly cold to a returned Indian. I stayed by my fire, and read Bulwer's Pompeii. It has eloquence and talent, like all his books. It has also more learning than I expected; but it labours under the usual faults of all works in which it is attempted to give moderns a glimpse of ancient manners. After all, between us and them there is a great gulf, which no learning will enable a man to clear. Strength of imagination may empower him to create a world unlike our own; but the chances are a thousand to one that it is not the world which has passed away. Perhaps those act most wisely who, in treating poetically of ancient events, stick to general human nature, avoid gross blunders of costume, and trouble themselves about little more. All attempts to exhibit Romans talking slang, and jesting with each other, however, clever, must be failures. There are a good many pretty obvious blots in Bulwer's book. Why in the name of common sense did Glaucus neglect to make himself a Roman citizen? He, a man of fortune and talents residing in Italy, intimate with Romans of distinction! Arbaces, too, is not a citizen. Rich, powerful, educated, subjects of Rome, dwelling in a considerable Italian town, and highly acceptable in all societies there, yet not citizens! The thing was never heard of, I imagine. The Christianity of Bulwer's book is not to my taste. The Trinity, the Widow's son, the recollections of the preaching of St. Paul, spoil the classical effect of the story. I do not believe that Christianity had, at that time, made the very smallest impression on the educated classes in Italy; some Jews, of course, excepted. Bulwer brings down the Greek valour and free spirit to too late an age. He carries back the modern feelings of philanthropy to too early an age. His Greeks are made up of scraps of the Athenian Republican, and scraps of the Parisian philosophe; neither of which suit with the smart, voluble, lying, cringing, jack-of-all-trades that a Greek under the Flavian family would have been. It is very clever, nevertheless.'

'*January* 12.—This was the King's birthday. The Court was attended by many foreigners. The King paid no attention to the English—not even to so great a man as the Duke of Buccleuch—but reserved his civilities for the Russians. Fool to think that either the lion or the bear cares which side the hare takes in these disputes! In the evening as I was sipping Marsala, and reading a novel called Crichton—by the author of Rookwood, and worse than Rookwood—in came Verney to beg me to take a seat in his opera-box at the Teatro di San Carlo, which was to be illuminated in honour of the day. I care little for operas; but, as this theatre is said to be the finest in Italy—indeed in Europe—and as the occasion was a great one, I agreed. The Royal Family were below us, so that we did not see them; and I am sure that I would not give a carlino to see every Bourbon, living and dead, of the Spanish branch. The performance tired me to death, or rather to sleep; and I actually dozed for half an hour. Home, and read Gil Blas. Charming. I am never tired of it.'

Macaulay returned from Naples to Marseilles by a coasting steamer, which touched at Civita Vecchia, where Mr. Goulburn, who was subsequently Sir Robert Peel's Chancellor of the Exchequer, came on board.

'He was very civil and friendly,' writes Macaulay. 'We chatted a good deal at dinner, and even got upon politics, and talked without the least acrimony on either side. Once I had him, and he felt it. He was abusing the Election Committees. "You really think then, Mr. Goulburn, that the decisions of the Election Committees are partial and unfair?" "I do," he said, "most decidedly." "Well then," said I, "I cannot but think that it was rather hard to pass a vote of censure on O'Connell for saying so." I never saw a man more completely at a nonplus. He quite coloured—face, forehead, and all—and looked

> As I have seen him in the Capitol,
> Being crossed in conference with some senators.

He had really nothing to say, except that he had given his opinion about Election Committees to me in private. I told him that I of course understood it so; and I was too generous and polite to press my victory. But, really, a vote of censure is a serious thing; and I do not conceive that any man is justified in voting for it unless he thinks it deserved. There is little difference between a dishonest vote in an Election Committee and a dishonest vote in a question of censure. Both are judicial proceedings. The oath taken by members of a Committee is merely a bugbear for old women and men like old women. A wise and honest man has other guides than superstition to direct his conduct. I like Goulburn's conversation and manners. I had a prejudice against him which, like most prejudices conceived merely on the ground of political difference, yields readily to a little personal intercourse. And this is a man whom I have disliked for years without knowing him, and who has probably disliked me with just as little reason! A lesson.

'I read Botta's History of the American War. The book interested me, though he is not a writer to my taste. He is fair enough; and, when he misrepresents, it is rather from ignorance than from partiality. But he is shallow, and his style is the most affected that can be imagined. I can better excuse his speeches, put into the mouths of his heroes, and his attempts to give a classical air to our English debates; his substitution of "Signor Giorgio Grenville" for "the right honourable gentleman," and "cari concittadini," Or "venerabili senatori," for "Mr. Speaker." But his efforts at naïveté move my disgust. The affectation of magnificence I can pardon; but the affectation of simplicity is loathsome: for magnificence may coexist with affectation, but simplicity and affectation are in their natures opposite. Botta uses so many odd old words that even Italians require a glossary to read him; and he is particularly fond of imitating the infantine style which is so delightful in Boccacio. He perpetually introduces into his narrative vulgar Florentine proverbs of the fourteenth century. He tells us that God, "who does not stay till Saturday to pay wages," took signal vengeance on the ravagers of Wyoming; and they they were repaid for their outrages "with colliers' measure." '

'*Paris, February* 2, 1839.—The sky was clear, though it was very cold, and the snow covered everything. I resolved to go to Versailles. The palace is a huge heap of littleness. On the side towards Paris the contrast between the patches of red brick in the old part and the attempt at classical magnificence in the later part is simply revolting. Enormous as is the size of the Place des Armes, it looks paltry beyond description. The statues which used to stand at Paris on the bridge in front of the Chamber of Deputies are ranged round this court. Wretched strutting things they were; heroes storming like captains of banditti blustering through a bad melodrama on a second-rate theatre. I had hoped never to have seen them again when I missed them on the bridge; and I fancied, more fool I, that the Government might have had the good taste to throw them into the Seine. In the middle of the court is an equestrian statue of Louis XIV. He showed his sense, at least, in putting himself where he could not see his own architectural performances. I was glad to walk through the Orangerie, and thence I went some little way into the gardens. The snow was several inches deep; but I saw enough to satisfy me that these famous grounds, in meanness and extravagance, surpassed my expectations; and my expectations were not moderate. The garden façade of the palace is certainly fine by contrast with the other front; but when the enormous means employed are compared with the effect, the disproportion is wonderful. This façade is about 2,000 feet in length and is elevated on a lofty terrace. It ought to be one of the most striking works of human power and art. I doubt whether there be anywhere any single architectural composition of equal extent. I do not believe that all the works of Pericles—nay, that even St. Peter's, colonnade and all—cost so much as was lavished on Versailles; and yet there are a dozen country houses of private individuals in England alone which have a greater air of majesty and splendour than this huge quarry. Castle Howard is immeasurably finer. I went inside, and was struck by the good sense—I would even say magnanimity—which the present King has shown in admitting all that does honour to the nation, without regard to personal or family considerations. The victories of Buonaparte furnish half the rooms. Even Charles the Tenth is fairly dealt with. Whatever titles he had to public respect—the African victories, Navarino, the Dauphin's exploits, such as they were, in Spain—all have a place here. The most interesting thing, however, in the whole palace, is Louis the Fourteenth's bedroom with its original furniture. I thought of all St. Simon's anecdotes about that room and bed.'

VOLUME II

CHAPTER VIII

1839–1841

Macaulay returns to London—He meets Lord Brougham—Letters to Mr. Napier and Mrs. Trevelyan—Correspondence with Mr. Gladstone—Heated state of politics—The hostility of the Peers to Lord Melbourne's Government—Macaulay's view of the situation—Verses by Praed—The Bedchamber question—Macaulay is elected for Edinburgh—Debate on the Ballot—Macaulay becomes a Cabinet Minister—The Times—Windsor Castle—Vote of Want of Confidence—The Chinese War—Irish Registration: scene in the House of Commons—Letters to Mr. Napier—Religious Difficulties in Scotland—Lord Cardigan—The Corn Laws—The Sugar Duties—Defeat of the Ministry, and Dissolution of Parliament—Macaulay is re-elected for Edinburgh—His love for street-ballads—The change of Government.

At the end of the first week in February, 1839, Macaulay was again in London.

'*Friday, February* 8.—I have been reading Lord Durham's Canadian Report, and think it exceedingly good and able. I learn with great concern, that the business has involved Lord Glenelg's resignation. Poor fellow! I love him and feel for him.[1] I bought Gladstone's book:[2] a capital shrovetide cock to throw at. Almost too good a mark.'

'*February* 13.—I read, while walking, a good deal of Gladstone's book. The Lord hath delivered him into our hand. I think I see my way to a popular, and at the same time gentleman-like, critique. I called on the Miss Berrys, who are very desirous to collect my articles. I gave them a list, and procured some numbers for them at a bookseller's near Leicester Square. Thence to Ellis, and repeated him Romulus, the alterations in Horatius, and the beginning of Virginia. He was much pleased. We walked away together to Lincoln's Inn Fields, and met Brougham: an awkward moment. But he greeted me just as if we had parted yesterday, shook hands, got between us, and walked with us some way. He was in extraordinary force, bodily and mental. He declared vehemently against the usage which Lord Glenelg has experienced, and said that it was a case for pistoling, an infamous league of eleven men to

[1] See vol. i, page 271.

[2] Mr. Gladstone's 'The State in its Relations with the Church.'

ruin one. It will be long enough before he takes to the remedy which he recommends to others. He talked well and bitterly of Lord Durham's report. It was, he said, a second-rate article for the Edinburgh Review. "The matter came from a swindler; the style from a coxcomb; and the dictator furnished only six letters, D-U-R-H-A-M." As we were talking, Allen the Quaker came by. Brougham hallooed to him, and began to urge him to get up the strongest opposition to Lord John Russell's Education plan. I was glad when we parted. Home, and thought about Gladstone. In two or three days I shall have the whole in my head, and then my pen will go like fire.'

3 Clarges Street: February 26, 1839.

Dear Napier,—

I can now promise you an article in a week, or ten days at furthest. Of its length I cannot speak with certainty. I should think it would fill about forty pages; but I find the subject grow on me. I think that I shall dispose completely of Gladstone's theory. I wish that I could see my way clearly to a good counter theory; but I catch only glimpses here and there of what I take to be truth.

I am leading an easy life; not unwilling to engage in the Parliamentary battle if a fair opportunity should offer, but not in the smallest degree tormented by a desire for the House of Commons, and fully determined against office. I enjoyed Italy intensely; far more than I had expected. By the bye, I met Gladstone at Rome. We talked and walked together in St. Peter's during the best part of an afternoon. He is both a clever and an amiable man.

As to politics, the cloud has blown over; the sea has gone down; the barometer is rising. The session is proceeding through what was expected to be its most troubled stage in the same quiet way in which it generally advances through the dog days towards its close. Everything and everybody is languid, and even Brougham seems to be somewhat mitigated. I met him in Lincoln's Inn Fields, the other day, when I was walking with Ellis. He greeted me as if we had breakfasted together that morning, and went on to declaim against everybody with even more than his usual parts, and with all his usual rashness and flightiness.

Ever yours

T. B. MACAULAY.

London: March 20, 1839.

Dearest Hannah,—

I have passed some very melancholy days since I wrote last. On Sunday afternoon I left Ellis tolerably cheerful. His wife's disorder was abating. The next day, when I went to him, I found the house shut up. I meant only to have asked after him; but he would see me. He gave way to very violent emotion; but he soon collected himself, and talked to me about her for hours. 'I was so proud of her,' he said. 'I loved so much to show her to anybody that I valued. And now, what good will it do me to be a Judge, or to make ten thousand a year? I shall not have her to go home to with the good news.' I could not speak, for I know what that feeling is as well as he. He talked much of the sources of happiness that were left to him—his children, his relations and hers, and my friendship. He ought, he said, to be very grateful that I had not died in India, but was at home to comfort him. Comfort him I could not, except by hearing him talk of her with tears in my eyes. I stayed till late. Yesterday I went again, and passed most of the day with him, and I shall go to him again to-day; for he says, and I see, that my company does him good. I would with pleasure give one of my fingers to get him back his wife, which is more than most widowers would give to get back their own.

I have had my proofs from Napier. He magnifies the article prodigiously. In a letter to Empson he calls it exquisite and admirable, and to me he writes that it is the finest piece of logic that ever was printed. I do not think it so; but I do think that I have disposed of all Gladstone's theories unanswerably; and there is not a line of the paper with which even so strict a judge as Sir Robert Inglis, or my uncle Babington, could quarrel at as at all indecorous. How is my dear little girl? Is she old enough to take care of a canary-bird or two? From her tenderness for the little fish, I think I may venture to trust her with live animals.

I have this instant a note from Lord Lansdowne, who was in the chair of *the* Club yesterday night, to say that I am unanimously elected.[1] Poor Ellis's loss had quite put it out of my head.

Ever yours
T. B. M.

On the 10th of April Macaulay received a letter from Mr. Gladstone, who in generous terms acknowledged the courtesy, and, with some reservations, the fairness of his article. 'I have been favoured,' Mr. Gladstone wrote, 'with a copy of the forthcoming number of the Edinburgh Review; and I perhaps too much presume upon the bare acquaintance with you, of which alone I can boast, in thus unceremoniously assuming you to be the author of the article entitled "Church and State," and in offering you my very warm and cordial thanks for the manner in which you have treated both the work, and the author on whom you deigned to bestow your attention. In whatever you write you can hardly hope for the privilege of most anonymous productions, a real concealment; but, if it had been possible not to recognise you, I should have questioned your authorship in this particular case, because the candour and singlemindedness which it exhibits are, in one who has long been connected in the most distinguished manner with political party,

[1] The Club, as it is invariably called, (for its members will not stoop to identify it by any distinctive title,) is the club of Johnson, Gibbon, Burke, Goldsmith, Garrick, and Reynolds. Under the date April 9, 1839, the following entry occurs in Macaulay's diary: 'I went to the Thatched House, and was well pleased to meet the Club for the first time. We had Lord Holland in the chair, the Bishop of London, Lord Mahon, Phillips the painter, Milman, Elphinstone, Sir Charles Grey. and Hudson Gurney. I was amused, in turning over the Records of the Club, to come upon poor Bozzy's signature, evidently affixed when he was too drunk to guide his pen.'

so rare as to be almost incredible. * * * In these lacerating times one clings to everything of personal kindness in the past, to husband it for the future; and, if you will allow me, I shall earnestly desire to carry with me such a recollection of your mode of dealing with a subject upon which the attainment of truth, we shall agree, so materially depends upon the temper in which the search for it is instituted and conducted.'

How much this letter pleased Macaulay is indicated by the fact of his having kept it unburned; a compliment which, except in this single instance, he never paid to any of his correspondents. 'I have very seldom,' he writes in reply to Mr. Gladstone, 'been more gratified than by the very kind note which I have just received from you. Your book itself, and everything that I heard about you, (though almost all my information came—to the honour, I must say, of our troubled times—from people very strongly opposed to you in politics,) led me to regard you with respect and good will, and I am truly glad that I have succeeded in marking those feelings. I was half afraid, when I read myself over again in print, that the button, as is too common in controversial fencing even between friends, had once or twice come off the foil.'

The emphatic allusions, which both these letters contain, to the prevailing bitterness and injustice of party feeling, have an unfamiliar sound to men, who have already for two sessions been living in that atmosphere of good temper and good manners which pervades the House of Commons whenever the Conservatives are contented and the Liberals despondent. It was a different matter in 1839. The closing years of the Whig Administration were one long political crisis, with all the disagreeable and discreditable accompaniments from which no political crisis is free. Public animosity and personal virulence had risen to a higher, or, at any rate, to a more sustained temperature than had ever been reached since the period when, amidst threats of impeachment, and accusations of treason, perfidy, and corruption, Sir Robert Walpole was tottering to his fall.

Lord Melbourne's Cabinet had rendered immense services to the country, and the greatest of those services was the fact of its own existence. In November, 1834, the King of his own will and pleasure, had imposed a Tory Government on a House of Commons which contained a large Whig majority. The fierce onslaught upon that Government, so gallantly and skilfully led by Lord John Russell, while it presented, (as it could not fail to present,) a superficial appearance of factious self-seeking, was in truth a struggle fought to establish, once and for ever, the most vital of all constitutional principles. Not a vote nor a speech was thrown away of all that were directed against Sir Robert Peel's first Ministry. It was worth any expenditure of time, and breath, and energy, to vindicate the right of the country to choose its rulers for itself, instead of accepting those who might be imposed upon it from above. The story of the session of 1835 reads strangely to us who have been born, and hope to grow old, within the reign of the monarch who, by a long course of loyal acquiescence in the declared wishes of her people, has brought about what is nothing less than another Great Revolution, all the more beneficent because it has been gradual and silent. We cannot, without an effort of the imagination, understand the indignation and disquietude of the Whig leaders, when they saw William the Fourth recurring to those maxims of personal government which his father had effectually practised, and after which his brother had feebly and fitfully hankered. To get Peel out was in their eyes the whole duty of public men; a duty which they strenuously and successfully accomplished. But, in pursuing their end with an audacity and determination which those who had not divined the real bearings of the situation mistook for want of scruple, they made hosts of new enemies, and embittered all their old ones. They roused against themselves the furies of resentment, alarm, and distrust, which attended them relentlessly until they in their turn succumbed. The passions heated during the debates of 1835 were cooled only in the deluge which overwhelmed the Whigs at the general election of 1841.

The Peers gave them no chance from the first. Those who have joined in the idle jubilation over the impotence and helplessness of the House of Lords, with which, in our own day, triumphant partisans celebrated the downfall of the Irish Church and the abolition of purchase in the Army, would do well to study the history of the decline and fall of Lord Melbourne's Administration. There they would learn how substantial and how formidable is the power of Conservative statesmen who, surveying the field of action from the secure stronghold of an assembly devoted to their interests, can discern through all the dust and clamour of a popular movement the exact strength and attitude of the hostile forces. An Upper Chamber, which will accept from Ministers whom it detests no measure that has not behind it an irresistible mass of excited public opinion, has, sooner or later, the fate of those Ministers in its hands. For, on the one hand, the friction generated by the process of forcing a Bill through a reluctant House of Lords annoys and scandalises a nation which soon grows tired of having a revolution once a twelvemonth; and, on the other hand, the inability of a Cabinet to conduct through both Houses that continuous flow of legislation which the ever-changing necessities of a country like ours demand—alienates those among its more ardent supporters who take little account of its difficulties, and see only that it is unable to turn its Bills into Acts.

Never was the game of obstruction played more ably, and to better purpose, than during the three sessions which preceded, and the three which followed, the accession of Queen Victoria. 'Lord Cadogan,' Macaulay writes, 'talked to me well of the exceedingly difficult situation of the Ministers in the Lords. They have against them Brougham, the first speaker of the age; the Duke, with the highest character of any public man of the age; Lyndhurst, Aberdeen, Ellenborough, and others, every one of whom is an overmatch for our best orator. And this superiority in debate is backed by a still greater superiority in number.' These advantages in point of votes and talents were utilised to the utmost by consummate Parliamentary strategy. The struggle was fought out over the destination of a sum of money expected to accrue from the improved management of Church property in Ireland. The Whigs proposed to appropriate this money to the education of the people at large, without distinction of religious persuasion; while the Opposition insisted on leaving it at the disposal of the Church, to be used exclusively for Church purposes. It was an admirable battle-ground for the Conservatives. The most exalted motives of piety and patriotism, the blindest prejudices of race and creed, were alike arrayed behind the impregnable defences which guarded the position so adroitly selected by the Tory leaders. In the fourth year of the contest the Ministers yielded, with a disastrous effect upon their own influence and reputation, from which they never recovered. But the victory had been dearly bought. In exchange for the reversion of a paltry hundred thousand pounds the Irish Establishment had bartered away what remained to it of the public confidence and esteem. The next sacrifice which it was called upon to make was of a very different magnitude; and it was fated to read by the light of a bitter experience the story of the Sibylline books—that fable the invention of which is in itself sufficient to stamp the Romans as a constitutional people.

Macaulay's letters from Calcutta prove with what profound uneasiness he watched the course of public affairs at home. A looker-on, who shares the passions of the combatants, is seldom inclined to underrate the gravity of the situation, or the drastic nature of the remedies that are required. 'I am quite certain,' so he writes to Mr. Ellis, 'that in a few years the House of Lords must go after Old Sarum and Gatton. What is now passing is mere skirmishing and manœuvring between two general actions. It seems to be of little consequence to the final result how these small operations turn out. When the grand battle comes to be fought, I have no doubt about the event.' At length his sense of coming evil grew so keen that he took the step of addressing to Lord Lansdowne a carefully reasoned letter, a State paper in all but the form; urging the imminent perils that threatened a constitution in which a reformed House of Commons found itself face to face with an unreformed House of Lords; and setting forth in detail a scheme for reconstructing the Upper Chamber on an elective basis. Macaulay's notions were not at all to his old friend's taste; and, after a single interchange of opinions, the subject never reappeared in their correspondence.

On the tactics pursued by Peel and Lyndhurst Macaulay expressed the sentiments of a Whig politician in the language of a student of history. 'Your English politics,' he writes from India during the first week of 1838, 'are in a singular state. The elections appear to have left the two parties still almost exactly equal in Parliamentary strength. There seems to be a tendency in the public mind to moderation; but there seems also to be a most pernicious disposition to mix up religion with politics. For my own part, I can conceive nothing more dangerous to the interests of religion than the new Conservative device of representing a reforming spirit as synonymous with an infidel spirit. For a short time the Tories may gain something by giving to civil abuses the sanctity of religion; but religion will very soon begin to contract the unpopularity which belongs to civil abuses. There will be, I am satisfied, a violent reaction; and ten years hence Christianity will be as unpopular a topic on the hustings as the duty of seeking the Lord would have been at the time of the Restoration. The world is governed by associations. That which is always appealed to as a defence for every grievance will soon be considered as a grievance itself. No cry which deprives the people of valuable servants, and raises jobbers and oppressors to power, will long continue to be a popular cry.'

There is something almost pathetic in this unbounded and unshaken faith in the virtues of a political party. The praise which in a confidential letter a man bestows upon his contemporaries is pretty sure to be sincere; and, when Macaulay described Lord Melbourne's Administration as a breakwater which stemmed the advancing tide of Tory jobbery, no one who knew him, or who knows his writings, can doubt that he believed what he said. And yet it required not a little courage to represent the Whigs of 1838 as deaf to the claims of private interests and family connections. So widespread, and so deeply rooted, was the conviction that the Ministers gave more thought to placing their dependents than to governing the country, that their best actions were beginning to be misconstrued by their oldest friends. The invaluable series of investigations, by Royal Commissions, into all that concerned the moral, social, and religious welfare of the people, which was conducted under Lord Melbourne's auspices, presented itself to all his opponents, and some of his allies, in the light of a gigantic machinery devised by the people in power with the express purpose of providing for briefless sons and nephews. Sydney Smith, whose appetite for reform was very soon satiated when the era of reform had once fairly set in, declared in a burst of humorous consternation that the whole earth was in Commission, and that mankind had been saved from the Flood only to be delivered over to barristers of six years' standing. The onus probandi, he declared, rested with any one who said that he was not a Commissioner; and the only doubt which a man felt on seeing a Whig whom he had never met before was, not whether he was a Commissioner or no, but what the department of human life might be into which he had been appointed to inquire.

That which was fussiness and nepotism in the eyes of an original founder of the Edinburgh Review, to a contributor to the Morning Post seemed little better than recklessness and rapacity. It was about this period that Praed assailed the Ministry in some of the most incisive couplets which a political satirist has ever penned.

> Sure none should better know how sweet [1]
> The tenure of official seat
> Than one who every session buys
> At such high rate the gaudy prize;
> One who for this so long has borne
> The scowl of universal scorn;
> Has seen distrust in every look;
> Has heard in every voice rebuke;
> Exulting yet, as home he goes
> From sneering friends and pitying foes,
> That, shun him, loathe him, if they will,
> He keeps the seals and salary still.
> And, truth to say, it must be pleasant
> To be a Minister at present:
> To make believe to guide the realm
> Without a hand upon the helm,
> And wonder what with such a crew
> A pilot e'er should find to do;
> To hold what people are content
> To fancy is the government,
> And touch extremely little of it
> Except the credit and the profit;
> When Follett presses, Sugden poses,
> To bid gay Stanley count the noses,[2]
> And leave the Cabinet's defence
> To Bulwer's wit and Blewitt's sense;
> To hear demands of explanation
> On India, Belgium, trade, taxation,
> And answer that perhaps they'll try
> To give an answer by and by;

[1] The little poem, from which these lines are taken, has hitherto remained unpublished, with the exception of the concluding appeal to the young Queen,—a passage which is marked by an elevation of tone unusual in Praed's political effusions.

[2] The late Lord Stanley of Alderley was Treasury Whip to the Melbourne Administration. The traditions of the lobby still point to his tenure of office as the culminating epoch in the art of Parliamentary management.

To save the Church, and serve the Crown
By letting others pull them down;
To promise, pause, prepare, postpone,
And end by letting things alone;
In short, to earn the people's pay
By doing nothing every day;
These tasks, these joys, the Fates assign
To well-placed Whigs in Thirty-nine.

A greater man than Praed or Sydney Smith has traced an indelible record of the impression produced upon himself, and others like him, by the events of that melancholy epoch. Carlyle had shared to the full in the ardour and enthusiasm which hailed the passing of the Great Reform Bill; and he now had rather more than his share of the disappointment and the gloom, which, after seven years' experience of a Reformed House of Commons, led by the Whigs and thwarted by the Peers, had begun to settle down upon the minds of all who loved their country better than their party. In more than one of his volumes he has told us the story of a 'young ardent soul, looking with hope and joy into a world infinitely beautiful to him, though overhung with falsities and foul cobwebs, which were to be swept away amidst heroic joy, and enthusiasm of victory and battle;' and of the discouragement that eclipsed these gallant anticipations, when one session after another was spent on getting, 'with endless jargoning, debating, motioning, and counter-motioning, a settlement effected between the Honourable Mr. This and the Honourable Mr. That as to their respective pretensions to ride the high horse.' The time had arrived when to the passion and energy of 1832 had succeeded the unedifying spectacle of 'hungry Greek throttling down hungry Greek on the floor of St. Stephen's, until the loser cried, "Hold! The place is thine."'

The responsibility for the continuance of this sterile and ignoble political ferment, which for some years had lain at the door of the House of Lords, began to be shared by the Whig Government soon after Macaulay's return from India. From that time forward Lord Melbourne and his brother Ministers could not have failed to perceive, by those signs which are so familiar to veteran politicians, that their popularity was waning; and that, with their popularity, their power for good was disappearing fast. When their measures were mangled and curtailed in the Commons and quashed in the Peers,—when one bye election after another told the same tale of general dissatisfaction and distrust,—it became incumbent on them to show themselves at least as ready to surrender office as, in 1835, they had been resolute in seizing it. The hour had arrived when statesmen should have caught eagerly at the first opportunity of proving that our unwritten constitution provides a key to that problem, on the right solution of which the prosperity, and even the existence, of a free community depends,—the problem how rulers, who have for a time lost the favour and confidence of the governed, may for a time be removed from power without impairing the force and the authority of the Executive Government. Unfortunately there were considerations, honourable in themselves, which deterred the Cabinet from that wise and dignified course; and the month of May 1839 saw the leaders of the great party, which had marched into office across the steps of a throne, standing feebly at bay behind the petticoats of their wives and sisters. Whether the part which they played was forced upon them by circumstances, or whether it was not, their example was disastrous in its effect upon English public life. Our standard of Ministerial duty was lower from that day forth; until, in June, 1866, it was raised to a higher point than ever by the refusal of Earl Russell and his colleagues to remain in power, after they had found themselves unable to carry in its integrity the measure of Reform which they had promised to the nation.

As soon as the Whigs had made up their minds to solve the Bedchamber difficulty by resuming office, they were, naturally enough, anxious to bring within the walls of the House of Commons all the ability and eloquence of their party. Times were coming when they were likely to find occasion for as much oratory as they could muster. Towards the end of May the elevation to the peerage of Mr. Abercromby, the Speaker, left a seat at Edinburgh vacant. The Ministers did all that could be done in London to get Macaulay accepted as the Liberal candidate, and the constituency gave a willing response. He introduced himself to the electors in a speech that in point of style came up to their expectations, and with the substance of which they were very well contented. He conciliated the Radicals by pledging himself to the ballot; the reminiscences of Lord Melville's despotism were still too fresh in Scotch memories to make it worth while for the Tories even to talk of contesting the representation of the Scotch capital; and the Whigs would have been monsters of ingratitude if they had not declared to a man in favour of one who was a Whig with the same intensity of conviction that Montrose had been a Royalist, or Carnot a Jacobin. 'I look with pride,' said Macaulay, 'on all that the Whigs have done for the cause of human freedom and of human happiness. I see them now hard pressed, struggling with difficulties, but still fighting the good fight. At their head I see men who have inherited the spirit and the virtues, as well as the blood, of old champions and martyrs of freedom. To those men I propose to attach myself. While one shred of the old banner is flying, by that banner will I, at least, be found. Whether in or out of Parliament,—whether speaking with that authority which must always belong to the representative of this great and enlightened community, or expressing the humble sentiments of a private citizen,—I will to the last maintain inviolate my fidelity to principles which, though they may be borne down for a time by senseless clamour, are yet strong with the strength, and immortal with the immortality, of truth; and which, however they may be misunderstood or misrepresented by contemporaries, will assuredly find justice from a better age.' Such fervour will provoke a smile from those who survey the field of politics with the serene complacency of the literary critic, more readily than from statesmen who have learned the value of party loyalty by frequent and painful experience of its opposite.

The first speech which Macaulay made after his re-appearance in Parliament was on Mr. Grote's motion for leave to introduce the Ballot Bill. That annual question, (to which the philosophical reasoning, and the classical erudition, of its champion had long ere this ceased to impart any charm more attractive than respectability,) in 1839 had recovered a certain flavour of novelty from the fact that Lord Melbourne's Cabinet, at its wits' end for something that might make it popular, had agreed that the more advanced among the Ministers might be at liberty to vote as they pleased. The propriety of this course was, naturally enough, challenged by their opponents. Macaulay had an admirable opportunity of giving the House, which was eager to hear him, a characteristic touch of his quality, as he poured forth a torrent of historical instances to prove that Governments, which had regard for their own stability, or for the consciences of their individual members, always had recognised, and always must recognise, the necessity of dealing liberally with open questions. 'I rejoice,' he said, 'to see that we are returning to the wise, the honest, the moderate maxims which prevailed in this House in the time of our fathers. If two men are brought up together from their childhood; if they follow the same studies, mix in the same society, and exercise a mutual influence in forming each other's minds, a perfect agreement between them on political subjects cannot even then be expected. But Governments are constructed in such a manner that forty or fifty gentlemen, some of whom have never seen each other's faces till they are united officially, or have been in hot opposition to each other all the rest of their lives, are brought all at once into intimate connection. Among such men unanimity would be an absolute miracle. "Talk of divided houses!" said Lord Chatham. "Why there never was an instance of an united Cabinet! When were the minds of twelve men ever cast in one and the same mould?" Within the memory of many persons now living the rule was this, that all questions whatever were open questions in a Cabinet, except those which came under two classes;—measures brought forward by the Government as a Government, which all the members of the Government were, of course, expected to support; and motions brought forward with the purpose of casting a censure, express or implied, on the Government, or any department of it, which all the members of the Government were, of course, expected to oppose.'

'Let Honourable Gentlemen,' said Macaulay, warming to his theme, 'run their minds over the history of Mr. Pitt's Administration:' and Honourable Gentlemen were reminded, or, not impossibly, informed, how, on Parliamentary Reform, Mr. Pitt and Mr. Dundas had voted against Lord Mulgrave and Lord Grenville; and how, on the question of the Slave-trade, Mr. Dundas and Lord Thurlow had voted against Lord Grenville and Mr. Pitt; and so on through the Law of Libel, and the impeachment of Warren Hastings, and the dropping of the impeachment of Warren Hastings, until the names of Mr. Pitt's Cabinet had been presented to the view of Honourable Gentlemen in every possible variation, and every conceivable combination. 'And was this the effect of any extraordinary weakness on the part of the statesman who was then Prime Minister? No. Mr. Pitt was a man whom even his enemies acknowledged to possess a brave, and commanding, spirit. And was the effect of his policy to enfeeble his Administration, to daunt his adherents, to render them unable to withstand the attacks of the Opposition? On the contrary, never did a Ministry present a firmer or more serried front; nor is there the slightest doubt but that their strength was increased in consequence of their giving each member more individual liberty.'

Sir Robert Peel, after expressing in handsome, and even chivalrous, terms, his satisfaction at finding himself once more confronted by so redoubtable an antagonist, proceeded to reply with a feeble and partial argument, set off by a fine quotation from Burke. To this day there remains unanswered Macaulay's protest against the cruelty of needlessly placing men in a position where they must be false, either to their personal convictions, or to a factitious theory of Ministerial obligation;—a protest which has still greater force when directed against the extravagant impolicy of bringing the immense weight and authority of the Treasury bench to influence the vote upon an abstract motion, which can have no possible value, except in so far as it affords a genuine and unbiassed indication of Parliamentary opinion.

London: July 4, 1839.

Dear Napier,—

I am sorry that you had set your heart on a paper from me. I was really not aware that you expected one, or I would have written earlier to tell you that it would be quite impossible for me to do anything of the kind at present. I mean to give you a life of Clive for October. The subject is a grand one, and admits of decorations and illustrations innumerable.

I meant to have spoken on the Education question; but the Ministers pushed up Vernon Smith just as I was going to rise, and I had no other opportunity till Goulburn sate down, having thoroughly wearied the House. Five hundred people were coughing and calling for the question; and, though some of our friends wanted me to try my fortune, I was too prudent. A second speech is a critical matter; and it is always hazardous to address an impatient audience after midnight.

I do not like to write for you on Education, or on other pending political questions. I have two fears,—one that I may commit myself, the other that I may unseat myself. I shall keep to history, general literature, and the merely speculative part of politics, in what I write for the Review.

Ever yours
T. B. M.

Edinburgh: September 2, 1839.

Dear Napier,—

I shall work on Clive as hard as I can, and make the paper as short as I can; but I am afraid that I cannot positively pledge myself either as to time or as to length. I rather think, however, that the article will take.

I shall do my best to be in London again on the 18th. God knows what these Ministerial changes may produce. Office was never, within my memory, so little attractive, and therefore, I fear, I cannot, as a man of spirit, flinch, if it is offered to me.

Ever yours
T. B. MACAULAY.

London: September 20, 1839.

Dear Napier,—

I reached town early this morning; having, principally on your account, shortened my stay at Paris, and crossed to Ramsgate in such weather that the mails could not get into the harbour at Dover. I hoped to have five or six days of uninterrupted work, in which I might finish my paper for the Review. But I found waiting for me—this is strictly confidential—a letter from Lord Melbourne with an offer of the Secretaryship at War, and a seat in the Cabinet. I shall be a good deal occupied, as you may suppose, by conferences and correspondence during some time; but I assure you that every spare minute shall be employed in your service. I shall hope to be able, at all events, to send you the article by the 30th. I will write the native names as clearly as I can, and trust to your care without a proof.

My historical plans must for the present be suspended;[1] but I see no reason to doubt that I shall

[1] '*Friday*, *March* 9.—I began my History with a sketch of

be able to do as much as ever for the Review. Again, remember, silence is the word.

Yours ever
T. B. M.

Macaulay accepted the Secretaryship at War without any show of reluctance; but he did not attain to this great elevation without incurring the penalties of success. A man who, having begun life without rank, fortune, or private interest, finds himself inside the Cabinet and the Privy Council before his fortieth birthday, must expect that the world will not be left in ignorance of anything that can be said against him. The Times, which had been faithful to Sir Robert Peel through every turn of fortune, grafted on to its public quarrel with the Whig Government a personal grudge against the New Minister. That grudge was vented in language that curiously marks the change which, between that day and this, has come over the tone of English journalism. For weeks together, even in its leading articles, the great newspaper could find no other appellation for the great man than that of 'Mr. Babbletongue Macaulay.' When, in company with Sheil he was sworn of the Privy Council, the disgust of the Times could only be expressed by ejaculations which even then were unusual in political controversy. 'These men Privy Councillors! These men petted at Windsor Castle! Faugh! Why they are hardly fit to fill up the vacancies that have occurred by the lamented death of her Majesty's two favourite monkeys.'

It so happened that, at this very moment, Macaulay got into a scrape which enabled his detractors to transfer their abuse from the general to the particular. When it became his duty to announce to his constituents that he had taken office, he was careless enough to date his address from Windsor Castle. The Times rose, or rather sank, to the occasion; but

the early revolutions of England. Pretty well; but a little too stately and rhetorical.'—Macaulay's Journal for 1839.

it would be an ungracious act to dignify the ephemeral scurrility of some envious scribbler, by reproducing it under the name of that famous journal, which, for a generation back, has seldom allowed a week to pass without an admiring reference to Macaulay's writings, or a respectful appeal to his authority.

Many months elapsed before the new Secretary at War heard the last of Windsor Castle. That unlucky slip of the pen afforded matter for comment and banter in Parliament, on the hustings, and through every corner of the daily and weekly press. It has obtained a chance of longer life than it deserves by reason of a passing allusion in the published works of Thackeray.[1] In later years the great novelist appears to have felt undue contrition for what was, after all, a very innocent, and not ill-natured, touch of satire. In his generous and affecting notice of Macaulay's death he writes: 'It always seemed to me that ample means, and recognised rank, were Macaulay's as of right. Years ago there was a wretched outcry raised because Mr. Macaulay dated a letter from Windsor Castle, where he was staying. Immortal Gods! Was this man not a fit guest for any palace in the world, or a fit companion for any man or woman in it? I dare say, after Austerlitz, the old court officials and footmen sneered at Napoleon for dating from Schönbrunn. But that miserable Windsor Castle outcry is an echo

[1] 'Time was when the author's trade was considered a very mean one, which a gentleman of family could not take up but as an amateur. This absurdity is pretty well worn out now, and I do humbly hope and pray for the day when the other shall likewise disappear. If there be any nobleman with a talent that way, why, why don't we see him among R.A.s?

501	The Schoolmaster (sketch taken abroad) . .	Brum, Henry, Lord, R.A., F.R.S., S.A. of the National Institute of France.
502	View of the Artist's residence at Windsor .	Maconkey, Right Honourable T. B.
503	Murder of the Babes in the Tower . .	Bustle, Lord J. Pill, Right Honourable Sir Robert.
504	A little Agitation . .	O'Carroll, Daniel, M.R.I.A.

Fancy, I say, such names as these figuring in the Catalogue of the Academy!'

out of fast-retreating old-world remembrances. The place of such a natural chief was amongst the first of the land; and that country is best, according to our British notion at least, where the man of eminence has the best chance of investing his genius and intellect.'

Macaulay took his promotion quietly, and paid little or no heed to the hard words which it brought him. He kept his happiness in his own hands, and never would permit it to depend upon the goodwill, or the forbearance, of others. His biographer has no occasion to indite those woful passages, in which the sufferings of misunderstood genius are commended to the indignant commiseration of posterity. In December 1839 he writes to Mr. Napier: 'You think a great deal too much about the Times. What does it signify whether they abuse me or not? There is nothing at all discouraging in their violence. It is so far from being a means or a proof of strength, that it is both a cause and a symptom of weakness.' This is the only instance, through his entire journals and correspondence, in which Macaulay even refers to a series of invectives extending over many months, and of a nature most unusual in the columns of a leading newspaper, when the subject of attack is a man of acknowledged eminence, and blameless character.

He was just now less disposed than ever to trouble himself about the justice, or injustice, of the treatment which he met with from the outside world. An event had occurred, most unexpectedly, which opened to him a long and secure prospect of domestic happiness. At the end of the year 1839, his brother-in-law, Mr. Charles Trevelyan, was appointed to the Assistant Secretaryship of the Treasury; one of the few posts in the English Civil Service which could fully compensate a man of energy and public spirit for renouncing the intensely interesting work, and the rare opportunities of distinction, presented by an Indian career. 'This event,' writes my mother, 'of course made England our home during your uncle's life. He could never afterwards speak of it without emotion. Throughout the autumn of 1839, his misery at the prospect of our return to India was the most painful and hourly trial; and, when the joy and relief came upon us, it restored the spring and flow of his spirits. He took a house in Great George Street, and insisted on our living together, and a most happy year 1840 was.'

Like other happy years, it was a busy year too. Macaulay, who had completely laid aside his History for the present, devoted his powers to his official work. He conducted the business of his department in Parliament with the unobstrusive assiduity, and the unvaried courtesy, by which a prudent Minister may do so much to shorten discussion and to deprecate opposition. And, indeed, the spirit of the age was such that he had every chance of an easy life. The House of Commons of 1840 spent upon the army very little of its own time, or of the nation's money. The paucity and insignificance of the questions, which it fell to Macaulay's lot to master, might well rouse the envy of a Secretary of State for War in these troubled days of alternate military reorganisation and reaction. He passed his Estimates, which were of an amount to make a modern reformer's mouth water, after a short grumble from Hume, and a single division, in which that implacable economist took with him into the lobby hardly as many adherents as the Government asked for millions. Mr. Charles Macaulay, who at this time was his brother's private secretary, is the authority for an anecdote which is worth recording. He remembers being under the gallery with Sulivan, the Assistant Secretary at War, and with the Estimate clerk of the War Office, when Macaulay was submitting to the House his first Army Estimate. In the course of his speech he made a statement to which the Estimate clerk demurred. 'That is a mistake,' said the clerk. 'No, it isn't,' said Sulivan, 'for a hundred pounds! I never knew him make a blunder in anything which he had once got up;' and it turned out that Sulivan was right.

On the 14th of March, 1840, Macaulay writes to

Mr. Ellis: 'I have got through my estimates with flying colours; made a long speech of figures and details without hesitation, or mistake, of any sort; stood catechising on all sorts of questions; and got six millions of public money in the course of an hour or two. I rather like the sort of work, and I have some aptitude for it. I find business pretty nearly enough to occupy all my time; and, if I have a few minutes to myself, I spend them with my sister and niece; so that, except while I am dressing and undressing, I get no reading at all. I do not know but that it is as well for me to live thus for a time. I became too mere a bookworm in India, and on my voyage home. Exercise, they say, assists digestion; and it may be that some months of hard official and Parliamentary work may make my studies more nourishing.'

But Macaulay's course in Parliament was not all plain-sailing when he ventured from the smooth waters of the War Office into the broken seas of general politics. The session of 1840 had hardly commenced, when Sir John Yarde Buller moved a Resolution professing want of confidence in the Ministry,—a motion which the Tories supported with all their strength both of vote and lung. For the first, and, as he himself willingly confessed, for the last time in his life Macaulay did not get a fair hearing. On the second night of the debate, Sir James Graham, speaking with the acrimony which men of a certain character affect when they are attacking old allies, by a powerful invective, spiced with allusions to the Windsor Castle address, had goaded the Opposition ranks into a fit of somewhat insolent animosity. When Macaulay rose to reply, the indications of that animosity were so manifest that he had almost to commence his remarks with an appeal for tolerance. 'I trust,' he said, 'that the first Cabinet Minister who, when the question is, whether the Government be or be not worthy of confidence, offers himself in debate, will find some portion of that generosity and good feeling which once distinguished English gentlemen.' The words 'first Cabinet Minister' were no sooner out of his mouth than the honourable gentlemen opposite, choosing wilfully to misconstrue those words as if he were putting forward an absurd claim to the leading place in the Cabinet, burst forth into a storm of ironical cheering which would have gone far to disconcert O'Connell. Macaulay, (who to speak his best, required the sympathy, or, at any rate, the indulgence of his audience,) said all that he had to say, but said it without spirit or spontaneity: and did not succeed in maintaining the enthusiasm either of himself, or his hearers, at the too high-pitched level of the only one of his Parliamentary efforts which could in any sense be described as a failure.[1]

Some days afterwards he met Sir James Graham in the Park, who expressed a hope that nothing which appeared rude or offensive had escaped his lips. 'Not at all,' said Macaulay; 'only I think that your speech would have been still more worthy of you, if you had not adopted the worn-out newspaper jests about my Windsor letter.' On the 7th of April, Sir James himself brought forward a vote of censure on the Government for having led the country into war with China; and Macaulay, who again followed him in the debate, achieved a brilliant and undoubted success in an oration crowned by a noble tribute to the majesty of the British flag,—quite incomparable as an example of that sort of rhetoric which goes straight to the heart of a British House of Commons.[2] When they met

[1] In 1853 Macaulay was correcting his speeches for publication. On the 28th of July of that year he writes in his journal:—'I worked hard, but without much heart; for it was that unfortunate speech on Buller's motion in 1840; one of the few unlucky things in a lucky life. I cannot conceive why it failed. It is far superior to many of my speeches which have succeeded. But, as old Demosthenes said, the power of oratory is as much in the ear as in the tongue.'

[2] 'I was much touched, and so, I dare say, were many other gentlemen, by a passage in one of Captain Elliot's despatches. I mean that passage in which he describes his arrival at the factory in the moment of extreme danger. As soon as he

again, Sir James said to him: 'In our last encounter none but polished weapons were used on both sides; and I am afraid that public opinion rather inclines to the belief that you had the best of it.' 'As to the polished weapons,' said Macaulay, 'my temptations are not so misleading as yours. You never wrote a Windsor letter.' His adversaries paid him a high compliment when they were reduced to make so much of a charge, which was the gravest that malice itself ever brought against him in his character of a public man.

Throughout the sessions of 1840, and 1841, a series of confused and angry discussions took place over a multitude of bills dealing with the Registration of Voters in Ireland, which were brought forward from every quarter of the House, and with every possible diversity of view. In these debates Macaulay gave marked proof of having profited by the severe legal training, which was not the least valuable and enduring reward of his Indian labours. Holding his own against Sugden in technical argument, he enforced his points with his customary wealth of language and illustration, much of which unfortunately perished between his lips and the reporters' gallery. 'Almost every clause of this Bill which is designed for keeping

landed he was surrounded by his countrymen, all in an agony of distress and despair. The first thing which he did was to order the British flag to be brought from his boat, and planted in the balcony. The sight immediately revived the hearts of those who had a minute before given themselves up for lost. It was natural that they should look up with hope and confidence to that victorious flag. For it reminded them that they belonged to a country unaccustomed to defeat, to submission, or to shame; to a country which had exacted such reparation for the wrongs of her children as had made the ears of all who heard it to tingle; to a country which had made the Dey of Algiers humble himself to the dust before her insulted consul; to a country which had avenged the victims of the Black Hole on the field of Plassey; to a country which had not degenerated since the great Protector vowed that he would make the name of Englishman as much respected as ever had been the name of Roman citizen. They knew that, surrounded as they were by enemies, and separated by great oceans and continents from all help, not a hair of their heads would be harmed with impunity.'

out the wrongful, acts just as effectually against the rightful, claimant. Let me suppose the case of a man of great wealth, and of imperious, obstinate, and arbitrary temper:—one of those men who thinks much of the rights of property, and little of its duties. Let me suppose that man willing to spend six or seven thousand a year in securing the command of a county,—an ambition, as everyone knows, not impossible even in England. I will not mention any recent transaction; nor do I wish to mix up personalities with this serious debate; but no one is ignorant how a certain man now dead, provoked by the opposition he received in a certain town, vowed that he would make the grass grow in its streets, and how that vow was kept. Another great person ejected four hundred voters in one shire, and entered two hundred and twenty-five civil actions. Such a man could easily command an Irish county. It would only be a picture the less in his gallery, or an antique gem the less in his collection.'

The conflict was not always carried on with such scrupulous abstinence from personalities.

'*Thursday*, *June* 11.—I went from the Office to the House, which was engaged upon Stanley's Irish Registration Bill. The night was very stormy. I have never seen such unseemly demeanour, or heard such scurrilous language in Parliament. Lord Norreys was whistling, and making all sorts of noises. Lord Maidstone was so ill-mannered that I hope he was drunk. At last, after much grossly indecent conduct, at which Lord Eliot expressed his disgust to me, a furious outbreak took place. O'Connell was so rudely interrupted that he used the expression "beastly bellowings." Then rose such an uproar as no O. P. mob at Covent Garden Theatre,—no crowd of Chartists in front of a hustings,—ever equalled. Men on both sides stood up, shook their fists, and bawled at the top of their voices. Freshfield, who was in the chair, was strangely out of his element. Indeed he knew his business so little that, when first he had to put a question, he fancied himself at Exeter Hall, or the Crown and Anchor, and said: "As many as are of that opinion please to signify the same by holding up their hands." He was quite unable to keep the smallest order when the storm came. O'Connell raged like a mad bull; and our people—I for one—while regretting and condemning his violence, thought it much extenuated by the provocation. Charles Buller spoke with talent, as he always does; and with earnestness, dignity, and propriety, which he scarcely ever does. A short and most amusing scene passed between O'Connell and Lord Maidstone, which in the tumult escaped the observation of many, but which I watched carefully. "If," said Lord Maidstone, "the word beastly is retracted, I shall be satisfied. If not, I shall not be satisfied." "I do not care whether the noble Lord be satisfied or not." "I wish you would give me satisfaction." "I advise the noble Lord to carry his liquor meekly." At last the tumult ended from absolute physical weariness. It was past one, and the steady bellowers of the Opposition had been howling from six o'clock with little interruption. I went home with a headache, and not in high spirits. But how different my frame of mind from what it was two years ago! How profoundly domestic happiness has altered my whole way of looking at life! I have my share of the anxieties, and vexations, of ambition; but it is only a secondary passion now.'

November 1839.

Dear Napier,—

I send back the paper on Clive. Remember to let me have a revise. I have altered the last sentence, so as to make it clearer and more harmonious; but I cannot consent to leave out the well-earned compliment to my dear old friend, Lord William Bentinck, of whom Victor Jacquemont said, as truly as wittily, that he was William Penn on the throne of the Mogul, and at the head of two hundred thousand soldiers.[1]

Ever yours

T. B. MACAULAY.

Lord William Bentinck, since his return from India, had taken an active, and sometimes even a turbid,

[1] 'To the warrior, history will assign a place in the same rank with Lucullus and Trajan. Nor will she deny to the reformer a share of that veneration with which France cherishes the memory of Turgot, and with which the latest generations of Hindoos will contemplate the statue of Lord William Bentinck.'

part in politics as member for Glasgow. Those who will turn to the last words of the Essay on Lord Clive, will understand Mr. Napier's uneasiness at the notion of placing on so conspicuous a literary pedestal the effigy of one who, for the time, had come to be regarded as the Radical representative of a large Scotch constituency is apt to be regarded during a period of Conservative reaction.

London: October 14, 1840.

Dear Napier,—

I am glad that you are satisfied.[1] I dare say that there will be plenty of abuse; but about that I have long ceased to care one straw.

I have two plans, indeed three, in my head. Two might, I think, be executed for the next number. Gladstone advertises another book about the Church. That subject belongs to me; particularly as he will very probably say something concerning my former article.

Leigh Hunt has brought out an edition of Congreve, Wycherley, and Farquhar. I see it in the windows of the booksellers' shops; but I have not looked at it. I know their plays, and the literary history of their time, well enough to make an amusing paper. Collier's controversy with Congreve, on the subject of the Drama, deserves to be better known than it is; and there is plenty of amusing and curious anecdote about Wycherley. If you will tell Longman to send me the book, I will see whether I can give you a short, lively, article on it.

My third plan cannot yet be executed. It is to review Capefigue's history of the Consulate and Empire of Napoleon. A character both of the man, and of the government, such as the subject deserves, has not yet, in my opinion, appeared. But there are still two volumes of Capefigue's book to come, if not more; and, though he writes with wonderful

[1] This refers to the article on Von Ranke's History of the Popes.

rapidity, he can hardly bring them out till the beginning of next year.

Ever yours
T. B. MACAULAY.

London: October 29, 1840.

Dear Napier,—

I have received Hunt's book, and shall take it down with me to Southampton, whither I hope to be able to make a short trip. I shall give it well to Hunt about Jeremy Collier, to whom he is scandalously unjust. I think Jeremy one of the greatest public benefactors in our history.

Poor Lord Holland! It is vain to lament. A whole generation is gone to the grave with him. While he lived, all the great orators and statesmen of the last generation were living too. What a store of historical information he has carried away! But his kindness, generosity, and openness of heart, were more valuable than even his fine accomplishments. I loved him dearly.

Ever yours truly
T. B. MACAULAY.

London: November 13, 1840.

Dear Napier,—

Yesterday evening I received Gladstone's book, and read it. I do not think that it would be wise to review it. I observed in it very little that had any reference to politics, and very little indeed that might not be consistently said by a supporter of the Voluntary system. It is, in truth, a theological treatise; and I have no mind to engage in a controversy about the nature of the sacraments, the operation of holy orders, the visibility of the Church, and such points of learning; except when they are connected, as in his former work they were connected, with questions of government. I have no disposition to split hairs about the spiritual reception of the body and blood of Christ in the Eucharist, or about baptismal regeneration. I shall try to give you a paper on a very different subject,—Wycherley, and the other good-for-nothing fellows, whose indecorous wit Leigh Hunt has edited.

I see that a Life of Warren Hastings is just coming out. I mark it for mine. I will try to make as interesting an article, though I fear not so flashy, as that on Clive.

The state of things at Edinburgh has greatly vexed me. Craig advises me not to go down, at least for some time. But, if I do not go soon, I shall not be able to go at all this year. What do you think about the matter?

Ever yours

T. B. MACAULAY.

There was, indeed, little to tempt him northwards. All Scotland was in a ferment between two great controversies; and the waves of religious passion, still surging with the excitement of the Church Extension agitation, already felt the first gusts of the rising storm which was soon to rage over the more momentous question of Patronage. Lord Melbourne and his colleagues were ignorant of the strength and meaning either of the one movement or the other. Incapable of leading the opinion of the country, they meddled from time to time only to make discords more pronounced, and difficulties more insoluble, than ever. The nation was split up into ill-defined, but not, on that account, less hostile, camps. On the platform and at the polling-booth,—in the pulpit, the press, the presbyteries, and the law courts,—churchmen were arrayed against dissenters, and against each other. The strife was one whose issues could never be finally determined, except in accordance with principles which Paisley weavers and Perthshire shepherds were beginning to understand much more clearly than ever did Her Majesty's Ministers. It was the general opinion of Macaulay's friends at Edinburgh that he would do well to avoid exposing himself to the blows, which were sure to fall about the head of a Parliamentary representative, at a time when his constituents were engaged in such fierce cross-fighting. He certainly consulted his comfort, and possibly his political interests, when he decided on refraining from an interference which would have offended most parties and satisfied none.

London: December 8, 1840.

Dear Napier,—

I shall work at my article on Hunt whenever I have a leisure hour, and shall try to make it amusing to lovers of literary gossip.

I will not plague you with arguments about the Eastern question. My own opinion has long been made up. Unless England meant to permit a virtual partition of the Ottoman Empire between France and Russia, she had no choice but to act as she has acted. Had the treaty of July not been signed, Nicholas would have been really master of Constantinople, and Thiers of Alexandria. The treaty once made, I never would have consented to flinch from it, whatever had been the danger. I am satisfied that the War party in France is insatiable and unappeasable; that concessions would only have strengthened and emboldened it; and that, after stooping to the lowest humiliations, we should soon have had to fight without allies, and at every disadvantage. The policy which has been followed I believe to be not only just and honourable, but eminently a pacific policy. Whether the peace of the world will long be preserved I do not pretend to say; but I firmly hold that the best chance of preserving it was to make the treaty of July, and, having made it, to execute it resolutely. For my own part, I will tell you plainly that, if the course of events had driven Palmerston to resign, I would have resigned with him, though I stood alone. Look at what the late Ministers of Louis Philippe have avowed with respect to the Balearic Islands. Were such designs ever proclaimed before, except in a crew of pirates, or a den of robbers? Look at Barrot's speeches about England. Is it for the sake of such friendships as this that our country is to abdicate her rank, and sink into a dependency? I like war quite as little as Sir William Molesworth, or Mr. Fonblanque. It is foolish and wicked to bellow for war, merely for war's sake, like the rump of the Mountain at Paris. I would never make offensive war. I would never offer to any other power a provocation which might be a fair ground for war. But I never would abstain from doing what I had a clear right to do, because a neighbour chooses to threaten me with an unjust war; first, because I believe that such a policy would, in the end, inevitably produce war; and secondly, because I think war, though a very great evil, by no means so great an evil as subjugation, and national humiliation.

In the present case, I think the course taken by the Government unexceptionable. If Guizot prevails,—that is to say, if reason, justice, and public law prevail,—we shall have no war. If the writers of the National, and the singers of the Marseillaise, prevail, we can have no peace. At whatever cost, at whatever risk, these banditti must be put down; or they will put down all commerce, civilisation, order, and the independence of nations.

Of course what I write to you is confidential: not that I should hesitate to proclaim the substance of what I have said on the hustings, or in the House of Commons; but because I do not measure my words in pouring myself out to a friend. But I have run on too long, and should have done better to have given the last half-hour to Wycherley.

Ever yours

T. B. MACAULAY.

London: January 11, 1841.

Dear Napier,—

As to my paper on the Dramatists, if you are content, so am I. I set less value on it than on anything I have written since I was a boy.

I have hardly opened Cleig's book on Warren Hastings, and I cannot yet judge whether I can review it before it is complete. I am not quite sure that so vast a subject may not bear two articles. The scene of the first would lie principally in India. The Rohilla War, the disputes of Hastings and his Council, the character of Francis, the death of Nuncomar, the rise of the Empire of Hyder, the seizure of Benares, and many other interesting matters, would furnish out such a paper. In the second, the scene would be changed to Westminster. There we should have the Coalition; the India Bill; the impeachment; the characters of all the noted men of that time, from Burke, who managed the prosecution of Hastings, down to the wretched Tony Pasquin, who first defended, and then libelled him. I hardly know a story so interesting, and of such various interest. And the central figure is in the highest degree striking and majestic. I think Hastings, though far from faultless, one of the greatest men that England ever produced. He had pre-eminent talents for government, and great literary talents too; fine taste, a princely spirit, and heroic equanimity in the midst of adversity and danger. He was a man for whom nature had done much of what the Stoic philosophy pretended, and only pretended, to do for its disciples. 'Mens æqua in arduis' is the inscription under his picture in the Government House at Calcutta; and never was there a more appropriate motto. This story has never been told as well as it deserves. Mill's account of Hastings's administration is indeed very able;—the ablest part, in my judgment, of his work; —but it is dry. As to Gleig, unless he has greatly improved since he wrote Sir Thomas Munro's life, he will make very little of his subject. I am not so vain as to think that I can do it full justice; but the success of my paper on Clive has emboldened me, and I have the advantage of being in hourly intercourse with Trevelyan, who is thoroughly well acquainted with the languages, manners, and diplomacy of the Indian Courts.

Ever yours
T. B. MACAULAY.

London: April 26, 1841.

Dear Napier,—

I have arranged with Leigh Hunt for a paper on the Colmans, which will be ready for the July number, He has written some very pretty lines on the Queen, who has been very kind to him both by sending him money, and by countenancing his play. It has occurred to me that, if poor Southey dies, (and his best friends must now pray for his death,) Leigh Hunt might very fitly have the laurel, if that absurd custom is to be kept up; or, at all events, the pension and the sack.

I wish that you could move Rogers to write a short character of Lord Holland for us. Nobody knew his house so well; and Rogers is no mean artist in prose.[1]

As to Lord Cardigan, he has deserved some abuse; he has had ten times as much as he deserved; and, as I do not choose to say a word more than I think just against him, I come in for a share. You may easily suppose that it troubles me very little.

Ever yours

T. B. MACAULAY.

During the session of 1841 Macaulay, as Secretary at War, had very little to do in the House of Commons except to defend Lord Cardigan; but that in itself was quite sufficient occupation for one Minister. Mr. Kinglake, who enjoyed large, and even over-abundant, opportunities for studying his Lordship, has described his character in a passage almost too well known for quotation. 'Having no personal ascendency, and no habitual consideration for the feelings of others, he was not, of course, at all qualified to exert easy rule over English gentlemen. There surely was cruelty in the idea of placing human beings under the military control of an officer at once so arbitrary and so narrow; but the notion of such a man having been able to purchase for himself a right to hold English-

[1] In a letter of May 4th, 1841, Macaulay writes: 'Lady Holland is so earnest with me to review her husband's "Protests in the House of Lords" that I hardly know what to do. I cannot refuse her.'

men in military subjection is, to my mind, revolting.' Lord Cardigan bought himself up from Cornet to Lieutenant-Colonel in the course of seven years; and by an expenditure, it is said, of four times as many thousand pounds. So open-handed a dealer had, of course, the pick of the market. He selected a fine cavalry regiment, which he proceeded to drag through a slough of scandal, favouritism, petty tyranny, and intrigue, into that glare of notoriety which to men of honour is even more painful than the misery which a commanding officer of Lord Cardigan's type has such unbounded power of inflicting upon his subordinates. Within the space of a single twelvemonth one of his captains was cashiered for writing him a challenge; he sent a coarse and insulting verbal message to another, and then punished him with prolonged arrest, because he respectfully refused to shake hands with the officer who had been employed to convey the affront; he fought a duel with a lieutenant who had left the corps, and shot him through the body; and he flogged a soldier on Sunday, between the services, on the very spot where, half an hour before, the man's comrades had been mustered for public worship. The Secretary at War had to put the best face he could on these ugly stories. When it was proposed to remove Lord Cardigan from the command of his regiment, Macaulay took refuge in a position which he justly regarded as impregnable. 'Honourable gentlemen should beware how they take advantage of the unpopularity of an individual to introduce a precedent which, if once established, would lead to the most fatal effects to the whole of our military system, and work a great injustice to all officers in Her Majesty's service. What is the case with officers in the army? They buy their commissions at a high price, the interest of which would be very nearly equal to the pay they receive; they devote the best years of their lives to the service, and are liable to be sent to the most unhealthy parts of the globe, where their health, and sometimes their lives, fall a sacrifice.

Is it to be expected that men of spirit and honour will consent to enter this service, if they have not, at least, some degree of security for the permanence of their situations:'—in other words, if they are not allowed to do as they will with their own.

Meanwhile the political crisis was approaching its agony. The Whig Government was now in such a plight that it could neither stand with decency nor fall with grace. Their great measure of the year, the Irish Registration Bill, narrowly escaped the perils of a second reading, and was ingloriously wrecked in Committee. Their last year's deficit, of something under one million, had this year grown to something over two; and they could no longer rely upon the wave of popular favour to tide them over their troubles. All the enthusiasm for progress which still survived had been absorbed into the ranks of those fiery reformers, who were urging the crusade against the Corn Laws under the guidance of leaders who sate elsewhere than on the Treasury bench, or did not sit in Parliament at all. As far back as 1839 Macaulay was writing in his diary: 'The cry for free-trade in corn seems to be very formidable. The Times has joined in it. I was quite sure that it would be so. If the Ministers play their game well, they may now either triumph completely or retire with honour. They have excellent cards, if they know how to use them.' Dire necessity had gradually brought even the most timid members of the Cabinet to acquiesce in these heroic sentiments, and the Whigs at length made up their minds to come before the country in the character of Freetraders. In a letter to Mr. Napier, on the 30th day of April, 1841, Macaulay says: 'All the chances of our party depend on to-night. We shall play double or quits. I do not know what to expect; and as far as I am concerned I rather hope for a defeat. I pine for liberty and ease, freedom of speech, and freedom of pen. I have all that I want; a small competence, domestic happiness, good health and spirits. If at forty I can get from under this yoke,

I shall not easily be induced to bear it again.' So wrote the Secretary at War in the morning; and, at four o'clock in the afternoon of the same day, Lord John Russell gave notice that, on the 31st of May, he should move that the House resolve itself into a Committee to consider the Acts relating to the trade in corn.

But it was too late to make a change of front in the face of the greatest Parliamentary captain of the age, and of a whole phalanx of statesmen, who were undoubtedly superior to the Ministers in debate, and who were generally believed to be far abler as administrators. A great deal was to happen between the 30th of April and the 31st of May. One main feature in the Budget was a proposal to reduce the duty on foreign sugar; a serious blow to the privilege which the free labour of our own colonies enjoyed, as against the slave labour of the Spanish plantations. Lord Sandon moved an amendment, skilfully framed to catch the votes of Abolitionist members of the Liberal party, and the question was discussed through eight livelong nights, with infinite repetition of argument, and dreariness of detail. Mr. Gladstone, who had early learned that habit of high-toned courtesy which is the surest presage of future greatness, introduced into the last sentences of a fine speech an allusion that pleased no one so much as him against whom it was directed. 'There is another name,' said he, 'strangely associated with the plan of the Ministry. I can only speak from tradition of the struggle for the abolition of slavery; but, if I have not been misinformed, there was engaged in it a man who was the unseen ally of Mr. Wilberforce, and the pillar of his strength; a man of profound benevolence, of acute understanding, of indefatigable industry, and of that self-denying temper which is content to work in secret, to forego the recompense of present fame, and to seek for its reward beyond the grave. The name of that man was Zachary Macaulay, and his son is a member of the existing Cabinet.'

In the early morning of the 19th of May Lord Sandon's amendment was carried by thirty-six votes; and, on the morrow, the House was crammed inside and out, in the confident expectation of such an announcement as generally follows upon a crushing Ministerial defeat. Neither the friends of the Government, nor its enemies, could believe their ears, when the Chancellor of the Exchequer, with the self-possessed air of a Minister who has a working majority and a financier who has an available surplus, gave notice that he should bring forward the usual sugar duties in Committee of Ways and Means; and, before the audience could recover its breath, Lord John Russell followed him with a motion that this House, on its rising, do adjourn to Monday. The Earl of Darlington, in a single sentence of contemptuous astonishment, asked on what day the noble Lord proposed to take the question of the Corn Laws. When that day had been ascertained to be the 4th of June, the subject dropped at once; and an unhappy Member began upon the grievances of the Royal Marines, amidst the buzz of conversation, expressive of gratified or disappointed curiosity, with which, after a thrilling episode, the House relieves its own nerves and tortures those of the wretch whose ambition or ill-luck has exposed him to the most formidable ordeal which can be inflicted on a public speaker.

But the matter was not to end thus. The 4th of June, instead of being the first day of the debate on the Corn Laws, was the fifth and last of an obstinate and and dubious conflict waged over a direct vote of want of confidence; which was proposed by the Conservative leader in a quiet and carefully reasoned speech, admirably worthy of the occasion and of himself. Macaulay, who had shown signs of immense interest while Sir Robert was unfolding his budget of historical parallels and ruling cases, replied on the same night with an ample roll of the instances in which Lord Sunderland, and Mr. Pitt, and Lord Liverpool had accepted defeat without resorting either to Resignation or Dissolution. But all the precedents in the Journals of Parliament, though collected by Hallam and set forth by Canning, would have failed to prove that the country had any interest whatsoever in the continued existence of a Ministry, which had long been powerless, and was rapidly becoming discredited. When Sir James Graham rose, there was a break in that tone of mutual forbearance which the principal speakers, on either side, had hitherto maintained. The Right Honourable Baronet could not resist the temptation of indulging himself in an invective which, as he proceeded towards his peroration, degenerated into a strain of downright ribaldry;[1] but the Government was already too far gone to profit by the mistakes, or the excesses, of its adversaries; and the Opposition triumphed by one vote, in a House fuller by twenty than that which, ten years before, had carried the second reading of the Reform Bill by exactly the same majority.

Within three weeks Parliament was dissolved, and the Ministers went to the country on the question of a fixed duty on foreign wheat. There could be but one issue to a general election which followed upon such a session, and but one fate in store for a party whose leaders were fain to have recourse to so feeble and perfunctory a cry. Lord Melbourne and his colleagues had touched the Corn Laws too late and too timidly for their reputation, and too soon for the public opinion of the constituencies. They sent their supporters on what was indeed a forlorn hope, when, as a sort of political afterthought, they bade them attack the most powerful interest in the nation.

[1] 'I cannot address the people of this country in the language of the quotation used by the noble Lord: "O passi graviora;"—for never was a country cursed with a worse, a more reckless, or a more dangerous Government. The noble Lord, the Secretary for Ireland, talks of "lubricity;" but, thank God, we have at last pinned you to something out of which you cannot wriggle; and, as we have the melancholy satisfaction to know that there is an end to all things, so I can now say with the noble Lord: "Dabit Deus his quoque finem; thank God we have at last got rid of such a Government as this." '

North of Trent the Whigs held their ground; but, throughout the southern districts of England, they were smitten hip and thigh from Lincoln to St. Ives. The adherents of the Government had to surrender something of their predominance in the boroughs, while those who sate for the counties were turned out by shoals. There were whole shires which sent back their writs inscribed with an unbroken tale of Protectionists. All the ten Essex members were Conservatives, in town and country alike; and so were all the twelve members for Shropshire. Before the Irish returns had come to hand, it was already evident that the Ministerial loss would be equivalent to a hundred votes on a stand and fall division. The Whigs had experienced no equally grave reverse since, in 1784, Pitt scattered to the winds the Coalition majority; and no such other was destined again to befall them,

> Until a day more dark and drear,
> And a more memorable year,

should, after the lapse of a generation, deliver over to misfortune and defeat

> A mightier host and haughtier name.

Scotland, as usual, was not affected by the contagion of reaction. Indeed, the troubles of candidates to the north of the Border proceeded rather from the progressive, than the retrogressive, tendencies of the electors. Macaulay was returned unopposed, in company with Mr. William Gibson Craig: though he had been threatened with a contest by the more ardent members of that famous party in the Scotch Church which, within two years from that time, was to give such a proof as history will not forget of its willingness to sacrifice, for conscience sake, things far more precious even than the honour of sending to St. Stephen's an eloquent and distinguished representative.[1]

[1] The disruption of the Scotch Church took place on the 18th of May, 1843.

To Miss F. Macaulay.

Edinburgh: June 28, 1841.

Dearest Fanny,—

We have had a meeting—a little stormy when church matters were touched on, but perfectly cordial on other points. I took the bull by the horns, and have reason to believe that I was right, both in principle, and in policy. A Non-intrusion opposition has been talked of. My language at the meeting displeased the violent churchmen, and they were at one time minded even to coalesce with the Tories against me. The leading Non-intrusionists, however, have had a conference with me; and, though we do not exactly agree, they own that they shall get more from me than from a Tory. I do not think that there is now any serious risk of a contest, and there is none at all of a defeat; but in the meantime I am surrounded by the din of a sort of controversy which is most distasteful to me. 'Yes, Mr. Macaulay; that is all very well for a statesman. But what becomes of the headship of our Lord Jesus Christ?' And I cannot answer a constituent quite as bluntly as I should answer any one else who might reason after such a fashion.

Ever yours

T. B. M.

London: July 12, 1841.

Dear Ellis,—

I cannot send you Virginius, for I have not a copy by me at present, and have not time to make one. When you return, I hope to have finished another ballad, on the Lake Regillus. I have no doubt that the author of the original ballad had Homer in his eye. The battle of the Lake Regillus is a purely Homeric battle. I am confident that the ballad-maker has heard of the fight over the body of Patroclus. We will talk more about this. I may, perhaps, publish a small volume next spring. I am encouraged by the approbation of all who have seen the little pieces. I find the unlearned quite as well satisfied as the learned.

I have taken a very comfortable suite of chambers in the Albany; and I hope to lead, during some years, a sort of life peculiarly suited to my taste,—college life at the West-end of London. I have an entrance hall, two sitting-rooms, a bedroom, a kitchen, cellars, and two rooms for servants,—all for ninety guineas a year; and this in a situation which no younger son of a Duke need be ashamed to put on his card. We shall have, I hope, some very pleasant breakfasts there, to say nothing of dinners. My own housekeeper will do very well for a few plain dishes, and the Clarendon is within a hundred yards.

I own that I am quite delighted with our prospects. A strong opposition is the very thing that I wanted. I shall be heartily glad if it lasts till I can finish a History of England, from the Revolution, to the Accession of the House of Hanover. Then I shall be willing to go in again for a few years. It seems clear that we shall be just about 300. This is what I have always supposed. I got through very triumphantly at Edinburgh, and very cheap. I believe I can say what no other man in the kingdom can say. I have been four times returned to Parliament by cities of more than a hundred and forty thousand inhabitants; and all those four elections together have not cost me five hundred pounds.

Your ballads are delightful. I like that of Ips,[1]

[1] Ips, Gips, and Johnson were three Northumbrian butchers; who, when riding from market, heard a cry for help, and came upon a woman who had been reduced to the distressful plight in which ladies were so often discovered by knights errant.

> Then Johnson, being a valiant man, a man of courage bold,
> He took his coat from off his back to keep her from the cold.
> As they rode over Northumberland, as hard as they could ride,
> She put her fingers in her ears, and dismally she cried.
> Then up there start ten swaggering blades, with weapons in their hands,
> And riding up to Johnson they bid him for to stand.
> 'It's I'll not stand,' says Ipson: 'then no indeed not I.'
> 'Nor I'll not stand,' says Gipson: 'I'll sooner live than die.'

Gips, and Johnson best. 'Napoleon' is excellent, but hardly equal to the 'Donkey wot wouldn't go.'

Ever yours
T. B. MACAULAY.

Macaulay's predilection for the Muse of the street has already furnished more than one anecdote to the newspapers.[1] It is, indeed, one of the few personal facts about him which up to this time has taken hold of the public imagination. He bought every half-penny song on which he could lay his hands; if only it was decent, and a genuine, undoubted poem of the people. He has left a scrap-book containing about eighty ballads; for the most part vigorous and picturesque enough, however defective they may be in rhyme and grammar; printed on flimsy, discoloured paper, and headed with coarsely executed vignettes, seldom bearing even the most remote reference to the subject which they are supposed to illustrate. Among the gems of his collection he counted 'Plato, a favourite song,' commencing with a series of questions

'Then I will stand,' says Johnson: 'I'll stand the while I can.
I never yet was daunted, nor afraid of any man.'

Johnson thereupon drew his sword, and had disposed of eight out of his ten assailants, when he was stabbed from behind by the woman, and died, upbraiding her with having killed

The finest butcher that ever the sun shone on.

It is not so easy to identify 'Napoleon' among a sheaf of ballads entitled 'The Island of St. Helena,' 'Maria Louisa's Lamentation,' and 'Young Napoleon, or the Bunch of Roses;' though from internal evidence there is reason to believe that the song in question was 'Napoleon's Farewell to Paris,' which commences with an apostrophe so gorgeous as to suggest the idea that the great Emperor's curious popularity with our troubadours of the kerbstone is of Irish origin.

Farewell, ye splendid citadel, Metropolis, called Paris,
Where Phœbus every morning shoots refulgent beams;
Where Flora's bright Aurora advancing from the Orient
With radiant light illumines the pure shining streams.

[1] Of these anecdotes the best known is the story of his being followed from the bookstall, where he had bought a parcel of ballads, by a crowd of children, whom he overheard discussing among themselves whether or not the gentleman was going to sing.

in which it certainly is not easy to detect traces of the literary style employed by the great dialectician:

> Says Plato, 'Why should man be vain,
> Since bounteous heaven has made him great?
> Why look with insolent disdain
> On those not decked with pomp or state?'

It is hardly too much to say that Macaulay knew the locality, and, at this period of his life, the stock in trade, of every book-stall in London.[1] 'After office hours,' says his brother Charles, 'his principal relaxation was rambling about with me in the back lanes of the City. It was then that he began to talk of his idea of restoring to poetry the legends of which poetry had been robbed by history; and it was in these walks that I heard for the first time from his lips the Lays of Rome, which were not published until some time afterwards. In fact, I heard them in the making. I never saw the hidden mechanism of his mind so clearly as in the course of these walks. He was very fond of discussing psychological and ethical questions; and sometimes, but more rarely, would lift the veil behind which he habitually kept his religious opinions.'

On the 19th of August Parliament met, to give effect to the verdict of the polling booths. An amendment on the Address, half as long as the Address itself, the gist of which lay in a respectful representation to Her Majesty that her present advisers did not possess the confidence of the country, was moved simultaneously in both Houses. It was carried on the first night of the debate by a majority of seventy-two in the Lords, and on the fourth night by a majority of ninety-one in the Commons. Macaulay of course voted with his colleagues; but he did not raise his voice to deprecate a consummation which on public grounds he could not desire to see postponed, and which, as far as his private inclinations were concerned, he had for some time past anticipated with unaffected, and all but unalloyed, delight.

[1] See Appendix III at the end of the second volume.

London: July 27, 1841.

Dear Napier,—

I am truly glad that you are satisfied. I do not know what Brougham means by objecting to what I have said of the first Lord Holland. I will engage to find chapter and verse for it all. Lady Holland told me that she could hardly conceive where I got so correct a notion of him.

I am not at all disappointed by the elections. They have, indeed, gone very nearly as I expected. Perhaps I counted on seven or eight votes more; and even these we may get on petition. I can truly say that I have not, for many years, been so happy as I am at present. Before I went to India, I had no prospect in the event of a change of Government, except that of living by my pen, and seeing my sisters governesses. In India I was an exile. When I came back, I was for a time at liberty; but I had before me the prospect of parting in a few months, perhaps for ever, with my dearest sister and her children. That misery was removed; but I found myself in office, a member of a Government wretchedly weak, and struggling for existence. Now I am free. I am independent. I am in Parliament, as honourably seated as man can be. My family is comfortably off. I have leisure for literature; yet I am not reduced to the necessity of writing for money. If I had to choose a lot from all that there are in human life, I am not sure that I should prefer any to that which has fallen to me. I am sincerely and thoroughly contented.

Ever yours

T. B. MACAULAY.

CHAPTER IX

1841–1844

Macaulay settles in the Albany—Letters to Mr. Napier—Warren Hastings, and the Vicar of Wakefield—Leigh Hunt—Macaulay's doubts about the wisdom of publishing his Essays—Lord Palmerston as a writer—The Lays of Rome—Handsome conduct of Professor Wilson—Republication of the Essays—Miss Aikin's Life of Addison—Macaulay in opposition—The Copyright Question—Recall of Lord Ellenborough—Macaulay as a public speaker: opinions of the Reporters' Gallery—Tour on the Loire—Letters to Mr. Napier—Payment of the Irish Roman Catholic Clergy—Barère.

THE change of Government was anything but a misfortune to Macaulay. He lost nothing but an income, which he could well do without, and the value of which he was ere long to replace many times over by his pen; and he gained his time, his liberty, the power of speaking what he thought, writing when he would, and living as he chose. The plan of life which he selected was one eminently suited to the bent of his tastes, and the nature of his avocations. Towards the end of the year 1840, Mr. and Mrs. Trevelyan removed to Clapham; and, on their departure, Macaulay broke up his establishment in Great George Street, and quartered himself in a commodious set of rooms on a second floor in the Albany; that luxurious cloister, whose inviolable tranquillity affords so agreeable a relief from the roar and flood of the Piccadilly traffic. His chambers, every corner of which was library, were comfortably, though not very brightly, furnished. The ornaments were few, but choice:—half a dozen fine Italian engravings from his favourite great masters; a handsome French clock, provided with a singularly melodious set of chimes, the gift of his friend and publisher, Mr. Thomas Longman; and the well-known bronze statuettes of Voltaire and Rousseau, (neither of them heroes of his own,)[1] which had been presented to him by Lady Holland as a remembrance of her husband.

The first use which Macaulay made of his freedom was in the capacity of a reviewer. Mr. Gleig, who had served with distinction during the last years of the great French war as a regimental officer, after having been five times wounded in action, had carried his merit into the Church, and his campaigning experiences into military literature. The author of one book which is good, and of several which are not amiss, he flew at too high game when he undertook

[1] Macaulay says in a letter to Lord Stanhope: 'I have not made up my mind about John, Duke of Bedford. Hot-headed he certainly was. That is a quality which lies on the surface of a character, and about which there can be no mistake. Whether a man is cold-hearted, or not, is a much more difficult question. Strong emotions may be hid by a stoical deportment. Kind and caressing manners may conceal an unfeeling disposition. Romilly, whose sensibility was morbidly strong, and who died a martyr to it, was by many thought to be incapable of affection. Rousseau, who was always soaking people's waistcoats with his tears, betrayed and slandered all his benefactors in turn, and sent his children to the Enfans Trouvés.'

Macaulay's sentiments with regard to Voltaire are pretty fully expressed in his essay on Frederick the Great. In 1853 he visited Ferney. 'The cabinet where Voltaire used to write looked, not towards Mont Blanc, of which he might have had a noble view, but towards a terrace and a grove of trees. Perhaps he wished to spare his eyes. He used to complain that the snow hurt them. I was glad to have seen a place about which I had read, and dreamed, so much; a place which, eighty years ago, was regarded with the deepest interest all over Europe, and visited by pilgrims of the highest rank and greatest genius. I suppose that no private house ever received such a number of illustrious guests during the same time as were entertained in Ferney between 1768 and 1778. I thought of Marmontel, and his "ombre chevalier;" of La Harpe, and his quarrel with the Patriarch; of Madame de Genlis, and of all the tattle which fills Grimm's Correspondence. Lord Lansdowne was much pleased. Ellis less so. He is no Voltairian; nor am I, exactly; but I take a great interest in the literary history of the last century." In his diary of the 28th of December, 1850, he writes: 'Read the "Physiology of Monkeys," and Collins's account of Voltaire;—as mischievous a monkey as any of them.'

to compile the Memoirs of Warren Hastings. In January 1841, Macaulay, who was then still at the War Office, wrote to the editor of the Edinburgh Review in these terms: 'I think the new Life of Hastings the worst book that I ever saw. I should be inclined to treat it mercilessly, were it not that the writer, though I never saw him, is as an Army chaplain in some sense placed officially under me; and I think that there would be something like tyranny and insolence in pouring contempt on a person who has a situation from which I could, for aught I know, have him dismissed, and in which I certainly could make him very uneasy. It would be far too Crokerish a proceeding for me to strike a man who would find some difficulty in retaliating. I shall therefore speak of him much less sharply than he deserves; unless indeed we should be out, which is not improbable. In that case I should, of course, be quite at liberty.'

Unfortunately for Mr. Gleig, the Whigs were relegated to private life in time to set Macaulay at liberty to make certain strictures; which, indeed, he was under an absolute obligation to make if there was any meaning in the motto of the Edinburgh Review.[1] The first two paragraphs of the Essay on Warren Hastings originally ran as follows:

'This book seems to have been manufactured in pursuance of a contract, by which the representatives of Warren Hastings, on the one part, bound themselves to furnish papers, and Mr. Gleig, on the other part, bound himself to furnish praise. It is but just to say that the covenants on both sides have been most faithfully kept; and the result is before us in the form of three big bad volumes, full of undigested correspondence and undiscerning panegyric.

'If it were worth while to examine this performance in detail, we could easily make a long article by merely pointing out inaccurate statements, inelegant expressions, and immoral doctrines. But it would be idle to waste criticism on a book-maker; and, whatever credit Mr. Gleig may have justly earned by former works, it is as a book-

[1] 'Judex damnatur cum nocens absolvitur.'

maker, and nothing more, that he now comes before us. More eminent men than Mr. Gleig have written nearly as ill as he, when they have stooped to similar drudgery. It would be unjust to estimate Goldsmith by the Vicar of Wakefield, or Scott by the Life of Napoleon. Mr. Gleig is neither a Goldsmith nor a Scott; but it would be unjust to deny that he is capable of something better than these Memoirs. It would also, we hope and believe, be unjust to charge any Christian minister with the guilt of deliberately maintaining some of the propositions which we find in this book. It is not too much to say that Mr. Gleig has written several passages which bear the same relation to the "Prince" of Machiavelli that the "Prince" of Machiavelli bears to the "Whole Duty of Man," and which would excite admiration in a den of robbers, or on board of a schooner of pirates. But we are willing to attribute these offences to haste, to thoughtlessness, and to that disease of the understanding which may be called the *Furor Biographicus*, and which is to writers of lives what the goître is to an Alpine shepherd, or dirt-eating to a negro slave.'

If this passage was unduly harsh, the punishment which overtook its author was instant and terrible. It is difficult to conceive any calamity which Macaulay would regard with greater consternation than that, in the opening sentences of an article which was sure to be read by everybody who read anything, he should pose before the world for three mortal months in the character of a critic who thought the Vicar of Wakefield a bad book.

Albany, London: October 26, 1841.

Dear Napier,—

I write chiefly to point out, what I dare say you have already observed, the absurd blunder in the first page of my article. I have not, I am sorry to say, the consolation of being able to blame either you or the printers: for it must have been a slip of my own pen. I have put the 'Vicar of Wakefield' instead of the 'History of Greece.' Pray be so kind as to correct this in the errata of the next number. I am, indeed, so much vexed by it that I could wish that the correction were made a little more prominent than usual, and introduced with two or three words of preface. But this I leave absolutely to your taste and judgment.

Ever yours truly

T. B. MACAULAY.

Dear Napier,— Albany, London: October 30, 1841.

I have received your letter, and am truly glad to find that you are satisfied with the effect of my article. As to the pecuniary part of the matter, I am satisfied, and more than satisfied. Indeed, as you well know, money has never been my chief object in writing. It was not so even when I was very poor; and at present I consider myself as one of the richest men of my acquaintance; for I can well afford to spend a thousand a year, and I can enjoy every comfort on eight hundred. I own, however, that your supply comes agreeably enough to assist me in furnishing my rooms, which I have made, unless I am mistaken, into a very pleasant student's cell.

And now a few words about Leigh Hunt. He wrote to me yesterday in great distress, and enclosed a letter which he had received from you, and which had much agitated him. In truth, he misunderstood you; and you had used an expression which was open to some little misconstruction. You told him that you should be glad to have a 'gentlemanlike' article from him, and Hunt took this for a reflection on his birth. He implored me to tell him candidly whether he had given you any offence, and to advise him as to his course. I replied that he had utterly misunderstood you; that I was sure you meant merely a literary criticism; that your taste in composition was more severe than his, more indeed than mine; that you were less tolerant than myself of little mannerisms springing from peculiarities of temper and training; that his style seemed to you too colloquial; that I myself thought that he was in danger of excess in that direction; and that, when you received a letter from him promising a very 'chatty' article, I was not surprised that you should caution him against his besetting sin. I said that I was sure that you wished him well, and would be glad of his assistance; but that he could not expect a person in your situation to pick his words very nicely; that you had during many years superintended great literary undertakings; that you had been under the necessity of collecting contributions from great numbers of writers, and that you were responsible to the public for the whole. Your credit was so deeply concerned that you must be allowed to speak plainly. I knew that you had spoken to men of the first consideration quite as plainly as to him. I knew that you had refused to insert passages written by so great a man as Lord Brougham. I knew that you had not scrupled to hack and hew articles on foreign politics which had been concocted in the Hotels of Ambassadors, and had received the *imprimatur* of Secretaries of State. I said that therefore he must, as a man of sense, suffer you to tell him what you might think, whether rightly or wrongly, to be the faults of his style. As to the sense which he had put on one or two of your expressions, I took it on myself, as your friend, to affirm that he had mistaken their meaning, and that you would never have used those words if you had foreseen that they would have been so understood. Between ourselves, the word 'gentlemanlike' was used in rather a harsh way.[1] Now I have told you what has passed between him and me; and I leave you to act as you think fit. I am sure that you will act properly and humanely. But I must add that I think you are too hard on his article.

As to the 'Vicar of Wakefield,' the correction must be deferred, I think, till the appearance of the next Number. I am utterly unable to conceive how I can have committed such a blunder, and failed to notice it in the proofs.

Ever yours

T. B. MACAULAY.

[1] It is worth notice that 'gentlemanlike' is the precise epithet which Macaulay applied to his own article on Gladstone's 'Church and State.' See vol. ii, page 1.

Albany, London: November 5, 1841.

Dear Napier,—

Leigh Hunt has sent me a most generous and amiable letter, which he has received from you. He seems much touched by it, and more than satisfied, as he ought to be.

I have at last begun my historical labours; I can hardly say with how much interest and delight. I really do not think that there is in our literature so great a void as that which I am trying to supply. English history, from 1688 to the French Revolution, is even to educated people almost a terra incognita. I will venture to say that it is quite an even chance whether even such a man as Empson, or Senior, can repeat accurately the names of the Prime Ministers of that time in order. The materials for an amusing narrative are immense. I shall not be satisfied unless I produce something which shall for a few days supersede the last fashionable novel on the tables of young ladies.

I should be very much obliged to you to tell me what are the best sources of information about the Scotch Revolution in 1688, the campaign of Dundee, the massacre of Glencoe, and the Darien scheme. I mean to visit the scenes of all the principal events both in Great Britain and Ireland, and also on the Continent. Would it be worth my while to pass a fortnight in one of the Edinburgh Libraries next summer? Or do you imagine that the necessary information is to be got at the British Museum?

By the bye, a lively picture of the state of the Kirk is indispensable.

Ever yours

T. B. MACAULAY.

Albany, London: December 1, 1841.

Dear Napier,—

You do not seem to like what I suggested about Henry the Fifth.[1] Nor do I, on full consideration. What

[1] Macaulay had written on the 10th of November: 'If Longman will send me Mr. Tyler's book on Henry the Fifth, I will see whether I cannot, with the help of Froissart and

do you say to an article on Frederic the Great? Tom Campbell is bringing out a book about His Majesty.

Now that I am seriously engaged in an extensive work, which will probably be the chief employment of the years of health and vigour which remain to me, it is necessary that I should choose my subjects for reviews with some reference to that work. I should not choose to write an article on some point which I should have to treat again as a historian; for, if I did, I should be in danger of repeating myself. I assure you that I a little grudge you Westminster Hall, in the paper on Hastings. On the other hand there are many characters and events which will occupy little or no space in my History, yet with which, in the course of my historical researches, I shall necessarily become familiar. There cannot be a better instance than Frederic the Great. His personal character, manners, studies, literary associates; his quarrel with Voltaire, his friendship for Maupertuis, and his own unhappy *métromanie* will be very slightly, if at all, alluded to in a History of England.[1] Yet in order to write the History of England, it will be necessary to turn over all the Memoirs, and all the writings, of Frederic, connected with us, as he was, in a most important war. In this way my reviews would benefit by my historical researches, and yet would not forestall my history, or materially impede its progress. I should not like to engage in any researches altogether alien from what is now my main object. Still less should I like to tell the same story over and over again, which I must do if I were to write on such a subject as the Vernon Correspondence, or Trevor's History of William the Third.

Ever yours

T. B. MACAULAY.

Monstrelet, furnish a spirited sketch of that short and most brilliant life.'

[1] At this period of his career Macaulay still purposed, and hoped, to write the history of England 'down to a time which is within the memory of men still living.'

In January 1842, Macaulay writes to Mr. Napier: 'As to Frederic, I do not see that I can deal with him well under seventy pages. I shall try to give a life of him after the manner of Plutarch. That, I think, is my forte. The paper on Clive took greatly. That on Hastings, though in my own opinion by no means equal to that on Clive, has been even more successful. I ought to produce something much better than either of those articles with so excellent a subject as Frederic. Keep the last place for me, if you can. I greatly regret my never having seen Berlin and Potsdam.'

Albany, London: April 18, 1842.

My dear Napier,—

I am much obliged to you for your criticisms on my article on Frederic. My copy of the Review I have lent, and cannot therefore refer to it. I have, however, thought over what you say, and should be disposed to admit part of it to be just. But I have several distinctions and limitations to suggest.

The charge to which I am most sensible is that of interlarding my sentences with French terms. I will not positively affirm that no such expression may have dropped from my pen in writing hurriedly on a subject so very French. It is, however, a practice to which I am extremely averse, and into which I could fall only by inadvertence. I do not really know to what you allude; for as to the words 'Abbé' and 'Parc-aux-Cerfs,' which I recollect, those surely are not open to objection. I remember that I carried my love of English in one or two places almost to the length of affectation. For example I called the 'Place des Victoires,' the 'place of Victories'; and the 'Fermier Général' D'Etioles, a 'publican.' I will look over the article again, when I get it into my hands, and try to discover to what you allude.

The other charge, I confess, does not appear to me to be equally serious. I certainly should not, in regular history, use some of the phrases which you censure. But I do not consider a review of this sort as regular history, and I really think that, from the highest and most unquestionable authority, I could vindicate my practice. Take Addison, the model of pure and graceful writing. In his Spectators I find 'wench,' 'baggage,' 'queer old put,' 'prig,' 'fearing that they should smoke the Knight.' All these expressions I met this morning, in turning over two or three of his papers at breakfast. I would no more use the word 'bore,' or 'awkward squad,' in a composition meant to be uniformly serious and earnest, than Addison would in a State paper have called Louis an 'old put,' or have described Shrewsbury and Argyle as 'smoking' the design to bring in the Pretender. But I did not mean my article to be uniformly serious and earnest. If you judge of it as you would judge of a regular history, your censure ought to go very much deeper than it does, and to be directed against the substance as well as against the diction. The tone of many passages, nay of whole pages, would justly be called flippant in a regular history. But I conceive that this sort of composition has its own character, and its own laws. I do not claim the honour of having invented it; that praise belongs to Southey; but I may say that I have in some points improved upon his design. The manner of these little historical essays bears, I think, the same analogy to the manner of Tacitus or Gibbon which the manner of Ariosto bears to the manner of Tasso, or the manner of Shakspeare's historical plays to the manner of Sophocles. Ariosto, when he is grave and pathetic, is as grave and pathetic as Tasso; but he often takes a light fleeting tone which suits him admirably, but which in Tasso would be quite out of place. The despair of Constance in Shakspeare is as lofty as that of Œdipus in Sophocles; but the levities of the bastard Faulconbridge would be utterly out place in Sophocles. Yet we feel that they are not out of place in Shakspeare.

So with these historical articles. Where the subject requires it, they may rise, if the author can manage it, to the highest altitudes of Thucydides. Then, again, they may without impropriety sink to the levity and colloquial ease of Horace Walpole's Letters. This is my theory. Whether I have succeeded in the execution is quite another question. You will, however, perceive that I am in no danger of taking similar liberties in my History. I do, indeed, greatly disapprove of those notions which some writers have of the dignity of history. For fear of alluding to the vulgar concerns of private life, they take no notice of the circumstances which deeply affect the happiness of nations. But I never thought of denying that the language of history ought to preserve a certain dignity. I would, however, no more attempt to preserve that dignity in a paper like this on Frederic than I would exclude from such a poem as Don Juan slang terms, because such terms would be out of place in Paradise Lost, or Hudibrastic rhymes, because such lines would be shocking in Pope's Iliad.

As to the particular criticisms which you have made, I willingly submit my judgment to yours, though I think that I could say something on the other side. The first rule of all writing,—that rule to which every other is subordinate,—is that the words used by the writer shall be such as most fully and precisely convey his meaning to the great body of his readers. All considerations about the purity and dignity of style ought to bend to this consideration. To write what is not understood in its whole force, for fear of using some word which was unknown to Swift or Dryden, would be, I think, as absurd as to build an Observatory like that at Oxford, from which it is impossible to observe, only for the purpose of exactly preserving the proportions of the Temple of the Winds at Athens. That a word which is appropriate to a particular idea, which everybody high and low uses to express that idea, and which expresses that idea with a completeness which is not equalled by any other single word, and scarcely by any circumlocution, should be banished from writing, seems to be a mere throwing away of power. Such a word as 'talented' it is proper to avoid; first, because it is not wanted; secondly, because you never hear it from those who speak very good English. But the word 'shirk' as applied to military duty is a word which everybody uses; which is the word, and the only word, for the thing; which in every regiment, and in every ship, belonging to our country, is employed ten times a day; which the Duke of Wellington, or Admiral Stopford, would use in reprimanding an officer. To interdict it, therefore, in what is meant to be familiar, and almost jocose, narrative seems to me rather rigid.

But I will not go on. I will only repeat that I am truly grateful for your advice, and that if you will, on future occasions, mark with an asterisk any words in my proof sheets which you think open to objection, I will try to meet your wishes, though it may sometimes be at the expense of my own.

Ever yours most truly
T. B. MACAULAY.

Albany, London: April 25, 1842.

Dear Napier,—

Thank you for your letter. We shall have no disputes about diction. The English language is not so poor but that I may very well find in it the means of contenting both you and myself.

I have no objection to try Madame D'Arblay for the October number. I have only one scruple,—that some months ago Leigh Hunt told me that he thought of proposing that subject to you, and I approved of his doing so. Now, I should have no scruples in taking a subject out of Brougham's hands, because he can take care of himself, if he thinks himself ill-used. But I would not do anything that could hurt the feelings of a man whose spirit seems to be quite broken by adversity, and who lies under some obligations to me.

By the way, a word on a subject which I should be much obliged to you to consider, and advise me upon. I find that the American publishers have thought it worth while to put forth two, if not three, editions of my reviews; and I receive letters from them, saying that the sale is considerable. I have heard that several people here have ordered them from America. Others have cut them out of old numbers of the Edinburgh Review, and have bound them up in volumes. Now, I know that these pieces are full of faults, and that their popularity has been very far beyond their merit; but, if they are to be republished, it would be better that they should be republished under the eye of the author, and with his corrections, than that they should retain all the blemishes inseparable from hasty writing and hasty printing. Longman proposed something of the kind to me three years ago; but at that time the American publication had not taken place, which makes a great difference. Give me your counsel on the subject.

Ever yours truly
T. B. MACAULAY.

Albany, London: June 24, 1842.

Dear Napier,—

I have thought a good deal about republishing my articles, and have made up my mind not to do so. It is rather provoking, to be sure, to learn that a third edition is coming out in America, and to meet constantly with smuggled copies. It is still more provoking to see trash, of which I am perfectly guiltless, inserted among my writings. But, on the whole, I think it best that things should remain as they are. The public judges, and ought to judge, indulgently of periodical works. They are not expected to be highly finished. Their natural life is only six weeks. Sometimes their writer is at a distance from the books to which he wants to refer. Sometimes he is forced to hurry through his task in order to catch the post. He may blunder; he may contradict himself; he may break off in the middle of a story; he may give an immoderate extension to one part of his subject, and dismiss an equally important part in a few words. All this is readily forgiven if there be a certain spirit and vivacity in his style. But, as soon as he republishes, he challenges a comparison with all the most symmetrical and polished of human compositions. A painter, who has a picture in the Exhibition of the Royal Academy, would act very unwisely if he took it down and carried it over to the National Gallery. Where it now hangs, surrounded by a crowd of daubs which are only once seen, and then forgotten, it may pass for a fine piece. He is a fool if he places it side by side with the master-pieces of Titian and Claude. My reviews are generally thought to be better written, and they certainly live longer, than the reviews of most other people; and this ought to content me. The moment I come forward to demand a higher rank, I must expect to be judged by a higher standard. Fonblanque may serve for a beacon. His leading articles in the Examiner were extolled to the skies, while they were considered merely as leading articles; for they were in style, and manner, incomparably superior to anything in the Courier, or Globe, or Standard; nay, to anything in the Times. People said that it was a pity that such admirable compositions should perish; so Fonblanque determined to republish them in a book. He never considered that in that form they would be compared, not with the rant and twaddle of the daily and weekly press, but with Burke's pamphlets, with Pascal's letters, with Addison's Spectators and Freeholders. They would not stand this new test a moment. I shall profit by the warning. What the Yankees may do I cannot help; but I will not found my pretensions to the rank of a classic on my reviews. I will remain, according to the excellent precept in the Gospel, at the lower end of the table, where I am constantly accosted with 'Friend, go up higher,' and not push my way to the top at the risk of being compelled with shame to take the lowest room. If I live twelve or fifteen years I may perhaps produce something which I may not be afraid to exhibit side by side with the performance of the old masters.

Ever yours truly

T. B. MACAULAY.

Albany, London: July 14, 1842.

Dear Napier,—

As to the next Number, I must beg you to excuse me. I am exceedingly desirous to get on with my History, which is really in a fair train. I must go down into Somersetshire and Devonshire to see the scene of Monmouth's campaign, and to follow the line of William's march from Torquay. I have also another plan of no great importance, but one which will occupy me during some days. You are acquainted, no doubt, with Perizonius's theory about the early Roman history; a theory which Niebuhr revived, and which Arnold has adopted as fully established. I have myself not the smallest doubt of its truth. It is, that the stories of the birth of Romulus and Remus, the fight of the Horatii and Curiatii, and all the other romantic tales which fill the first three or four books of Livy, came from the lost ballads of the early Romans. I amused myself in India with trying to restore some of these long-perished poems. Arnold saw two of them,[1] and wrote to me in such terms of eulogy that I have been induced to correct and complete them. There are four of them, and I think that, though they are but trifles, they may pass for scholarlike and not inelegant trifles. I must prefix short prefaces to them, and I think of publishing them next November in a small volume. I fear, therefore, that just at present I can be of no use to you. Nor, indeed should I find it easy to select a subject. Romilly's Life is a little stale. Lord Cornwallis is not an attractive subject. Clive and Hastings were great men, and their history is full of great events. Cornwallis was a respectable specimen of

[1] Dr. Arnold never saw the Lays in print. Just a month previous to the date of this letter Macaulay wrote to his sister Fanny: 'But poor Arnold! I am deeply grieved for him, and for the public. It is really a great calamity, and will be felt as such by hundreds of families. There was no such school: and from the character of the Trustees, who almost all are strong, and even bitter, Tories, I fear that the place is likely to be filled by somebody of very different spirit.'

mediocrity. His wars were not brilliantly successful; fiscal reforms were his principal measures; and to interest English readers in questions of Indian finance is quite impossible.

I am a little startled by the very careless way in which the review on Duelling has been executed. In the historical part there are really as many errors as assertions. Look at page 439. Ossory never called out Clarendon. The Peer whom he called out, on the Irish Cattle Bill, was Buckingham. The provocation was Buckingham's remark that whoever opposed the Bill had an Irish interest, or an Irish understanding. It is Clarendon who tells the whole story. Then, as to the scuffle between Buckingham and a free-trading Lord Dorchester in the lobby, the scuffle was not in the lobby, but at a Conference in the Painted Chamber; nor had it anything to do with free trade; for at a Conference all the Lords are on one side. It was the effect of an old quarrel, and of an accidental jostling for seats. Then, a few lines lower, it is said that Lady Shrewsbury dissipated all her son's estate, which is certainly not true; for, soon after he came of age, he raised 40,000*l.* by mortgage, which at the then rate of interest he never could have done unless he had a good estate. Then, in the next page, it is said that Mohun murdered rather than killed the Duke of Hamilton,—a gross blunder. Those who thought that the Duke was murdered always attributed the murder not to Mohun, but to Mohun's second, Macartney. The fight between the two principals was universally allowed to be perfectly fair. Nor did Steele rebuke Thornhill for killing Dering, but on the contrary did his best to put Thornhill's conduct in the most amiable light, and to throw the whole blame on the bad usages of society. I do not know that there ever was a greater number of mistakes as to matters of fact in so short a space. I have read only those two pages of the article. If it is all of a piece, it is a prodigy indeed.

Let me beg that you will not mention the little literary scheme which I have confided to you. I should be very sorry that it were known till the time of publication arrives.

Ever yours truly
T. B. MACAULAY.

Albany, London: July 20, 1842.

Dear Napier,—

I do not like to disappoint you; and I really would try to send you something, if I could think of a subject that would suit me. My objections to taking Romilly's Life are numerous. One of them is that I was not acquainted with him, and never heard him speak, except for a few minutes when I was a child. A stranger, who writes a description of a person whom hundreds still living knew intimately, is almost certain to make mistakes; and, even if he makes no absolute mistake, his portrait is not likely to be thought a striking resemblance by those who knew the original. It is like making a bust from a description. The best sculptor must disappoint those who knew the real face. I felt this even about Lord Holland; and nothing but Lady Holland's request would have overcome my unwillingness to say anything about his Parliamentary speaking, which I had never heard. I had, however, known him familiarly in private; but Romilly I never saw except in the House of Commons.

You do not quite apprehend the nature of my plan about the old Roman ballads; but the explanation will come fast enough. I wish from my soul that I had written a volume of my History. I have not written half a volume; nor do I consider what I have done as more than rough hewn.

I hear with some concern that Dickens is going to publish a most curious book against the Yankees. I am told that all the Fearons, Trollopes, Marryats, and Martineaus together have not given them half so much offence as he will give. This may be a more serious affair than the destruction of the Caroline, or the mutiny in the Creole.[1]

Ever yours
T. B. MACAULAY.

[1] The Caroline was an American steamboat which had been

In a subsequent letter Macaulay says: 'I wish Dickens's book to be kept for me. I have never written a word on that subject; and I have a great deal in my head. Of course I shall be courteous to Dickens, whom I know, and whom I think both a man of genius, and a good-hearted man, in spite of some faults of taste.'

Mr. Napier was very anxious to turn the enforced leisure of the Whig leaders to some account, by getting an article for his October Number from the Foreign Secretary of the late Administration. In August 1842 Macaulay writes: 'I had a short talk about the Edinburgh Review with Palmerston, just before he left London. I told him what is quite true, that there were some public men of high distinction whom I would never counsel to write, both with a view to the interests of the Review, and to their own; but that he was in no danger of losing by his writings any part of the credit which he had acquired by speech and action. I was quite sincere in this, for he writes excellently.' Lord Palmerston, after thinking the matter over, sent Macaulay a letter promising to think it over a little more; and stating, in his free pleasant style, the difficulties which made him hesitate about acceding to the proposal. 'If one has any good hits to make about the present state of foreign affairs, one feels disposed to reserve them for the House of Commons; while, in order to do justice to the British Government, it might now and then be necessary to say things about some foreign Governments which would not come altogether well from anybody who had been, and might be thought likely again at some future time to be, concerned in the management of affairs. Perhaps you will say that the

employed to convey arms and stores to the Canadian insurgents. A party of loyalists seized the vessel, and sent her down the falls of Niagara. The Creole difficulty arose from the mutiny of a ship-load of Virginian slaves, who, in an evil hour for their owner, bethought themselves that they were something better than a cargo of cattle.

last consideration need not restrain the pen of any of us, according to present appearances.'

Albany, London: August 22, 1842.

Dear Ellis,—

For the ballads many thanks. Some of them are capital.

I have been wishing for your advice. My little volume is nearly finished, and I must talk the prefaces over with you fully. I have made some alterations which I think improvements, and, in particular, have shortened the Battle of Regillus by nearly thirty lines without, I think, omitting any important circumstance.

It is odd that we never, in talking over this subject, remembered that, in all probability, the old Roman lays were in the Saturnian metre; and it is still more odd that my ballads should, by mere accident, be very like the Saturnian metre; quite as like, indeed, as suits the genius of our language. The Saturnian metre is catalectic dimeter Iambic, followed by three trochees. A pure Saturnian line is preserved by some grammarian:

Dabunt malum Metelli Nævio poetæ.

Now, oddly enough, every tetrastich, and almost every distich, of my ballads opens with a catalectic dimeter Iambic line.

Lars Porsena of Clusium

is precisely the same with

Dabunt malum Metelli.

I have not kept the trochees, which really would be very unpleasing to an English ear. Yet there are some verses which the omission of a single syllable would convert into pure Saturnian metre as

In Alba's lake no fisher
(His) nets to-day is flinging.

Is not this an odd coincidence?

The only pure Saturnian line, that I have been able to call to mind, in all English poetry, is in the nursery song,

> The Queen was in her parlour
> Eating bread and honey.

Let me know when you come to town. I shall be here. Fix a day for dining with me next week, the sooner after your arrival the better. I must give you one good boring about these verses before I deliver them over to the printer's devils.

Have you read Lord Londonderry's Travels? I hear that they contain the following pious expressions of resignation to the divine will: 'Here I learned that Almighty God, for reasons best known to Himself, had been pleased to burn down my house in the county of Durham.' Is not the mixture of vexation with respect admirable?

Ever yours
T. B. M.

In a later letter to Mr. Ellis, Macaulay says: 'Your objection to the lines,

> 'By heaven,' he said, 'yon rebels
> Stand manfully at bay,'

is quite sound. I also think the word 'rebels' objectionable, as raising certain modern notions about allegiance, divine right, Tower Hill, and the Irish Croppies, which are not at all to the purpose. What do you say to this couplet?

> Quoth he, 'The she-wolf's litter
> Stand savagely at bay.'

"Litter" is used by our best writers as governing the plural number.'

Albany: September 29, 1842.

Dear Ellis,—

Many thanks for the sheets. I am much obliged to Adolphus for the trouble which he has taken. Some of his criticisms are quite sound. I admit that the line about bringing Lucrece to shame is very bad, and the worse for coming over so often.[1] I will try to mend it. I admit, also, that the inventory of spoils in the last poem is, as he says, too long. I will see what can be done with it. He is not, I think, in the right about 'the true client smile.' 'The true client smile' is not exactly in the style of our old ballads; but it would be dangerous to make these old ballads models, in all points, for satirical poems which are supposed to have been produced in a great strife between two parties, crowded together within the walls of a republican city. And yet even in an old English ballad I should not be surprised to find an usurer described as having the 'righte Jew grinne.'

I am more obliged to Adolphus than I can express for his interest in these trifles. As to you, I need say nothing. But pray be easy. I am so, and shall be so. Every book settles its own place. I never did, and never will, directly or indirectly take any step for the purpose of obtaining praise, or deprecating censure. Longman came to ask what I wished him to do before the volume appeared. I told him that I stipulated for nothing but that there should be no puffing of any sort. I have told Napier that I ask it, as a personal favour, that my name and writings may never be mentioned in the Edinburgh Review. I shall certainly leave this volume as the ostrich leaves her eggs in the sand.

T. B. MACAULAY.

Albany: October 19, 1842.

Dear Napier,—

This morning I received Dickens's book. I have now read it. It is impossible for me to review it; nor do I think that you would wish me to do so. I cannot praise it, and I will not cut it up. I cannot praise it,

[1] It is evident from this letter that the line

That brought Lucrece to shame

originally stood wherever the line

That wrought the deed of shame

stands now.

though it contains a few lively dialogues and descriptions; for it seems to me to be on the whole a failure. It is written like the worst parts of Humphrey's Clock. What is meant to be easy and sprightly is vulgar and flippant, as in the first two pages. What is meant to be fine is a great deal too fine for me, as the description of the Fall of Niagara. A reader who wants an amusing account of the United States had better go to Mrs. Trollope, coarse and malignant as she is. A reader who wants information about American politics, manners, and literature had better go even to so poor a creature as Buckingham. In short, I pronounce the book, in spite of some gleams of genius, at once frivolous and dull.

Therefore I will not praise it. Neither will I attack it; first, because I have eaten salt with Dickens; secondly, because he is a good man, and a man of real talent; thirdly, because he hates slavery as heartily as I do; and, fourthly, because I wish to see him enrolled in our blue and yellow corps, where he may do excellent service as a skirmisher and sharp-shooter.

Ever yours truly

T. B. MACAULAY.

My little volume will be out, I think, in the course of the week. But all that I leave to Longman, except that I have positively stipulated that there shall be no puffing.

The sails of the little craft could dispense with an artificial breeze. Launched without any noise of trumpets, it went bravely down the wind of popular favour. Among the first to discern its merits was Macaulay's ancient adversary, Professor Wilson of Edinburgh, who greeted it in Blackwood's Magazine with a pæan of hearty, unqualified panegyric; which was uttered with all the more zest because the veteran gladiator of the press recognised an opportunity for depreciating, by comparison with Macaulay, the reigning verse-writers of the day.

'What! Poetry from Macaulay? Ay, and why not? The House hushes itself to hear him, even though Stanley is the cry? If he be not the first of critics, (spare our blushes,) who is! Name the Young Poet who could have written the Armada. The Young Poets all want fire; Macaulay is full of fire. The Young Poets are somewhat weakly; he is strong. The Young Poets are rather ignorant; his knowledge is great. The Young Poets mumble books; he devours them. The Young Poets dally with their subject: he strikes its heart. The Young Poets are still their own heroes; he sees but the chiefs he celebrates. The Young Poets weave dreams with shadows transitory as clouds without substance; he builds realities lasting as rocks. The Young Poets steal from all and sundry, and deny their thefts; he robs in the face of day. Whom? Homer.'

Again and again in the course of his article Christopher North indulges himself in outbursts of joyous admiration, which he had doubtless repressed, more or less consciously, ever since the time when, 'twenty years ago, like a burnished fly in pride of May, Macaulay bounced through the open windows of Knight's Quarterly Magazine.' He instructs his readers that a war-song is not to be skimmed through once, and then laid aside like a pamphlet on the Corn Laws.

'Why, Sir Walter kept reciting his favourite ballads almost every day for forty years, and with the same fire about his eyes, till even they grew dim at last. Sir Walter would have rejoiced in Horatius as if he had been a doughty Douglas.

> Now by our sire Quirinus
> It was a goodly sight
> To see the thirty standards
> Swept down the tide of flight.

That is the way of doing business! A cut and thrust style, without any flourish. Scott's style when his blood was up, and the first words came like a vanguard impatient for battle.'

The description of Virginia's death is pronounced by the Reviewer to be 'the only passage in which Mr. Macaulay has sought to stir up pathetic emotion. Has he succeeded? We hesitate not to say that he has, to our heart's desire. This effect has been wrought simply by letting the course of the great natural affections flow on, obedient to the promptings of a sound manly heart.' Slight as it is, this bit of criticism shows genuine perspicacity. Frequent allusions in Macaulay's journals leave no doubt that in these lines he intended to embody his feelings towards his little niece Margaret, now Lady Holland,[1] to whom then, as always, he was deeply and tenderly attached.

By making such cordial amends to an author whom in old days he had unjustly disparaged, Professor Wilson did credit to his own sincerity; but the public approbation needed no prompter, either then or thereafter. Eighteen thousand of the Lays of Ancient Rome were sold in ten years; forty thousand in twenty years; and, by June 1875, upwards of a hundred thousand copies had passed into the hands of readers. But it is a work of superfluity to measure by statistics the success of poems every line of which is, and long has been, too hackneyed for quotation.

Albany, London: November 16, 1842.

Dear Napier,—

On my return from a short tour I found your letter on my table. I am glad that you like my Lays, and the more glad because I know that, from good-will to me, you must have been anxious about their fate. I do not wonder at your misgivings. I should have felt similar misgivings if I had learned that any person, however distinguished by talents and knowledge, whom I knew as a writer only by prose works, was about to publish a volume of poetry. Had I seen advertised a poem by Mackintosh, by Dugald Stewart, or even by Burke, I should have augured nothing but failure; and I am far from putting myself on a level even with the least of the three. So much the better for me. Where people look for no merit, a little merit goes a long way; and, without the smallest affectation of modesty, I confess that the success of my little book

[1] Afterwards Viscountess Knutsford.

has far exceeded its just claims. I shall be in no hurry to repeat the experiment; for I am well aware that a second attempt would be made under much less favourable circumstances. A far more severe test would now be applied to my verses. I shall, therefore, like a wise gamester, leave off while I am a winner, and not cry Double or Quits.

As to poor Leigh Hunt, I wish that I could say, with you, that I heard nothing from him. I have a letter from him on my table asking me to lend him money, and lamenting that my verses want the true poetical aroma which breathes from Spenser's Faery Queen. I am much pleased with him for having the spirit to tell me, in a begging letter, how little he likes my poetry. If he had praised me, knowing his poetical creed as I do, I should have felt certain that his praises were insincere.

Ever yours

T. B. MACAULAY.

Albany, London: December 3, 1842.

Dear Napier,—

Longman has earnestly pressed me to consent to the republication of some of my reviews. The plan is one of which, as you know, I had thought; and which, on full consideration, I had rejected. But there are new circumstances in the case. The American edition is coming over by wholesale.[1] To keep out the American copies by legal measures, and yet to refuse to publish an edition here, would be an odious course, and in the very spirit of the dog in the manger. I am, therefore, strongly inclined to accede to Longman's proposition. And if the thing is to be done, the sooner the better.

I am about to put forth a second edition of my

[1] In a subsequent letter Macaulay writes: 'The question is now merely this, whether Longman and I, or Carey and Hart of Philadelphia, shall have the supplying of the English market with these papers. The American copies are coming over by scores, and measures are being taken for bringing them over by hundreds.'

Roman Lays. They have had great success. By the bye, Wilson, whom I never saw but at your table, has behaved very handsomely about them. I am not in the habit of returning thanks for favourable criticism; for, as Johnson says in his Life of Lyttleton, such thanks must be paid either for flattery or for justice. But, when a strong political opponent bestows fervent praise on a work which he might easily depreciate by means of sly sneer and cold commendations, and which he might, if he chose, pass by in utter silence, he ought, I think, to be told that his courtesy and good feeling are justly appreciated. I should be really obliged to you, if, when you have an opportunity, you will let Professor Wilson know that his conduct has affected me as generous conduct affects men not ungenerous.

Ever yours

T. B. MACAULAY.

Macaulay spent the first weeks of 1843 in preparing for the republication of his Essays. 'I find from many quarters,' he writes to Mr. Longman on the 25th of January, 'that it is thought that the article on Southey's edition of Bunyan ought to be in the collection. It is a favourite with the Dissenters.' And again: 'Pray omit all mention of my Prefatory Notice. It will be very short and simple, and ought by no means to be announced beforehand as if it were anything elaborate and important.' The world was not slow to welcome, and, having welcomed, was not in a hurry to shelve, a book so unwillingly and unostentatiously presented to its notice. Upwards of a hundred and twenty thousand copies have been sold in the United Kingdom alone by a single publisher. Considerably over a hundred and thirty thousand copies of separate essays have been printed in the series known by the name of the Travellers' Library. And it is no passing, or even waning, popularity which these figures represent. Between the years 1843 and 1853, the yearly sales by Messrs. Longman of the collected editions averaged 1,230 copies; between 1853 and 1864, they rose to an average of 4,700; and, since 1864, more than six thousand copies have, one year with another, been disposed of annually. The publishers of the United States are still pouring forth reprints by many thousands at a time; and in British India, and on the Continent of Europe, these productions, which their author classed as ephemeral, are so greedily read and so constantly reproduced, that, taking the world as a whole, there is probably never a moment when they are out of the hands of the compositor. The market for them in their native country is so steady, and apparently so inexhaustible, that it perceptibly falls and rises with the general prosperity of the nation; and it is hardly too much to assert that the demand for Macaulay varies with the demand for coal. The astonishing success of this celebrated book must be regarded as something of far higher consequence than a mere literary or commercial triumph. It is no insignificant feat to have awakened in hundreds of thousands of minds the taste for letters, and the yearning for knowledge; and to have shown by example that, in the interests of its own fame, genius can never be so well employed as on the careful and earnest treatment of serious themes.

Albany, London: January 18, 1843.

Dear Napier,—

Another paper from me is at present out of the question. One in half a year is the very utmost of which I can hold out any hopes. I ought to give my whole leisure to my History; and I fear that, if I suffer myself to be diverted from that design as I have done, I shall, like poor Mackintosh, leave behind me the character of a man who would have done something, if he had concentrated his powers, instead of frittering them away. I do assure you that, if it were not on your account, I should have already given up writing for the Review at all. There are people who can carry on twenty works at a time. Southey would write the

History of Brazil before breakfast, an ode after breakfast, then the History of the Peninsular War till dinner, and an article for the Quarterly Review in the evening. But I am of a different temper. I never write to please myself until my subject has for the time driven every other out of my head. When I turn from one work to another, a great deal of time is lost in the mere transition. I must not go on dawdling, and reproaching myself, all my life.

Ever yours

T. B. MACAULAY.

Albany, London: April 19, 1843.

Dear Napier,—

You may count on an article from me on Miss Aikin's Life of Addison. Longman sent me the sheets as they were printed. I own that I am greatly disappointed. There are, to be sure, some charming letters by Addison which have never yet been published; but Miss Aikin's narrative is dull, shallow, and inaccurate. Either she has fallen off greatly since she wrote her former works, or I have become much more acute since I read them. By the bye, I have an odd story to tell you. I was vexed at observing in a very hasty perusal of the sheets, a great number of blunders, any of which singly was discreditable, and all of which united were certain to be fatal to the book. To give a few specimens, the lady called Evelyn 'Sir John Evelyn;' transferred Christ Church from Oxford to Cambridge; confounded Robert Earl of Sunderland, James the Second's Minister, with his son Charles, Earl of Sunderland, George the First's Minister; confounded Charles Montague, Earl of Halifax, with George Savile, Marquis of Halifax; called the Marquis of Hertford 'Earl of Hertford,' and so forth. I pointed the grossest blunders out to Longman, and advised him to point them out to her without mentioning me. He did so. The poor woman could not deny that my remarks were just; but she railed most bitterly, both at the publishers, and at the Mr. Nobody, who had

had the insolence to find any blemish in her writings. At first she suspected Sedgwick. She now knows that she was wrong in that conjecture, but I do not think that she has detected me. This, you will say, is but a bad return to me for going out of my way to save her book from utter ruin. I am glad to learn that, with all her anger, she has had the sense to cancel some sheets in consequence of Mr. Nobody's criticisms.

My collected reviews have succeeded well. Longman tells me that he must set about a second edition. In spite, however, of the applause and of the profit, neither of which I despise, I am sorry that it had become necessary to republish these papers. There are few of them which I read with satisfaction. Those few, however, are generally the latest, and this is a consolatory circumstance. The most hostile critic must admit, I think, that I have improved greatly as a writer. The third volume seems to me worth two of the second, and the second worth ten of the first.

Jeffrey is at work on his collection. It will be delightful, no doubt; but to me it will not have the charm of novelty; for I have read, and re-read, his old articles till I know them by heart.

Ever yours

T. B. MACAULAY.

Albany: June 15, 1843.

Dear Napier,—

I mistrust my own judgment of what I write so much, that I shall not be at all surprised if both you and the public think my paper on Addison a failure; but I own that I am partial to it. It is now more than half finished. I have some researches to make before I proceed; but I have all the rest in my head, and shall write very rapidly. I fear that I cannot contract my matter into less than seventy pages. You will not, I think, be inclined to stint me.

I am truly vexed to find Miss Aikin's book so very bad, that it is impossible for us, with due regard to our own character, to praise it. All that I can do is to speak civilly of her writings generally, and to express regret that she should have been nodding. I have found, I will venture to say, not less than forty gross blunders as to matters of fact in the first volume. Of these I may, perhaps, point out eight or ten as courteously as the case will bear. Yet it goes much against my feelings to censure any woman, even with the greatest lenity. My taste and Croker's are by no means the same. I shall not again undertake to review any lady's book till I know how it is executed.

Ever yours

T. B. MACAULAY.

Albany, London: July 22, 1843.

Dear Napier,—

I hear generally favourable opinions about my article. I am much pleased with one thing. You may remember how confidently I asserted that 'little Dicky' in the Old Whig was the nickname of some comic actor.[1] Several people thought that I risked too much

[1] 'One calumny, which has been often repeated, and never yet contradicted, it is our duty to expose. It is asserted, in the Biographia Britannica, that Addison designated Steele as "little Dicky." This assertion was repeated by Johnson, who had never seen the Old Whig, and was therefore excusable. It has also been repeated by Miss Aikin, who has seen the Old Whig, and for whom therefore there is less excuse. Now, it is true that the words "little Dicky" occur in the Old Whig, and that Steele's name was Richard. It is equally true that the words "little Isaac" occur in the Duenna, and that Newton's name was Isaac. But we confidently affirm that Addison's little Dicky had no more to do with Steele, than Sheridan's little Isaac with Newton. If we apply the words "little Dicky" to Steele, we deprive a very lively and ingenious passage, not only of all its wit, but of all its meaning. Little Dicky was evidently the nickname of some comic actor who played the usurer Gomez, then a most popular part, in Dryden's Spanish Friar.'

This passage occurs in Macaulay's Articles on Miss Aikin's Life and Writings of Addison, as it originally appeared in July 1843. There is a marked difference of form between this and all his previous contributions to the Edinburgh Review. The text of the article on Addison is, with few and slight variations, the text of the Collected Edition; while all that relates to Miss Aikin is relegated to the foot-notes. Thus in the

in assuming this so strongly on mere internal evidence. I have now, by an odd accident, found out who the actor was. An old prompter of Drury Lane Theatre, named Chetwood, published in 1749 a small volume, containing an account of all the famous performers whom he remembered, arranged in alphabetical order. This little volume I picked up yesterday, for sixpence, at a book-stall in Holborn; and the first name on which I opened was that of Henry Norris, a favourite comedian, who was nicknamed Dicky, because he first obtained celebrity by acting the part of Dicky in the Trip to the Jubilee. It is added that his figure was very diminutive. He was, it seems, in the height of his popularity at the very time when the Old Whig was written. You will, I think, agree with me that this is decisive. I am a little vain of my sagacity, which I really think would have dubbed me a 'vir clarissimus' if it had been shown on a point of Greek or Latin learning; but I am still more pleased that the vindication of Addison from an unjust charge, which has been universally believed since the publication of the Lives of the Poets, should thus be complete. Should you have any objection to inserting a short note at the end of the next Number? Ten lines would suffice; and the matter is really interesting to all lovers of literary history.

As to politics, the Ministers are in a most unenviable

note on page 239 we read: 'Miss Aikin says that the Guardian was launched in November 1713. It was launched in March 1713, and was given over in the following September.' And in the note on page 247: 'Miss Aikin has been most unfortunate in her account of this Rebellion. We will notice only two errors, which occur in one page. She says that the rebellion was undertaken in favour of James the Second, who had been fourteen years dead, and that it was headed by Charles Edward, who was not born.'

Macaulay was now no longer able to conceal from himself the fact, that, whether he liked it or not, his Essays would live; and he accordingly took pains to separate the part of his work, which was of permanent literary value, from those passing strictures upon his author which as a Reviewer he was bound to make, in order to save himself the trouble of subsequent revision and expurgation.

situation; and, as far as I can see, all the chances are against them. The immense name of the Duke, though now only a 'magni nominis umbra,' is of great service to them. His assertion, unsupported by reasons, saved Lord Ellenborough. His declaration that sufficient precautions had been taken against an outbreak in Ireland has done wonders to calm the public mind. Nobody can safely venture to speak in Parliament with bitterness, or contempt, of any measure which he chooses to cover with his authority. But he is seventy-four, and, in constitution, more than seventy-four. His death will be a terrible blow to these people. I see no reason to believe that the Irish agitation will subside of itself, or that the death of O'Connell would quiet it. On the contrary, I much fear that his death would be the signal for an explosion. The aspect of foreign politics is gloomy. The finances are in disorder. Trade is in distress. Legislation stands still. The Tories are broken up into three or more factions, which hate each other more than they hate the Whigs, the faction which stands by Peel, the faction which is represented by Vyvyan and the Morning Post, and the faction of Smythe and Cochrane. I should not be surprised if, before the end of the next session, the Ministry were to fall from mere rottenness.

Ever yours

T. B. MACAULAY.

Macaulay was right in thinking that the Government was rotten, and Lord Palmerston[1] in believing that it was safe. Sir Robert Peel was not the first Minister, and perhaps he is not destined to be the last, who has been chained down to office by the passive weight of an immense but discontented majority. Unable to retire in favour of his opponents and compelled to disgust his supporters at every turn, he had still before him three more years of public usefulness and personal mortification. One, at any

[1] See vol. ii, page 63.

rate, among his former antagonists did much to further his measures, and little or nothing to aggravate his difficulties. The course which Macaulay pursued between the years 1841 and 1846 deserves to be studied as a model of the conduct which becomes a statesman in opposition. In following that course he had a rare advantage. The continuous and absorbing labours of his History filled his mind and occupied his leisure, and relieved him from the craving for occupation and excitement that lies at the root of half the errors to which politicians out of office are prone;—errors which the popular judgment most unfairly attributes to lack of patriotism, or excess of gall. In the set party fights, that from time to time took place, he spoke seldom, and did not speak his best; but, when subjects came to the front on which his knowledge was great, and his opinion strongly marked, he interfered with decisive and notable effect.

It has been said of Macaulay, with reference to this period of his political career, that no member ever produced so much effect upon the proceedings of Parliament who spent so many hours in the Library, and so few in the House. Never has any public man, unendowed with the authority of a Minister, so easily moulded so important a piece of legislation into a shape which so accurately accorded with his own views, as did Macaulay the Copyright Act of 1842. In 1814 the term, during which the right of printing a book was to continue private property, had been fixed at twenty-eight years from the date of publication. The shortness of this term had always been regarded as a grievance by authors and by publishers, and was beginning to be so regarded by the world at large. 'The family of Sir Walter Scott,' says Miss Martineau in her History of England, 'stripped by his great losses, might be supposed to have an honourable provision in his splendid array of works, which the world was still buying as eagerly as ever: but the copyright of Waverley was about to expire; and there was no one who could not see the injustice of transferring to the public a property so evidently sacred as theirs.'

An arrangement which bore hardly upon the children of the great Scotchman, whose writings had been popular and profitable from the first, was nothing less than cruel in the case of authors who, after fighting a lifelong battle against the insensibility of their countrymen, had ended by creating a taste for their own works. Wordsworth's poetry was at length being freely bought by a generation which he himself had educated to enjoy it; but as things then stood, his death would at once rob his representatives of all share in the produce of the Sonnets and the Ode on Immortality, and would leave them to console themselves as they best might with the copyright of the Prelude. Southey, (firmly possessed, as he was, with the notion that posterity would set the highest value upon those among his productions which living men were the least disposed to purchase,) had given it to be understood that, in the existing state of the law, he should undertake no more works of research like the History of Brazil, and no more epic poems on the scale of Madoc and Roderick. But there was nothing which so effectually stirred the sympathies of men in power, and persuaded their reason, as a petition presented to the House of Commons by 'Thomas Carlyle, a writer of books;' which began by humbly showing 'That your petitioner has written certain books, being incited thereto by certain innocent and laudable considerations;' which proceeded to urge 'that this his labour has found hitherto, in money or money's worth, small recompense or none: that he is by no means sure of its ever finding recompense: but thinks that, if so, it will be at a distant time, when he, the labourer, will probably no longer be in need of money, and those dear to him will still be in need of it;' and which ended by a prayer to the House to forbid 'extraneous persons, entirely unconcerned in this adventure of his, to steal from him his small winnings, for a space of sixty years at the shortest. After sixty years, unless your Honourable House provide otherwise, they may begin to steal.'

In the session of 1841 Serjeant Talfourd brought in a measure devised with the object of extending the term of copyright in a book to sixty years, reckoned from the death of the author. Macaulay, speaking with wonderful force of argument and brilliancy of illustration, induced a thin House to reject the bill by a few votes. Talfourd, in the bitterness of his soul, exclaimed that Literature's own familiar friend, in whom she trusted, and who had eaten of her bread, had lifted up his heel against her. A writer of eminence has since echoed the complaint; but none can refuse a tribute of respect to a man who, on high grounds of public expediency, thought himself bound to employ all that he possessed of energy and ability on the task of preventing himself from being placed in a position to found a fortune, which, by the year 1919, might well have ranked among the largest funded estates in the country.

Admonished, but not deterred, by Serjeant Talfourd's reverse, Lord Mahon next year took up the cause of his brother authors, and introduced a bill in which he proposed to carry out the objectionable principle, but to carry it less far than his predecessor. Lord Mahon was for giving protection for five-and-twenty years, reckoned from the date of death; and his scheme was regarded with favour, until Macaulay came forward with a counter-scheme, giving protection for forty-two years, reckoned from the date of publication. He unfolded his plan in a speech, terse, elegant, and vigorous; as amusing as an essay of Elia, and as convincing as a proof of Euclid.[1]

[1] 'But this is not all. My noble friend's plan is not merely to institute a lottery in which some writers will draw prizes and some will draw blanks. His lottery is so contrived that, in the vast majority of cases, the blanks will fall to the best books, and the prizes to books of inferior merit.

'Take Shakespeare. My noble friend gives a longer protection than I should give to Love's Labour Lost, and Pericles,

When he resumed his seat, Sir Robert Peel walked across the floor, and assured him that the last twenty minutes had radically altered his own views on the

Prince of Tyre; but he gives a shorter protection than I should give to Othello and Macbeth.

'Take Milton. Milton died in 1674. The copyrights of Milton's great works would, according to my noble friend's plan, expire in 1699. Comus appeared in 1634, the Paradise Lost in 1668. To Comus, then, my noble friend would give sixty-five years of copyright, and to Paradise Lost only thirty-one years. Is that reasonable? Comus is a noble poem; but who would rank it with the Paradise Lost? My plan would give forty-two years both to the Paradise Lost, and to Comus.

'Let us pass on from Milton to Dryden. My noble friend would give more than sixty years of copyright to Dryden's worst works; to the encomiastic verses on Oliver Cromwell, to the Wild Gallant, to the Rival Ladies, to other wretched pieces as bad as anything written by Flecknoe or Settle: but for Theodore and Honoria, for Tancred and Sigismunda, for Cimon and Iphigenia, for Palamon and Arcite, for Alexander's Feast, my noble friend thinks a copyright of twenty-eight years sufficient. Of all Pope's works, that to which my noble friend would give the largest measure of protection is the volume of Pastorals, remarkable only as the production of a boy. Johnson's first work was a Translation of a Book of Travels in Abyssinia, published in 1735. It was so poorly executed that in his later years he did not like to hear it mentioned. Boswell once picked up a copy of it, and told his friend that he had done so. "Do not talk about it," said Johnson: "it is a thing to be forgotten." To this performance my noble friend would give protection during the enormous term of seventy-five years. To the Lives of the Poets he would give protection during about thirty years. * * *

'I have, I think, shown from literary history that the effect of my noble friend's plan would be to give to crude and imperfect works a great advantage over the highest productions of genius. What I recommend is that the certain term, reckoned from the date of publication, shall be forty-two years instead of twenty-eight years. In this arrangement there is no uncertainty, no inequality. The advantage which I propose to give will be the same to every book. No work will have so long a copyright as my noble friend gives to some books, or so short a copyright as he gives to others. No copyright will last ninety years. No copyright will end in twenty-eight years. To every book published in the last seventeen years of a writer's life I give a longer term of copyright than my noble friend gives; and I am confident that no person versed in literary history will deny this,—that in general the most valuable works of an author are published in the last seventeen years of his life. To Lear, to Macbeth, to Othello, to the Faery

law of copyright. One member after another confessed to an entire change of mind; and, on a question which had nothing to do with party, each change of mind brought a vote with it. The bill was remodelled on the principle of calculating the duration of copyright from the date of publication, and the term of forty-two years was adopted by a large majority. Some slight modifications were made in Macaulay's proposal; but he enjoyed the satisfaction of having framed according to his mind a Statute which may fairly be described as the charter of his craft, and of having added to Hansard what are by common consent allowed to be among its most readable pages.

There was another matter, of more striking dimensions in the eyes of his contemporaries, on which, by taking an independent course and persevering in it manfully, Macaulay brought round to his own opinion first his party, and ultimately the country. The Afghan war had come to a close in the autumn of 1842. The Tories claimed for Lord Ellenborough the glory of having saved India; while the Opposition held that he had with difficulty been induced to refrain from throwing obstacles in the way of its being saved by others. Most Whigs believed, and one Whig was ready on all fit occasions to maintain, that his Lordship had done nothing to deserve national admiration in the past, and a great deal to arouse the gravest apprehensions for the future. Macaulay had persuaded himself, and was now bent on persuading

Queen, to the Paradise Lost, to Bacon's Novum Organum and De Augmentis, to Locke's Essay on the Human Understanding, to Clarendon's History, to Hume's History, to Gibbon's History, to Smith's Wealth of Nations, to Addison's Spectators, to almost all the great works of Burke, to Clarissa and Sir Charles Grandison, to Joseph Andrews, Tom Jones, and Amelia, and, with the single exception of Waverley, to all the novels of Sir Walter Scott, I give a longer term of copyright than my noble friend gives. Can he match that list? Does not that list contain what England has produced greatest in many various ways, poetry, philosophy, history, eloquence, wit, skilful portraiture of life and manners? I confidently therefore call on the Committee to take my plan in preference to the plan of my noble friend.'

others, that, as long as Lord Ellenborough continued Governor-General, the peace of our Eastern Empire was not worth six months' purchase.

Albany, February, 1843.

Dear Ellis,—

I never thought that I should live to sympathise with Brougham's abuse of the Whigs; but I must own that we deserve it all. I suppose that you have heard of the stupid and disgraceful course which our leaders have resolved to take. I really cannot speak or write of it with patience. They are going to vote thanks to Ellenborough, in direct opposition to their opinion, and with an unanswerable case against him in their hands, only that they may save Auckland from recrimination. They will not save him, however. Cowardice is a mighty poor defence against malice. And to sacrifice the whole weight and respectability of our party to the feelings of one man is—but the thing is too bad to talk about. I cannot avert the disgrace of our party; but I do not choose to share it. I shall therefore go to Clapham quietly, and leave those, who have cooked this dirt-pie for us, to eat it. I did not think that any political matter would have excited me so much as this has done. I fought a very hard battle, but had nobody except Lord Minto and Lord Clanricarde to stand by me. I could easily get up a mutiny among our rank and file, if I choose; but an internal dissension is the single calamity from which the Whigs are at present exempt. I will not add it to all their other plagues.

Ever yours

T. B. MACAULAY.

On the 20th of February the House of Commons was called upon to express its gratitude to the Governor-General. The speeches from the front Opposition bench were as good as could be made by statesmen who had assumed an attitude such that they could not very well avoid being either insincere, or ungracious. The Vote of Thanks was unanimously passed; and within three weeks' time the Whigs were, almost to a man, engaged in hot support of a motion of Mr. Vernon Smith involving a direct and crushing censure on Lord Ellenborough. Lord Stanley, (making, as he was well able, the most of the opportunity,) took very good care that there should be no mistake about the consistency of men who, between the opening of the Session and the Easter holidays, had thanked a public officer for his 'ability and judgment,' and had done their best to stigmatise him as guilty of conduct 'unwise, indecorous, and reprehensible.' Happily Macaulay's conscience was clear; and his speech, in so far as the reader's pleasure is a test of excellence, will bear comparison with anything that still remains of those orations against Warren Hastings in which the great men of a former generation contested with each other the crown of eloquence.

The division went as divisions go, in the most good-natured of all national assemblies, when the whole strength of a powerful Government is exerted to protect a reputation. On the 14th of March the Duke of Wellington wrote to Lord Ellenborough: 'Nothing could have been more satisfactory than the debate in the House of Lords, and I am told it was equally so in the Commons.' The Duke's informant could not have seen far below the surface. Macaulay's measured and sustained denunciation of Lord Ellenborough's perilous levity had not fallen on inattentive ears. He had made, or at any rate had implied, a prophecy. 'Who can say what new freak we may hear of by the next mail? I am quite confident that neither the Court of Directors, nor Her Majesty's Ministers, can look forward to the arrival of that mail without uneasiness.' He had given a piece of advice. 'I cannot sit down without addressing myself to those Directors of the East India Company who are present. I exhort them to consider the heavy responsibility which rests on them. They have the power to recall Lord Ellenborough; and I trust that they will not hesitate to exercise that power.' The prophecy came true, and the advice was adopted to the letter. Before another twelvemonth had elapsed, Lord Ellenborough was in a worse scrape than ever. This time, Macaulay resolved to take the matter in hand himself. He had a notice of motion on the books of the House, and his speech was already in his head, when on the 26th of April, 1844, Sir Robert Peel announced that Her Majesty's Government had received a communication from the Court of Directors 'stating that they had exercised the power which the law gives them to recall at their will and pleasure the Governor-General of India.'

Macaulay's reputation and authority in Parliament owed nothing to the outward graces of the orator. On this head, the recollections of the Reporters' Gallery, (which have been as gratefully accepted as they were kindly offered,) are unanimous and precise. Mr. Clifford, of the Times, says: 'His action,—the little that he used—was rather ungainly. His voice was full and loud; but it had not the light and shade, or the modulation, found in practised speakers. His speeches were most carefully prepared, and were repeated without the loss, or omission, of a single word.'

This last observation deserves a few sentences of comment. Macaulay spoke freely enough on the spur of the moment; and some excellent judges were of opinion that, on these occasions, his style gained more in animation than it lost in ornament. Even when he rose in his place to take part in a discussion which had been long foreseen, he had no notes in his hand, and no manuscript in his pocket. If a debate was in prospect, he would turn the subject over while he paced his chamber, or tramped along the streets. Each thought, as it rose in his mind, embodied itself in phrases, and clothed itself in an appropriate drapery of images, instances, and quotations; and when, in the course of his speech, the thought recurred, all the words which gave it point and beauty spontaneously recurred with it.

'He used scarcely any action,' says a gentleman on the staff of the Standard. 'He would turn round on his heel, and lean slightly on the table; but there was nothing like demonstrative or dramatic action. He spoke with great rapidity; and there was very little inflection in the voice, which, however, in itself, was not unmusical. It was somewhat monotonous, and seldom rose or fell. The cadences were of small range. He spoke with very great fluency, and very little emphasis. It was the matter and the language, rather than the manner, that took the audience captive.'[1]

[1] Lord Lytton, in his poem on 'St. Stephen's,' amply confirms this view of Macaulay:

> Perhaps so great an orator was ne'er
> So little of an actor; half the care
> Giv'n to the speaking which he gave the speech
> Had raised his height beyond all living reach.
> Ev'n as it was, a master's power he proved
> In the three tests:—he taught, he charmed, he moved.
> Few compass one; whate'er their faults may be
> Great orators alone achieve the three.

This generous testimony of a political opponent is repeated in prose, at greater length, but hardly with more precision, than in the verse:—

'However carefully prepared, Lord Macaulay's parliamentary speeches were composed as orations, not as essays. Indeed, many years ago, before he went to India, he observed to the author of the lines which render so inadequate a tribute to his honoured name, that he himself never committed to writing words intended to be spoken,—upon the principle that, in the process of writing, the turn of diction, and even the mode of argument, might lose the vivacity essential to effective oration, and, in fact, fall into *essay*. His wonderful powers of memory enabled him to compose, correct, and retain, word by word, the whole of a speech, however long, without the aid of the pen. * * *

'It was certainly, however, the brilliant art with which his speeches were composed upon *oratorical* principles, both as to arrangement of argument and liveliness of phraseology, that gave them that prodigious effect which they, (at least the earlier ones,) produced upon a mixed audience, and entitles this eminent personage to the fame of a very considerable orator. I may be pardoned for insisting upon this, since in the various obituary notices of Lord Macaulay there has appeared to me a disposition to depreciate his success as an orator, while doing the amplest justice to his merits as a writer. He was certainly not a debater, nor did he ever attempt to be so;

Mr. Downing of the Daily News writes: 'It was quite evident that Macaulay had not learned the art of speaking from the platform, the pulpit, the forum, or any of the usual modes of obtaining a fluent diction. He was at once too robust, and too recondite, for these methods of introduction to the oratorical art. In all probability it was that fulness of mind, which broke out in many departments, that constituted him a born orator. Vehemence of thought, vehemence of language, vehemence of manner, were his chief characteristics. The listener might almost fancy he heard ideas and words gurgling in the speaker's throat for priority of utterance. There was nothing graduated, or undulating, about him. He plunged at once into the heart of the matter, and continued his loud resounding pace from beginning to end, without halt or pause. This vehemence and volume made Macaulay the terror of the reporters; and, when he engaged in a subject outside their ordinary experience, they were fairly nonplussed by the display of names, and dates, and titles. He was not a long-winded speaker. In fact, his earnestness was so great that it would have failed under a very long effort. He had the faculty, possessed by every great orator, of compressing a great deal in a short space.'

A fourth witness, after confirming the testimony of his colleagues, concludes with the remark: 'Macaulay was wonderfully telling in the House of Commons. Every sentence was perfectly devoured by the listeners.'

As soon as the session of 1843 ended, Macaulay started for a trip up and down the Loire. Steaming from Orleans to Nantes, and back again from Nantes to Angers, he indulged to the full his liking for river travel and river scenery, and his passion for old cities which had been the theatre of memorable events. His letters to his sisters abundantly prove that

but in the higher art of sustained, elaborate oration, no man in our age has made a more vivid effect upon an audience.'

he could have spoken off a very passable historical handbook for Central France, without having trained himself for the feat by a course of special reading. His catalogue of the successive occupants of Chambord is marvellously accurate and complete, from Francis the First and his Italian architects, to the time when 'the royalists got up a subscription to purchase it for the Duke of Berri's posthumous son, whom they still call Henry the Fifth. The project was not popular; but, by dint of bullying, and telling all who objected that they would be marked men as long as they lived, a sufficient sum was extorted.' There are touches that mark the historian in his description of the Castle of Blois, when he speaks of 'the chimney at which Henry Duke of Guise sate down for the last time to warm himself,' and 'the observatory of Catherine de' Medici, designed rather for astrological than for astronomical observations;' but, taken as a whole, the letters have too much of the tourist's journal about them to bear printing in their integrity.

Paris: August 21, 1843.

'Dearest Hannah,—

What people travel for is a mystery. I have never during the last forty-eight hours had any wish so strong as to be at home again. To be sure, those forty-eight hours have hardly been a fair specimen of a traveller's life. They have been filled with little miseries, such as made Mr. Testy roar, and Mr. Sensitive sigh. I could very well add a chapter to the "Miseries of Human Life." For example:—

'Groan 1. The Brighton railway; in a slow train; a carriage crowded as full as it would hold; a sick lady smelling of æther; a healthy gentleman smelling of brandy; the thermometer at 102° in the shade, and I not in the shade, but exposed to the full glare of the sun from noon till half after two, the effect of which is that my white trowsers have been scorched into a pair of very serviceable nankeens.

'Groan 2;—and for this Fanny is answerable, who made me believe that the New Steyne Hotel at Brighton was a good one. A coffee-room ingeniously contrived on the principle of an oven, the windows not made to open; a dinner on yesterday's pease-soup, and the day before yesterday's cutlets; not an ounce of ice; and all beverages, wine, water, and beer,—in exactly the state of the Church of Laodicea.

'Groan 3. My passage to Dieppe. We had not got out of sight of the Beachy Head lights, when it began to rain hard. I was therefore driven into the cabin, and compelled to endure the spectacle, and to hear the unutterable groans and gasps, of fifty sea-sick people. I went out when the rain ceased; but everything on deck was soaked. It was impossible to sit; so that I walked up and down the vessel all night. The wind was in our faces, and the clear grey dawn was visible before we entered the harbour of Dieppe. Our baggage was to be examined at seven; so that it was too late to go to bed, and yet too early to find any shop open, or anything stirring. All our bags and boxes were in the custody of the authorities, and I had to pace sulkily about the pier for a long time, without even the solace of a book.

'Groan 4. The custom-house. I never had a dispute with custom-house officers before, having found that honesty answered in England, France, and Belgium, and corruption in Italy. But the officer at Dieppe finding among my baggage some cotton stockings which had not been yet worn, threatened to confiscate them, and exacted more than they were worth—between thirteen and fourteen francs—by way of duty. I had just bought these unlucky stockings to do honour to our country in the eyes of foreigners; being unwilling that the washerwomen of Paris and Orleans should see an English Member of Parliament's stockings either in holes or darned. See what the fruits of patriotism are!

'Groan 5. Mine inn at Dieppe. I need not describe it, for it was the very same at which we stopped for a night in 1840, and at which you ate of a gigot as memorable as Sam Johnson's shoulder of mutton.[1] I did not discover where I was till too late. I had a cup of coffee worse than I thought any French cook could make for a wager. In the bedroom, where I dressed, there was a sort of soap which I had half a mind to bring away, that men of science might analyse it. It would be, I should think, an excellent substitute for

[1] In the review on Croker, Macaulay calls it a leg of mutton. As a matter of fact, Boswell does not specify whether it was a leg or a shoulder. Whatever the joint may have been, Dr. Johnson immortalised it in these words: 'It is as bad as bad can be—it is ill-fed, ill-killed, ill-kept, and ill-dressed.'

Spanish flies in a blister. I shaved with it, and the consequence is that I look as if I had that complaint which our mother held in such horror. If I used such cosmetics often, I should be forced to beg Queen Victoria to touch me.

'The cathedral, which was my chief object at Chartres, rather disappointed me; not that it is not a fine church; but I had heard it described as one of the most magnificent in Europe. Now, I have seen finer Gothic churches in England, France, and Belgium. It wants vastness; and its admirers make the matter worse by proving to you that it is a great deal larger than it looks, and by assuring you that the proportions are so exquisite as to produce the effect of littleness. I have heard the same cant canted about a much finer building,—St. Peter's. But, surely, it is impossible to say a more severe thing of an architect than that he has a knack of building edifices five hundred feet long which look as if they were only three hundred feet long. If size be an element of the sublime in architecture, —and this, I imagine, everybody's feelings will prove,— then a great architect ought to aim, not at making buildings look smaller than they are, but at making them look larger than they are. If there be any proportions which have the effect of making St. Paul's look larger than St. Peter's, those are good proportions. To say that an artist is so skilful that he makes buildings, which are really large, look small, is as absurd as it would be to say that a novelist has such skill in narration as to make amusing stories dull, or to say that a controversialist has such skill in argument that strong reasons, when he states them, seem to be weak ones.'

'September 1, 1843.

'I performed my journey to Bourges, comfortably enough, in the coupée of the diligence. There was a prodigious noise all night of people talking in English on the roof. At Vierzon I found that this noise proceeded from seven English labourers, good-looking fellows enough, who were engaged to work on a line of railroad, and were just going to quit the coach. I asked them about their state and prospects, told them that I hoped they would let a countryman treat them to breakfast, and gave them a Napoleon for that purpose. They were really so pleased and grateful for being noticed in that way that I was almost too strongly moved by their thanks. Just before we started, one of them, a very intelligent man and a sort of spokesman, came to the window, and asked me with great earnestness to tell them my name, which I did. "Ah, sir, we have all heard of you. You have always been a good friend to the country at home, and it will be a great satisfaction to us all to know this." He told me to my comfort, that they did very well,—being, as he said, sober men; that the wages were good; and that they were well treated, and had no quarrels with their French fellow-labourers.

'I could not, after this, conceal my name from a very civil, good-natured, Frenchman, who travelled in the coupée with me, and with whom I had already had some conversation. He insisted on doing the honours of Bourges to me, and has really been officiously kind and obliging. Indeed, in this city I have found nothing but courtesy worthy of Louis the Fourteenth's time. Queer old-fashioned country gentlemen of long descent, who recovered part of their estates on their return from emigration, abound in the neighbourhood. They have hotels in Bourges, where they often pass the winter, instead of going up to Paris. The manners of the place are most ceremonious. Hats come off at every word. If you ask your way, a gentleman insists on escorting you. Did you ever read Georges Dandin? If not, read it before you sleep. There you will see how Molière has portrayed the old-fashioned provincial gentry. I could fancy that many Messieurs and Mesdames de Sotenville were to be found at Bourges.'

'September 6.

'I know nothing about politics except what I glean from French newspapers in the coffee-houses. The people here seem to be in a very ill-humour about the Queen's visit; and I think it, I must own, an ill-judged step. Propriety requires that a guest, a sovereign, and a woman, should be received by Louis Philippe with something of chivalrous homage, and with an air of deference. To stand punctiliously on his quality in intercourse with a young lady would be uncourteous, and almost insulting. But the French have taken it strongly into their heads that their Government is acting a servile part towards England, and they are therefore disposed to consider every act of hospitality and gallantry on the part of the King as a national humiliation. I see that the journals are crying out that France is for ever degraded because the band of a French regiment played "God Save the Queen" when Her Majesty landed. I fear that Louis Philippe cannot possibly behave on this occasion so as at once to gratify his guest and his subjects. They are the most unreasonable people which exists; that is the truth; and they will never be wiser until they have had another lesson like that of 1815.'

'September 9, 1843.

'It was just four in the morning when I reached Angers; but I found a café open, made a tolerable breakfast, and before five was on board a steamer for Tours. It was a lovely day. The banks were seen to every advantage, and, without possessing beauty of the highest class, presented an endless succession of pretty and cheerful landscapes. With the scenery, and a book, I was in no want of company. A Frenchman, however, began to talk to me, and proved a sensible and well-bred man. He had been in England, and, when ill, had been kindly treated by the people among whom he found himself. He always therefore, he said, made a point of paying attention to Englishmen. I could not help telling him that he might easily get himself into a scrape with some swindler, or worse, if he carried his kindness to our nation too far. "Sans doute," said he, "il faut distinguer;" and then he paid me the highest compliment that ever was paid me in my life; for he said that nobody who knew the world could fail to perceive that I was what the English call a gentleman, "homme comme il faut." That you may fully appreciate the value of this compliment I must tell you that, having travelled all the preceding night, I had a beard of two days' growth, that my hair was unbrushed, my linen of yesterday, my coat like a miller's, and my waistcoat, which had been white when I left Nantes, in a state which filled me with self-abhorrence. Nor had he the least notion who I was; for I gave no hint, and my name was not on my baggage. I shall, therefore, henceforward consider myself as a person of singularly noble look and demeanour.

'Will you let me recommend you a novel? Try Sœur Anne, by Paul de Kock. It is not improper, and the comic parts are really delightful. I have laughed over them till I cried. There are tragic parts which I skipped for fear of crying in another sense.'

Albany, London: November 25, 1843.

Dear Napier,—

Many thanks for your excellent letter. I have

considered it fully, and I am convinced that by visiting Edinburgh at present I should do unmixed harm.

The question respecting the Catholic clergy is precisely in that state in which a discussion at a public meeting can do no good, and may do great mischief. It is in a state requiring the most painful attention of the ablest heads; nor is it by any means certain that any attention, or any ability, will produce a satisfactory solution of the problem.

My own view is this. I do not on principle object to the paying of the Irish Catholic priests. I regret that such a step was not taken in 1829. I would, even now, gladly support any well digested plan which might be likely to succeed. But I fear that the difficulties are insurmountable. Against such a measure there are all the zealots of the High Church, and all the zealots of the Low Church; the Bishop of Exeter, and Hugh Macneile; Oxford, and Exeter Hall; all the champions of the voluntary system; all the English Dissenters; all Scotland; all Ireland, both Orangemen and Papists. If you add together the mass which opposed the late Government on the Education question, the mass which opposed Sir James Graham's Education clauses last year,[1] and the mass which is crying out for repeal in Ireland, you get something like a notion of the force which will be arrayed against a Bill for paying the Irish Catholic clergy.

What have you on the other side? You have the statesmen, both Tory and Whig; but no combination of statesmen is a match for a general combination of fools. And, even among the statesmen, there is by no means perfect concord. The Tory statesmen are for paying the Catholic priests, but not for touching one farthing of the revenue of the Protestant Church. The Liberal statesmen, (I for one, if I may lay claim to the name,) would transfer a large part of the Irish Church revenues from the Protestants to the Catholics.

[1] In 1843, Sir James Graham, speaking for the Government, proposed a scheme for educating the population of our great towns which was defeated by the opposition of the Nonconformists.

For such a measure I should think it my duty to vote, though I were certain my vote would cost me my seat in Parliament. Whether I would vote for a measure which, leaving the Protestant Church of Ireland untouched, should add more than half a million to our public burdens for the maintenance of the Popish priesthood, is another question. I am not ashamed to say that I have not quite made up my mind, and that I should be glad, before I made it up, to hear the opinions of others.

As things stand, I do not believe that Sir Robert or Lord John, or even Sir Robert and Lord John united, could induce one third part of the members of the House of Commons to vote for any plan whatever of which the object should be the direct payment of the Irish Catholic priests. Thinking thus, I have turned my mind to the best indirect ways of effecting this object, and I have some notions which may possibly bear fruit. I shall probably take an opportunity of submitting them to the House of Commons. Now I can conceive nothing more inexpedient than that, with these views, I should at the present moment go down to Edinburgh. If I did, I should certainly take the bull by the horns. I should positively refuse to give any promise. I should declare that I was not, on principle, opposed to the payment of Catholic priests; and I should reserve my judgment as to any particular mode of payment till the details were before me. The effect would be a violent explosion of public feeling. Other towns would follow the example of Edinburgh. Petitions would pour in by thousands as soon as Parliament had assembled, and the difficulties with which we have to deal, and which are great enough as it is, would be doubled.

I do not, however, think that the Edinburgh Review ought to be under the same restraints under which a Whig Cabinet is necessarily placed. The Review has not to take the Queen's pleasure, to count votes in the Houses, or to keep powerful supporters in good humour. It should expound and defend the

Whig theory of government; a theory from which we are forced sometimes to depart in practice. There can be no objection to Senior's arguing in the strongest manner for the paying of the Catholic priests. I should think it very injudicious to lay down the rule that the Whig Review should never plead for any reforms except such as a Whig Ministry could prudently propose to the Legislature.

I have a plan in my head which I hope you will not dislike. I think of reviewing the Memoirs of Barère. I really am persuaded that I could make something of that subject.

Ever yours

T. B. MACAULAY.

Albany, London: December 13, 1843

Dear Napier,—

You shall have my paper on Barère before Parliament meets. I never took to writing anything with more hearty goodwill. If I can, I will make the old villain shake even in his grave. Some of the lies in which I have detected him are such as you, with all your experience in literary matters, will find it difficult to believe without actual inspection of the authorities.[1]

What do you hear of Jeffrey's book?[2] My own general impression is that the selection is ill made, and that a certain want of finish, which in a periodical work is readily excused, and has sometimes even the effect of a grace, is rather too perceptible in many passages. On the other hand, the variety and versatility of Jeffrey's mind seems to me more extraordinary than ever. I think that there are few things in the four volumes which one or two other men could not have done as well; but I do not think that any one man except Jeffrey, nay that any three men, could

[1] 'As soon as he ceases to write trifles, he begins to write lies; and such lies! A man who has never been within the tropics does not know what a thunderstorm means; a man who has never looked on Niagara has but a faint idea of a cataract; and he who has not read Barère's Memoirs may be said not to know what it is to lie.'—Macaulay's Article on Barère.

[2] Lord Jeffrey's Contributions to the Edinburgh Review.

have produced such diversified excellence. When I compare him with Sydney and myself, I feel, with humility perfectly sincere, that his range is immeasurably wider than ours. And this is only as a writer; but he is not only a writer; he has been a great advocate, and he is a great Judge. Take him all in all, I think him more nearly an universal genius than any man of our time; certainly far more nearly than Brougham, much as Brougham affects the character. Brougham does one thing well, two or three things indifferently, and a hundred things detestably. His Parliamentary speaking is admirable; his forensic speaking poor; his writings, at the very best, second-rate. As to his hydrostatics, his political philosophy, his equity judgments, his translations from the Greek, they are really below contempt. Jeffrey, on the other hand, has tried nothing in which he has not succeeded, except Parliamentary speaking; and there he obtained what to any other man would have been great success, and disappointed his hearers only because their expectations were extravagant.

Ever yours

T. B. MACAULAY.

Albany, London: April 10, 1844.

Dear Napier,—

I am glad that you like my article. It does not please me now, by any means, as much as it did while I was writing it. It is shade, unrelieved by a gleam of light.[1] This is the fault of the subject rather than of the painter; but it takes away from the effect of the portrait. And thus, to the many reasons which all honest men have for hating Barère I may add a reason personal to myself, that the excess of his rascality has spoiled my paper on him.

Ever yours

T. B. MACAULAY.

[1] 'Whatsoever things are false, whatsoever things are dishonest, whatsoever things are unjust, whatsoever things are impure, whatsoever things are hateful, whatsoever things are of evil report, if there be any vice, and if there be any infamy, all these things were blended in Barère.'

CHAPTER X
1844–1847

Letters to Mr. Napier—Macaulay remodels his design for an article on Burke and his Times into a sketch of Lord Chatham's later years—Tour in Holland—Scene off Dordrecht—Macaulay on the Irish Church—Maynooth—The Ministerial crisis of December 1845: letters to Mrs. Trevelyan—Letter to Mr. Macfarlan—Fall of Sir Robert Peel—Macaulay becomes Paymaster-General—His re-election at Edinburgh—His position in the House of Commons—General election of 1847—Macaulay's defeat at Edinburgh.

Albany, London: August 14, 1844.

Dear Napier,—

I have been working hard for you during the last week, and have covered many sheets of foolscap; and now I find that I have taken a subject altogether unmanageable.[1] There is no want of materials. On the contrary, facts and thoughts, both interesting and new, are abundant. But this very abundance bewilders me. The stage is too small for the actors. The canvas is too narrow for the multitude of figures. It is absolutely necessary that I should change my whole plan. I will try to write for you, not a History of England during the earlier part of George the Third's reign, but an account of the last years of Lord Chatham's life. I promised or half promised this ten years ago, at the end of my review of Thackeray's book. Most of what I have written will come in very well. The fourth volume of the Chatham Correspondence has not, I think, been reviewed. It will furnish a heading for the article.

Ever yours truly

T. B. MACAULAY.

[1] The unmanageable subject was a review of Burke's Life and Writings. 'I should wish,' Macaulay writes, 'to say a good deal about the Ministerial revolutions of the early part of George the Third's reign; about the characters of Bute, Mansfield, Chatham, Townsend, George Grenville, and many others; about Wilkes's and Churchill's lampoons, and so forth. I should wish also to go into a critical examination of the Essay

A week later Macaulay writes: 'The article on Chatham goes on swimmingly. A great part of the information which I have is still in manuscript;—Horace Walpole's Memoirs of George the Third's reign, which were transcribed for Mackintosh; and the first Lord Holland's Diary, which Lady Holland permitted me to read. I mean to be with you on Saturday the 31st. I would gladly stay with you till the Tuesday; but I shall not be quite my own master. It is certainly more agreeable to represent such a place as Paisley, or Wolverhampton, than such a place as Edinburgh. Hallam or Everett can enjoy the society and curiosities of your fine city; but I am the one person to whom all those things are interdicted.'

Shortly before Macaulay's arrival in India, a Civil Servant of the Company, employed as Resident at a native court, came under the suspicion of having made use of his position to enrich himself by illicit means. Bills came to hand through Persia, drawn in his favour for great sums of money on the Company itself. The Court of Directors naturally took the alarm, and sent a hint to the Governor-General, who wrote to the officer in question inviting him to clear his character before a Commission of Inquiry. But the bird had already flown. The late Resident was well on his way to Europe; and his answer to Lord William Bentinck, in which the offer of an investigation was civilly but most positively declined, was actually addressed from the Sandheads at the mouth of the Hooghly. The following letters will sufficiently indicate the aspect under which the transaction presented itself to Macaulay. His behaviour on this occasion may seem unnecessarily harsh to that section of society which, in its dealings with gilded rogues, takes very good care not to err on

on the Sublime and Beautiful, and to throw out some hints on the subject which have long been rolling up and down in my mind. But this would be enough for a long article; and, when this is done, we have only brought Burke to the threshold of the House of Commons. The American War, the Coalition, the Impeachment of Hastings, the French Revolution, still remain.'

the side of intolerance; but most readers will think the better of him because, when he found himself in questionable company, he obeyed the instinct which prompted him to stand on his dignity as an honest man.

Rotterdam: October 9, 1844.

Dear Hannah,—

After a very pleasant day at Antwerp, I started at seven yesterday morning by the steamer for Rotterdam. I had an odd conversation on board, and one which, I think, will amuse both you and Trevelyan. As we passed Dordrecht, one of the passengers, an Englishman, said that he had never seen anything like it. Parts of it reminded me of some parts of Cape Town; and I said so. An elderly gentleman immediately laid hold of me. 'You have been at the Cape, Sir?' 'Yes, Sir.' 'Perhaps you have been in India?' 'Yes, Sir.' 'My dear, here is a gentleman who has been in India.' So I became an object of attention to an ill-looking vulgar woman, who appeared to be the wife of my questioner; and to his daughter, a pretty girl enough, but by no means ladylike. 'And how did you like India? Is it not the most delightful place in the world?' 'It is well enough,' I said, 'for a place of exile.' 'Exile!' says the lady. 'I think people are exiled when they come away from India.' 'I have never,' said the old gentleman, 'had a day's good health since I left India.' A little chat followed about mangoes and mango-fish, punkahs and palanquins, white ants and cockroaches. I maintained, as I generally do on such occasions, that all the fruits of the tropics are not worth a pottle of Covent Garden strawberries, and that a lodging up three pair of stairs in London is better than a palace in a compound at Chowringhee. My gentleman was vehement in asserting that India was the only country to live in. 'I went there,' he said, 'at sixteen, in 1800, and stayed till 1830, when I was superannuated. If the Company had not chosen to superannuate me, I should have been there still. I should like to end my days there.' I could not conceive what he meant by being superannuated at a time when he could have been only forty-six years old, and consequently younger than most of the field-officers in the Indian army, and than half the Senior Merchants in the Civil Service; but I was too polite to interrogate him.

That was a politeness, however, of which he had no notion. 'How long,' he asked, 'were you in India?' 'Between four and five years.' 'A clergyman, I suppose?' Whether he drew this inference from the sanctity of my looks, or from my olive-coloured coat and shawl waistcoat, I do not pretend to guess; but I answered that I had not the honour to belong to so sacred a profession. 'A mercantile gentleman, no doubt?' 'No.' Then his curiosity got the better of all the laws of good breeding, and he went straight to the point. 'May I ask, Sir, to whom I have the honour of talking?' I told him. 'Oh, Sir,' said he, 'you must often have heard of me. I am Mr. ——. I was long at Lucknow.' 'Heard of you!' thought I. 'Yes; and a pretty account I have heard of you!' I should have at once turned on my heel, and walked away, if his daughter had not been close to us; and, scoundrel as he is, I could not affront him in her presence. I merely said, with the coldest tone and look: 'Certainly I have heard of Mr. ——.' He went on: 'You are related, I think, to a civil servant who made a stir about ———.' It was just on my lips to say: 'Yes. It was by my brother-in-law's means that ——— was *superannuated*;' but I commanded myself, and merely said that I was nearly related to Mr. Trevelyan; and I then called to the steward, and pretended to be very anxious to settle with him about some coffee that I had taken. While he was changing me a gold William I got away from the old villain; went to the other end of the poop; took out my book; and avoided looking towards him during the rest of the passage. And yet I could not help thinking a little better of him for what had happened, for it reminded me of what poor Macnaghten once said to me at Ootacamund. '——— has certain excuses which ——— and others have not had; for he is really so great a fool that he can hardly be called a responsible agent.' I certainly never knew such an instance of folly as that to which I had just been witness. Had he been a man of common sense he would have avoided all allusion to India, or, at any rate, would have talked about India only to people who were likely to be unacquainted with his history. He must have known that I was Secretary to the Board of Control when that Board expressed its entire concurrence in the measures taken by the Company against him.

Ever yours
T. B. M.

Four days later Macaulay writes from Amsterdam: 'I have been pestered by those ——s all the way from Rotterdam hither, and shall probably be pestered by them the whole way back. We are always in the same inns; we always go to Museums at the same hour, and we have been as near as possible to travelling in the same diligence. I resolutely turn away from the old rogue, and pretend not to see him. He perfectly comprehends my meaning, and looks as if he were in the pillory. But it is not pleasant to have such scenes daily in the presence of his wife and daughter.'

During 1844 and 1845 Macaulay pretty frequently addressed the House of Commons. He earned the gratitude of the Unitarians by his successful vindication of their disputed title to their own chapels and cemeteries. By his condemnation of theological tests at Scotch Universities, and his adventurous assault upon the Church of Ireland, he appealed to the confidence of those Edinburgh dissenters whose favour he for some time past had been most undeservedly losing. It is hard to conceive how United Presbyterians, and Free Churchmen fresh from the Disruption, could have found it in their hearts to quarrel with a representative who was able to compose, and willing to utter, such a declaration as this: 'I am not speaking in anger, or with any wish to excite anger in others; I am not speaking with rhetorical exaggeration; I am calmly and deliberately expressing, in the most appropriate terms, an opinion which I formed many years ago, which all my observations and reflections have confirmed, and which I am prepared to support by reasons, when I say that, of all the institutions of the civilised world, the Established Church of Ireland seems to me the most absurd.'

When Sir James Graham was called to account for opening Mazzini's envelopes, Macaulay attacked that unlucky statesman in a speech, which, in writing to a correspondent, he mentions as having fallen 'like a shell in a powder magazine.' He likewise was active and prominent in the controversy that raged over the measure by which the question of Maynooth College was sent to an uneasy sleep of five-and-twenty years. The passage in which he drew a contrast, glowing with life and colour, between the squalor of the Irish Seminary and the wealth of the Colleges at Cambridge and Oxford, will rank higher than any other sample of his oratory in the estimation of schoolboys; and especially of such schoolboys as are looking forward longingly to the material comforts of an university career.[1] But men, who are acquainted with those

[1] 'When I think of the spacious and stately mansions of the heads of houses, of the commodious chambers of the fellows and scholars, of the refectories, the combination rooms, the bowling greens, the stabling, of the state and luxury of the great feast days, of the piles of old plate on the tables, of the savoury steam of the kitchens, of the multitude of geese and capons which turn at once on the spits, of the oceans of excellent ale in the butteries; and when I remember from whom all this splendour and plenty is derived; when I remember what was the faith of Edward the Third and of Henry the Sixth, of Margaret of Anjou and Margaret of Richmond, of William of Wykeham and William of Waynefleet, of Archbishop Chicheley and Cardinal Wolsey; when I remember what we have taken from the Roman Catholics,—King's College, New College, Christ Church, my own Trinity; and when I look at the miserable Dotheboys Hall which we have given them in exchange, I feel, I must own, less proud than

temptations and anxieties which underlie the glitter of Parliamentary success, will give their preference to the closing sentences;—sentences more honourable to him who spoke them than the most finished and famous among all his perorations. 'Yes, Sir, to this bill, and to every bill which shall seem to me likely to promote the real Union of Great Britain and Ireland, I will give my support, regardless of obloquy, regardless of the risk which I may run of losing my seat in Parliament. For such obloquy I have learned to consider as true glory; and as to my seat, I am determined that it never shall be held by an ignominious tenure; and I am sure that it can never be lost in a more honourable cause.' These words were not the idle flourish of an adroit speaker, certain of impunity, and eager only for the cheer which is the unfailing reward of a cheap affectation of courage and disinterestedness. They were given forth in grave earnest, and dictated by an expectation of impending trouble which the event was not slow to justify.

In September 1853, when Macaulay, much against his will, was preparing his speeches for publication, he notes in his diary: 'After breakfast I wrote out the closing passages of Maynooth. How white poor Peel looked while I was speaking! I remember the effect of the words, "There you sit ——." I have a letter from my Dutch translator. He is startled by the severity of some of my speeches, and no wonder. He knows nothing of the conflict of parties.'

Peel might well look white beneath the flood of unanswerable taunts which was poured forth by his terrible ally. Even in his utmost need, it was a heavy price to pay for the support of Macaulay and his party. 'There is too much ground for the reproaches of those who, having, in spite of a bitter experience, a second time trusted the Right Honourable Baronet, now find themselves a second time deluded. It has been too much his practice, when in Opposition, to make use of

I could wish of being a Protestant and a Cambridge man.'—Page 175 of Macaulay's Speeches (People's Edition).

passions with which he has not the slightest sympathy, and of prejudices which he regards with a profound contempt. As soon as he is in power a change takes place. The instruments which have done his work are flung aside. The ladder by which he has climbed is kicked down. . . . Can we wonder that the eager, honest, hot-headed Protestants, who raised you to power in the confident hope that you would curtail the privileges of the Roman Catholics, should stare and grumble when you propose to give public money to the Roman Catholics? Can we wonder that, from one end of the country to the other, everything should be ferment and uproar; that petitions should, night after night, whiten all our benches like a snow-storm? Can we wonder that the people out of doors should be exasperated by seeing the very men who, when we were in office, voted against the old grant to Maynooth, now pushed and pulled into the House by your whippers-in to vote for an increased grant? The natural consequences follow. All those fierce spirits, whom you hallooed on to harass us, now turn round and begin to worry you. The Orangeman raises his war-whoop; Exeter Hall sets up its bray; Mr. Macneile shudders to see more costly cheer than ever provided for the priests of Baal at the table of the Queen; and the Protestant operatives of Dublin call for impeachments in exceedingly bad English. But what did you expect? Did you think, when, to serve your turn, you called the devil up, that it was as easy to lay him as to raise him? Did you think, when you went on, session after session, thwarting and reviling those whom you knew to be in the right, and flattering all the worst passions of those whom you knew to be in the wrong, that the day of reckoning would never come? It has come. There you sit, doing penance for the disingenuousness of years.'

Between the House of Commons and his History, Macaulay had no time to spare for writing articles. Early in 1845 a rumour had found its way into the newspapers, to the effect that he had discontinued his connection with the Edinburgh Review. He at once assured Mr. Napier that the rumour in question had not been set on foot by himself; but, in the same letter, he announced his resolution to employ himself exclusively upon his History, until the first portion of it was completed. 'If I had not taken that resolution, my History would have perished in embryo, like poor Mackintosh's. As soon as I have finished my first two volumes, I shall be happy to assist you again. But when that will be it is difficult to say.[1] Parliamentary business, at present, prevents me from writing a line. I am preparing for Lord John's debate on Sugar, and for Joseph Hume's debate on India; and it is one of my infirmities—an infirmity, I grieve to say, quite incurable—that I cannot correctly and heartily apply my mind to several subjects together. When an approaching debate is in my head, it is to no purpose that I sit down at my desk to write history, and I soon get up again in disgust.'

London: December 11, 1845.

Dear Hannah,—

I am detained for a few minutes at Ellis's chambers with nothing to do. I will therefore employ my leisure in writing to you on a sheet of paper meant for some plea or replication. Yesterday morning I learned that the Ministers had gone down to the Isle of Wight for the purpose of resigning, and that Lord John had been sent for. This morning, all the world knows it. There are many reports; but my belief is that the Duke of Wellington, after having consented to support Peel, was alarmed by the symptoms of opposition among the Lords of the Tory party, and retracted. How this is we shall probably soon learn. In the meantime, London is in confusion. The politicians run from club to club picking up and circulating rumours, and nobody knows exactly what to expect. All discerning men, among whom I rank myself, are anxious and melancholy. What is to befall the country? Will Lord John attempt to form a Government? Can such a Government abolish the Corn duties? Can it stand three

[1] Macaulay never again wrote for the Edinburgh Review.

months with the present House of Commons? Would even a dissolution give the Whigs a working majority in the Commons? And, even if we had such a majority in the Commons, what could we do with the Lords? Are we to swamp them, as Lord Grey's Ministry proposed to do? Have we sufficient support in the country to try so extreme a measure? Are we to go on, as Lord Melbourne's Ministry did—unable to carry our own bills, and content with holding the executive functions, and distributing the loaves and fishes? Or are we, after an unsuccessful attempt to settle the Corn question, to go out? If so, do we not leave the question in a worse position than at present? Or are Peel and Lord John to unite in one Government? How are personal pretensions to be adjusted in such an arrangement? How are questions of Foreign policy, and of Irish policy, to be settled? How can Aberdeen and Palmerston pull together? How can Lord John himself bear to sit in the same Cabinet with Graham? And, supposing all these difficulties got over, is it clear that a coalition between Peel and the Whigs could carry the repeal of the Corn Law through the Lords? What then remains, except an Ultra-Tory Administration composed of such men as the Dukes of Buckingham and Richmond? Yet how can such an Administration look in the face an Opposition, which will contain every statesman and orator in the House of Commons? What, too, will be the effect produced out of doors by such an Administration? What is there that may not be apprehended if we should have a year of severe distress, and if the manufacturers should impute all their sufferings to the selfish tyranny and rapacity of the Ministers of the Crown? It is difficult, I think, to conceive a darker prospect than that which lies before us. Yet I have a great confidence in the sense, virtue, and self-command of the nation; and I therefore hope that we shall get out of this miserable situation, as we have got out of other situations not less miserable.

I have spent some hours in carefully considering my own position, and determining on my own course. I have at last made up my mind; and I send you the result of my deliberations.

If, which is not absolutely impossible, though improbable, Peel should still try to patch up a Conservative Administration, and should, as the head of that Administration, propose the repeal of the Corn Laws, my course is clear. I must support him with all the energy that I have, till the question is carried. Then I am free to oppose him. If an Ultra-Tory Ministry should be framed, my course is equally clear. I must oppose them with every faculty that God has given me.

If Lord John should undertake to form a Whig Ministry, and should ask for my assistance, I cannot in honour refuse it. But I shall distinctly tell him, and tell my colleagues and constituents, that I will not again go through what I went through in Lord Melbourne's Administration. I am determined never again to be one of a Government which cannot carry the measures which it thinks essential. I am satisfied that the great error of Lord Melbourne's Government was, that they did not resign as soon as they found that they could not pass the Appropriation Clause. They would have gone out with flying colours, had they gone out then. This was while I was in India. When I came back, I found the Liberal Ministry in a thoroughly false position; but I did not think it right to separate myself from them. Now the case is different. Our hands are free. Our path is still clear before us; and I never will be a party to any step which may bring us into that false position again. I will therefore, supposing that Lord John applies to me, accept office on this express condition,—that, if we find that we cannot carry the total repeal of the Corn Laws, we will forthwith resign; or, at all events, that I shall be at liberty forthwith to resign. I am quite sure that this is the right course; and I am equally sure that, if I take it, I shall be out of office at Easter.

There remains another possible case. What if Lord John and Peel should coalesce, and should offer me a place in their Cabinet? I have fully made up my mind to refuse it. I should not at all blame them for coalescing. I am willing, as an independent Member, to support them as far as I can; and, as respects the question of the Corn Laws, to support them with all my heart and soul. But, after the language which I have held respecting Peel, and which I am less than ever disposed to retract, I feel that I cannot, without a loss of personal dignity, and without exposing myself to suspicions and insinuations which would be insupportable to me, hold any situation under him. The circumstance that my fortune, though amply sufficient for my wants, is small when compared with the fortunes of all the other Cabinet Ministers of our time, makes it fit that I should avoid with punctilious care everything which the multitude may attribute to sordid motives. There are other reasons which do not apply to Lord John, to Lord Lansdowne, to Palmerston, to Baring, to Labouchere, and to Grey; but which would prevent me from holding office in such an arrangement. My opinions about the Irish Church are stronger than those of my friends, and have recently been expressed in a manner which has excited attention. The question of the ballot would also be an insuperable obstacle. I have spoken and voted for it; I will not vote against it for a place; and I am certain that Peel will never consent to let it be an open question. This is an objection which does not apply to Lord John, and to others whom I have named; for they always opposed the ballot. My full resolution therefore is, if a Coalition Ministry should be formed, to support it, but not to be a member of it.

I hope you will not be dissatisfied with this long exposition of my views and intentions. I must now make haste home, to dress for dinner at Milman's, and for the Westminster Play.

Ever yours
T. B. M.

Albany: December 13, 1845.

Dear Hannah.—

I am glad that you sympathise with me, and approve

of my intentions. I should have written yesterday; but I was detained till after post-time at a consultation of Whigs, which Lord John had summoned. We were only five,—Lord John, Lord Cottenham, Clarendon, Palmerston, and myself. This morning we met again at eleven, and were joined by Baring, by Lord Lansdowne, and by the Duke of Bedford. The posture of affairs is this. Lord John has not consented to form a Ministry. He has only told the Queen that he would consult his friends, and see what could be done. We are all most unwilling to take office, and so is he. I have never seen his natural audacity of spirit so much tempered by discretion, and by a sense of responsibility, as on this occasion. The question of the Corn Laws throws all other questions into the shade. Yet, even if that question were out of the way, there would be matters enough to perplex us. Ireland, we fear, is on the brink of something like a servile war,—the effect, not of Repeal agitation, but of the severe distress endured by the peasantry. Foreign politics look dark. An augmentation of the army will be necessary. Pretty legacies to leave to a Ministry which will be in a minority in both Houses! I have no doubt that there is not a single man among us who would not at once refuse to enlist, if he could do so with a clear conscience. Nevertheless, our opinion is that, if we have a reasonable hope of being able to settle the all-important question of the Corn Laws in a satisfactory way, we ought, at whatever sacrifice of quiet and comfort, to take office, though only for a few weeks. But can we entertain such a hope? That is the point; and, till we are satisfied about it, we cannot positively accept or refuse. A few days must pass before we are able to decide.

It is clear that we cannot win the battle with our own unassisted strength. If we win it at all, it must be by the help of Peel, Graham, and their friends. Peel has not seen Lord John; but he left with the Queen a memorandum, containing a promise to support a Corn Bill founded on the principles of Lord John's famous letter to the electors of London.[1] Graham has had both a correspondence, and a personal conference, with Lord John and with Lord Lansdowne, and has given similar assurances. But we all feel that this is too vague, and that we may still be left in the lurch. Lord John has asked for a sketch of Peel's own plan. This we cannot get. In fact, strange as it seems, the plan was never drawn up in a distinct form, or submitted to the late Cabinet in detail. As soon as the general nature of it was stated, the opposition became so strong that nothing was said as to minor points. We have therefore determined on the following course. All our friends who are likely to be Cabinet Ministers are summoned to London, and will, with scarcely an exception, be here in a day or two. We shall then resolve on the heads of a Corn Law, such as we think that we can with honour introduce. When this is done, we shall send it to Peel and Graham, and demand categorically whether they will cordially support such a Bill, aye or no. If they refuse, or use vague language, we shall at once decline to form a Government. If they pledge themselves to stand by us, we must undertake the task.

This is a very strange, indeed an unprecedented, course. But the situation is unprecedented. We are not coming into office as conquerors, leading a majority in Parliament, and driving out our predecessors. Our predecessors, at a most critical moment, throw up the reins in confusion and despair, while they have a strong majority in both Houses, and implore us, who are a minority, to extricate the country from its troubles. We are therefore entitled, if we consent, to demand their honest support as a right, not to supplicate it as a favour. My hope is that Peel will not accede to our terms, and that we shall be set at liberty.

[1] 'The imposition of any duty at present, without a provision for its extinction within a short period, would but prolong a contest already sufficiently fruitful of animosity and discontent.' Such was the cardinal sentence of Lord John Russell's celebrated letter.

He will then be forced to go on with a Ministry patched up as well as he can patch it up. In the meantime, nothing can be more public-spirited or disinterested than the feelings of all our friends who have yet been consulted. This is a good sign.

If I do come in, I shall take a carriage by the month from Newman, and remain at the Albany for some weeks. I have no doubt that we shall all be out by Easter in any event. If we should remain longer, I must, of course, take a house; but nobody can expect that I should be provided with a house at a day's notice.

Ever yours
T. B. M.

Albany: December 19, 1845.

Dear Hannah,—

It is an odd thing to see a Ministry making. I never witnessed the process before. Lord John has been all day in his inner library. His ante-chamber has been filled with comers and goers, some talking in knots, some writing notes at tables. Every five minutes somebody is called into the inner room. As the people who have been closeted come out, the cry of the whole body of expectants is 'What are you?' I was summoned almost as soon as I arrived, and found Lord Auckland and Lord Clarendon sitting with Lord John. After some talk about other matters, Lord John told me that he had been trying to ascertain my wishes, and that he found that I wanted leisure and quiet more than salary and business. Labouchere had told him this. He therefore offered me the Pay Office, one of the three places which, as I have often told you, I should prefer. I at once accepted it. The tenure by which I shall hold it is so precarious that it matters little what its advantages may be; but I shall have two thousand a year for the trouble of signing my name. I must indeed attend Parliament more closely than I have of late done; but my mornings will be as much my own as if I were out of office. If I give to my History the time which I used to pass in transacting business when I was Secretary at War, I shall get on nearly as fast as when I was in Opposition. Some other arrangements promise to be less satisfactory. Palmerston will hear of nothing but the Foreign Office, and Lord Grey therefore declines taking any place. I hope that Lord John will give one of the Secretaryships of State to George Grey. It would be a great elevation; but I am sure that it is the right thing to do. I have told Grey that I look to him as our future leader in the Commons, and that no pretensions of mine shall ever interfere with this. Labouchere feels exactly as I do. Labouchere and Baring are at least as good men of business as Grey; and I may say without vanity that I have made speeches which were out of the reach of any of the three. But, taking the talent for business and the talent for speaking together, Grey is undoubtedly the best qualified among us for the lead; and we are perfectly sensible of this. Indeed, I may say that I do not believe that there was ever a set of public men who had less jealousy of each other, or who formed a more correct estimate of themselves, than the younger members of this Cabinet.

Ever yours

T. B. M.

Albany, London: December 20, 1845.

Dear Hannah,—

All is over. Late at night, just as I was undressing, a knock was given at the door of my chambers. A messenger had come from Lord John with a short note. The quarrel between Lord Grey and Lord Palmerston had made it impossible to form a Ministry. I went to bed, and slept sound. In the morning I went to the corner of Belgrave Square, which is now the great place for political news, and found that Lord John had gone to Windsor to resign his trust into the Queen's hands.

I have no disposition to complain of the loss of office. On the contrary, my escape from the slavery of a placeman is my only consolation.[1] But I feel that we are in an ignominious position as a party. After agreeing on the principles of our measure, after agreeing that our public duty required us to take office, we have now thrown the game up, not on account of any new matter affecting the national interests, but solely because we are, as the French say, *mauvais coucheurs*, and cannot adjust ourselves to accommodate each other. I do not blame Lord John; but Lord Grey and Lord Palmerston are both at fault. I think Lord Grey, highly as I esteem his integrity and ability, chiefly responsible for the unfortunate situation in which we are now placed; but I suspect that Palmerston will be made the scapegoat. He is no favourite with the public. A large portion of our own friends think him a dangerous Minister. By the whole continental and American press he has been represented as the very Genius of War and Discord. People will now say that, when every other place was within his reach; when he might have had the Home Office, the Colonies, the Admiralty, a peerage,—in short, his own terms,—he declared that, unless he was allowed to be where he was generally considered as a firebrand, he would blow up his party, at a crisis when the fate of his party involved the fate of his country. I suspect that a great storm of public indignation will burst upon him, and that he will sink under it. In the meantime what is to happen?

I have had an anxious time since you were away; but I can truly say that I have done nothing through all these troubles which I should be ashamed to hear proclaimed at Charing Cross, or which I would not do again.

Ever yours

T. B. M.

[1] 'On the whole,' Macaulay wrote to Mr. Ellis, 'I am inclined to think that what has happened will do more good than harm. Perhaps the pleasure with which I have this morning looked round my chambers, and resumed my History, has something to do in making me thus cheerful. Let me advise you to put forth a little tract, after the fashion of the seven-

Macaulay's readiness to brave publicity was soon put to a most unpleasant test. Mr. Macfarlan, a constituent who was much in his confidence, had transmitted to him for presentation a memorial to the Queen praying for the removal of all restriction on the importation of corn. Macaulay replied by a letter which commenced as follows: 'You will have heard the termination of our attempt to form a Government. All our plans were frustrated by Lord Grey. I hope the public interests will not suffer. Sir Robert Peel must now undertake the settlement of the question. It is certain that he can settle it. It is by no means certain that we could have done so: for we shall to a man support him; and a large proportion of those who are now in office would have refused to support us. On my own share in these transactions I reflect with unmixed satisfaction. From the first, I told Lord John that I stipulated for one thing only,—total and immediate repeal of the Corn Laws; that my objections to gradual abolition were insurmountable; but that, if he declared for total and immediate repeal, I would be, as to all other matters, absolutely in his hands; that I would take any office or no office, just as it suited him best; and that he should never be disturbed by any personal pretensions or jealousies on my part. If everybody else had acted thus, there would now have been a Liberal Ministry. However, as I said, perhaps it is best as it is.'

It unfortunately happened that Mr. Macfarlan, forgetting both prudence and propriety in his eagerness to seize so good an opportunity of establishing his Member's character as an uncompromising free-trader, thought the letter much too good to be kept to himself. It accordingly appeared in the columns of the Scotsman, and was copied into all the newspapers of the country, to the heartfelt, and, as his diaries prove, the lifelong, regret of Macaulay. He was deeply pained at

teenth century, entitled "A Secret History of some Late Passages, as they were communicated by a Person of Honour to T. F. E., a Gentleman of the Inner Temple." '

being paraded before the world as the critic of an old friend and colleague.[1]

My dear Napier,— Bowood: January 4, 1846.

I am, as ever, grateful for your kindness. Of course you were perfectly right in supposing that I was altogether taken by surprise when I saw my letter to Macfarlan in print. I do not think that I was ever more astonished or vexed. However, it is very little my way to brood over what is done and cannot be helped.

I am not surprised that many should blame me; and yet I cannot admit that I was much to blame. I was writing to an active friendly constituent who had during some years been in almost constant communication with me. We had corresponded about Edinburgh intrigues, about the Free Church, about Maynooth; and I had always written with openness, and had never found any reason to complain of indiscretion. After all, I wrote only what everybody at Brooks's, and at the Reform Club, was saying from morning till night. I will venture to affirm, that, if the post-bags of the last fortnight were rummaged, it would appear that Lord John, Lord Morpeth, Lord Grey himself,—in fact, everybody concerned in the late negotiations,—has written letters quite as unfit for the public eye as mine. However, I well know that the world always judges by the event; and I must be content to be well abused till some new occurrence puts Macfarlan's prank out of people's heads.

I should be much obliged to you, whenever an opportunity offers, to say from me that I am surprised and

[1] 'May 17, 1850. Macfarlan called; a man who did me a great injury; but he meant no harm, and I have long forgiven him; though to the end of my life I shall occasionally feel twinges of a very painful sort at the recollection.'

And again: 'July 4, 1851. I stayed at home all the morning, and wrote not amiss. Macfarlan called. What harm that man did me! What misery for a time he caused me! In my happy life that was one of the calamities which cut deep. There is still a scar.' So keenly did Macaulay feel the only circumstance which ever threw a momentary doubt upon the loyalty of his friendship.

indignant at the unauthorised publication of a private letter unguardedly written; but that, whatever I have written, guardedly or unguardedly, is the truth by which I am prepared to stand.

Ever yours truly

T. B. MACAULAY.

Albany, London: January 10, 1846.

Dear Napier,—

Thanks for all your kindness. I am sorry to be the cause of so much trouble to my friends. I have received a penitent letter from Macfarlan, offering to do anything in his power.

The business is very disagreeable, but might have been worse. To say of a man that he has talents and virtue, but wants judgment and temper, is no very deadly outrage. I declare that I should not have scrupled to put this unlucky sentence,[1] with a little softening, into the Edinburgh Review. For example: 'We cannot but regret that a nobleman, whose talents and virtues we fully acknowledge, should have formed so high an estimate of his own pretensions, and should be so unwilling to make any concession to the opinions of others, that it is not easy to act in concert with him.' There is nothing here which I would not say in the House of Commons.

I do not know whether it is worth while to mention the following circumstance. Macfarlan, soon after he got this unlucky letter, wrote to tell me that he thought the publication of it would be of use to me. I instantly wrote to beg that he would not think of such a thing, and gave as my reason the great esteem and admiration which, in spite of recent events, I felt for Lord Grey. Whether any good use can be made of this fact I do not know. I am very unwilling to be on bad terms with a man whom I greatly respect and value. I rely implicitly on your discretion.

Ever yours truly

T. B. MACAULAY.

[1] The sentence which referred to 'personal pretensions' and 'jealousies.'

At this period of his life Macaulay was still a hard hitter; but he timed his blows with due regard for the public interests. In January 1845 he writes to Mr. Napier: 'Many thanks for your kind expressions about the last session. I have certainly been heard with great favour by the House whenever I have spoken. As to the course which I have taken, I feel no misgivings. Many honest men think that there ought to be no retrospect in politics. I am firmly convinced that they are in error, and that much better measures than any which we owe to Peel would be very dearly purchased by the utter ruin of all public virtue which must be the consequence of such immoral lenity.'

So much for Maynooth, and for the past. With regard to the future, and the Corn Laws, he says: 'As to any remarks which I may make on Peel's gross inconsistency, they must wait till his Bill is out of all danger. On the Maynooth question he ran no risk of a defeat; and therefore I had no scruple about attacking him. But to hit him hard while he is fighting the landowners would be a very different thing. It will be all that he can do to win the battle with the best help that we can give him. A time will come for looking back. At present our business is to get the country safe through a very serious and doubtful emergency.'

But no aid from his opponents, however loyally rendered, could keep Sir Robert Peel in office when once that emergency was at an end. On the 26th of June, 1846, the Corn Law Bill passed the Peers; and, before the night was over, the Government had received its coup-de-grâce in the Commons. Lord John Russell was again commanded to form an Administration. Macaulay obtained the post which he preferred, as the least likely to interfere with his historical labours; and, as Paymaster-General of the Army, he went down to Scotland to ask for re-election. On the 9th of July he wrote to Mrs. Trevelyan from the Royal Hotel: 'I reached Edinburgh last night, and found the city in a storm. The dissenters and Free Churchmen have got up an opposition on the old ground of Maynooth, and have sent for Sir Culling Eardley Smith. He is to be here this evening. Comically enough, we shall be at the same inn; but the landlord, waiters, chambermaid, and boots are all with me. I have no doubt about the result. We had to-day a great meeting of electors. The Lord Provost presided. Near three thousand well-dressed people, chiefly voters, were present. I spoke for an hour,—as well, they tell me, as I ever spoke in my life, and certainly with considerable effect. There was immense cheering, mingled with a little hissing. A show of hands was called for. I had a perfect forest, and the other side not fifty. I am exceedingly well and in high spirits. I had become somewhat effeminate in literary repose and leisure. You would not know me again now that my blood is up. I am such as when, twelve years ago, I fought the battle with Sadler at Leeds.' This ardour for the fray augured badly for Sir Culling Eardley. He proved no match for Macaulay, who out-talked him on the hustings; beat him by two to one at the poll; and returned to the Albany in triumph, none the worse for his exhilarating, though rather expensive, contest.

We are told by Gibbon, in the most delightful of autobiographies, that he never found his mind more vigorous, nor his composition more happy, than in 'the winter hurry of society and Parliament.' The historian of the Roman Empire found a gentle stimulus and a salutary distraction in the discharge of his functions as Commissioner of Trade and Plantations, and in the debates on Burke's measures of Economical Reform. In like manner the routine of the Pay Office, and the obligations of the Treasury Bench in the House of Commons, were of benefit to Macaulay while he was engaged upon Monmouth's invasion, and the Revolution of 1688. The new Paymaster-General discovered his duties to be even less burdensome than he had been given to suppose. An occasional Board day at Chelsea, passed in checking off lists of names and signing grants of pension, made very moderate demands upon his time and energy; and in Parliament his brother Members treated him with a respectful indulgence on which he very seldom trespassed. Lord Lytton must have been thinking of this period in his career, when he ascribed to him

> A royal Eloquence, that paid, in state,
> A ceremonious visit to Debate.

Macaulay spoke only five times in all during the sessions of 1846 and 1847; but whenever, and on whatever subject, he opened his lips, the columns of Hansard are thickly studded with compliments paid to him either in retrospect or by anticipation. His intention to take part in a discussion was, as it were, advertised beforehand by the misgivings of the speakers who differed from him. When the Ten Hours' Bill was under consideration, one of its most resolute opponents, fearing the effect which would be produced upon the House by a dissertation from Macaulay in favour of the principle of the Factory Acts, humorously deprecated the wrath of 'his Right Honourable friend, under whose withering eloquence he would, there was little doubt, be very speedily extinguished.'[1] On another occasion

[1] On the 8th of October 1853, Macaulay says, with the frankness of a man who is speaking about his own performances without the fear of being overheard: 'I worked at the Factory speech, but did little. I like the speech amazingly. I rather think that it is my very best.'

At all events, it has proved a mine of wealth to those who, since Macaulay's day, have argued for extending the Factory Acts. He made an effective use of the analogy of the Sunday in order to defend the principle of regulating the hours of labour by law. 'Man, man is the great instrument that produces wealth. The natural difference between Campania and Spitzbergen is trifling when compared with the difference between a country inhabited by men full of bodily and mental vigour, and a country inhabited by men sunk in bodily and mental decrepitude. Therefore it is that we are not poorer but richer, because we have, through many ages, rested from our labour one day in seven. That day is not lost. While industry is suspended, while the plough lies in the furrow, while the Exchange is silent, while no smoke ascends from the factory, a process is going on quite as important to the wealth of nations as any process which is performed on more busy days. Man, the machine of machines, the machine compared with which all the contrivances of the Watts and the Arkwrights are

he was unexpectedly called upon his feet to account for a letter, in which he had expressed an opinion about the propriety of granting a pardon to the leaders of the Welsh Chartists. When the House had heard his explanation, (into which he contrived to bring an allusion to Judge Jeffreys and the Bloody Assize,—a reminiscence, in all probability, of his morning's study,) Mr. Disraeli gracefully enough expressed the general sentiment of the audience. 'It is always, to me at least, and I believe to the House, so agreeable to listen to the Right Honourable gentleman under any circumstances, that we must have been all gratified to-night that he has found it necessary to vindicate his celebrated epistle.'

In October 1846, Macaulay writes to one of his sisters: 'I have received the most disgusting letter, by many degrees, that I ever read in my life from old Mrs. ——. I can convey to you no idea of it but by transcribing it, and it is too long to transcribe. However, I will give you the opening. "My dear friend,—Many years have passed away, since my revered husband, and your excellent father, walked together as Christian friends, and since I derived the sweetest comfort and pleasure from a close friendship with both your blessed parents." After a great deal more about various revered and blessed people, she comes to the real object of her epistle, which is to ask for three livings and a bishopric. I have been accustomed to

worthless, is repairing and winding up, so that he returns to his labours on the Monday with clearer intellect, with livelier spirits, with renewed corporal vigour. Never will I believe that what makes a population stronger, and healthier, and wiser, and better, can ultimately make it poorer. You try to frighten us by telling us that, in some German factories, the young work seventeen hours in the twenty-four; that they work so hard that among thousands there is not one who grows to such a stature that he can be admitted into the army; and you ask whether, if we pass this bill, we can possibly hold our own against such competition as this. Sir, I laugh at the thought of such competition. If ever we are forced to yield the foremost place among commercial nations, we shall yield it, not to a race of degenerate dwarfs, but to some people pre-eminently vigorous in body and mind.'

unreasonable and importunate suitors; but I protest that this old hag's impudence fairly took away my breath. She is so moderate as to say that for her son she will accept,—nay, very thankfully accept,—even a living of five hundred a year. Another proof of her moderation is that, before she asks for a bishopric, she has the grace to say, "I am now going to be very bold." Really the comedy of actual life is beyond all comedy.'

The repugnance which this deluge of unctuous importunity aroused in Macaulay's breast was not aggravated by any prepossession in favour of doctrines the opposite of Evangelical. This is clearly proved, if proof be wanting, by the last sentence of a letter bearing upon what was perhaps the most important piece of business which it fell to him to transact as Paymaster-General of the Army.

Dear Ellis,—

I have at this moment the disposal of a tolerable piece of patronage, the Chaplainship of Chelsea Hospital; light duty, a nice house, coal, candles, and three hundred pounds a year. It would be an exceedingly pleasant situation for a literary man. But he must also be a man of piety and feeling; for, the Hospital being full of old battered soldiers, the duty, though by no means onerous, consists chiefly in attending sick beds, and I would not for any consideration assign such a duty to a person who would hurry through it in a perfunctory manner. Is there any among the junior Fellows of Trinity who would suit? I do not want a politician; and nothing shall induce me to take a Puseyite.

Yours very truly
T. B. M.

In Parliament, in society, and in literary and political circles throughout the country, Macaulay already enjoyed that general respect and goodwill which attach themselves to a man who has done great things, and from whom something still greater is expected. But there was one city in the kingdom where he had ceased to be popular, and unfortunately that city was Edinburgh. The causes of his unpopularity were in part external and temporary, and in part can be detected only after an attentive review of his personal character.

In the year 1847 the disruption of the Scotch Church was already an accomplished and accepted fact; but that momentous crisis had left bitter feelings behind it. Our leading public men had displayed an indifference to the tendencies of religious opinion in Scotland, and a scandalous ignorance of her religious affairs, which had alienated from Whigs and Englishmen the confidence and attachment of the population north of Tweed. Macaulay, the most eminent Whig, and far the most eminent Englishman, who then sat for a Scotch constituency, was made the scapegoat for the sins of all his colleagues. He might have averted his fate by subservience, or mitigated it by prudence; but the necessity of taking a side about Maynooth obliged him to announce his views on the question of religious endowments, and his nature did not allow him to soften down those views by the use of dainty and ambiguous phraseology. He wished all the world to know that, however much the people whom he represented might regard ecclesiastical matters from the standpoint of the Church, he regarded them, and would always continue to regard them, exclusively from the standpoint of the State.

Radicalism, again, then as always, was stronger in Scotland than in any other portion of the United Kingdom, and stronger in Edinburgh than in any other town of Scotland; for in Edinburgh the internal differences of the Liberal party were intensified by local circumstances. 'Twenty years ago,' writes a former supporter of Macaulay, 'there was among us a great deal of what in Oxford is called Town and Gown. The Parliament House, Literature, and the University made the Gown. The tradesmen, as a class, maintained that the high Whigs, though calling themselves the friends of the people, were exclusive and overbearing; and there was some truth in this. The Whigs were always under terror of being coupled with Cobbett, Hunt, and their kind.' Macaulay had his full share of this feeling. In May 1842, when the People's Charter was presented to Parliament, he spoke, with an emphasis which nothing but sincere conviction could supply, against Mr. Thomas Duncombe's motion that the petitioners should be heard at the Bar of the House. 'Sir,' he said, 'I cannot conscientiously assent to the motion. And yet I must admit that the Honourable Member for Finsbury has framed it with considerable skill. He has done his best to obtain the support of all those timid and interested politicians who think much more about the security of their seats than about the security of their country. It would be very convenient to me to give a silent vote with him. I should then have it in my power to say to the Chartists of Edinburgh, "When your petition was before the House I was on your side: I was for giving you a full hearing." I should at the same time be able to assure my Conservative constituents that I never had supported and never would support the Charter. But, Sir, though this course would be very convenient, it is one which my sense of duty will not suffer me to take.' In a letter to Mr. Napier, dated the 10th of August 1844, he writes: 'I must put off my journey northward for a week. One of my reasons for this postponement, (but let it rest between ourselves,) is that, on Wednesday the 21st, Hume is to lay the first stone of a monument to the Republicans who were transported by Pitt and Dundas. Now, though I by no means approve of the severity with which those people were treated, I do not admire their proceedings, nor should I choose to attend the ceremony. But, if I arrived just before it, I should certainly be expected by a portion of my constituents either to attend or explain the reasons of my absence, and thus we should have another disagreeable controversy.'

But Macaulay might have been as much of a Whig

and an Erastian as he chose if he had had in his composition more of the man of the world and less of the man of the study. There was a perceptible want of lightness of touch in his method of doing the ordinary business which falls to the lot of a Member of Parliament. 'The truth is,' wrote Lord Cockburn in July 1846, 'that Macaulay, with all his admitted knowledge, talent, eloquence, and worth, is not popular. He cares more for his History than for the jobs of his constituents, and answers letters irregularly, and with a brevity deemed contemptuous; and, above all other defects, he suffers severely from the vice of over-talking, and consequently of under-listening. A deputation goes to London to enlighten their representative. They are full of their own matter, and their chairman has a statement bottled and ripe, which he is anxious to draw and decant; but, instead of being listened to, they no sooner enter the audience chamber than they find themselves all superseded by the restless ability of their eloquent Member, who, besides mistaking speaking for hearing, has the indelicate candour not even to profess being struck by the importance of the affair.'

Macaulay had exalted, and, as some would hold, overstrained ideas of the attitude which a representative should adopt in his pecuniary relations with the electors who have sent him to Parliament. Although one of the most generous of men,—who knew no delight like giving, and who indulged himself in that respect with an indiscriminate and incautious facility which was at times little short of blameworthy,—he was willing, when Edinburgh was in question, to be called stingy if he could only make it clear to his own conscience that he was not tampering with corruption.

London: July 14, 1841.

My dear Mr. Black,—

I am much gratified by what you say about the race-cup. I had already written to Craig to say that I should not subscribe, and I am glad that my determination meets your approbation. In the first place,

I am not clear that the object is a good one. In the next place, I am clear that by giving money for such an object in obedience to such a summons, I should completely change the whole character of my connection with Edinburgh. It has been usual enough for rich families to keep a hold on corrupt boroughs by defraying the expense of public amusements. Sometimes it is a ball; sometimes a regatta. The Derby family used to support the Preston races. The Members for Beverley, I believe, find a bull for their constituents to bait. But these were not the conditions on which I undertook to represent Edinburgh. In return for your generous confidence, I offer Parliamentary service, and nothing else. I am indeed most willing to contribute the little that I can spare to your most useful public charities. But even this I do not consider as matter of contract. Nor should I think it proper that the Town Council should call on me to contribute even to an hospital or a school. But the call that is now made is one so objectionable that, I must plainly say, I would rather take the Chiltern Hundreds than comply with it.

I should feel this if I were a rich man. But I am not rich. I have the means of living very comfortably according to my notions, and I shall still be able to spare something for the common objects of our party, and something for the distressed. But I have nothing to waste on gaieties which can at best only be considered harmless. If our friends want a Member who will find them in public diversions, they can be at no loss. I know twenty people who, if you will elect them to Parliament, will gladly treat you to a race or a race-ball once a month. But I shall not be very easily induced to believe that Edinburgh is disposed to select her representatives on such a principle.

Ever yours truly

T. B. MACAULAY.

Macaulay was so free from some faults to which literary men are proverbially inclined, that many of those who had claims upon his time and services were too apt to forget that, after all, he possessed the literary temperament. In the heyday of youth he relished the bustle of crowds, and could find amusement in the company of strangers; but as years went forward,—as his spirits lost their edge and his health its spring,—he was ever more and more disposed to recoil from publicity. Insatiable of labour, he regarded the near approach, and still more the distant prospect, of worry with an exaggerated disquietude which in his case was a premonitory symptom of the disease that was to kill him. Perpetually overworked by his History, (and there is no overwork like that of a task which has grown to be dearer to a man than life itself,) he no longer had the nerve required to face the social efforts, and to undergo the minute and unceasing observation, to which he was, or fancied himself to be, exposed when on a visit to the city which he represented. 'If the people of Edinburgh,' he wrote to Mr. Napier, 'were not my constituents, there is no place in the island where I should like so much to pass a few weeks: but our relation imposes both such constant exertion and such constant reserve that a trip thither is neither pleasant nor prudent.' And again: 'I hope to be at Edinburgh on August the 19th or 20th. At so dead a time of the year I should think that it might be possible for me to escape speeches and meetings, particularly as I mean to go quietly, and without sending notice to any of our political managers. It is really very hard that I cannot visit your city as any other gentleman and man of letters can do. My intention is to stay about a fortnight and I should like to go out to you from Edinburgh on Saturday the 20th, and to return on the Monday. I wish to avoid passing a Sunday in the good town, for to whatever church I go, I shall give offence to somebody.'

Whatever may have been the origin and the extent of Macaulay's shortcomings as representative of Edinburgh, there were men at hand who were anxious, and very well able, to turn them to their own account. But the injuries which he forgave I am forbidden to resent. No drop of ink from this pen shall resuscitate the memory of the intrigues that preceded and brought about the catastrophe of 1847; a catastrophe which was the outcome of jealousies which have long been dead, and the stepping-stone of ambitions which have ere this been gratified. But justice demands that on one point a protest should be made. There are some still alive who have persuaded themselves into the belief that they opposed Macaulay because he was not sound on the Corn Laws;—and this in the teeth of the facts that from the year 1843 onward he was a consistent and hearty supporter of the uncompromising Resolution annually brought forward by Mr. Charles Villiers; and that, (as his letter to Mr. Macfarlan made only too notorious,) at the crowning moment of the Free Trade controversy he statedly and resolutely refused to lend his assistance in forming any Ministry which did not pledge itself to the total and immediate removal of the duty upon corn.[1] If such an early and signal repentance as this,—(and I will not enter into the question whether or not his previous conduct had been such as called for repentance,)—was ineffectual to clear him in the eyes of his constituents, then indeed the authority of an elector over his representative would be a tyranny which no man of right feeling would desire to exercise, and no man of honour could be expected to endure.

When Parliament was dissolved in the summer of 1847, all the various elements of discontent, political, ecclesiastical, and personal alike, mustered round the standard that was raised by Sir Culling Eardley's former committee, 'which,' says Lord Cockburn, 'contained Established Churchmen and wild Voluntaries, intense Tories and declamatory Radicals, who agreed in nothing except in holding their peculiar religion as the scriptural, and therefore the only safe, criterion of fitness for public duty. These men would have preferred Blackadder to Marlborough for the command

[1] See vol. ii, pages 105 and 114.

of an army.' 'The struggle,' wrote Hugh Miller, 'is exciting the deepest interest, and, as the beginning of a decided movement on the part of Christians of various denominations to send men of avowed Christian principle to Parliament, may lead to great results.' The common sense of the Scotch people brought this movement, such as it was, to a speedy close; and it led to no greater result than that of inflicting a transient scandal upon the sacred name of religion, and giving Macaulay the leisure which he required in order to put the finishing touch to the first two volumes of his History.

The leaders of the agitation judged it necessary to select a stronger candidate than Sir Culling Eardley; and their choice fell upon Mr. Charles Cowan, a son of one of the most respected citizens of Edinburgh, and himself a man of high private character, though not very conversant with public affairs. The gentleman who introduced Mr. Cowan to the electors at his first public meeting recommended him on the express ground that 'Christian men ought to send Christian men to represent them.' But, when people inspired by these exemplary motives had once begun to move, others whose views were of a more temporal and mundane complexion were not behindhand in following their example. A deputation of spirit-dealers waited upon Macaulay to urge the propriety of altering the method of levying the excise duties. They failed to convince him; and he told them plainly that he would do nothing for them, and most probably should do something against them. The immediate consequence of this unsatisfactory interview was the appearance of a fourth candidate in the person of Mr. Blackburn, who was described by his own proposer as one who 'came forward for the excise trader, which showed that his heart was with the people,'—or at any rate with that section of the people whose politics consisted in dislike to the whisky-duty.

The contest was short, but sharp. For ten days the city was white with broadsides, and the narrow courts off the High Street rang with the dismal strains of innumerable ballad-singers. The opposition was nominally directed against both the sitting Members; but from the first it was evident that all the scurrility was meant exclusively for Macaulay. He came scatheless even out of that ordeal. The vague charge of being too much of an essayist and too little of a politician was the worst that either saint or sinner could find to say of him. The burden of half the election-songs was to the effect that he had written poetry, and that one who knew so much about Ancient Rome could not possibly be the man for Modern Athens. The day of nomination was the 29th of July. The space in front of the hustings had been packed by the advocates of cheap whisky. Professor Aytoun, who seconded Mr. Blackburn, was applauded to his heart's content, while Macaulay was treated with a brutality the details of which are painful to read, and would be worse than useless to record. The polling took place on the morrow. A considerable number of the Tories, instead of plumping for Blackburn, or dividing their favours with the sitting Members, (who were both of them moderate Whigs and supporters of the Establishment,) thought fit to give their second votes to Mr. Cowan, an avowed Voluntaryist in Church matters, and the accepted champion of the Radical party. 'I waited with Mr. Macaulay,' says Mr. Adam Black, 'in a room of the Merchants' Hall, to receive at every hour the numbers who had polled in all the districts. At ten o'clock we were confounded to find that he was 150 below Cowan, but still had faint hopes that the next hour might turn the scale. The next hour came, and a darker prospect. At twelve o'clock he was 340 below Cowan. It was obvious now that the field was lost; but we were left from hour to hour under the torture of a sinking poll, till at four o'clock it stood thus: Cowan, 2,063; Craig, 1,854; Macaulay, 1,477; Blackburn, 980.'

Edinburgh: July 30, 1847.

Dearest Hannah,—

I hope that you will not be much vexed; for I am not vexed, but as cheerful as ever I was in my life. I have been completely beaten. The poll has not closed; but there is no chance that I shall retrieve the lost ground. Radicals, Tories, Dissenters, Voluntaries, Free Churchmen, spirit drinkers who are angry because I will not pledge myself to repeal all taxes on whisky, and great numbers of persons who are jealous of my chief supporters here, and think that the patronage of Edinburgh has been too exclusively distributed among a clique, have united to bear me down. I will make no hasty resolutions; but everything seems to indicate that I ought to take this opportunity of retiring from public life.

Ever yours
T. B. M.

Edinburgh: July 30, 1847.

Dear Ellis,—

I am beaten, but not at all the less happy for being so. I think that having once been manumitted, after the old fashion, by a slap in the face, I shall not take to bondage again. But there is time to consider that matter.

Ever yours
T. B. MACAULAY.

That same night, while the town was still alive with jubilation over a triumph that soon lost its gloss even in the eyes of those who won it, Macaulay, in the grateful silence of his chamber, was weaving his perturbed thoughts into those exquisite lines which tell within the compass of a score of stanzas the essential secret of the life whose outward aspect these volumes have endeavoured to portray.

The day of tumult, strife, defeat, was o'er.
  Worn out with toil, and noise, and scorn, and spleen,
I slumbered, and in slumber saw once more
  A room in an old mansion, long unseen.

That room, methought, was curtained from the light;
  Yet through the curtains shone the moon's cold ray
Full on a cradle, where, in linen white,
  Sleeping life's first soft sleep, an infant lay.

*　　*　　*　　*

And lo! the fairy queens who rule our birth
  Drew nigh to speak the new-born baby's doom:
With noiseless step, which left no trace on earth,
  From gloom they came, and vanished into gloom.

Not deigning on the boy a glance to cast
  Swept careless by the gorgeous Queen of Gain.
More scornful still, the Queen of Fashion passed,
  With mincing gait and sneer of cold disdain.

The Queen of Power tossed high her jewelled head,
  And o'er her shoulder threw a wrathful frown.
The Queen of Pleasure on the pillow shed
  Scarce one stray rose-leaf from her fragrant crown.

Still fay in long procession followed fay;
  And still the little couch remained unblest:
But, when those wayward sprites had passed away,
  Came One, the last, the mightiest, and the best.

Oh! glorious lady, with the eyes of light,
  And laurels clustering round thy lofty brow,
Who by the cradle's side didst watch that night,
  Warbling a sweet strange music, who wast thou?

'Yes, darling; let them go,' so ran the strain:
  'Yes; let them go, gain, fashion, pleasure, power,
And all the busy elves to whose domain
  Belongs the nether sphere, the fleeting hour.

'Without one envious sigh, one anxious scheme,
  To nether sphere, the fleeting hour resign.
Mine is the world of thought, the world of dream,
  Mine all the past, and all the future mine.

* * * *

'Of the fair brotherhood who share my grace,
  I, from thy natal day, pronounce thee free;
And, if for some I keep a nobler place,
  I keep for none a happier than for thee.

'There are who, while to vulgar eyes they seem
  Of all my bounties largely to partake,
Of me as of some rival's handmaid deem
  And court me but for gain's, power's, fashion's sake.

'To such, though deep their lore, though wide their fame,
  Shall my great mysteries be all unknown:
But thou, through good and evil, praise and blame,
  Wilt not thou love me for myself alone?

'Yes; thou wilt love me with exceeding love;
And I will tenfold all that love repay:
Still smiling, though the tender may reprove;
Still faithful, though the trusted may betray.

* * * *

'In the dark hour of shame, I deigned to stand
Before the frowning peers at Bacon's side;
On a far shore I smoothed with tender hand,
Through months of pain, the sleepless bed of Hyde.

'I brought the wise and brave of ancient days
To cheer the cell where Raleigh pined alone.
I lighted Milton's darkness with the blaze
Of the bright ranks that guard the eternal throne.

'And even so, my child, it is my pleasure
That thou not then alone shouldst feel me nigh,
When in domestic bliss and studious leisure,
Thy weeks uncounted come, uncounted fly.

* * * *

'No; when on restless night dawns cheerless morrow,
When weary soul and wasting body pine,
Thine am I still, in danger, sickness, sorrow,
In conflict, obloquy, want, exile, thine;

'Thine where on mountain waves the snowbirds scream,
Where more than Thule's winter barbs the breeze,
Where scarce, through lowering clouds, one sickly gleam
Lights the drear May-day of Antarctic seas.

'Thine, when around thy litter's track all day
White sandhills shall reflect the blinding glare;
Thine, when, through forests breathing death, thy way
All night shall wind by many a tiger's lair;

'Thine most, when friends turn pale, when traitors fly
When, hard beset, thy spirit, justly proud,
For truth, peace, freedom, mercy, dares defy
A sullen priesthood and a raving crowd.[1]

[1] 'I cannot,' said Macaulay on the hustings, 'ask pardon for my conduct. I cannot ask pardon for being in the right. I come here to state what I have done clearly, and to defend it.' The address to his late constituents, which he put forth after his defeat, contained the following sentence. 'I shall always be proud to think that I once enjoyed your favour; but permit me to say that I shall remember not less proudly how I risked, and how I lost it.'

'Amidst the din of all things fell and vile,
  Hate's yell, and envy's hiss, and folly's bray,
Remember me; and with an unforced smile
  See riches, baubles, flatterers, pass away.

'Yes; they will pass away; nor deem it strange;
  They come and go, as comes and goes the sea:
And let them come and go; thou, through all change,
  Fix thy firm gaze on virtue and on me.'

CHAPTER XI

1847–1849

Macaulay retires into private life—Extracts from Lord Carlisle's journal—Macaulay's conversation—His memory—His distaste for general society—His ways with children—Letters to his niece Margaret—The judicious poet—Valentines — Sight-seeing — Eastern tours — Macaulay's method of work—His diligence in collecting his materials—Glencoe—Londonderry—Macaulay's accuracy: opinions of Mr. Bagehot and Mr. Buckle—Macaulay's industry at the desk—His love for his task—Extracts from his diary—His attention to the details of the press—The History appears—Congratulations—Lord Halifax; Lord Jeffrey; Lord Auckland; Miss Edgeworth—The popularity of the work—Extract from 'Punch'—Macaulay's attitude in relation to his critics—The Quarterly Review—The sacrifices which Macaulay made to literature.

After a few nights of sound sleep, and a few days of quiet among his books, Macaulay had recovered both from the fatigues of the contest and the vexation of the defeat. On the 6th of August 1847, he writes to his sister Fanny: 'I am here in solitude, reading and working with great satisfaction to myself. My table is covered with letters of condolence, and with invitations from half the places which have not yet chosen members. I have been asked to stand for Ayr, for Wigton, and for Oxfordshire. At Wigton, and in Oxfordshire, I was actually put in nomination without my permission, and my supporters were with difficulty prevented from going to the poll. From the Sheffield Iris, which was sent me to-day, I see that a party wishes to put me up for the West Riding. Craig tells me that there is a violent reaction at Edinburgh, and that those who voted against me are very generally ashamed of themselves, and wish to have me back again. I did not know how great a politician I was till my Edinburgh friends chose to dismiss me from politics. I never can leave public life with more dignity and grace than at present.'

Such consolations as private life had to offer, Macaulay possessed in abundance. He enjoyed the pleasures of society in their most delightful shape, for he was one of a circle of eminent and gifted men who were the warm friends of himself and of each other. How brilliantly these men talked is already a matter of tradition. No report of their conversation has been published, and in all probability none exists. Scattered and meagre notices in the leaves of private diaries form the sole surviving record of many an Attic night, and still more agreeable morning. Happily Lord Carlisle's journal has preserved for us, (as may be seen in the extracts which follow,) at least the names of those with whom Macaulay lived, the houses which he frequented, and some few of the topics which he discussed. That journal proves, by many an affectionate and admiring expression, how highly my uncle was esteemed by one whose approbation and regard were never lightly given.[1]

[1] Macaulay's acquaintance with the Howard family was of old standing, as may be gathered from a passage in a letter of the year 1833. This exceedingly droll production is too thickly strewn with personal allusions to admit of its being published except in a fragmentary condition which would be unjust to the writer, and not very interesting to the reader.

'I dined at Holland House yesterday.

DRAMATIS PERSONÆ.

Lord Holland . . . A fine old gentleman, very gouty and good-natured.

Earl Grey . . . Prime Minister; a proud and majestic, yet polite and affable person.

The Rev. Sydney Smith A holy and venerable ecclesiastic, director of the consciences of the above-named lords.

* * * * * *

Lady Dover . . . A charming woman, like all the Howards of Carlisle.'

'*June* 27, 1843.—I breakfasted with Hallam, John Russell, Macaulay, Everett, Van de Weyer, Mr. Hamilton, U S., and Mahon. Never were such torrents of good talk as burst and sputtered over from Macaulay and Hallam. A great deal about Latin and Greek inscriptions. They think the first unrivalled for that purpose: so free from articles and particles. Hallam read some wondrous extracts from the Lives of the Saints now being edited by Newman.[1] Macaulay repeated, after the Yankees were gone, an egregious extract from a Natchez repudiation Paper, making out our Saviour to be the first great repudiator, when he overthrew the seats of the money-changers.'

'*March* 4, 1848.—Macaulay says that they' (the Parisian republicans) 'are refuting the doctrines of political economy in the way a man would refute the doctrine of gravitation by jumping off the Monument.'

'*January* 6, 1849.—Finished Macaulay's two volumes. How admirable they are, full of generous impulse, judicial impartiality, wide research, deep thought, picturesque description, and sustained eloquence! Was history ever better written? Guizot[2] praises Macaulay. He says that he has truly hit the ruling passion of William the Third: his hatred for Louis the Fourteenth.'

'*February* 12.—Breakfasted with Macaulay. There were Van de Weyer, Hallam, Charles Austin, Panizzi, Colonel Mure, and Dicky Milnes, but he went to Yorkshire after the first cup. The conversation ranged the world; art,

[1] About this period Macaulay writes to Mr. Napier: 'Newman announces an English Hagiology in numbers, which is to contain the lives of such blessed saints as Thomas à Becket and Dunstan. I should not dislike to be the Avvocato del Diavolo on such an occasion.' And again: 'I hear much of the miracles of the third and fourth centuries by Newman. I think that I could treat that subject without giving scandal to any rational person, and I should like it much. The times require a Middleton.'

[2] Guizot was then a refugee in England. Shortly before this date Macaulay writes to his sister Selina: 'I left a card with Guizot, but did not ask to see him. I purposely avoided meeting him on Friday at Lord Holland's. The truth is that I like and esteem the man: but I think the policy of the Minister both at home and abroad detestable. At home it was all corruption, and abroad all treachery. I could not hold to him the language of entire respect and complacency without a violation of truth; and, in his present circumstances, I could not bear to show the least disapprobation.'

ancient and modern; the Greek tragedians; characters of the orators,—how Philip and Alexander probably felt towards them as we do towards a scurrilous newspaper editor. It is a refreshing break in the common-place life. I stayed till past twelve. His rooms at the top of the Albany are very liveable and studious-looking.'

'*May* 25.—Breakfasted with Rogers. It was a beautiful morning, and his house, view, and garden looked lovely. It was extremely pleasant. Mahon tried to defend Clarendon, but was put down by Hallam and Macaulay. Macaulay was very severe on Cranmer. Then we all quoted a good deal; Macaulay, (as I had heard him before,) four very fine lines from the Tristia, as being so contrary to their usual whining tone, and of even a Miltonic loftiness of sentiment.

> En ego, quum patriâ caream, vobisque, domoque;
> Raptaque sint, adimi quæ potuere, mihi;
> Ingenio tamen ipse meo comitorque, fruorque.
> Cæsar in hoc potuit juris habere nihil.

I think we must have rather shot beyond Rogers sometimes.'

'*October* 11.—(Dinner at Lord Carlisle's.) The evening went off very cosily and pleasantly, as must almost always happen with Macaulay. He was rather paradoxical, as is apt to be his manner, and almost his only social fault. The greatest marvel about him is the quantity of trash he remembers. He went off at score with Lord Thurlow's poetry.'

'*March* 5, 1850.—Dined at the Club. Dr. Holland in the chair. Lord Lansdowne, Bishop of London, Lord Mahon, Macaulay, Milman, Van de Weyer, I, David Dundas, Lord Harry Vane, Stafford O'Brien. The Bishop talked of the wit of Rowland Hill. One day his chapel, with a thinner attendance than usual, suddenly filled during a shower of rain. He said: "I have often heard of religion being used as a cloak, but never before as an umbrella." In his later life he used to come to his chapel in a carriage. He got an anonymous letter rebuking him for this because it was not the way his heavenly Master travelled. He read the letter from the pulpit, said it was quite true, and that if the writer would come to the vestry afterwards with a saddle and bridle he would ride him home. They talked a good deal of French authors. The Tartuffe was thought Molière's best play; then the Misanthrope. Macaulay prefers

L'Avare. We recited Johnson's beautiful epitaphs on Philips and Levett. Macaulay's flow never ceased once during the four hours, but it is never overbearing.'

'*March* 23.—Breakfast with Macaulay. On being challenged, he repeated the names of the owners of the several carriages that went to Clarissa's funeral. We chiefly talked of Junius, and the irresistible proofs for Sir Philip Francis.'[1]

'*May* 9.—Breakfast with Macaulay. We talked of Thiers and Lamartine as historians; Thiers not having any moral principle; Lamartine a great artist, but without the least care for truth. They were just passing to the Jesuits and Pascal when I thought it right (and I must claim some merit in this) to go to the Ascension morning service at St. James's. After I went, the conversation got upon moral obligations, and was so eagerly carried on by Hallam, Whewell, and Macaulay, though without the slightest loss of temper, that not one sentence could any of them finish.'

'*November* 11.—Breakfasted with Macaulay, Charles Greville, Hobhouse, Sir R. Murchison, and Charles (Howard). The talk was even more than usually agreeable and interesting, and it got on very high themes. Macaulay argued very forcibly against Hobhouse and Charles Greville for the difference between the evidence of Christ's miracles and of the truth of transubstantiation. To put them on a level, Lazarus ought to have remained inanimate, colourless, and decomposing in the grave, while we should be called upon to believe that he had at the word of Christ become alive. He does not consider the doctrine of the Trinity opposed to reason. He was rather less opposed to the No Popery cry, so rife at present, than I might have expected. He thinks the nonsense of people may be advantageously made use of to set them against the real mischief of Popish interference.'[2]

[1] Two days previously Macaulay and Carlyle had met at Lord Ashburton's house. It was perhaps on this occasion that Carlyle was wofully bored by the irresistible proofs for Sir Philip Francis. 'As if it could matter the value of a brass farthing to any living human being who was the author of Junius!'

[2] Four days after this breakfast Macaulay wrote to his sister Fanny: 'If I told you all that I think about these disputes I should write a volume. The Pope hates the English nation and government. He meant, I am convinced, to insult and annoy the Queen and her Ministers. His whole conduct in

'*May* 13.—Dined at the Club. Bishop of Oxford, Dean of St. Paul's, Whewell, Macaulay, Lord Overstone, Dr. Holland, Sir G. Staunton, George Lewis. A good company, and it was most agreeable. They were very droll about Sir John Sinclair;—his writing to Pitt that it was very desirable that the President of the Scotch Agricultural Society' (which office he then held) 'should be a Peer. Pitt answered that he quite agreed with him; accepted his resignation, and appointed Lord Somerville. The Bishop said he remembered his complaining of it at his father's, at Kensington Gore;—it had been "such a wilful misunderstanding." Macaulay said that there are in his works two distinctions, the one the most complete, the other the most incomplete, that he remembers. The first is: "There are two kinds of sleep: one with the your nightcap, and the other without it." The second: "There are three kinds of bread: white bread, brown bread, and rolls." At the end

Ireland has evidently been directed to that end. Nevertheless the reasons popularly urged against this Bull seem to me absurd. We always knew that the Pope claimed spiritual jurisdiction, and I do not see that he now claims temporal jurisdiction. I could wish that Lord John had written more guardedly; and that, I plainly see, is the wish of some of his colleagues, and probably by this time is also his own. He has got much applause in England: but, when he was writing, he should have remembered that he had to govern several millions of Roman Catholics in Ireland; that to govern them at all is no easy task; and that anything which looks like an affront to their religion is certain to call forth very dangerous passions. In the meantime these things keep London all alive. Yesterday the ballad-singers were entertaining a great crowd under my windows with bawling:

> Now all the old women are crying for fear,
> "The Pope is a-coming: oh dear! oh dear!"

The wall of Burlington Gardens is covered with "No Popery," "No Wafer Gods." I cannot help enjoying the rage and terror of the Puseyites, who are utterly prostrated by this outbreak of popular feeling.'

And again, some days later, he says: 'A deputation of my parish, St. James's, came to me yesterday to ask me to move a Resolution at a public meeting. I refused, took their Resolutions in my hand, and criticised them in such a way as, for the time at least, converted the delegates. They told me, at parting, that the whole should be recast; that intolerant sentiments should be expunged; and that, instead of calling for laws to punish avowed Roman Catholics, the parish would express its dislike of the concealed Roman Catholics who hold benefices in the Established Church.'

the Bishop and I fought a mesmeric and electro-biological battle against the scornful opposition of all the rest.' [1]

'*May* 15.—Breakfasted with the Bishop of Oxford, It was remarkably pleasant; a little on derivations.[2] As an instance of unlucky quotation I gave Lord Fitzwilliam's, when calling on the Dissenters to join the Established Clergy in subscribing for the rebuilding of York Minster,

Flectere si nequeo superos Acheronta movebo.

Van de Weyer remarked on the English horror of false quantities, which Macaulay defended justly on the plea that no one is bound to quote. No one resents the Duke of Wellington, in the theatre at Oxford, having called it Carōlus, after being corrected for saying Jacŏbus. It was the Duke's advice to Sir George Murray, when he said he never should be able to get on with speaking in the Commons, "Say what you have to say, don't quote Latin, and sit down."'

'*May* 27.—Dined at the Club. The talk ran for some time on whether the north or south of different countries had contributed most to their literature. I remained on with Macaulay and Milman. The first gave a list of six poets, whom he places above all others, in the order of his preference: Shakespeare, Homer, Dante, Æschylus, Milton, Sophocles. Milman, on the whole, acquiesced. I fought some battle for Virgil coming before Sophocles: but "What," said Macaulay, "did Virgil ever write like the Philoctetes?" He would place Lucretius and Ariosto before him. He thinks the first part of Henry the Fourth Shakespeare's best comic play; then the second part; then Twelfth Night: but Shakespeare's plays are not to be classed into Tragedy and Comedy. It was the object of the Elizabethan drama, the highest form of composition he can conceive, to represent life as it is.'

'*February* 14, 1852.—Dined at Mrs. Drummond's. Trevelyans, Strutts, Fords, Merivales, Macaulay. It was very pleasant. Macaulay and Mrs. Strutt both own to the

[1] Macaulay's account of the evening is: 'Pleasant party at the Club: but we got a little too disputatious at last about Mesmerism and Clairvoyance. It is difficult to discuss such matters without using language which seems to reflect on the understanding of those who believe what you think absurd. However, we kept within tolerable bounds.'

[2] Lord Carlisle elsewhere says: 'The conversation rather etymological, as perhaps it is too apt to be in this society.'

feeling Doctor Johnson had, of thinking oneself bound sometimes to touch a particular rail or post, and to tread always in the middle of the paving-stone. I certainly have had this very strongly. Macaulay wished that he could spend a day of every century in London since the Romans; though of the two he would rather spend a day in it 1800 years hence, than 1800 years ago, as he can less easily conceive it. We agreed there can never have been thirty years in which all mechanical improvements have made so much progress as in the last thirty, but he looks on printing as a greater discovery than steam, but not near so rapid in its obvious results. He told us of two letters he had received from America;—one from a Mr. Crump, offering him 500 dollars if he could introduce the name of Crump into his History; another from a Young Men's Philosophical Society in New York, beginning, "Possibly our fame has not pinioned the Atlantic." '

'*May* 4.—Dined with the Club. Very pleasant, though select. Something led to my reminding Lord Aberdeen that we both put Macbeth the first of Shakespeare's great plays. Lord Lansdowne quite concurred. Macaulay thinks it may be a little owing to our recollections of Mrs. Siddons. He is much inclined to rank them thus: Othello, Lear, Macbeth, Hamlet.' [1]

'*November* 29.—Breakfasted with Macaulay. He thinks that, though the last eight books of Paradise Lost contain incomparable beauties, Milton's fame would have stood higher if only the first four had been preserved. He would then have been placed above Homer.'

There is nothing very attractive in a memorandum which barely chronicles the fact that on a certain day,

[1] In the course of the next month there was a breakfast at the Bishop of Oxford's. 'Extremely agreeable,' writes Lord Carlisle, 'and would have been still more so, but there was a tendency to talk very loud, and all at once.' On this occasion Macaulay told a story about one of the French prophets of the seventeenth century, who came into the Court of King's Bench, and announced that the Holy Ghost had sent him to command Lord Holt to enter a nolle prosequi. 'If,' said Lord Holt, 'the Holy Ghost had wanted a nolle prosequi he would have bade you apply to the Attorney-General. The Holy Ghost knows that I cannot enter a nolle prosequi. But there is one thing which I can do. I can lay a lying knave by the heels;' and thereupon he committed him to prison.

five-and-twenty years ago, Hallam, and Milman, and Macaulay undertook to classify in order of excellence the Greek Tragedians or the Elizabethan Dramatists. But it must be remembered that every one of these entries represents an hour of glowing declamation and sparkling repartee, interspersed with choice passages from the writer whose merits were in question, recited as poetry is recited by men who learn without effort and admire without affectation. 'When I praise an author,' Macaulay used to say, 'I love to give a sample of his wares.' That sample was sometimes only too favourable. He had so quick an eye for literary effect,—so grateful was he to any book which had pleased him even for a moment,—that he would pick out from such a book, and retain for ever in his memory, what was perhaps the single telling anecdote or well-turned couplet which could be discovered in its pages. A pointed story, extracted from some trumpery memoir of the eighteenth century, and then re-told in his own words,—a purple patch from some third-rate sermon or political treatise, woven into the glittering fabric of his talk with that art which in his case was a second nature,—have often and often tempted his younger hearers into toiling through volume after volume of prosy or flippant trash in which a good paragraph was as rare as a silver spoon in a dust-heap.[1]

Whatever fault might be found with Macaulay's gestures as an orator, his appearance and bearing in conversation were singularly effective. Sitting bolt upright, his hands resting on the arms of his chair or folded over the handle of his walking-stick;—knitting

[1] 'My father,' says Sara Coleridge, 'had a way of seizing upon the one bright thing out of long tracts of dull and tedious matter. I remember a great campanula which grew in a wood at Keswick. Two or three such I found in my native vale during the course of my flower-seeking days. As well might we present one of these as a sample of the blue-bells of bonny Cumberland, or the one or two oxlips which may be found among a multitude of cowslips in a Somersetshire meadow, as specimens of the flowerhood of the field,—as give these extracts for proof of what the writer was generally wont to produce.'

his great eyebrows if the subject was one which had to be thought out as he went along, or brightening from the forehead downwards when a burst of humour was coming; his massive features and honest glance suited well with the manly sagacious sentiments which he set forth in his pleasant sonorous voice, and in his racy and admirably intelligible language. To get at his meaning people had never the need to think twice, and they certainly had seldom the time. And with all his ardour, and all his strength and energy of conviction, he was so truly considerate towards others,—so delicately courteous with the courtesy which is of the essence, and not only in the manner! However eager had been the debate, and however prolonged the sitting, no one in the company ever had personal reasons for wishing a word of his unsaid, or a look or a tone recalled. His good things were never long in the making. During the Caffre war, at a time when we were getting rather the worst of it, he opened the street door for a walk down Westbourne Terrace. 'The blacks are flying,' said his companion. 'I wish they were in South Africa,' was the instant reply. His quotations, both in verse and prose, were at all times ready, and never off the mark. Sometimes he would re-cast his thoughts, and give them over again in the shape of an epigram. 'You call me a Liberal,' he said; 'but I don't know that in these days I deserve the name. I am opposed to the abolition of standing armies. I am opposed to the abrogation of capital punishment. I am opposed to the destruction of the National Church. In short, I am in favour of war, hanging, and Church Establishments.'

He was always willing to accept a friendly challenge to a feat of memory. One day, in the Board-room of the British Museum, Sir David Dundas saw him hand to Lord Aberdeen a sheet of foolscap, covered with writing arranged in three parallel columns down each of the four pages. This document, of which the ink was still wet, proved to be a full list of the Senior Wranglers at Cambridge, with their dates and colleges, for the hundred years during which the names of Senior Wranglers had been recorded in the University Calendar. On another occasion Sir David asked: 'Macaulay, do you know your Popes?' 'No,' was the answer; 'I always get wrong among the Innocents.' 'But can you say your Archbishops of Canterbury?' 'Any fool,' said Macaulay, 'could say his Archbishops of Canterbury backwards;' and thereupon he went off at score, drawing breath only once in order to remark about the oddity of there having been both an Archbishop Sancroft and an Archbishop Bancroft, until Sir David stopped him at Cranmer.[1]

Macaulay could seldom be tempted to step outside his own immediate circle of friends and relations. His distaste for the chance society of a London drawing-room increased as years went on. Like Casaubon of old, he was well aware that a man cannot live with the idlers, and with the Muses too. 'He was peculiarly susceptible,' says Lady Trevelyan, 'of the feeling of ennui when in company. He really hated staying out even in the best and most agreeable houses. It was with an effort that he even dined out, and few of those who met him, and enjoyed his animated conversation, could guess how much rather he would have remained at home, and how much difficulty I had to force him to accept invitations and prevent his growing a recluse. But, though he was very easily bored in general society, I think he never felt ennui when he was alone, or when he was with those he loved. Many people are very fond of children, but he was the only person I ever knew who never tired of being with them. Often has he come to our house, at Clapham or in Westbourne Terrace, directly after breakfast, and, finding me out, has dawdled away the whole morning with the children; and then, after sitting with me at lunch, has taken Margaret a long walk through the City which

[1] Macaulay was proud of his good memory, and had little sympathy with people who affected to have a bad one. In a note on the margin of one of his books he reflects upon this not uncommon form of self-depreciation: 'They appear to reason thus: The more memory, the less invention.'

lasted the whole afternoon. Such days are always noted in his journals as especially happy.'

It is impossible to exaggerate the pleasure which Macaulay took in children, or the delight which he gave them. He was beyond all comparison the best of playfellows; unrivalled in the invention of games, and never wearied of repeating them. He had an inexhaustible repertory of small dramas for the benefit of his nieces, in which he sustained an endless variety of parts with a skill that at any rate was sufficient for his audience. An old friend of the family writes to my sister, Lady Holland: 'I well remember that there was one never-failing game of building up a den with newspapers behind the sofa, and of enacting robbers and tigers; you shrieking with terror, but always fascinated and begging him to begin again: and there was a daily recurring observation from him that, after all, children were the only true poets.'

Whenever he was at a distance from his little companions he consoled himself and them by the exchange of long and frequent letters. The earliest in date of those which he wrote in prose begins as follows:

September 15, 1842.

My dear Baba,[1]—

Thank you for your very pretty letter. I am always glad to make my little girl happy, and nothing pleases me so much as to see that she likes books. For when she is as old as I am she will find that they are better than all the tarts, and cakes, and toys, and plays, and sights in the world. If anybody would make me the greatest king that ever lived, with palaces, and gardens, and fine dinners, and wine, and coaches, and beautiful clothes, and hundreds of servants, on condition that I would not read books, I would not be a king. I would rather be a poor man in a garret with plenty of books than a king who did not love reading.

Five years later on he writes: 'I must begin sooner or

[1] Baba was a pet name for his niece Margaret, derived from the Indian nursery.

later to call you "Margaret;" and I am always making good resolutions to do so, and then breaking them. But I will procrastinate no longer.

> Procrastination is the thief of time,

says Dr. Young. He also says,

> Be wise to-day. 'Tis madness to defer,

and,

> Next day the fatal precedent will plead.

That is to say, if I do not take care, I shall go on calling my darling "Baba" till she is as old as her mamma, and has a dozen Babas of her own. Therefore I will be wise to-day, and call her "Margaret." I should very much like to see you and Aunt Fanny at Broadstairs: but I fear, I fear, that it cannot be. Your Aunt asks me to shirk the Chelsea Board. I am staying in England chiefly in order to attend it. When Parliament is not sitting, my duty there is all that I do for two thousand four hundred pounds a year. We must have some conscience.

'Michaelmas will, I hope, find us all at Clapham over a noble goose. Do you remember the beautiful Puseyite hymn on Michaelmas day? It is a great favourite with all the Tractarians. You and Alice should learn it. It begins:

> Though Quakers scowl, though Baptists howl,
> Though Plymouth Brethren rage,
> We Churchmen gay will wallow to-day
> In apple sauce, onions, and sage.
>
> Ply knife and fork, and draw the cork,
> And have the bottle handy:
> For each slice of goose will introduce
> A thimbleful of brandy.

Is it not good? I wonder who the author can be. Not Newman, I think. It is above him. Perhaps it is Bishop Wilberforce.'

The following letter is in a graver tone, as befits the correspondent of a young lady who has only two years of the schoolroom still before her.

October 14, 1851.

Dear Margaret,—

Tell me how you like Schiller's Mary Stuart. It is not one of my favourite pieces. I should put it fourth among his plays. I arrange them thus: Wallenstein, William Tell, Don Carlos, Mary Stuart, the Maid of Orleans. At a great interval comes the Bride of Messina; and then, at another great interval, Fieschi. 'Cabal and Love' I never could get through. 'The Robbers' is a mere schoolboy rant below serious criticism, but not without indications of mental vigour which required to be disciplined by much thought and study. But, though I do not put Mary Stuart very high among Schiller's works, I think the Fotheringay scenes in the fifth act equal to anything that he ever wrote,—indeed equal to anything dramatic that has been produced in Europe since Shakspeare. I hope that you will feel the wonderful truth and beauty of that part of the play.

I cannot agree with you in admiring Sintram. There is an age at which we are disposed to think that whatever is odd and extravagant is great. At that age we are liable to be taken in by such orators as Irving, such painters as Fuseli, such plays as the Robbers, such romances as Sintram. A better time comes, when we would give all Fuseli's hobgoblins for one of Reynolds's little children, and all Sintram's dialogues with Death and the Devil for one speech of Mrs. Norris or Miss Bates. Tell me however, as of course you will, quite truly what you think of Sintram.

I saw a description of myself yesterday in a New York paper. The writer says that I am a stout man with hazel eyes; that I always walk with an umbrella; that I sometimes bang the umbrella against the ground; that I often dine in the Coffee-room of the Trafalgar on fish; that once he saw me break a decanter there, but that I did not appear to be at all ashamed of my awkwardness, but called for my bill as coolly as if nothing had happened. I have no recollection of such an occurrence; but, if it did take place, I do not think that it would have deprived me of my self-possession. This is fame. This is the advantage of making a figure in the world.

This has been the last week of the Great Exhibition. It makes me quite sad to think of our many, many happy walks there. To-morrow I shall go to the final ceremony, and try to hear the Bishop of London's thanksgiving, in which I shall very cordially join. This will long be remembered as a singularly happy year, of peace, plenty, good feeling, innocent pleasure, national glory of the best and purest sort.

I have bespoken a Schiller for you. It is in the binder's hands, and will be ready, I hope, before your return.

Ever yours
T. B. MACAULAY.

His poetical, no less than his epistolary, style was carefully adapted to the age and understanding of those whom he was addressing. Some of his pieces of verse are almost perfect specimens of the nursery lyric. From five to ten stanzas in length, and with each word carefully formed in capitals,—most comforting to the eyes of a student who is not very sure of his small letters,—they are real children's poems, and they profess to be nothing more. They contain none of those strokes of satire, and allusions to the topics and personages of the day, by which the authors of what is now called Juvenile Literature so often attempt to prove that they are fit for something better than the task on which they are engaged. But this very absence of pretension, which is the special merit of these trifles, renders them unworthy of a place in a book intended for grown-up readers. There are, however, few little people between three and five years old who would not care to hear how

There once was a nice little girl,
With a nice little rosy face.
She always said 'Our Father,'
And she always said her grace:

and how as the reward of her good behaviour

> They brought the browned potatoes,
> And minced veal, nice and hot,
> And such a good bread-pudding
> All smoking from the pot!

And there are still fewer who would be indifferent to the fate which befell the two boys who talked in church, when

> The Beadle got a good big stick,
> Thicker than uncle's thumb.
> Oh, what a fright those boys were in
> To see the Beadle come!
>
> And they were turned out of the church
> And they were soundly beat:
> And both those wicked, naughty boys
> Went bawling down the street.

All his rhymes, whether written or improvised, he put down to the credit of the Judicious Poet. The gravity with which he maintained the innocent delusion was too much for children, who more than half believed in the existence of a writer for whose collected works they searched the library in vain; though their faith was from time to time shaken by the almost miraculous applicability of a quotation to the most unexpected circumstances of the moment. St. Valentine's Day brought Macaulay's nieces a yearly offering of rhyme, until he thought them too old to care for verses which he himself pronounced to be on a level with the bellman's, but which are certainly as good, and probably as sincere, as nine-tenths of the pastoral poetry that has been written during the last two centuries. In 1847 the annual effusion ran as follow:—

> And canst thou spurn a kneeling bard,
> Mine own, mine only Valentine?
> The heart of beauty still is hard;
> But ne'er was heart so hard as thine.
> Each year a shepherd sings thy praise,
> And sings it in no vulgar strain.
> Each year a shepherd ends his days,
> A victim to thy cold disdain.

In forty-five, relentless maid,
  For thee melodious Strephon died.
For thee was gentle Thyrsis laid,
  In forty-six, by Strephon's side.
The swain who to thy footstool bears
  Next spring the tribute of his verses
Will tell thee that poor Damon shares
  The grave of Strephon and of Thyrsis.

Then will the whole Arcadian quire
  Their sweetest songster's fate bemoan,
Hang o'er his tomb his crook and lyre,
  And carve this ditty on the stone:
'Stop, passenger. Here Damon lies,
  Beloved of all the tuneful nine;
The third who perished by the eyes
  Of one too charming Valentine.'

THE BROKEN-HEARTED DAMON.

The longest and the most elaborate of these little compositions was addressed to the daughter of Earl Stanhope, now the Countess Beauchamp. The allusion to the statue of Mr. Pitt in Hanover Square is one of the happiest touches that can be found in Macaulay's writings.

* * * *

Good morrow, gentle Child, and then
Again good morrow, and again;
Good morrow following still good morrow,
Without one cloud of strife or sorrow.
And when the god to whom we pay
In jest our homages to-day
Shall come to claim, no more in jest,
His rightful empire o'er thy breast,
Benignant may his aspect be,
His yoke the truest liberty:
And if a tear his power confess,
Be it a tear of happiness!
It shall be so. The Muse displays
The future to her votary's gaze.
Prophetic rage my bosom swells.
I taste the cake! I hear the bells!
From Conduit Street the close array
Of chariots barricades the way

To where I see, with outstretched hand,
Majestic, thy great kinsman stand,
And half unbend his brow of pride,
As welcoming so fair a bride.

* * * *

The feelings with which Macaulay regarded children were near akin to those of the great writer to whom we owe the death of little Paul, and the meeting between the schoolboy and his mother in the eighth chapter of David Copperfield. 'Have you seen the first number of Dombey?' he writes. 'There is not much in it; but there is one passage which made me cry as if my heart would break. It is the description of a little girl who has lost an affectionate mother, and is unkindly treated by everybody. Images of that sort always overpower me, even when the artist is less skilful than Dickens.' In truth, Macaulay's extreme sensibility to all which appealed to the sentiment of pity, whether in art or in nature, was nothing short of a positive inconvenience to him.[1] He was so moved by the visible representation of distressing scenes that he went most unwillingly to the theatre, for which during his Cambridge days he had entertained a passionate, though passing, fondness.[2] I remember well how, during the performance of Masks and Faces, the sorrows of the broken-down author and his starving family in their Grub Street garret entirely destroyed the pleasure which he otherwise would have taken in Mrs. Stirling's admirable acting. And he was hardly less easily affected to tears by that which was sublime and stirring in literature, than by that which was melancholy and pathetic. In August 1851, he writes from Malvern to his niece Mar-

[1] '*April* 17, 1858.—In the Times of this morning there was an account of a suicide of a poor girl which quite broke my heart. I cannot get it out of my thoughts, or help crying when I think of it.'

[2] I recollect hearing Macaulay describe the wonder and delight with which, during a long vacation spent at the University, he saw his first play acted by a strolling company in the Barnwell Theatre. 'Did you, then, never go to the play as a boy?' asked some one who was present. 'No,' said he; 'after the straitest sect of our religion I was bred a Pharisee.'

garet: 'I finished the Iliad to-day. I had not read it through since the end of 1837, when I was at Calcutta, and when you often called me away from my studies to show you pictures and to feed the crows. I never admired the old fellow so much, or was so strongly moved by him. What a privilege genius like his enjoys! I could not tear myself away. I read the last five books at a stretch during my walk to-day, and was at last forced to turn into a by-path lest the parties of walkers should see me blubbering for imaginary beings, the creations of a ballad-maker who has been dead two thousand seven hundred years. What is the power and glory of Cæsar and Alexander to that? Think what it would be to be assured that the inhabitants of Monomotapa would weep over one's writings Anno Domini 4551!'

Macaulay was so devoid of egotism, and exacted so little deference and attention from those with whom he lived, that the young people around him were under an illusion which to this day it is pleasant to recall. It was long, very long, before we guessed that the world thought much of one who appeared to think so little of himself. I remember telling my schoolfellows that I had an uncle who was about to publish a History of England in two volumes, each containing 650 pages; but it never crossed my mind that the work in question would have anything to distinguish it except its length. As years went on, it seemed strange and unnatural to hear him more and more frequently talked of as a great man; and we slowly, and almost reluctantly, awoke to the conviction that 'Uncle Tom' was cleverer, as well as more good-natured, than his neighbours.

Among other tastes which he had in common with children was an avidity for sight-seeing. 'What say you,' he asks Mr. Ellis, 'to a visit to the Chinese Museum? It is the most interesting and curious sight that I know. If you like the plan, I will call on you at four. Or will you call on me? For I am halfway between the Temple and the wonders of the Celestial

Empire.' And again: 'We treated the Clifton Zoo much too contemptuously. I lounged thither, and found more than sixpennyworth of amusement.' 'After breakfast I went to the Tower,' he writes in his journal of 1839. 'I found great changes. The wild beasts were all gone. The Zoological Gardens have driven paved courts and dark narrow cages quite out of fashion. I was glad for the sake of the tigers and leopards.'

He was never so happy as when he could spend an afternoon in taking his nieces and nephews a round of London sights, until, to use his favourite expression, they 'could not drag one leg after the other.' If he had been able to have his own way, the treat would have recurred at least twice a week. On these occasions we drove into London in time for a sumptuous midday meal, at which everything that we liked best was accompanied by oysters, caviare, and olives, some of which delicacies he invariably provided with the sole object of seeing us reject them with contemptuous disgust. Then off we set under his escort, in summer to the bears and lions; in winter to the Panorama of Waterloo, to the Colosseum in Regent's Park, or to the enjoyment of the delicious terror inspired by Madame Tussaud's Chamber of Horrors. When the more attractive exhibitions had been exhausted by too frequent visits, he would enliven with his irrepressible fun the dreary propriety of the Polytechnic, or would lead us through the lofty corridors of the British Museum, making the statues live and the busts speak by the spirit and colour of his innumerable anecdotes paraphrased offhand from the pages of Plutarch and Suetonius. One of these expeditions is described in a letter to my mother in January 1845. 'Fanny brought George and Margaret, with Charley Cropper, to the Albany at one yesterday. I gave them some dinner; fowl, ham, marrow-bones, tart, ice, olives, and champagne. I found it difficult to think of any sight for the children: however, I took them to the National Gallery, and was excessively amused with the airs of connoisseurship which Charley and Margaret gave themselves, and with Georgy's honestly avowed weariness. "Let us go. There is nothing here that I care for at all." When I put him into the carriage, he said, half sulkily: "I do not call this seeing sights. I have seen no sight to-day." Many a man who has laid out thirty thousand pounds on paintings would, if he spoke the truth, own that he cared as little for the art as poor Georgy.'

Regularly every Easter, when the closing of the public offices drove my father from the Treasury for a brief holiday, Macaulay took our family on a tour among Cathedral-towns, varied by an occasional visit to the Universities. We started on the Thursday; spent Good Friday in one city and Easter Sunday in another, and went back to town on the Monday. This year it was Worcester and Gloucester; the next, York and Lincoln; then Lichfield and Chester, Norwich and Peterborough, Ely and Cambridge, Salisbury and Winchester. Now and then the routine was interrupted by a trip to Paris, or to the great churches on the Loire; but in the course of twenty years we had inspected at least once all the Cathedrals of England, or indeed of England and Wales, for we carried our researches after ecclesiastical architecture as far down in the list as Bangor. 'Our party just filled a railway carriage,' says Lady Trevelyan, 'and the journey found his flow of spirits unfailing. It was a return to old times; a running fire of jokes, rhymes, puns, never ceasing. It was a peculiarity of his that he never got tired on a journey. As the day wore on he did not feel the desire to lie back and be quiet, and he liked to find his companions ready to be entertained to the last.'

Any one who reads the account of Norwich and Bristol in the third chapter, or the account of Magdalen College in the eighth chapter, of the History, may form an idea of Macaulay's merits as a Cicerone in an old English provincial capital. To walk with him round the walls of York, or through the Rows of Chester; to look up at the towers of Lichfield from the spot where Lord Brook received his death-wound, or down upon Durham from the brow of the hill behind

Neville's Cross; to hear him discourse on Monmouth and Bishop Ken beneath the roof of Longleat Hall, or give the rein to all the fancies and reminiscences, political, personal, and historical, which were conjured up by a drive past Old Sarum to Stonehenge, were privileges which a child could appreciate, but which the most learned of scholars might have envied.

When we returned to our inn in the evening, it was only an exchange of pleasures. Sometimes he would translate to us choice morsels from Greek, Latin, Italian, or Spanish writers, with a vigour of language and vivacity of manner which communicated to his impromptu version not a little of the air and the charm of the original. Sometimes he would read from the works of Sterne, or Smollett, or Fielding those scenes to which ladies might listen, but which they could not well venture to pick out for themselves. And when we had heard enough of the siege of Carthagena in 'Roderick Random,' or of Lieutenant Le Fever's death in 'Tristram Shandy,' we would fall to capping verses, or stringing rhymes, or amusing ourselves with some game devised for the occasion which often made a considerable demand upon the memory or invention of the players. Of these games only a single trace remains. One of his nieces, unable to forecast the future of her sex, had expressed a regret that she could never hope to go in for a college examination. Macaulay thereupon produced what he was pleased to call a paper of questions in Divinity, the contents of which afford a curious proof how constantly the lighter aspects of English sectarianism were present to his thoughts. The first three questions ran as follows:

1. And this is law, I will maintain
   Until my dying day, Sir,
That whatsoever king shall reign,
   I'll be the Vicar of Bray, Sir.

Then read Paul's epistles,
   You rotten Arminian.
You won't find a passage
   To support your opinion.

When the lads of the village so merrily, ah!
Sound their tabors, I'll hand thee along.
And verily, verily, verily, ah!
Thou and I will be first in the throng.

To what sects did the three persons belong who express their sentiments in the three passages cited above? Is there anything in the third passage at variance with the usages of the sect to which it relates? Which of those three sects do you prefer? Which of the three bears the closest resemblance to Popery? Where is Bray? Through what reigns did the political life of the Vicar of Bray extend?

2. Define 'Jumper,' 'Shaker,' 'Ranter,' 'Dunker.'

3. Translate the following passage into the Quakeric dialect: 'You and Sir Edward Ryan breakfasted with me on Friday the eleventh of December.'

Like all other men who play with a will, and who work to a purpose, Macaulay was very well aware of the distinction between work and play. He did not carry on the business of his life by desultory efforts, or in the happy moments of an elegant inspiration. Men have disputed, and will long continue to dispute, whether or not his fame was deserved; but no one who himself has written books will doubt that at any rate it was hardly earned. 'Take at hazard,' says Thackeray, 'any three pages of the Essays or History: and, glimmering below the stream of the narrative, you, an average reader, see one, two, three, a half-score of allusions to other historic facts, characters, literature, poetry, with which you are acquainted. Your neighbour, who has *his* reading and *his* little stock of literature stowed away in his mind, shall detect more points, allusions, happy touches, indicating, not only the prodigious memory and vast learning of this master, but the wonderful industry, the honest, humble previous toil of this great scholar. He reads twenty books to write a sentence; he travels a hundred miles to make a line of description.'

That this praise, though high, was not excessive, is amply proved by that portion of Macaulay's papers which extends over the period when his History was in course of preparation. Justice demands that, even at the risk of being tedious, a specimen should be given of the scrupulous care and the unflagging energy with which he conducted his investigations.

Dear Ellis, July 17, 1848.

Many thanks for your kindness. Pray let Dr. Hook know, whenever you have an opportunity, how much I am obliged to him.[1] The information which he has procured for me, I am sorry to say, is not such as I can use. But you need not tell him so. I feel convinced that he has made some mistake: for he sends me only a part of the Leeds burials in 1685; and yet the number is double that of the Manchester burials in the same year. If the ordinary rules of calculation are applied to these data, it will be found that Leeds must in 1685 have contained 16,000 souls or thereabouts. Now at the beginning of the American war Leeds contained only 16,000 souls, as appears from Dr. Hook's own letter. Nobody can suppose that there had been no increase between 1685 and 1775. Besides, neither York nor Exeter contained 16,000 inhabitants in 1685, and nobody who knows the state of things at that time can believe that Leeds was then a greater town than York or Exeter. Either some error has been committed, or else there was an extraordinary mortality at Leeds in 1685. In either case the numbers are useless for my purpose.

Ever yours
T. B. M.

Dear Ellis,— July 27, 1848.

Many thanks. Wardell[2] is the man. He gives a much better thing than a list of burials; a list of the houses returned by the hearthmoney collectors. It appears that Leeds contained, in 1663, just 1,400 houses. And observe; all the townships are included. The average number of people to a house in a country town was, according to the best statistical writers of the seventeenth century, 4·3. If that estimate be just, Leeds must, in 1663, have contained about 6,000 souls. As it increased in trade and wealth during the reign of Charles II, we may well suppose that in 1685 the population was near 8,000; that is to say, about

[1] Mr. Ellis was Recorder of Leeds, and Dr. Hook its vicar.

[2] The author of the Municipal History of the Borough of Leeds.

as much as the population of Manchester. I had expected this result from observing that by the writers of that time Manchester and Leeds are always mentioned as of about the same size. But this evidence proves to demonstration either that there was some mistake about the number of burials, or that the year 1685 was a singularly unhealthy year from which no inference can be drawn. One person must have died in every third house within twelve months; a rate of mortality quite frightful.

Ever yours

T. B. MACAULAY.

It must be remembered that these letters represent only a part of the trouble which Macaulay underwent in order to ensure the correctness of five and a half lines of print. He had a right to the feeling of self-satisfaction which, a month later on, allowed him to say: 'I am working intensely, and, I hope, not unsuccessfully. My third chapter, which is the most difficult part of my task, is done, and, I think, not ill done.' Any one who will turn to the description of the town of Leeds, and will read the six paragraphs that precede it, and the three that follow it, may form a conception of the pains which those clear and flowing periods must have cost an author who expended on the pointing of a phrase as much conscientious research as would have provided some writers, who speak of Macaulay as showy and shallow, with at least half a dozen pages of ostentatious statistics.

On the 8th of February 1849, after the publication of his first two volumes, he writes in his journal: 'I have now made up my mind to change my plan about my History. I will first set myself to know the whole subject:—to get, by reading and travelling, a full acquaintance with William's reign. I reckon that it will take me eighteen months to do this. I must visit Holland, Belgium, Scotland, Ireland, France. The Dutch archives and French archives must be ransacked. I will see whether anything is to be got from other diplomatic collections. I must see Londonderry, the Boyne, Aghrim, Limerick, Kinsale, Namur again,

Landen, Steinkirk. I must turn over hundreds, thousands, of pamphlets. Lambeth, the Bodleian and the other Oxford Libraries,[1] the Devonshire Papers, the British Museum, must be explored, and notes made: and then I shall go to work. When the materials are ready, and the History mapped out in my mind, I ought easily to write on an average two of my pages daily. In two years from the time I begin writing I shall have more than finished my second part. Then I reckon a year for polishing, retouching, and printing. This brings me to the autumn of 1853. I like this scheme much. I began to-day with Avaux's despatches from Ireland, abstracted almost a whole thick volume, and compared his narrative with James's. There is much to be said as to these events.'

This programme was faithfully carried out. He saw Glencoe in rain and in sunshine: 'Yet even with sunshine what a place it is! The very valley of the shadow of death.' He paid a second visit to Killiecrankie for

[1] '*October* 2, 1854.—I called on the Warden of All Souls', who was the only soul in residence. He was most kind; got me the manuscript of Narcissus Luttrell's Diary,—seven thick volumes in cramped writing,—put me into a comfortable room; and then left me to myself. I worked till past five; then walked for an hour or so, and dined at my inn, reading Cooper's "Pathfinder." '

'*October* 3.—I went to All Souls' at ten, and worked till five. Narcissus is dreadfully illegible in 1696; but that matters the less, as by that time the newspapers had come in. I found some curious things. The Jacobites had a way of drinking treasonable healths by limping about the room with glasses at their lips.

To limp meant L. Lewis XIV.
I. James.
M. Mary of Modena.
P. Prince of Wales.

'*October* 4.—I have done with All Souls'. At ten I went to the Bodleian. I got out the Tanner MSS., and worked on them two or three hours. Then the Wharton MSS. Then the far more remarkable Nairne MSS. At three they rang me out. I do think that from ten to three is a very short time to keep so noble a library open.

'*October* 5.—Pamphlets in abundance; but pamphlets I can get elsewhere; so I fell on the Nairne MSS. again. I could amuse myself here ten years without a moment of ennui.'

the special purpose of walking up the old road which skirts the Garry, in order to verify the received accounts of the time spent by the English army in mounting the pass which they were to descend at a quicker rate. The notes made during his fortnight's tour through the scenes of the Irish war are equal in bulk to a first-class article in the Edinburgh or Quarterly Reviews. He gives four closely-written folio pages to the Boyne, and six to Londonderry. It is interesting to compare the shape which each idea took, as it arose in his mind, with the shape in which he eventually gave it to the world. As he drove up the river from Drogheda he notices that 'the country looked like a flourishing part of England. Cornfields, gardens, woods, succeeded each other just as in Kent and Warwickshire.' And again: 'Handsome seats, fields of wheat and clover, noble trees:—it would be called a fine country even in Somersetshire.' In the sixteenth chapter of the History these hasty jottings have been transmuted into the sentences: 'Beneath lay a valley now so rich and so cheerful that an Englishman who gazes on it may imagine himself to be in one of the most highly favoured parts of his own highly favoured country. Fields of wheat, woodlands, meadows bright with daisies and clover, slope gently down to the edge of the Boyne.'

Macaulay passed two days in Londonderry, and made the most of each minute of daylight. He penetrated into every corner where there still lurked a vestige of the past, and called upon every inhabitant who was acquainted with any tradition worth the hearing. He drove through the suburbs; he sketched a ground-plan of the streets; alone or in company, he walked four times round the walls of the city for which he was to do what Thucydides had done for Platæa. A few extracts from the voluminous records of those two days will give some notion of what Macaulay meant by saying that he had seen a town.

'*August* 31, 1849.—I left a card for Captain Leach of

the Ordnance Survey, and then wandered round the walls, and saw the Cathedral. It has been spoiled by architects who tried to imitate the Gothic style without knowing what they were about.[1] The choir, however, is neat and interesting. Leach came,—a sensible, amiable young officer, as far as I could judge. I went again round the walls with him. The circuit is a short one. It may be performed, I should say, in twenty minutes. Then we got into a car, crossed the wooden bridge, and took a view of the city from the opposite bank of the river. Walker's pillar is well placed, and is not contemptible.[2] The honest divine, in his canonicals, haranguing with vehemence, is at the top, and makes a tolerable figure at some distance. Then we crossed again, and drove to Boom Hall, so called from the memorable boom. The mistress of the house, a very civil lady, came out and acted as Cicerone. We walked down to the very spot where the boom was fastened. It was secured by a chain which passed through the earth of the bank, and was attached to a huge stone. Our hospitable guide would insist that an iron ring, fixed in one of the rocks close by, had been part of the apparatus to secure the boom. I felt very sceptical, and my doubts were soon changed into certainties: for I lifted up my eyes, and, about fifty yards off, I saw just such another ring fastened to another rock. I did not tell the good lady what I thought, but, as soon as we had taken our leave, I told Leach that these rings were evidently put there for the same purpose, that of

[1] 'On the highest ground stood the Cathedral, a church which, though erected when the secret of Gothic architecture was lost, and though ill qualified to sustain a comparison with the awful temples of the middle ages, is not without grace and dignity.'—Macaulay's History of England, Chapter XII.

[2] 'A lofty pillar, rising from a bastion which bore during many weeks the heaviest fire of the enemy, is seen far up and far down the Foyle. On the summit is the statue of Walker, such as when, in the last and most terrible emergency, his eloquence roused the fainting courage of his brethren. In one hand he grasps a Bible. The other, pointing down the river, seems to direct the eyes of his famished audience to the English topmasts in the distant bay.'

securing shipping. He quite agreed with me, and seemed to admire my sagacious incredulity a great deal more than it at all deserved.'

'*Saturday, September* 1.—As soon as I had breakfasted, Sir R. Ferguson came, and walked round the walls with me. Then he took me to the reading-room, where I met Captain Leach, and a Mr. Gilmour, a great man here. They walked with me round the walls, which I have thus gone over four times. The bastions are planted as gardens. The old pieces of ordnance lie among the flowers and shrubs: strange antique guns of the time of Elizabeth and Charles the First; Roaring Meg, a present of the Fishmongers with the date 1642; another piece of the same date given by the Vintners; and another by the Merchant Tailors. The citizens are to the last degree jealous of the integrity of these walls.[1] No improvement which would deface them would be proposed without raising a storm: and I do not blame them. Every stone has some fact, or at least some legend, connected with it. I found no difficulty, sometimes, in separating the facts from the legends. The picture of the whole is in my mind, and I do not know that there would be any advantage in putting the plan on paper.'

Put it on paper, however, he did; and indeed, when employed upon his History, he habitually preserved in writing such materials as were gathered elsewhere than

[1] 'The wall is carefully preserved; nor would any plea of health or convenience be held by the inhabitants sufficient to justify the demolition of that sacred enclosure which, in the evil time, gave shelter to their race and their religion. . . . It is impossible not to respect the sentiment which indicates itself by these tokens. It is a sentiment which belongs to the higher and purer part of human nature, and which adds not a little to the strength of States. A people which takes no pride in the noble achievements of remote ancestors will never achieve anything to be remembered with pride by remote descendants. Yet it is impossible for the moralist or the statesman to look with unmixed complacency on the solemnities with which Londonderry commemorates her deliverance, and on the honours which she pays to those who saved her.'

from the shelves of his own library, instead of continuing the facile, though hazardous, course which he had pursued as a Reviewer, and trusting to his memory alone. The fruits of many a long hour passed among the Pepysian bookcases, the manuscripts at Althorp, or the archives of the French War Office, were garnered into a multitude of pocketbooks of every possible shape and colour. Of these a dozen still remain, ready to the hands of any among Macaulay's remote heirs who may be tempted to commit the posthumous treachery of publishing the commonplace book of a great writer.

His industry has had its reward. The extent and exactness of his knowledge have won him the commendation of learned and candid writers who have travelled over ground which he has trod before. Each, in his own particular field, recognises the high quality of Macaulay's work; and there is no testimonial so valuable as the praise of an enlightened specialist. Such praise has been freely given by Mr. Bagehot, the Editor of the Economist, in that very attractive treatise which goes by the name of 'Lombard Street.' He commences one important section of his book with a sentence in which, except for its modesty, I am unwilling to find a fault. 'The origin of the Bank of England has been told by Macaulay, and it is never wise for an ordinary writer to tell again what he has told so much better.' And Mr. Buckle, who was as well acquainted with the social manners of our ancestors as is Mr. Bagehot with their finance, appends the following note to what is perhaps the most interesting chapter in his History of Civilisation: 'Everything Mr. Macaulay has said on the contempt into which the clergy fell in the Reign of Charles the Second is perfectly accurate;[1] and, from evidence which I have collected, I know that this very able writer, of whose

[1] 'I shall soon have done this ecclesiastical part of my narrative. Some people may imagine that I infer too much from slight indications; but no one who has not soaked his mind with the transitory literature of the day is really entitled to judge.'—Macaulay's Journal.

immense research few people are competent judges, has rather under-stated the case than over-stated it. On several subjects I should venture to differ from Mr. Macaulay; but I cannot refrain from expressing my admiration of his unwearied diligence, of the consummate skill with which he has arranged his materials, and of the noble love of liberty which animates his entire work. These are qualities which will long survive the aspersions of his puny detractors,—men who, in point of knowledge and ability, are unworthy to loosen the shoe-latchet of him they foolishly attack.'

The main secret of Macaulay's success lay in this, that to extraordinary fluency and facility he united patient, minute, and persistent diligence. He well knew, as Chaucer knew before him, that

> There is na workeman
> That can bothe worken wel and hastilie.
> This must be done at leisure parfaitlie.

If his method of composition ever comes into fashion, books probably will be better, and undoubtedly will be shorter. As soon as he had got into his head all the information relating to any particular episode in his History, (such, for instance, as Argyll's expedition to Scotland, or the attainder of Sir John Fenwick, or the calling in of the clipped coinage,) he would sit down and write off the whole story at a headlong pace; sketching in the outlines under the genial and audacious impulse of a first conception; and securing in black and white each idea, and epithet, and turn of phrase, as it flowed straight from his busy brain to his rapid fingers. His manuscript, at this stage, to the eyes of any one but himself, appeared to consist of column after column of dashes and flourishes, in which a straight line, with a half-formed letter at each end, and another in the middle, did duty for a word. It was from amidst a chaos of such hieroglyphics that Lady Trevelyan, after her brother's death, deciphered that account of the last days of William which fitly closes the History.[1]

[1] Lord Carlisle relates how Mr. Prescott, as a brother

As soon as Macaulay had finished his rough draft, he began to fill it in at the rate of six sides of foolscap every morning; written in so large a hand, and with such a multitude of erasures,[1] that the whole six pages were, on an average, compressed into two pages of print. This portion he called his 'task,' and he was never quite easy unless he completed it daily. More he seldom sought to accomplish; for he had learned by long experience that this was as much as he could do at his best; and except when at his best, he never would work at all. 'I had no heart to write,' he says in his journal of March 6, 1851. 'I am too self-indulgent in this matter, it may be: and yet I attribute much of the success which I have had to my habit of writing only when I am in the humour, and of stopping as soon as the thoughts and words cease to flow fast. There are therefore few lees in my wine. It is all the cream of the bottle.'[2]

historian, was much interested by the sight of these manuscript sheets, 'in which words are as much abbreviated as "cle" for "castle."'

[1] Mr. Woodrow, in the preface to his collection of the Indian Education minutes, says: 'Scarcely five consecutive lines in any of Macaulay's minutes will be found unmarked by blots or corrections. He himself, in a minute dated November 3, 1835, says, "After blotting a great deal of paper I can recommend nothing but a reference to the Governor-General in Council." My copyist was always able instantly to single out his writing by the multiplicity of corrections and blots which mark the page. These corrections are now exceedingly valuable. When the first master of the English language corrects his own composition, which appeared faultless before, the correction must be based on the highest rules of criticism.'

[2] In small things as well as in great, Macaulay held that what was worth doing at all was worth doing well. He had promised to compose an epitaph for his uncle, Mr. Babington. In June 1851, he writes: 'My delay has not arisen from any want of respect or tenderness for my uncle's memory. I loved and honoured him most sincerely. But the truth is, that I have not been able to satisfy myself. People who are not accustomed to this sort of literary exercise often imagine that a man can do it as he can work a sum in rule of three, or answer an invitation to dinner. But these short compositions, in which every word ought to tell strongly, and in which there ought to be at once some point and much feeling, are not to be produced by mere labour. There must be a concurrence of

Macaulay never allowed a sentence to pass muster until it was as good as he could make it. He thought little of recasting a chapter in order to obtain a more lucid arrangement, and nothing whatever of reconstructing a paragraph for the sake of one happy stroke or apt illustration. Whatever the worth of his labour, at any rate it was a labour of love.

> Antonio Stradivari has an eye
> That winces at false work, and loves the true.

Leonardo da Vinci would walk the whole length of Milan that he might alter a single tint in his picture of the Last Supper. Napoleon kept the returns of his army under his pillow at night, to refer to in case he was sleepless; and would set himself problems at the Opera, while the overture was playing. 'I have ten thousand men at Strasburg; fifteen thousand at Magdeburg; twenty thousand at Wurtzburg. By what stages must they march so as to arrive at Ratisbon on three successive days?' What his violins were to Stradivarius, and his fresco to Leonardo, and his campaigns to Napoleon, that was his History to Macaulay. How fully it occupied his thoughts did not appear in his conversation; for he steadily and successfully resisted any inclination to that most subtle form of selfishness, which often renders the period of literary creation one long penance to all the members of an author's family. But none the less his book was always in his mind; and seldom indeed did he pass a day, or turn over a volume, without lighting upon a suggestion which could be applied to an useful purpose. In May 1851, he writes: 'I went to the Exhibition and lounged there during some hours. I never knew a sight which extorted from all

luck with industry. It is natural that those who have not considered the matter should think that a man, who has sometimes written ten or twelve effective pages in a day, must certainly be able to write five lines in less than a year. But it is not so; and if you think over the really good epitaphs which you have read, and consider how small a proportion they bear to the thousands that have been written by clever men, you will own that I am right.'

ages, classes, and nations, such unanimous and genuine admiration. I felt a glow of eloquence, or something like it, come on me from the mere effect of the place, and I thought of some touches which will greatly improve my Steinkirk.' It is curious to trace whence was derived the fire which sparkles through every line of that terse and animated narrative, which has preserved from unmerited oblivion the story of a defeat more glorious to the British arms than not a few of our victories.

Macaulay deserved the compliment which Cecil paid to Sir Walter Raleigh as the supreme of commendations: 'I know that he can labour terribly.' One example will serve for many in order to attest the pains which were ungrudgingly bestowed upon every section of the History.

'*March* 21.—To-morrow I must begin upon a difficult and painful subject, Glencoe.'

'*March* 23.—I looked at some books about Glencoe. Then to the Athenæum, and examined the Scotch Acts of Parliament on the same subject. Walked a good way, meditating. I see my line. Home, and wrote a little, but thought and prepared more.'

'*March* 25.—Wrote a little. Mr. Lovell Reeve, editor of the Literary Gazette, called, and offered to defend me about Penn. I gave him some memoranda. Then to Glencoe again, and worked all day with energy, pleasure, and, I think, success.'

'*March* 26.—Wrote much. I have seldom worked to better purpose than on these three days.'

'*March* 27.—After breakfast I wrote a little, and then walked through April weather to Westbourne Terrace, and saw my dear little nieces.[1] Home, and wrote more. I am getting on fast with this most horrible story. It is even worse than I thought. The Master of Stair is a perfect Iago.'

'*March* 28.—I went to the Museum, and made some extracts about Glencoe.'

[1] In the summer of 1849 my father changed house from Clapham Common to 20 Westbourne Terrace.

On the 29th, 30th, and 31st of March, and the 1st and 2nd of April, there is nothing relating to the History except the daily entry, 'Wrote.'

'*April* 3.—Wrote. This Glencoe business is infernal.'

'*April* 4.—Wrote; walked round by London Bridge, and wrote again. To-day I finished the massacre. This episode will, I hope, be interesting.'

'*April* 6.—Wrote to good purpose.'

'*April* 7.—Wrote and corrected. The account of the massacre is now, I think, finished.'

'*April* 8.—I went to the Museum, and turned over the Gazette de Paris, and the Dutch despatches of 1692. I learned much from the errors of the French Gazette, and from the profound silence of the Dutch ministers on the subject of Glencoe. Home, and wrote.'

'*April* 9.—A rainy and disagreeable day. I read a Life of Romney, which I picked up uncut in Chancery Lane yesterday: a quarto. That there should be two showy quarto lives of a man who did not deserve a duodecimo! Wrote hard, re-writing Glencoe.'

'*April* 10.—Finished Don Carlos. I have been long about it; but twenty pages a day in bed while I am waiting for the newspaper will serve to keep up my German. A fine play, with all its faults. Schiller's good and evil genius struggled in it; as Shakspeare's good and evil genius, to compare greater things with smaller, struggled in Romeo and Juliet. Carlos is half by the author of the Robbers and half by the author of Wallenstein; as Romeo and Juliet is half by the author of Love's Labour 's Lost and half by the author of Othello. After Romeo and Juliet Shakspeare never went back, nor Schiller after Carlos. Wrote all the morning, and then to Westbourne Terrace. I chatted, played chess, and dined there.'

'*April* 11.—Wrote all the morning. Ellis came to dinner. I read him Glencoe. He did not seem to like it much, which vexed me, though I am not partial to it. It is a good thing to find sincerity.'

That author must have had a strong head, and no very exaggerated self-esteem, who, while fresh from a literary success which had probably never been equalled, and certainly never surpassed,—at a time when the booksellers were waiting with almost feverish eagerness for anything that he chose to give them,—spent nineteen working days over thirty octavo pages, and ended by humbly acknowledging that the result was not to his mind.

When at length, after repeated revisions, Macaulay had satisfied himself that his writing was as good as he could made it, he would submit it to the severest of all tests, that of being read aloud to others. Though he never ventured on this experiment in the presence of any except his own family, and his friend Mr. Ellis, it may well be believed that even within that restricted circle he had no difficulty in finding hearers. 'I read,' he says in December 1849, 'a portion of my History to Hannah and Trevelyan with great effect. Hannah cried, and Trevelyan kept awake. I think what I have done as good as any part of the former volumes: and so thinks Ellis.'

Whenever one of his books was passing through the press, Macaulay extended his indefatigable industry, and his scrupulous precision, to the minutest mechanical drudgery of the literary calling. There was no end to the trouble that he devoted to matters which most authors are only too glad to leave to the care and experience of their publisher. He could not rest until the lines were level to a hair's breadth, and the punctuation correct to a comma; until every paragraph concluded with a telling sentence, and every sentence flowed like running water.[1] I remember the pleasure

[1] Macaulay writes to Mr. Longman about the Edition of 1858: 'I have no more corrections to make at present. I am inclined to hope that the book will be as nearly faultless, as to typographical execution, as any work of equal extent that is to be found in the world.'

On another occasion he says: 'I am very unwilling to seem captious about such a work as an Index. By all means let Mr. —— go on. But offer him, with all delicacy and courtesy, from me this suggestion. I would advise him to have very few heads, except proper names. A few there must be, such as Convocation, Nonjurors, Bank of England, National Debt. These are heads to which readers who wish for information on those subjects will naturally turn. But I think that Mr. ——

with which he showed us a communication from one of the readers in Mr. Spottiswoode's office, who respectfully informed him that there was one expression, and one only, throughout the two volumes of which he did not catch the meaning at a glance. And it must be remembered that Macaulay's punctilious attention to details was prompted by an honest wish to increase the enjoyment, and smooth the difficulties, of those who did him the honour to buy his books. His was not the accuracy of those who consider it necessary to keep up a distinction, in small matters, between the learned and the unlearned. As little of a purist as it is possible for a scholar to be, his distaste for Mr. Grote's exalted standard of orthography interfered sadly with his admiration for the judgment, the power, and the knowledge of that truly great historian. He never could reconcile himself to seeing the friends of his boyhood figure as Kleon, and Alkibiadês, and Poseidôn, and Odysseus; and I tremble to think of the outburst of indignation with which, if he had lived to open some of the most recent editions of the Latin poets, he would have lighted upon the Dialogue with Lydia, or the Ode to Lyce, printed with a small letter at the head of each familiar line.

Macaulay's correspondence in the summer and autumn of 1848 is full of allusions to his great work, the first volumes of which were then in the hands of the publisher. On the 22nd of June he writes to Mr. Longman: 'If you wish to say, "History of England from the Accession of James II.," I have no objection; but I cannot consent to put in anything about an Introductory Essay. There is no Introductory Essay, unless you call the first Book of Davila, and the first three

will on consideration perceive that such heads as Priestcraft, Priesthood, Party Spirit, Insurrection, War, Bible, Crown, Controversies, Dissent, are quite useless. Nobody will ever look at them; and, if every passage in which party-spirit, dissent, the art of war, and the power of the Crown are mentioned, is to be noticed in the Index, the size of the volumes will be doubled. The best rule is to keep close to proper names, and never to deviate from that rule without some special occasion.'

chapters of Gibbon, Introductory Essays.' In a letter to his sister Selina he says: 'Longman seems content with his bargain. Jeffrey, Ellis, and Hannah all agree in predicting that the book will succeed. I ought to add Marian Ellis's judgment; for her father tells me that he cannot get the proof-sheets out of her hand. These things keep up my spirits: yet I see every day more and more clearly how far my performance is below excellence.' On the 24th of October 1848 he writes to my mother: 'I do not know whether you have heard how pleasant a day Margaret passed with me. We had a long walk, a great deal of chat, a very nice dinner, and a quiet, happy evening. That was my only holiday last week. I work with scarcely any intermission from seven in the morning to seven in the afternoon, and shall probably continue to do so during the next ten days. Then my labours will become lighter, and, in about three weeks, will completely cease. There will still be a fortnight before publication. I have armed myself with all my philosophy for the event of a failure. Jeffrey, Ellis, Longman, and Mrs. Longman seem to think that there is no chance of such a catastrophe. I might add Macleod, who has read the third chapter, and professes to be on the whole better pleased than with any other history that he has read. The state of my own mind is this: when I compare my book with what I imagine history ought to be, I feel dejected and ashamed; but when I compare it with some histories which have a high repute, I feel reassured.'

He might have spared his fears. Within three days after its first appearance the fortune of the book was already secure. It was greeted by an ebullition of national pride and satisfaction which delighted Macaulay's friends, and reconciled him to most who remained of his old political adversaries. Other hands than his have copied and preserved the letters of congratulation and approval which for months together flowed in upon him from every quarter of the compass; but prudence forbids me to admit into these pages more than a very few samples of a species of correspondence which forms the most uninviting portion of only too many literary biographies. It is, however, worth while to reproduce the phrases in which Lord Halifax expressed the general feeling that the History was singularly well timed. 'I have finished,' he writes, 'your second volume, and I cannot tell you how grateful all lovers of truth, all lovers of liberty, all lovers of order and of civilised freedom, ought to be to you for having so set before them the History of our Revolution of 1688. It has come at a moment when the lessons it inculcates ought to produce great practical effects on the conduct of the educated leaders of what is now going on abroad; but I fear that the long education in the working of a constitution such as ours is not to be supplied by any reading or meditation. Jameses we may find; but Europe shows no likeness of William.'

'My dear Macaulay,' says Lord Jeffrey, 'the mother that bore you, had she been yet alive, could scarcely have felt prouder or happier than I do at this outburst of your graver fame. I have long had a sort of parental interest in your glory; and it is now mingled with a feeling of deference to your intellectual superiority which can only consort, I take it, with the character of a female parent.'

A still older friend than Lord Jeffrey,—Lord Auckland, the Bishop of Sodor and Man,—wrote of him in more racy, but not less affectionate, language. 'Tom Macaulay should be embalmed and kept. I delight in his book, though luckily I am not half through it, for I have just had an ordination, and my house is pervaded by Butler's Analogy and young priests. Do you think that Tom is not a little hard on old Cranmer? He certainly brings him down a peg or two in my estimation. I had also hated Cromwell more than I now do; for I always agree with Tom; and it saves trouble to agree with him at once, because he is sure to make you do so at last. Since I have had this book I have hated the best Insular friend we have for coming in and breaking up the evening. At any other crisis we should have embraced him on both sides of his face.'

Among all the incidents connected with the publication of his History nothing pleased Macaulay so much as the gratification that he contrived to give to Maria Edgeworth, as a small return for the enjoyment which, during more than forty years, he had derived from her charming writings.[1] That lady, who was then in her eighty-third winter, and within a few months of her death, says in the course of a letter addressed to Dr. Holland: 'And now, my good friend, I require you to believe that all the admiration I have expressed of Macaulay's work is quite uninfluenced by the self-satisfaction, vanity, pride, surprise, I had in finding my own name in a note!!!!! I had formed my opinion and expressed it to my friends who were reading the book to me, before I came to that note.[2] Moreover, there was a mixture of shame, and a twinge of pain, with the pleasure and the pride I felt in having a line in this immortal History given to *me*, when there is no mention of Sir Walter Scott throughout the work, even in places where it seems impossible that the historian could resist paying the becoming tribute which genius owes, and loves to pay, to genius. Perhaps he reserves himself for the '45; and I hope in heaven it is so. Meanwhile be so good as to make my grateful and deeply felt thanks to the great author for the honour which he has done me.'

Macaulay's journal will relate the phases and gradations which marked the growing popularity of his book, in so far as that popularity could be measured by the figures in a publisher's ledger. But, over and above Mr. Longman's triumphant bulletins, every day brought to his ears a fresh indication of the hold which

[1] Macaulay on one occasion pronounces that the scene in the Absentee, where Lord Colambre discovers himself to his tenantry and to their oppressor, is the best thing of the sort since the opening of the Twenty-second book of the Odyssey.

[2] This note is in the sixth chapter, at the bottom of a page describing the habits of the old native Irish proprietors in the seventeenth century. 'Miss Edgeworth's King Corny belongs to a later and much more civilised generation; but whoever has studied that admirable portrait can form some notion of what King Corny's great-grandfather must have been.'

the work had taken on the public mind. Some of the instances which he has recorded are quaint enough. An officer of good family had been committed for a fortnight to the House of Correction for knocking down a policeman. The authorities intercepted the prisoner's French novels, but allowed him to have the Bible, and Macaulay's History.[1] At Dukinfield, near Manchester, a gentleman, who thought that there would be a certain selfishness in keeping so great a pleasure to himself, invited his poorer neighbours to attend every evening after their work was finished, and read the History aloud to them from beginning to end. At the close of the last meeting, one of the audience rose, and moved, in north-country fashion, a vote of thanks to Mr. Macaulay, 'for having written a history which working men can understand.'[2]

The people of the United States were even more eager than the people of the United Kingdom to read about their common ancestors; with the advantage that, from the absence of an international copyright, they were able to read about them for next to nothing. On the 4th of April, 1849, Messrs. Harper of New York wrote to Macaulay: 'We beg you to accept herewith a copy of our cheap edition of your work. There have been three other editions published by different houses, and another is now in preparation; so there will be six different editions in the market. We have already sold 40,000 copies, and we presume that over 60,000 copies have been disposed of. Probably, within three months of this time, the sale will amount to two hundred thousand copies. No work, of any kind, has ever so completely taken our whole country by storm.'

[1] London gossip went on to say that the gallant captain preferred picking oakum to reading about the Revolution of 1688;—gossip which avenged Guicciardini for the anecdote told by Macaulay in the second paragraph of his Essay on Burleigh.

'There was, it is said, a criminal in Italy, who was suffered to make his choice between Guicciardini and the galleys. He chose the history. But the war of Pisa was too much for him. He changed his mind, and went to the oar.'

[2] Macaulay says in his journal: 'I really prize this vote.'

An indirect compliment to the celebrity of the book was afforded by a desperate, and almost internecine, controversy which raged throughout the American newspapers as to whether the Messrs. Harper were justified in having altered Macaulay's spelling to suit the orthographical canons laid down in Noah Webster's dictionary.

Nor were the enterprising publishers of Paris and Brussels behindhand in catering for readers whose appetite for cheap literature made them less particular than they should have been as to the means by which they gratified it. 'Punch' devoted the half of one of his columns to a serio-comic review of Galignani's edition of the History.

'This is an extraordinary work. A miracle of cheapness. A handsomely printed book, in royal octavo, (if anything be royal in republican France,) and all that at the low charge of some 7*s*. 6*d*. of English money. Many thousands of this impression of Mr. Macaulay's works—it must delight his *amour propre* as an author to know it—have been circulated in England. "Sir," said a Boulogne bookseller, his voice slightly trembling with emotion, "Sir, it is impossible to supply travellers; but we expect a few thousand kilogrammes more of the work by to-morrow's train, and then, for a week, we may rub on." It is cheering to find that French, Belgian, and American booksellers are doing their best to scatter abroad, and at home too, the seeds of English literature. "Sir," said the French bookseller, holding up the tome, "you will smuggle it thus: Divide the book in two; spread it over your breast; button your waistcoat close; and, when you land, look the picture of innocence in the face of the searchers." '

It is a characteristic trait in Macaulay that, as soon as his last proof-sheet had been despatched to the printers, he at once fell to reading a course of historians from Herodotus downwards. The sense of his own inferiority to Thucydides did more to put him out of conceit with himself than all the unfavourable comments which were bestowed upon him, (sparingly enough, it must be allowed,) by the newspapers and reviews of the day. He was even less thin-skinned as a writer than as a politician. When he felt conscious that he had done his very best,—when all that lay in his own power had been faithfully and diligently performed,—it was not his way to chafe under hostile criticism, or to waste time and temper by engaging in controversies on the subject of his own works. Like Dr. Johnson, 'he had learned, both from his own observation, and from literary history, in which he was deeply read, that the place of books in the public estimation is fixed, not by what is written about them, but by what is written in them; and that an author whose works are likely to live is very unwise if he stoops to wrangle with detractors whose works are certain to die.'[1] 'I have never been able,' Macaulay says in a letter dated December 1849, 'to discover that a man is at all the worse for being attacked. One foolish line of his own does him more harm than the ablest pamphlets written against him by other people.'

It must be owned that, as far as his History was concerned, Macaulay had not occasion to draw largely upon his stock of philosophy. Some few notes of disapprobation and detraction might here and there be heard; but they were for the most part too faint to mar the effect produced by so full a chorus of eulogy; and the only loud one among them was harsh and discordant to that degree that all the bystanders were fain to stop their ears. It was generally believed that Mr. Croker had long been praying that he might be spared to settle accounts with his old antagonist. His opportunity had now arrived; and people gave themselves up with a safer conscience to the fascination of the historian's narrative, because the Quarterly Review would be certain to inform them of all that could be said either against the book or against the author. But Macaulay's good fortune attended him even here. He could not have fared better had he been privileged to choose his own adversary, and to select the very weapons with which the assault was to be conducted.

[1] This passage is taken from Macaulay's article on Dr. Johnson in the Encyclopædia Britannica.

After spending four most unprofitable months in preparing his thunder, Mr. Croker discharged it in an article so bitter, so foolish, and, above all, so tedious, that scarcely anybody could get through it, and nobody was convinced by it. Many readers, who looked to professional critics for an authoritative opinion on the learning and accuracy of a contemporary writer, came to the not unreasonable conclusion that the case against Macaulay had irretrievably broken down, when they saw how little had been made of it by so acrimonious and so long-winded an advocate. Nothing would have opened the pages of the Quarterly Review to that farrago of angry trash except the deference with which its proprietor thought himself bound to treat one who, forty years before, had assisted Canning to found the periodical. The sole effect which the article produced upon the public was to set it reading Macaulay's review of Croker's Boswell, in order to learn what the injury might be which, after the lapse of eighteen years, had sting enough left to provoke a veteran writer, politician, and man of the world into such utter oblivion of common sense, common fairness, and common courtesy.

The Whig press, headed by the Times and the Scotsman, hastened to defend the historian; and the Tory press was at least equally forward to disown the critic. A subsequent page in this volume will show that Croker's arrow did not go very far home. Indeed, in the whole of Macaulay's journal for the year 1849 there can be detected but one single indication of his having possessed even the germ of an author's sensibility. '*February* 17.—I went to the Athenæum, and saw in a weekly literary journal a silly, spiteful attack on what I have said about Procopius in the first pages of my first chapter. I was vexed for a moment, but only for a moment. Both Austin and Mahon had looked into Procopius, and were satisfied that I was right;—as I am. I shall take no notice.' A year later he wrote to Mr. Longman: 'I have looked through the tenth volume of Lingard's History in the new edition.

I am not aware that a single error has been pointed out by Lingard in my narrative. His estimate of men and of institutions naturally differs from mine. There is no direct reference to me, but much pilfering from me, and a little carping at me. I shall take no notice either of the pilfering or the carping.' After once his judgment had become mature, Macaulay, at all times and under all temptations, acted in strict accordance with Bentley's famous maxim, (which in print and talk alike he dearly loved to quote,) that no man was ever written down, except by himself.[1]

'Lord Macaulay,' said an acute observer, who knew him well, 'is an almost unique instance of a man of transcendent force of character, mighty will, mighty energy, giving all that to literature instead of to practical work;' and it cannot be denied that, in his vocation of historian, he showed proof of qualities which would have commanded success in almost any field. To sacrifice the accessory to the principal; to plan an extensive and arduous task, and to pursue it without remission and without misgiving; to withstand resolutely all counter-attractions, whether they come in the shape of distracting pleasures or of competing duties;—such are the indispensable conditions for attaining to that high and sustained excellence of artistic

[1] Bentley's career was one long exemplification of his famous saying. In the year 1856 Macaulay writes, after what was perhaps his tenth re-perusal of Bishop Monk's life of the great critic: 'Bentley seems to me an eminent instance of the extent to which intellectual powers of a most rare and admirable kind may be impaired by moral defects. It was not on account of any obscuration of his memory, or of any decay in his inventive faculties, that he fell from the very first place among critics to the third or fourth rank. It was his insolence, his arrogance, his boundless confidence in himself, and disdain of everybody else, that lowered him. Instead of taking subjects which he thoroughly understood, and which he would have treated better than all the other scholars in Europe together, he would take subjects which he had but superficially studied. He ceased to give his whole mind to what he wrote. He scribbled a dozen sheets of Latin at a sitting, sent them to the press without reading them over, and then, as was natural, had to bear the baiting of word-catching pedants who were on the watch for all his blunders.'

performance which, in the beautiful words of George Eliot, 'must be wooed with industrious thought and patient renunciation of small desires.' At a period when the mere rumour of his presence would have made the fortune of an evening in any drawing-room in London, Macaulay consented to see less and less, and at length almost nothing, of general society, in order that he might devote all his energies to the work which he had in hand. He relinquished that House of Commons which the first sentence of his speeches hushed into silence, and the first five minutes filled to overflowing. He watched, without a shade of regret, or a twinge of envy, men, who would never have ventured to set their claims against his, rise one after another to the summit of the State. 'I am sincerely glad,' said Sir James Graham, 'that Macaulay has so greatly succeeded. The sacrifices which he has made to literature deserve no ordinary triumph; and, when the statesmen of this present day are forgotten, the historian of the Revolution will be remembered.' Among men of letters, there were some who maintained that the fame of Macaulay's volumes exceeded their deserts; but his former rivals and colleagues in Parliament, one and all, rejoiced in the prosperous issue of an undertaking for the sake of which he had surrendered more than others could ever hope to win.[1]

[1] Macaulay sacrificed to the demands of literature an exceptional, and most enviable, position in the House of Commons; where he exercised a commanding influence over his brother-members on all matters which lay outside party politics. His speeches on Copyright, on the Government of India, and on the Dissenters' Chapels Bill, turned votes by the score, and in some cases by the hundred. A respected statesman, who had made a speciality of the Factory Laws, and of popular Education, used to declare that everything worth saying about the principle of those two great questions might be found in Macaulay's two re-published speeches. His argument for the Anatomy Bill,—an indispensable, but, (at the time when it was proposed,) a most unpopular measure,—is a model of persuasive reasoning, and apt illustration, packed into fewer than forty sentences.

His oratory had a warm, and lifelong, admirer in Mr. Gladstone, who frequently in after years discoursed to me

CHAPTER XII

1848–1852

Extracts from Macaulay's diary—Herodotus—Mr. Roebuck—Anticipations of failure and success—Appearance of the History—Progress of the sale—The Duke of Wellington—Lord Palmerston—Letters to Mr. Ellis—Lord Brougham on Euripides—Macaulay is elected Lord Rector of Glasgow University—His inaugural address—Good resolutions—Croker—Dr. Parr—The Historical Professorship at Cambridge—Byron—Tour in Ireland—Althorp—Lord Sidmouth—Lord Thurlow—Death of Jeffrey—Mr. Richmond's portrait of Macaulay—Dinner at the Palace—Robert Montgomery—Death of Sir Robert Peel—The Prelude—Ventnor—Letters to Mr. Ellis—Plautus—Fra Paolo—Gibbon—The Papal Bull—Death of Henry Hallam—Porson's Letters to Archdeacon Travis—Charles Mathews—Windsor Castle—Macaulay sets up his carriage—Opening of the great Exhibition of 1851—Cobbett—Malvern—Letters to Mr. Ellis—Wilhelm Meister—The battle of Worcester—Palmerston leaves the Foreign Office—Macaulay refuses an offer of the Cabinet—Windsor Castle—King John—Scene of the Assassination Plot—Royal Academy dinner.

'*NOVEMBER* 18, 1848. *Albany.*—After the lapse of more than nine years, I begin my journal again.[1]

about Macaulay,—and always in very much the same words, as is the wont of an old man when talking to a younger one. On one occasion his own Chancellor of the Exchequer, speaking within three feet of us as we sat together on the Treasury Bench, expressed himself as endorsing his opponent's argument 'to a certain extent.' 'Endorse to a certain extent!' said Mr. Gladstone. 'What a phrase! We want your uncle back among us. He was a famous purist; a jealous guardian of the English language.' I then asked his opinion of Macaulay's manner of Parliamentary speaking; and he described it as unaffected, forcible, and quite sufficiently impressive. 'But the House,' (so Mr. Gladstone added,) 'cared nothing about his manner. Our one and only thought was not to miss a single word that he said.' (1908.)

[1] It must be remembered that whatever was in Macaulay's mind may be found in his diary. That diary was written, throughout, with the unconscious candour of a man who freely and frankly notes down remarks which he expects to be read by himself alone; and with the copiousness natural to one who, except where it was demanded for the purpose of literary effect, did not willingly compress anything which he had to say. It may, therefore, be hoped that the extracts presented

What a change! I have been, since the last lines were written, a member of two Parliaments, and of two Cabinets. I have published several volumes with success. I have escaped from Parliament, and am living in the way best suited to my temper. I lead a college life in London, with the comforts of domestic life near me; for Hannah and her children are very dear to me. I have an easy fortune. I have finished the first two volumes of my History. Yesterday the last sheets went to America, and within a fortnight, I hope, the publication will take place in London. I am pretty well satisfied. As compared with excellence, the work is a failure: but as compared with other similar books I cannot think it so. We shall soon know what the world says. To-day I enjoyed my new liberty, after having been most severely worked during three months in finishing my History and correcting proofs. I rose at half after nine, read at breakfast Fearon's Sketches of America, and then finished Lucian's critique on the bad historians of his time, and felt my own withers unwrung. Ellis came to dinner at seven. I gave him a lobster curry, woodcock, and macaroni. I think that I will note dinners as honest Pepys did.'

'*Monday, November* 20.—Read Pepys at breakfast, and then sate down to Herodotus, and finished Melpomene at a sitting. I went out, looked into the Athenæum, and walked about the streets for some time; came home, and read Terpsichore, and began Erato. I never went through Herodotus at such a pace before. He is an admirable artist in many respects; but undoubtedly his arrangement is faulty.'

'*November* 23.—I received to-day a translation of Kant from Ellis's friend at Liverpool. I tried to read

in these volumes possess those qualities in which, as he has himself pronounced, the special merit of a private journal lies. In a letter dated August 4, 1853, he says: 'The article on the Life of Moore is spiteful. Moore, however, afforded but too good an opportunity to a malevolent assailant. His diary, it is evident to me, was written to be published, and this destroys the charm proper to diaries.'

it, but found it utterly unintelligible, just as if it had been written in Sanscrit. Not one word of it gave me anything like an idea except a Latin quotation from Persius. It seems to me that it ought to be possible to explain a true theory of metaphysics in words which I can understand. I can understand Locke, and Berkeley, and Hume, and Reid, and Stewart. I can understand Cicero's Academics, and most of Plato: and it seems odd that in a book on the elements of metaphysics by a Liverpool merchant I should not be able to comprehend a word. I wrote my acknowledgments with a little touch of the Socratic irony.

'Roebuck called, and talked to me about the West Riding. He asked me to stand. I told him that it was quite out of the question; that I had made up my mind never again to make the smallest concession to fanatical clamour on the subject of Papal endowment. I would not certainly advise the Government to propose such endowment, but I would say nothing tending to flatter the absurd prejudices which exist on that subject. I thanked him for his goodwill, and asked him to breakfast on Monday. I find that Macculloch and Hastie have a wager on the sale of my History. Macculloch has betted that it will sell better than Lord Campbell's book. Hastie bets on Lord Campbell. Green of Longman's house is to be arbiter.'

'*November* 25.—Read my book while dressing, and thought it better than Campbell's, with all deference to Mr. Hastie. But these things are a strange lottery. After breakfast I went to the British Museum. I was in the chair. It is a stupid useless way of doing business. An hour was lost in reading trashy minutes. All boards are bad, and this is the worst of boards. If I live, I will see whether I cannot work a reform here. Home, and read Thucydides. I admire him more than ever. He is the great historian. The others one may hope to match: him, never.'

'*November* 29, 1848, *Wednesday*.—I was shocked to

learn the death of poor Charles Buller. It took me quite by surprise. I could almost cry for him.[1] I found copies of my History on my table. The suspense must now soon be over. I read my book, and Thucydides's, which, I am sorry to say, I found much better than mine.'

'*November* 30.—Tufnell[2] sent for me, and proposed Liskeard to me. I hesitated; and went home, leaving the matter doubtful. Roebuck called at near seven to ask about my intentions, as he had also been thought of. This at once decided me; and I said that I would not stand, and wrote to Tufnell telling him so. Roebuck has on more than one occasion behaved to me with great kindness and generosity; and I did not choose to stand in his way.'

'*December* 4, 1848.—Stayed at home all the day, making corrections for the second edition. Shaw, the printer, came to tell me that they are wanted with speed, and that the first edition of 3,000 is nearly out. Then I read the eighth book of Thucydides. On the whole he is the first of historians. What is good in him is better than anything that can be found elsewhere. But his dry parts are dreadfully dry; and his arrangement is bad. Mere chronological order is not the order for a complicated narrative.

'I have felt to-day somewhat anxious about the fate of my book. The sale has surpassed expectation: but that proves only that people have formed a high idea of what they are to have. The disappointment, if there is disappointment, will be great. All that I

[1] 'In Parliament I shall look in vain for virtues which I loved, and for abilities which I admired. Often in debate, and never more than when we discuss those questions of colonial policy which are every day acquiring a new importance, I shall remember with regret how much eloquence and wit, how much acuteness and knowledge, how many engaging qualities, how many fair hopes, are buried in the grave of poor Charles Buller.'—Macaulay's Speech at Edinburgh in 1852.

[2] Mr. Tufnell was then Patronage Secretary, or, in more familiar parlance, Treasury Whip.

hear is laudatory. But who can trust to praise which is poured into his own ear? At all events, I have aimed high; I have tried to do something that may be remembered; I have had the year 2000, and even the year 3000, often in my mind; I have sacrificed nothing to temporary fashions of thought and style; and, if I fail, my failure will be more honourable than nine-tenths of the successes that I have witnessed.'

'*December* 12, 1848.—Longman called. A new edition of 3,000 copies is preparing as fast as they can work. I have reason to be pleased. Of the Lay of the Last Minstrel two thousand two hundred and fifty copies were sold in the first year; of Marmion two thousand copies in the first month; of my book three thousand copies in ten days. Black says that there has been no such sale since the days of Waverley. The success is in every way complete beyond all hope, and is the more agreeable to me because expectation had been wound up so high that disappointment was almost inevitable. I think, though with some misgivings, that the book will live. I put two volumes of Foote into my pockets, and walked to Clapham. They were reading my book again. How happy their praise made me, and how little by comparison I care for any other praise! A quiet, happy, affectionate evening. Mr. Conybeare makes a criticism, in which Hannah seems to agree, that I sometimes repeat myself. I suspect there is truth in this. Yet it is very hard to know what to do. If an important principle is laid down only once, it is unnoticed or forgotten by dull readers, who are the majority. If it is inculcated in several places, quick-witted persons think that the writer harps too much on one string. Probably I have erred on the side of repetition. This is really the only important criticism that I have yet heard.

'I looked at the Life of Campbell by a foolish Dr. Beattie; a glorious specimen of the book-making of this age. Campbell may have written in all his life three hundred good lines, rather less than more. His letters, his conversation, were mere trash.[1] A life such as Johnson has written of Shenstone, or Akenside, would have been quite long enough for the subject; but here are three mortal volumes. I suppose that, if I die to-morrow, I shall have three volumes. Really, I begin to understand why Coleridge says that Life in Death is more horrible than Death.[2]

'I dined with Miss Berry. She and her guests made an idol of me; but I know the value of London idolatry, and how soon these fashions pass away.'[3]

'*January* 11, 1849.—I am glad to find how well my book continues to sell. The second edition of three thousand was out of print almost as soon as it appeared, and one thousand two hundred and fifty of the third edition are already bespoken. I hope all this will not make me a coxcomb. I feel no intoxicating

[1] This was rather ungrateful to Campbell, who had provided Macaulay with an anecdote, which he told well and often, to illustrate the sentiment with which the authors of old days regarded their publishers. At a literary dinner Campbell asked leave to propose a toast, and gave the health of Napoleon Bonaparte. The war was at its height, and the very mention of Napoleon's name, except in conjunction with some uncomplimentary epithet, was in most circles regarded as an outrage. A storm of groans broke out, and Campbell with difficulty could get a few sentences heard. 'Gentlemen,' he said, 'you must not mistake me. I admit that the French Emperor is a tyrant. I admit that he is a monster. I admit that he is the sworn foe of our own nation, and, if you will, of the whole human race. But, gentlemen, we must be just to our great enemy. We must not forget that he once shot a bookseller.' The guests, of whom two out of every three lived by their pens, burst into a roar of laughter, and Campbell sate down in triumph.

[2] See Coleridge's 'Ancient Mariner;' Part the third.

[3] 'There is nothing,' Macaulay says elsewhere, 'more pitiable than an ex-lion or ex-lioness. London, I have often thought, is like the sorceress in the Arabian Nights, who, by some mysterious law, can love the same object only forty days. During forty days she is all fondness. As soon as they are over, she not only discards the poor favourite, but turns him into some wretched shape,—a mangy dog or spavined horse. How many hundreds of victims have undergone this fate since I was born! The strongest instances, I think, have been Betty, who was called the young Roscius; Edward Irving; and Mrs. Beecher Stowe.'

effect; but a man may be drunk without knowing it. If my abilities do not fail me, I shall be a rich man; as rich, that is to say, as I wish to be. But that I am already if it were not for my dear ones. I am content, and should have been so with less. On the whole I remember no success so complete, and I remember all Byron's poems and all Scott's novels.'

'*Saturday, January* 27.—Longman has written to say that only sixteen hundred copies are left of the third edition of five thousand, and that two thousand more copies must be immediately printed, still to be called the third edition. I went into the City to discuss the matter, and found William Longman and Green. They convinced me that the proposed course was right; but I am half afraid of this strange prosperity. Thirteen thousand copies, they seem quite confident, will have been taken off in less than six months.[1] Of such a run I had never dreamed. But I had thought that the book would have a permanent place in our literature; and I see no reason to alter that opinion. Yet I feel extremely anxious about the second part. Can it possibly come up to the first? Does the subject admit of such vivid description and such exciting narrative? Will not the judgment of the public be unduly severe? All this disturbs me. Yet the risk must be run; and whatever art and labour can do shall be done.'

'*February* 2.—Mahon sent me a letter from Arbuthnot saying that the Duke of Wellington was enthusiastic in admiration of my book. Though I am almost callous to praise now, this praise made me happy for two minutes. A fine old fellow! The Quakers have fixed Monday at eleven for my opportunity.[2] Many a man, says Sancho, comes for wool, and goes home shorn. To dinner at Lansdowne House. All were

[1] As a matter of fact they were taken off in less than four months.

[2] A deputation from the Society of Friends proposed to wait upon Macaulay to remonstrate with him about his treatment of William Penn in the fifth and eighth chapters of the History.

kind and cordial. I thought myself agreeable, but perhaps I was mistaken. Lord Lansdowne almost made up his mind to come to the interview with the Quakers; but a sense of decorum withheld him. Lord Shelburne begged so hard to be admitted that I could not refuse him, though I must provide myself with a different kind of second in such a combat. Milman will come if he can.'

'*Saturday*, *February* 3.—Longman came. He brought two reviews of my book, North British and British Quarterly. When he was gone I read both. They are more than sufficiently eulogistic. In both there are squeezes of acid. Part of the censure I admit to be just, but not all. Much of the praise I know to be undeserved. I began my second part, and wrote two foolscap sheets. I am glad to see how well things are going in Parliament. Stanley is surely very foolish and inconsiderate. What would he have done if he had succeeded? He is a great debater: but as to everything else he is still what he was thirty years ago, a clever boy. All right in the Commons. Excellent speech of Palmerston. What a knack he has for falling on his feet! I never will believe, after this, that there is any scrape out of which his cleverness and his good fortune will not extricate him. And I rejoice in his luck most sincerely; for, though he now and then trips, he is an excellent Minister, and I cannot bear the thought of his being a sacrifice to the spite of foreign powers.'

Of all English statesmen, Macaulay liked Lord Palmerston the best; and never was that liking stronger than during the crisis through which the nations of the Continent were passing in 1848 and 1849. His heart was entirely with the Minister who, whenever and wherever the interests of liberty and humanity were at stake, was eager to prove that those to whom the power of England was committed did not wield the pen, and on occasion did not bear the sword, in vain. But Palmerston's foreign policy was little to the taste of some among his political opponents. They had not been able to digest his civility to Republican Governments; nor could they forgive him for having approved the conduct of the Admiral who anchored British men-of-war between the broadsides of the King of Naples' ships and the defenceless streets of Palermo. An amendment on the Address was moved in both Houses, humbly representing to her Majesty that her affairs were not in such a state as to justify Parliament in addressing her in the language of congratulation. The Peers, dazzled by Lord Stanley's reckless eloquence, ran the Ministry within two votes of a defeat which, in the then existing condition of affairs abroad, would have been nothing short of a European calamity. In the Commons Lord Palmerston opposed the amendment in a speech of extraordinary spirit,[1] which at once decided the for-

[1] 'If you say that you cannot congratulate us, I say, "Wait till you are asked." It would be highly improper to ask the House to express on the present occasion any opinion on the foreign relations of the country. * * * The real fault found with her Majesty's Government is that we are not at war with some of our allies. Our great offence is that we have remained on amicable terms with the Republican Government of France. There are those who think that the Government of a Republic is not sufficiently good company for the Government of a Monarchy. Now, I hold that the relations between Governments are, in fact, the relations between those nations to which the Governments belong. What business is it of ours to ask whether the French nation thinks proper to be governed by a king, an emperor, a president, or a consul? Our object, and our duty, is to cement the closest ties of friendship between ourselves and our nearest neighbour—that neighbour who in war would be our most formidable enemy, and in peace our most useful ally. * * * This, then, is the state of the matter. We stand here charged with the grave offence of having preserved a good understanding with the Republic of France, and of having thereby essentially contributed to the maintenance of peace in Europe. We are charged with having put an end to hostilities in Schleswig-Holstein which might have led to a European war. We are accused of having persuaded Austria and Sardinia to lay down their arms, when their differences might have involved the other powers of Europe in contention. We are reproached with having prevented great calamities in Sicily, and with labouring to restore friendly relations between the King of Naples and his subjects. These are the charges

tune of the debate; a motion for adjournment was thrown out by 221 votes to 80; and Mr. Disraeli, rightly interpreting the general feeling of the House, took the judicious course of withdrawing the hostile amendment.

'*Sunday, February* 4.—I walked out to Clapham yesterday afternoon; had a quiet happy evening; and went to church this morning. I love the church for the sake of old times. I love even that absurd painted window with the dove, the lamb, the urn, the two cornucopias, and the profusion of sunflowers, passion-flowers, and peonies. Heard a Puseyite sermon, very different from the oratory which I formerly used to hear from the same pulpit.'

'*February* 5, 1849.—Lord Shelburne, Charles Austin, and Milman to breakfast. A pleasant meal. Then the Quakers, five in number. Never was there such a rout. They had absolutely nothing to say. Every charge against Penn came out as clear as any case at the Old Bailey. They had nothing to urge but what was true enough, that he looked worse in my History than he would have looked on a general survey of his whole life. But that is not my fault. I wrote the History of four years during which he was exposed to great temptations; during which he was the favourite of a bad king, and an active solicitor in a most corrupt court. His character was injured by his associations. Ten years before, or ten years later, he would have made a much better figure.[1] But was I to begin

which the House is called upon to determine for, or against, us. We stand here as men who have laboured assiduously to prevent war, and, where it had broken out, to put an end to it as soon as was practicable. We stand here as the promoters of peace under charges brought against us by the advocates of war. I leave it to the house to decide between us and our accusers, and I look forward with confidence to the verdict which the House will give.'

[1] If Macaulay's History was not a Life of William Penn, this book is still less so. Those who are honourably jealous for Penn's reputation will forgive me if I do not express an opinion of my own with regard to the controversy; an opinion which, after all, would be valueless. In my uncle's papers there can

my book ten years earlier or ten years later for William Penn's sake? The Quakers were extremely civil. So was I. They complimented me on my courtesy and candour.'

This will, perhaps, be the most convenient place to insert some extracts from Macaulay's letters to Mr. Ellis.

'Albany: January 10, 1849.

'I have had a pastoral epistle in three sheets from St. Henry of Exon, and have sent him three sheets in answer. We are the most courteous and affectionate of adversaries. You cannot think how different an opinion I entertain of him since he has taken to subscribing himself, "with very high esteem,

"My admiring reader."

How is it possible to hold out against a man whose censure is conveyed in the following sort of phrase? "Pardon me if I say that a different course would have been more generous, more candid, more philosophical; all which I may sum up in the words, more like yourself." This is the extreme point of his severity. And to think how long I denied to this man all share of Christian charity!'[1]

'March 6, 1849.

'Pray tell Adolphus how much obliged I am to him for his criticisms. I see that I now and then fell into error. I

be found no trace of his ever having changed his mind on the merits of the question.

[1] Unfortunately these were only the preliminaries of the combat. When the Bishop passed from compliments to arguments, he soon showed that he had not forgotten his swashing blow. Macaulay writes with the air of a man whose sole object is to be out of a controversy on the shortest and the most civil terms. 'Before another edition of my book appears, I shall have time to weigh your observations carefully, and to examine the works to which you have called my attention. You have convinced me of the propriety of making some alterations. But I hope that you will not accuse me of pertinacity if I add that, as far as I can at present judge, the alterations will be slight, and that on the great point at issue my opinion is unchanged.' To this the Bishop rejoins: 'Do not think me very angry, when I say that a person *willing* to come to such a conclusion would make an invaluable foreman of a jury to convict another Algernon Sidney. Sincerely, I never met so monstrous an attempt to support a foregone conclusion.'

got into a passion with the Stuarts, and consequently did less damage than I should have done if I had kept my temper.

'I hear that Croker has written a furious article against me, and that Lockhart wishes to suppress it, declaring that the current of public opinion runs strongly on my side, and that a violent attack by a personal enemy will do no harm to me and much harm to the Quarterly Review. How they settle the matter I care not, as the Duke says, one twopenny damn.'[1]

'March 8, 1849.

'At last I have attained true glory. As I walked through Fleet Street the day before yesterday, I saw a copy of Hume at a bookseller's window with the following label: "only 2*l.* 2*s*. Hume's History of England in eight volumes, highly valuable as an introduction to Macaulay." I laughed so convulsively that the other people who were staring at the books took me for a poor demented gentleman. Alas for poor David! As for me, only one height of renown yet remains to be attained. I am not yet in Madame Tussaud's waxwork. I live, however, in hope of seeing one day an advertisement of a new group of figures; Mr. Macaulay, in one of his own coats, conversing with Mr. Silk Buckingham in Oriental costume, and Mr. Robert Montgomery in full canonicals.'

'March 9, 1850.

'I hope that Roebuck will do well. If he fails it will not be from the strength of his competitors. What a nerveless, milk-and-water set the young fellows of the present day are! —— —— declares that there is not in the whole House of Commons any stuff, under thirty-five, of which a Junior Lord of the Treasury can be made. It is the same in literature, and, I imagine, at the bar. It is odd that the last twenty-five years, which have witnessed the greatest progress ever made in physical science,—the greatest victories ever achieved by man over matter,—should have produced hardly a volume that will be remembered in 1900, and should have seen the breed of great advocates and Parliamentary orators become extinct among us.

'One good composition of its kind was produced yesterday; the judgment in Gorham's case.[2] I hope you like it.

[1] It was the Duke of Wellington who invented this oath, so disproportioned to the greatness of its author.

[2] On March 8, 1850, Lord Langdale delivered the judgment of the Judicial Committee of the Privy Council.

I think it excellent, worthy of D'Aguesseau or Mansfield. I meant to have heard it delivered: but, when I came to Whitehall, I found the stairs, the passages, and the very street so full of parsons, Puseyite and Simeonite, that there was no access even for Privy Councillors; and, not caring to elbow so many successors of the Apostles, I walked away.

'I have seen the hippopotamus, both asleep and awake; and I can assure you that, awake or asleep, he is the ugliest of the works of God. But you must hear of my triumphs. Thackeray swears that he was eye-witness and ear-witness of the proudest event of my life. Two damsels were just about to pass that doorway which we, on Monday, in vain attempted to enter, when I was pointed out to them. "Mr. Macaulay!" cried the lovely pair. "Is that Mr. Macaulay? Never mind the hippopotamus." And having paid a shilling to see Behemoth, they left him in the very moment at which he was about to display himself to them, in order to see—but spare my modesty. I can wish for nothing more on earth, now that Madame Tussaud, in whose Pantheon I hoped once for a place, is dead.'

'*February* 12.—I bought a superb sheet of paper for a guinea, and wrote on it a Valentine for Alice. I dined at Lady Charlotte Lindsay's with Hallam and Kinglake. I am afraid that I talked too much about my book. Yet really the fault was not mine. People would introduce the subject. I will be more guarded; yet how difficult it is to hit the right point! To turn the conversation might look ungracious and affected.'

'*February* 13, 1849.—I sent off Alice's Valentine to Fanny to be forwarded.[1] The sale keeps up; eighty or more a day. It is strange. People tell me that Miss Aikin abuses my book like a fury, and cannot forgive my treatment of her Life of Addison. Poor creature! If she knew how little I deserve her ill-will, and how little I care for it, she would be quieter. If she would have let me save her from exposing herself, I would

[1] The Miss Macaulays resided at Brighton. The many weeks which their brother spent there in their company added much to his health and comfort. For the most part he lived at the Norfolk Hotel; but he sometimes took a lodging in the neighbourhood of their house. His article on Bunyan in the Encyclopædia Britannica was written in one of the houses in Regency Square.

have done so;[1] and, when she rudely rejected my help, and I could not escape from the necessity of censuring her, I censured her more leniently, I will venture to say, than so bad a book was ever censured by any critic of the smallest discernment. From the first word to the last I never forgot my respect for her petticoats. Even now, I do not reprint one of my best reviews for fear of giving her pain. But there is no great magnanimity in all this.'

'*February* 14.—At three came Fanny and the children. Alice was in perfect raptures over her Valentine. She begged quite pathetically to be told the truth about it. When we were alone together she said, "I am going to be very serious." Down she fell before me on her knees, and lifted up her hands: "Dear uncle, do tell the truth to your little girl. Did you send the Valentine?" I did not choose to tell a real lie to a child even about such a trifle, and so I owned it.'

'*February* 15.—To dinner with Baron Parke. Brougham was noisily friendly. I know how mortally he hates and how bitterly he reviles me. But it matters little. He has long outlived his power to injure. He has not, however, outlived his power to amuse. He was very pleasant, but, as usual, excessively absurd, and exposed himself quite ludicrously on one subject. He maintained that it was doubtful whether the tragic poet was Eurip̆ides or Euripīdes. It was Euripīdes in his Ainsworth. There was, he said, no authority either way. I answered by quoting a couple of lines from Aristophanes. I could have overwhelmed him with quotations. "Oh!" said this great scholar, "those are Iambics. Iambics are very capricious and irregular: not like hexameters." I kept my countenance, and so did Parke. Nobody else who heard the discussion understood the subject.'

In November 1848 Macaulay had been elected Lord Rector of the University of Glasgow. The time

[1] See Vol. ii, pages 73 and 74.

was now approaching for the ceremony of his Installation: one of those occasions which are the special terror of an orator, when much is expected, and everything has been well said many times before. His year of office fortunately chanced to be the fourth centenary of the body over which he had been chosen to preside; and he contrived to give point and novelty to his inaugural Address by framing it into a retrospect of the history and condition of the University at the commencement of each successive century of its existence.

'*March* 12.—I called on the Lord Advocate, settled the date of my journey to Glasgow, and consulted him about the plan of my speech. He thought the notion very good; grand, indeed, he said; and I think that it is striking and original without being at all affected or eccentric. I was vexed to hear that there is some thought of giving me the freedom of Glasgow in a gold box. This may make it necessary for me to make a speech on which I had not reckoned. It is strange, even to myself, to find how the horror of public exhibitions grows on me. Having made my way in the world by haranguing, I am now as unwilling to make a speech as any timid stammerer in Great Britain.'

The event proved that his apprehensions were superfluous. 'I took the oath of office,' he writes in his journal of March 21, 1849; 'signed my name; and delivered my Address. It was very successful; for, though of little intrinsic value, it was not unskilfully framed for its purpose, and for the place and time. The acclamations were prodigious.'

'*March* 22.—Another eventful and exciting day. I was much annoyed and anxious, in consequence of hearing that there were great expectations of a fine oration from me at the Town Hall. I had broken rest, partly from the effect of the bustle which was over, and partly from the apprehension of the bustle which was to come. I turned over a few sentences in my head, but was very ill satisfied with them. Well or ill satisfied, however, I was forced to be ready when the Lord Provost called for me. I felt like a man going to be hanged; and, as such a man generally does, plucked up courage to behave with decency. We went to the City Hall, which is a fine room, and was crowded as full as it could hold. Nothing but huzzaing and clapping of hands. The Provost presented me with a handsome box, silver gilt, containing the freedom of the City, and made a very fair speech on the occasion. I returned thanks with sincere emotion, and, I hope, with propriety. What I said was very well received, and I was vehemently applauded at the close. At half-past two I took flight for Edinburgh, and, on arriving, drove straight from the station to Craig Crook. I had a pleasant, painful, half-hour with Jeffrey;—perhaps the last. He was in almost hysterical excitement. His kindness and praise were quite overwhelming. The tears were in the eyes of both of us.'

'*March* 26.—Longman has written to say that the third edition is all sold off to the last copy. I wrote up my journal for the past week: an hour for fourteen pages, at about four minutes a page. Then came a long call from Macleod, with whom I had much good talk, which occupied most of the morning. I must not go on in this dawdling way. Soon the correspondence to which my book has given occasion will be over; the correcting of proof-sheets for fresh editions will also be over; the mornings will be mild: the sun will be up early; and I will try to be up early too. I should like to get again into the habit of working three hours before breakfast. Once I had it, and I may easily recover it. A man feels his conscience so light during the day when he has done a good piece of work with a clear head before leaving his bed-room. I think I will fix Easter Tuesday for the beginning of this new system. It is hardly worth while to make the change before we return from our tour.'[1]

'*April* 13.—To the British Museum. I looked over the Travels of the Duke of Tuscany, and found the passage the existence of which Croker denies. His blunders are really incredible. The article has been received with general contempt. Really Croker has done me a great service. I apprehended a strong reaction, the natural effect of such a success; and, if hatred had left him free to use his very slender faculties to the best advantage, he might have injured me much. He should have been large in acknowledgment; should have taken a mild and expostulatory tone; and should have looked out for real blemishes, which, as I too well know, he might easily have found. Instead of that he has written with such rancour as to make everybody sick. I could almost pity him. But he is a bad, a very bad man: a scandal to politics and to letters.

'I corrected my article on Addison for insertion in the collected Essays. I shall leave out all the animadversions on Miss Aikin's blunders. She has used me ill, and this is the honourable and gentlemanlike revenge.'

'*Friday, May* 5, 1849.—A lucky day on which to begin a new volume of my journal. Glorious weather. A letter from Lord John to say that he has given my brother John the living of Aldingham, worth 1,100*l.* a year, in a fine country, and amidst a fine population. Was there ever such prosperity? I wrote a few lines of warm thanks to Lord John. To Longman's. A thousand of the fifth edition bespoken. Longman has sent me Southey's Commonplace Book;—trash, if ever there was trash in a bookseller's shop.

'I read some of Dr. Parr's correspondence while I dressed. I have been dawdling, at odd moments, over his writings, and over the memoirs of him, during the last week. He certainly was very far from being all humbug. Yet the proportion of humbug was so great that one is tempted to deny him the merit which he

[1] At Easter 1849 he went to Chester, Bangor, and Lichfield.

really possessed. The preface to the Warburtonian Tracts is, I think, the best piece.'

'*June* 28.—After breakfast to the Museum, and sate till three, reading and making extracts. I turned over three volumes of newspapers and tracts; Flying Posts, Postboys, and Postmen. I found some curious things which will be of direct service; but the chief advantage of these researches is that the mind is transported back a century and a half, and gets familiar with the ways of thinking, and with the habits, of a past generation. I feel that I am fast becoming master of my subject; at least, more master of it than any writer who has yet handled it.'

'*June* 29.—To the British Museum, and read and extracted there till near five. I find a growing pleasure in this employment. The reign of William the Third, so mysterious to me a few weeks ago, is beginning to take a clear form. I begin to see the men, and to understand all their difficulties and jealousies.'

'*June* 30.—To-day my yearly account with Longman is wound up. I may now say that my book has run the gauntlet of criticism pretty thoroughly. I have every reason to be content. The most savage and dishonest assailant has not been able to deny me merit as a writer. All critics who have the least pretence to impartiality have given me praise which I may be glad to think that I at all deserve. My present enterprise is a more arduous one, and will probably be rewarded with less applause. Yet I feel strong in hope.

'I received a note from Prince Albert. He wants to see me at Buckingham Palace at three to-morrow. I answered like a courtier; yet what am I to say to him? For of course he wants to consult me about the Cambridge Professorship.[1] How can I be just at once to Stephen and to Kemble?'

'*Saturday*, *July* 1.—To the Palace. The Prince, to my extreme astonishment, offered me the Professor-

[1] The Professorship of Modern History. The Chair was eventually filled by Sir James Stephen.

ship; and very earnestly, and with many flattering expressions, pressed me to accept it. I was resolute, and gratefully and respectfully declined. I should have declined, indeed, if only in order to give no ground to anybody to accuse me of foul play; for I have had difficulty enough in steering my course so as to deal properly both by Stephen and by Kemble; and, if I had marched off with the prize, I could not have been astonished if both had entertained a very unjust suspicion of me. But, in truth, my temper is that of the wolf in the fable. I cannot bear the collar, and I have got rid of much finer and richer collars than this. It would be strange if, having sacrificed for liberty a seat in the Cabinet and 2,500*l*. a year, I should now sacrifice liberty for a chair at Cambridge and 400*l*. a year. Besides, I never could do two things at once. If I lectured well, my History must be given up; and to give up my History would be to give up much more than the emoluments of the Professorship—if emolument were my chief object, which it is not now, nor ever was. The Prince, when he found me determined, asked me about the other candidates.'

'*July* 21.—I went to a shop near Westminster Bridge, where I yesterday remarked some volumes of the Morning Chronicle, and bought some of them to continue my set. I read the Morning Chronicle of 1811. How scandalously the Whig Press treated the Duke of Wellington, till his merit became too great to be disputed! How extravagantly unjust party spirit makes men!

'Some scribbler in the Morning Post has just now a spite to Trevelyan, and writes several absurd papers against him every week. He will never hear of them probably, and will certainly not care for them. They can do him no harm; and yet I, who am never moved by such attacks on myself, and who would not walk across the room to change all the abuse that the Morning Post has ever put forth against me into panegyric, cannot help being irritated by this low, dirty wickedness. To the Museum, and passed two or three hours usefully and agreeably over maps and tracts relating to Londonderry. I can make something of that matter, unless I have lost my cunning.'

'*August* 3.—I am now near the end of Tom Moore's Life of Byron. It is a sad book. Poor fellow! Yet he was a bad fellow, and horribly affected. But then what, that could spoil a character, was wanting? Had I at twenty-four had a peerage, and been the most popular poet and the most successful Lovelace of the day, I should have been as great a coxcomb, and possibly as bad a man. I passed some hours over Don Juan, and saw no reason to change the opinion which I formed twenty-five years ago. The first two cantos are Byron's masterpiece. The next two may pass as not below his average. Then begins the descent, and at last he sinks to the level of his own imitators in the Magazines.'

Macaulay spent the last half of August in Ireland,[1] and, as his custom was, employed himself during the days that preceded his tour in studying the literature of the country. He turned over Swift's Correspondence, and at least a shelf-full of Irish novels; and read more carefully Moore's Life of Sheridan, and the Life of Flood, which did not at all meet his fancy. 'A stupid, ill-spelt, ill-written book it is. He was a remarkable man; but one not much to be esteemed or loved. I looked through the Memoirs of Wolfe Tone. In spite of the fellow's savage, unreasonable hatred of England, there is something about him which I cannot help liking. Why is it that an Irishman's, or Frenchman's, hatred of England does not excite in me an answering hatred? I imagine that my national pride prevents it. England is so great that an Englishman cares little what others think of her, or how they talk of her.'

'*August* 16, 1849.—The express train reached Holyhead about seven in the evening. I read, between

[1] See Vol. ii, pages 157–159.

London and Bangor, the Lives of the Emperors, from Maximin to Carinus inclusive, in the Augustan History, and was greatly amused and interested. It is a pity that Philip and Decius are wanting to the series. Philip's strange leaning towards Christianity, and the vigour and ability of Decius, and his inveterate hostility to the new religion, would be interesting even in the worst history; and certainly worse historians than Trebellius Capitolinus and Vopiscus are not easily to be found. Yet I like their silliest garrulity. It sometimes has a Pepys-like effect.

'We sailed as soon as we got on board. The breeze was fresh and adverse, and the sea rough. The sun set in glory, and then the starlight was like the starlight of the Trades. I put on my great-coat and sate on deck during the whole voyage. As I could not read, I used an excellent substitute for reading. I went through Paradise Lost in my head. I could still repeat half of it, and that the best half. I really never enjoyed it so much. In the dialogue at the end of the fourth book Satan and Gabriel became to me quite like two of Shakspeare's men. Old Sharp once told me that Henderson the actor used to say to him that there was no better acting scene in the English drama than this. I now felt the truth of the criticism. How admirable is that hit in the manner of Euripides:

> But wherefore thou! Wherefore with thee
> Came not all hell broke loose?

I will try my hand on the passage in Greek Iambics; or set Ellis to do it, who will do it better.

'I had got to the end of the conversation between Raphael and Adam, admiring more than ever the sublime courtesy of the Archangel, when I saw the lights of Dublin Bay. I love entering a port at night. The contrast between the wild, lonely sea, and the life and tumult of a harbour when a ship is coming in, have always impressed me much.'

'*August* 17.—Off to Dublin by railway. The public buildings, at this first glance, struck me as very fine;

and would be considered fine even at Paris. Yet the old Parliament House, from which I had expected most, fell below my expectations. It is handsome, undoubtedly; indeed, more than handsome; but it is too low. If it were twice as high as it is, it would be one of the noblest edifices in Europe. It is remarkable that architecture is the only art in which mere bulk is an element of sublimity. There is more grandeur in a Greek gem of a quarter of an inch diameter, than in the statue of Peter the Great at Petersburg. There is more grandeur in Raphael's Vision of Ezekiel than in all West's and Barry's acres of spoiled canvas. But no building of very small dimensions can be grand, and no building as lofty as the Pyramids or the Colosseum can be mean. The Pyramids are a proof: for what on earth could be viler than a pyramid thirty feet high?

'The rain was so heavy that I was forced to come back in a covered car. While in this detestable vehicle I looked rapidly through the correspondence between Pliny and Trajan, and thought that Trajan made a most creditable figure. I saw the outside of Christ Church Cathedral, and felt very little inclination to see the inside. Not so with St. Patrick's. Ruinous, and ruinous in the worst way,—undergoing repairs which there are not funds to make,—it is still a striking church; but the interest which belongs to it is chiefly historical. In the choir I saw Schomberg's grave, and Swift's furious libel written above.[1] Opposite hang the spurs of St. Ruth, and the chain-ball which killed him; not a very Christian-like ornament for the neighbourhood of an altar. In the nave Swift and Stella are buried. Swift's bust is much the best likeness of him that I ever saw; striking and full of character. Going away through Kevin

[1] The inscription on Schomberg's tablet relates, in most outspoken phrases, how the Dean and Chapter of St. Patrick's in vain importuned the Duke's heirs to erect him a monument, and how at length they were reduced to erect one themselves. The last line runs thus: 'Plus potuit fama virtutis apud alienos, quam sanguinis proximitas apud suos.'

Street I saw the Deanery; not Swift's house, though on the same site. Some of the hovels opposite must have been standing in his time; and the inmates were probably among the people who borrowed small sums of him, or took off their hats to him in the street.'

'*August* 24. *Killarney.*—A busy day. I found that I must either forego the finest part of the sight or mount a pony. Ponies are not much in my way. However, I was ashamed to flinch, and rode twelve miles, with a guide, to the head of the Upper Lake, where we met the boat which had been sent forward with four rowers. One of the boatmen gloried in having rowed Sir Walter Scott and Miss Edgeworth, twenty-four years ago. It was, he said, a compensation to him for having missed a hanging which took place that very day. Nothing can exceed the beauty of the Upper Lake.[1] I got home after a seven hours' ramble, during which I went twelve miles on horseback, and about twenty by boat. I had not crossed a horse since in June 1834 I rode with Captain Smith through the Mango Garden near Arcot. I was pleased to find that I had a good seat; and my guide, whom I had apprised of my unskilfulness, professed himself quite an admirer of the way in which I trotted and cantered. His flattery pleased me more than many fine compliments which have been paid to my History.'[2]

[1] 'Killarney is worth some trouble,' Macaulay writes to Mr. Ellis. 'I never in my life saw anything more beautiful; I might say, so beautiful. Imagine a fairer Windermere in that part of Devonshire where the myrtle grows wild. The ash-berries are redder, the heath richer, the very fern more delicately articulated than elsewhere. The wood is everywhere. The grass is greener than anything that I ever saw. There is a positive sensual pleasure in looking at it. No sheep is suffered to remain more than a few months on any of the islands of the lakes. I asked why not. I was told that they would die of fat; and, indeed, those that I saw looked like Aldermen who had passed the Chair.'

[2] In a letter written from Dublin on his way home Macaulay says: 'I was agreeably disappointed with what I saw of the condition of the people in Meath and Louth, when I went to the Boyne, and not much shocked by anything that I fell in with in going by railway from Dublin to Limerick. But from

After his fortnight in Ireland, Macaulay took another fortnight in France, and then applied himself sedulously and continuously to the completion of his twelfth chapter. For weeks together the account of each day ends or begins with the words: 'My task'; 'Did my task;' 'My task, and something over.'

'*September* 22.—Wrote my regular quantity,—six foolscap pages of my scrawl, which will be about two pages in print. I hope to hold on at this pace through the greater part of the year. If I do this, I shall, by next September, have rough-hewn my third volume. Of course the polishing and retouching will be an immense labour.'

'*October* 2.—Wrote fast, and long. I do not know that I ever composed with more ease and pleasure than of late. I have got far beyond my task. I will only mention days when I fall short of it; and I hope that it will be long before I have occasion to make such an entry.'

'*October* 9.—Sate down again to write, but not in the vein. I hope that I shall not break my wholesome practice to-day, for the first time since I came back from France. A Frenchman called on me, a sort of man of letters, who has translated some bits of my History. When he went, I sate down doggedly, as Johnson used to say, and did my task, but somewhat against my will.'

Limerick to Killarney, and from Killarney to Cork, I hardly knew whether to laugh or cry. Hundreds of dwellings in ruins, abandoned by the late inmates who have fled to America; the labouring people dressed literally, not rhetorically, worse than the scarecrows of England; the children of whole villages turning out to beg of every coach and car that goes by. But I will have done. I cannot mend this state of things, and there is no use in breaking my heart about it. I am comforted by thinking that between the poorest English peasant and the Irish peasant there is ample room for ten or twelve well-marked degrees of poverty. As to political agitation, it is dead and buried. Never did I see a society apparently so well satisfied with its rulers. The Queen made a conquest of all hearts.'

'*October* 25, 1849.—My birthday. Forty-nine years old. I have no cause of complaint. Tolerable health; competence; liberty; leisure; very dear relations and friends; a great, I may say a very great, literary reputation.

> Nil amplius oro,
> Maiâ nate, nisi ut propria hæc mihi munera faxis.[1]

But how will that be? My fortune is tolerably secure against anything but a great public calamity. My liberty depends on myself, and I shall not easily part with it. As to fame, it may fade and die; but I hope that mine has deeper roots. This I cannot but perceive, that even the hasty and imperfect articles which I wrote for the Edinburgh Review are valued by a generation which has sprung up since they were first published. While two editions of Jeffrey's papers, and four of Sydney's, have sold, mine are reprinting for the seventh time. Then, as to my History, there is no change yet in the public feeling of England. I find that the United States, France, and Germany confirm the judgment of my own country. I have seen not less than six German reviews, all in the highest degree laudatory. This is a sufficient answer to those detractors who attribute the success of my book here to the skill with which I have addressed myself to mere local temporary feelings. I am conscious that I did not mean to address myself to such feelings, and that I wrote with a remote past, and a remote future, constantly in my mind. The applause of people at Charleston, people at Heidelberg, and people at Paris has reached me this very week; and this consent of men so differently situated leads me to hope that I have really achieved the high adventure which I undertook, and produced something which will live. What a long rigmarole! But on a birthday a man may be excused for looking backwards and forward.'

[1] 'My only prayer is, O son of Maia, that thou wilt make these blessings my own.'

'Not quite my whole task; but I have a grand purple patch to sew on,[1] and I must take time. I have been delighted to hear of Milman's appointment to St. Paul's:—honestly delighted, as much as if a good legacy had been left me.'

'*December* 5.—In the afternoon to Westbourne Terrace. I read my Irish narrative to Hannah. Trevelyan came in the middle. After dinner I read again. They seemed much, very much, interested. Hannah cried. I could not at all command my voice. I think that, if I ever wrote well, I have done so here. But this is but a small part of my task. However, I was pleased at the effect which I produced; and the more so as I am sensible that I do not read my own compositions well.'

'*December* 7.—I bought Thiers's new volume, and read it in the street. He is fair enough about Vimiera and Corunna, and just to the English officers, but hardly so to the private soldiers. After dinner I read Thiers again, and finished him. I am afraid of saying to other people how much I miss in historians who pass for good. The truth is that I admire no historians much except Herodotus, Thucydides, and Tacitus. Perhaps, in his way, a very peculiar way, I might add Fra Paolo. The modern writers who have most of the great qualities of the ancient masters of history are some memoir writers; St. Simon for example. There is merit, no doubt, in Hume, Robertson, Voltaire, and Gibbon. Yet it is not the thing. I have a conception of history more just, I am confident, than theirs. The execution is another matter. But I hope to improve.'

In a letter of December 19, 1849, Macaulay writes: 'Lord Spencer has invited me to rummage his family papers; a great proof of liberality, when it is considered that he is the lineal descendant of Sunderland and Marlborough. In general, it is ludicrous to notice how sore people are at the truth being told about their

[1] The Relief of Londonderry.

ancestors. I am curious to see that noble library; the finest private library, I believe, in England.'

'*December* 20. *Althorp.*—This is a very early house. We had breakfast at nine, preceded by prayers in the chapel. I was just in time for them. After breakfast I went to the library. The first glance showed what a vast collection it was. Mr. Appleyard was Cicerone. Though not much given to admire the merely curious parts of libraries, I was greatly pleased with the old block-printing; the very early specimens of the art at Mentz; the Caxtons; the Florence Homer; the Alduses; the famous Boccaccio. I looked with particular interest into the two editions of Chaucer by Caxton, and at the preface of the latter. Lord Spencer expressed his regret that his sea education had kept him ignorant of much that was known to scholars, and said that his chief pleasure in his library was derived from the pleasure of his friends. This he said so frankly and kindly that it was impossible not to be humbled by his superiority in a thing more important even than learning. He reminded me of his brother, my old friend and leader.'

'*December* 21.—After breakfast to-day I sate down to work. Appleyard showed me the pamphlet corner, and I fell to vigorously. There is here a large collection of pamphlets formerly the property of General Conway. The volumes relating to William's reign cannot have been fewer than fourteen or fifteen; the pamphlets, I should think, at least a dozen to a volume. Many I have, and many are to my knowledge at the British Museum. But there were many which I had never seen; and I found abundant, and useful, and pleasing occupation for five or six hours. I filled several sheets of paper with notes. Though I do not love country-house society, I got pleasantly through the evening. In truth, when people are so kind and so honest, it would be brutal not to be pleased. To-day I sent 10*l.* to poor ——'s family. I do not complain of such calls; but I must save in other things in order to meet them.'

'*December* 26.—I bought Thackeray's Rebecca and Rowena,—a very pretty, clever piece of fooling: but I doubt whether everybody will taste the humour as I do. I wish him success heartily. I finished the Life of Lord Sidmouth. Addington seems to me to have had more pluck than I had given him credit for. As to the rest, he was narrow-minded and imbecile, beyond any person who has filled such posts since the Revolution. Lord Sidmouth might have made a highly creditable figure, if he had continued to be Speaker, as he well might have done, twenty years longer. He would then have left as considerable a name as Onslow's. He was well qualified for that sort of work. But his sudden elevation to the highest place in the State not only exposed his incapacity, but turned his head. He began to think highly of himself exactly at the moment when everybody else began to think meanly of him. There is a punctiliousness, a sense of personal dignity, an expectation of being consulted, a disposition to resent slights, to the end of his life. These were the effects, I apprehend, of his having been put above his station. He had a dream like Abou Hassan's, and was the worse for it all his days. I do not wonder at the contempt which Pitt felt for him: but it was below Pitt to be angry.'

'*December* 27.—Disagreeable weather, and disagreeable news. —— is in difficulty again. I sent 50*l*., and I shall send the same to ——, who does not ask it. But I cannot help being vexed. All the fruits of my book have for this year been swallowed up. It will be all that I can do to make both ends meet without breaking in upon capital. In the meantime, people who know my incomings, and do not know the drains, have no scruple about boring me for subscriptions and assistance.

'I read Romilly's Memoirs. A fine fellow; but too stoical for my taste. I love a little of the Epicurean element in virtue.'

'*January* 12, 1850.—To the Board at the Museum, and shook hands with Peel. We did business,—board-fashion. Would it were otherwise! I went home, worked some hours, and got on tolerably. No doubt what I am writing will require much correction; but in the main, I think, it will do. How little the all-important art of making meaning pellucid is studied now! Hardly any popular writer, except myself, thinks of it. Many seem to aim at being obscure. Indeed, they may be right enough in one sense; for many readers give credit for profundity to whatever is obscure, and call all that is perspicuous shallow. But coraggio! and think of A.D. 2850. Where will your Emersons be then? But Herodotus will still be read with delight. We must do our best to be read too.

'A letter from Campbell with news that I am a bencher of Lincoln's Inn. I am pleased, and amused.[1] I read some of Campbell's lives. To Thurlow's abilities he is surely unjust. It is idle to question powers of mind which a generation of able men admitted. Thurlow was in the House of Commons when Fox and Burke were against him, and made a great figure there. He dominated over the Lords, in spite of Camden, Mansfield, and Loughborough. His talents were acknowledged by the writers of the Rolliad, and even by Peter Pindar. It is too late to dispute them now.'

'*January* 28.—Jeffrey is gone. Dear fellow! I loved him as much as it is easy to love a man who belongs to an older generation. And how good, and kind, and generous he was to me! His goodness, too, was the more precious because his perspicacity was so great. He saw through and through you. He marked every

[1] A Benchership of Lincoln's Inn has rarely fallen to a stuff gown;—and to a stuff gown whose wearer had, in the course of his life, earned but one solitary guinea. The notion of conferring this high honour upon Macaulay was mooted by Lord Justice Knight Bruce, who had been one of his most determined adversaries in the House of Commons during the heat of the great controversies of 1832.

fault of taste, every weakness, every ridicule; and yet he loved you as if he had been the dullest fellow in England. He had a much better heart than Sydney Smith. I do not mean that Sydney was in that respect below par. In ability I should say that Jeffrey was higher, but Sydney rarer. I would rather have been Jeffrey; but there will be several Jeffreys, before there is a Sydney. After all, dear Jeffrey's death is hardly matter for mourning. God grant that I may die so! Full of years; full of honours; faculties bright, and affections warm to the last; lamented by the public, and by many valuable private friends. This is the euthanasia.

'I dined at home, and read in the evening Rousseau's Letter to the Archbishop of Paris, and Letter to D'Alembert. In spite of my hatred of the fellow, I cannot deny that he had great eloquence and vigour of mind. At the same time, he does not amuse me, and to me a book which is not amusing wants the highest of all recommendations.'

'*February* 19.—Went with Hannah to Richmond's studio, to see my picture. He seemed anxious and excited; but at last, when he produced his work, she pronounced it excellent. I am no judge of the likeness; but the face is characteristic. It is the face of a man of considerable mental powers, great boldness and frankness, and a quick relish for pleasure. It is not unlike Mr. Fox's face in general expression. I am quite content to have such a physiognomy. Home, and counted my books. Those which are in front are, in round numbers, 6,100. There are several hundreds behind, chiefly novels. I may call the whole collection at least 7,000. It will probably amount to 10,000 by the time that my lease of these chambers expires; unless, indeed, I expire first, which I think very probable. It is odd how indifferent I have become to the fear of death; and yet I enjoy life greatly. I looked at some Spanish ballads, and was struck by the superiority of Lockhart's versions to the originals.

'To dinner at the Club,[1] and very pleasant it was.'

'*March* 2.—I was pained by hearing at Westbourne Terrace that —— is deeply hurt by the failure of his portrait of me.[2] I am very sorry for it. He seemed a good fellow, and a pleasing painter; and I have a great tenderness for the sensibility of artists whose bread depends on their success. I have had as few checks to my vanity in my own line as most men; but I have felt enough to teach me sympathy. I have been reading a book called "Les Gentilshommes Chasseurs." The old régime would have been a fine thing if the world had been made only for gentlemen, and if gentlemen had been made only for hunting.'

'*March* 9, 1850.—To dinner at the Palace. The Queen was most gracious to me. She talked much about my book, and owned that she had nothing to say for her poor ancestor, James the Second. "Not your Majesty's ancestor," said I; "your Majesty's predecessor." I hope this was not an uncourtly correction. I meant it as a compliment, and she seemed to take it so.'

In the year 1839 Macaulay dined at the Palace for the first time, and described his entertainment in a letter to one of his sisters. 'We all spoke in whispers; and, when dinner was over, almost everybody went to cards or chess. I was presented; knelt down; kissed her Majesty's hand; had the honour of a conversation with her of about two minutes, and assured her that India was hot, and that I kept my health there.' It may well be believed that Macaulay did not

[1] Lord Carlisle says, in his diary of February 19, 1850: 'Dined at the Club. Hallam in the Chair. It was remarkably pleasant, except once, when we got on Scotch entails. I saw Pemberton Leigh look amused when Macaulay turned on him: "Don't you remember"—as he always begins—then something in Don Gusman d'Alfarache. He said Dryden had three great dialogues in his plays: Sebastian and Dorax; Antony and Ventidius; (I forget the third;) but he considers all immeasurably below the Brutus and Cassius.' The third dialogue was Tröilus and Hector.

[2] This does not refer to Mr. Richmond's picture.

relish a society where he fancied himself bound to condense his remarks into the space of two minutes, and to speak in the nearest approach to a whisper which he had at his command. But, in truth, the restraint under which he found himself was mainly due to his own inexperience of court life; and, as time went on, he began to perceive that he could not make himself more acceptable than by talking as he talked elsewhere. Before long, a lady who met him frequently at the Palace, both in the character of a Cabinet Minister and of a private guest, writes: 'Mr. Macaulay was very interesting to listen to; quite immeasurably abundant in anecdote and knowledge.'

'*March* 11.—I wrote the arrival of the news of the Boyne at Whitehall. I go on slowly, but, I think, pretty well. There are not many weeks in which I do not write enough to fill seven or eight printed pages. The rule of never going on when the vein does not flow readily would not do for all men, or for all kinds of work. But I, who am not tied to time, who do not write for money, and who aim at interesting and pleasing readers whom ordinary histories repel, can hardly do better. How can a man expect that others will be amused by reading what he finds it dull to compose?

'Still North-east wind. Alas for the days when N.E. and S.W. were all one to me! Yet I have compensations, and ought to be contented, and so I am, though now and then I wince for a moment.'

'*March* 21.—I have been plagued to know what to do about a letter from that poor creature, Robert Montgomery. He has written to me begging, in fact, that I will let him out of the pillory. I wrote, and re-wrote my answer. It was very difficult to hit the exact point:—to refuse all concession without offering any new offence, and, without any fresh asperity, to defend the asperity of my article.'

'*April* 15.—After breakfast I fell to work on the conspiracy of the Jacobites in 1690. This is a tough chapter. To make the narrative flow along as it ought, every part naturally springing from that which precedes,—to carry the reader backward and forward across St. George's Channel without distracting his attention,—is not easy. Yet it may be done. I believe that this art of transition is as important, or nearly so, to history, as the art of narration. I read the last volume of Clarissa, which I have not opened since my voyage from India in the Lord Hungerford. I nearly cried my eyes out.'

'*April* 27.—To Westbourne Terrace, and passed an hour in playing with Alice. A very intelligent and engaging playfellow I found her. I was Dando at a pastry-cook's, and then at an oyster-shop.[1] Afterwards I was a dog-stealer, who had carried away her little spaniel Diamond, while she was playing in Kensington Gardens, and who came to get the reward advertised in the Times. Dear little creature! How such things twine themselves about our hearts!

'To dinner with Inglis. Hardinge told some good campaigning stories; and, among others, the cold language which the Duke used about a brave officer on the staff, who was killed by exposing himself injudiciously. "What business had he larking there? I shall not mention his name. I shall teach officers that, dead or alive, they shall not be praised if they throw their lives away." William the Third all over.[2]

'Longman gives a capital account of the sale of my

[1] A generation has arisen of whom not one in fifty knows Dando; the 'bouncing, seedy swell;' hero of a hundred ballads; who was at least twice in every month brought before the magistrates for having refused to settle his bill after overeating himself in an oyster-shop.

[2] 'Walker was treated less respectfully. William thought him a busybody who had been properly punished for running into danger without any call of duty, and expressed that feeling with characteristic bluntness, on the field of battle. "Sir," said an attendant, "the Bishop of Derry has been killed by a shot at the ford." "What took him there?" growled the king.' See likewise, in the twenty-first chapter of the History, the whole paragraph containing the account of the death of Mr. Godfrey at the siege of Namur.

works. The sixth edition of the History is gone. That makes 22,000 copies.'

'*May* 9.—To the British Museum. We put Peel into the Chair. Very handy he is, to use the vulgar phrase. A capital man of business. We got on fast.'

'*May* 14.—To the Museum. Peel brought his project of a report. I admire the neatness and readiness with which he does such things. It is of a piece with his Parliamentary performances. He and I get on wonderfully well together.'

'*June* 1.—Dined with Peel. How odd!'[1]

Three weeks afterwards, Macaulay started for his tour to Glencoe and Killiecrankie.

'*July* 3.—As we drove into Glasgow, I saw "Death of Sir Robert Peel" placarded at a newsman's. I was extremely shocked. Thank God, I had shaken hands cordially with the poor fellow, after all our blows given and received.'[2]

'*July* 4.—Poor Peel's death in the Times. I have been more affected by it than I could have believed. It was in the dining-room that he died. I dined with him there for the first, and the last, time about a

[1] The strangeness consisted in Macaulay's dining under Sir Robert Peel's roof. He had, at least once before this, met his old antagonist at the house of a common friend. '*April* 2 (1839).—I dined at Inglis's, and met Peel. He was pleasant enough; not a brilliant talker, but conversible and easy, with a little turn in private, as in public, to egotism. We got on very well. I recollect only his account of Sir William Scott's excessive timidity about speaking in Parliament. "My dear young friend, how does the House seem? Is Brougham there? Does he look very savage?" '

[2] 'I shall hardly know the House of Commons without Sir Robert Peel. * * * His figure is now before me: all the tones of his voice are in my ears; and the pain with which I think that I shall never hear them again would be embittered by the recollection of some sharp encounters which took place between us, were it not that at last there was an entire and cordial reconciliation, and that, only a very few days before his death, I had the pleasure of receiving from him marks of kindness and esteem of which I shall always cherish the recollection.'—Macaulay's Speech at Edinburgh in 1852.

month ago. If he is buried publicly, I will certainly follow his coffin. Once I little thought that I should have cried for his death.'

'*July* 28.—My account of the Highlands is getting into tolerable shape. To-morrow I shall begin to transcribe again, and to polish. What trouble these few pages will have cost me! The great object is that, after all this trouble, they may read as if they had been spoken off, and may seem to flow as easily as table talk. We shall see.

'I brought home, and read, the "Prelude." It is a poorer "Excursion;" the same sort of faults and beauties; but the faults greater, and the beauties fainter both in themselves, and because faults are always made more offensive, and beauties less pleasing by repetition. The story is the old story. There are the old raptures about mountains and cataracts; the old flimsy philosophy about the effect of scenery on the mind; the old crazy mystical metaphysics; the endless wildernesses of dull, flat, prosaic twaddle; and here and there fine descriptions and energetic declamations interspersed. The story of the French Revolution, and of its influence on the character of a young enthusiast, is told again at greater length, and with less force and pathos, than in the Excursion. The poem is to the last degree Jacobinical, indeed Socialist. I understand perfectly why Wordsworth did not choose to publish it in his lifetime.

'I looked over Coleridge's Remains. What stuff some of his criticisms on style are! Think of his saying that scarcely any English writer before the Revolution used the Saxon genitive, except with a name indicating a living being, or where a personification was intended! About twenty lines of Shakspeare occurred to me in five minutes. In King John:

> In dreadful trial of our kingdom's king:

Again:

> Nor let my kingdom's rivers take their course.

In Hamlet:

The law's delay.

In Romeo and Juliet:

My bosom's lord sits lightly on his throne.

In Richard the Third, strongest of all:

Why then All Souls' day is my body's doomsday.'

Macaulay spent the September of 1850 in a pleasant villa on the south coast of the Isle of Wight. The letters in which he urges Mr. Ellis to share his retreat may lack the poetical beauty of Horace's invitation to Mæcenas, and Tennyson's invitation to Mr. Maurice; but it is probable that the entertainment, both material and intellectual, which awaited a guest at Madeira Hall, did not yield in quality to that provided either at Tibur or at Freshwater.

Madeira Hall, Ventnor: September 3, 1850.

Dear Ellis,—

Here I am, lodged most delightfully. I look out on one side to the crags and myrtles of the Undercliff, against which my house is built. On the other side I have a view of the sea, which is at this moment as blue as the sky, and as calm as the Serpentine. My little garden is charming. I wish that I may not, like Will Honeycomb, forget the sin and sea-coal of London for innocence and haycocks. To be sure, innocence and haycocks do not always go together.

When will you come? Take your own time; but I am rather anxious that you should not lose this delicious weather, and defer your trip till the equinoctial storms are setting in. I can promise you plenty of water and of towels; good wine; good tea; good cheese from town; good eggs, butter, and milk from the farm at my door; a beautiful prospect from your bedroom window; and, (if the weather keeps us within doors,) Plautus's Comedies, Plutarch's Lives, twenty or thirty Comedies of Calderon, Fra Paolo's History, and a little library of novels—to say nothing of my own compositions, which, like Ligurinus, I will read to you stanti, sedenti, &c., &c.

I am just returned from a walk of near seven hours, and of full fifteen miles; part of it as steep as the Monument.

Indeed, I was so knocked up with climbing Black Gang Chine that I lay on the turf at the top for a quarter of an hour.

Ever yours

T. B. MACAULAY.

Ventnor: September 8, 1850.

Dear Ellis,—

I shall be at Ryde to meet you next Saturday. I only hope that the weather may continued to be just what it is. The evenings are a little chilly out of doors; but the days are glorious. I rise before seven; breakfast at nine; write a page; ramble five or six hours over rocks, and through copsewood, with Plutarch in my hand; come home; write another page; take Fra Paolo, and sit in the garden reading till the sun sinks behind the Undercliff. Then it begins to be cold; so I carry my Fra Paolo into the house and read on till dinner. While I am at dinner the Times comes in, and is a good accompaniment to a delicious dessert of peaches, which are abundant here. I have also a novel of Theodore Hook by my side, to relish my wine. I then take a short stroll by starlight, and go to bed at ten. I am perfectly solitary; almost as much so as Robinson Crusoe before he caught Friday. I have not opened my lips, that I remember, these six weeks, except to say, 'Bread if you please,' or 'Bring me a bottle of soda-water;' yet I have not had a moment of ennui. Nevertheless I am heartily glad that you can give me nine days. I wish it were eighteen.

Ever yours

T. B. MACAULAY.

'*September* 9.—Up soon after six, and read Cobbett with admiration, pleasure, and abhorrence.[1] After

[1] 'I read Cobbett,' Macaulay writes. 'Interesting; but the impression of a prolonged perusal of such venomous invective, and gross sophistry, becomes painful. After he came into Parliament he was nothing. He spoke feebly there when I heard him, which was often. He made, I believe, one successful speech—mere banter on Plunkett—when I was absent. He proved that he was quite incapable of doing anything great in debate; and his Parliamentary attendance prevented him from doing anything great with his pen. His Register became as stupid as the Morning Herald. In truth, his faculties were impaired by age; and the late hours of the House probably assisted to enfeeble his body, and consequently his mind. His

breakfast I gave orders about culinary preparations for Ellis, who is more of an Apicius than I am. Then, after writing a little, I put a volume of Plautus in my pocket, and wandered through the thickets under Bonchurch. I sate down here and there, and read the Pœnulus. It is amusing; but there is a heavy, lumbering way about honest Plautus which makes him as bad a substitute for the Attic masters of the later Comedy as the ass was for the spaniel in the fable. You see every now and then that what he does coarsely and blunderingly was done in the original with exquisite delicacy. The name of Hanno in the play reminded me of Hanno in my lay of Virginia,[1] and I went through it all during the rest of my ramble, and was pretty well pleased with it. Those poems have now been eight years published. They still sell, and seem still to give pleasure. I do not rate them high; but I do not remember that any better poetry has been published since.

'On my return home I took Fra Paolo into the garden. Admirable writer! How I enjoy my solitude; the sunshine, the fresh air, the scenery, and quiet study! I do not know why I have suffered myself to get into the habit of thinking that I could not live out of London. After dinner I walked again, looking at the stars, and thinking how I used to watch them on board the Asia. Those were unhappy times compared with these. I find no disposition in myself to regret the past by comparison with the present.'

'*September* 16.—I walked again in the beautiful thicket under Bonchurch, and turned the dialogue in the Rudens between Gripus and Dæmones, "O Gripe, Gripe," back again into Greek:—nineteen lines, which I should not be ashamed to send in for a University

egotism, and his suspicion that everybody was in a plot against him, increased, and at last attained such a height that he was really as mad as Rousseau. I could write a very curious article on him, if I chose.'

[1] The money-changer Crispus, with his long silver hairs,
And Hanno from the stately booth glittering with Punic wares.

Scholarship, or a Medal. They were made under every disadvantage, for there is no Greek book within my reach except a Plutarch and a New Testament, neither of which is of much use here.'[1]

Macaulay was of opinion that men, the business of whose lives lies elsewhere than among the classics, may easily amuse themselves to more purpose than by turning good English poetry into Greek and Latin verses which may have merit, but cannot possibly have any value. It has been well said that 'Greek Iambics, of which Euripides wrote ten at a sitting,—Latin Hexameters, of which Virgil wrote five in a day,—are not things to be thrown off by dozens' in the course of an afternoon's walk by an English lawyer or statesman who is out for a holiday. Indeed, Macaulay went farther still, and held that the incongruities between modern and ancient modes of feeling and expression are such as to defy the skill of the most practised and industrious translator,—working, as he must work, in a language which is not his own. It was in accordance with this notion that the only experiment in Greek composition, which he made since the day that he left college, took the shape of an attempt to reproduce a lost antique original.

'*September* 28.—I read part of the Life of Fra Paolo prefixed to his history. A wonderful man; but the biographer would have done better to have softened down the almost incredible things which he relates. According to him Fra Paolo was Galileo's predecessor in mathematics, Locke's in metaphysics,—this last, I think, is true,—and the real discoverer of the Circulation of the Blood. This is a little too much. To have written the History of the Council of Trent, and the tracts on the Venetian Dispute with Rome, is enough for one man's fame. As to the attempt to make out that he was a real Roman Catholic, even according

[1] These lines may be found at the end of the Miscellaneous Writings. A Greek drama, which is no longer extant, by the poet Diphilus, is supposed to have been the original of the Rudens.

to the lowest Gallican notions, the thing is impossible. Bossuet, whom the Ultramontane divines regard as little better than a heretic, was himself a bigoted Ultramontane when compared with Fra Paolo.'[1]

'*October* 9.—I picked up Whitaker's criticism on Gibbon. Pointless spite, with here and there a just remark. It would be strange if in so large a work as Gibbon's there were nothing open to just remark. How utterly all the attacks on his History are forgotten![2] this of Whitaker; Randolph's; Chelsum's; Davies's; that stupid beast Joseph Milner's;[3] even

[1] Macaulay says in a letter dated September 1850: 'Fra Paolo is my favourite modern historian. His subject did not admit of vivid painting; but, what he did, he did better than anybody. I wish that he had not kept his friar's gown; for he was undoubtedly at heart as much a Protestant as Latimer.'

[2] 'A victory,' says Gibbon, 'over such antagonists was a sufficient humiliation. They were, however, rewarded in this world. Poor Chelsum is indeed neglected; and I dare not boast the making Dr. Watson a bishop. He is a prelate of a large mind and liberal spirit. But I enjoyed the pleasure of giving a royal pension to Dr. Davies, and of collating Dr. Apthorpe to an archiepiscopal living.'

[3] Macaulay's view of Milner is pretty strongly expressed on the margin of his copy of the 'History of the Church.' 'My quarrel with you,' he says in one place, 'is that you are ridiculously credulous; that you wrest everything to your own purpose in defiance of all the rules of sound construction; that you are profoundly ignorant of your subject; that your information is second-hand, and that your style is nauseous.' On the margin of the passage where Basil says of Gregory Thaumaturgus, (in whose miraculous powers Milner devoutly believed,) 'He never allowed himself to call his Brother fool,' Macaulay writes: 'He never knew such a fool as Milner then.'

Dean Milman, writing for the public eye, indicates the same opinion in terms more befitting the pen of a clergyman; 'Milner's History of the Church enjoys an extensive popularity with a considerable class of readers, who are content to accept fervent piety and an accordance with their own religious views, instead of the profound original research, the various erudition, and dispassionate judgment which more rational Christians consider indispensable to an historian. In his answer to Gibbon, Milner unfortunately betrays the incapacity of his mind for historical criticism. When he enters into detail, it is in general on indefensible points, long abandoned by sound scholars.'

Watson's. And still the book, with all its great faults of substance and style, retains, and will retain, its place in our literature; and this though it is offensive to the religious feeling of the country, and really most unfair where religion is concerned. But Whitaker was as dirty a cur as I remember.'

'*October* 14.—In the morning —— called. He seems to be getting on well. He is almost the only person to whom I ever gave liberal assistance without having reason to regret it. Of course I do not speak of my own family; but I am confident that, within the last ten years, I have laid out several hundreds of pounds in trying to benefit people whose own vices and follies have frustrated every attempt to serve them. I have had a letter from a Miss ——, asking me to lend, that is to give her, a hundred pounds. I never saw her; I know nothing of her; her only claim on me is that I once gave her money. She will, of course, hate me and abuse me for not complying with this modest request. Except in the single case of ——, I never, as far as I know, reaped anything in return for charities, which have often been large for my means, except positive ill-will. My facility has tempted those whom I have relieved to make one unreasonable request after another. At last I have been forced to stop, and then they thought themselves wronged.

'I picked up a tract on the Blockade of Norway, by Sir Philip Francis:—Junius all over, but Junius grown old. Among other things I read Newman's Lectures, which have just been published. They are ingenious enough, and, I dare say, cogent to those people who call themselves Anglo-Catholics; but to me they are futile as any Rabbinical tradition. One lecture is evidently directed against me, though not by name: and I am quite willing that the public should judge between us.

'I walked to Westbourne Terrace, and talked with Hannah about setting up a brougham. I really shall do it. The cost will be small, and the comfort great.

It is but fair, too, that I should have some of the advantage of my own labour.'

'*October* 25, 1850.—My birthday. I am fifty. Well, I have had a happy life. I do not know that anybody, whom I have seen close, has had a happier. Some things I regret: but, on the whole, who is better off? I have not children of my own, it is true; but I have children whom I love as if they were my own, and who, I believe, love me. I wish that the next ten years may be as happy as the last ten. But I rather wish it than hope it.'

'*November* 1.—I was shocked to find a letter from Dr. Holland, to the effect that poor Harry Hallam is dying at Sienna. What a trial for my dear old friend! I feel for the lad himself too. Much distressed. I dined, however. We dine, unless the blow comes very, very, near the heart indeed.

'Holland is angry and alarmed about the Papal Bull, and the Archbishop of Westminster. I am not; but, I am not sorry that other people take fright, for such fright is an additional security to us against that execrable superstition. I begin to feel the same disgust at the Anglo-Catholic, and Roman Catholic cant, which people after the Restoration felt for the Puritan cant. Their Saints' Days affect me as the Puritan Sabbath affected drunken Barnaby. Their dates of letters,—the Eve of St. Bridget,—the Octave of St. Swithin,—provoke me as I used to be provoked by the First Month and First Day of the Quakers. I shall not at all wonder if this feeling should become general, and these follies should sink amidst a storm of laughter. Oh, for a Butler!'[1]

'*November* 2.—At breakfast I was comforted by a line from Holland saying that young Hallam is better, and likely to do well, God sent it! To Brooks's, and talked on the Wiseman question. I made my hearers very merry.'

[1] It is, perhaps, needless to say that this prayer refers to the author of Hudibras, and not to the author of the Analogy.

'*November* 4.—I am deeply concerned to hear that poor Harry Hallam is gone. Alas! alas! He died on my birthday. There must have been near a quarter of a century between us. I could find it in my heart to cry. Poor Hallam! what will he do? He is more stoical than I am, to be sure. I walked reading Epictetus in the streets. Anointing for broken bones! Let him try how Hallam will be consoled by being told that the lives of children are οὐκ ἐφ' ἡμῖν.'[1]

'*November* 5.—I went to poor Hallam's. The servants had heard from him to-day. He was at Florence, hastening home, perhaps with the body. He brought home his son Arthur. Alas![2] Looked at the Life of Hugh Blair;—a stupid book, by a stupid man, about a stupid man. Surely it is strange that so poor a creature as Blair should ever have had any literary reputation at all. The Life is in that very vile fashion which Dugald Stewart set;—not a life, but a series of disquisitions on all sorts of subjects.'

'*December* 2.—To poor Hallam's. He was much as before. At first he wept, and was a good deal affected. Then he brightened up, and we talked, as in old times, for the best part of an hour.'

'*December* 10.—I wrote, or rather transcribed and corrected, much. The declamatory disquisition, which I have substituted for the orations of the ancient historians, seems to me likely to answer.[3] It is a sort of composition which suits my style, and will probably take with the public. I met Sir Bulwer Lytton, or Lytton Bulwer. He is anxious about some scheme for some association of literary men. I detest all such

[1] 'Matters beyond our control.'

[2]
Fair ship, that from the Italian shore
    Sailest the placid ocean's plains
    With my lost Arthur's loved remains,
Spread thy full wings, and waft him o'er.

In Memoriam.

[3] Macaulay was then employed upon the controversy about the lawfulness of swearing allegiance to William and Mary, which split the High Church divines of 1689 into two parties. See Chapter XIV of the History.

associations. I hate the notion of gregarious authors. The less we have to do with each other the better.'

'*December* 25.—In bed, and at breakfast, I read Porson's Letters to Archdeacon Travis, and compared the collected letters with the Gentleman's Magazine, in which they originally appeared. The book has a little suffered from the awkwardness of turning what were letters to Sylvanus Urban into letters to Archdeacon Travis; but it is a masterly work.[1] A comparison between it and the Phalaris would be a comparison between Porson's mind and Bentley's mind: Porson's more sure-footed, more exact, more neat; Bentley's far more comprehensive and inventive. While walking I read Bishop Burgess's trash in answer to Porson. Home, and read Turton's defence of Porson against Burgess; an impenetrable dunce, to reason with whom is like kicking a woolpack. Was there ever such an instance of the blinding power of bigotry as the fact that some men, who were not absolute fools, continued after reading Porson and Turton, to believe in the authenticity of the text of the Three Witnesses?'

'*January* 10, 1851.—Rain. Rain. Wrote a little, but am out of heart. The events take new shapes. I find that what I have done must be done over again. Yet so much the better. This is the old story. How many times it was so with the first two volumes, and how well it ended at last! I took heart again, and worked.

'I finished the Life of Mathews. It is a strange book; too much of it, but highly interesting. A singular man; certainly the greatest actor that I ever saw; far greater than Munden, Dowton, Liston, or Fawcett; far greater than Kean, though there it is not so easy to make a comparison. I can hardly believe Garrick to have had more of the genuine mimetic genius than Mathews. I often regret that I did not see him more

[1] Sylvanus Urban was the *nom de plume* adopted by the editor of the Gentleman's Magazine. In another part of his diary Macaulay says: 'Read Porson's letters to Travis. I am never weary of them.'

frequently. Why did I not? I cannot tell; for I admired him, and laughed my sides sore whenever I saw him.'

'*January* 13.—At breakfast came a summons to Windsor Castle for to-morrow. I feel a twinge at the name. Was ever man so persecuted for such a trifle as I was about that business. And, if the truth were known, without the shadow of a reason. Yet my life must be allowed to have been a very happy one, seeing that such a persecution was among my greatest misfortunes.'

'*January* 14.—To Windsor, and walked up to the Castle. I found my room very comfortable, and read a volume of Jacobite pamphlets by a blazing fire. At eight, I went into the Corridor, and was struck by its immense length, and the number and beauty of the objects which it contains. It is near twelve years since I was here. How changed is everything, and myself among other things! I had a few words with the Prince about the Regius Professorship of Medicine at Cambridge, now vacant by Haviland's death. I remarked that it was impossible to make either Oxford or Cambridge a great medical school. He said, truly enough, that Oxford and Cambridge are larger towns than Heidelberg, and yet that Heidelberg is eminent as a place of medical education. He added, however, something which explained why this was. There was hardly, he said, a physician in Germany, even at Berlin, even at Vienna, who made 1,000*l.* a year by his profession. In that case a professorship at Heidelberg may well be worth as much as the best practice in the great cities. Here, where Brodie and Bright make more than 10,000*l.* a year, and where, if settled at Cambridge or Oxford, they probably could not make 1,500*l.*, there is no chance that the Academic chairs will be filled by the heads of the profession.

'At table I was between the Duchess of Norfolk and a foreign woman who could hardly speak English intelligibly. I got on as well as I could. The band covered the talk with a succession of sonorous tunes. "The Campbells are coming" was one.[1] When we went into the drawing-room the Queen came to me with great animation, and insisted on my telling her some of my stories, which she had heard at second-hand from George Grey. I certainly made her laugh heartily. She talked on for some time, most courteously and pleasantly. Nothing could be more sensible than her remarks on German affairs. She asked me about Merle d'Aubigné's book; and I answered that it was not to be implicitly trusted; that the writer was a strong partisan, and too much of a colourist; but that his work well deserved a perusal, and would greatly interest and amuse her. Then came cards, during which I sate and chatted with two maids of honour. The dinner was late, and, consequently, the evening short. At eleven precisely the Queen withdrew.'

'*January* 16.—To the station. Lord Aberdeen and George Grey went with me. Throughout this visit we have been inseparable, and have agreed perfectly. We talked much together till another party got into the carriage; a canting fellow, and a canting woman. Their cant was not religious, but philanthropical and phrenological. I never heard such stuff. It was all that we could do to avoid laughing out loud. The lady pronounced that the Exhibition of 1851 would enlarge her ideality, and exercise her locality. Lord Aberdeen had a little before told us some droll stories of the old Scotch Judges. Lord Braxfield, at whist, exclaimed to a lady with whom he was playing: "What are ye doing, ye damned auld ——?" and then, recollecting himself: "Your pardon's begged, madam. I took ye for my ain wife."

'At half-past seven the brougham came, and I went to dine at Lord John Russell's, pleased and proud, and thinking how unjustly poor Pepys was abused for noting in his diary the satisfaction it gave him to ride

[1] This is the only authentic instance on record of Macaulay's having known one tune from another.

in his own coach. This is the first time I ever had a carriage of my own, except when in office.'

'*February* 5.—At breakfast I read the correspondence between Voltaire and Frederic; a precious pair! I looked over my paper on Frederic. It contains much that is just, and much that is lively and spirited; but, on the whole, I think I judged rightly in not reprinting it.[1] I bought a superb Valentine in the Colonnade, and wrote my lines to Miss Stanhope. Pretty lines they are. Then to Westbourne Terrace, and picked up by the way a well-remembered volume, which I had not seen for many years; a translation of some Spanish Comedies,—one of the few bright specks in our very sullen library at Clapham. Hannah was in delight at seeing it again.

'I read a good deal of what I have written, and was not ill pleased, especially with the account of the Treason Trials Bill in the eighteenth chapter. These abstracts of Parliamentary debates will be a new, and, I hope, a striking feature in the book.'

'*Thursday, May* 1, 1851.—A fine day for the opening of the Exhibition. A little cloudy in the morning, but generally sunny and pleasant. I was struck by the number of foreigners in the streets. All, however, were respectable and decent people. I saw none of the men of action with whom the Socialists were threatening us. I went to the Park, and along the Serpentine. There were immense crowds on both sides of the water. I should think that there must have been near three hundred thousand people in Hyde Park at once. The sight among the green boughs was delightful. The boats, and little frigates, darting across the lake; the flags; the music; the guns;—everything was exhilarating, and the temper of the multitude the best possible. I fell in with Punch Greville, and walked with him for an hour. He, like me, thought the outside spectacle better worth seeing than the pageant under cover.

[1] Macaulay changed his mind before long, and the essay on Frederic took its place in the Collected Edition.

He showed me a letter from Madame de Lieven, foolish, with an affectation of cleverness and profundity, just like herself. She calls this Exhibition a bold, a rash, experiment. She apprehends a horrible explosion. "You may get through it safe; and, if you do, you will give yourselves more airs than ever." And this woman is thought a political oracle in some circles! There is just as much chance of a revolution in England as of the falling of the moon.

'I made my way into the building; a most gorgeous sight; vast; graceful; beyond the dreams of the Arabian romances.[1] I cannot think that the Cæsars ever exhibited a more splendid spectacle. I was quite dazzled, and I felt as I did on entering St. Peter's. I wandered about, and elbowed my way through the crowd which filled the nave, admiring the general effect, but not attending much to details.

'Home, and finished "Persuasion." I have now read over again all Miss Austen's novels. Charming they are; but I found a little more to criticise than formerly. Yet there are in the world no compositions which approach nearer to perfection.'

'*May* 26.—To-day the Exhibition opens at a shilling. It seems to be the fate of this extraordinary show to confound all predictions, favourable and unfavourable. Fewer people went on the shilling day than on the five-shilling day. I got a letter from ——, who is in great distress about his son's debts. I am vexed and sorry; but I wrote, insisting on being allowed to settle the matter; and I was pleased that, (though there have been, and will be, other calls on me,) I made this offer from the heart, and with the wish to have it accepted.

'I finished Joan of Arc. The last act is absurd beyond description. The monstrous violation of

[1] In October Macaulay writes: 'As the Exhibition is drawing towards its close the crowd becomes greater and greater. Yesterday I let my servants go for the last time. I shall go no more. Alas! alas! It was a glorious sight; and it is associated in my mind with all whom I love most. I am glad that the building is to be removed. I have no wish to see the corpse when the life has departed.'

history which everybody knows is not to be defended. Schiller might just as well have made Wallenstein dethrone the Emperor, and reign himself over Germany,—or Mary become Queen of England, and cut off Elizabeth's head,—as make Joan fall in the moment of victory.'

'*June* 12.—After breakfast —— called. I must make one more effort to save him, and it shall be the last.[1] Margaret came, to take me to Thackeray's lecture. He is full of humour and imagination, and I only wish that these lectures may answer both in the way of fame and money. He told me, as I was going out, that the scheme had done wonders for him; and I told him, and from my heart, that I wished he had made ten times as much. Dear Lord Lansdowne was there, looking much better; much. I dined at Baron Parke's. It was pleasant, and I thought that I pleased; but perhaps was mistaken. Then to Lady Granville's rout, where I found many friends, and all kind. I seldom appear, and therefore am the better received. This racketing does not suit me; but civility requires me to go once for ten times that I am asked to parties.'

'*June* 9.—I picked up the volumes of 1832 and 1833 of Cobbett's Register. His style had then gone off, and the circumstance that he was in Parliament was against him. His mind was drawn away from that which he did well to that which he did very poorly. My own name often appears in these volumes. Many people thought that he had a peculiar animosity to me; but I doubt it. He abuses me; but less than he abused almost every other public man whom he mentioned.

'An American has written to me from Arkansas, and sent me a copy of Bancroft's History. Very civil and kind; but by some odd mistake he directs to me at

[1] It was not the last, by a good many. The person of whom Macaulay writes thus had no claim whatever upon him except their common humanity.

Abbotsford. Does he think that all Britishers who write books live there together?'

Macaulay spent August and September at Malvern, in a pleasant villa, embowered in 'a wood full of blackbirds.' Mr. Ellis gave him ten days of his company; timing his visit so as to attend the Musical Festival at Worcester.

Malvern: August 21, 1851.

Dear Ellis,—

I shall expect you on Wednesday next. I have got the tickets for the Messiah. There may be some difficulty about conveyances during the festival. But the supply here is immense. On every road round Malvern coaches and flys pass you every ten minutes, to say nothing of irregular vehicles. For example, the other day I was overtaken by a hearse as I was strolling along, and reading the night expedition of Diomede and Ulysses. 'Would you like a ride, Sir?' said the driver. 'Plenty of room.' I could not help laughing. 'I dare say I shall want such a carriage some day or other. But I am not ready yet.' The fellow, with the most consummate professional gravity, answered, 'I meant, Sir, that there was plenty of room on the box.'

I do not think that I ever, at Cambridge or in India, did a better day's work in Greek than to-day. I have read at one stretch fourteen books of the Odyssey, from the Sixth to the Nineteenth inclusive.[1] I did it while walking to Worcester and back. I have a great deal to say about the old fellow. I admire him more than ever; but I am now quite sure that the Iliad is a piece of mosaic, made very skilfully, long after his time, out of several of his lays, with bits here and there of the compositions of inferior minstrels.

I am planning various excursions. We can easily see Hereford between breakfast and dinner one day, and Gloucester on another. Cheltenham, and Tewkesbury, with its fine church, are still more accessible. The rain is

[1] In his journal of August 19 Macaulay writes: 'I walked far into Herefordshire, and read, while walking, the last five books of the Iliad, with deep interest and many tears. I was afraid to be seen crying by the parties of walkers that met me as I came back; crying for Achilles cutting off his hair; crying for Priam rolling on the ground in the courtyard of his house; mere imaginary beings, creatures of an old ballad-maker who died near three thousand years ago.'

over; the afternoon has been brilliant, and I hope that we have another glorious month before us. You shall have water in plenty. I have a well-polished ἀσάμινθος[1] for you, into which going you may wash, and out of which you may come, looking like a god.

Ever yours

T. B. MACAULAY.

Dear Ellis,— Malvern: September 12, 1851.

I have sent William to look after your business. In the meantime I must own that your ill-luck rather titillates the malicious parts of my nature. The taking of a place by a railway train, which the vulgar, myself included, perform in thirty seconds, is with you an operation requiring as much thought and time as the purchase of an estate. On two successive days did I kick my heels in the street, first before the Railway Office, and then before the Bellevue Hotel, while you were examining and cross-examining the book-keepers and arranging and rearranging your plans. I must say that your letter is well calculated to make me uneasy as to my own return to London. For if all your forethought and anxiety, your acute inquiries and ingenious combinations, have ended thus, how can such a careless fellow as I am hope to reach town without immeasurable disappointment and losses?

Here is William at last with a letter, from the coach office, but no money. As to the three shillings, οὔποτε ἥξουσι πρὸς σε· οὔποτε ἥξουσιν.[2] I send the book-keeper's explanation. You took your place in one coach: you rode to Worcester in another: you have paid the full fare to both: and you will not recover a halfpenny from either. Your case, if that is any comfort, is not a rare one. Indeed it seems to be the common practice at Malvern to travel in this way. And here we have an explanation of the extraordinary number of coaches at this place. There is room for a great many rival establishments, when passengers pay both for the conveyance by which they go and for that by which they do not go.

Good-bye; I miss you much, and console myself as well as I can with Demosthenes, Goethe, Lord Campbell, and Miss Ferrier.

Ever yours

T. B. MACAULAY.

[1] The Homeric word for a bath. The sentence is, of course, a ludicrously literal translation from the Greek.

[2] 'You will never get them back: never.'

'*September* 19.—I put Wilhelm Meister into my pocket; walked to the Cleaveland Ferry; crossed the Severn, and rambled along the eastern bank to Upton. The confessions of the pious Stiftsdame interested me, as they have always done, more than I can well explain. I felt this when I read them first on the Indian Ocean, and I felt it again when I read them at the inn at Hereford in 1844. I think that the cause of the interest which I feel in them is that Goethe was here exerting himself to do, as an artist, what, as far as I know, no other mere artist has ever tried to do. From Augustin downward, people strongly under religious impressions have written their confessions, or, in the cant phrase, their experience; and very curious many of their narratives are. John Newton's; Bunyan's; Will Huntington's; Cowper's; Wesley's; Whitefield's; Scott's; there is no end of them. When worldly men have imitated these narratives it has almost always been in a satirical and hostile spirit. Goethe is the single instance of an unbeliever who has attempted to put himself into the person of one of these pious autobiographers. He has tried to imitate them, just as he tried to imitate the Greek dramatists in his Iphigenia, and the Roman poets in his elegies. A vulgar artist would have multiplied texts and savoury phrases. He has done nothing of the kind; but has tried to exhibit the spirit of piety in the highest exaltation; and a very singular performance he has produced.[1]

'What odd things happen! Two gentlemen, or at least two men in good coats and hats, overtook me as I was strolling through one of the meadows close to the river. One of them stared at me, touched his hat, and said, "Mr. Macaulay, I believe." I admitted

[1] When Macaulay was at Frankfort he went to Goethe's house, and 'found it with some difficulty. I was greatly interested; not that he is one of my first favourites; but the earlier books of his life of himself have a great charm for me; and the old house plays a great part in the narrative. The house of Wilhelm Meister's father, too, is evidently this house at Frankfort.'

the truth of the imputation. So the fellow went on. "I suppose, Sir, you are come here to study the localities of the battle of Worcester. We shall expect a very fine account of the battle of Worcester." I hinted with all delicacy that I had no more to do with the battle of Worcester than with the battle of Marathon. "Of course not, Sir, of course not. The battle of Worcester certainly does not enter into your plan." So we bowed and parted. I thought of the proverb,[1] and I thought, too, that on this occasion the name of Tom Fool might be properly applied to more than one of the parties concerned.'

'*September* 21.—I saw in the hedge the largest snake that I remember to have seen in wild natural liberty. I remember the agonies of terror into which the sight of a snake, creeping among the shrubs at Barley Wood, threw me when I was a boy of six. It was a deep, and really terrible, impression. My mother feared that it would make me ill. It was to no purpose that they told me, and that I told myself, that there was no danger. A serpent was to me like a giant or a ghost,—a horrible thing which was mentioned in story books, but which had no existence in England; and the actual sight affected me as if a hobgoblin had really appeared. I followed the snake of to-day for some distance. He seemed as much afraid of me as I was of his kinsman forty-four years ago. During this long walk I read Wilhelm Meister occasionally. I never liked it so little. Even the account of Aurelia's and Marianne's deaths, which used to break my heart, moved me as little as it moved those brutes Lothario and Wilhelm.'

At the close of 1851 Palmerston was ejected from the Foreign Office. The Government needed no small accession of prestige in order to balance so heavy a loss, and overtures were made, without much hope of success, to induce Macaulay to accept a seat in the Cabinet.

[1] More people know Tom Fool than Tom Fool knows.

'*December* 24.—Palmerston is out. It was high time; but I cannot help being sorry. A daring, indefatigable high-spirited man; but too fond of conflict, and too ready to sacrifice everything to victory when once he was in the ring. Lord Granville, I suppose, will succeed. I wish him well. 1851 has done a great deal for him.'

'*December* 25.—I met Lord Granville at Brooks's. I congratulated him, and gave him good wishes warmly, and sincerely; but I spoke kindly, and with regret, as I felt, about Palmerston. From Granville's answer, guarded as it very properly was, I judge that we have not yet seen the true explanation. He told me that anxiety had kept him awake two nights.'

'*December* 31.—I met Peacock; a clever fellow, and a good scholar.[1] I am glad to have an opportunity of being better acquainted with him. We had out Aristophanes, Æschylus, Sophocles, and several other old fellows, and tried each other's quality pretty well. We are both strong enough in these matters for gentlemen. But he is editing the Supplices. Æschylus is not to be edited by a man whose Greek is only a secondary pursuit.'

'*January* 18, 1852.—At dinner I received a note from Lord John, asking to see me to-morrow at eleven.'

'*January* 19.—I was anxious; but determined, if I found myself hard pressed, to beg a day for consideration, and then to send a refusal in writing. I find it difficult to refuse people face to face. I went to Chesham Place. He at once asked me to join the Cabinet. I refused, and gave about a quarter of my reasons, though half a quarter would have been sufficient. I told him that I should be of no use; that I was not a debater; that it was too late for me to become one; that I might once have turned out effective in that way, but that now my literary habits,

[1] This passage refers to the author of 'Headlong Hall,' and not to the Dean of Ely, as some readers might possibly suppose.

and my literary reputation, had made it impossible. I pleaded health, temper, and tastes.[1] He did not urge me much, and I think has been rather induced by others, than by his own judgment, to make the proposition. I added that I would not sit for any nomination borough, and that my turn of mind disqualified me for canvassing great constituent bodies. I might have added that I did not wish to be forced to take part against Palmerston in a personal dispute; that I much doubt whether I should like the new Reform Bill; and that I had no reason to believe that all that I think right will be done as respects national defence. I did speak very strongly on this point, as I feel.'

'*January* 31.—I see that Lord Broughton retires, and that Maule goes to the India Board. I might have had that place, I believe; the pleasantest in the Government, and the best suited to me; but I judged far better for my reputation and peace of mind.'

In February Macaulay paid another visit to Windsor Castle.

'*February* 6.—We breakfasted at nine. I strolled up and down the fine gallery for an hour; then with Mahon to the Library; and then to the top of the Round Tower, and enjoyed a noble view. In the Library, taking up by the merest chance, a finely bound book, it proved to be Ticknor's;—a presentation copy, with a letter from the author to the Queen, saying that he had sent his volumes because he had been told by the American Minister that an eminent literary man had recommended them to her Majesty. I was the eminent literary man; and I dare say that I could find the day in my journal. It is an odd coincidence that I should light on his letter. Dinner was

[1] In another passage of his diary he writes, 'Shall I leave my oil, shall I leave my wine, for this wretched magistracy over the trees? No, as I said once before, let them go to the bramble.'

at a quarter to seven on account of the play which was to follow. The theatre was handsome, the scenery good, and the play "King John." There were faults in the acting, as there are great faults in the play, considered as an acting play; but there was great effect likewise. Constance made me cry. The scene between King John and Hubert, and that between Hubert and Arthur, were very telling. Faulconbridge swaggered well. The allusions to a French invasion, and to the Popish encroachments, would have been furiously applauded at Drury Lane or Covent Garden. Here we applauded with some reserve. The little girl who acted Arthur did wonders.[1] Lord Salisbury seemed not to like the part which his namesake performed in the play.[2]'

'*February* 16.—To Van de Weyer's to breakfast. Thiers, Duvergier de Hauranne, Hallam, Mahon, Milnes. I hate talking French before men of eminence whom I don't know well. I feel that I speak it worse than at other times. I made one hit, however. Speaking of Palmerston, I said: "Après avoir été l'apôtre des idées libérales, il a été le martyr du pouvoir arbitraire." "Mon Dieu!" said Thiers, "et c'est un Anglais qui a dit ça." He and I were very civil, and promised to exchange our works.

'I finished St. Simon's Memoirs, and am more struck with the goodness of the good parts than ever. To be sure, the road from fountain to fountain lies through a very dry desert.'

'*May* 1.—A cold 1st of May. After breakfast I went to Turnham Green, to look at the place. I found it

[1] It is almost worth while to be past middle life in order to have seen Miss Kate Terry in Arthur.

[2] *Sal.* Stand by, or I shall gall you, Faulconbridge.
Bast. Thou wert better gall the devil, Salisbury:
If thou but frown on me, or stir thy foot,
Or teach thy hasty spleen to do me shame,
I'll strike thee dead. Put up thy sword betime;
Or I'll so maul you and your toasting-iron
That you shall think the devil is come from hell.

after some search; the very spot beyond all doubt, and admirably suited for an assassination.[1]

'On my return I looked into Shakspeare, and could not get away from him. I passed the whole day, till it was time to dress, in turning him over. Then to dine with the Royal Academy.[2] A great number of my friends, and immense smiling and shaking of hands. I got a seat in a pleasant situation near Thesiger, Hallam, and Inglis. The scene was lively, and many of the pictures good. I was charmed by Stanfield's Rochelle, and Roberts's three paintings. It is the old Duke's birthday; he is eighty-three to-day. I never see him now without a painful interest. I look at him every time with the thought that this may be the last. We drank his health with immense shouting and table-banging. He returned thanks and spoke of the loss of the Birkenhead. I remarked, (and Lawrence, the American Minister, said that he had remarked the same thing) that, in his eulogy of the poor fellows who were lost, the Duke never spoke of their courage, but always of their discipline and subordination. He repeated it several times over. The courage, I suppose, he treated as a thing of course. Lord Derby spoke with spirit, but with more hesitation than on any occasion on which I have heard him. Disraeli's speech was clever. In defiance of all rule he gave Lord John Russell's health. Lord John answered good-humouredly and well. I was glad of it. Although a speech at the Royal Academy is not much, it is important that, whatever he does now, should be well done.'

[1] See the account of the Assassination Plot in Chapter XXI of the History. 'The place and time were fixed. The place was to be a narrow and winding lane leading from the landing-place on the north of the river to Turnham Green. The spot may still easily be found. The ground has since been drained by trenches. But in the seventeenth century it was a quagmire, through which the royal coach was with difficulty tugged at a foot's pace. The time was to be the afternoon of Saturday the fifteenth of February.'

[2] Macaulay attended the dinner in his character of Professor of Ancient Literature to the Royal Academy.

CHAPTER XIII

1852–1856

The magnetoscope, and table-turning—Macaulay's re-election for Edinburgh, and the general satisfaction which it occasioned—He has a serious attack of illness—Clifton—Extracts from Macaulay's journal—His strong feelings for old associations—Barley Wood—Letters to Mr. Ellis—Great change in Macaulay's health and habits—His speech at Edinburgh—The House of Commons—Mr. Disraeli's Budget—Formation of Lord Aberdeen's Ministry—The Judges' Exclusion Bill—The India Bill—The Annuity Tax—Macaulay ceases to take an active part in politics—Letters to Mr. Ellis—Mrs. Beecher Stowe—Tunbridge Wells—Plato—Mr. Vizetelly—Macaulay's patriotism—The Crimean War—Open competition—The History—Thames Ditton—Publication of Macaulay's Third and Fourth Volumes—Statistics of the sale of the History—Honours conferred on Macaulay—The British Museum.

THE year 1852 opened very pleasantly for Macaulay. From January to July his diary presents a record of hopeful and uninterrupted literary labour, and of cheerful dinners and breakfasts at the houses which he cared to frequent. About this period the friends among whom he lived were much given to inquiries into fields of speculation that may not unfairly be classed under the head of the Occult Sciences; allusions to which more than once occur both in Lord Carlisle's and in Macaulay's journals. Lord Carlisle writes:

'*May* 19,. 1852.—Breakfasted with the Mahons. We talked a good deal of the magnetoscope, which has received a staggerer from Dufferin, who went rather disguised a second time, and got quite a different character. The man told Macaulay that he was an historical painter, which the Bishop of Oxford thinks a very just character. Macaulay, I hear, denounces the wretched quack without measure. At twelve there was a large assemblage at the Bishop's to see a clairvoyante, brought by Sir David Brewster very much for the purpose of encountering Whewell, who is an arch-sceptic. About twelve of us in turns put our hands upon her eyes, and in every instance she read without mistake one, two, or three lines from books taken at random. We believed, except Whewell; who has very resilient eyes himself, which he thinks can see through everything.'

Macaulay held the same opinion about his own eyes, at any rate so far as concerned the magnetoscope, as the following extract from his diary will show:

'*May* 18, 1852.—Mahon came, and we went to a house in —— Street, where a Dr. —— performs his feats of phrenology and mesmerism. I was half ashamed of going; but Mahon made a point of it. The Bishop of Oxford, and his brother Robert, came soon after us. Never was there such paltry quackery. The fraud was absolutely transparent. I cannot conceive how it could impose upon a child. The man knew nothing about me, and therefore his trickery completely failed him. He made me out to be a painter,—a landscape painter or a historical painter. He had made out Hallam to be a musician. I could hardly restrain myself from expressing my contempt and disgust while he was pawing my head, and poring over the rotations and oscillations of his pendulum, and the deviations to different points of the compass. Dined at the Club. We have taught Lord Aberdeen to talk. He is really quite gay.'

'*May* 19.—To dine with the Bishop of London. The party should have been pleasant;—the Bishop of Oxford, Milman, Hallam, and Rajah Brooke. But unluckily we got into a somewhat keen argument about clairvoyance. The two bishops lost their temper. Indeed, we were all too disputatious, though I hope I was not offensively so. The ladies, who wanted to be off to the Queen's Ball, wished us, I dare say, at Jericho.'

Macaulay writes on a subsequent occasion: 'A breakfast-party at my chambers. There was talk about electricity, and the rotatory motion of tables under electrical influence. I was very incredulous. We tried the experiment on my table, and there certainly was a rotatory motion, but probably impressed by the Bishop of Oxford, though he declared that he was not quite certain whether he had pushed or not.

We tried again; and then, after we had given it up, he certainly pushed, and caused a rotatory motion exactly similar to what we had seen before. The experiment therefore failed. At the same time I would not confidently say in this case, as I say in cases of clairvoyance, that there must be deception. I know too little of electricity to judge.'[1]

Equable and tranquil as was the course of Macaulay's life during the earlier months of 1852, that year had still both good and evil in store for him. The Parliamentary Session had been fruitful in events. 'I met Greville in the street,' Macaulay writes. 'He is going to Broadlands, and seems persuaded that Palmerston has nothing but revenge on Lord John in his head and heart, and that he will soon be leader of the House of Commons under Lord Derby. I doubt.' He might well doubt. The late Foreign Secretary was not the man to sit down under a grievance; but he knew how to pay off old scores in accordance with the rules of political decency. By his powerful aid, the Conservatives succeeded in defeating the Ministry on a detail of the Militia Bill; and Lord Derby came in with a minority, and scrambled through the Session as best he might. While the summer was yet young,

[1] Macaulay did not love charlatans; and he included in that category some who pretty confidently arrogated to themselves the title of philosophers. 'There came,' he once writes to Lady Trevelyan, 'a knock at my door, and in walked that miserable old impostor, ——, who, I hoped, had been hanged or guillotined years ago. You must have heard of him. He is a votary of Spurzheim; a compound of all the quackeries, physiological and theological, of half a century. I always detested the fellow; but I could not turn him out of the room; for he came up with, "Do you not remember? You are so like the dear man, Zachary. It was just so that he used to look on me." (I looked by-the-bye, as sulky as a bear.) "I felt your dear skull when you was a child, and I prophesied that you should be a Minister of State. Paff! That is a demonstration. I keep my eye on you ever since. Paff! It come true!" So I desired the man to sit down, and was as civil as I could be to one whom I know to be a mere Dousterswivel.' Macaulay, very characteristically, ended his letter by regretting that his visitor did not ask for pecuniary assistance, in order that he might have given him a ten-pound note.

Parliament was dissolved, and the General Election took place in July, with no very great issue definitely at stake. The Ministerial programme was not of a nature to arouse enthusiasm. Lord Derby confined himself to vague hints, which might be construed to mean either that Protection was capable of being revived, or that he personally had not ceased to be a mourner for its death; but he made up for his reticence on the question of the day by entreating the country to believe that his Government had every intention of upholding the Established Church. The country, which was very well aware that the Church could keep on its feet without the assistance of a Tory Administration, but which was sincerely anxious to be reassured that the Cabinet had no wish to tamper with Free Trade, did not respond to the appeal, and the electioneerers of the Carlton failed to make any marked impression upon the borough constituencies.

Edinburgh was one of the places where the Conservatives resolved to try an almost desperate chance. The Liberals of that city were at odds among themselves; and the occurrences of 1847 had not been such as to attract any candidate who enjoyed the position and reputation which would have enabled him to unite a divided party. Honourably ambitious to obtain a worthy representative for the capital of Scotland, and sincerely desirous to make amends for their harsh usage of a great man who had done his best to serve them, the electors turned their eyes towards Macaulay. A resolution in favour of taking the necessary measures for furthering his return was carried in a crowded public meeting by unanimous acclamation. The speeches in support of that resolution did honour to those who made them. 'No man,' said Mr. Adam Black, 'has given stronger pledges than Mr. Macaulay that he will defend the rights of the people against the encroachments of despotism, and the licentiousness of democracy. His pledges have not been given upon the hustings, during the excitement of an election; but they have been published to the world in the calm deliberation of the closet; and he stands and falls by them. If Mr. Macaulay has a fault, it is that he is too straightforward; too open; that he uses no ambiguities to disarm opposition. By many his early, his eloquent, his constant, his consistent advocacy of civil liberty is forgotten, while a few unconsidered words are harped upon. Will you lose the most powerful defender for a piece of etiquette? Will you rob the British Senate of one of its brightest ornaments? Will you deprive Edinburgh of the honour of association with one of the most illustrious men of the day? Will you silence that voice whose tones would sustain the sinking spirits of the friends of constitutional liberty in Europe? No. I know the inhabitants of Edinburgh are not so unwise. It is in their power to secure the most able advocate of their own cause, and of the cause of truth and liberty in the world; and they will secure him.' The resolution, advocated in these words by the chief of the Edinburgh Whigs, was seconded by another citizen; a fine fellow, whose remarks were very brief, as is almost universally the case, in Scotland and in the North of England, with local leaders who have any real influence over the political conduct of their fellow citizens. 'The vexatious question,' he said, 'being long ago settled upon which alone I, along with several hundred other electors, felt reluctantly constrained to withhold our support from Mr. Macaulay at the last election, I have great pleasure in having this opportunity afforded me of returning to my first love by seconding the nomination of that illustrious historian and statesman.'

To Miss Macaulay.

Albany: June 19, 1852.

Dear Fanny,—

I have not made, and do not mean to make, the smallest move towards the people of Edinburgh. But they, to my great surprise, have found out that they treated me ill five years ago, and that they are now paying the penalty. They can get nobody to stand who is likely to do them credit; and it seemed as if they were in danger of having Members who would have made them regret not only me, but Cowan. Then, without any communication with me, it was suggested by some of the most respectable citizens that the town might solve its difficulties by electing me without asking me to go down, or to give any pledges, or even any opinion, on political matters. The hint was eagerly taken up; and I am assured that the feeling in my favour is strong, and that I shall probably be at the head of the poll. All that I have been asked to do is to say that, if am chosen on those terms, I will sit. On full consideration, I did not think that I could, consistently with my duty, decline the invitation.

To me, personally, the sacrifice is great. Though I shall not make a drudge of myself, and though I certainly shall never, in any event, accept office, the appearance of my next volumes may be postponed a year, or even two. But it seems to me to be of the highest importance that great constituent bodies should learn to respect the conscience, and the honour, of their representatives; should not expect slavish obedience from men of spirit and ability; and should, instead of catechising such men, and cavilling at them, repose in them a large confidence. The way in which such bodies have of late behaved has driven many excellent persons from public life, and will, unless a remedy is found, drive away many more. The conduct of Edinburgh towards me was not worse than that of several other places to their Members; but it attracted more notice, and has been often mentioned in Parliament, and out of Parliament, as a flagrant instance of the caprice and perverseness of even the most intelligent bodies of electors. It is, therefore, not an unimportant nor an undesirable thing that Edinburgh should, quite spontaneously, make a signal, I may say, an unprecedented, reparation.

Do not talk about this more than you find absolutely necessary; but treat it lightly, as I do in all companies where I hear it mentioned.

Ever yours

T. B. MACAULAY.

Macaulay's diary amply proves that in this letter to his sister he had written about the Edinburgh election exactly as he had felt; if, indeed, he had been capable of writing otherwise to any person, or on any subject.

'*May* 15.—I met Dundas in Bond Street, and went with him to Brooks's. Craig showed me a letter from Adam Black, by which it appears that some of the people at Edinburgh think of putting me up without applying to me. I said a little to discourage the notion, but thought it best not to appear to treat it seriously. I dined with Lord Broughton. Lord John and I sate together, and got on very well. I cannot help loving him; and I regret the diminution of his weight and popularity both for his own sake, and for that of the country.'

'*May* 27.—Breakfast with Mahon. Very pleasant it was. I had a letter from Hannah, enclosing one from Craig about Edinburgh. She has acquitted herself with true feminine skill and tact. I feel quite indifferent about the matter. I should like the *amende*. I should dislike the trouble. The two feelings balance each other; so I have only to follow a perfectly straightforward course, which indeed is always best.'

'*June* 9.—I received a letter from James Simpson about the election, and answered him as I resolved. I am fully determined that no trace of vacillation or inconsistency shall be discerned in what I write and say. I shall stick to one plain story.'

Little as he wished it, Macaulay soon had to tell that story to the public at large. The Committee of the Scottish Reformation Society, insisting on their privilege as electors, wrote to him in respectful terms to inquire whether, in the event of his being returned to Parliament, he was prepared to vote against the grant to Maynooth. He replied as follows:

To the Secretary of the Scottish Reformation Society.

June 23, 1852.

Sir,—

I must beg to be excused from answering the questions which you put to me. I have great respect for the gentlemen in whose name you write, but I have nothing to ask of them; I am not a candidate for their suffrages; I have no desire to sit again in Parliament, and I certainly shall never again sit there, except in an event which I did not till very lately contemplate as possible, and which even now seems to me highly improbable. If, indeed, the electors of such a city as Edinburgh should, without requiring from me any explanation or any guarantee, think fit to confide their interests to my care, I should not feel myself justified in refusing to accept a public trust offered me in a manner so honourable and so peculiar. I have not, I am sensible, the smallest right to expect that I shall on such terms be chosen to represent a great constituent body; but I have a right to say that on no other terms can I be induced to leave that quiet and happy retirement in which I have passed the last four years.

I have the honour to be
Yours &c.

T. B. MACAULAY.

The dignified minuteness with which Macaulay defined his position did not altogether meet the views of his supporters; and yet it is not easy to see how, under circumstances of such extreme delicacy, the letter could have been better written.

'*June* 30.—I heard from Adam Black, who is alarmed about the effect which my answer to the Reformation Society may have upon the election. It is very odd that, careless as I am about the result of the whole business, a certain disagreeable physical excitement was produced by Black's letter. All day I have felt unstrung; a weight at my heart; and an indescribable sense of anxiety. These are the penalties of advancing life. My reason is as clear as ever, and tells me that I have not the slightest cause for uneasiness. I answered Adam, using language much gentler than I should have used except out of consideration for him.'

'*July* 5.—I see in the Scotsman my answer to Adam,

or most of it. I hardly like this; but no doubt it was done for the best. I cannot bear anything that looks like stooping.'

It is difficult to imagine how even Macaulay could discern any trace of obsequiousness in the language which he had employed when writing to Mr. Black. 'I despair' (so the letter ran) 'of being able to use words which will not be distorted. How stands the case? I say that such a distinction is so rare that I lately thought it unattainable, and that even now I hardly venture to expect that I shall attain it; and I am told that I hold it cheap. I say that to be elected Member for Edinburgh, without appearing as a candidate, would be a high and peculiar honour,—an honour which would induce me to make a sacrifice such as I would in no other case,—and I am told that this is to treat the electors contemptuously. My language, naturally construed, was respectful,—nay, humble. If any person finds an insult in it, the reason must be that he is determined to find an insult in everything I write.'

'*July* 7.—Broken sleep at night, and then an eventful day. The Times is full of election oratory. All is right, on the whole. The City is well; the Tower Hamlets well; at Greenwich a check, but very slight; gains at Reading, Aylesbury, Horsham, and Hertford; but for the gain at Hertford I am sorry, from personal regard for Mahon. I am glad that Strutt heads the poll at Nottingham.'

'*July* 8.—Another day of excitement, following another bad night. Immediately after breakfast I went to Golden Square, and polled for Shelley and Evans. All the day was taken up with questioning and answering questions; waiting for news; and devouring it. Brooks's was quite like a beehive. We were anxious to the last about Westminster. I have had news from Black and Craig,—welcome and unwelcome. My success, if it is to be so called, seems certain. I shall not go down to the Declaration of the poll. I cannot travel all night in my present state of health; and, as to starting on Tuesday morning, and going as far as Berwick with the chance of having to turn back in case of a reverse, the thing is not to be thought of. I have held my head pretty high; and this would be a humiliation aggravated tenfold by the reserve, approaching to haughtiness, which I have hitherto maintained.'

In spite of Mr. Black's friendly apprehensions, Macaulay's high and rigid bearing had not been distasteful to the Edinburgh electors. They justly considered that the self-respect of a Member of Parliament reflects itself upon his constituents; and they were rather proud, than not, of voting for a candidate who was probably the worst electioneerer since Coriolanus. The enthusiasm in his favour was not confined to his own party. Professor Wilson, the most distinguished survivor from the old school of Scotch Toryism, as Toryism was understood by Lord Melville and Sir Walter Scott, performed the last public act of his bustling and jovial existence by going to the poll for Macaulay. At the close of the day the numbers stood:

Macaulay	1,846
Cowan	1,753
M'Laren	1,561
Bruce	1,068
Campbell	625

It is no exaggeration to say that from one end of the island to the other the tidings were received with keen, and all but universal, satisfaction.[1] Amidst the passions, and ambitions, and jealousies of a General Election that was to decide the fate of a Ministry, the combatants on both sides found time to rejoice over an event which was regarded, not as a party victory,

[1] 'All over the country the news of his election was received with a burst of joy. Men congratulated each other as if some dear friend or relation of their own had received so signal an honour. People who had never seen his face shook hands with one another in an unreasoning way on the receipt of such glorious news.'—The Public Life of Lord Macaulay. By the Rev. Frederick Arnold, B.A.

but as the triumph of intellectual eminence and political integrity. I well remember blushing and trembling with a boy's delight when Albert Smith, in two or three dashing couplets inserted offhand into the best of his admirable songs, announced that Edinburgh had at last put itself right with Mr. Macaulay; and I still seem to hear the prolonged and repeated cheering that broke forth from every corner of an audience which, unless it differed from every other London audience of its class, must have been at least three-fourths Tory.

But the very same week which honoured Macaulay with so marked a proof of the esteem and admiration of his countrymen, brought with it likewise sad and sure indications that the great labours to which his fame was due had not been undertaken with impunity. 'In the midst of my triumphs,' he writes, ' I am but poorly;' and he was one who never complained lightly. For some months past such ominous passages as these had been frequent in his journal: 'I turned over the new volumes of Thiers's book; the Austrian campaign of 1809. It is heavy. I hope that my volumes will be more attractive reading. I am out of sorts, however, at present; and cannot write. Why? I cannot tell. I will wait a day or two and then try anew.' And again: 'I wrote some of my History; not amiss; but I am not in the stream yet. I feel quite oppressed by the weight of the task. How odd a thing the human mind is! Mine, at least. I could write a queer Montaignish essay on my morbidities. I sometimes lose months, I do not know how; accusing myself daily, and yet really incapable of vigorous exertion. I seem under a spell of laziness. Then I warm, and go on working twelve hours at a stretch. How I worked a year ago! And why cannot I work so now?'

He was soon to know. On the 15th of July, two days after the election was decided, he describes himself as extremely languid and oppressed; hardly able to walk or breathe. A week later he says: 'I was not well today; something the matter with the heart. I felt a load on my breast. I was much unstrung, and could hardly help shedding tears of mere weakness: but I did help it. I shrink from the journey to Edinburgh, and the public appearance. I am sure that, in the state in which I am, I shall be forced to sit down in five minutes; if, indeed, I do not faint, which I have repeatedly expected to do of late.'

The day on which he was to address his constituents was close at hand, and there was no time to be lost. 'I sent for Bright. He came with a stethoscope; pronounced that the action of the heart was much deranged, and positively forbade me to think of going to Edinburgh. I went out, but could hardly get along with the help of my stick; so I took a cab to Westbourne Terrace, and returned in the same way. Their society and kindness keep up my spirits, which are but low. I am vexed with myself for having suffered myself to be enticed back to public life. My book seems to me certain to be a failure. Yet, when I look up any part, and read it, I cannot but see that it is better than the other works on the same subject. That, to be sure, is not saying much; for Ralph, Smollett, Kennett, Somerville, Belsham, Lord Dungannon, are all of them wretched writers of history; and Burnet, who down to the Revolution is most valuable and amusing, becomes dull as soon as he reaches the reign of William. I should be sorry to leave that reign unfinished.'

For some weeks to come Macaulay was very ill indeed; and he never recovered the secure and superabundant health which he had hitherto enjoyed. It is needless to say that the affection, which he had passed his life in deserving, did not fail him now. Lady Trevelyan saw Dr. Bright, and learned that the case was more serious than she believed her brother himself to be aware of;—a belief which was quite erroneous, as his journal proves; but under which he very willingly allowed her to lie. She took upon herself the arrangements necessary for the postponement of the Edinburgh meeting, and then accompanied Macaulay down to Clifton; where she saw him comfortably settled, and stayed with him until he began to mend.

'*Clifton*, *August* 8, 1852.—I went out, reading Julius Cæsar in Suetonius, and was overtaken by heavy rain and thunder. I could not get under a tree for fear of lightning, and could not run home for fear of bringing on the palpitation; so I walked through the rain as slowly and gravely as if I had been a mourner in a funeral. The slightest excitement or anxiety affects the play of my heart. In spite of myself my spirits are low; but my reason tells me that hardly any man living has so much to be thankful for. And I will be thankful, and firm, as far as I am master of myself. Hannah and I did not venture out after dinner, but chatted over old times, affectionately, and very pleasantly.'

'*Sunday*, *August* 15.—To Christ Church. I got a place among the free seats, and heard not a bad sermon on the word "Therefore." The preacher disclaimed all intention of startling us by oddity, after the fashion of the seventeenth century; but I doubt whether he did not find in St. Paul's "therefore," much more than St. Paul thought of. There was a collection for church building, and I slipped my sovereign into the plate the more willingly because the preacher asked for our money on sensible grounds, and in a manly manner.'

'*August* 16.—The Times brought the news of Sir James Parker's death. He died of heart-complaint. Poor fellow! I feel for him. The attack came on just as he was made Vice Chancellor. Mine came on just as I was elected for Edinburgh. Mine may, very likely, end as his has ended; and it may be for the best that it should do so. My eyes fill with tears when I think of those whom I must leave; but there is no mixture of pusillanimity in my tenderness. I long to see Hannah and Margaret. I wish that they were back again from the Continent; but I do not think that the end is so near. To-day I wrote a pretty fair quantity of History. I should be glad to finish William before I go. But this is like the old excuses that were made to Charon.'

Some fastidious critics think it proper to deny Macaulay the title of a poet; and it was a title which he did not claim. No one was more ready than himself to allow that the bay-tree does not grow kindly in the regions among which his lot had been cast. He had lived in the world, and had held his own there; and a man who would hold his own in the world must learn betimes to think, as well as write, in prose. Downing Street and Calcutta, the Edinburgh Review and the House of Commons, had exercised his judgment and curbed his fancy; but those who knew his inner mind never doubted that, however much it had been overlaid by the habits and the acquirements of an active and varied career, the poetic nature was there. If any one will read the story of the copying-clerk who found himself unexpectedly transformed into a poet, as told in Hans Andersen's exquisite little fairy tale, he will get an exact picture of the manner in which Macaulay's memory and imagination worked during the greater part of his idler hours. He positively lived upon the associations of his own past. A sixpenny print which had hung in a Clapham nursery or schoolroom gave him more real delight than any masterpiece of Reynolds. The day on which he detected, in the darkest recesses of a Holborn bookstall, some trumpery romance that had been in the Cambridge circulating libraries of the year 1820, was a date marked with a white stone in his calendar. He exults in his diary over the discovery of a wretched novel called Conscience, which he himself confesses to be 'execrable trash,' as triumphantly as if it had been a first folio edition of Shakspeare with an inch and a half of margin. But nothing caused him so much pleasure, (a pleasure which frequent repetition did not perceptibly diminish,) as a visit to any scene that he had known in earlier years. It mattered not with what period of his existence that scene was connected, or whether the reminiscences which it conjured up were gay or gloomy, utterly trivial or profoundly interesting. The inn at Durham, where he had dined badly when on circuit; the court-house at Lancaster, where as a briefless barrister he had listened to Brougham exchanging retorts with Pollock; the dining-room in Great George Street, in a corner of which he had written his articles on Lord Holland and Warren Hastings; the church at Cheddar, where as a child he had sate of a Sunday afternoon, longing to get at the great black letter volume of the Book of Martyrs which was chained to the neighbouring reading-desk, while the vicar, whom Mrs. Hannah More had pronounced to be a 'poor preacher, and not at all a Gospel minister,' was droning unheeded overhead;—these, and others such as these, were localities possessing, in his eyes, a charm far surpassing that which the most stately and famous cities derive from historic tradition or architectural splendour. Never had he a better opportunity of indulging himself in his favourite amusement of hunting up old recollections, than when he was living at Clifton, within a short drive of the cottage which had once been Mrs. Hannah More's, and under the strictest orders from his physicians to do nothing but amuse himself.

'*August* 21.—A fine day. At eleven the Harfords of Blaise Castle called in their barouche to take Margaret and me to Barley Wood. The valley of Wrington was as rich and lovely as ever. The Mendip ridge, the church tower, the islands in the distance were what they were forty years ago, and more. But Barley Wood itself is greatly changed. There has been no want of care, or taste, or respect for old recollections; but the trees would grow, and the summer-houses would decay. The cottage itself, once visible from a considerable distance, is now so completely surrounded with wood that you do not see it until you actually drive up to the door. The shrubs, which were not as high as I was at eleven years old, have become great masses of verdure; and at many points from which there once was an extensive prospect nothing can now be seen. The house, and the esplanade of turf just before it, are the least changed. The dining-room and drawing-room are what they were, the old engravings excepted, the place of almost every one of which I well remembered. The old roses run up the old trellis-work, or up trellis-work very like the old. But the Temple of the Winds is in ruins; and the root-house, which was called the "Tecta pauperis Evandri," has quite disappeared. That was my favourite haunt. The urn of Locke has been moved. The urn of Porteus stands where it did. The place is improved; but it is not the place where I passed so many happy days in my childhood.'

'*Thursday*, *August* 26.—The day rather better. I finished Herodian, and passed some hours, oddly enough, in poring on the river while the tide ran first down, and then up. After lunch to the station; met ——, and brought him home.[1] Yet I doubt whether, separated as we long have been, a close friendship can now be knitted between us. Esteem there is, and good will; and on my side a great sensibility to old recollections, and a great effusion of feeling. But he, though an excellent fellow, is so dry and cold that he never uttered, as far as I know, a word indicative of tenderness in his life. In old days I always had to make all the advances; and so it is still. He is, however, a man of learning, of ability, and of excellent principles. I learn much from his conversation; but it is only by constant effort on my part that any conversation at all is kept up between us.'

'*August* 28.—Immediately after breakfast we set off for Cheddar. My orders were not obeyed. However, I pardoned the disobedience when we came to the pass; for I never was more delighted by any scenery. The gradual rising of the heights, till the defile, from a rather tame valley, became the most awful of ravines, was wonderful. We lunched at Cheddar. To the church. I remembered the old pulpit of stone painted. I saw a book fastened to a desk, and instantly recollected that it was the Book of Martyrs. So it was. I had not been there during more than forty years. That is the only copy of the Book of Martyrs that I ever saw

[1] The following passages refer to an old school, and college, contemporary of Macaulay.

in a parish church. It is in tatters, thumbed to pieces —the first edition in black letter; but I could make out the account of Tyndal, and some prints of burnings. The parsonage was said, in 1812, to be the oldest in England, and was doubtless very old, with a hall as high as the house. It has since been pulled down. A new one has been built in very good taste, but I would rather have seen the old one. The parson, whom I remember rather shabbily dressed, and looking like a farmer, and whom Hannah More described as a poor preacher, and "not at all a Gospel minister," as the phrase ran, is now lying under a stone near his pulpit. The sexton told me that some old women of Hannah More's club were still alive; but the institution has sunk into insignificance. Home by Axbridge. Saw dear Barley Wood from the road.'

'*August* 31.—I took —— to the station, and saw him off. I respect his character and attainments, and should be delighted to be able to serve him. But, if ever there was a man who resembled the well which Wordsworth opposed to the fountain, it is ——.[1] Even at parting, after five days, during which I have been labouring to please him in every way, he did not say a word about the renewal of our old intimacy, or bid me

[1] There is a change, and I am poor;
  Your love hath been, nor long ago,
A fountain at my fond heart's door,
  Whose only business was to flow;
And flow it did; not taking heed
Of its own bounty, or my need.

What happy moments did I count!
  Bless'd was I then, all bliss above.
Now, for this consecrated fount
  Of murmuring, sparkling, living love,
What have I,—shall I dare to tell?
A comfortless and hidden well.

A well of love. It may be deep,—
  I trust it is,—and never dry.
What matter? if the waters sleep
  In silence and obscurity.
Such change, and at the very door
Of my fond heart, hath made me poor.

good bye in any other tone than that in which he would have taken leave of any common acquaintance. The truth is that we were not made for each other. The accident of our being together at school and college during seven or eight years, and having the same pursuits, produced a close intercourse, which on my side was really affectionate; on his, never. I remember how I used to follow him, to humour him, to court him; he always cold and dry. He vexed me sometimes; but I soon, from habit, and real respect for his character and attainments, came back to him, concealed my ill-temper, and defended him vehemently against some who told me that he did not use me well. As a young man he was, I think, generally regarded as quite my match, till the Union, and Charles Knight's Magazine, made a distinction between us which has ever since been widening. I have tried at fifty-one to renew the old tie, and I have found exactly the same difficulty. I have done.'

'*September* 14.—A beautiful day. After breakfast Ellis and I drove to Wrington in an open carriage and pair. We first paid a visit to the church. I recognised the old pew, and one of the epitaphs; but I missed the pulpit cloth of scarlet velvet, with an inscription in remarkably long gold letters. The sexton recollected it. There were the books chained to the desks; and, to my surprise, the Book of Martyrs was among them. I did not remember that there was one here, though I perfectly remember that at Cheddar. I saw my dear old friend's grave, with a foolish canting inscription. We then walked to Barley Wood. They very kindly asked me to go upstairs. We saw Mrs. Hannah More's room. The bed is where her sofa and desk used to stand. The old bookcases, some of them at least, remain. I could point out the very place where the Don Quixote, in four volumes, stood, and the very place from which I took down, at ten years old, the Lyrical Ballads. With what delight and horror I read the Ancient Mariner! Home, much pleased with this second visit.'

'*September* 16.—A knock, and a carriage. Who should it be but my old Trinity Tutor, Monk, the Bishop of the Diocese? I was really glad to see him, and to shake hands with him; for he was kind to me when I was young, and I was ungrateful and impertinent to him.'

'*October* 4.—I finished Uncle Tom's Cabin; a powerful and disagreeable book; too dark and Spagnoletto-like for my taste, when considered as a work of art. But, on the whole, it is the most valuable addition that America has made to English Literature.'

While in the West of England Macaulay read as much as ever, but he wrote little except his weekly letter to Mr. Ellis.

16 Caledonian Place, Clifton.

Here I am; not the worse, on the whole, for the journey. I already feel the influence of this balmy air. Remember that you are booked for the 10th of September. You will find a good bedroom; a great tub; a tolerably furnished bookcase; lovely walks; fine churches; a dozen of special sherry; half-a-dozen of special hock; and a tureen of turtle soup. I read this last paragraph to Hannah, who is writing at the table beside me. She exclaimed against the turtle: 'Such gluttons men are!' 'For shame!' I said; 'when a friend comes to us, we ought to kill the fatted calf.'' 'Yes,' says she: 'but from the fatted calf you will get only mock turtle.'

Rely on it that I shall never be in office again. Every motive is against it; avarice and ambition, as well as the love of ease and the love of liberty. I have been twice a Cabinet Minister, and never made a farthing by being so. I have now been four years out of office; and I have added ten thousand pounds to my capital. So much for avarice. Then, as for ambition, I should be a far greater man as M.P. for Edinburgh, supporting a Liberal Government cordially, but not servilely, than as Chancellor of the Duchy, or Paymaster of the Forces. I receive congratulations from all quarters. The most fervent, perhaps, are from Graham. My own feelings are mixed. If I analyse them strictly, I find that I am glad and sorry; glad to have been elected, sorry to have to sit. The election was a great honour. The sitting will be a great bore.

August 12, 1852.

I am better than when I left town, but still far from well. The weather has been against me as yet. During the last forty-eight hours I have been close prisoner to the house. The Deluge, which Lord Maidstone told us was to come after Lord Derby, has come already; so that we are cursed with Derby and the Deluge too. I have very little to complain of. I suffer no pain. My mind is unclouded. My temper is not soured. I sleep sound. I eat and drink heartily. Nothing that care or tenderness can do for me is wanting. Indeed, it would be unjust and selfish in me to accept all the sacrifices which those whom I love are eager to make.

September 25, 1852.

On Thursday I walked to Leigh Court, on the other side of the Ferry, to see the famous collection of pictures, and found that report had not done them justice. Nothing struck me so much as Rubens's Woman taken in Adultery. The figures have a look of life which I do not know that I ever saw elsewhere on canvas. On the road between Leigh Court and the Ferry, however, I saw a more delightful picture than any in the collection. In a deep shady lane was a donkey-cart driven by a lad; and in it were four very pretty girls from eleven to six, evidently sisters. They were quite mad with spirits at having so rare a treat as a ride; and they were laughing and singing in a way that almost made me cry with mere sense of the beautiful. They saw that I was pleased, and answered me very prettily when I made some inquiry about my route. I begged them to go on singing; and they all four began carolling in perfect concert, and in tones as joyous as a lark's. I gave them the silver that I had about me to buy dolls. I should like to have a picture of the cart and the cargo. Gainsborough would have been the man. But I should not like to have an execrably bad poem on the subject, such as Wordsworth would have written. I am really quite well; though my Clifton doctor adjures me not to take liberties, and Bright writes, advising me to ask for the Chiltern Hundreds.

Dr. Bright had good reason for the advice which he gave. So far from being quite well, it may be said that Macaulay never was well again. 'Last July was a crisis in my life,' he writes in March 1853. 'I became twenty years older in a week. A mile is more to me now than ten miles a year ago.' In the winter that followed his re-election at Edinburgh he had a severe attack of bronchitis; and during all his remaining years he suffered from confirmed asthma, and was tormented by frequent and distressing fits of violent coughing. One after another, in quick succession, his favourite habits were abandoned, without any prospect of being resumed. His day-long rambles, in company with Homer or Goethe, along river banks, and over ridge and common; his afternoons spent in leisurely explorations of all the bookstalls and printshops between Charing Cross and Bethnal Green; his Sunday walks from the Albany to Clapham, and from Clapham to Richmond or Blackwall, were now, during long periods together, exchanged for a crawl along the sunny side of the street in the middle hours of any day which happened to be fine. Instead of writing, as on a pinch he loved to write, straight on from his late and somewhat lazy breakfast until the moment of dinner found him hungry and complacent, with a heavy task successfully performed, he was condemned, for the first time in his life, to the detested necessity of breaking the labours of the day by luncheon. He was forced, sorely against his will, to give up reading aloud, which, ever since he was four years old, he had enjoyed even more than reading to himself. He was almost totally debarred from general society; for his doctor rarely permitted him to go out of an evening, and often forbade him to go out at all. In February 1855 he writes to Mr. Ellis: 'I am still a prisoner; I have now had nearly three months of it, with rather less range than Sir Francis Burdett had in the Tower, or Leigh Hunt at Newgate.' In May 1854 Lord Carlisle writes: 'I met Macaulay at a few breakfasts, and was sorry to think his health less good.' And again: 'It was tolerably pleasant;—always so, when Macaulay talked. The "flashes of silence" come much more frequently now.'[1]

[1] 'Yes,' said Sydney Smith, 'he is certainly more agreeable

The change for the worse in Macaulay's health was apparent even to those who watched him less closely and less anxiously than did Lord Carlisle; but, though that change might be read on his countenance, it was seldom, indeed, that any allusion to it passed his lips. Sufficient for himself, he made no demands upon the compassion of others. His equanimity had never been found wanting amidst the difficulties and reverses of a not unchequered public career; and it now stood the severer test of a life, which, for long periods together, was the life of an invalid who had to depend largely upon his own fortitude for support, and upon his own mental resources for occupation and amusement. It might have been expected that he would have made his private journal the safety-valve for that querulousness which an egotist vents upon his relatives, and a self-conscious author upon his readers. But, as each birthday and each New Year recurs, instead of peevishly mourning over the blessings which had departed from him, he records in manly terms his gratitude for those that had been left to him.

'*December* 31, 1853.—Another day of work and solitude. I enjoy this invalid life extremely. In spite of my gradually sinking health, this has been a happy year. My strength is failing. My life will not, I think, be long. But I have clear faculties, warm affections, abundant sources of pleasure.'

At very distant intervals, he gives expression, in two or three pathetic sentences, to the dejection which is the inevitable attendant upon the most depressing of all ailments. 'I am not what I was, and every month my heart tells it me more and more clearly. I am a little low; not from apprehension; for I look forward to the inevitable close with perfect serenity; but from regret for what I love. I sometimes hardly command my tears when I think how soon I may leave them. I

since his return from India. His enemies might perhaps have said before (though I never did so) that he talked rather too much; but now he has occasional flashes of silence, that make his conversation perfectly delightful.'

feel that the fund of life is nearly spent.' But, throughout the volumes of his journals, Macaulay never for a single instant assumes the air of an unfortunate or an ill-used man. One or two of his contemporaries, who grudged him his prosperity, have said that discontent was a sin to which he had small temptation. At any rate, it was a sin of which he never was guilty. Instead of murmuring and repining, we find him exhorting himself to work while it was day, and to increase his exertions as the sand sank ever lower in the glass; rescuing some from the poverty from which he long ago had set himself free, and consoling others for the pangs of disappointed ambition from which he had never suffered; providing the young people around him only too lavishly with the pleasures that he could no longer enjoy, and striving by every possible method to make their lives all the brighter, as the shadows deepened down upon his own. To admit the world unreservedly behind the scenes of Macaulay's life would be an act which the world itself would blame; but those who have special reason to cherish his memory may be allowed to say that, proud as they are of his brilliant and elaborate compositions, which in half a score of languages have been the delight of a million readers, they set a still higher value upon the careless pages of that diary which testifies how, through seven years of trying and constant illness, he maintained his industry, his courage, his patience, and his benevolence, unimpaired and unbroken to the last.

By the end of October 1852 Macaulay had recovered his health sufficiently to fulfil his engagements with the people of Edinburgh. After spending some days there in the society of his friends, both old and new, he delivered an Address in the Music Hall on the 2nd of November. He began, as became an historian, by reviewing the events of the past five years, both foreign and domestic, in a strain of lofty impartiality, to which his audience listened with respectful and not dissatisfied attention; and then, of a sudden, he changed his tone, and did his best to satisfy the expectations of his constituents by giving them forty minutes of as rattling a party speech as ever was delivered from the Westminster Hustings, or the platform of the Free Trade Hall at Manchester. And yet, party speech as it was, it occasioned very little offence in any quarter; for its easy flow of raillery was marked by an absence of asperity which betokened to experienced eyes that Macaulay, as far as modern politics were concerned, had ceased to be at heart a party man. As an author, he had met with so much indulgence from his Conservative fellow-countrymen that he was thenceforward most unwilling, as a statesman, to say anything which could hurt their feelings, or shock their sincere convictions. The most determined Tory found little to quarrel with in the spirit of the speech, and thought himself justified in laughing, as heartily as if he had been a Whig, over the jokes about Lord Maidstone's Hexameters, and the enfranchising clause which Lord Derby's Cabinet had proposed to tack on to the Militia Bill.[1]

[1] This clause gave a vote to every man who had served for two years in the militia. 'And what,' said Macaulay, 'is the qualification? Why, the first qualification is youth. These electors are not to be above a certain age; but the nearer you can get them to eighteen, the better. The second qualification is poverty. The elector is to be a person to whom a shilling a day is an object. The third qualification is ignorance; for I venture to say that, if you take the trouble to observe the appearance of those young fellows who follow the recruiting sergeant in the streets, you will at once say that, among your labouring classes, they are not the most educated, they are not the most intelligent. And then a young man who goes from the ploughtail into the army is generally rather thoughtless, and disposed to idleness. Oh! but there is another qualification which I had forgotten; the voter must be five feet two. There is a qualification for you! Only think of measuring a man for the franchise! And this is the work of a Conservative Government, this plan which would swamp all the counties in England with electors who possess the qualifications of youth, poverty, ignorance, a roving disposition, and five feet two. Why, what right have people who have proposed such a change as this to talk about—I do not say Lord John Russell's imprudence—but the imprudence of Ernest Jones, or of any other Chartist? The Chartists, to do them justice, would give the franchise to wealth as well as to poverty, to knowledge as well as to

'*Sunday, October* 31, *Edinburgh.*—This is a Sunday—a Presbyterian Sunday,—a Presbyterian Sacrament Sunday. The town is as still as if it were midnight. Whoever opposes himself to the prevailing humour would run a great risk of being affronted. There was one person, whom Christians generally mention with respect, who, I am sure, could not have walked Prince's Street in safety, and who would have addressed some very cutting rebukes to my grave constituents.[1]

'I have just been to Guthrie's Church. I had once before seen the Presbyterian administration of the Eucharist, in July 1817. There was much appearance of devotion, and even of religious excitement, among the communicants; and the rite was decently performed; but, though Guthrie is a man of considerable powers, his prayers were at a prodigious distance from those of our liturgy. There was nothing which, even for a moment, rose to the level of "Therefore with angels and archangels." There were some fine passages, in the midst of much that was bad, in his sermon. The man is a noble, honest, courageous specimen of humanity.[2] I stayed at home all the afternoon; dined

ignorance, to mature age as well as to youth. But to make a qualification compounded of disqualifications is a feat of which the whole glory belongs to our Conservative rulers.'

[1] 'Your old parson is a dunce,' Macaulay writes to one of his sisters. 'There is nothing in Homer, or in Hesiod either, about the observation of every seventh day. Hesiod, to be sure, says that the seventh day of every month (a very different thing) is a holiday; and the reason which he gives is that, on the seventh day of the month, Latona brought Apollo into the world. A pretty reason for Christians!'

[2] Some years before this, Macaulay had found himself in Scotland on a Fast-day, without the luck of being in the same town with Guthrie. 'A Kirk-fast. The place had all the aspect of a Puritan Sunday. Every shop was shut, and every church open. I heard the worst and longest sermon that I ever remember. Every sentence was repeated three or four times over, and nothing in any sentence deserved to be said once. I withdrew my attention, and read the Epistle to the Romans. I was much struck by the eloquence and force of some passages, and made out the connection and argument of some others which had formerly seemed to me unmeaning; but

alone; and stole out in the dark for a walk. The view of the Old Town at night from my windows is the finest thing in the world. They have taken to lighting their houses with gas, and the effect is wonderful.'

'*Tuesday, November* 2.—A great day. Very fine; a splendid specimen of St. Martin's little summer. I was pretty well prepared for the exhibition, and doubted only about my bodily strength. People were too considerate to call this morning. At half-past twelve came my escort, and brought me to the Hall, which was as full as it could hold. Multitudes had gone away, unable to find room. At one we went in. A vast gathering. They received me with a prodigious uproar of kindness. Black took the chair, on Craig's motion, and said a very few words. Then I rose, and spoke more than an hour; always with the sympathy and applause of the whole audience. I found that I could not go on longer; so I contrived to leave off at a good moment, and to escape from some dangerous topics. Nothing could be more successful. There was immense acclamation, in the midst of which I retired, exhausted, but relieved from a weight which has been pressing on my heart during four months. I dined at Moncreiff's with a large party. Lord Ivory talked loud, with Cowan at his elbow, about the disgrace of 1847, and the recovered character of the city. I felt for Cowan, who has been very civil to me, and to whom I have not, and never had, any unkind feeling. As I was undressing, came the proofs of the Scotsman's report of my speech. I was too much exhausted to correct them, and sent them back with a civil line to the editor, who is both a good and a clever fellow.'

The new Parliament assembled early in November, and on the 3rd of December Mr. Disraeli opened his Budget. 'It was well done,' writes Macaulay, 'both as to manner and language. The statement was lucid,

there were others, again, which I was still quite unable to comprehend. I know few things finer than the end of the First Chapter, and the "Who shall separate us from the love of Christ?"'

though much too long. I could have said the whole as clearly, or more clearly, in two hours; and Disraeli was up five. The plan was nothing but taking money out of the pockets of the people in towns, and putting it into the pockets of growers of malt. I greatly doubt whether he will be able to carry it; but he has raised his reputation for practical ability.'

During the first six weeks of his renewed experience of the House of Commons, Macaulay, as befitted a re-enlisted veteran, thought that the tone of speaking was lower than of old. But he soon had reason to change his mind. 1832 itself could boast few more animated and exciting scenes than that which was enacted during the first three hours in the morning of the 17th of December, 1852; when the Tory leader, more formidable than ever in the audacity of despair, turned to bay in defence of his doomed Budget; and when, at the moment that friends and foes alike thought that the last word had been spoken on either side, Mr. Gladstone bounded on to the floor amidst a storm of cheering and counter-cheering such as the walls of Parliament have never re-echoed since, and plunged straight into the heart of an oration which, in a single day, doubled his influence in Parliament and his popularity in the country. 'At half-past ten,' says Macaulay, 'I went to the House, and stayed till near four; generally in the library, or the division lobby, reading. I heard a little of Disraeli, who was clever, but inconclusive; and most unhandsome. A little of Gladstone, gravely and severely bitter. At last came the division. There was an immense crowd; a deafening cheer, when Hayter took the right hand of the row of tellers; and a still louder cheer when the numbers were read;—305 to 286. In the midst of the shouting I stole away, got to my carriage, and reached home just at four much exhausted.'

Then came the change of Government, with all that accompanies the process of forming a Cabinet. The stir; the gossip; the political clubs, swarming with groups of talkers, who exchange morsels of news and of criticism in eager whispers; the hansom cabs dashing about Belgravia and Mayfair, or waiting for hours together at the door of the in-coming Premier; the ever increasing discomfort of eminent statesmen who sit in their studies, waiting for the possible arrival of a Treasury messenger; the cosy dinners at the houses of the new ministers, growing larger and merrier daily, as another, and yet another Right Honourable gentleman is added to the number of the elect. 'I doubt,' says Macaulay, 'whether so many members of the two Houses have been in town on Christmas day since 1783, sixty-nine years ago. Then, as now, there was a change of Ministry in Christmas week. Indeed, there was a great debate in a full House of Commons on the 22nd of December, and Lord North made, on that occasion, a very celebrated speech.'

'*December* 20.—An eventful day. After breakfast at the Athenæum, I met Senior, who told me that he had been at my chambers to beg me to go to Lansdowne House;—that Lord Lansdowne wished to see me before half-past twelve. I went. I found him and Lord John closeted together. Lord John read us a letter which he had received from the Queen; very good, like all her letters that I have seen. She told him that she saw hope of making a strong and durable Government, at once conservative and reforming; that she had asked Lord Aberdeen to form such a Government; that great exertions and sacrifices would be necessary, and that she relied on the patriotism of Lord John not to refuse his valuable aid. They asked me what I thought. I said that I could improve the Queen's letter neither in substance nor in language, and that she had expressed my sentiments to a tittle. Then Lord John said that of course he should try to help Lord Aberdeen;—but how? There were two ways. He might take the lead of the Commons with the Foreign Office, or he might refuse office, and give his support from the back benches. I adjured him not to think of the last course, and I argued it with him during a quarter of an hour with, I thought, a great flow of thoughts and words. I was encouraged by Lord Lansdowne, who nodded, smiled, and rubbed his hands at everything that I said. I reminded him that the Duke of Wellington had taken the Foreign Office, after having been at the Treasury, and I quoted his own pretty speech on the Duke. "You said, Lord John, that we could not all win battles of Waterloo; but that we might all imitate the old man's patriotism, sense of duty, and indifference to selfish interests and vanities when the public welfare was concerned; and now is the time for you to make a sacrifice. Your past services, and your name, give us a right to expect it." He went away evidently much impressed by what had been said, and promising to consult others. When he was gone, Lord Lansdowne told me that I had come just as opportunely as Blucher did at Waterloo. He told me also, what affected me, and struck me exceedingly, that, in the last resort, he would himself, in spite of the danger to his health and the destruction of his comfort, take the Treasury, if in no other way Lord John could be induced to lead the Commons. But this he keeps wisely secret for the present.'

When the question of the leadership in the Commons had once been settled, Macaulay's interest in the personal arrangements of Lord Aberdeen's Ministry did not go further than the sympathy, not unmixed with amusement, with which he listened to the confidences of his old Whig colleagues. 'I went to Brooks's,' he says, 'and heard not a little grumbling about the large share of the spoil which has been allotted to the Peelites. I myself think that we ought to have had either the Lord Lieutenant, or the Secretary for Ireland. How glad I am that I so positively announced at Edinburgh my resolution never again to hold office! Otherwise people might fancy that I was disappointed. I went home, but wrote nothing. I never can work in these times of crisis.'

Macaulay did well to stand aside from official life.

He never opened his lips in Parliament without receiving a fresh proof that his authority there could gain nothing even from a seat in the Cabinet. Lord Hotham, a much respected member of the Conservative party, had introduced a measure whose chief object was to exclude the Master of the Rolls from the House of Commons. He had brought it unopposed through all its stages but the last; and when, on the 1st of June, 1853, he rose to move the Third Reading, he was full justified in regarding his success as a foregone conclusion. But the ultimate fate of the bill was curiously at variance with the anticipations which were entertained by its promoter, and, indeed, by all other Members of Parliament who knew that such a bill was in existence. The story was told at the time in the Leader newspaper, with a minuteness of circumstance which calls for some degree of abridgment.

'It was pleasanter talking on Wednesday, when the position of Mr. Macaulay in Great Britain was measured in a great way. On a Wednesday the House, and the Committees, are sitting at once. The talk was not interesting;—on a Wednesday it seldom is;—and you were loitering along the Committee lobby upstairs, wondering which of the rooms you should take next, when, as you paused uncertain, you were bumped against by somebody. He begged your pardon, and rushed on;—a Member; a stout Member; a man you couldn't conceive in a run, and yet he's running like mad. You are still staring at him, when two more men trot past you, one on each side, and they are Members too. The door close to you, marked "Members' Entrance," is flung open, and five Members dash from it, and plunge furiously down the lobby. More doors open; more Members rush out; Members are tearing past you, from all points, but in one direction. Then wigs and gowns appear. Their owners tell you, with happy faces, that their committees have adjourned; and then come a third class, the gentlemen of the Press, hilarious. Why, what's the matter? Matter? Macaulay is up. It was an announcement that one had not heard for years; and the passing of the word had emptied the committee rooms, as, of old, it emptied clubs.

'You join the runners in a moment, and are in the gallery

in time to see the senators, who had start of you, perspiring into their places. It was true. He was up, and in for a long speech. He was in a new place; standing in the second row above the Treasury Bench; and looking and sounding all the better for the elevation, and the clearer atmosphere for an orator. The old voice, the old manner, and the old style;—glorious speaking! Well prepared, carefully elaborated, confessedly essayish; but spoken with perfect art, and consummate management;—the grand conversation of a man of the world, confiding his learning, his recollections, and his logic, to a party of gentlemen, and just raising his voice enough to be heard through the room. Such it was while he was only opening his subject, and waiting for his audience; but, as the House filled, which it did with marvellous celerity, he got prouder and more oratorical; and then he poured out his speech, with rapidity increasing after every sentence, till it became a torrent of the richest words, carrying his hearers with him into enthusiasm, and yet not leaving them time to cheer. A torrent of words;—that is the only description of Macaulay's style, when he has warmed into speed. And such words! Why, it wasn't four in the afternoon; lunch hardly digested; and the quiet reserved English gentlemen were as wild with delight as an Opera House, after Grisi, at ten. You doubt it? See the division; and yet, before Mr. Macaulay had spoken, you might have safely bet fifty to one that Lord Hotham would have carried his bill. After that speech the bill was not thrown out, but pitched out. One began to have a higher opinion of the House of Commons, seeing, as one did, that, if the Macaulay class of minds would bid for leadership, they would get it. But it was not all congratulation. Mr. Macaulay had rushed through his oration of forty minutes with masterly vigour; but the doubts about his health, which arise when you meet him in the street,—when you take advantage of his sphinx-like reverie,

Staring right on with calm, eternal eyes,

to study the sickly face,—would be confirmed by a close inspection on Wednesday. The great orator was trembling when he sat down; the excitement of a triumph overcame him; and he had scarcely the self-possession to acknowledge the eager praises which were offered by the Ministers and others in the neighbourhood.'

Lord Hotham, with the courage of a man who had been wounded at Salamanca, did his best, in his reply, to stem the cataract of arguments and illustrations with which his unfortunate measure had been overwhelmed. But all was in vain. There were at least two hundred men in the House who had been brought there to hear Macaulay, and who knew nothing about the question except what he had thought fit to tell them. The bill was thrown out by 224 votes to 123. After the lapse of twenty years, the Act which created the Supreme Court of Judicature at length gave effect to Lord Hotham's policy. That portion of the Act, which provided for the exclusion of the Master of the Rolls from the House of Commons, was carried through the Parliament of 1873 without opposition and without discussion. 'Clauses 9 to 11, inclusive, agreed to,' is the sole notice which Hansard takes of the proceedings which reversed the decision of 1853. The enthusiastic adhesion to Macaulay's views of a House of Commons which had heard those views stated by himself, as compared with the silent unanimity, in the opposite direction, of a House of Commons which he was not there to persuade, together constitute as high, and, at the same time, as unintentional a compliment as ever was paid to the character and the genius of an orator.

The pages of Macaulay's diary prove how short a time he gave to the preparation of a speech, conspicuous even among his speeches, for wealth of material and perfection of finish. He spent exactly two mornings' work over the arrangement of what he intended to say on an occasion which he regarded as critical, for personal, as well as for public, reasons. On the evening preceding the debate, he writes: 'I thought of Lord Hotham's Bill. Craig called, and sate for two hours. His account of the state of things at Edinburgh is as good as possible. In the evening I again thought of the bill. I was anxious, and apprehensive of complete failure; and yet I must stand the hazard.'

'*Wednesday, June* 1.—A day of painful anxiety, and great success. I thought that I should fail; and, though no failure can now destroy my reputation, which rests on other than Parliamentary successes, it would have mortified me deeply. I was vexed to find how much expectation had been excited. I was sure that I should not speak well enough to satisfy that expectation. However, down I went. First we were three hours on an Irish criminal bill, and then the Judges Exclusion Bill came on. Drummond moved to put off the third reading for six months, and spoke tersely and keenly, but did not anticipate anything at all important that had occurred to me. When he sate down, nobody rose. There was a cry of "Divide!" Then I stood up. The House filled, and was as still as death;—a severe trial to the nerves of a man returning, after an absence of six years, to an arena where he had once made a great figure. I should have been more discomposed if I had known that my dear Hannah and Margaret were in the gallery. They had got tickets, but kept their intention strictly secret from me, meaning, if I failed, not to let me know that they had witnessed my failure. I spoke with great ease to myself; great applause; and, better than applause, complete success. We beat Lord Hotham by more than a hundred votes, and everybody ascribes the victory to me. I was warmly congratulated by all my friends and acquaintances. In the midst of the first tumult of applause, a note was handed to me from Margaret, to say that she and her mamma were above. I went up to them, and they were very kind, and very happy. To have given them pleasure is to me the best part of this triumph. To be sure, I am glad to have stopped a most mischievous course of legislation, and to find that, even for public conflict, my faculties are in full vigour and alertness. Craig, I hear, was in the gallery; and his kind heart will be pleased with my success. But I was knocked up.'

Just twenty years had passed since Macaulay won his spurs as a Minister by the workmanlike style in which he conducted through Parliament the India Bill of 1833. In 1853 the time had again come round for the periodical revision of our relations with our Eastern dependency; and Sir Charles Wood, as President of the Board of Control, introduced a bill which met with Macaulay's warmest approbation. He recognised the courage and public spirit which prompted the Minister to call upon Parliament to enact that a nomination for the Civil Service of India should thenceforward become the reward of industry and ability, instead of being the price of political support, or the appanage of private interest and family connection. He had himself imported into the Act of 1833 clauses which rearranged the system of appointment to the Civil Service on a basis of Competition.[1]

[1] The passage in which Macaulay explained and defended these clauses is still worth reading: 'It is said, I know, that examinations in Latin, in Greek, and in mathematics are no tests of what men will prove to be in life. I am perfectly aware that they are not infallible tests; but that they are tests I confidently maintain. Look at every walk of life, at this House, at the other House, at the Bar, at the Bench, at the Church, and see whether it be not true that those who attain high distinction in the world were generally men who were distinguished in their academic career. Indeed, Sir, this objection would prove far too much even for those who use it. It would prove that there is no use at all in Education. Education would be a mere useless torture, if, at two or three-and-twenty, a man who had neglected his studies were exactly on a par with a man who had applied himself to them,—exactly as likely to perform all the offices of public life with credit to himself and with advantage to society. Whether the English system of Education be good or bad is not now the question. Perhaps I may think that too much time is given to the ancient languages and to the abstract sciences. But what then? Whatever be the languages, whatever be the sciences, which it is, in any age or country, the fashion to teach, the persons who become the greatest proficients in those languages and those sciences will generally be the flower of the youth; the most acute, the most industrious, the most ambitious of honourable distinctions. If the Ptolemaic system were taught at Cambridge instead of the Newtonian, the senior wrangler would, nevertheless, be in general a superior man to the wooden spoon. If, instead of learning Greek, we learned the Cherokee, the man who understood the Cherokee best, who made the most correct and melodious Cherokee verses, who comprehended most accurately the effect of the Cherokee particles, would generally be a superior

But the Directors of the East India Company had then been too strong for him. They were not going to resign without a struggle the most valuable patronage which had existed in the world since the days when the Roman senate sent proconsuls and proprætors to Syria, Sicily, and Egypt. Backstairs influence in Leadenhall Street contrived that the clauses embodying Macaulay's plan lay dormant in a pigeon-hole at the Board of Control, until backstairs influence in Parliament at length found an opportunity to procure their repeal.

Unfortunately, the India Bill of 1853 fell short of Mr. Bright's expectations. That statesman, in his generous enthusiasm for the welfare of the Indian people, pronounced that the Ministerial scheme did little or nothing to promote those salutary reforms which, in his opinion, our duty as a nation imperatively demanded of us to effect without delay. The discussion in the House of Commons on the First Reading damaged the prospects of Sir Charles Wood's measure. The effect of cold water, when thrown by Mr. Bright, is never very bracing; and Macaulay was seriously alarmed for the future of a bill, the positive advantages of which, in his opinion, outweighed all defects and shortcomings whatsoever. 'I read Wood's speech,' he writes on the 6th of June; 'and thought the plan a great improvement on the present system. Some of Bright's objections are groundless, and others exaggerated; but the vigour of his speech will do harm. On the Second Reading I will try whether I cannot deal with the Manchester champion.'

The Second Reading of the India Bill was moved on

man to him who was destitute of those accomplishments. If astrology were taught at our universities, the young man who cast nativities best would generally turn out a superior man. If alchymy were taught, the young man who showed most activity in the pursuit of the philosopher's stone would generally turn out a superior man.'

When Macaulay was correcting this speech for the Press in 1853, he says with pardonable complacency: 'Every subject has a striking and interesting side to it, if people could find it out.'

the 23rd of June. Sir Charles Wood urged Macaulay to speak as early in the debate as possible; but his health was already in a state which required that special arrangements should be made in order to enable him to speak at all. The oppression on his chest would not allow him to exert his voice for some hours after eating; and, on the other hand, with his tendency to faintness, he could not go far into the evening without the support of food. There was a general wish that he should take the first place on the afternoon of the 24th; but the Ministers were not sufficiently on the alert; and, late at night on the 23rd, Mr. Joseph Hume moved the adjournment, and secured the precedence for himself.

When the morrow came, the House was crammed. Every one who could venture to remonstrate with the Member for Montrose on so delicate a subject entreated him not to stand between Macaulay and his audience; but Mr. Hume replied that his own chest was weak; that his health was as important as that of any other person; that he knew just as much about India as Mr. Macaulay; and, in short, that speak he would. In spite of his assurances that he would detain Honourable Gentlemen for no 'great length of time,' the House, who had very little compassion for an invalid who had been on his legs six times within the last ten days, received him with signs of impatience so marked that Hansard has thought it incumbent upon him to record them with greater minuteness than he has bestowed upon the speech itself. Hume, and his hearers, had different notions as to what a 'great length of time' meant; and the clock was well on towards eight before Macaulay rose. 'It was the deadest time of the evening,' he writes; 'but the House was very well filled. I spoke for an hour and a half, pretty well,—others say very well. I did not satisfy myself; but, on the whole, I succeeded better than I expected. I was much exhausted, though I had by no means exhausted my subject.'

As a consequence of his having been forced to bring

his speech to an abrupt and premature conclusion, Macaulay did not judge it worthy of a place in the Collected Edition. He was too much an artist to consent to rest his reputation upon unfinished work, and too much a man of the world to print what he had never spoken. But it would have been well if he had done some violence to his literary taste, by publishing, as a fragment, the most masterly vindication of the principle of Appointment of Competition that ever was left unanswered. He began by a few remarks about the relations between the Board of Control and the Court of Directors, and then glided off, by a happy transition, from that portion of the bill which related to the men who were to rule India from home, to that portion which related to the men who were to rule it on the spot. 'The test,' he said, 'by which I am inclined to judge of the present bill, is the probable effect it will have upon the Civil Service in India. Is it likely to raise, or is it likely to lower, the character and spirit of that distinguished body which furnishes India with its Judges and Collectors?' The question for the House to consider was the process by which these functionaries were henceforward to be selected. There had been talk of giving the Governor-General an unlimited power of appointing whom he chose.

'There is something plausible in the proposition that you should allow him to take able men wherever he finds them. But my firm opinion is, that the day on which the Civil Service of India ceases to be a close service will be the beginning of an age of jobbing,—the most monstrous, the most extensive, and the most perilous system of abuse in the distribution of patronage that we have ever witnessed. Every Governor-General would take out with him, or would soon be followed by, a crowd of nephews, first and second cousins, friends, sons of friends, and political hangers on; while every steamer arriving from the Red Sea would carry to India some adventurer bearing with him testimonials from people of influence in England. The Governor-General would have it in his power to distribute Residencies, Seats at the Council Board, Seats at the Revenue Board, places of from 4,000*l.* to 6,000*l.* a year, upon men without the least acquaintance with the character or habits of the natives, and with only such knowledge of the language as would enable them to call for another bottle of pale ale, or desire their attendant to pull the punkah faster. In what way could you put a check on such proceedings? Would you, the House of Commons, control them? Have you been so successful in extirpating nepotism at your own door, and in excluding all abuses from Whitehall and Somerset House, that you should fancy that you could establish purity in countries the situation of which you do not know, and the names of which you cannot pronounce? I believe most fully that, instead of purity resulting from that arrangement to India, England itself would soon be tainted; and that before long, when a son or brother of some active member of this House went out to Calcutta, carrying with him a letter of recommendation from the Prime Minister to the Governor-General, that letter would really be a Bill of Exchange, drawn on the revenues of India for value received in Parliamentary support in this House.

'We are not without experience on this point. We have only to look back at those shameful and lamentable years which followed the first establishment of our power in Bengal. If you turn to any poet, satirist, or essayist of those times, you may see in what manner that system of appointment operated. There was a tradition in Calcutta that, during Lord Clive's second administration, a man came out with a strong letter of recommendation from one of the Ministers. Lord Clive said in his peculiar way, "Well, chap, how much do you want?" Not being accustomed to be spoken to so plainly, the man replied that he only hoped for some situation in which his services might be useful. "That is no answer, chap," said Lord Clive. "How much do you want? will a hundred thousand pounds do?"[1] The person replied, that he should be delighted if, by laborious service, he could obtain that competence. Lord Clive at once wrote out an order for the sum, and told the applicant

[1] I have kept the amount of money as it stands in Hansard; but it is more than probable that Macaulay had said 'a hundred thousand rupees,' in accordance with the version which in his day was current at Calcutta. A hundred thousand rupees was a favourite sum with Lord Clive. When, in obedience to the absurd custom which then prevailed in society, he was called upon for a sentiment after dinner, he used to give 'Alas, and a-lackaday!' (a lass, and a lac a day).

to leave India by the ship he came in, and, once back in England, to remain there. I think that the story is very probable, and I also think that India ought to be grateful for the course which Lord Clive pursued; for, though he pillaged the people of Bengal to enrich this lucky adventurer, yet, if the man had received an appointment, they would have been pillaged and misgoverned as well. Against evils like these there is one security, and, I believe, but one; and that is, that the Civil Service should be kept close.'

Macaulay then referred to Sir Charles Wood's proposal that admissions to the Civil Service of India should be distributed according to the result of an open Competitive Examination. He expressed his satisfaction at the support which that proposal had received from the present Earl of Derby, and the surprise and disappointment which had been aroused in his mind by the nature of Lord Ellenborough's opposition to it.

'If I understand the opinions imputed to that noble Lord, he thinks that the proficiency of a young man in those pursuits which constitute a liberal education is not only no indication that he is likely to make a figure in after life, but that it positively raises a presumption that he will be passed by those whom he overcame in these early contests. I understand that the noble Lord holds that young men who gain distinction in such pursuits are likely to turn out dullards, utterly unfit for an active career; and I am not sure that the noble Lord did not say that it would be wiser to make boxing or cricket a test of fitness than a liberal education. It seems to me that there never was a fact proved by a larger mass of evidence, or a more unvaried experience than this;—that men, who distinguish themselves in their youth above their contemporaries, almost always keep to the end of their lives the start which they have gained. This experience is so vast that I should as soon expect to hear any one question it, as to hear it denied that arsenic is poison, or that brandy is intoxicating. Take down in any library the Cambridge Calendar. There you have the list of honours for a hundred years. Look at the list of wranglers and of junior optimes; and I will venture to say that, for one man who has in after life distinguished himself among the junior optimes, you will find twenty among the wranglers. Take the Oxford Calendar, and compare the list of first-class men with an equal number of men of the third class. Is not our history full of instances which prove this fact? Look at the Church, or the Bar. Look at Parliament, from the time that Parliamentary government began in this country;—from the days of Montague and St. John to those of Canning and Peel. Look to India. The ablest man who ever governed India was Warren Hastings, and was he not in the first rank at Westminster? The ablest civil servant I ever knew in India was Sir Charles Metcalfe, and was he not of the first standing at Eton? The most eminent member of the aristocracy who ever governed India was Lord Wellesley. What was his Eton reputation? What was his Oxford reputation? I must also mention,—I cannot refrain from mentioning,—another noble and distinguished Governor-General. A few days ago, while the memory of the speech to which I have alluded was still fresh in my mind, I read in the *Musæ Cantabrigienses* a very eloquent and classical ode by a young poet of seventeen, which the University of Cambridge rewarded with a gold medal; and with pleasure, not altogether unmingled with pain, I read at the bottom of that composition the name of the Honourable Edward Law, of St. John's College. I saw with pleasure that the name of Lord Ellenborough may be added to the long list of men who, in early youth, have by success in academical studies given the augury of the part which they were afterwards to play in public life; and, at the same time, I could not but feel some concern and surprise that a noblemen, so honourably distinguished in his youth by attention to those studies, should, in his maturer years, have descended to use language respecting them which would have better become the lips of Ensign Northerton,[1] or the Captain in Swift's poem, who says:

> A scholard when first from his college broke loose
> Can hardly tell how to cry *boh!* to a goose.

[1] It was Ensign Northerton who, on a certain famous occasion, commented over the mess-table upon Homer and Corderius in language far too strong for quotation, and with an audacious misapplication of epithets as ludicrous as anything in Fielding. It cannot be said that the young officer's impertinence was unprovoked. Tom Jones's observations about the Greeks and Trojans would have been voted a gratuitous piece of pedantry even in a college common-room.

Your Noveds, and Bluturchs, and Omurs, and stuff,
By George, they don't signify this pinch of snuff.
To give a young gentleman right education
The army's the only good school in the nation.
My schoolmaster called me a dunce and a fool;
But at cuffs I was always the cock of the school.

If a recollection of his own early triumphs did not restrain the noble Earl from using this language, I should have thought that his filial piety would have had that effect. I should have thought that he would have remembered how splendid was the academical career of that great and strong-minded magistrate, the late Lord Ellenborough. * * * It is no answer to say that you can point,—as it is desirable that you should be able to point,—to two or three men of great powers who, having idled when they were young, stung with remorse and generous shame have afterwards exerted themselves to retrieve lost time. Such exceptions should be noted; for they seem intended to encourage those who, after having thrown away their youth from levity or love of pleasure, may be inclined to throw their manhood after it from despair; but the general rule is, beyond all doubt, that the men who were first in the competition of the schools have been first in the competition of the world.'

Macaulay clearly explained to the House how a system of Competitive Examination, by an infallible and self-acting process, maintains, and even raises, the standard of excellence; and how a system of pass examination tends surely and constantly to lower it. He supported his view by a chain of reasoning which has often been employed since, but to which no advocate of the old mode of appointment by private interest has even so much as attempted to reply.[1] He said some-

[1] His argument ran thus: Under a system of Competition every man struggles to do his best; and the consequence is that, without any effort on the part of the examiner, the standard keeps itself up. But the moment that you say to the examiner, not, 'Shall A or B go to India?' but 'Here is A. Is he fit to go to India?' the question becomes altogether a different one. The examiner's compassion, his good nature, his unwillingness to blast the prospects of a young man, lead him to strain a point in order to let the candidate in if he possible can. That would be the case even if we suppose the dispensers of patronage left merely to the operation of their own minds; but you would have them subjected to solicitations of a sort which it would be impossible to resist. The father comes with tears in his

thing against the superstition that proficiency in learning implies a want of energy and force of character; which, like all other superstitions, is cherished only by those who are unwilling to observe facts, or unable to draw deductions. A man who has forced his way to the front of English politics has afforded at least a strong presumption that he can hold his own in practical affairs; and there has been a Cabinet, in which six out of the seven Ministers in the House of Commons, who had been educated at the English Universities, were either first class, or double first class, men.

Macaulay did not vouchsafe more than a passing allusion to the theory that success in study is generally attended by physical weakness, and dearth of courage and animal spirits. As if a good place in an examination list was any worse test of a sound constitution than the possession of family or political interest! As if a young fellow, who can get the heart out of a book, and concentrate his faculties over a paper of questions, must needs be less able to sit a horse, or handle a bat, and, if need be, to lead a forlorn hope or take charge of a famine-stricken district, than the son of a person of fashion who has the ear of a Minister, or the nephew of an influential constituent who owns twenty public-houses in a Parliamentary borough! The Royal Engineers, the select of the select,—every one of whom, before he obtains his commission, has run the gauntlet of an almost endless series of intellectual contests,—for years together could turn out the best football eleven in the kingdom, and within the last twelvemonth gained a success at cricket absolutely unprecedented in the annals of the game.[1] But special

eyes; the mother writes the most pathetic and heart-breaking letters. Very firm minds have often been shaken by appeals of that sort. But the system of Competition allows nothing of the kind. The parent cannot come to the examiner, and say: 'I know very well that the other boy beat my son; but please be good enough to say that my son beat the other boy.'

[1] The match in question was played on the 20th and 21st of August, 1875, against an eleven of I Zingari. Eight wickets of the Royal Engineers fell for an average of more than ninety

examples are not needed in order to confute the proposition that vigour of mind necessarily, or even frequently, goes with feebleness of body. It is not in deference to such sophistry as this that the fathers of Great Britain will ever surrender what is now the acknowledged birthright of their sons,—the privilege of doing their country's work, and eating their country's bread, if only, in a fair and open trial, they can win for themselves the right to be placed on the roll of their country's servants.

Before he sate down, Macaulay had shown how little faith his opponents themselves had in their own arguments. 'The noble Lord,' he said, 'is of opinion that by encouraging natives to study the arts and learning of Europe, we are preparing the way for the destruction of our power in India. I am utterly at a loss to understand how, while contemning education when it is given to Europeans, he should regard it with dread when it is given to natives. This training, we are told, makes a European into a bookworm, a twaddler, a man unfit for the active duties of life; but give the same education to the Hindoo, and it arms him with such an accession of intellectual strength, that an established Government, with an army of 250,000 men, backed by the whole military and naval force of England, are to go down inevitably before its irresistible power.'

Macaulay had done his duty by India; and it now remained for him to show his gratitude to his constituents. The Established Church in Edinburgh was mainly supported by the proceeds of a local impost which went by the name of the Annuity Tax. This tax was paid as reluctantly as Church Rates were paid in England during the ten years that preceded their abolition; and, indeed, even more reluctantly; for it was levied on an inequitable and oppressive system. In the Session of 1853 a bill was before Parliament which embodied a scheme for providing the stipends

runs a wicket; and this stupendous score was made against good bowling and excellent fielding.

of the Edinburgh clergy by a less unjust, or, at any rate, a less invidious method. The bill was supported on grounds of expediency by the Lord Provost and the majority of the Town Council; but it was vigorously opposed by that party which objected on principle to making grants of public money for religious purposes, of any amount, and under any disguise, whatsoever. Macaulay, who, as might be expected, took the Whig view of the matter, was very glad to have an opportunity of obliging his supporters, and not sorry to say his say on the general question of Church and State. On the 18th of July, (during which month he was rusticating at Tunbridge Wells,) he records his intention of trying 'to make a Lysias-like speech on it.' It is not easy for a Scotch member, who knows by experience what an Annuity Tax debate is, to picture for himself the figure which an old Greek orator would make in so grim an argument. There is, indeed, very little in common between the controversies which engage the British Parliament on a Wednesday afternoon, and the glowing topics of war, and diplomacy, and high imperial statecraft, that were discussed on a spring or autumn morning beneath the shadow of the Parthenon, and in full view of Pentelicus and Hymettus.[1]

'*July* 19.—I was early at the railway station. On reaching town, I drove instantly to the House of Commons, and found the Lord Provost, Baillie Morrison, and Maitland, in the lobby, and had a short talk with them. There is a ridiculous mistake in the votes. Some fool has given an absurd notice about yachting,

[1] It is probable that, by the epithet 'Lysias-like,' Macaulay meant nothing more than a short, unpretentious speech, on which he should bestow less pains than usual. He only began to think the subject over on the day preceding the debate; and on that day he likewise wrote out a good part of his speech of the 28th of February 1832, on the Representation of the Tower Hamlets; finished the Nigrinus of Lucian; and began to read Plato's Gorgias, which he pronounced to be 'my favourite dialogue, or nearly so, since my college days.'

and my name has been put to it. At twelve business began. The Lord Advocate opened the matter; and then Smith, the member for Stockport, made a strong speech against the Edinburgh clergy, and proposed to read the bill again on that day three months. Hadfield seconded him; and I followed Hadfield, speaking without any preparation as to language, but with perfect fluency, and with considerable effect. I was heartily glad to have got it over. I have now done the handsome thing by my constituents. The bitterness of the voluntaries surprised me. I have no particular love for establishments, or for priests; but I was irritated, and even disgusted, by the violence with which the bill was assailed.'

It was the old Maynooth difficulty under a new aspect. 'There is a rumour,' said Mr. Hadfield, 'that the Right Honourable and eloquent Gentleman, the Member for Edinburgh, intends to give his support to the bill; and curious shall I be to hear a defence of it from such eloquent lips. No man has more to lose in character, either in this House or the country, than the Right Honourable Gentleman.' 'The Honourable Member for Sheffield,' replied Macaulay, 'must expect to hear nothing that deserves the name of eloquence from me.' In truth his speech was framed with the view of convincing, rather than of dazzling, his audience; and the peroration, (if so it might be called,) contained nothing which could arouse the disapprobation of even the most resolute voluntary. 'The unpopularity of an Established Church is a very different thing from the unpopularity of the preventive service, of the army, of the police. The police, the army, and the coastguard may be unpopular from the nature of the work which they have to do; but of the Church it may be said that it is worse than useless if it is unpopular; for it exists only to inspire affection and respect; and, if it inspires feelings of a character opposite to respect and affection, it had better not exist at all. Most earnestly, therefore, I implore the House not to support an institution, which is useless unless it is beloved, by means which can only cause it to be hated.'

These were the last words which Macaulay spoke in the House of Commons. It would have been well for his comfort if, to use a favourite quotation of his own, he had never again quitted for politics 'la maison d'Aristippe, le jardin d'Epicure.' The first two debates in which he took part after his return to Parliament proved to him by infallible indications that he must renounce the career of an orator, unless he was prepared to incur a risk which no man has a right to run. The biographer of another famous student [1] has told us that 'when the brain is preoccupied, and the energy is drawn off into books, calls for efforts of external attention alarm and distress;' and to distress of that nature the state of his heart rendered Macaulay peculiarly susceptible. He had at every period of his career his full share in those tremors of anticipation from which no good speaker is free,—the nature of which it is hard to analyse, and harder still to reconcile with reason and experience; and during his later years his strength was quite unequal to the exertion and excitement of the speech itself.[2] When he re-entered the House of Commons in 1852, he had no intention of again aspiring to be a leader; and he very soon was taught that he must not even hope to count as an effective among the rank and file of politicians. He was slow to learn so painful a lesson. As regarded his attendance at Westminster, the indulgence of his constituents knew no bounds; but he himself had very little inclination to presume upon that indulgence. In the matter of party divisions, Macaulay's conscience was still that of a Whig who had served through the Committee of the Great Reform Bill, and who had sat in the Parliament of Lord Melbourne, when a vote

[1] Isaac Casaubon.

[2] 'This speech,' he writes when the Indian debate of June 1853 was in prospect, 'which I must make, and which for many reasons cannot be good, troubles me.' And again: 'I thought all day over my speech. I was painfully anxious; although, as usual, I recovered courage as the time drew near.'

was a vote, and the fate of the Ministry trembled daily in the balance. But the very first late night in the winter session of 1852 showed him that he was no longer the man of 1832 and 1841. On the 26th of November he writes: 'We divided twice, and a very wearisome business it was. I walked slowly home at two in the morning, and got to bed much exhausted. A few such nights will make it necessary for me to go to Clifton again.' After the defeat of Mr. Disraeli's Budget, he says: 'I did not seem to be much the worse for yesterday's exertion until I went out; and then I found myself very weak, and felt as I used to do at Clifton.' On an evening in January he writes: 'I was in pain and very poorly. I went down to the House, and paired. On my return, just as I was getting into bed, I received a note from Hayter to say that he had paired me. I was very unwilling to go out at that hour, and afraid of the night air; but I have a horror of the least suspicion of foul play; so I dressed, and went again to the House; settled the matter about the pairs; and came back at near twelve o'clock.' [1]

If it had been a question of duty, Macaulay would have cared little whether or not his constitution could stand the strain of the House of Commons. He was no niggard of health and ease. To lavish on his work all that he had to give; to toil on against the advice of physicians, and the still surer and more urgent warning of his own bodily sensations; to shorten, if need be, his life by a year, in order that his History might be longer by a volume,—were sacrifices which he was ready to make, like all men who value their time on earth for the sake of what they accomplish, and not of what they enjoy. But he could not conceal from himself, and his friends would not suffer him to do so, that it was grievous waste, while the reign of Anne still remained unwritten, for him to consume his scanty stock of vigour in the tedious but exhausting routine of a political existence; waiting whole evenings for the

[1] It would, of course, be highly irregular for one member to be paired against two of his opponents.

vote, and then walking half a mile at a foot's pace round and round the crowded lobbies; dining amidst clamour and confusion, with a division of twenty minutes long between two of the mouthfuls; trudging home at three in the morning through the slush of a February thaw; and sitting behind Ministers in the centre of a closely packed bench during the hottest weeks of a London summer.

It was, therefore, with good reason that Macaulay spared himself as a Member of Parliament. He did not economise his energies in order to squander them in any other quarter. The altered character of his private correspondence henceforward indicates how carefully he husbanded his powers with the view of employing them exclusively upon his books. When writing to publishers or editors, he never again allowed his pen to revel in that picturesque amplitude of literary detail which rendered many of his business letters to Mr. Napier as readable as so many passages from Sainte-Beuve. When writing to his relations, he never again treated them to those spirited imitations of Richardson, in which he described to his delighted sisters the routs, the dinner-parties, and the debates of the London season of 1831. With Mr. Ellis he continued to correspond as frequently as ever. His letters sometimes consisted in little more than an invitation to dinner embedded in a couple of racy sentences; but for the most part they were not deficient in length. Flowing, or rather meandering on, in the easy and almost desultory style of an unrestrained familiarity,—like the talk of a bachelor, in dressing gown and slippers, over his morning coffee,—they contain occasional passages which may be read with pleasure by those who care to know Macaulay as he showed himself to his chosen friend.

'Albany: December 8, 1852.

'Dear Empson,—

I meant dear Ellis; but my mind is full of poor Empson. He is dying. I expect every hour to hear that all is over. Poor fellow! He was a most kind, generous friend to me, and as unselfish and unenvious as yourself. Longman has just been here;—sorry for Empson, and anxious about the Review.[1] I recommended Cornewall Lewis; and I have little doubt that the offer will be made to him.'

'December 13, 1852.

'Poor Empson died with admirable fortitude and cheerfulness. I find that his wife was lately brought to bed. He spoke to her, to his friends, and to his other children, with kindness, but with perfect firmness; but, when the baby was put on his bed, he burst into tears. Poor fellow! for my part I feel that I should die best in the situation of Charles the First, or Lewis the Sixteenth, or Montrose;—I mean, quite alone, surrounded by enemies, and nobody that I cared for near me. The parting is the dreadful thing. I do not wonder at Russell's saying "The bitterness of death is past." '[2]

'December 30, 1852.

'I am glad that you like Beaumarchais. The result was that the Goëzmans were utterly ruined; the husband forced to quit his office; the wife driven to a convent. Beaumarchais was *blâmé* by the Court. The effect of that *blâme* was very serious. It made a man legally infamous, I believe, and deprived him of many civil rights. But the public feeling was so strongly with Beaumarchais that he paraded his stigma as if it had been a mark of honour. He gave himself such airs that somebody said to him, "Monsieur, ce n'est pas assez que d'être blâmé: il faut être modeste." Do you see the old finesse of this untranslatable *mot*? What a quantity of French words I have used! I suppose that the subject Frenchifies my style.[3]

[1] Mr. Empson had succeeded Mr. Napier as editor of the Edinburgh Review.

[2] The famous scene between Lord Russell and his wife is described, briefly enough, by Hume. 'With a tender and decent composure they took leave of each other on the day of his execution. "The bitterness of death is now past," said he, when he turned from her.'

[3] M. Goëzman was the judge who threw Beaumarchais over after Madame Goëzman had accepted a present from him. The unsuccessful suitor got his present back, 'and those who had disappointed him probably thought that he would not, for the mere gratification of his malevolence, make public a transaction which was discreditable to himself as well as to them. They knew little of him. He soon taught them to

'I am disengaged all next week. Fix some day for dining with me in honour of 1853. I hope that it will be as happy a year as, in spite of some bodily suffering, 1852 has been to me. It is odd that, though time is stealing from me perceptibly, my vigour and my pleasures, I am growing happier and happier. As Milnes says, It is shocking, it is scandalous, to enjoy life as I do.'

'Albany: July 11, 1853.

'Read Haydon's memoirs. Haydon was exactly the vulgar idea of a man of genius. He had all the morbid peculiarities which are supposed by fools to belong to intellectual superiority,—eccentricity, jealousy, caprice, infinite disdain for other men; and yet he was as poor, commonplace, a creature as any in the world. He painted signs, and gave himself more airs than if he had painted the Cartoons. * * * Whether you struck him or stroked him, starved him or fed him, he snapped at your hand in just the same way. He would beg you in piteous accents to buy an acre and a half of canvas that he had spoiled. Some good-natured Lord asks the price. Haydon demands a hundred guineas. His Lordship gives the money out of mere charity, and is rewarded by some such entry as this in Haydon's journal: "A hundred guineas, and for such a work! I expected that, for very shame, he would have made it a thousand. But he is a mean, sordid wretch." In the meantime the purchaser is looking out for the most retired spot in his house to hide the huge daub which he has bought, for ten times its value, out of mere compassion.'

'Tunbridge Wells: July 28, 1853.

'I hope that you are looking forward to our tour. On Tuesday the 23rd I shall be at the Albany, and shall proceed to hire a courier, and to get passports. My present notion of a route is Dover; Ostend; Cologne; the Rhine to Strasburg; the railway to Basle; voiture or diligence to Berne, and from Berne to Lausanne; steamboat on the Lake of Geneva; post to Lyons; up the Saône by steam to Châlons; railway to Paris; three or four days at Paris, and back to London in one day. But I shall readily agree to

curse the day in which they had dared to trifle with a man of so revengeful and turbulent a spirit, of such dauntless effrontery, and of such eminent talents for controversy and satire.' Macaulay's account of the Goëzman scandal, in his essay on Bacon, makes it evident that to write about Beaumarchais did not necessarily Frenchify his style.

any modification which you may propose. We could easily, I think, do all this, and be in town on the 18th of September with a great stock of pleasant recollections, and images of fine objects, natural and artificial. I dare say you will despise me for saying that, on the whole, I expect more pleasure from the Cathedrals of Cologne, and Strasburg, than from the Bernese Alps, or the Lake of Geneva.'[1]

'Tunbridge Wells: August 16, 1853.

'I am glad to find that we shall have three clear weeks for our expedition. I hope to secure Wolmar. At all events I shall have a good courier. I can afford to indulge myself; for Longman informs me that he shall have more than thirteen hundred pounds to pay me on the 1st of December, besides five hundred pounds in the first week of January; so that my whole income this year will be about three thousand six hundred pounds, clear of property tax. Like Dogberry, I shall have two gowns, and everything handsome about me. But alas! like Dogberry I have had losses. The East India Company is going to pay me off some thousands; and I must take four per cent. instead of five, and be thankful even to get four. How justly has an ancient poet observed that

Crescentem sequitur cura pecuniam!

However, as my Lord Smart says, "Hang saving! We'll have a penn'orth of cheese."[1] I say, "Hang saving! We'll have a jolly three weeks on the Continent."

[1] Like many other people, Macaulay was disappointed with the Cathedral of Cologne. 'My expectations,' he says in his journal, 'had been raised too high, and perhaps nothing could quite have satisfied me. It will never be equal to St. Ouen, and, I think, hardly to York Minster.' Of the tower at Strasburg he writes: 'I thought it the most exquisite morsel of Gothic architecture that I ever saw. The interior is grand, but has faults. The side aisles are too broad for their height. Even the central aisle would be better if it were narrower. The end of the vista is wretched. Nevertheless, it is a Church of the first rank.' He thoroughly enjoyed his tour. 'So ends this journal of my travels. Very pleasant travels they were. I had good health, generally good weather, a good friend, and a good servant.'

[2] Lord Smart is one of the characters in Swift's 'Polite Conversations;' a book strangely neglected by a generation which ransacks the world from California to Calcutta for something to laugh at.

'I send you a treasure. I do believe that it is the autograph of the great Robert Montgomery. Pray let me have it again. I would not lose such a jewel on any account. I have read it, as Mr. Montgomery desires, in the presence of God; and in the presence of God I pronounce it to be incomparable.[1]

'Glorious news! Robert Montgomery writes to Longman that there is a point at which human patience must give way. Since the resignation and Christian fortitude of a quarter of a century have made no impression on the hard heart and darkened conscience of Mr. Macaulay, an injured poet must appeal to the laws of his country, which will doubtless give him a redress the more signal because he has been so slow to ask for it. I retain you. Consider yourself as fee'd. You shall choose your own junior. I shall put nobody over your head in this cause. Will he apply for a criminal information? Imagine Jack![2] "I have *thee graitest* respect for the very eminent poet who makes this application, and for the very eminent critic against whom it is made. It must be very satisfactory to Mr. Montgomery to have had an opportunity of denying on oath the charge that he writes nonsense. But it is not the practice of this Court to grant criminal informations against libels which have been a quarter of a century before the world."

'I send you some exquisite lines which I saw placarded on a wall the other day. The versification and diction seem to me perfect. Byrom's "My time, oh ye Muses," is not so complete in its kind.[3]

[1] 'Robert Montgomery,' Macaulay says in his journal, 'has written to ask that he may be taken out of the pillory. Never, with my consent. He is the silliest scribbler of my time; and that his book sells among a certain class is a reason for keeping my protest on record. Besides, he has calumniated me in print; and I will not seem to be bullied into a concession.'

[2] It is to be feared that this unceremonious reference is to no less a personage than Lord Campbell.

[3] Byrom's lines,

> My time, oh ye Muses, was happily spent
> When Phœbe went with me wherever I went,

were addressed to Joanna Bentley, the daughter of the great critic, and constitute the 603rd paper of the Spectator. The effect which this little poem produces upon the reader may best be described by one of its prettiest couplets; for it resembles

> The fountain that wont to run sweetly along,
> And dance to soft murmurs the pebbles among.

Although it is wrong, I must frankly confess,
To judge of the merits of folks by their dress,
I cannot but think that an ill-looking hat
Is a very bad sign of a man, for all that;
Especially now, when James Johnson is willing
To touch up our old ones in style for a shilling,
And gives them a gloss of so silky a hue
As makes them look newer than when they were new.'

In the spring of 1853 the expectation of Mrs. Beecher Stowe's visit to England created some apprehension in the minds of those eminent men who were pretty sure to come within the circuit of her observation, and quite sure to find themselves in her book of travels.

'*March* 16, 1853.—To dinner, after a long interval, at Westbourne Terrace. Gladstone, Lord Glenelg, and Goulburn. There was much laughing about Mrs. Beecher Stowe, and what we were to give her. I referred the ladies to Goldsmith's poems for what I should give. Nobody but Hannah understood me; but some of them have since been thumbing Goldsmith to make out the riddle.'[1]

A year later, Macaulay writes: 'A mighty foolish, impertinent book this of Mrs. Stowe. She puts into my mouth a great deal of stuff that I never uttered, particularly about Cathedrals. What blunders she makes! Robert Walpole for Horace Walpole. Shaftesbury, the author of the Habeas Corpus Act, she confounds with Shaftesbury, the author of the Characteristics. She cannot even see. Palmerston, whose eyes are sky-blue, she calls dark-eyed. I am glad that I met her so seldom, and sorry that I met her at all.' The passage in Mrs. Stowe's book, to which Macaulay took exception, runs as follows:

'Macaulay made some suggestive remarks on cathedrals generally. I said that I thought that we so seldom know who were the architects that designed these great buildings; that they appeared to me the most sublime efforts of human genius.

[1] The riddle is not difficult; and its solution is well worth the pleasing trouble of turning over the few dozen pages of Goldsmith's poems.

'He said that all the cathedrals of Europe were undoubtedly the result of one or two minds; that they rose into existence very nearly contemporaneously, and were built by travelling companies of masons, under the direction of some systematic organisation. Perhaps you knew all this before, but I did not; and so it struck me as a glorious idea. And, if it is not the true account of the origin of cathedrals, it certainly ought to be; and, as our old grandmother used to say, "I'm going to believe it!" '[1]

Macaulay spent part of the summer of 1853 at Tunbridge Wells. On the 11th of July he writes to Mr. Ellis that he has taken a 'house in a delightful situation. The drawing-room is excellent; the dining-room so much overshadowed by trees and a verandah that it is dark even in the brightest noon. The country looks lovely. The heath is close to the door. I have a very pleasant room for you; a large tub; half a dozen of the best sherry, and a dozen of good champagne; and Plato and Lucian.' Macaulay had known Tunbridge Wells in his boyhood; and he now found a plentiful source of enjoyment in reviving his recollections of the past. He was pleased at feeling once more beneath his feet the red brick pavement of the Pantiles; an ancient centre of social resort which, with a strange disregard for literary and historical associations whereof any town might well be proud, the inhabitants have lately rechristened by the title of 'the Parade.' As if a name that satisfied Johnson and Garrick, Richardson and Cibber, the Earl of Chatham and Mr. Speaker Onslow, was not good enough to serve for us![2] On Sundays Macaulay went to church 'in the well-remembered old building; the same that was erected in Charles the Second's days, and which the Tantivies wished to dedi-

[1] 'Sunny Memories of Foreign Lands,' Letter xix. It certainly would be difficult even to manufacture a less adequate representation than this of Macaulay's talk, either as regarded manner or matter. But Mrs. Beecher Stowe has unfortunately shown herself only too ready to rush into print when she has lighted upon what she conceives to be curious information about the private life of a great English author.

[2] The old name was restored in consequence of this remonstrance. (1908.)

cate to St. Charles the Martyr.'[1] And on more than one week-day he sat 'in Nash's reading-room, in the old corner looking out upon the heath,' and was 'amused by finding among the books the "Self-Tormentor," published in 1789, and Sally More's novel, unseen since 1816.'

But, during his stay at Tunbridge Wells, he was better engaged than in renewing his acquaintance with the dogs-eared romances of a former day which still lingered on the back shelves of the circulating library. 'I have determined,' he writes to Mr. Ellis, 'to read through Plato again. I began with the Phædrus yesterday; one of the most eloquent, ingenious, fantastic, and delicately ironical of the dialogues. I doubt whether there be any of Plato's works which has left so many traces in the literature and philosophy of Europe. And this is the more remarkable, because no ancient work is so thoroughly tainted with what in modern times is regarded as the most odious of all kinds of immorality.'[2] Some days later he says: 'I have read a good deal of Plato; and the more I read, the more I admire his style, and the less I admire his reasonings.'

[1] 'In 1665 a subscription had just been raised among those who frequented the wells for building a church, which the Tories, who then domineered everywhere, insisting on dedicating to St. Charles the Martyr.' The Third Chapter of the History contains, within the compass of a page, a pleasant little picture of the Tunbridge Wells of the Restoration, as brightly coloured as one of Turner's vignettes.

[2] 'I read Plato's Phædrus,' he says in his journal. 'Wonderful irony, eloquence, ingenuity, fancy. But what a state of morals! What a distortion of the imagination!' Macaulay felt a hearty detestation for the perverted sentiment, (to use the mildest phrase,) which disfigures some of the most beautiful works of antiquity. Below the 12th Idyl of Theocritus he writes, 'A fine poem on an odious subject;' and at the end of the 3rd Idyl, 'A pretty little poem; but it is inferior to Virgil's 2nd Eclogue, in spite of the great inferiority of Virgil's subject.' When Demosthenes rebuked his brother ambassadors by the words, '*οὐκ εἶπον ὡς καλὸς εἶ· γυνὴ γὰρ τῶν ὄντων ἐστι κάλλιστον*.' Macaulay expresses in the margin his delight at meeting with a Greek who had the feelings of a man, and who was not ashamed to avow them. 'I am glad,' he writes, 'that Demosthenes had so good a taste.'

Macaulay's diary for the month of July 1853 is full of Plato. 'I read the Protagoras at dinner. The childish quibbling of Socrates provokes me. It is odd that such trumpery fallacies should have imposed on such powerful minds. Surely Protagoras reasoned in a better and more manly strain. I am more and more convinced that the merit of Plato lies in his talent for narrative and description, in his rhetoric, in his humour, and in his exquisite Greek. The introductions to the Phædrus, the Lysis, and the Protagoras are all three first-rate; the Protagoras best.'[1] And again: 'I

[1] For the sake of readers who do not know Greek, I venture to give a very inadequate translation, or rather paraphrase, of some portion of what Macaulay calls the 'introduction' to the Protagoras. Socrates, and his friend Hippocrates, had gone to call at the house of Callias, an Athenian person of quality, much given to letters. The purpose of their visit was to have a look at three famous sophists from foreign parts, Protagoras of Abdera, Hippias of Elis, and Prodicus of Ceos. 'When we had arrived within the porch,' says Socrates, 'we stopped there to finish a discussion which had been started in the course of our walk. And I suppose that the porter heard us talking away outside the threshold; which was unfortunate; as he was already in a bad temper on account of the number of sophists who were about the premises. So, when we knocked, he opened the door, and directly he saw us he cried, "More sophists! eh! Master's not at home," and slammed the door to. We, however, persevered, and beat the panels vigorously with both hands: upon which he bawled through the keyhole. "I tell you, master's not at home." "But my good fellow," said I, "we don't want your master, and we do not happen to be sophists. We have come to see Protagoras; so just send in our names!" And then he grumbled a good deal, and let us in.

'And, when we were inside, we found Callias and his friends walking about in the corridor, seven a-breast, with Protagoras in the middle. And behind them came a crowd of his disciples, chiefly foreigners, whom the great man drags about in his train from city to city, listening with all their ears to whatever was said. And what amused me most was to observe how carefully these people avoided getting in the way of their master; for, whenever he and the rest of the vanguard came to the end and turned round, his followers parted to right and left, let him pass through, and then wheeled about, and fell into the rear with admirable regularity and discretion.

'"And after him I was aware," as Homer says, of Hippias sitting on a chair in the opposite corridor; and around him were seated on footstools Eryximachus and Phædrus, and a group of citizens and strangers. And they appeared to be

came home, and finished the Apology, and looked through the Crito. Fine they are; but the stories of the Oracle, the divine monitor, and the dream are absurd. I imagine that, with all his skill in Logomachy, Socrates was a strange, fanciful, superstitious old fellow. Extreme credulity has often gone with extreme logical subtlety. Witness some of the schoolmen. Witness John Wesley. I do not much wonder at the violence of the hatred which Socrates had provoked. He had, evidently, a thorough love for making men look small. There was a meek maliciousness about him which gave wounds such as must have smarted long, and his command of temper was more provoking than noisy triumph and insolence would have been.' Macaulay, who loved Plato for the sake of what he called the 'setting' of his dialogues, ranked them according to their literary beauty rather than their philosophical excellence. By the time that he had got through the Hippias Major and the best part of the Republic,—and had nothing before him more entertaining than the Laws, the Philebus, and the Sophistes,—he allowed his attention once more to be diverted by modern books. 'I walked on the heath,' he says, 'in glorious weather, and read the Mystères de Paris. Sue has quite put poor Plato's nose out of joint.'

The month that Macaulay passed at Tunbridge Wells was not all playtime. An event had occurred which gave him great and just annoyance, and im-

putting questions to Hippias concerning natural science, and the celestial bodies; and he, sitting on his chair, answered them in turn, and cleared up their several difficulties. And Prodicus was occupying a closet, which Callias ordinarily uses as a still-room; but, on this occasion, what with his sophists and their disciples, he was so hard put to it for space, that he had turned out all his stores, and made it into a bedchamber. So Prodicus was lying there, rolled up in an immense number of blankets and counterpanes; while his hearers had planted themselves on the neighbouring beds. But, without going in, I could not catch the subject of their conversation, though I was anxious to hear what was said, (for I consider Prodicus a wonderfully wise personage,) because his voice was so deep that the closet seemed full of a sort of humming noise which rendered his words indistinguishable.'

posed upon him a considerable amount of unexpected, though well invested, labour. 'I have,' he writes, 'some work to do at Tunbridge Wells which I had not reckoned upon. A bookseller named Vizetelly, a sort of Curll,[1] has advertised an edition of my speeches "*by Special License*," and had the brazen impudence to write to Lord Lansdowne, and to ask his Lordship to accept the dedication.' In order to checkmate this proceeding Mr. Longman advised Macaulay to prepare forthwith for publication a selection of his best speeches; and, under the stress of circumstances, he had no choice but to give an instant, though reluctant, assent. 'I found,' he says, 'that people really wished to have the speeches. I therefore, much against my will, determined to give a revised and corrected edition. The preparing of this edition will occupy me two or three hours a day during my holiday. Many of the speeches must be re-written from memory, and from the hints given by the reports. I think of adding two or three State Papers,—my minute on the education of the natives of India, and my minute on the Black Act.'[2] 'It will take some time,' he writes in his diary; 'but I do not know that I should have given that time to my History. I can retouch a speech as well in the country as in town. The History is quite a different matter.' The day after his arrival at Tunbridge Wells he fell to work, transcribing every speech from beginning to end, at the rate of from nine to fifteen printed pages a day. On July the 14th he says: 'Heaps

[1] Macaulay, who took a warm interest in the great historical scandals and mysteries of literature, had at his fingers' ends all that was known in his own day concerning the relations between Pope and the notorious publisher whom he accused of having printed his correspondence;—relations which were of a far more dubious character than his own with Mr. Vizetelly. He had a strong relish for Pope's celebrated pasquinade, the Poisoning of Edmund Curll, Bookseller; which, in its own rather questionable class, he held to be inferior only to Voltaire's 'Diatribe of Doctor Akakia.'

[2] In January 1853 he notes in his journal: 'I got from Westbourne Terrace a copy of my Education Minute of 1835, and was pleased to see it again after eighteen years. It made a great revolution.'

of letters. I sent eight or nine answers, and then employed myself upon the Reform speech of July the 5th, 1831. I wrote vigorously during several hours. I could not go out; for the rain was falling by pailfuls, and the wind blowing a hurricane. I wrote with spirit, as it seemed to me, and made a speech very like the real one in language, and in substance exactly the real one. I had half performed my task at five.' And again on the 4th of August: 'I went on with the Somnauth speech, which is among my very best. I cannot help expecting that the volume will have some success. At all events it will, I really think, deserve success.'

It was not until Mr. Vizetelly's publication appeared that his victim knew the full extent of the injury which had so gratuitously been inflicted upon him. How serious that injury was, and how peculiarly it was adapted to mortify and provoke Macaulay, may be seen in the preface to Mr. Longman's edition of the Speeches. Readers, who have a taste for strong food, will find that the time which they may spend over that preface will not be thrown away. 'The substance of what I said,' writes Macaulay, 'is perpetually misrepresented. The connection of the arguments is altogether lost. Extravagant blunders are put into my mouth in almost every page. An editor who was not grossly ignorant would have perceived that no person to whom the House of Commons would listen could possibly have been guilty of such blunders. An editor who had the smallest regard for truth, or for the fame of the person whose speeches he had undertaken to publish, would have had recourse to the various sources of information which were readily accessible, and, by collating them, would have produced a book which would at least have contained no absolute nonsense. But I have unfortunately had an editor whose only object was to make a few pounds, and who was willing to sacrifice to that object my reputation and his own.'

* * * * * *

I could fill a volume with instances of the injustice

with which I have been treated. But I will confine myself to a single speech, the speech on the Dissenters' Chapels Bill. I have selected that speech, not because Mr. Vizetelly's version of that speech is worse than his version of thirty or forty other speeches, but because I have before me a report of that speech which an honest and diligent editor would have thought it his first duty to consult. The report of which I speak was published by the Unitarian Dissenters, who were naturally desirous that there should be an accurate record of what had passed in a debate deeply interesting to them.' Macaulay, infusing into his style a certain grim humour which was not usual with him, then proceeds to give a detailed list of absurdities which had been deliberately presented to the world as having been spoken by himself. 'These samples,' he goes on to say, 'will probably be found sufficient. They all lie within the compass of seven or eight pages. It will be observed that all the faults which I have pointed out are grave faults of substance. Slighter faults of substance are numerous. As to faults of syntax and of style, hardly one sentence in a hundred is free from them.'

'I cannot permit myself to be exhibited, in this ridiculous and degrading manner, for the profit of an unprincipled man. I therefore unwillingly, and in mere self-defence, give this volume to the public. * * * I have only, in conclusion, to beg that the readers of this preface will pardon an egotism which a great wrong has made necessary, and which is quite as disagreeable to myself as it can be to them.'

By the time that Macaulay's speeches were in print he had already ceased to be a politician. Absorbed in his History, he paid little attention to what was passing at Westminster. Mr. Gladstone's plan for the consolidation of the national debt was far less to him than Montague's scheme for restoring the standard of the coinage by calling in the clipped silver; and the abortive Triennial Bill of 1692 was far more to him than the abortive Reform Bill of 1854. 'To-day,' he writes on the 13th of February, 'Lord John is to bring in his new Reform Bill. I had meant to go down, but did not venture. This east wind keeps me a prisoner. How different a world from that which was convulsed by the first Reform Bill! How different a day this from the 1st of March, 1831, an epoch in my life as well as in that of the nation!' He now was so seldom at the House of Commons that his presence there was something of an event. Old members recollect how, if ever he was seen standing behind the Speaker's Chair, some friend or acquaintance would undertake the easy task of drawing him into conversation; and very soon the space around him was as crowded as during the five minutes which precede a stand-and-fall division. He was very unwilling to continue to call himself a Member of Parliament. 'The feeling that I ought not to be in the House of Commons,' (so he wrote to Mr. Black,) 'preys upon my mind. I think that I am acting ungenerously and ungratefully to a constituent body which has been most indulgent to me.' But the people of Edinburgh thought otherwise; and the earnest and repeated solicitations of his leading supporters prevailed upon him to retain for a while the title of Representative of their city.

Although, as a statesman, his day was past and gone, Macaulay watched with profound emotion the course of his country's fortunes during the momentous years, 1854 and 1855. He was a patriot, if ever there was one.[1] It would be difficult to find anybody, whether great or small, who more heartily and more permanently enjoyed the consciousness of being an Englishman. 'When I am travelling on the Continent,' he used to say, 'I like to think that I am a citizen of no

[1] '*August* 28, 1859.—M. de C—— has thrown some scurrilous reflections on the national character of the English into one of his pamphlets. He ought not to have sent such a work to me. I was a good deal perplexed, being unwilling to act uncourteously towards a person who to me personally has shown the most marked civility; and being, on the other hand, unwilling to put up with affronts to my country in consideration of compliments to myself. I wrote him a letter which, I am sure, ought not to offend him, but which, I really think, must make him a little ashamed of himself.'

mean city.' He hailed every sign which told that the fighting strength of the nation was undecayed, and its spirit as high as ever. Long before affairs in the east of Europe had assumed a threatening aspect he had been unfeignedly anxious about the condition of our armaments. In November 1852 he writes: 'Joe Hume talked to me very earnestly about the necessity of a union of Liberals. He said much about Ballot and the Franchise. I told him that I could easily come to some compromise with him and his friends on these matters, but that there were other questions about which I feared that there was an irreconcileable difference, particularly the vital question of national defence. He seemed quite confounded, and had absolutely nothing to say. I am fully determined to make them eat their words on that point, or to have no political connection with them.'

Macaulay followed the progress of the Russian war through all its stages with intense but discriminating interest. He freely expressed his disdain of the gossip which accused Prince Albert of having played an underhand part in the negotiations that preceded the outbreak of hostilities. In a letter dated the 17th of January 1854 he says: 'The yelping against Prince Albert is a mere way of filling up the time till Parliament meets. If he has the sense and fortitude to despise it, the whole will blow over and be forgotten. I do not believe that he has done anything unconstitutional; and I am sure that those who are loudest in bawling know neither what he has done nor what is unconstitutional.' And, on the day that the Queen opened Parliament, he writes in his diary: 'I was pleased to find that the Prince was not ill received. The late attacks on him have been infamous and absurd to the last degree. Nothing so shameful since the Warming Pan story. I am ashamed for my country. However, the reaction has begun.'

The Baltic fleet sailed early in March, under the command of Sir Charles Napier, who, a few days before his departure, had been entertained at a public banquet, which was attended by some leading members of the Government. The speeches which were made upon this occasion cannot even now be read without a sensation of shame. Their tone and substance are best described by the epithet 'un-English.' It has never been the habit of British statesmen to declaim boastfully and passionately against a foreign power with whom war has not been declared, and still less has it been the way with British sailors to exult beforehand over a victory which is yet to be won. Mr. Bright referred in the House of Commons to the fact that Cabinet Ministers had been present at this unlucky festival. 'I have read,' he said, 'the proceedings of that banquet with pain and humiliation. The reckless levity displayed is, in my own opinion, discreditable to the grave and responsible statesmen of a civilised and Christian nation.' There was very little trace either of statesmanship or Christianity in Lord Palmerston's reply. He began by alluding to Mr. Bright as 'the honourable and reverend gentleman.' He was called to order for this gross violation of the ordinary courtesies of debate; but, instead of taking advantage of the interruption to recover his temper and self-respect, he continued his remarks in a strain which, though it did not justify the interference of the Speaker, was most repugnant to the taste and feeling of his brother Members. For the first and last time in his life Macaulay had nothing to say in defence of his hero. 'I went to the House on Monday,' he writes; 'but, for any pleasure I got, I might as well have stayed away. I heard Bright say everything that I thought; and I heard Palmerston and Graham expose themselves lamentably. Palmerston's want of temper, judgment, and good breeding was almost incredible. He did himself more harm in three minutes than all his enemies and detractors throughout the world would have been able to do him in twenty years. I came home quite dispirited.'

Though Macaulay was not inclined by premature jubilation to discount triumphs which were still in the future, no one was more ready to feel an Englishman's pride as soon as our army should give him something to be proud of. He had not long to wait. 'Glorious news!' he says, on the 4th of October 1854. 'Too glorious, I am afraid, to be all true. However, there is room for a large abatement. One effect, and a most important one, of these successes, is that the war, which has not yet been national in France, will become so; and that, consequently, neither the death of the Emperor, nor any revolution which may follow, will easily dissolve the present alliance.' Throughout the winter months his journal shows how constantly the dangers and sufferings of our soldiers were present to his mind, and with what heartfelt admiration he regarded each successive proof of the discipline, the endurance, and the intrepidity which those dangers and sufferings so cruelly but so effectually tested. 'I am anxious,' he writes on the 13th of November, 'about our brave fellows in the Crimea, but proud for the country, and glad to think that the national spirit is so high and unconquerable. Invasion is a bugbear indeed while we retain our pluck.' Macaulay viewed with great and increasing satisfaction the eagerness of his fellow-countrymen to make all the sacrifices which the war demanded. He was fond of reminding himself and others that the prosperity and the independence of England had not been bought for nothing, and could be retained only so long as we were willing to pay the price. A full and clear expression of this sentiment was evoked from him by the tidings of the great battle that tried, more severely than it had been tried since Albuera, that British courage, which to use his own words, 'is never so sedate and stubborn as towards the close of a doubtful and murderous day.' These were the terms in which he wrote, with the gazette containing the account of Inkermann on the table before him: 'The interest excited by the war is as great as that which in my boyish days used to be excited by the Duke of Wellington's operations. I am well pleased on the whole. It is impossible not to regret so many brave men, and to feel for the distress of so many families. But it is a great thing that, after the longest peace ever known, our army should be in a higher state of efficiency than at the end of the last war. The spirit of the soldiers, and of the whole country, is a complete guarantee against those dangers with which we were threatened two or three years ago. Nobody will be in a hurry to invade England for a long time to come.'[1]

The occasion had now arrived for carrying into effect that part of the India Act of 1853 which related to the appointment of Civil Servants by open competition. Sir Charles Wood entrusted the duty of making the necessary arrangements to a Committee of distinguished men, with Macaulay as Chairman.[2] 'I am to draw the Report,' he writes on the 1st July 1854. 'I must and will finish it in a week.' He completed his rough draft on the 7th of July; wrote it out fair on Saturday the 8th; and read it to his brother-in-law on the Sunday. 'Trevelyan,' he says, 'was much pleased;' and no wonder; for Macaulay had so framed his plan as to bring out all the strong points of the

[1] Macaulay says in a letter dated August 1857: 'Lord Panmure has asked me to write an inscription for a column which is building at Scutari, in honour of our soldiers and sailors who died in the East during the last war. It is no easy task, as you may guess. Give me your opinion of what I have written. It is, as you will see, concise and austerely simple. There is not a single adjective. So far I believe that I am right. But whether the execution be in other respects good is a matter about which I feel great misgivings.

TO THE MEMORY
OF THE BRITISH SOLDIERS AND SAILORS
WHO
DURING THE YEARS 1854 AND 1855
DIED FAR FROM THEIR COUNTRY
IN DEFENCE OF THE LIBERTIES OF EUROPE
THIS MONUMENT IS ERECTED
BY THE GRATITUDE
OF QUEEN VICTORIA AND HER PEOPLE
1857.'

[2] Macaulay's colleagues were Lord Ashburton; the Rev. Henry Melvill, the Principal of Haileybury College; Mr. Jowett; and Sir John Shaw Lefevre.

competitive system, and avoid its perils. He provided a simple but effective machinery for admitting into the service men of energy and ability, whose faculties were keen and whose acquirements were solid, and for excluding those who rested their hopes of success upon masses of half-digested heterogeneous learning.

'Nothing,' he wrote, 'can be further from our wish than to hold out premiums for knowledge of wide surface and of small depth. We are of opinion that a candidate ought to be allowed no credit at all for taking up a subject in which he is a mere smatterer. Profound and accurate acquaintance with a single language ought to tell more than bad translations and themes in six languages. A single paper which shows that the writer thoroughly understands the principles of the differential calculus ought to tell more than twenty superficial and incorrect answers to questions about chemistry, botany, mineralogy, metaphysics, logic, and English history. * * *

'The marks ought, we conceive, to be distributed among the subjects of examination, in such a manner that no part of the kingdom, and no class of schools, shall exclusively furnish servants to the East India Company. It would be grossly unjust, for example, to the great academical institutions of England, not to allow skill in Greek and Latin versification to have a considerable share in determining the issue of the competition. Skill in Greek and Latin versification has indeed no direct tendency to form a judge, a financier, or a diplomatist. But the youth who does best what all the ablest and most ambitious youths about him are trying to do well, will generally prove a superior man; nor can we doubt that an accomplishment by which Fox and Canning, Grenville and Wellesley, Mansfield and Tenterden first distinguished themselves above their fellows, indicates powers of mind, which, properly trained and directed, may do great service to the State. On the other hand, we must remember that in the north of this island the art of metrical composition in the ancient languages is very little cultivated, and that men so eminent as Dugald Stewart, Horner, Jeffrey, and Mackintosh would probably have been quite unable to write a good copy of Latin alcaics, or to translate ten lines of Shakspeare into Greek iambics. We wish to see such a system of examination established as shall not exclude from the service of the East India Company either a Mackintosh or a Tenterden, either a Canning or a Horner. We have, with an anxious desire to deal fairly by all parts of the United Kingdom, and by all places of liberal education, framed the following scale, which we venture to submit to your consideration.—'

There follows hereupon a complete list of subjects of examination, with the proportion of marks that was to be allotted to each. The Indian Government adopted this list in its integrity; and the same very practical compliment was paid to all the recommendations of the Committee, whether they related to the age of the candidates, the abolition of the Company's college at Haileybury, or to the training of the probationers during the two years which were to intervene between their first selection and their final departure for India. One other passage in the Report deserves quotation, as testifying to the confidence with which Macaulay anticipated that in nicety of honour and uprightness of character the young Civilians of the future would be inferior to no class of public servants in the world.

'We hope and believe, also, that it will very rarely be necessary to expel any probationer from the service on account of grossly profligate habits, or of any action unbecoming a man of honour. The probationers will be young men superior to their fellows in science and literature; and it is not among young men superior to their fellows in science and literature that scandalous immorality is generally found to prevail. It is notoriously not once in twenty years that a student who has attained high academical distinction is expelled from Oxford or Cambridge. Indeed, early superiority in science and literature generally indicates the existence of some qualities which are securities against vice,—industry, self-denial, a taste for pleasures not sensual, a laudable desire of honourable distinction, a still more laudable desire to obtain the approbation of friends and relations. We therefore believe that the intellectual test which is about to be established will be found in practice to be also the best moral test that can be desired.'

Macaulay had hopes, but not very strong hopes,

that the example of the Indian Government would be followed in the offices at Whitehall. 'There is good public news,' he writes in January 1864. 'The plan for appointing public servants by competition is to be adopted on a large scale, and mentioned in the Queen's Speech.' 'I had a long talk,' he says again, 'about the projected examination with Trevelyan. I am afraid that he will pay the examiners too high, and turn the whole thing into a job.[1] I am anxious on this head. If the thing succeeds it will be of immense benefit to the country.' Civil Service reform had Mr. Gladstone for a champion in the Cabinet; and the introduction of open competition had been earnestly recommended in a Report drawn up by Sir Charles Trevelyan and Sir Stafford Northcote, who had been associated together in a comprehensive and searching revision of our public departments. But it soon became evident that very few of our leading politicians had their hearts in the matter. It was one thing for them to deprive the East India Directors of their patronage, and quite another to surrender their own. The outcry of the dispensers and expectants of public employment was loud and fierce, and the advocates of the new system were forced to admit that its hour had not yet come. 'I went to Brooks's,' says Macaulay on the 4th of March, 'and found everybody openmouthed, I am sorry to say, against Trevelyan's plans about the Civil Service. He has been too sanguine. The pear is not ripe. I always thought so. The time will come, but it is not come yet. I am afraid that he will be much mortified.'

He was mortified, and had good cause to be alarmed, for his career was seriously threatened by the hostility of some of the most powerful men of the day. But he

[1] Any such danger was eventually obviated by the appointment of Sir Edward Ryan to the post of Chief Civil Service Commissioner. That truly eminent man, who to the authority and experience of age united the vigour and enthusiasm which too seldom survive the prime of life, nursed the infant system through its troubled childhood, until from a project and an experiment it had grown into an institution.

did not lose his courage or composure. Accustomed, according to the frequent fate of permanent officials, to be pushed to the front in the moment of jeopardy, and thrust into the rear in the moment of triumph, he had weathered more formidable storms than that which was now growling and blustering through all the clubs and board-rooms between Piccadilly and Parliament Street. Macaulay, who lived sufficiently behind the scenes to discern the full gravity of the situation, was extremely uneasy on his brother-in-law's account. 'The news is worse,' he writes, 'about Trevelyan. There is a set made at him by men who will not scruple to do their utmost. But he will get through his difficulties, which he feels less than I should in his place; less, indeed, than I feel them for him. I was nervous about him, and out of spirits the whole evening.' During the next few weeks Macaulay was never so depressed as when he had been spending part of his afternoon at Brooks's. Such were the views which then prevailed at the head-quarters of the great party that has long ere this identified itself with the maintenance of a system, to which, more than to any other cause, we owe it that our political morality grows purer as our political institutions become more popular;—a system which the most far-seeing of American statesmen already regard with a generous envy, knowing, as they have only too good reason to know, that it is the one and only specific against the jobbery and corruption which are fast undermining the efficiency of their administration, and debasing their standard of national virtue.[1]

[1] The whole question of patronage, as bearing upon the official system of the United States, is most ably and frankly discussed in the North American Review of January 1871. The author of the article, speaking of the proposal to introduce Competition into his own country, says distinctly: 'There should be no attempt to disguise the fact that it is the purpose of this theory of administration to prevent the public service from being used in any manner, or to any extent, as a means of party success.' It is to be hoped that this is a case in which, instead of Americanising our own institutions, we shall induce our transatlantic cousins to Anglicise theirs.

When Macaulay had finished the business of preparing his Speeches for the press, he returned to his History, and continued to work upon it almost without intermission for two years, from November 1853 onward. His labours, during this period of his life, were always too severe for his strength, and sometimes even for his happiness. He felt the strain most painfully during the early months of 1854.

'*Sunday, January* 1, 1854.—This will, I hope, be a year of industry. I began pretty well. Chapter XIV will require a good deal of work. I toiled on it some hours, and now and then felt dispirited. But we must be resolute, and work doggedly, as Johnson said. I read some of his Life with great delight, and then meditated a new arrangement of my History. Arrangement and transition are arts which I value much, but which I do not flatter myself I have attained. I amused myself with making out a Laponian New Testament by the help of a Norwegian Dictionary. With time I could learn a good deal of the two languages in this way.'

'*February* 6.—I worked hard at altering the arrangement of the first three chapters of the third volume. What labour it is to make a tolerable book, and how little readers know how much trouble the ordering of the parts has cost the writer! I have now finished reading again most of Burke's works. Admirable! The greatest man since Milton.'

'*Thursday, February* 16.—I stayed at home and did nothing. An unprofitable day. I tried to write, but had a feeling of impotency and despondency to which I am subject, but which I have not had now for some time. I sent 20*l.* to ——, and ——. I thought that these high prices might pinch them. Then I sat down doggedly to work and got on very tolerably; the state of England at the time of William's return from the Continent in 1692. I read Monk Lewis's life. A very odd fellow! One of the best of men, if he had not had a trick of writing profane and indecent books. Excellent son; excellent master; and in the most trying circumstances; for he was the son of a vile brace of parents, and the master of a stupid, ungrateful gang of negroes.'

'*March* 3.—I stayed at home all day. In the morning there was a fog which affected my breath, and made me cough much. I was sad and desponding all day. I thought that my book would be a failure; that I had written myself out; that my reputation would go down in my lifetime; and that I should be left like Hayley and other such men, among people who would wonder why I had ever been thought much of. These clouds will pass away, no doubt.'

They passed away when the warm weather came, and did not return with the returning winter. Macaulay's health was confirmed by a fine summer, spent under circumstances which exactly suited his notions of enjoyment; and, for a good while to come, he was a stronger man than he had been since his first great illness. His brother-in-law had taken a house in the village of Esher; and Macaulay accordingly settled himself, with infinite content, exactly in the middle of the only ugly square mile of country which can be found in that delightful neighbourhood. 'I am pretty well pleased,' he says, 'with my house. The cabin, for a cabin it is, is convenient.' 'Here I am,' he writes to Mr. Ellis, 'in a pleasant small dwelling, surrounded by geraniums and roses; the house so clean that you might eat off the floor. The only complaint I have to make is that the view from my front windows is blocked by a railway embankment. The Trevelyans have a very pleasant place only a mile and a half off.' Macaulay's cottage, which stood in Ditton Marsh, by the side of the high road from Kingston to Esher, was called Greenwood Lodge. An occasional extract from his journal will show how smoothly ran the current of his days.

'*July* 23, 1854.—Tremendous heat. I put the first volume of Wilberforce's Life into my pocket, went by ferry across the Thames to Hampton Court, and lounged under the shade of the palace gardens and of Bushey Park during some hours. A hot walk back. I don't know that I ever felt it hotter.'

'*August* 12.—I wrote to Longman. I think that I must take till October next. By that time the book may be not what I wish, but as good as I can hope to make it.[1] I read Dickens's "Hard Times." One excessively touching, heartbreaking passage, and the rest sullen socialism. The evils which he attacks he caricatures grossly, and with little humour. Another book of Pliny's letters. Read "Northanger Abbey;" worth all Dickens and Pliny put together. Yet it was the work of a girl. She was certainly not more than twenty-six. Wonderful creature! Finished Pliny. Capital fellow, Trajan, and deserving of a better Panegyric.'

'*September* 22.—I am glad that our troops have landed in the Chersonese. As I walked back from Esher a shower came on. Afraid for my chest, which, at best, is in no very good state, I turned into a small ale-house, and called for a glass of ginger-beer. I found there a party of hop-pickers come back from the neighbourhood of Franham. They had had but a bad season, and were returning nearly walked off their legs. I liked their looks, and thought their English remarkably good for their rank in life. It was in truth the Surrey English, the English of the suburbs of London, which is to the Somersetshire and Yorkshire what Castilian is to Andalusian, or Tuscan to Neapolitan. The poor people had a foaming pot before them; but, as soon as they heard the price, they rose, and were going to leave it untasted. They could not, they said, afford so much. It was but fourpence-halfpenny. I laid the money down; and their delight and gratitude quite affected me. Two more of the party soon arrived. I ordered another pot, and, when the rain was over,

[1] He underrated by full three-quarters of a year the duration of the work which was still before him.

left them, followed by more blessings than, I believe, were ever purchased for ninepence. To be sure the boon, though very small, was seasonable; and I did my best to play the courteous host.'

During his residence in Surrey Macaulay kept Mr. Ellis regularly informed of all that a friend would wish to know; but his letters contain little of general interest. On the 11th of July he writes:

'I have been working four or five days at my Report on the Indian Civil Service, and have at last finished it. It is much longer than I anticipated that it would be, and has given me great trouble. To-morrow I go vigorously to work on my History. I have been so busy here with my Report that I have read nothing but Comedies of Goldoni and novels of Eugene Sue.

'I walked yesterday to Hampton Court along the Middlesex bank of the Thames, and lounged among the avenues and flower beds, about an hour. I wonder that no poet has thought of writing a descriptive poem on the Thames. Particular spots have been celebrated; but surely there is no finer subject of the sort than the whole course of the river from Oxford downward;—the noble University; Clifden; Windsor; Chertsey, the retreat of Cowley; St. Anne's Hill, the retreat of Fox; Hampton Court with all the recollections of Wolsey, Cromwell, William and Mary, Belinda's hair, the Cartoons, the Beauties; then Strawberry Hill; then Twickenham and Pope's grotto; then Richmond; and so on to the great City, the forest of masts, the Tower, Greenwich Hospital, Tilbury Fort, and the Armada. Is there any river in the world which, in so short a space, affords such subjects for poetry? Not the Tiber, I am sure, nor the Seine.'

From the summer of 1854, until his third and fourth volumes were published, the composition of his History was to Macaulay a source of almost unmingled interest and delight;—'a work which never presses, and never ceases,' as he called it in a letter to his sister; 'a work which is the business and the pleasure of my life,' as he described it in the preface to his Speeches. By September 1854 he was so far forward that he thought himself justified in saying, after a visit to the Windsor collection: 'I was told that there was scarcely anything of earlier date than George I. A good hearing. I have now got to a point at which there is no more gratifying discovery than that nothing is to be discovered.' As the months went on he worked harder, and ever harder. His labour, though a labour of love, was immense. He almost gave up letter-writing; he quite gave up society; and at last he had not leisure even for his diary.

'*January* 1, 1855.—A new year. May it be as happy as the last! To me it will probably be more eventful, as it will see, if I live and am well, the publication of the second part of my History.'

'*January* 10.—I find that I am getting out of the habit of keeping my journal. I have, indeed, so much to do with my History that I have little inclination for any other writing. My life, too, is very uneventful. I am a prisoner to my room, or nearly so. I do nothing but write or read. I will, however, minute down interesting things from time to time. Some day the taste for journalising may return.'

'*January* 29, 1855.—I open this book again after an interval of near three weeks; three weeks passed by the fireside. Once I dined out,—on Tuesday the 16th at Westbourne Terrace to meet Gladstone. Nothing could be more lamentable than his account of affairs in the Crimea.

'To-night there will, I suppose, be a vote against the Government, and to-morrow a change of Administration.[1] I am content that it should be so, and well pleased that my illness dispenses me from voting. I have made great progress with my book of late, and see no reason to doubt that I shall go to press in the summer. I am now deep in Chapter XIX. Odd that

[1] On January 29 Mr. Roebuck carried his motion for a Committee of Inquiry into the condition of our army before Sebastopol, by 305 votes to 148. Lord Aberdeen at once resigned.

here, within a few yards of all the bustle of politics, I should be as quiet as a hermit; as quiet as Cowper was at Olney; much more quiet, thank God, than my old friend Hannah More at Barley Wood; buried in old pamphlets and broadsides; turning away from the miseries of Balaklava to the battle of Steinkirk, on which I was busied to-day. The fates have spun me not the coarsest thread, as old Ben says. Hannah, Margaret, Alice, Trevelyan, and George are as kind as possible. I want no more; but I have other very kind visitors. I cannot think that this can go on long. But I hope that I shall bring out my two volumes. I am conscious of no intellectual decay. My memory I often try, and find it as good as ever; and memory is the faculty which it is most easy to bring to decisive tests, and also the faculty which gives way first.'

'*November* 6, 1855.—After an interval of eight months I begin my journal again. My book is almost printed. It will appear before the middle of December, I hope. It will certainly make me rich, as I account riches. As to success I am less certain; but I have a good hope. I mean to keep my journal as regularly as I did seven years ago when the first part came out. To-day I went to call on poor Hallam. How much changed! In the evening a proof of Chapter XX came from Spottiswoode's.'

During the ensuing fortnight the entries in Macaulay's diary relate almost exclusively to the proof sheets, which generally occupied him both morning and afternoon, and to the books which he turned over for his amusement after the appearance of the lamp had given him the signal to leave his desk, and draw his easy chair to the hearth-rug. On the 13th of November, to take an instance, he read 'Welsted's Life and Remains; mostly trash. At Dinner the Love Match. In the evening Jesse's Selwyn Correspondence, Skelton's Deism Revealed, and a great deal of Bolingbroke's stupid infidelity.'

At length, on the 21st of November, he writes: 'I looked over and sent off the last twenty pages. My work is done, thank God; and now for the result. On the whole, I think that it cannot be very unfavourable. At dinner I finished Melpomene.' The first effect upon Macaulay of having completed an instalment of his own History was now, as in 1848, to set him reading Herodotus.

'*November* 23.—Longman came. All the twenty-five thousand copies are ordered. Monday, the 17th of December, is to be the day; but on the evening of the preceding Saturday those booksellers who take more than a thousand are to have their books. The stock lying at the bookbinders' is insured for ten thousand pounds. The whole weight is fifty-six tons. It seems that no such edition was ever published of any work of the same bulk. I earnestly hope that neither age nor riches will narrow my heart.'

'*November* 27.—I finished Prescott's Philip the Second. What strikes me most about him is that, though he has had new materials, and tells his story well, he does not put anything in a light very different from that in which I had before seen it; and I have never studied that part of history deeply. To-day I received from Longman the first copy of my book in the brown livery. I sent him yesterday the list of presentation copies.'

'*November* 28.—I dawdled over my book most of the day, sometimes in good, sometimes in bad spirits about it. On the whole, I think that it must do. The only competition which, as far as I perceive, it has to dread, is that of the two former volumes. Certainly no other history of William's reign is either so trustworthy or so readable.'

'*November* 29.—I was again confined to my room all day, and again dawdled over my book. I wish that the next month were over. I am more anxious than I was about the first part, for then I had no highly raised expectations to satisfy, and now people expect so much that the Seventh Book of Thucydides would hardly content them. On the other hand, the general sterility, the miserably enervated state of literature, is all in my favour. We shall see. It is odd that I should care so very little about the money, though it is full as much as I made by banishing myself for four and a half of the best years of my life to India.'

'*December* 4.—Another bleak day passed in my chambers. I am never tired of reading. Read some of Swift's Polite Conversations, and Arbuthnot's John Bull. One never wearies of these excellent pieces.'[1]

'*December* 6.—Fine, but cold. I stayed at home all day, read ten Cantos of the Morgante Maggiore, and was languidly amused. A Yankee publisher sends me very coolly an enormous folio in two closely printed columns, a Dictionary of Authors, and asks me to give my opinion of it;—that opinion of course to be printed as a puff. He has already used the opinions of Everett, Washington Irving, and others, in that way. I sent it back with a note saying that I could not form an opinion of such a work at a glance, and that I had not time for a full examination. I hate such tricks. À propos of puffing, I see that Robert Montgomery is gathered to Bavius and Blackmore. How he pestered me with his alternate cries for mercy and threats of vengeance!'

'*December* 9.—Colder and more gloomy than ever. I stayed at home, and enjoyed my liberty, though a prisoner to my room. I feel much easier about my

[1] In Chapter XXIV of his History, Macaulay calls the History of John Bull 'the most ingenious and humorous political satire in our language.' His own imitation of it well deserves a reading. It appeared first in Knight's Quarterly Magazine, in April 1824, under the title: 'Some Account of the great Lawsuit between the Parishes of St. Dennis and St. George in the Water,' and may now be found in his Miscellaneous Writings.

book; very much. I read a great deal of Photius with much zest.[1] His account of Isocrates induces me to take down Isocrates again. I have not read him since I was in India. I looked at several speeches. He was never a favourite of mine, and I see no reason to change my opinion. I have found one serious mistake in my History. I wonder whether anybody else will find it out.'

The presentation copies were delivered on the 15th of December. On Sunday the 16th, which Macaulay, as usual, spent within doors, 'Sir Henry Holland called; very kind. He had read the first chapter, and came to pay compliments, which were the more welcome because my chief misgivings are about that chapter.'

'*Monday, December* 17.—An article on my book in the Times; in tone what I wished, that is to say, laudatory without any appearance of puffing. I had letters from Stephen and Adolphus; kind; but neither of them can as yet have read enough to judge. Longman called today, and told me that they must print more copies. He was for five thousand. I insisted that there should be only two thousand.'

'*December* 18.—There came one of Longman's clerks, with news that the first two volumes of the History must be reprinted at once, as the sale of them has during the last few days been very great.[2] I wrote to

[1] Macaulay had first attacked Photius during his country rambles round Thames Ditton, without the aid of notes or of a Latin version. 'I do not get on with Photius,' he says. 'I read chiefly while walking, and my copy is not one which I can conveniently carry in my hand.' The rumour that he read Photius for pleasure was current in the Athenæum Club, and was never mentioned without awe. The very name of the Patriarch's great work, the 'Myriobiblon,' or 'Bibliotheca,' is enough for most scholars of our degenerate day.

[2] The sale of the first two volumes rose, from eleven hundred and seventy-two copies in 1854–5, to four thousand nine hundred and one copies in 1855–6; and this, be it observed, in the large library edition.

——, and ——, about money matters. I am glad that I am now able to make them quite comfortable.'

'*Sunday, December* 23.—More of Photius. He sent me to Lysias; and I read with the greatest delight some of those incomparable speeches;—incomparable I mean, in their kind, which is not the highest kind. They are wonderful,—Scarlett speaking in the style of Addison.'

'*Wednesday, December* 26.—Read Cicero de Divinatione. The second book is excellent. What a man he was! To think that the Divinatione, the De Fato, and the De Officiis, should all have been the fruits of his leisure during the few months that he outlived the death of Cæsar. During those months Cicero was leader of the Senate, and as busy a man as any in the republic. The finest of his Senatorial speeches, spoken or not, belongs to that time. He seems to have been at the head of the minds of the second order.'[1]

'*Tuesday, January* 1, 1856.—A new year. I am happy in fame, fortune, family affection,—most eminently so. Under these heads I have nothing to ask more; but my health is very indifferent. Yet I have no pain. My faculties are unimpaired. My spirits are very seldom depressed; and I am not without hopes of being set up again. I read miscellaneous trifles from the back rows of my books; Nathan's Reminiscences of Byron; Colman's Broad Grins; Strange's Letter to Lord Bute; Gibbon's Vindication, and his answer to Warburton about the 6th Æneid. Letters and criticisms still pour in. Praise greatly preponderates, but there is a strong admixture of censure. I can, however, see no sign that these volumes excite less interest than their predecessors. Fanny tells me that a sermon was preached at Brighton to my praise and glory last Sunday, and the Londonderry people seem in great glee.'

[1] Macaulay had of late been reading Cicero's De Finibus. 'I always liked it,' he says, 'the best of his philosophical works; and I am still of the same mind.'

'*Friday, January* 4.—To-day I gave a breakfast to Jowett;—Ellis; Hannah; Margaret; and Montagu Butler, and Vaughan Hawkins, young Fellows of Trinity. A pleasant party; at least I thought so. After long silence and solitude I poured myself out very freely and generally. They stayed till past one; a pretty good proof that they were entertained. I have a letter from Guizot, full of kind compliments. He asks a question about the place where the Lords received Charles the Second on May 29, 1660. It is odd that a foreigner should trouble himself about so minute a matter. I went to the Royal Institution, got down the Journals, and soon found that the Lords were in the drawing-room at Whitehall. The Commons were in the Banqueting House.'

'*Monday, January* 7.—Yesterday and to-day I have been reading over my old journals of 1852 and 1853. What a strange interest they have! No kind of reading is so delightful, so fascinating, as this minute history of a man's self. I received another heap of criticisms,—praise and blame. But it matters little. The victory is won. The book has not disappointed the very highly-raised expectations of the public. The first fortnight was the time of peril. Now all is safe.'

The event more than justified Macaulay's confidence. The ground which his book then gained has never been lost since. 'I shall not be satisfied,' he wrote in 1841, 'unless I produce something which shall for a few days supersede the last fashionable novel on the tables of young ladies.' It may be said, for the credit of his countrymen no less than for his own, that the annual sale of his History has frequently since 1857 surpassed the sale of the fashionable novel of the current year. How firm a hold that History has obtained on the estimation of the reading world is well known to all whose business makes them acquainted with the intellectual side of common English life; but the figures which testify to Macaulay's stable and increasing popularity may well surprise even the guardian of a Free Library, or the secretary of a Mechanics' Institute. Those figures shall be given in the simplest and the most precise shape. 'Round numbers are always false,' said Dr. Johnson; and a man need not be as conversant as Dr. Johnson with the trade secrets of literature in order to be aware that what are called 'New Editions' are sometimes even more misleading than round numbers. Messrs. Longman's books show that, in an ordinary year, when nothing is done to stimulate the public appetite by novelty of form or reduction of price, their stock of the History goes out of their hands at the rate of seventy complete copies a week. But a computation founded on this basis would give a very inadequate notion of the extent to which Macaulay's most important work is bought and read; for no account would have been taken of the years in which large masses of new and cheap editions were sold off in the course of a few months. 12,024 copies of a single volume of the History were put into circulation in 1858, and 22,925 copies of a single volume in 1864. During the nine years ending with the 25th of June 1857, Messrs. Longman disposed of 30,478 copies of the first volume of the History; 50,783 copies during the nine years ending with June 1866; and 52,392 copies during the nine years ending with June 1875. Within a generation of its first appearance, upwards of a hundred and forty thousand copies of the History will have been printed and sold in the United Kingdom alone.

But the influence of the work, and the fame of its author, are not confined to the United Kingdom. 'I have,' writes Macaulay, 'a most intoxicating letter from Everett. He says that no book has ever had such a sale in the United States, except, (note the exception,) the Bible and one or two school books of universal use. This, he says, he has been assured by booksellers of the best authority.'[1] On the continent of Europe, within

[1] With reference to the first two volumes of the History Macaulay wrote to Mr. Everett: 'It would be mere affectation

six months after the third and fourth volumes appeared, Baron Tauchnitz had sold near ten thousand copies; 'which proves,' writes Macaulay, 'that the number of persons who read English in France and Germany is very great.' 'The incomparable man,' (says of him Professor Von Ranke,) 'whose works have a European, or rather a world-wide circulation, to a degree unequalled by any of his contemporaries.' Six rival translators were engaged at one and the same time on the work of turning the History into German. It has been published in the Polish, the Danish, the Swedish, the Italian, the French, the Dutch, the Spanish, the Hungarian, the Russian, the Bohemian languages; and is at this moment in course of translation into Persian.

Macaulay received frequent and flattering marks of the respect and admiration with which he was regarded by the foreigner. He was made a member of the Academies of Utrecht, Munich, and Turin. The King of Prussia named him a Knight of the Order of Merit, on the presentation of the Royal Academy of Sciences at Berlin; and his nomination was communicated to him in a letter from the Baron Von Humboldt, the Chancellor of the Order.[1] Guizot wrote to inform him that he had himself proposed him for the Institute

in me not to own that I am greatly pleased by the success of my History in America. But I am almost as much puzzled as pleased; for the book is quite insular in spirit. There is nothing cosmopolitan about it. I can well understand that it might have an interest for a few highly educated men in your country; but I do not at all understand how it should be acceptable to the body of a people who have no King, no Lords, no established Church, no Tories, nay, (I might say,) no Whigs in the English sense of the word. The Dispensing power, the Ecclesiastical supremacy, the doctrines of Divine right and passive obedience, must all, I should have thought, have seemed strange, unmeaning, things to the vast majority of the inhabitants of Boston and Philadelphia. Indeed, so very English is my book, that some Scotch critics, who have praised me far beyond my deserts, have yet complained that I have said so much of the crotchets of the Anglican High-Churchmen,—crotchets which scarcely any Scotchman seems able to comprehend.'

[1] The Prussian Order of Merit is, to other honours, what its

of France. On one and the same day of February 1853 the official announcement of his election came from Paris, and his badge of the Order of Merit from Berlin.

In the following June Macaulay was presented to the degree of Doctor of Civil Law at Oxford; where he was welcomed enthusiastically by the crowd in the body of the theatre, and not unkindly even by the undergraduates, who almost forgot to enter a protest against the compliment that their University had thought fit to bestow on the great Whig writer.[1] In 1854 he was chosen President of the Philosophical Institution of Edinburgh, to the duties of which post he could give little of his time, though the institution owes to his judgment and liberality some important additions to its stock of curious and valuable books. He showed himself, however, most assiduous in his attendance at the British Museum, both as a Trustee and as a student. His habit was to work in the King's Library; partly for quiet, and partly in order to have George the Third's wonderful collection of pamphlets

founder Frederic the Great was to other kings. The following paragraph appeared lately in the 'Academy:'

'It has excited some surprise that Mr. Carlyle should have declined the Grand Cross of the Bath, after having accepted the *Ordre pour le Mérite*. There is, however, a great difference between the two. The *Ordre pour le Mérite* is not given by the Sovereign or the Minister, but by the Knights themselves. The king only confirms their choice. The number of the Knights of the *Order pour le Mérite* is strictly limited,—(there are no more than thirty German and thirty foreign Knights,)—so that every knight knows who will be his peers. In Germany, not even Bismarck is a Knight of the *Ordre pour le Mérite*. Moltke was elected simply as the best representative of military science, nor does he rank higher as a Knight of that Order than Bunsen, the representative of physical science, or Ranke the historian.'

[1] The batch of New Doctors included Mr. Grote, Mr. Disraeli, Sir Edward Bulwer Lytton, and the present Lord Derby. 'I congratulated Grote with special warmth,' says Macaulay, 'for, with all his faults of style, he has really done wonders. * * * I was pleased with Lord Derby's reception of his son. "Fili mi dilectissime," he called him. When I entered somebody called out "History of England!" Then came a great tumult of applause and hissing; but the applause greatly predominated.'

within an easy walk of his chair. He did his writing at one of the oak tables which stand in the centre of the room, sitting away from the outer wall, for the sake of the light. He availed himself of his official authority to search the shelves at pleasure without the intervention of a librarian; and, (says the attendant,) 'when he had taken down a volume, he generally looked as if he had found something in it.' A manuscript page of his History, thickly covered with dashes and erasures,—it is the passage in the twenty-fifth Chapter where Sir Hans Sloane is mentioned as 'the founder of the magnificent museum which is one of the glories of our country,' —is preserved at that museum in a cabinet, which may truly be called the place of honour; within whose narrow limits are gathered together a rare collection of objects such as Englishmen of all classes and parties regard with a common reverence and pride. There may be seen Nelson's hasty sketch of the line of battle at the Nile; and the sheet of paper on which Wellington computed the strength of the cavalry regiments that were to fight at Waterloo; and the note-book of Locke; and the autographs of Samuel Johnson's Irene, and Ben Jonson's Masque of Queens; and the rough copy of the translation of the Iliad, written, as Pope loved to write, on the margin of frayed letters and the backs of tattered envelopes. It is pleasant to think what Macaulay's feelings would have been, if, when he was rhyming and castle-building among the summer-houses at Barley Wood, or the laurel-walks at Aspenden, or under the limes and horse-chesnuts in the Cambridge Gardens, he could have been assured that the day would come when he should be invited to take his place in such a noble company.

CHAPTER XIV

1856–1858

Macaulay resigns his seat for Edinburgh—He settles himself at Holly Lodge—His house and garden—His notions of hospitality—L'Almanach des Gourmands—Country visits—Continental tours—Chateaubriand—Macaulay as a man of business—His generosity in money matters—His kindness to his relations and towards children—Picture galleries—Macaulay as an instructor—He pays a compliment to Lord Palmerston—Macaulay is made a Peer—His attachment to his old University—He is elected Lord High Steward of the Borough of Cambridge—Macaulay in the House of Lords—French politics—The Indian Mutiny—The National Fast-day—The capture of Delhi, and the relief of Lucknow—Professor Owen, and the British Museum—Literary ease—The Fifth Volume of the History—Macaulay's contributions to the Encyclopædia Britannica—His habit of learning by heart—Foreign languages—Macaulay's modes of amusing himself—The consequences of celebrity—Extracts from Macaulay's journal—His literary Conservatism—His love for Theology and Church History—His devotion to literature.

Macaulay's first care in the year 1856 was to make his arrangements for retiring from Parliament. He bade farewell to the electors of Edinburgh in a letter which, as we are told by his successor in the representation of the city, was received by them with 'unfeigned sorrow.' 'The experience,' he writes, 'of the last two years has convinced me that I cannot reasonably expect to be ever again capable of performing, even in an imperfect manner, those duties which the public has a right to expect from every Member of the House of Commons. You meanwhile have borne with me in a manner which entitles you to my warmest gratitude. Had even a small number of my constituents hinted to me a wish that I would vacate my seat, I should have thought it my duty to comply with that wish. But from not one single elector have I received a line of reproach or complaint.' This letter was despatched on the 19th of January; on the 21st he applied for the Chiltern Hundreds; and on the 2nd of February he notes in his journal: 'I received a letter from the Lord Provost of Edinburgh, enclosing an Address from the electors unanimously voted in a great meeting. I was really touched.'

And now Macaulay, yielding a tardy obedience to the advice of every one who had an interest in his welfare, began to enjoy the ease which he had so laboriously earned. He had more than once talked of shifting his quarters to some residence less unsuited to his state of health than a set of chambers on a second floor between Vigo Street and Piccadilly. At one time he amused himself with the idea of renting one of the new villas on Weybridge Common; and at another he was sorely tempted to become the purchaser of a large mansion and grounds at 'dear old Clapham.' But in January 1856 Dean Milman wrote to inform him that the lease of a very agreeable house and garden at Kensington was in the market. The immediate effect of this letter was to suggest to Macaulay the propriety of giving his old friend's book another reading. 'I began,' he says, 'Milman's Latin Christianity, and was more impressed than ever by the contrast between the substance and the style. The substance is excellent. The style very much otherwise.'[1] On the morrow he heard from the Duchess of Argyll, who, knowing the place in question as only a next-door neighbour could, urged him not to miss what was indeed an excellent opportunity. Accordingly, on the 23rd of January, he says: 'I went with Hannah and Margaret to see the house about which the Duchess and the Dean had written to me. It is in many respects the very thing; but I must know more, and think more; before I decide.' He soon made up his mind that he had lighted on the home which he wanted. Without more ado, he bought the lease; and with great deliberation, and after many a pleasant family discussion, he re-furnished his

[1] A few months after this Macaulay writes: 'I was glad to hear that a new edition of Milman's History is called for. It is creditable to the age. I began to read it again.'

new abode in conformity with his sister's taste and his own notions of comfort.

'*May* 1, 1856.—The change draws very near. After fifteen happy years passed in the Albany I am going to leave it, thrice as rich a man as when I entered it, and far more famous; with health impaired, but with affections as warm and faculties as vigorous as ever. I have lost nothing that was very near my heart while I was here. Kind friends have died, but they were not part of my daily circle. I do not at all expect to live fifteen years more. If I do, I cannot hope that they will be so happy as the last fifteen. The removal makes me sad, and would make me sadder but for the extreme discomfort in which I have been living during the last week. The books are gone, and the shelves look like a skeleton. To-morrow I take final leave of this room where I have spent most of the waking hours of so many years. Already its aspect is changed. It is the corpse of what it was on Sunday. I hate partings. To-day, even while I climbed the endless steps, panting and weary, I thought that it was for the last time, and the tears would come into my eyes. I have been happy at the top of this toilsome stair. Ellis came to dinner;—the last of probably four hundred dinners, or more, that we have had in these chambers. Then to bed. Everything that I do is coloured by the thought that it is for the last time. One day there will come a last in good earnest.'

I well remember that, about this period, my uncle used to speak of the affinity which existed between our feeling for houses and our feeling for people. 'Nothing,' he said, 'would at one time have reconciled me to the thought of leaving the Albany; but, when I go home, and see the rooms dismantled, and the bookcases empty, and the whole place the ghost of its former self, I acknowledge that the end cannot come too soon.' And then he spoke of those sad changes, the work of age and illness, which prepare us gradually, and even mercifully, for the loss of those from whom it once seemed as if we could never have borne to part. He was thinking of a very dear friend who was just then passing quietly, and very slowly, through the ante-chamber of death. On the 13th of February in this year he says: 'I went to call on poor Hallam. I found him quite prisoner to his sofa, unable to walk. To write legibly he has long been unable. But in the conversation between us,—not, to be sure, a trying conversation,—he showed no defect of memory or apprehension. Poor dear fellow! I put a cheerful face on the matter; but I was sad at heart.

> Let me not live
> After my flame lacks oil, to be the scoff
> Of meaner spirits.

Mean they must be indeed who scoff in such a case.'[1]

Macaulay was thenceforward lodged as his friends wished to see him. He could not well have bettered his choice. Holly Lodge, now called 'Airlie Lodge,'[2] occupies the most secluded corner of the little labyrinth of bye-roads, which, bounded to the east by Palace Gardens and to the west by Holland House, constitutes the district known by the name of Campden Hill. The villa, for a villa it is, stands in a long and winding lane, which, with its high black paling concealing from the passer-by everything except a mass of dense and varied foliage, presents an appearance as rural as Roehampton and East Sheen present still, and as Wandsworth and Streatham presented twenty years ago. The only entrance into the lane for carriages was at the end furthest from Holly Lodge; and Macaulay had no one living beyond him except

[1] Mr. Hallam lived into 1859. In the January of that year Macaulay wrote: 'Poor Hallam! To be sure, to me he died some years ago. I then missed him much and often. Now the loss is hardly felt. I am inclined to think that there is scarcely any separation, even of those separations which break hearts and cause suicides, which might not be made endurable by gradual weaning. In the course of that weaning there will be much suffering; but it will at no moment be very acute.'

[2] The old name has been restored by the present occupier, Mr. Stephen Winkworth. (1881.)

the Duke of Argyll, who loved quiet as much as himself, and for the same reasons.

The rooms in Holly Lodge were for the most part small. The dining-room was that of a bachelor who was likewise something of an invalid; and the drawing-room, which, from old habit, my uncle could seldom bring himself to use, was little more than a vestibule to the dining-room. But the house afforded in perfection the two requisites for an author's ideal of happiness, a library and a garden. The library was a spacious and commodiously shaped room, enlarged, after the old fashion, by a pillared recess. It was a warm and airy retreat in winter; and in summer it afforded a student only too irresistible an inducement to step from among his bookshelves on to a lawn whose unbroken slope of verdure was worthy of the country house of a Lord Lieutenant. The sward was graced by two rare and beautiful variegated elms, a noble willow, and a mulberry tree, which a century hence it will be said that he planted. Nothing else in the garden exceeded thirty feet in height; but there was in abundance all that hollies, and laurels, and hawthorns, and groves of standard roses, and bowers of lilacs and laburnums could give of shade, and scent, and colour. The charms of the spot were not thrown away upon its owner. 'How I love,' he says, 'my little paradise of shrubs and turf!' 'I remember no such May,' he writes in 1857. 'It is delicious. The lilacs are now completely out; the laburnums almost completely. The brilliant red flowers of my favourite thorn tree began to show themselves yesterday. To-day they are beautiful. To-morrow, I dare say, the whole tree will be in a blaze.' And again, a few days later: 'The rhododendrons are coming out; the mulberry tree, which, though small, is a principal object in the view of the garden from my library window, is starting into leaf.' In the following September, when fresh from a tour down the Moselle and up the Rhine, through the glen of Vaucluse, and across the pastures of the Italian Alps, he writes in high content, after his return to Holly Lodge: 'My garden is really charming. The flowers are less brilliant than when I went away; but the turf is perfect emerald. All the countries through which I have been travelling could not show such a carpet of soft rich green herbage as mine.'

The beauty of the objects around him, combined with the novel sense of possession, inspired Macaulay with an interest in small everyday matters to which he had hitherto been a stranger. He began to feel the proprietor's passion for seeing things in order within doors and without. He says in one place: 'To-day I cleared my tables of a vast accumulation of books and pamphlets. This process I must carry a good deal further. The time so spent is not time lost. It is, as Bacon would say, *luciferum*, if not directly *fructiferum*.' One of the most fortunate consequences arising from his change of residence was that, if it were only for ten minutes in the day, he accustomed himself to do something besides write, and talk, and read. It must be admitted that his efforts at gardening were sufficiently humble. Far beneath anything which is recorded of such scientific horticulturists as Pope and Shenstone, his first attempts might have aroused the mild scorn even of Wordsworth and of Cowper. 'I have ordered,' he says, 'the dead sprigs to be cleared from the lilacs, and the grass to be weeded of dandelions;' and, shortly after: 'I had an hour's walk, and exterminated all the dandelions which had sprouted up since yesterday.'[1] But he soon became more ambitious. 'I chose places for rhododendron beds,

[1] These unlucky weeds play a leading part in Macaulay's correspondence with his youngest niece. 'My dear little Alice,' he writes: 'I quite forgot my promised letter, but I assure you that you were never out of my mind for three waking hours together. I have, indeed, had little to put you and yours out of my thoughts; for I have been living, these last ten days, like Robinson Crusoe in his desert island. I have had no friends near me, but my books and my flowers, and no enemies but those execrable dandelions. I thought that I was rid of the villains; but the day before yesterday, when I got up and looked out of my window, I could see five or six of their great,

and directed the workmen to set creepers in my xystus.'[1] On Christmas Day, 1856, he writes to his sister Fanny: 'The holiday interrupts my gardening. I have turned gardener; not indeed working gardener, but master gardener. I have just been putting creepers round my windows, and forming beds of rhododendrons round my fountain. In three or four summers, if I live so long, I may expect to see the results of my care.' The easier life, which Macaulay henceforward led, gave him a fresh lease of health, or, at any rate, of comfort. 'I am wonderfully well,' he writes; 'my sleep is deeper and sweeter than it has been for years.' And again: 'I had an excellent night. What a blessing to regain, so late, the refreshing sleep of early years! I am altogether better than I have been since 1852.'

The hospitality of Holly Lodge had about it a flavour of pleasant peculiarity. Macaulay was no epicure on his own account. In his Reform Bill days, as many passages in his letters show, he enjoyed a banquet at the house of a Cabinet Minister, or a City magnate, with all the zest of a hungry undergraduate; but there never was a time when his daily wants would not have been amply satisfied by a couple of eggs with his coffee in the morning, and a dinner such as is served at a decent seaside lodging-house. He could not, however, endure to see guests, even of the most tender age, seated round his board, unless there was upon it something very like a feast. He generally selected, by a half-conscious preference, dishes of an established, and, if so it may be called, an historical reputation. He was fond of testifying to his friendliness for Dissenters by treating his friends to a fillet of

impudent, flaring, yellow faces turned up at me. "Only you wait, till I come down," I said. How I grubbed them up! How I enjoyed their destruction! Is it Christianlike to hate a dandelion so savagely? That is a curious question of casuistry.'

[1] The word 'xystus' was a reminiscence from the letters of Cicero and Pliny. According to Dr. William Smith it signifies 'an open colonnade or portico, for recreation, conversation, and philosophical discussion.'

veal, which he maintained to be the recognised Sunday dinner in good old Nonconformist families. He liked still better to prove his loyalty to the Church by keeping her Feasts, and keeping them in good company; and by observing her Fasts, so far, that is to say, as they could be observed by making additions to the ordinary bill of fare. A Michaelmas Day on which he did not eat goose, or ate it in solitude, was no Michaelmas to him; and regularly on Christmas Eve there came to our house a cod-fish, a barrel of oysters, and a chine, accompanied by the heaviest turkey which diligence could discover, and money could purchase. If he was entertaining a couple of schoolboys who could construe their fourth satire of Juvenal, he would reward them for their proficiency with a dish of mullet that might have passed muster on the table of an augur or an Emperor's freedman. If he succeeded in collecting a party of his own Cambridge contemporaries, he took care that they should have no cause to remember with regret the Trinity butteries.[1] 'I should be much obliged to you,' so he writes to Mr. Ellis, 'to lend me a bottle or two of that excellent audit ale which you produced the last time that I dined with you. You shall have in return two bottles which still require time to make them perfect. I ask this, because our party on Tuesday will consist exclusively of old fellows and scholars of Trinity; and I should like to give them some of our own nectar.'[2]

[1] Macaulay liked nothing better than a Trinity gathering. In February, 1852, he says: 'To the Clarendon at seven, where I had ordered dinner for a party of ex-fellows of the dear old College. Malden came first; then the Lord Chief Baron, Baron Parke, Waddington, Lefevre, and Ellis. We had an excellent dinner. The Dean of Durham's favourite dish, Filet de bœuf sauté au vin de Madère aux Truffes, was there. We all tried it, applauded it, and drank his health in champagne recommended by him.'

[2] The party in question turned out a complete success. '*November* 9.—Lord Mayor's Day; and I had a dinner as well as the Lord Mayor. I did my best as host. The dinner was well cooked; the audit ale perfect. We had so much to say about auld lang syne that great powers of conversation were not wanted. I have been at parties of men celebrated for wit

With regard to the contents of his cellar, Macaulay prided himself on being able to say with Mr. John Thorpe, 'Mine is famous good stuff, to be sure;' and, if my mother took him to task for his extravagance, he would reply, in the words used by another of their favourite characters in fiction, that there was a great deal of good eating and drinking in seven hundred a year, if people knew how to manage it.'[1]

But he never was so amusing as when it pleased him to season a family repast by a series of quotations from the Almanach des Gourmands;—that wonderful monument of the outrageous self-indulgence prevalent in French society during the epoch of luxury and debauchery which succeeded to the surly discomfort of the Revolution,[2] and ushered in the vulgar magnificence of the First Empire. He had by heart the choice morsels of humour and extravagance that are so freely scattered through the eight fat little volumes; and he was at all times ready to undertake the feat of detailing the ceremonies of a Parisian banquet, from those awkward complications of arrangement, 'que les personnes bien avisées ont l'attention d'abréger en mettant d'avance le nom de chaque convive sur chaque couvert, dans l'ordre de leur appétit connu ou présumé,' to the 'visite de digestion' on the morrow, the length of which was supposed to be proportioned to the excellence of the entertainment. He could follow the repast through the whole series of delicacies, from the 'potage brûlant, tel qu'il doit être,' on to the 'biscuit d'ivrogne;' taking care to impress upon the unwilling ears of his younger hearers that 'tout bon mangeur a fini son dîner après le rôti.' He would assure us on the same high authority that, after the

and eloquence which were much less lively. Everybody seemed to be pleased.'

[1] See Miss Ferrier's 'Marriage,' Chapter XX.

[2] 'Les Tables d'Hôte,' says the Almanach, speaking of the Reign of Terror, 'ne se rouvrirent point alors. On continua d'aller manger isolément et tristement chez les restaurateurs, où chacun, assis à une petite table, et séparé des autres, consomme en silence sa portion, sans se mêler de ce que dit ou de ce que fait son voisin.'

sixth dozen, oysters ceased to whet the appetite; and he would repeat with infinite gusto the sentence that closes the description of a breakfast such as, during the last years of the century, a high official of the Republic took pride in giving: 'Ceux qui veulent faire grandement les choses, finissent par parfumer la bouche de leurs convives, (ou plutôt de leurs amis, car c'est ainsi que s'appellent les convives d'un déjeûner,) avec deux ou trois tasses de glaces; on se la rince ensuite avec un grand verre de marasquin; et puis chacun se retire en hâte chez soi—pour aller manger la soupe.'[1]

It must be owned that even a 'grand déjeûner' at the hôtel of Cambacérès or Barras could hardly have lasted longer than a breakfast at Holly Lodge; but Macaulay's guests were detained at table by attractions less material than those which were provided by the Amphitryons of the Directory and the Consulate. Long after the cutlets and the potted char had been forgotten the circle would sit entranced, while their host disposed of topic after topic, and fetched from his shelves volume after volume, until the noon-day sun invited the party to spare yet another hour for a stroll round the garden, so gay in its winter dress of scarlet berries, that it seemed 'very enjoyable' even to the master of Castle Howard. Lord Carlisle says in his journal of December 19, 1856. 'Walked to Campden Hill on a beautiful morning. David Dundas had invited me to breakfast there. Was received with surprise, but with warm welcome, by Macaulay. I never knew his memory more brilliant or surprising. A casual mention of the lion on the Howard shield brought down a volume of Skelton with his finger on

[1] Macaulay's favourite passage in the Almanach des Gourmands was that which prescribes the period, (varying from a week to six months according to the goodness of the dinner,) during which the guests may not speak ill of their host; who has, moreover, the privilege of chaining their tongues afresh by sending out a new set of invitations before the full time has expired. 'On conviendra que, de toutes les manières d'empêcher de mal parler de soi, celle-ci n'est pas la moins aimable.'

the passage. Then there was a long charade on Polyphemus, which he remembered from an Age newspaper in 1825. He seemed to me to have gained in health by his transfer to his pleasant villa.'

So pleasant was it that its occupant did not care to seek for pleasure elsewhere. Months would pass away without Macaulay's having once made his appearance in London society; and years, during which he refused all invitations to stay with friends or acquaintances in the country. One or two nights spent at Windsor Castle, and one or two visits to Lord Stanhope's seat in Kent, formed almost the sole exceptions to a rule which the condition of his health imperatively prescribed, and against which his inclinations did not lead him to rebel.

'*Chevening*, *July* 16, 1856.—After breakfast Lord Stanhope very kindly and sensibly left me to rummage his library. A fine old library it is, of, I should guess, fifteen thousand volumes: much resembling a college library both in appearance and in the character of the books. I was very agreeably entertained till two in the afternoon. Then we set off for Mountstuart Elphinstone's, six miles off. I saw him probably for the last time; still himself, though very old and infirm. A great and accomplished man as any that I have known. In the evening Darwin, a geologist and traveller, came to dinner.'

'*July* 17.—The morning again in the library. In the afternoon to a pretty spot of common land which has fallen to Lord Stanhope under a late enclosure act;—fine wood and heath, and a fine prospect. My Valentine[1] was with us, dancing about among the flowers; gathering foxgloves and whortle-berries, and very gay and happy. I love all little girls of that age for the sake of my own nieces; and Lady Mary is a very amiable child. In the evening Lord Stanhope produced a Tragedy written by Pitt, and his brother Lord Chatham, in 1772; detestable, of course, but

[1] See vol. ii, page 149.

well enough for a boy of thirteen. Odd that there was no love at all in the plot:—a dispute about a Regency, during the absence of the King, and the minority of his son Prince Florus. There were several passages which reminded me of 1789.'

There is a characteristic notice in Macaulay's diary of a winter visit to Bowood.

'*January* 31.—A fine frosty day. Lord Lansdowne proposed a walk, and we went up to the hill where the old moat and the yew tree are. The way lay through a perfect Slough of Despond. I, like Pliable, should have turned back, but Lady Mahon's courage shamed me. After lunch I went to walk alone in the pleasure ground, but was pestered by a most sociable cur who would not be got rid of. I went into a plantation, railed off with gates at each end, and shut the brute out; but he perfectly understood my tactics,—curse his intelligence!—and waited for me at the other gate. After vainly trying to escape him in this way, I shut him in, and stayed outside myself. When I walked away he saw that he had been out-generalled by human reason, and set up the most ludicrous howl that I ever heard in my life.'

It is to be hoped, for Macaulay's sake, that the biographers of great men who were partial to the company of animals overstate their case when they assert that the love of dogs is the surest test of a good heart. In 1850, when staying with some friends in the country, he writes: 'After breakfast I walked with the young ladies;—nice, intelligent girls they are. A couple of ill-conditioned curs went with us, whom they were foolish enough to make pets of; so that we were regaled by a dog-fight, and were very near having on our hands two or three other fights. How odd that people of sense should find any pleasure in being accompanied by a beast who is always spoiling conversation!'[1] It must be said that my uncle was very

[1] In July, 1856, Macaulay writes: 'I went to Oatlands and walked with Margaret and Alice to a most singular monument

kind to the only dog which ever depended on him for kindness; a very pretty and very small Mexican spaniel, that belonged to one of his nieces. He treated the little animal exactly as he treated children, bringing it presents from the toy-shops, and making rhymes about it by the quarter of an hour together. 'I bought,' he says, 'a stuffed bird for Cora, and laughed to see how the poor brute was surprised and amused.'

'Little as Macaulay liked to spend his time under other people's roofs, he had no objection to hotels, and to foreign hotels least of all. Nothing short of a Continental war, or the impossibility of getting Mr. Ellis's company, would ever have prevented him from taking his autumn tour. In 1856 he once more crossed the Alps, and was at Milan by the end of August. 'From the balcony we caught a sight of the Cathedral, which made us impatient to see the whole. We went. I

of human folly. The Duchess of York had made a cemetery for her dogs. There is a gateway like that under which coffins are laid in the churchyards of this part of the country; there is a sort of chapel; and there are the gravestones of sixty-four of her Royal Highness's curs. On some of these mausoleums were inscriptions in verse. I was disgusted by this exceeding folly. Humanity to the inferior animals I feel and practise, I hope, as much as any man; but seriously to make friends of dogs is not my taste. I can understand, however, that even a sensible man may have a fondness for a dog. But sixty-four dogs! Why, it is hardly conceivable that there should be warm affection in any heart for sixty-four human beings. I had formed a better opinion of the Duchess.' It is difficult to say whether his opinion of the Duchess was raised or lowered by some information which reached him a few days later, when he was dining with Lord Lyveden, 'very agreeably seated between two clever women, Lady Morley and Lady Dufferin.' The latter told him that she and Mrs. Norton had been much at Oatlands when they were girls of twelve or thirteen; that the epitaphs were not, as Macaulay had supposed, the mature efforts of Monk Lewis's genius, but the childish productions of herself and her sister; and that the great multitude of the graves might be accounted for by the fact that the Duchess was plagued to death with presents of dogs, which she did not like to refuse, and which would have turned her house into a kennel, if she had not given them a dose of opium, and sent them to the cemetery.

never was more delighted and amazed by any building except St. Peter's. The great façade is undoubtedly a blunder; but a most splendid and imposing blunder. I wish to heaven that our Soanes, and Nashes, and Wilkinses had blundered in the same way.' Venice, with which, ever since his boyhood, he had been as familiar as book and picture could make him, when seen at length in her own sad grandeur, seemed to him 'strange beyond all words.' He did not fail to admire 'the succession of palaces, towering out of the green salt water; now passing into decay, yet retaining many traces of their ancient magnificence,—rich carvings, incrustations of rare marbles, faint remains of gilding and fresco-painting. Of these great mansions there is scarcely one so modern as the oldest house in St. James's Square. Many were built, and crowded with brilliant company, in the days of Henry the Eighth and Elizabeth; some as far back as the days of Richard the Second and Henry the Fourth. For Venice then was to London what London now is to Sydney or Toronto.'

St. Mark's Church, without impairing his loyalty to the great Roman basilica, affected him in a manner which was beyond, or rather beside, his expectations. 'I do not think it, nobody can think it, beautiful, and yet I never was more entertained by any building. I never saw a building except St. Peter's, where I could be content to pass so many hours in looking about me. There is something attractive to me in the very badness of the rhyming monkish hexameters, and in the queer designs and false drawing of the pictures. Everything carries back the mind to a remote age; to a time when Cicero and Virgil were hardly known in Italy; to a time compared with which the time of Politian, and even the time of Petrarch, is modern. I returned in the course of the day, and spent an hour in making out the histories of Moses and Joseph, and the mottoes. They amused me as the pictures in very old Bibles used to amuse me when I was a child.'

After his first visit to the Academy, Macaulay makes

some remarks which, with the fear of Mr. Ruskin before my eyes, I almost tremble to transcribe: 'The glow, the blaze, of warm Venetian colouring produces a wonderful effect. But there are few pieces, which, considered separately as works of art, give me much pleasure. There is an eternal repetition of the same subjects;—nine Holy Families, for example, in one small room. Then the monstrous absurdity of bringing Doges, Archangels, Cardinals, Apostles, persons of the Trinity, and members of the Council of Ten into one composition, shocks and disgusts me. A spectator who can forgive such faults for the sake of a dexterous disposition of red tints and green tints must have improved his eye, I think, at the expense of his understanding.' Macaulay's last day at Venice was devoted to the Ducal Palace. 'I was more indignant,' he writes, 'than I chose to show, when I found, not only that Petrarch's legacy of books had been suffered to perish, but that the public library of Venice did not contain a copy of one of Aldus's great editions of the Greek classics. I am sorry to leave this fascinating city; for ever, I suppose. I may now often use the words "for ever" when I leave things.'

He had brought with him instructions from his nieces to report at length upon Juliet's tomb; and he accordingly writes to them from Verona to express his delight at finding himself in a city so rich in its matchless variety of beauties and associations. 'You have an amphitheatre which very likely Pliny may have frequented; huge old palaces and towers, the work of princes who were contemporary with our Edward the First; and most charming and graceful architecture of the time of Michel Angelo and Raphael;—and all this within a space not larger than Belgrave Square.' At the same time he threatens them with a Popish aunt, who will be able to assist them in their Italian studies. 'But perhaps the questions of religion and residence may be as hard to get over in the case of the Chevalier Macaulay as in the case of the Chevalier Grandison; and I may be forced to leave the too charming

Guiseppa here with a blister on her head, and a strait-waistcoat on her back.'

During his journeys abroad Macaulay always made a point of reading the literature of the country. He began his Italian tour with Cicero's Letters,[1] and ended it with I Promessi Sposi. 'I finished Manzoni's novel, not without many tears. The scene between the Archbishop and Don Abbondio is one of the noblest that I know. The parting scene between the lovers and Father Cristoforo is most touching. If the Church of Rome really were what Manzoni represents her to be, I should be tempted to follow Newman's example.'

The next year, while travelling through France to the cities of the Rhine and the Moselle, he bought on the way Chateaubriand's Génie du Christianisme. 'I was astonished,' he says, 'at the utter worthlessness of the book, both in matter and manner. The French may be beautiful, as far as mere selection and arrangement of words go. But in the higher graces of style, —those graces which affect a foreigner as much as a native,—those graces which delight us in Plato, in Demosthenes, and in Pascal,—there is a lamentable deficiency. As to the substance, it is beneath criticism. Yet I have heard men of ten times Chateaubriand's powers talk of him as the first of French writers. He was simply a great humbug.'

On the last day of February 1856, Macaulay writes in his journal: 'Longman called. It is necessary to reprint. This is wonderful. Twenty-six thousand five hundred copies sold in ten weeks! I should not wonder if I made twenty thousand pounds clear this year by literature. Pretty well, considering that, twenty-two years ago, I had just nothing when my debts were paid; and all that I have, with the exception of a small part left me by my uncle the General, has been made

[1] 'I have been reading,' he says, 'those letters of Cicero which were written just after Cæsar had taken up arms. What materials for history! What a picture of a mind which well deserves to be studied! No novel ever interested me more. Often as I have read them, every sentence seems new.'

by myself, and made easily and honestly, by pursuits which were a pleasure to me, and without one insinuation from any slanderer that I was not even liberal in all my pecuniary dealings.'

'*March* 7.—Longman came, with a very pleasant announcement. He and his partners find that they are overflowing with money, and think that they cannot invest it better than by advancing to me, on the usual terms of course, part of what will be due to me in December. We agreed that they shall pay twenty thousand pounds into Williams's Bank next week. What a sum to be gained by one edition of a book! I may say, gained in one day. But that was harvest-day. The work had been near seven years in hand. I went to Westbourne Terrace by a Paddington omnibus, and passed an hour there, laughing and laughed at. They are all much pleased. They have, indeed, as much reason to be pleased as I, who am pleased on their account rather than on my own, though I am glad that my last years will be comfortable. Comfortable, however, I could have been on a sixth part of the income which I shall now have.'

The cheque is still preserved as a curiosity among the archives of Messrs. Longman's firm. 'The transaction,' says Macaulay, 'is quite unparalleled in the history of the book-trade; and both the people at Smith, Payne, and Smiths' who are to pay the money, and my friends who are to receive it, have been much amused. I went into the City to-day to give instructions, and was most warmly congratulated on being a great moneyed man. I said that I had some thoughts of going to the Chancellor of the Exchequer as a bidder for the next loan.'

My uncle was a great favourite with his bankers. Mr. Henry Thornton, who was, and is, a partner in Messrs. Williams and Deacon's, carefully encouraged him in his fixed idea that business could only be done by word of mouth; and many a pleasant half-hour the two old college friends had together in the back-parlour of Birchin Lane. On one occasion Mr. Thornton, by Macaulay's request, explained to him at some length the distinction between the different classes of Spanish Stock,—Active, Passive, and Deferred. 'I think,' said my uncle, 'that I catch your meaning. Active Spanish Bonds profess to pay interest now, and do not. Deferred Spanish Bonds profess to pay interest at some future time, and will not. Passive Spanish Bonds profess to pay interest neither now, nor at any future time. I think that you might buy a large amount of Passive Spanish Bonds for a very small sum.'

It mattered nothing to Macaulay personally whether or not Spain pretended to be solvent; for he never touched crazy securities. He was essentially an investor, and not a speculator. 'He had as sound a judgment in City matters,' said Mr. Thornton, 'as I ever met with. You might safely have followed him blindfold.' 'I have,' my uncle writes in his journal, 'a great turn for finance, though few people would suspect it. I have a pleasure in carrying on long arithmetical operations in my head. I used to find amusement, when I was Secretary at War, in the Army Estimates. I generally went through my pecuniary statements without book, except when it was necessary to come to pence and farthings.'

Macaulay so arranged his affairs that their management was to him a pastime, instead of being a source of annoyance and anxiety. His economical maxims were of the simplest; to treat official and literary gains as capital,[1] and to pay all bills within the twenty-

[1] Macaulay had good historical authority for this method of proceeding. We are told by an admirer of the Right Honourable George Grenville that it was the unvaried practice of that statesman, in all situations, to live upon his private fortune, and save the emoluments of whatever office he possessed. 'He had early accustomed himself to a strict appropriation of his income, and an exact economy in its expenditure, as the only sure ground on which to build a reputation for public and private integrity, and to support a dignified independence.' The moral results which were expected to flow from the observance of these excellent precepts were not

four hours. 'I think,' he says, 'that prompt payment is a moral duty; knowing, as I do, how painful it is to have such things deferred.' Like other men who have more money than time, his only account-book was that which his banker kept for him; and, to assist himself in making up his yearly balance-sheet, he embodied a list of his investments, and the main items of his expenditure, in a couple of irregular, but not inharmonious stanzas.

North-West; South-West; South-East; Two Irish Greats;
Denmark; Bengal; Commercial; London Dock;
Insurance; Steam-ship; and United States;
Slave-State; and Free-State; and Old English Stock.

Taxes; Rent; Sisters; Carriage; Wages; Clo'es;
Coals; Wine; Alms; Pocket-cash; Subscriptions; Treats;
Bills, weekly these, and miscellaneous those.
Travel the list completes.

The wealth which Macaulay gathered prudently he spent royally; if to spend royally is to spend on others rather than yourself. From the time that he began to feel the money in his purse almost every page in his diary contains evidence of his inexhaustible and sometimes rather carelessly regulated, generosity. 'Mrs. X—— applied to me, as she said, and as I believe, without her husband's knowledge, for help in his profession. He is a clergyman; a good one, but too Puritanical for my taste. I could not promise to ask any favours from the Government; but I sent him twenty-five pounds to assist him in supporting the orphan daughters of his brother. I mean to let him have the same sum annually.' 'I have been forced to refuse any further assistance to a Mrs. Y——, who has had thirty-five pounds from me in the course of a few months, and whose demands come thicker and thicker. I suppose that she will resent my refusal bitterly. That is all that I ever got by conferring

very visible in the case of Grenville, who ratted more shamefully than any public man even of his own century.

benefits on any but my own nearest relations and friends.' 'H—— called. I gave him three guineas for his Library subscription. I lay out very little money with so much satisfaction. For three guineas a year, I keep a very good, intelligent young fellow out of a great deal of harm, and do him a great deal of good.'[1] 'I suppose,' he writes to one of his sisters, 'that you told Mrs Z—— that I was not angry with her; for to-day I have a letter from her begging for money most vehemently, and saying that, if I am obdurate, her husband must go to prison. I have sent her twenty pounds; making up what she has had from me within a few months to a hundred and thirty pounds.' As a matter of fact, the language in which some of Macaulay's most regular pensioners were accustomed to address him contrasts almost absurdly with the respect paid towards him by the public at large. 'That wretched K——,' he writes, 'has sent a scurrilous begging letter in his usual style. He hears that I have made thirty thousand pounds by my malignant abuse of good men. Will I not send some of it to him?'

To have written, or to pretend to have written, a book, whether good or bad, was the surest and shortest road to Macaulay's pocket. 'I sent some money to Miss ——, a middling writer, whom I relieved some time ago. I have been giving too fast of late;—forty pounds in four or five days. I must pull in a little.' 'Mrs. —— again, begging and praying. "This the last time; an execution; &c., &c." I will send her five pounds more. This will make fifty pounds in a few months to a bad writer whom I never saw.' 'I have received,' he writes to Mr. Longman, 'a rather queer letter, purporting to be from the wife of Mr. D——, the author of ——, and dated from Greenwich. Now, I have once or twice received similar letters which have afterwards turned out to be forgeries. I sent ten

[1] This 'intelligent young fellow' was afterwards Sir Robert G. C. Hamilton, K.C.B.,—a worthy kinsman of Macaulay, and one of the most eminent public servants of his generation. (1908.)

pounds to a sham Mary Howitt, who complained that an unforeseen misfortune had reduced her to poverty; and I can hardly help suspecting that there may be a sham Mrs. D——. If, however, the author of —— is really in distress, I would gladly assist him, though I am no admirer of his poetry. Could you learn from his publishers whether he really lives at Greenwich? If he does, I will send him a few pounds. If he does not, I will set the police to work.' The Rev. Mr. Frederick Arnold tells the story of a German gentleman, the husband of a lady honourably connected with literature, who had fallen from affluence to unexpected poverty. He applied to Macaulay for assistance, and, instead of the guinea for which he had ventured to hope, he was instantly presented with thirty pounds. During the last year of my uncle's life, I called at Holly Lodge to bid him good-bye before my return to the University. He told me that a person had presented himself that very morning, under the name of a Cambridge Fellow of some mark, but no great mark, in the learned world. This gentleman, (for such he appeared to be,) stated himself to be in distress, and asked for pecuniary aid. Macaulay, then and there, gave him a hundred pounds. The visitor had no sooner left the room than my uncle began to reflect that he had never set eyes on him before. He accordingly desired me, as soon as I got back to Cambridge, to make, with all possible delicacy, such inquiries as might satisfy him that, when wishing to relieve the necessities of a brother scholar, he had not rewarded the audacity of a professional imposter.[1]

If he was such with regard to people whose very faces were strange to him, it may well be believed that

[1] *September* 14, 1859.—A Dr. —— called, and introduced himself as a needy man of letters. I was going to give him a sovereign, and send him away, when I discovered that he was the philologist, whom I should never have expected to see in such a plight. I felt for him, and gave him a hundred pounds. A hard pull on me, I must say. However, I have been prosperous beyond the common lot of men, and may well assist those who have been out of luck.'

every valid claim upon his liberality was readily acknowledged. He was handsome in all his dealings, both great and small. Wherever he went, (to use his own phrase,) he took care to make his mother's son welcome. Within his own household he was positively worshipped; and with good reason; for Sir Walter Scott himself was not a kinder master. He cheerfully and habitually submitted to those petty sacrifices by means of which an unselfish man can do so much to secure the comfort and to earn the attachment of those who are around him;—marching off in all weathers to his weekly dinner at the club, in order to give his servants their Sunday evening; going far out of his way to make such arrangements as would enable them to enjoy and to prolong their holidays; or permitting them, if so they preferred, to entertain their relations under his roof for a month together. 'To-day,' he says, 'William and Elizabeth went off to fetch William's father. As I write, here come my travellers; the old man with a stick. Well! It is good to give pleasure and show sympathy. There is no vanity in saying that I am a good master.'

It would be superfluous to dwell upon Macaulay's conduct towards those with whom he was connected by the ties of blood, and by the recollections of early days which had not been exempt from poverty and sorrow. Suffice it to say that he regarded himself as the head of his family; responsible, (to speak plainly,) for seeing that all his brothers and sisters were no worse off than if his father had died a prosperous man. It was only in this respect that he assumed the paternal relation. In his ordinary behaviour there was nothing which betokened that he was the benefactor of all with whom he had to do. He never interfered; he never obtruded advice; he never demanded that his own tastes or views should be consulted, and he was studiously mindful of the feelings, and even the fancies, of others. With the omission of only two words, we may justly apply to him the eulogy pronounced upon another famous author by one who certainly had the best of reasons for knowing that it was deserved. 'It is Southey's almost unexampled felicity to possess the best gifts of talent and genius, free from all their characteristic defects. A son, brother, husband, father, master, friend, he moves with firm yet light steps, alike unostentatious, and alike exemplary.'[1]

It is pleasant to reflect that Macaulay's goodness was repaid, as far as gratitude and affection could suffice to repay it. He was contented with the share of domestic felicity which had fallen to his lot. 'To-morrow,' he says in one place, 'the Trevelyans go to Weybridge. I feel these separations, though they are for short times, and short distances; but a life is happy of which these are the misfortunes.'[2] From graver calamities and longer partings he was mercifully spared;—most mercifully, because, as will soon be seen, he was quite unfitted to bear them. Already he was painfully aware that the maladies under which he suffered had relaxed the elasticity of his spirits; had sapped his powers of mental endurance; and had rendered his happiness more dependent than ever upon the permanence of blessings which no human foresight could secure. The prayer that most often came to his lips was that he might not survive those whom he loved. 'God grant,' he writes on the 1st of January 1858, 'that, if my dear little circle is to be diminished this year by any death, it may be mine! Not that I am weary of life. I am far from insensible to the pleasure of having fame, rank, and this opulence

[1] This passage is from a letter written by Coleridge, which forms part of the extraordinarily interesting collection published by Mr. Cottle, the Bristol bookseller. The correspondence presents a winning picture of Southey's silent and unconscious heroism. 'I feel,' he once said, (and his life showed how truly he felt it,) 'that duty and happiness are inseparable.' Neither he nor Macaulay laid claim to what are called the 'privileges of genius.' In a note on the margin of Nichols's 'Literary Anecdotes' my uncle says: 'Genius! What had Perceval Stockdale to do with genius? But, as it is, the plea of genius is but a poor one for immorality, and nine-tenths of those who plead it are dunces.'

[2] He consoled himself on this occasion by reading Crabbe 'during some hours, with pleasure ever fresh.'

which has come so late.' His imagination was deeply impressed by an old Roman imprecation, which he had noticed long ago in a Gallery of Inscriptions: '"Ultimus suorum moriatur!" An awful curse.'

Once, and once only, during many years, he had any real ground for alarm.

'*January* 29, 1855.—The severest shock that I have had since January 1835.[1] A note from Margaret to say that Hannah has scarlet fever. Margaret, too, is exposed. I was quite overset. They begged me not to go, but I could not stay away. I saw them both, and was much relieved. It seems that the crisis is over, and that the worst was past before the nature of the disease was known.' A few days afterwards he says; 'I went to Westbourne Terrace, and saw Margaret. I begin to be nervous about her now that her mother is safe. Alas, that I should have staked so much on what may be so easily lost! Yet I would not have it otherwise.'

He assuredly had no cause to wish it otherwise; for he enjoyed the satisfaction of feeling, not only that his affection was appreciated and returned, but that those of whom he was fondest never wearied of his company. Full and diversified always, and often impassioned or profound, his conversation was never beyond the compass of his audience; for his talk, like his writing, was explanatory rather than allusive; and, born orator that he was, he contrived without any apparent effort that every sentence which he uttered should go home to every person who heard it. He was admirable with young people. Innumerable passages in his journals and correspondence prove how closely he watched them; how completely he understood

[1] It was in January 1835 that he heard of his younger sister's death. He writes, in April 1856: 'I passed the day in burning and arranging papers. Some things that met my eyes overcame me for a time. Margaret. Alas! Alas! And yet she might have changed to me. But no; that could never have been. To think that she has been near twenty-two years dead; and I am crying for her as if it were yesterday.'

them; and how, awake or asleep, they were for ever in his thoughts. On the fragment of a letter to Mr. Ellis there is mention of a dream he had about his younger niece, 'so vivid that I must tell it. She came to me with a penitential face, and told me that she had a great sin to confess; that Pepys's Diary was all a forgery, and that she had forged it. I was in the greatest dismay. "What! I have been quoting in reviews, and in my History, a forgery of yours as a book of the highest authority. How shall I ever hold my head up again?" I woke with the fright, poor Alice's supplicating voice still in my ears.' He now and then speaks of his wish to have some serious talk with one or another of the lads in whom he was specially interested 'in a quiet way,' and 'without the forms of a lecture.' His lectures were, indeed, neither frequent nor formidable. I faintly remember his once attempting to shame me out of a fit of idleness by holding himself up as an awful example of the neglect of mathematics. It must not, however, be supposed that Macaulay spoiled the children of whom he was fondest. On the contrary, he had strict notions of what their behaviour should be; and, in his own quiet way, he took no little pains to train their dispositions. He was visibly pained by any outbreak on their part of wilfulness, or bad temper, or, above all, of selfishness. But he had very seldom occasion to give verbal expression to his disapprobation. His influence over us was so unbounded;—there was something so impressive in the displeasure of one whose affection for us was so deep, and whose kindness was so unfailing;—that no punishment could be devised one half as formidable as the knowledge that we had vexed our uncle. He was enabled to reserve his spoken reproofs for the less heinous sins of false rhymes, misquotations, and solecisms, (or what he chose to consider as such,) in grammar, orthography, and accentuation;—for saying 'The tea is being made,' and not 'The tea is a-making;' for writing 'Bosphorus' instead of 'Bosporus,' and 'Syren' instead of 'Siren;' and, above all, for pronouncing the penultimate of 'Metamorphosis' short. This was the more hard upon us because, in conforming to the fashion of the world, we were acting in accordance with the moral of the best among his many stories about Dr. Parr. A gentleman, who had been taken to task for speaking of the ancient capital of Egypt as 'Alexandrīa,' defended himself by the authority and example of Dr. Bentley. 'Dr. Bentley and I,' replied Dr. Parr, 'may call it Alexandrīa; but I think you had better call it Alexandrĭa.'

It was a grievous loss to Macaulay when we grew too old for sight-seeing;—or, at any rate, for seeing the same sight many times over. As the best substitute for Madame Tussaud and the Panoramas, he used in later years to take his nieces the round of the picture-galleries; and, though far from an unimpeachable authority on matters of art, he was certainly a most agreeable Cicerone. In painting, as in most things, he had his likes and dislikes, and had them strongly. In 1857 he writes: 'Preraphaelitism is spreading, I am glad to see;—glad, because it is by spreading that such affectations perish.' He saw at the Frankfort Museum 'several chefs-d'œuvre, as they are considered, of modern German art; all, to my thinking, very poor. There is a Daniel in the den of lions which it is a shame to exhibit. I did not even like the John Huss, and still less Overbeck's trashy allegory. One of Stanfield's landscapes, or of Landseer's hunting pieces, is worth all the mystic daubs of the Germans.'

Macaulay looked at pictures as a man of letters, rather than as a connoisseur; judging them less by their technical merits than with reference to the painter's choice and treatment of his subject. 'There was a Salvator,' he says in one place, 'which I was pleased to see, because the thought had occurred to me in Horatius;—an oak struck by lightning, with the Augurs looking at it in dismay.' In 1853 he writes: 'The exhibition was very good indeed; capital Landseers; one excellent Stanfield; a very good Roberts. Ward was good; but I was struck by one obvious fault in his picture of Montrose's execution;—a fault, perhaps, inseparable from such subjects. Montrose was a mean-looking man, and Ward thought it necessary to follow the likeness, and perhaps he was right. But all the other figures are imaginary, and each is, in its own way, striking. The consequence is that the central figure is not only mean in itself, but is made meaner by contrast. In pictures where all the figures are imaginary this will not occur, nor in pictures where all the figures are real.' Macaulay's sentence about Dr. Johnson's literary verdicts might perhaps be applied to his own criticisms on art: 'At the very worst, they mean something; a praise to which much of what is called criticism in our time has no pretensions.'[1]

Macaulay may not have been a reliable guide in the regions of high art; but there was one department of education in which, as an instructor, he might have challenged comparison with the best. A boy whose classical reading he watched, and in some degree directed, might indeed be lazy, but could not be indifferent to his work. The dullest of tiros would have been inspired by the ardour of one whose thoughts were often for weeks together more in Latium and Attica than in Middlesex; who knew the careers and the characters of the great men who paced the forum, and declaimed in the Temple of Concord, as intimately

[1] Macaulay had a great admiration for that fine picture, the Lady's Last Stake, which, strange to say, is not included in the ordinary editions of Hogarth. He suggested that an engraving of it should be prefixed as frontispiece to a collection of Mrs. Piozzi's papers which Mr. Longman talked of publishing. 'There is a great deal,' he writes, 'about that picture in Mrs. Piozzi's Life of herself. The Lady who is reduced to the last stake was a portrait of her; and the likeness was discernible after the lapse of more than fifty years.' The expression of puzzled amusement on the Lady's face is as good as anything in the breakfast scene of the Marriage à la Mode; and the effect of the background,—a plain parlour, with the ordinary furniture of the day,—is a remarkable instance of the amount of pleasure that may be afforded to the spectator by the merest accessories of a picture which is the careful work of a great artist.

as those of his own rivals in Parliament, and his own colleagues in the Cabinet; to whom Cicero was as real as Peel, and Curio as Stanley; who was as familiar with his Lucian, and his Augustan Histories, as other men of letters are with their Voltaire and their Pepys; who cried over Homer with emotion, and over Aristophanes with laughter, and could not read the 'De Coronâ' even for the twentieth time without striking his clenched fist, at least once a minute, on the arm of his easy chair. As he himself says of Lord Somers, 'he had studied ancient literature like a man;' and he loved it as only a poet could. No words can convey a notion of the glamour which Macaulay's robust and unaffected enthusiasm threw over the books or the events which had aroused and which fed it; or of the permanent impression which that enthusiasm left upon the minds of those who came within its influence. All the little interviews that took place between us as master and pupil, to which a multitude of notices in his diary refer, are as fresh in my memory as if they had occurred last summer, instead of twenty years ago. 'Home, and took a cabfull of books to Westbourne Terrace for George;—Scapula, Ainsworth, Lucian, Quintus Curtius.' And again: 'George was at home, with a hurt which kept him from returning to school. I gave him a lecture on the tragic metres, which will be well worth a day's schooling to him, if he profits by it.' Macaulay's care of my classics ceased with the holidays; for he knew that at school I was in safe hands. He writes to his sister in December 1856: 'I am truly glad that Vaughan remains for the present at Harrow. After next October, the sooner he is made a Bishop the better.' This last opinion was shared by all who wished well to the Church of England, with the most unfortunate exception of Dr. Vaughan himself.

Macaulay wrote to me at Harrow pretty constantly, sealing his letters with an amorphous mass of red wax, which, in defiance of post-office regulations, not unfrequently concealed a piece of gold. 'It is said,' (so he once began,) 'that the best part of a lady's letter is the postscript. The best part of an uncle's is under the seal.'

Tunbridge Wells: August 1, 1853.

Dear George,—

I am glad that you are working hard. Did you ever read Paradise Lost? If not, I would advise you to read it now; for it is the best commentary that I know on the Prometheus. There was a great resemblance between the genius of Æschylus and the genius of Milton; and this appears most strikingly in those two wonderful creations of the imagination, Prometheus and Satan. I do not believe that Milton borrowed Satan from the Greek drama. For, though he was an excellent scholar after the fashion of his time, Æschylus was, I suspect, a little beyond him. You cannot conceive how much the facilities for reading the Greek writers have increased within the last two hundred years, how much better the text is now printed, and how much light the successive labours of learned men have thrown on obscure passages. I was greatly struck with this when, at Althorp, I looked through Lord Spencer's magnificent collection of Aldine editions. Numerous passages which are now perfectly simple, were mere heaps of nonsense. And no writer suffered more than Æschylus.

Note particularly in the Prometheus the magnificent history of the origin of arts and sciences. That passage shows Æschylus to have been, not only a poet of the first order, but a great thinker. It is the fashion to call Euripides a philosophical poet; but I remember nothing in Euripides so philosophical as that rapid enumeration of all the discoveries and inventions which make the difference between savage and civilised man. The latter part of the play is glorious.

I am very busy here getting some of my speeches ready for the press; and during the day I get no reading, except while I walk on the heath, and then I read Plato, one of the five first-rate Athenians. The other four are your friends Æschylus and Thucydides, Sophocles and Demosthenes. I know of no sixth Athenian who can be added to the list. Certainly not Euripides, nor Xenophon, nor Isocrates, nor Æschines. But I forgot Aristophanes. More shame for me. He makes six, and I can certainly add nobody else to the six. How I go on gossiping about these old fellows when I should be thinking of other things!

Ever yours

T. B. MACAULAY.

During my last year at school, my uncle did me the honour of making me the vehicle for a compliment to Lord Palmerston. 'George's Latin Poem,' he writes to Mr. Ellis in the spring of 1857, 'is an account of a tour up the Rhine in imitation of the fifth Satire of Horace's first Book. The close does not please Vaughan, and, indeed, is not good. I have suggested what I think a happier termination. The travellers get into a scrape at Heidelberg, and are taken up. How to extricate them is the question. I advise George to represent himself as saying that he is an Englishman, and that there is one who will look to it that an Englishman shall be as much respected as a Roman citizen. The name of Palmerston at once procures the prisoners their liberty. Palmerston, you remember, is a Harrow man. The following termination has occurred to me:

Tantum valuit prænobile nomen,
Quod noster collis, nostra hæc sibi vindicat aula;
Quod Scytha, quod tortâ redimitus tempora mitrâ
Persa timet, diroque gerens Ser bella veneno.[1]

Do not mention this. It might lead people to think

[1] It is necessary, in order to explain the allusions in Macaulay's lines, to remind the reader that in July 1857, Palmerston's Russian laurels were still fresh; and that he had, within the last few months, brought the Persian difficulty to a successful issue, and commenced a war with China. Hostilities began with an attempt on the part of a Hong-Kong baker, of the suggestive name of A-lum, to poison Sir John Bowring.

that I have helped George; and there is not a line in any of his exercises that is not his own.'

It may be imagined amidst what a storm of applause these spirited verses, (redolent, perhaps, rather of Claudian than of Horace,) were declaimed on the Harrow speech-day, to an audience as proud of Palmerston as ever an Eton audience was of Canning.

'*August* 28, 1857.—A great day in my life. I stayed at home, very sad about India.[1] Not that I have any doubt about the result; but the news is heart-breaking. I went, very low, to dinner, and had hardly begun to eat when a messenger came with a letter from Palmerston. An offer of a peerage; the Queen's pleasure already taken. I was very much surprised. Perhaps no such offer was ever made without the slightest solicitation, direct or indirect, to a man of humble origin and moderate fortune, who had long quitted public life. I had no hesitation about accepting, with many respectful and grateful expressions; but God knows that the poor women at Delhi and Cawnpore are more in my thoughts than my coronet. It was necessary for me to choose a title offhand. I determined to be Baron Macaulay of Rothley. I was born there; I have lived much there; I am named from the family which long had the manor; my uncle was Rector there. Nobody can complain of my taking a designation from a village which is nobody's property now.'

Macaulay went abroad on the 1st of September. After his return from the Continent he says: 'On my way from the station to Holly Lodge yesterday, I called at the Royal Institution, and saw the papers of the last fortnight. There is a general cry of pleasure at my elevation. I am truly gratified by finding how well I stand with the public, and gratified by finding that Palmerston has made a hit for himself in bestow-

[1] The Sepoy Mutiny was then at its very worst. Something like the truth of the Cawnpore story was beginning to be known in England.

ing this dignity on me.' 'I think,' (so my mother writes,) 'that his being made a peer was one of the very few things that everybody approved. I cannot recall any opinion adverse to it. He enjoyed it himself, as he did everything, simply and cordially. We were making a tour in the Tyrol that summer; and, on our return, we stopped at Paris, I and my children, to spend a few days at the Louvre Hotel with your uncle and Mr. Ellis. I often think of our arrival at eleven at night;—the well-spread board awaiting us; his joyous welcome; and then his desiring us to guess what his news was, and my disappointing him by instantly guessing it. Then a merry time together; the last unbroken circle; for change began the following year, and change has since been the order of my life.'

To the Rev. Dr. Whewell.

Holly Lodge, Kensington: October 9, 1857.

My dear Master,—

Thanks for your kindness, which is what it has always been. Unhappily I have so bad a cold, and Trevelyan has so much to do, that neither of us will be able to accompany our boy,—for we are equally interested in him,—to Cambridge next week. It is pleasant to me to think that I have now a new tie to Trinity.

Ever yours
MACAULAY.

My uncle had long been looking forward to the period of my residence at the University as an opportunity for renewing those early recollections and associations which he studiously cultivated, and which, after the lapse of five-and-thirty years, filled as large a space as ever in his thoughts. I have at this moment before me his Cambridge Calendar for 1859. The book is full of his handwriting. He has been at the pains of supplementing the Tripos lists, between 1750 and 1835, with the names of all the distinguished men who took their degrees in each successive year, but who, failing to go out in honours, missed such immortality as the Cambridge Calendar can give. He has made an elaborate computation, which must have consumed a whole morning in order to ascertain the collective annual value of the livings in the gift of the several colleges; from the twenty-four thousand pounds a year of St. John's and the eighteen thousand of Trinity, down to the hundreds a year of St. Catherine's and of Downing. Many and many an entry in his diary proves that he never ceased to be proud of having won for himself a name at Cambridge. On the 11th of June 1857 he writes: 'I dined with Milnes, and sate between Thirwall and Whewell;—three Trinity fellows together; and not bad specimens for a college to have turned out within six years, though I say it.'

If Macaulay's reverence for those personal anecdotes relating to the habits and doings of famous students, which have come down to us from the golden age of classical criticism, was any indication of his tastes, he would willingly have once more been a member of his old college, leading the life of a senior fellow, such as it was, or such as he imagined it to have been, in the days of Porson, Scholefield, or Dobree. Gladly, (at least so he pretended to believe,) would he have passed his summers by the banks of the Cam,—editing the Pharsalia, collating[1] the manuscripts of the Hecuba which are among the treasures of the University Library, and 'dawdling over Tryphiodorus, Callimachus's Epigrams, and Tacitus's Histories.' He was always ready for a conversation, and even for a correspondence, on a nice point of scholarship; and I have seldom seen him more genuinely gratified than by the intelligence that an emendation which he had suggested upon an obscure passage in Euripides was

[1] Macaulay had a sincere admiration for that old scholar, who, when condoled with upon the misfortune of an illness which had injured his sight, thanked God that he had kept his 'collating eye.'

favourably regarded in the Trinity combination room.[1]

During the May term of 1858 he paid me the first of those visits which he had taught me to anticipate with delight ever since I had been old enough to know what a college was. He detained a large breakfast party of undergraduates far into the day, while he rolled out for their amusement and instruction his stores of information on the history, customs, and traditions of the University; and I remember that after their departure he entertained himself with an excessively droll comparison of his own position with that of Major Pendennis among the young heroes of St. Boniface. But, proud as I was of him, I can recall few things more painful than the contrast between his strength of intellect and of memory, and his extreme weakness of body. In July 1858 Lord Carlisle expressed himself as distressed 'to see and hear Macaulay much broken by cough;' and in the previous May the symptoms of failing health were not less clearly discernible. With a mind still as fresh as when in 1820 he wore the blue gown of Trinity, and disputed with Charles Austin till four in the morning over the comparative merits of the Inductive and the *à priori* method in politics, it was already apparent that a journey across Clare bridge, and along the edge of the great lawn at King's, performed at the rate of half a mile in the hour, was an exertion too severe for his feeble frame.[2]

[1] *τί δῆτ' ἔτι ζῶ; τιν' ὑπολείπομαι τύχην;*
γάμους ἑλομένη τῶν κακῶν ὑπαλλαγὰς,
μετ' ἀνδρὸς οἰκεῖν βαρβάρου, πρὸς πλουσίαν
τράπεζαν ἵζουσ'; ἀλλ' ὅταν πόσις πικρὸς
ξυνῇ γυναικὶ, καὶ τὸ σῶμ' ἐστὶν πικρόν.

The difficulty of this passage lies in the concluding line. One editor reads '*τὸ σῶν ἐστίν*,' and another '*τὸ σῶζεσθαι.*' Macaulay proposed to substitute '*βρῶμ'*' for '*σῶμ'*.'

[2] In November 1857 Macaulay received invitations from Edinburgh and Glasgow to take part in the ceremony of the Burns centenary. 'I refused both invitations,' he says, 'for fifty reasons; one of which is that, if I went down in the depth

In the autumn of 1857 the High Stewardship of the Borough of Cambridge became vacant by the death of Earl Fitzwilliam, and Macaulay was elected in his place by the unanimous vote of the Town Council. 'I find,' he says, 'that the office has been held by a succession of men of the highest eminence in political and literary history;—the Protector Somerset; Dudley Duke of Northumberland; Ellesmere; Bacon; Coventry; Finch; Oliver Cromwell; Clarendon; and Russell, the La Hogue man. Very few places have been so filled.' The ceremony of Macaulay's inauguration as High Steward was deferred till the warm weather of 1858.

'*Tuesday*, *May* 11.—I was at Cambridge by ten. The mayor was at the station to receive me; and most hospitable he was, and kind. I went with him to the Town Hall, was sworn in, and then was ushered into the great room where a public breakfast was set out. I had not been in that room since 1820, when I heard Miss Stephens sing there, and bore part in a furious contest between "God save the King" and "God save the Queen." I had been earlier in this room. I was there at two meetings of the Cambridge Bible Society; that of 1813, and that of 1815. On the latter occasion I bought at Deighton's Scott's "Waterloo," just published, and read it on a frosty journey back to Aspenden Hall. But how I go on wandering! The room now looked smaller than in old times. About forty municipal functionaries, and as many guests, chiefly of the University, were present. The mayor gave my health in a very graceful manner. I replied concisely, excusing myself, with much truth, on the plea of health, from haranguing longer. I was well received; very well. Several speeches followed; the Vice-Chancellor saying very handsomely that I was a pledge of the continuance of the present harmony between town and gown.'

Macaulay had good reason to shrink from the exer-

of winter to harangue in Scotland, I should never come back alive.'

tion of a long speech, as was only too evident to his audience in the Cambridge Assembly-room. There was a touch of sadness in the minds of all present as they listened to the brief but expressive phrases in which he reminded them that the time had been when he might have commanded a hearing 'in larger and stormier assemblies,' but that any service which he could henceforward do for his country must be done in the quiet of his own library. 'It is now five years,' he said, 'since I raised my voice in public; and it is not likely—unless there be some special call of duty—that I shall ever raise it in public again.'

That special call of duty never came. Macaulay's indifference to the vicissitudes of party politics had by this time grown into a confirmed habit of mind. His correspondence during the spring of 1857 contains but few and brief allusions even to catastrophes as striking as the ministerial defeat upon the China war, and the overwhelming reverse of fortune which ensued when the question was transferred to the polling booths. 'Was there ever anything,' he writes, 'since the fall of the rebel angels, like the smash of the Anti-Corn Law League? How art thou fallen from Heaven, O Lucifer! I wish that Bright and Cobden had been returned.' Macaulay's opinion in the matter, as far as he had an opinion, was in favour of the Government, and against the coalition. 'I am glad,' he wrote on the eve of the debate, 'that I have done with politics. I should not have been able to avoid a pretty sharp encounter with Lord John.' But his days for sharp encounters were over, and his feelings of partisanship were reserved for the controversies about Standing Armies and Royal Grants which convulsed the last two Parliaments of the seventeenth century. He was, to describe him in his own words, 'a vehement ministerialist of 1698,' who thought 'more about Somers and Montague than about Campbell and Lord Palmerston.'

A faint interest, rather personal than political, in the proceedings of the Upper House, was awakened in his breast when, sitting for the first time on the red benches, he found himself in the presence of the most eminent among his ancient rivals, adversaries, and allies. 'Lord Derby,' he writes, 'was all himself,—clever, keen, neat, clear; never aiming high, but always hitting what he aims at.' A quarter of a century had not changed Macaulay's estimate of Lord Brougham, nor softened his mode of expressing it. 'Strange fellow! His powers gone. His spite immortal. A dead nettle.'[1]

During his first Session the new Peer more than once had a mind to speak upon matters relating to India. In February 1858 Lord Ellenborough gave notice of a motion for papers, with the view, as was presumed, of eliciting proofs that the Sepoy Mutiny had been provoked by the proselytising tendencies of the British Government. Macaulay, prompted by an Englishman's sense of fair-play, resolved to give the eloquent and redoubtable ex-Governor General a chance of paying off outstanding scores. But it all came to nothing. '*February* 19.—I worked hard, to make ready for a discussion of the great question of religion and education in India. I went down to the House. Lord Ellenborough's speech merely related to a petty question about the report of a single inspector—a very silly one, I am afraid—in Bahar. Lord Granville answered well, and much more than sufficiently. Then the debate closed. Many people thought that Lord Ellenborough would have been much longer and more vehement if he had not been taken aback by seeing me ready to reply. They say that he has less pluck than his warm and somewhat petulant manner indicates.

[1] Macaulay's disapprobation of Lord Brougham had been revived and intensified by a recent occurrence. '*April* 27, 1856.—I had a short conversation with Lord Lansdowne about a disagreeable matter;—that most cruel and calumnious attack which Brougham had made on Lord Rutherford in a paper which had been printed and circulated among the peers who form the Committee on Life Peerages. I was glad to find that there was no chance that the paper would be published. Should it be published, poor Rutherford will not want defenders.'

I can only say that I was quite as much afraid of him as he could be of me. I thought of Winkle and Dowler in the Pickwick Papers.'[1] On the 1st of May in the same year Macaulay says: 'I meant to go to the Museum; but seeing that Lord Shaftesbury has given notice of a petition which may produce a discussion about Christianity in India, I stayed at home all day, preparing myself to speak if there should be occasion. I shall drop no hint of my intention. I cannot help thinking that I shall succeed, if I have voice enough to make myself heard.' But, when the day arrived, he writes: 'Shaftesbury presented the petition with only a few words. Lord Ellenborough said only a few words in answer.[2] To make a long set speech in such circumstances would have been absurd; so I went quietly home.'

In the course of the year 1858 several of those eminent Frenchmen who refused to bow the knee before the Second Empire had frequent and friendly conversations with Macaulay on the future of their unhappy country; but they failed to convince the historian of our great Revolution that the experiment of 1688 could be successfully repeated on Gallic soil. 'I argued strongly,' he writes on one occasion, 'against the notion that much good was likely to be done by insurrection even against the bad governments of the Continent. What good have the revolutions of 1848 done? Or, rather, what harm have they not done? The only revolutions which have turned out well have been defensive revolutions;—ours of 1688; the French of 1830. The American was, to a great extent, of the same kind.' On the 15th of May he says: 'Montalembert called. He talked long, vehemently, and with feeling, about the degraded state of France. I could have said a good deal on the

[1] ' "Mr. Winkle, Sir, be calm. Don't strike me. I won't bear it. A blow! Never!" said Mr. Dowler looking meeker than Mr. Winkle had expected from a gentleman of his ferocity.'

[2] Between February and May Lord Ellenborough had become President of the Indian Board of Control.

other side; but I refrained. I like him much.' A fortnight later: 'Duvergier d'Hauranne called, and brought his son. How he exclaimed against the French Emperor! I do not like the Emperor or his system; but I cannot find that his enemies are able to hold out any reasonable hope, that, if he is pulled down, a better government will be set up. I cannot say to a Frenchman what I think;—that the French have only themselves to thank; and that a people which violently pulls down constitutional governments, and lives quiet under despotism, must be, and ought to be, despotically governed. We should have reformed the government of the House of Orleans without subverting it. We should not have borne the yoke of *Celui-ci* for one day. However, I feel for men like Duvergier d'Hauranne and Montalembert, who are greatly in advance of the body of their countrymen.'

Macaulay had little attention to spare for the politics of the Westminster lobbies or the Parisian boulevards; but it must not be thought that he was growing indifferent to the wider and more permanent interests of the British nation and the British empire. The honour of our flag, and the welfare of our people, were now, as ever, the foremost objects of his solicitude. 'England,' he writes, 'seems to be profoundly quiet. God grant that she may long continue so, and that the history of the years which I may yet have to live may be the dullest portion of her history! It is sad work to live in times about which it is amusing to read.' The fervour of this prayer for public tranquillity was prompted by the recollections of 1857, which were still fresh in Macaulay's mind. On the 29th of June in that terrible year he notes in his diary: 'To breakfast with Milnes. Horrible news from India; massacre of Europeans at Delhi, and mutiny. I have no apprehensions for our Indian Empire; but this is a frightful event. Home; but had no heart to work. I will not try at present.' Again he says, and yet again: 'I cannot settle to work while the Delhi affair is undecided.' His correspondence during the coming months overflows with allusions to India. 'No more news; that is to say, no later news than we had before you started; but private letters are appearing daily in the newspapers. The cruelties of the sepoys have inflamed the nation to a degree unprecedented within my memory. Peace Societies, and Aborigines Protection Societies, and Societies for the Reformation of Criminals, are silenced. There is one terrible cry for revenge. The account of that dreadful military execution at Peshawur,—forty men blown at once from the mouths of cannon,—their heads, legs, arms flying in all directions,—was read with delight by people who three weeks ago were against all capital punishment. Bright himself declares for the vigorous suppression of the mutiny. The almost universal feeling is that not a single sepoy within the walls of Delhi should be spared; and I own that it is a feeling with which I cannot help sympathising.'

When Macaulay was writing these words, the crimes of the mutineers were still unpunished, and their power unbroken. The belief that mercy to the sepoy was no mercy, as long as Delhi remained in rebel hands, was sternly carried into action in the Punjaub and the North-west Provinces of India by men who were sincerely humane both by temperament and by religious conviction. That belief was almost universal among people of our race on both sides of the Atlantic. The public opinion even of philanthropic and abolitionist Boston did not differ on this point from the public opinion of London. 'The India mail,' wrote Dr. Oliver Wendell Holmes, 'brings stories of women and children outraged and murdered. The royal stronghold is in the hands of the babe-killers. England takes down the Map of the World, which she has girdled with empire, and makes a correction thus: DELHI. *Dele*. The civilised world says, Amen!'

'*September* 19, 1857.—The Indian business looks ill. This miserable affair at Dinapore may produce serious inconvenience.[1] However, the tide is near the turn.

[1] The Dinapore Brigade, a force of twenty-five hundred

Within a month the flood of English will come in fast. But it is painful to be so revengeful as I feel myself. I, who cannot bear to see a beast or bird in pain, could look on without winking while Nana Sahib underwent all the tortures of Ravaillac. And these feelings are not mine alone. Is it possible that a year passed under the influence of such feelings should not have some effect on the national character? The effect will be partly good and partly bad. The nerves of our minds will be braced. Effeminate, mawkish philanthropy will lose all its influence. But shall we not hold human life generally cheaper than we have done? Having brought ourselves to exult in the misery of the guilty, shall we not feel less sympathy for the sufferings of the innocent? In one sense, no doubt, in exacting a tremendous retribution we are doing our duty, and performing an act of mercy. So is Calcraft when he hangs a murderer. Yet the habit of hanging murderers is found to injure the character.'

Macaulay did everything which lay in his power to show that at such a crisis he felt a citizen's concern in the fortunes of the commonwealth. At the invitation of the Lord Mayor he became a member of the Committee for the relief of the Indian sufferers. On the day appointed for national humiliation and prayer he writes as follows:

'*October* 7.—Wind and rain. However, I went to church, though by no means well. Nothing could be more solemn or earnest than the aspect of the congregation, which was numerous. The sermon was detestable; ignorance, stupidity, bigotry. If the maxims of this fool, and of others like him, are followed, we shall soon have, not the mutiny of an

bayonets, mutinied on the 25th of July, and a few days later routed, and well-nigh destroyed, an ill-conducted expedition which had been despatched to relieve the European garrison at Arrah. The glorious defence of the little house, and its equally glorious relief, have thrown into shade the memory of the lamentable blunders which gave occasion for that display of intelligent and heroic valour.

army, but the rebellion of a whole nation, to deal with. He would have the Government plant missionaries everywhere, invite the sepoy to listen to Christian instruction, and turn the Government schools into Christian seminaries. Happily there is some security against such mischievous doctrines in the good sense of the country, and a still stronger security in its nonsense. Christianity in teaching sounds very well; but the moment that any plan is proposed, all the sects in the kingdom will be together by the ears. We who are for absolute neutrality shall be supported against such fools as this man by all the Dissenters, by the Scotch, and by the Roman Catholics.'

'*October* 25, 1857.—My birthday. Fifty-seven. I have had a not unpleasant year. My health is not good, but my head is clear and my heart is warm. I receive numerous marks of the good opinion of the public;—a large public, including the educated men both of the old and of the new world. I have been made a peer, with, I think, as general an approbation as I remember in the case of any man that in my time has been made a peer. What is much more important to my happiness than wealth, titles, and even fame, those whom I love are well and happy, and very kind and affectionate to me. These are great things. I have some complaints, however, to make of the past year. The Indian troubles have affected my spirits more than any public events in the whole course of my life. To be sure, the danger which threatened the country at the beginning of April 1848 came nearer to me. But that danger was soon over, and the Indian Mutiny has now lasted several months, and may last months still. The emotions which it excites, too, are of a strong kind. I may say that, till this year, I did not know what real vindictive hatred meant. With what horror I used to read in Livy how Fulvius put to death the whole Capuan Senate in the Second Punic War! And with what equanimity I could hear that the whole garrison of Delhi, all the Moulavies and Mussulman

Doctors there, and all the rabble of the bazaar had been treated in the same way! Is this wrong? Is not the severity which springs from a great sensibility to human suffering a better thing than the lenity which springs from indifference to human suffering? The question may be argued long on both sides.'

'*October* 27.—Huzza! Huzza! Thank God! Delhi is taken. A great event. Glorious to the nation, and one which will resound through all Christendom and Islam. What an exploit for that handful of Englishmen in the heart of Asia to have performed!'[1]

'*November* 11.—Huzza! Good news! Lucknow relieved. Delhi ours. The old dotard a prisoner. God be praised! Another letter from Longman. They have already sold 7,600 more copies. This is near 6,000*l*., as I reckoned, in my pocket. But it gratified me, I am glad to be able to say with truth, far, very far, less than the Indian news. I could hardly eat my dinner for joy.'

The lovers of ballad-poetry may be permitted to wonder how it was that the patriotic ardour which passing events aroused in Macaulay did not find vent in strains resembling those with which he celebrated Ivry and the Armada. It is still more remarkable that, (if we except the stanzas which he wrote after his defeat at Edinburgh,) he never embodied in verse any of those touching expressions of personal emotion which so constantly recur in the pages of his journal. The explanation probably lies in the fact that, from the time when he became a regular contributor to the Edinburgh Review, he always had on hand some weighty and continuous employment which concentrated his imagination, and consumed all his productive energies. There was but one short break in his labours; and that break gave us the Lays of Ancient Rome. 'If,' said Goethe, 'you have a great

[1] On the 28th October Macaulay writes from Holly Lodge to Mr. Ellis, asking him to name a day to 'come out, and drink a glass of claret to the conquerors of Delhi.'

work in your head, nothing else thrives near it.'[1] The truth of this aphorism, representing, as it does, the life-long experience of the greatest master who ever consciously made an art of literature, was at first not very acceptable to Macaulay. But he soon discovered that Clio was a mistress who would be satisfied with no divided allegiance; and her sister muses thenceforward lost the homage of one who might fairly have hoped to be numbered among their favoured votaries.

Long after Macaulay had abandoned all other public business he continued to occupy himself in the administration of the British Museum. In February 1856 he wrote to Lord Lansdowne, with the view of securing that old friend's potent influence in favour of an arrangement by which Professor Owen might be placed in a position worthy of his reputation and of his services. The circumstance which gave rise to the letter was the impending appointment of Signor Panizzi to the post of Secretary and Principal Librarian to the Museum. 'I am glad of this,' writes Macaulay, 'both on public and private grounds. Yet I fear that the appointment will be unpopular both within and without the walls of the Museum. There

[1] This remark was addressed to Eckermann. The whole conversation is highly interesting. 'Beware,' Goethe said, 'of attempting a large work. It is exactly that which injures our best minds, even those distinguished by the finest talents, and the most earnest efforts. I have suffered from this cause, and know how much it has injured me. What have I not let fall into the well! If I had written all that I well might, a hundred volumes would not contain it.

'The Present will have its rights. The thoughts which daily press upon the poet will and should be expressed. But, if you have a great work in your head, nothing else thrives near it; all other thoughts are repelled, and the pleasantness of life itself is for the time lost. What exertion and expenditure of mental force are required to arrange and round off a great whole; and then what powers, and what a tranquil, undisturbed situation in life, to express it with the proper fluency. * * * But if he [the poet] daily seizes the present, and always treats with a freshness of feeling what is offered him, he always makes sure of something good, and, if he sometimes does not succeed, has, at least, lost nothing.'

The English of this passage is that of Mr. Oxenford's translation.

is a growing jealousy among men of science, which, between ourselves, appears even at the Board of Trustees. There is a notion that the Department of Natural History is neglected, and that the library and the sculpture gallery are unduly favoured. This feeling will certainly not be allayed by the appointment of Panizzi, whose great object, during many years, has been to make our library the best in Europe, and who would at any time give three Mammoths for an Aldus.'

Macaulay then went on to propose that, simultaneously with Signor Panizzi's nomination to the Secretaryship, Professor Owen should be constituted Superintendent of the whole department of Natural History, including geology, zoology, botany, and mineralogy. 'I cannot but think,' he says, 'that this arrangement would be beneficial in the highest degree to the Museum. I am sure that it would be popular. I must add that I am extremely desirous that something should be done for Owen. I hardly know him to speak to. His pursuits are not mine. But his fame is spread over Europe. He is an honour to our country, and it is painful to me to think that a man of his merit should be approaching old age amidst anxieties and distresses. He told me that eight hundred a year, without a house in the Museum, would be opulence to him. He did not, he said, even wish for more. His seems to me to be a case for public patronage. Such patronage is not needed by eminent literary men or artists. A poet, a novelist, an historian, a painter, a sculptor, who stood in his own line as high as Owen stands among men of science, could never be in want except by his own fault. But the greatest natural philosopher may starve, while his countrymen are boasting of his discoveries, and while foreign Academies are begging for the honour of being allowed to add his name to their list.'[1]

[1] On the 26th of May, 1856, Professor Owen was appointed Superintendent of the Department of Natural History with a salary of 800*l*. a year.

From the moment when, in the summer of 1854, Macaulay had definitely and deliberately braced himself to the work of completing the second great instalment of the History, he went to his daily labours without intermission and without reluctance until his allotted task had been accomplished. When that result had been attained,—when his third and fourth volumes were actually in the hands of the public,—it was not at first that he became aware how profoundly his already enfeebled health had been strained by the prolonged effort which the production of those volumes had cost him. At every previous epoch in his life the termination of one undertaking had been a signal for the immediate commencement of another; but in 1856 summer succeeded to spring, and gave place to autumn, before he again took pen in hand. For many weeks together he indulged himself in the pleasure of loitering over those agreeable occupations which follow in the train of a literary success;—answering letters of congratulation; returning thanks, more or less sincere, for the suggestions and criticisms which poured in from the most opposite, and sometimes the most unexpected, quarters; preparing new editions; and reading everything that the Reviews had to say about him with the placid enjoyment of a veteran author.

'I bought the British Quarterly Review;—an article on my book, praise and blame. Like other writers I swallow the praise, and think the blame absurd. But in truth I do think that the fault-finding is generally unreasonable, though the book is, no doubt, faulty enough. It is well for its reputation that I do not review it, as I could review it.' 'Fraser's Magazine. Very laudatory. The author evidently John Kemble. He is quite right in saying that I have passed lightly over continental politics. But was this wrong? I think I could defend myself. I am writing a History of England; and as to grubbing, as he recommends, in Saxon and Hessian archives for the purpose of ascertaining all the details of the continental negotiations of that time, I should have doubled my labour, already severe enough. That I have not given a generally correct view of our continental relations he certainly has not shown.' 'After breakfast to the Athenæum, and saw articles on my book in the Dublin Review, and the National Review. Very well satisfied to find that the whole skill and knowledge of Maynooth could make no impression on my account of the Irish war.' 'I received the Allgemeine Zeitung, and found in it a long article on my book, very laudatory, and to me very agreeable; for I hold the judgment of foreigners to be a more sure prognostic of what the judgment of posterity is likely to be than the judgment of my own countrymen.' 'I made some changes in my account of James's Declaration of 1692. If my critics had been well informed, they might have worried me about one paragraph on that subject. But it escaped them, and now I have put everything to rights.' 'To-day I got a letter from ——, pointing out what I must admit to be a gross impropriety of language in my book;—an impropriety of a sort rare, I hope with me. It shall be corrected; and I am obliged to the fellow, little as I like him.'

At length, on the 1st of October, 1856, Macaulay notes in his diary: 'To the Museum, and turned over the Dutch despatches for information about the fire of Whitehall. Home, and wrote a sheet of foolscap, the first of Part III. God knows whether I shall ever finish that part. I begin it with little heart or hope.' In the summer of 1857 he remarks: 'How the days steal away, and nothing done! I think often of Johnson's lamentations repeated every Easter over his own idleness. But the cases differ. Often I have felt this morbid incapacity to work; but never so long and so strong as of late;—the natural effect of age and ease.' On the 14th of July in the same year: 'I wrote a good deal to-day; Darien. The humour has returned, and I shall woo it to continue. What better amusement can I have, if it should prove no more than an amusement?' And again: 'Read about the Darien affair. It will be impossible to tell the truth as to that matter without putting the Scotch into a rage. But the truth shall be told.'

The intrinsic importance of the work on which Macaulay was now engaged could hardly be overrated; for the course of his History had brought him to a most momentous era in the political annals of our country. It was his business to tell the story, and to point the lesson, of the years from 1697 to 1701; —those years when the majority in the House of Commons was already the strongest force in the State, but when the doctrine that the executive administration must be in the hands of Ministers who possessed the confidence of that majority had not as yet been recognised as a constitutional axiom. Nothing which he has ever written is more valuable than his account of the grave perils which beset the kingdom during that period of transition, or than his vivid and thoughtful commentary upon our method of government by alternation of parties. No passage in all his works more clearly illustrates the union of intellectual qualities which formed the real secret of his strength, —the combination in one and the same man of literary power, historical learning, and practical familiarity with the conduct of great affairs.[1]

Nor again, as specimens of narrative carefully planned and vigorously sustained, has he produced anything with which his descriptions of the visit of the Czar, the trial of Spencer Cowper,[2] and, above

[1] See especially the two paragraphs in Chapter XXIV which commence with the words, 'If a Minister were now to find himself thus situated—.' There is little doubt that Lord Carlisle had something of this in his mind when he wrote in his diary of the 28th of March, 1861: 'I finished Macaulay's fifth volume, and felt in despair to close that brilliant pictured page. I think it even surpasses in interest and animation what had gone before; and higher praise no man can give. The leading reflection is, how as a nation we have been rescued, led, and blessed; by the side of this, how much of the old faults and leaven still remain.'

[2] The page of Macaulay's manuscript, which is preserved in the British Museum, is taken from his account of the trial of Spencer Cowper.

all, the fatal hallucination of Darien, may not fairly rank. And yet, however effective were the episodes which thickly strew the portion of his History that he did not live to publish, there can be no question that the alacrity with which he had once pursued his great undertaking had begun to languish. 'I find it difficult,' he writes in February 1857, 'to settle to my work. This is an old malady of mine. It has not prevented me from doing a good deal in the course of my life. Of late I have felt this impotence more than usual. The chief reason, I believe, is the great doubt which I feel whether I shall live long enough to finish another volume of my book.' He already knew, to use the expression which he applied to the dying William of Orange, 'that his time was short, and grieved, with a grief such as only noble spirits feel, to think that he must leave his work but half finished.'

Gradually and unwillingly Macaulay acquiesced in the conviction that he must submit to leave untold that very portion of English history which he was competent to treat as no man again will treat it. Others may study the reign of Anne with a more minute and exclusive diligence; the discovery of materials hitherto concealed cannot fail from time to time to throw fresh light upon transactions so extensive and complicated as those which took place between the rupture of the Peace of Ryswick and the accession of the House of Brunswick; but it may safely be affirmed that few or none of Macaulay's successors will be imbued like him with the enthusiasm of the period. There are phases of literary taste which pass away, never to recur; and the early associations of future men of letters will seldom be connected with the Rape of the Lock and the Essay on Criticism,—with the Spectator, the Guardian, the Freeholder, the Memoirs of Martinus Scriblerus, and the History of John Bull. But Macaulay's youth was nourished upon Pope, and Bolingbroke and Atterbury, and Defoe. Everything which had been written by them, or about them, was as familiar to him as the Lady of the Lake, and the Bride of

Abydos, were to the generation which was growing up when Lockhart's Life of Scott and Moore's Life of Byron were making their first appearance in the circulating libraries. He had Prior's burlesque verses, and Arbuthnot's pasquinades, as completely at his fingers'-ends as a clever public-school boy of fifty years ago had the Rejected Addresses or the poetry of the Anti-Jacobin. He knew every pamphlet which had been put forth by Swift, or Steele, or Addison as well as Tories of 1790 knew their Burke, or Radicals of 1820 knew their Cobbett. There were times when he amused himself with the hope that he might even yet be permitted to utilise these vast stores of information, on each separate fragment of which he could so easily lay his hand. His diary shows him to have spent more than one summer afternoon 'walking in the portico, and reading pamphlets of Queen Anne's time.' But he had no real expectation that the knowledge which he thus acquired would ever be turned to account. Others, who could not bring themselves to believe that such raciness of phrase, and such vivacity of intellect, belonged to one whose days were already numbered, confidently reckoned upon his making good the brave words which form the opening sentence of the first chapter of his History. One old friend describes himself in a letter as looking forward to the seventh and eight volumes in order to satisfy his curiosity about the reigns of the first two Georges; which, he says, 'are to me the dark ages.' Another is sanguine enough to anticipate the pleasure of reading what Macaulay would have to say about 'the great improvement of the steam-engine, and its consequences.' But, by the time that he had written a few pages of his fifth volume, the author himself would have been well content to be assured that he would live to carry his History, in a complete and connected form, down to the death of his hero, William of Orange.

During the later years of his life Macaulay sent an occasional article to the Encyclopædia Britannica.

'He had ceased,' says Mr. Adam Black, 'to write for the reviews or other periodicals, though often earnestly solicited to do so. It is entirely to his friendly feeling that I am indebted for those literary gems, which could not have been purchased with money; and it is but justice to his memory that I should record, as one of the many instances of the kindness and generosity of his heart, that he made it a stipulation of his contributing to the Encyclopædia that remuneration should not be so much as mentioned.' The articles in question are those on Atterbury, Bunyan, Goldsmith, Doctor Johnson, and William Pitt. The last of these, which is little more than seventy octavo pages in length, was on hand for three quarters of a year. Early in November 1857 Macaulay writes: 'The plan of a good character of Pitt is forming in my mind;' and, on the 9th of August 1858: 'I finished and sent off the paper which has caused me so much trouble. I began it, I see, in last November. What a time to have been dawdling over such a trifle!'

The conscientious and unsparing industry of his former days now brought Macaulay a reward of a value quite inestimable in the eyes of every true author. The habit of always working up to the highest standard within his reach was so ingrained in his nature, that, however sure and rapid might be the decline of his physical strength, the quality of his productions remained the same as ever. Instead of writing worse, he only wrote less. Compact in form, crisp and nervous in style, these five little essays are everything which an article in an Encyclopædia should be. The reader, as he travels softly and swiftly along, congratulates himself on having lighted upon what he regards as a most fascinating literary or political memoir; but the student, on a closer examination, discovers that every fact, and date, and circumstance is distinctly and faithfully recorded in its due chronological sequence. Macaulay's belief about himself as a writer was that he improved to the last; and the question of the superiority of his later over his earlier manner may securely be staked upon a comparison between the article on Johnson in the Edinburgh Review, and the article on Johnson in the Encyclopædia Britannica. The latter of the two is indeed a model of that which its eminent subject pronounced to be the essential qualification of a biographer,—the art of writing trifles with dignity.[1]

Macaulay was under no temptation to over-write himself; for his time never hung heavy on his hands. He had a hundred devices for dissipating the monotony of his days. Now that he had ceased to strain his faculties, he thought it necessary to assure himself from time to time that they were not rusting; like an old Greek warrior who continued to exercise in the Gymnasium the vigour which he no longer expended in the field. 'I walked in the portico,' he writes in October, 1857, 'and learned by heart the noble Fourth Act of the Merchant of Venice. There are four hundred lines, of which I knew a hundred and fifty. I made myself perfect master of the whole, the prose letter included, in two hours.' And again: 'I learned the passage in which Lucretius represents Nature expostulating with men, who complain of the general law of mortality. Very fine it is; but it strikes me that the Epicureans exaggerated immensely the effect which religious terrors and the fears of future punishment had on their contemporaries, for the purpose of exalting their master, as having delivered mankind from a horrible mental slavery. I see no trace of such feelings in any part of the literature of those times except in these Epicurean declamations.' 'I have pretty nearly learned all that I like best in Catullus. He grows on me with intimacy. One thing he has,—I do not know whether it belongs to him, or to something in myself,—but there are some chords of

[1] A gentleman once observed to Doctor Johnson that he excelled his competitors in writing biography. 'Sir,' was the complacent reply, 'I believe that is true. The dogs don't know how to write trifles with dignity.'

my mind which he touches as nobody else does. The first lines of "Miser Catulle;" the lines to Cornificius, written evidently from a sick bed;[1] and part of the poem beginning "Si qua recordanti" affect me more than I can explain. They always move me to tears.' 'I have now gone through the first seven books of Martial, and have learned about 360 of the best lines. His merit seems to me to lie, not in wit, but in the rapid succession of vivid images. I wish he were less nauseous. He is as great a beast as Aristophanes. He certainly is a very clever, pleasant writer. Sometimes he runs Catullus himself hard. But besides his indecency, his servility and his mendicancy disgust me. In his position,—for he was a Roman Knight,—something more like self-respect would have been becoming. I make large allowance for the difference of manners; but it never can have been *comme il faut* in any age or nation for a man of note,—an accomplished man,—a man living with the great,—to be constantly asking for money, clothes, and dainties, and to pursue with volleys of abuse those who would give him nothing.'

In September 1857 Macaulay writes: 'I have at odd moments been studying the Peerage. I ought to be better informed about the assembly in which I am to sit.' He soon could repeat off book the entire roll of the House of Lords; and a few days afterwards comes the entry, 'more exercise for my memory,—Second titles.' When he had done with the Peerage, he turned to the Cambridge, and then to the Oxford, Calendars. 'I have now,' he says, 'the whole of our University Fasti by heart; all, I mean, that is worth remembering. An idle thing, but I wished to try whether my memory is as strong as it used to be, and I perceive no decay.'

'*June* 1, 1858.—I am vexed to think I am losing my German. I am resolved to win it back. No sooner said than done. I took Schiller's History of the War in the

[1] Male est, Cornifici, tuo Catullo.
Male est, mehercule, et laboriose.

Netherlands out into the garden and read a hundred pages. I will do the same daily all the summer.' Having found the want of Italian on his annual tours, Macaulay engaged a master to assist him in speaking the language. 'We talked,' he says, 'an hour and a quarter. I got on wonderfully; much better than I at all expected.' I well remember my uncle's account of the interview. As long as the lessons related to the ordinary colloquialisms of the road, the rail, and the hotel, Macaulay had little to say and much to learn; but, whenever the conversation turned upon politics or literature, his companion was fairly bewildered by the profusion of his somewhat archaic vocabulary. The preceptor could scarcely believe his ears when a pupil, who had to be taught the current expressions required for getting his luggage through the custom-house or his letters from the Poste Restante, suddenly fell to denouncing the French occupation of Rome in a torrent of phrases that might have come straight from the pen of Fra Paolo.

The zest with which Macaulay pursued the amusements that beguiled his solitary hours contributed not a little to his happiness and his equanimity. During his last two years he would often lay aside his book, and bury himself in financial calculations connected with the Stock Market, the Revenue Returns, the Civil Service Estimates, and, above all, the Clergy List. He would pass one evening in comparing the average duration of the lives of Archbishops, Prime Ministers, and Lord Chancellors; and another in tracing the careers of the first half-dozen men in each successive Mathematical Tripos, in order to ascertain whether, in the race of the world, the Senior Wrangler generally contrived to keep ahead of his former competitors. In default of any other pastime, he would have recourse to the retrospect of old experiences and achievements, or would divert himself by giving the rein to the vagaries of his fancy. 'I took up Knight's Magazine the other day, and, after an interval of perhaps thirty years, read a Roman novel which I wrote at Trinity. To be sure, I was a smart lad, but a sadly unripe scholar for such an undertaking.'[1] And again: 'I read my own writings during some hours, and was not ill-pleased on the whole. Yet, alas, how short life, and how long art! I feel as if I had but just begun to understand how to write; and the probability is that I have very nearly done writing.' 'I find,' he says in another place, 'that I dream away a good deal of time now; not more perhaps than formerly; but formerly I dreamed my day-dreams chiefly while walking. Now I dream, sitting or standing by my fire. I will write, if I live, a fuller disquisition than has ever yet been written on that strange habit,—a good habit, in some respects. I, at least, impute to it a great part of my literary success.'[2]

And so Macaulay dwelt at ease in his pleasant retreat, a classic in his own lifetime. His critics, and still more his readers, honoured him with a deferential indulgence which is seldom exhibited towards a contemporary. One or another of the Magazines occasionally published an article reflecting upon his partiality as an historian; but he held his peace, and the matter, whatever it might be, soon died away. The world apparently refused to trouble itself with any misgivings that might impair the enjoyment which it derived from its pages. People were as little disposed to resent his disliking James, and admiring William, as they would have been to quarrel with Tacitus for making Tiberius a tyrant and Germanicus a hero. Macaulay, in his diary, mentions a circumstance illustrating the position which he already occupied in the popular estimation. A gentleman moving in

[1] The 'Fragments of a Roman Tale' are printed in Macaulay's Miscellaneous Writings.

[2] 'I went yesterday to Weybridge,' he says in a letter to Mr. Ellis. 'We talked about the habit of building castles in the air, a habit in which Lady Trevelyan and I indulge beyond any people that I ever knew. I mentioned to George what, as far as I know, no critic has observed, that the Greeks called this habit *κενὴ μακαρία* (empty happiness).'

good, and even high, society,—as thorough a man of the world as any in London,—who had the misfortune to be a natural son, called on him in order to make a formal remonstrance on his having used the term 'bastard' in his History, and earnestly entreated him not to sanction so cruel an epithet with his immense authority.[1]

It may easily be supposed that Macaulay's literary celebrity attracted round him his full share of imitators and plagiarists, assailants and apologists, busybodies and mendicants. 'A new number of the Review. There is an article which is a mocking-bird imitation of me. Somehow or other, the mimic cannot catch the note, but many people would not be able to distinguish. Sometimes he borrows outright. "Language so pure and holy that it would have become the lips of those angels——." This is rather audacious. However, I shall not complain. A man should have enough to spare something for thieves.' 'I looked through ——'s two volumes. He is, I see, an imitator of me. But I am a very unsafe model. My manner is, I think, and the world thinks, on the whole a good one; but it is very near to a very bad manner indeed, and those characteristics of my style which are most easily copied, are the most questionable.' 'There are odd instances of folly and impertinence. A clergyman of the Scotch Episcopal Church is lecturing at Windsor. He wrote to me three weeks ago to ask the meaning of the allusion to St. Cecilia in my account of the trial of Warren Hastings. I answered him civilly, and he wrote to thank me. Now he writes again to say that he has forgotten a verse of my Horatius, and begs me to write it for him; as if there was nobody in the kingdom, except me, to apply to. There is a fool at Wiesbaden, who sent me some days ago, a heap of execrable verses. I told him that they were bad, and advised him to take to some other pursuit. As

[1] The word in question is applied to the Duc du Maine, in Macaulay's account of the siege of Namur in his twenty-first Chapter.

examples illustrating my meaning, I pointed out half-a-dozen lines. Now he sends me twice as many verses, and begs me to review them. He has, he assures me, corrected the lines to which I objected. I have sent him back his second batch with a letter which he cannot misunderstand.' 'A letter from a man in Scotland, who says that he wants to publish a novel, and that he will come up and show me the manuscript if I will send him fifty pounds. Really, I can get better novels cheaper.' 'What strange begging letters I receive! A fellow has written to me telling me that he is a painter, and adjuring me, as I love the fine arts, to hire or buy him a cow to paint from.'

'A schoolmaster at Cheltenham,' writes Macaulay to his sister, 'sent me two years and a half ago a wretched pamphlet about British India. In answering him, I pointed out two gross blunders into which he had fallen, and which, as he proposed to publish a small edition for the use of schools, I advised him to correct. My reward was that his book was advertised as "revised and corrected by Lord Macaulay." It is idle to be angry with people of this sort. They do after their kind. One might as well blame a fly for buzzing.' 'An article on me in Blackwood. The writer imagines that William the Third wrote his letters in English, and takes Coxe's translations for the original. A pretty fellow to set me to rights on points of history!' 'I was worried by ——, who, in spite of repeated entreaties, pesters me with his officious defences of my accuracy against all comers. Sometimes it is the Saturday Review; then Paget; and now it is Blackwood. I feel that I shall be provoked at last into saying something very sharp.' 'Some great fool has sent me a card printed with a distich, which he calls an Impromptu on two bulky histories lately published:

> Two fabulists; how different the reward!
> One justly censured, t'other made a Lord.

Whom he means by the other I have not the slightest

notion. That a man should be stupid enough to take such a couplet to a printer, and have it printed, purely in order to give pain, which, after all, he does not give! I often think that an extensive knowledge of literary history is of inestimable value to a literary man; I mean as respects the regulating of his mind, the moderating of his hopes and of his fears, and the strengthening of his fortitude. I have had detractors enough to annoy me, if I had not known that no writer equally successful with myself has ever suffered so little from detraction; and that many writers, more deserving and less successful than myself, have excited envy which has appeared in the form of the most horrible calumnies. The proper answer to abuse is contempt, to which I am by nature sufficiently prone; and contempt does not show itself by contemptuous expressions.'

Now and again, when Macaulay happened to be in a mood for criticism, he would fill a couple of pages in his journal with remarks suggested by the book which he had in reading at the time. A few of these little essays are worth preserving.

'I cannot understand the mania of some people about Defoe. They think him a man of the first order of genius, and a paragon of virtue. He certainly wrote an excellent book,—the first part of Robinson Crusoe,—one of those feats which can only be performed by the union of luck with ability. That awful solitude of a quarter of a century,—that strange union of comfort, plenty, and security with the misery of loneliness,—was my delight before I was five years old, and has been the delight of hundreds of thousands of boys. But what has Defoe done great except the first part of Robinson Crusoe? The second part is poor in comparison. The History of the Plague, and the Memoirs of a Cavalier, are in one sense curious works of art. They are wonderfully like true histories; but, considered as novels, which they are, there is not much in them. He had undoubtedly a knack at making fiction look like truth. But is such a knack much to be admired? Is it not of the same sort with the knack of a painter who takes in the birds with his fruit? I have seen dead game painted in such a way that I thought the partridges and pheasants real;

but surely such pictures do not rank high as works of art. Villemain, and before him Lord Chatham, were deceived by the Memoirs of a Cavalier; but, when those Memoirs are known to be fictitious, what are they worth? How immeasurably inferior to Waverley, or the Legend of Montrose, or Old Mortality! As to Moll Flanders, Roxana, and Captain Jack, they are utterly wretched and nauseous; in no respect that I can see beyond the reach of Afra Behn.[1] As a political writer Defoe is merely one of the crowd. He seems to have been an unprincipled hack, ready to take any side of any question. Of all writers he was the most unlucky in irony. Twice he was prosecuted for what he meant to be ironical; but he was so unskilful that everybody understood him literally. Some of his tracts are worse than immoral; quite beastly. Altogether I do not like him.'

'Lord Stanhope sent me the first volume of the Peel papers. I devoured them. The volume relates entirely to the Catholic question. It contains some interesting details which are new; but it leaves Peel where he was. I always noticed while he was alive, and I observe again in this his posthumous defence, an obstinate determination not to understand what the charge was which I, and others who agreed with me, brought against him. He always affected to think that we blamed him for his conduct in 1829, and he produced proofs of what we were perfectly ready to admit,—that in 1829 the State would have been in great danger if the Catholic disabilities had not been removed. Now, what we blamed was his conduct in 1825, and still more in 1827. We said: "Either you were blind not to foresee what was coming, or you acted culpably in not settling the question when it might have been settled without the disgrace of yielding to agitation and to the fear of insurrection; and you acted most culpably in deserting and persecuting Canning." To this, which was our

[1] 'Take back your bonny Mrs. Behn,' said Mrs. Keith of Ravelstone to her grand-nephew Sir Walter Scott; 'and, if you will take my advice, put her in the fire, for I found it impossible to get through the very first novel. But is it not a very odd thing that I, an old woman of eighty and upwards, sitting alone, feel myself ashamed to read a book which, sixty years ago, I have heard read aloud for the amusement of large circles, consisting of the first and most creditable society in London?'

real point, he does not even allude. He is a debater even in this book.'[1]

'I walked in the garden, and read Cicero's speeches for Sextius and Cœlius, and the invective against Vatinius. The egotism is perfectly intolerable. I know nothing like it in literature. The man's self-importance amounted to a monomania. To me the speeches, tried by the standard of English forensic eloquence, seem very bad. They have no tendency to gain a verdict. They are fine lectures, fine declamations, excellent for Exeter Hall or the Music Room at Edinburgh; but not to be named with Scarlett's or Erskine's speeches, considered as speeches meant to convince and persuade juries. We ought to know, however, what the temper of those Roman tribunals was. Perhaps a mere political harangue may have had an effect on the Forum which it could not have in the Court of King's Bench. We ought also to know how far in some of these cases Hortensius and others had disposed of questions of evidence before Cicero's turn came. The peroration seems to have been reserved for him. But imagine a barrister now, defending a man accused of heading a riot at an election, telling the jury that he thought this an excellent opportunity of instructing the younger part of the audience in the galleries, touching the distinction between Whigs and Tories; and then proceeding to give an historical dissertation of an hour on the Civil War, the Exclusion Bill, the Revolution, the Peace of Utrecht, and heaven knows what! Yet this is strictly analogous to what Cicero did in his defence of Sextius.'

'I went to the Athenæum, and stayed there two hours to read John Mill on Liberty and on Reform. Much that is good in both. What he says about individuality in the treatise on Liberty is open, I think, to some criticism. What is meant by the complaint that there is no individuality now? Genius takes its own course, as it always did. Bolder invention was never known in science than in our time. The steam-ship, the steam-carriage, the electric telegraph, the gas lights, the new military engines, are instances. Geology is quite a new true science. Phrenology is quite a new false one. Whatever may be thought of the

[1] Macaulay writes elsewhere: 'I read Guizot's Sir Robert Peel. Hardly quite worthy of Guizot's powers, I think; nor can it be accepted as a just estimate of Peel. I could draw his portrait much better, but for many reasons I shall not do so.'

theology, the metaphysics, the political theories of our time, boldness and novelty is not what they want. Comtism, St. Simonianism, Fourierism, are absurd enough, but surely they are not indications of a servile respect for usage and authority. Then the clairvoyance, the spirit-rapping, the table-turning, and all those other dotages and knaveries indicate rather a restless impatience of the beaten paths than a stupid determination to plod on in those paths. Our lighter literature, as far as I know it, is spasmodic and eccentric. Every writer seems to aim at doing something odd,—at defying all rules and canons of criticism. The metre must be queer; the diction queer. So great is the taste for oddity that men who have no recommendation but oddity hold a high place in vulgar estimation. I therefore do not like to see a man of Mill's excellent abilities recommending eccentricity as a thing almost good in itself —as tending to prevent us from sinking into that Chinese, that Byzantine, state which I should agree with him in considering as a great calamity. He is really crying "Fire!" in Noah's flood.'

'I read the Quarterly Reviews of 1830, 1831, and 1832, and was astonished by the poorness and badness of the political articles. I do not think that this is either personal or political prejudice in me, though I certainly did not like Southey, and though I had a strong antipathy to Croker, who were the two chief writers. But I see the merit of many of Southey's writings with which I am far from agreeing;—Espriella's Letters, for example, and the Life of Wesley; and I see the merit of the novels of Theodore Hook, whom I held in greater abhorrence than even Croker, stuffed as those novels are with scurrility against my political friends. Nay, I can see merit in Warren's Ten Thousand a Year. I therefore believe that my estimate of these political papers in the Quarterly Review is a fair one; and to me they seem to be mere trash—absurd perversions of history; parallels which show no ingenuity, and from which no instruction can be derived; predictions which the event has singularly falsified; abuse substituted for argument; and not one paragraph of wit or eloquence. It is all forgotten, all gone to the dogs. The nonsense which Southey talks about political economy is enough to settle my opinion of his understanding. He says that no man of sense ever troubles himself about such pseudo-scientific questions as what rent is, or what wages are. Surely he could not be such a dunce as not to know that a part of the produce of a landed estate goes to the proprietor, and a part to the cultivator; and he must, unless he had a strange sort of skull, have supposed that there was some law or other which regulated the distribution of the produce between these parties. And, if there be such a law, how can it be unworthy of a man of sense to try to find out what it is? Can any inquiry be more important to the welfare of society? Croker is below Southey; for Southey had a good style, and Croker had nothing but italics and capitals as substitutes for eloquence and reason.'

'I read a great deal of the Memoirs of Southey by his son;—little more than Southey's own letters for the most part. I do not know how it happened that I never read the book before. It has not at all altered my opinion of Southey. A good father, husband, brother, friend, but prone to hate people he did not know, solely on account of differences of opinion, and in his hatred singularly bitter and rancorous. Then he was arrogant beyond any man in literary history; for his self-conceit was proof against the severest admonitions. The utter failure of one of his books only confirmed him in his opinion of its excellence. Then he had none of that dissatisfaction with his own performances which I, perhaps because I have a great deal of it, am prone to believe to be a good sign. Southey says, some time after Madoc had been published, and when the first ardour of composition must have abated, that the execution is perfect; that it cannot be better. I have had infinitely greater success as a writer than Southey, and, though I have not written a fifth part, not a tenth part, of what he wrote, have made more thousands by literature than he made hundreds. And yet I can truly say that I never read again the most popular passages of my own works without painfully feeling how far my execution has fallen short of the standard which is in my mind. He says that Thalaba is equal or superior to the Orlando Furioso, and that it is the greatest poem that has appeared during ages;—and this over and over again, when nobody would read it, and when the copies were heaped up in the booksellers' garrets. His History of Brazil is to be immortal—to be a mine of wealth to his family under an improved system of copyright. His Peninsular War, of which I never could get through the first volume, is to live for ever. To do him justice, he had a fine manly spirit where money was concerned. His conduct about Chatteron and Kirke

White, at a time when a guinea was an object to himself, was most honourable. I could forgive him a great deal for it.'

Macaulay had a very slight acquaintance with the works of some among the best writers of his own generation. He was not fond of new lights, unless they had been kindled at the ancient beacons; and he was apt to prefer a third-rate author, who had formed himself after some recognised model, to a man of high genius whose style and method were strikingly different from anything that had gone before. In books, as in people and places, he loved that, and that only, to which he had been accustomed from boyhood upwards.[1] Very few among the students of Macaulay will have detected the intensity and, in some cases, (it must be confessed,) the wilfulness of his literary conservatism; for, with the instinctive self-restraint of a great artist, he permitted no trace of it to appear in his writings. In his character of a responsible critic, he carefully abstained from giving expression to prejudices in which, as a reader, he freely indulged. Those prejudices injured nobody but himself; and the punishment which befel him, from the very nature of the case, was exactly proportioned to the offence. To be blind to the merits of a great author is a sin which brings its own penalty; and, in Macaulay's instance, that penalty was severe indeed. Little as he was aware of it, it was no slight privation that one who had by heart the Battle of Marathon, as told by Herodotus, and the Raising of the Siege of

[1] The remarks in Macaulay's journal on the 'History of Civilisation' curiously illustrate the spirit in which he approached a new author. What he liked best in Buckle was that he had some of the faults of Warburton. '*March* 24, 1858.—I read Buckle's book all day, and got to the end, skipping of course. A man of talent and of a good deal of reading, but paradoxical and incoherent. He is eminently an anticipator, as Bacon would have said. He wants to make a system before he has got the materials; and he has not the excuse which Aristotle had, of having an eminently systematising mind. The book reminds me perpetually of the Divine Legation. I could draw the parallel out far.'

Syracuse, as told by Thucydides, should have passed through life without having felt the glow which Mr. Carlyle's story of the charge across the ravine at Dunbar could not fail to awake even in a Jacobite; that one who so keenly relished the exquisite trifling of Plato should never have tasted the description of Coleridge's talk in the Life of John Stirling,—a passage which yields to nothing of its own class in the Protagoras or the Symposium; that one who eagerly and minutely studied all that Lessing has written on art, or Goethe on poetry, should have left unread Mr. Ruskin's comparison between the landscape of the Odyssey and the landscape of the Divine Comedy, or his analysis of the effect produced on the imagination by long continued familiarity with the aspect of the Campanile of Giotto.

Great, beyond all question, was the intellectual enjoyment that Macaulay forfeited by his unwillingness to admit the excellence of anything which had been written in bold defiance of the old canons; but, heavy as the sacrifice was, he could readily afford to make it. With his omnivorous and insatiable appetite for books there was, indeed, little danger that he would ever be at a loss for something to read. A few short extracts, taken at random from the last volume of his journals, will sufficiently indicate how extensive and diversified were the regions of literature over which he roved at will. 'I turned over Philo, and compared his narrative with Josephus. It is amusing to observe with what skill those Jews, trained in Greek learning, exhibited the philosophical side of their religion to the Pagan scholars and statesmen, and kept out of sight the ceremonial part. It was just the contrary, I imagine, with the lower class of Jews, who became, in some sense, the spiritual directors of silly women at Rome.' 'Letters to Père Daniel. Odd how all the controversial books to which the Lettres Provinciales gave occasion have perished and been forgotten, and the Lettres remain.[1] Accurate or

[1] On December 7, 1852, Macaulay writes in his diary: 'To

inaccurate, they form the opinion of mankind touching the Jesuit morality.' 'I read a good deal of Fray Gerundio. A good book. The traits of manners are often interesting. There is something remarkable in the simple plenty and joyousness of the life of the rustics of Old Castile.' 'I read some of a novel about sporting;—a Mr. Sponge the hero. It was a new world to me, so I bore with the hasty writing, and was entertained.' 'I read some of Tieck; the Brothers, and the Preface to the collected works. He complains that his countrymen are slow to take a joke. He should consider that the jokes which he, and some of his brother writers, are in the habit of producing are not laughing matters. Then Sir Walter Scott's Life. I had Rokeby out, and turned it over. Poor work; and yet there are gleams of genius few and far between. What a blunder to make the scenery the foreground, and the human actors the background, of a picture! In the Lay the human actors stand out as they should; and the Aill, and the Tweed, and Melrose Abbey are in proper subordination. Even in the Lady of the Lake, Loch Katrine does not throw Fitzjames and Roderic into the shade; but Rokeby is primarily a descriptive poem like Grongar Hill. There was some foundation for Moore's sarcastic remark that Scott meant to do all the gentlemen's seats from Edinburgh to London. The only good thing in the poem is the Buccaneer.' 'I read Ælian for the first time. Odd that it should be for the first time! I despatched the whole volume in a few hours, skimming and reading sometimes the Greek, and sometimes the Latin translation, which I thought more than usually well written. The most interesting fact which I learned from this very miscellaneous collection of information was that there were said to be translations of Homer into the Persian and Indian languages, and that those translations

dine with Van de Weyer. A Frenchman, or Fleming, said that the word *pudeur* was modern, and could not be found in the writers of Lewis XIV's age. I floored him with the Provincial Letters.'

were sung by the barbarians. I had never heard this mentioned. The thing is really not impossible. The conquests of Alexander must have made the Greek language well known to men whose mother tongue was the Persian or the Sanskrit. I wish to Heaven that the translation could be found.'

Some of the great metaphysical philosophers, both ancient and modern, were among the authors with whom Macaulay was most familiar; but he read them for the pleasure of admiring the ingenuity of their arguments or the elegance of their literary manner, and not from any sympathy with the subject-matter of their works. He was, in fact, very much inclined towards the opinion expressed by Voltaire in Zadig: 'Il savait de la métaphysique ce qu'on a su dans tous les âges,—c'est à dire, fort peu de chose.' But there was another field of inquiry and discussion in which he was never tired of ranging. He had a strong and enduring predilection for religious speculation and controversy, and was widely and profoundly read in ecclesiastical history. His partiality for studies of this nature is proved by the full and elaborate notes with which he has covered the margin of such books as Warburton's Julian, Middleton's Free Inquiry, Middleton's Letters to Venn and Waterland, and all the rest of the crop of polemical treatises which the Free Inquiry produced.[1]

[1] 'Middleton,' writes Macaulay, 'does not shine in any of his strictly controversial pieces. He is too querulous and egotistical. Above all, he is not honest. He knew that what alarmed the Church was not his conclusion, but the arguments by which he arrived at that conclusion. His conclusion might be just, and yet Christianity might be of Divine origin; but his arguments seem to be quite as applicable to the miracles related by St. Luke as to those related by Jerome. He was in a deplorable predicament. He boasted of his love of truth and of his courage, and yet he was paltering and shamming through the whole controversy. He should have made up his mind from the beginning, whether he had the courage to face obloquy and abuse, to give up all hopes of preferment, and to speak plainly out. If, from selfish motives, (or, as I rather believe and hope, from a real conviction that, by attacking the Christian religion, he should do more harm than good to mankind,) he determined to call himself a Christian, and to

But nowhere are there such numerous and deeply-marked traces of his passion for Church history as in the pages of Strype's biographies of the bishops who played a leading part in the English Reformation. Those grim folios of six generations back,—the lives of Cranmer, and Grindal, and Whitgift, and Parker, acquire all the interest of a contemporary narrative if read with the accompaniment of Macaulay's vivid and varied comments. When, at the commencement of the Life of Cranmer, Strype apologises for employing phraseology which even in his own day was obsolete and uncouth, he obtained an easy pardon from his assiduous student. 'I like,' says Macaulay, 'his old-fashioned style. He writes like a man who lived with the people of an earlier age. He had thoroughly imbued himself with the spirit of the sixteenth century.'[1] And again: 'Strype was an honest man and a most valuable writer. Perhaps no person with so slender abilities has done so much to improve our knowledge of English history.' Somewhat later in the same volume, when Gardiner first appears upon the scene, Macaulay writes: 'Gardiner had very great vices. He was a dissembler and a persecutor. But he was, on the whole, the first public man of his generation in England. He had, I believe, a real love for his country. He showed a greater respect for Parliaments than any statesman of that time. He opposed the Spanish match. When forced to consent to it, he did his best to obtain such terms as might secure the

respect the sacred books, he should have kept altogether out of a controversy which inevitably brought him into the necessity of either declaring himself an infidel, or resorting to a thousand dishonest shifts, injurious to his arguments, and discreditable to his character.'

Macaulay says elsewhere: 'No man in English literature had a clearer and more just understanding, or a style which more exactly and agreeably expressed his meaning. The Free Inquiry is Middleton's masterpiece. He settled the authority of the Fathers for ever with all reasonable men.'

[1] Strype himself was well enough aware that his style was suited to his subject. 'In truth,' he writes, 'he that is a lover of antiquity loves the very language and phrases of antiquity.'

independence of the realm. He was a far more estimable man than Cranmer.' Of Latimer he says: 'He was the Cobbett of the Reformation, with more honesty than Cobbett, and more courage; but very like him in the character of his understanding.' At the foot of a fine letter addressed by Ridley from his prison in 'Bocardo in Oxenford, to his former steward who had complied with the Romish Religion,' Macaulay notes 'A stout-hearted, honest, brave man.' Grindal he more than once pronounces to be 'the best Archbishop of Canterbury since the Reformation, except Tillotson.' Indeed, it may safely be asserted that, in one corner or another of Macaulay's library, there is in existence his estimate of every famous or notorious English prelate from the beginning of the sixteenth to the end of the eighteenth century. The most concise of these sketches of episcopal character may be found in his copy of the letters from Warburton to Hurd, the first of which is headed in pencil with the words, 'Bully to Sneak.'

Valuable, indeed, is the privilege of following Macaulay through his favourite volumes, where every leaf is plentifully besprinkled with the annotations of the most lively of scholiasts; but it would be an injustice towards his reputation to separate the commentary from the text, and present it to the public in a fragmentary condition. Such a process could give but a feeble idea of the animation and humour of that species of running conversation which he frequently kept up with his author for whole chapters together. Of all the memorials of himself which he has left behind him, these dialogues with the dead are the most characteristic. The energy of his remonstrances, the heartiness of his approbation, the contemptuous vehemence of his censure, the eagerness with which he urges and reiterates his own opinions, are such as to make it at times difficult to realise that his remarks are addressed to people who died centuries, or perhaps tens of centuries, ago. But the writer of a book which had lived was always alive for Macaulay. This sense of personal relation between himself and the men of the past increased as years went on,—as he became less able and willing to mix with the world, and more and more thrown back upon the society which he found in his library. His way of life would have been deemed solitary by others, but it was not solitary to him. While he had a volume in his hands he never could be without a quaint companion to laugh with or laugh at; an adversary to stimulate his combativeness; a counsellor to suggest wise or lofty thoughts, and a friend with whom to share them. When he opened for the tenth or fifteenth time some history, or memoir, or romance,—every incident, and almost every sentence of which he had by heart,—his feeling was precisely that which we experience on meeting an old comrade, whom we like all the better because we know the exact lines on which his talk will run. There was no society in London so agreeable that Macaulay would have preferred it at breakfast or at dinner to the company of Sterne, or Fielding, or Horace Walpole, or Boswell; and there were many less distinguished authors with whose productions he was very well content to cheer his repasts. 'I read,' he says, 'Henderson's Iceland at breakfast; a favourite breakfast book with me. Why? How oddly we are made! Some books which I never should dream of opening at dinner please me at breakfast, and vice versâ.' In choosing what he should take down from his shelves he was guided at least as much by whim as by judgment. There were certain bad writers whose vanity and folly had a flavour of peculiarity which was irresistibly attractive to Macaulay. In August 1859 he says to Lady Trevelyan: 'The books which I had sent to the binder are come; and Miss Seward's letters are in a condition to bear twenty more re-perusals.' But, amidst the infinite variety of lighter literature with which he beguiled his leisure, 'Pride and Prejudice,' and the five sister novels, remained without a rival in his affections. He never for a moment wavered in his allegiance to Miss Austen. In

1858 he notes in his journal: 'If I could get materials, I really would write a short life of that wonderful woman and raise a little money to put up a monument to her in Winchester Cathedral.' Some of his old friends may remember how he prided himself on a correction of his own in the first page of 'Persuasion,' which he maintained to be worthy of Bentley, and which undoubtedly fulfils all the conditions required to establish the credit of an emendation; for, without the alteration of a word, or even of a letter, it turns into perfectly intelligible common-sense a passage which has puzzled, or which ought to have puzzled, two generations of Miss Austen's readers.[1]

Of the feelings which he entertained towards the great minds of bygone ages it is not for any one except himself to speak. He has told us how his debt to them was incalculable; how they guided him to truth; how they filled his mind with noble and graceful images; how they stood by him in all vicissitudes,—comforters in sorrow, nurses in sickness, companions in solitude, 'the old friends who are never seen with new faces; who are the same in wealth and in poverty, in glory and in obscurity.' Great as were the honours and possessions which Macaulay acquired by his pen, all who knew him were well aware that the titles and rewards, which he gained by his own works, were as nothing in the balance as compared with the pleasure which he derived from the works of others. That knowledge has largely contributed to the tenderness with which he has been treated by writers whose views on books, and events, and politics past and present, differ widely from his own. It has been well said that even the most hostile of his critics cannot

[1] A slight change in the punctuation effects all that is required. According to Macaulay, the sentence was intended by its author to run thus: 'There, any unwelcome sensations, arising from domestic affairs, changed naturally into pity and contempt as he turned over the almost endless creations of the last century; and there, if every other leaf were powerless, he could read his own history with an interest which never failed. This was the page at which the favourite volume opened:—'

help being 'awed and touched by his wonderful devotion to literature.' And, while his ardent and sincere passion for letters has thus served as a protection to his memory, it was likewise the source of much which calls for admiration in his character and conduct. The confidence with which he could rely upon intellectual pursuits for occupation and amusement assisted him not a little to preserve that dignified composure, with which he met all the changes and chances of his public career; and that spirit of cheerful and patient endurance, which sustained him through years of broken health and enforced seclusion. He had no pressing need to seek for excitement and applause abroad, when he had beneath his own roof a never-failing store of exquisite enjoyment. That 'invincible love of reading,' which Gibbon declared that he would not exchange for the treasures of India, was with Macaulay a main element of happiness in one of the happiest lives that it has ever fallen to the lot of a biographer to record.[1]

[1] Macaulay amused himself, among other forms of relaxation, by touching up some of Doctor Parr's rather clumsy epitaphs. An amended version of Parr's own translation of his long-drawn panegyric on Sir John Moore, as it stands on a blank page of my uncle's copy of Parr's biography, is a fine example of stately and nervous English,—the vigour of which is intensified, it must be allowed, by Whig prejudices and resentments. Doctor Parr had composed a Latin inscription on King Richard's Well in Bosworth Field. In the ultimate shape which it assumed under Macaulay's pencil that inscription is an almost perfect production of its own class.

Hoc fonte
Ultimam sitim sedavit,
Acie jam commissâ,
Ricardus Tertius Rex Angliæ,
Et vitâ pariter et sceptro
Ante noctem cariturus.

The manner in which Macaulay was wont to divert himself with the follies of a silly author is illustrated by the Fourth Appendix. A selection from his more serious and valuable marginal notes is now given in the closing chapter which has been added to this book. The reflections suggested to him by the reading of Shakspeare, Cicero, and Plato have already found favour with true lovers of choice literature. 'They are

CHAPTER XV

1859

Melancholy anticipations—Visit to the English Lakes, and to Scotland—Extracts from Macaulay's Journal—His death and funeral.

WHEN the year 1859 opened, it seemed little likely that any event was at hand which would disturb the tranquil course of Macaulay's existence. His ailments, severe as they were, did not render him discontented on his own account, nor diminish the warmth of his interest in the welfare of those who were around him. Towards the close of the preceding year, his niece Margaret Trevelyan had been married to the son of his old friend Sir Henry Holland; an event which her uncle regarded with heartfelt satisfaction. Mr. Holland resided in London; and consequently the marriage, so far from depriving Macaulay of one whom he looked on as a daughter, gave him another household where he was as much at home as in his own. But a most unexpected circumstance now occurred which changed in a moment the whole complexion of his life. Early in January 1859 the Governorship of Madras was offered to my father. He accepted the post, and sailed for India in the third week of February. My mother remained in England for a while; but she was to follow her husband after no very long interval, and Macaulay was fully convinced that, when he and his sister parted, they would part for ever. Though he derived his belief from his own sensations, and not from any warning of physicians, he was none the less firmly persuaded that the end was now not far off. 'I

as interesting,' (Lord Rosebery has written,) 'as any of his works, so full of enthusiasm and keen discrimination. He is a sublime guide to sublime things.' And John Morley has pronounced Macaulay's marginalia 'the most splendid literary *nugæ* that ever were; if indeed that be at all the right word for things so stirring, provocative, challenging, and fertile in suggestion.' (1908.)

took leave of Trevelyan,' he says on the 18th of February. 'He said, "You have always been a most kind brother to me." I certainly tried to be so. Shall we ever meet again? I do not expect it. My health is better; but another sharp winter would probably finish me.' In another place he writes: 'I am no better. This malady tries me severely. However, I bear up. As to my temper, it never has been soured, and, while I keep my understanding, will not, I think, be soured, by evils for which it is evident that no human being is responsible. To be angry with relations and servants because you suffer something which they did not inflict, and which they are desirous to alleviate, is unworthy, not merely of a good man, but of a rational being. Yet I see instances enough of such irritability to fear that I may be guilty of it. But I will take care. I have thought several times of late that the last scene of the play was approaching. I should wish to act it simply, but with fortitude and gentleness united.'

The prospect of a separation from one with whom he had lived in close and uninterrupted companionship since his childhood and his own early manhood, —a prospect darkened by the thought that his last hour would surely come when she was thousands of miles away,—was a trial which weighed heavily on Macaulay's sinking health. He endured it manfully, and almost silently; but his spirits never recovered the blow. During the spring and summer of 1859 his journal contains a few brief but significant allusions to the state of his feelings; one of which, and one only, may fitly be inserted here. '*July* 11, 1859.—A letter from Hannah; very sad and affectionate. I answered her. There is a pleasure even in this exceeding sorrow; for it brings out the expression of love with a tenderness which is wanting in ordinary circumstances. But the sorrow is very, very bitter. The Duke of Argyll called, and left me the sheets of a forthcoming poem of Tennyson. I like it extremely;—notwithstanding some faults, extremely. The parting of Lancelot and Guinevere, her penitence, and Arthur's farewell, are all very affecting. I cried over some passages; but I am now ἀρτίδακρυς,[1] as Medea says.'

Towards the end of July my uncle spent a week with us at Lowood Hotel, on the shore of Windermere; and thence he accompanied my mother and my younger sister on a fortnight's tour through the Western Highlands, and by Stirling to Edinburgh. Every stage of the journey brought some fresh proof of the eager interest which his presence aroused in the minds of his fellow-countrymen, to whom his face and figure were very much less familiar than is usual in the case of a man of his eminence and reputation. He now so rarely emerged from his retirement that, whenever he appeared abroad, he was attended by a respect which gratified, and a curiosity which did not annoy him. 'I went the day before yesterday,' he writes to Mr. Ellis, 'to Grasmere Churchyard, and saw Wordsworth's tomb. I thought of announcing my intention of going, and issuing guinea tickets to people who wished to see me there. For a Yankee who was here a few days ago, and heard that I was expected, said that he would give the world to see that most sublime of all spectacles, Macaulay standing by the grave of Wordsworth.' 'In Scotland,' my mother writes, 'his reception was everywhere most enthusiastic. He was quickly recognised on steamers and at railway stations. At Tarbet we were escorted down to the boat by the whole household; and, while they surrounded your uncle, finding a seat for him, and making him comfortable, I sat modestly in the shade next a young woman, who called a man to her, and asked who they were making such a fuss about. He replied that it was the great Lord Macaulay, who wrote the History. "Oh," said she, "I thought it was considered only a romance!" However, she added herself to the group of starers. When we went to Dr. Guthrie's church in Edinburgh, the congregation made a line for us through which to walk away.' At the hotels, one not uncommon form of doing Macaulay honour consisted in serving up a better

[1] 'With the tears near the eyes.'

dinner than had been ordered,—no easy matter when he was catering for others besides himself,—and then refusing to accept payment for his entertainment. At Inverary he writes: 'The landlord insisted on treating us to our drive of yesterday, but I was peremptory. I was half sorry afterwards, and so was Hannah, who, at the time, took my part. It is good to accept as well as to give. My feeling is too much that of Calderon's hero:

> Cómo sabrá pedir
> Quien solo ha sabido dar? [1]

I shrink too much from receiving services which I love to render.'

During this visit to the North my uncle was still the same agreeable travelling companion that we had always known him;—with the same readiness to please and be pleased, and the same sweet and even temper. When one of us happened to be alone with him, there sometimes was a touch of melancholy about his conversation which imparted to it a singular charm; but, when the whole of our little circle was assembled, he showed himself as ready as ever to welcome any topic which promised to afford material for amusing and abundant talk. I especially remember our sitting at the window through the best part of an afternoon, looking across Windermere, and drawing up under his superintendence a list of forty names for an imaginary English Academy. The result of our labours, in the shape in which it now lies before me, bears evident marks of having been a work of compromise; and cannot therefore be presented to the world as a faithful and authentic expression of Macaulay's estimate of his literary and scientific contemporaries.

In a letter to Mr. Ellis, written on the 24th of October 1859, Macaulay says: 'I have been very well in body since we parted; but in mind I have suffered

[1] 'How will he know how to ask who has only known how to give?'

much, and the more because I have had to put a force upon myself in order to appear cheerful. It is at last settled that Hannah and Alice are to go to Madras in February. I cannot deny that it is right; and my duty is to avoid whatever can add to the pain which they suffer. But I am very unhappy. However, I read, and write, and contrive to forget my sorrow for whole hours. But it recurs, and will recur.'

The trial which now at no distant date awaited Macaulay was one of the heaviest that could by any possibility have been allotted to him, and he summoned all his resources in order to meet it with firmness and resignation. He thenceforward made it a duty to occupy his mind, and fortify his powers of self-control, by hard and continuous intellectual exertion. 'I must drive away,' he says, 'these thoughts by writing;' and with diminished strength he returned to his labours, purposing not to relax them until he had completed another section of the History. In October he tells Mr. Longman that he is working regularly, and that he designs to publish the next volume by itself. On the 14th of December he writes: 'Finished at last the session of 1699–1700. There is a good deal in what I have written that is likely to interest readers. At any rate, this employment is a good thing for myself, and will be a better soon when I shall have little else left.' Influenced by the same settled determination forcibly to divert the current of his reflections from the sombre channel in which they were now prone to run, Macaulay, even during his hours of leisure, began to read on system. On the second day after he had received the unwelcome announcement of my mother's plans with regard to India, he commenced the perusal of Nichols's Literary Anecdotes,—a ponderous row of nine volumes, each containing seven or eight hundred closely-printed pages. He searched and sifted this vast repertory of eighteenth century erudition and gossip with a minute diligence such as few men have the patience to bestow upon a book which they do not intend to re-edit;—

correcting blunders, supplying omissions, stigmatising faults in taste and grammar, and enriching every blank space, which invited his pencil, with a profusion of valuable and entertaining comments. Progressing steadily at the rate of a volume a week, he had read and annotated the entire work between the 17th day of October and the 21st of December.

During this period of his life Macaulay certainly was least unhappy when alone in his own library;[1] for, in the society of those whom he was about to lose, the enjoyment of the moment could not fail to be overclouded by sad presentiments. 'I could almost wish,' he writes, 'that what is to be were to be immediately. I dread the next four months more than even the months which will follow the separation. This prolonged parting,—this slow sipping of the vinegar and the gall,—is terrible.' The future was indeed dark before him; but God, who had so blessed him, dealt kindly with him even to the end, and his burden was not permitted to be greater than his strength could bear.

'*Friday, December* 16.—From this morning I reckon some of the least agreeable days of my life. The physic was necessary, but I believe it brought me very low. The frost was more intense than ever, and arrested my circulation.[2] Bating the irregularity of the pulse, I suffered all that I suffered when, in 1852, I was forced to go to Clifton. The depression, the weakness, the sinking of the heart, the incapacity to do anything that required steady exertion, were very distressing. To write, though but a few words, is disagreeable to me. However, I read German, Latin, and English, and got through the day tolerably.'

'*December* 17.—Very hard frost. The weather has

[1] On the 16th of October he notes in his diary: 'I read, and found, as I have always found, that an interesting book acted as an anodyne.'

[2] Macaulay's habitual ill health had been aggravated by a walk which he took in a bitter east wind, from the British Museum to the Athenæum Club.

seldom been colder in this latitude. I sent for Martin, and told him my story.[1] He says that there is no organic affection of the heart, but that the heart is weak.'

'*December* 19.—Still intense frost. I could hardly use my razor for the palpitation of the heart. I feel as if I were twenty years older since last Thursday;—as if I were dying of old age. I am perfectly ready, and shall never be readier. A month more of such days as I have been passing of late would make me impatient to get to my little narrow crib, like a weary factory child.'

'*Wednesday, Dec.* 21.—Everything changed; the frost and frozen snow all gone; heavy rain falling; clouds from the south-west driving fast through the sky. The sun came, and it was so mild that I ventured into the verandah; but I was far from well. My two doctors, Watson and Martin, came to consult. They agreed in pronouncing my complaint a heart-complaint simply. If the heart acted with force, all the plagues would vanish together. They may be right. I am certainly very poorly;—weak as a child. Yet I am less nervous than usual. I have shed no tears during some days, though with me tears ask only leave to flow, as poor Cowper says. I am sensible of no intellectual decay;—not the smallest.'

'*Friday, December* 23.—"In the midst of life ——." This morning I had scarcely left my closet when down came the ceiling in large masses. I should certainly have been stunned, probably killed, if I had stayed a few minutes longer. I stayed by my fire, not exerting myself to write, but making Christmas calculations, and reading. An odd declaration by Dickens that he did not mean Leigh Hunt by Harold Skimpole. Yet he owns that he took the light externals of the character from Leigh Hunt, and surely it is by those light externals that the bulk of mankind will always recognise character. Besides, it is to be observed that the

[1] Sir Ranald Martin had been Macaulay's physician in Calcutta.

vices of Harold Skimpole are vices to which Leigh Hunt had, to say the least, some little leaning, and which the world generally imputed to him most unsparingly. That he had loose notions of *meum* and *tuum*, that he had no high feeling of independence, that he had no sense of obligation, that he took money wherever he could get it, that he felt no gratitude for it, that he was just as ready to defame a person who had relieved his distress as a person who had refused him relief,—these were things which, as Dickens must have known, were said, truly or falsely, about Leigh Hunt, and had made a deep impression on the public mind. Indeed, Leigh Hunt had said himself: "I have some peculiar notions about money. They will be found to involve considerable difference of opinion with the community, particularly in a commercial country. I have not that horror of being under obligation which is thought an essential refinement in money matters." This is Harold Skimpole all over. How then could D. doubt that H. S. would be supposed to be a portrait of L. H.?'

At this point Macaulay's journal comes to an abrupt close. Two days afterwards he wrote to Mr. Ellis: 'The physicians think me better; but there is little change in my sensations. The day before yesterday I had a regular fainting-fit, and lay quite insensible. I wish that I had continued to be so; for if death be no more ——. Up I got, however; and the doctors agree that the circumstance is altogether unimportant.' Nevertheless, from this time forward there was a marked change for the worse in Macaulay. 'I spent Christmas Day with him,' my mother writes. 'He talked very little, and was constantly dropping asleep. We had our usual Christmas dinner with him, and the next day I thought him better. Never, as long as I live, can I lose the sense of misery that I ever left him after Christmas Day. But I did not feel alarmed. I thought the accident to the ceiling had caused a shock to his nerves from which he was gradually recovering; and, when we were alone together, he gave way to so much emotion that, while he was so weak, I rather avoided being long with him.' It may give occasion for surprise that Macaulay's relatives entertained no apprehension of his being in grave and immediate danger; but the truth is that his evident unhappiness, (the outward manifestations of which, during the last few days of his life, he had no longer the force to suppress,) was so constantly present to the minds of us all that our attention was diverted from his bodily condition. His silence and depression,—due, in reality, to physical causes,—were believed by us to proceed almost entirely from mental distress.

In a contemporary account of Macaulay's last illness [1] it is related that on the morning of Wednesday, the 28th of December, he mustered strength to dictate a letter addressed to a poor curate, enclosing twenty-five pounds;—after signing which letter he never wrote his name again. Late in the afternoon of the same day I called at Holly Lodge, intending to propose myself to dinner; an intention which was abandoned as soon as I entered the library. My uncle was sitting, with his head bent forward on his chest, in a languid and drowsy reverie. The first number of the Cornhill Magazine lay unheeded before him, open at the first page of Thackeray's story of 'Lovel the Widower.' He did not utter a word, except in answer; and the only one of my observations, that at this distance of time I can recall, suggested to him painful and pathetic reflections which altogether destroyed his self-command.

On hearing my report of his state, my mother resolved to spend the night at Holly Lodge. She had just left the drawing-room to make her preparations for the visit, (it being, I suppose, a little before seven

[1] This account, which is very brief, but apparently authentic, is preserved among the Marquis of Lansdowne's papers. Macaulay writes, on the 19th of August 1859: 'I grieve to hear about my dear old friend, Lord Lansdowne. I owe more to him than any man living; and he never seemed to be sensible that I owed him anything. I shall look anxiously for the next accounts.' Lord Lansdowne recovered from this illness, and survived Macaulay more than three years.

in the evening,) when a servant arrived with an urgent summons. As we drove up to the porch of my uncle's house, the maids ran crying out into the darkness to meet us, and we knew that all was over. We found him in the library, seated in his easy chair, and dressed as usual; with his book on the table beside him, still open at the same page. He had told his butler that he should go to bed early, as he was very tired. The man proposed his lying on the sofa. He rose as if to move, sat down again, and ceased to breathe. He died as he had always wished to die;—without pain; without any formal farewell; preceding to the grave all whom he loved; and leaving behind him a great and honourable name, and the memory of a life every action of which was as clear and transparent as one of his own sentences. It would be unbecoming in me to dwell upon the regretful astonishment with which the tidings of his death were received wherever the English language is read; and quite unnecessary to describe the enduring grief of those upon whom he had lavished his affection, and for whom life had been brightened by daily converse with his genius, and ennobled by familiarity with his lofty and upright example. 'We have lost,' (so my mother wrote,) 'the light of our home, the most tender, loving, generous, unselfish, devoted of friends. What he was to me for fifty years how can I tell? What a world of love he poured out upon me and mine! The blank, the void he has left,—filling, as he did, so entirely both heart and intellect,—no one can understand. For who ever knew such a life as mine, passed as the cherished companion of such a man?'

He was buried in Westminster Abbey, on the 9th of January 1860. The pall was borne by the Duke of Argyll, Lord John Russell, Lord Stanhope, Lord Carlisle, Bishop Wilberforce, Sir David Dundas, Sir Henry Holland, Dean Milman, Sir George Cornewall Lewis, the Lord Chancellor, and the Speaker of the House of Commons. 'A beautiful sunrise,' wrote Lord Carlisle. 'The pall-bearers met in the Jerusalem Chamber. The last time I had been there on a like errand was at

Canning's funeral. The whole service and ceremony were in the highest degree solemn and impressive. All befitted the man and the occasion.'

He rests with his peers in Poets' Corner, near the west wall of the South Transept. There, amidst the tombs of Johnson, and Garrick, and Handel, and Goldsmith, and Gay, stands conspicuous the statue of Addison; and, at the feet of Addison, lies the stone which bears this inscription:

THOMAS BABINGTON, LORD MACAULAY,

BORN AT ROTHLEY TEMPLE, LEICESTERSHIRE,
OCTOBER 25, 1800.

DIED AT HOLLY LODGE, CAMPDEN HILL,
DECEMBER 28, 1859.

'HIS BODY IS BURIED IN PEACE,
BUT HIS NAME LIVETH FOR EVERMORE.'

CHAPTER XVI [1]

Macaulay's marginal notes—Ben Jonson—Pope—Swift—Gibbon — Conyers Middleton — Shakspeare — Cicero — Plato.

It is a rare privilege to journey in Macaulay's track through the higher regions of literature. The margins of his favourite volumes are illustrated and enlivened by innumerable entries, of which none are prolix, pointless, or dull; while interest and admiration are expressed by lines drawn down the sides of the text,—and even by double lines, for whole pages together, in the case of Shakspeare and Aristophanes, Demosthenes and Plato, Paul Louis Courier and Jonathan Swift. His standard of excellence was always at the same level, his mind always on the alert, and his sense of enjoyment always keen. Frederic Myers, himself a fine scholar and an eager student, once said to me: 'He

[1] From *Marginal Notes by Lord Macaulay*. Copyright, 1907, by Longmans, Green, & Co.

seems habitually to have read as I read only during my first half-hour with a great author.' Macaulay began with the frontispiece, if the book possessed one. 'Said to be very like, and certainly full of the character. Energy, acuteness, tyranny, and audacity in every line of the face.' Those words are written above the portrait of Richard Bentley, in Bishop Monk's biography of that famous writer. The blank spaces are frequently covered with little spurts of criticism, and outbursts of warm appreciation. 'This is a very good Idyll. Indeed it is more pleasing to me than almost any other pastoral poem in any language. It was my favourite at College. There is a rich profusion of rustic imagery about it which I find nowhere else. It opens a scene of rural plenty and comfort which quite fills the imagination, —flowers, fruits, leaves, fountains, soft goatskins, old wine, singing birds, joyous friendly companions. The whole has an air of reality which is more interesting than the conventional world which Virgil has placed in Arcadia.' So Macaulay characterises the Seventh Idyll of Theocritus. Of Ben Jonson's Alchemist he writes: 'It is very happily managed indeed to make Subtle use so many terms of alchemy, and talk with such fanatical warmth about his "great art," even to his accomplice. As Hume says, roguery and enthusiasm run into each other. I admire this play very much. The plot would have been more agreeable, and more rational, if Surly had married the widow whose honor he has preserved. Lovewit is as contemptible as Subtle himself. The whole of the trick about the Queen of Fairy is improbable in the highest degree. But, after all, the play is as good as any in our language out of Shakspeare.' Ben Jonson, in the preface to his Catiline, appeals from 'the reader in ordinary' to 'the reader extraordinary' against the charge of having borrowed too largely and undisguisedly from Cicero's speeches. 'I,' said Macaulay, 'am a reader in ordinary, and I cannot defend the introduction of the First Catilinarian oration, at full length, into a play. Catiline is a very middling play. The characters are certainly discriminated, but with no delicacy. Jonson makes Cethegus a mere vulgar ruffian. He quite forgets that all the conspirators were gentlemen, noblemen, politicians, probably scholars. He has seized only the coarsest peculiarities of character. As to the conduct of the piece, nothing can be worse than the long debates and narratives which make up half of it.'

Of Pope's Rape of the Lock, Macaulay says: 'Admirable indeed! The fight towards the beginning of the last book is very extravagant and foolish. It is the blemish of a poem which, but for this blemish, would be as near perfection in its own class as any work in the world.' He thus remarks on the Imitations of Horace's Satires: 'Horace had perhaps less wit than Pope, but far more humour, far more variety, more sentiment, more thought. But that to which Horace chiefly owes his reputation, is his perfect good sense and self-knowledge, in which he exceeded all men. He never has attempted anything for which his powers did not qualify him. There is not one disgraceful failure in all his poems. The case with Pope was widely different. He wrote a moral didactic poem. He wrote odes. He tried his hand at comedy. He meditated an epic. All these were failures. Horace never would have fallen into such mistakes.'

That view is enforced in Macaulay's remarks on Pope's paraphrase of the Ninth Ode in the Fourth Book of Horace.

> Sages and Chiefs long since had birth
> Ere Cæsar was, or Newton, named.
> These raised new Empires o'er the Earth;
> And those new Heavens and Systems framed.
> Vain was the Chief's, the Sage's, pride!
> They had no Poet, and they died.
> In vain they schemed, in vain they bled!
> They had no poet, and are dead.

'I do not see,' writes Macaulay, 'the smallest merit in this affected verse, which I suppose was meant to be very striking and sublime. Besides, what in Horace, like everything in his works, is excellent sense, is false and ridiculous in the imitation. It *is* true that the warriors who lived before Agamemnon are almost utterly forgotten, and excite no interest, while Agamemnon is remembered as Homer's hero. But it is *not* true that the Chiefs who preceded Cæsar, or the Sages who preceded Newton, are forgotten. Nor is it true that either Cæsar or Newton owes his fame to poetry. Every verse, in which either of them is mentioned, might be burned without any diminution of their fame.'

Horace, again, made a fine and apt allusion to the old song, which Curius and Camillus used to sing as boys in the streets of Rome, telling their companions that, if they did right, they would all be kings together. This was how Pope translated the passage:

> Yet every child another song will sing;
> 'Virtue, brave boys! 'Tis Virtue makes a king.'
>
> * * * *
>
> And say, to which shall our applause belong,
> This new Court jargon, or the good old song?
> The modern language of corrupted Peers,
> Or what was spoke at Cressy and Poitiers?

Bishop Warburton, with the partiality of an editor, thought Pope's version superior to the Latin original. 'Why so?' asked Macaulay. 'Horace refers to a real old Roman song which boys sang at play. Pope's imitation is only an imaginary allusion. Who ever heard an English boy sing that Virtue made kings? And what song to that effect existed at the time of Cressy and Poitiers?'

And, once more, in the First Satire of the Second Book, Horace's friend, the famous counsellor Trebatius, warns the poet that his satirical writing brings him within the grasp of the law.

> *Trebatius*: Si mala condiderit in quem quis carmina, jus est Judiciumque.
> *Horatius*: Esto, si quis *mala*. Sed *bona* si quis Judice condiderit laudatus Cæsare?

Pope's adaptation ran as follows:

> It stands on record that in Richard's times
> A man was hanged for very honest rhymes.
> Consult the Statute. *Quart.*, I think, it is
> *Edwardi Sext.*, or *prim. et quint. Eliz.*

'The legal opinion,' Warburton remarked, 'is here more justly and decently taken off than in the original. Horace evades the force of it with a quibble.' 'I think the original,' said Macaulay, 'far better, by Warburton's leave. For Horace really recites a law from the Twelve Tables; but there is nothing about satires in the laws of Edward the Sixth. Horace's turn of expression about *bona* and *mala* is not a mere idle quibble. It raises the whole question of legitimate and illegitimate satire.'

Macaulay thought Paul Louis Courier the prince of all pamphleteers, and 'Le Simple Discours' his best pamphlet. 'A most powerful piece of rhetoric,' (so he called it,) 'as ever I read;' and he used to read Courier aloud to his sister at Calcutta of a June afternoon,—in the darkened upstairs chamber, with the punkah swinging overhead, with as much enjoyment as ever Charles James Fox read the romances of Voltaire to his wife in the garden at St. Anne's Hill, though with a less irreproachable accent. Macaulay was strangely moved by Courier's terrible invective against the harsh and inquisitorial Church of the French Restoration.[1] 'Worthy of Demosthenes,' he said. 'It makes my blood boil against that accursed tyranny.' He marked with a triple line of appreciation the attack upon those courtiers of Louis the Eighteenth and the Comte d'Artois, who cajoled the people out of their savings in the name of the King, but for the sake of their own pockets. 'Ces domaines, ces apanages, ces listes civiles, ces budgets ne sont guères autrement pour le roi que le revenu des abbayes n'est pour Jésus Christ. * * * * L'offrande n'est jamais pour le saint, ni nos épargnes pour les rois, mais pour cet essaim

[1] *Réponse aux Anonymes; No. 2. Véretz, 6 février*, 1823.

dévorant qui sans cesse bourdonne autour d'eux depuis leur berceau jusqu'à Saint-Denis.' 'Very fine!' wrote Macaulay. 'Quite Greek as to the energy and the beauty of the expression.' When Courier was brought before the Court of Assizes on the charge of having written disrespectfully about the royal mistresses of past generations, he defended himself in a strain of irony which impressed his reader as being 'in the exact manner of Blaise Pascal.'[1] The report of a Socratic conversation, held in the Neapolitan palace of the Countess of Albany, about the respective value and merit of a great artist, and a great general, is thus characterised by Macaulay. 'This is one of the finest dialogues ever written, in my opinion. It reminds me more of Plato's manner than anything that has been produced since the earlier Provinciales. The painter pushes his argument too far;[2] but he is not wrong in the main. April 19, 1835.'

Macaulay made every allowance for the disadvantages under which Paul Louis Courier had picked up the fragments of an education. A subaltern of artillery in the armies of the Republic, and afterwards of Napoleon,—serving through campaign after campaign in the wildest and most disturbed regions of Europe, with a single Greek volume packed into his slender baggage,—having his Herodotus captured by the Austrian Hussars, and his Homer by the Calabrian brigands,—that wonderful genius could not, in after life, be expected to discuss political and religious questions with precise and all-embracing knowledge. And yet, however little Macaulay was inclined to bear hard upon the deficiencies of his author and, however much he was fascinated by his wit and eloquence, he seldom allowed a blunder to pass unnoticed. 'If we lost the

[1] *Procès de Paul Louis Courier:* 28 *août* 1821, *au lieu ordinaire des séances de la Cour d'Assises.*

[2] 'Tandis qu'il y aura,' wrote Courier, 'quelques tacticiens qui s'écrieront, "Oh! La belle bataille! Le beau siège!" tout le reste du genre humain, noyé dans les pleurs, chargera d'exécrations l'auteur de la bataille ou du siège.' 'This,' said Macaulay, 'is not true. Perhaps it might be well if it were.'

day at Malplaquet,' (so Courier wrote,) 'we took our revenge at Oudenarde.' 'Very slovenly history,' said Macaulay. 'The French were beaten first at Oudenarde, and afterwards at Malplaquet.' When Courier enumerated an imperfect list of the famous publicists of history, 'Odd,' remarked Macaulay, 'that he should not have mentioned Junius. But it is plain that he knew little about England, and that little inaccurately.' 'Whence comes,' asked Courier, 'our indifference to religion? We are dead cold in our feelings, and are not even among the lukewarm ones whom God would spue out of His mouth, to use the words of Saint Paul.' 'Saint John!' wrote Macaulay. 'The Greek Testament, Monsieur Courier, is not one of your favourite classics.'[1]

Macaulay was fond of inditing observations on human character, and on the conduct of life, which have about them a perceptible flavour of autobiography. Swift had pronounced that discretion in statesmen was 'usually attended with a strong desire for money, with a want of public spirit and principle, with servile flattery and submission, and with a perpetual wrong judgment, when the owners came into power and high place, how to dispose of favour and preferment.' 'I doubt this,' said Macaulay. 'Swift wrote with all the spleen of a man of genius who had been outstripped by dunces in the career of preferment. Neither my own experience, nor history, leads me to think that the discretion which so often raises men of mediocrity to high posts is necessarily, or generally, connected with avarice, want of principle, or servility. Take, as instances, Cardinal Fleury, Pelham, the late Lord Liverpool, and the present Lord Spencer.'[2] In

[1] *Conversation chez la Comtesse d'Albany. Pamphlet des Pamphlets. Pétition à la chambre des Députés, pour les villageois que l'on empêche de danser.*

[2] These words were written in July 1835, not many months after the time when Lord Althorp,—in the course of nature, and to the infinite distress of the Whigs,—was removed from the leadership of the Commons, and translated, as Earl Spencer, into the House of Lords.

the 'Essay on the Fates of Clergymen,' Swift related the disappointments of his own career under the transparent mask of the brilliant and unsuccessful Eugenio. 'People,' wrote Macaulay, 'speak of the world as they find it. I have been more fortunate or prudent than Swift or Eugenio.' What business, (he then asked, in language of unusual, and quite unproducible, emphasis,) had such men in such a profession?

Edward Gibbon, on an early page of his thrice admirable 'Vindication,' explains his reason for condescending to notice the attacks upon his History. 'Fame,' he says, 'is the motive, it is the reward, of our labours: nor can I easily comprehend how it is possible that we should remain cold and indifferent with regard to the attempts which are made to deprive us of the most valuable object of our possessions, or, at least, of our hopes.' 'But what,' wrote Macaulay, 'if you are confident that these attempts will be vain, and that your book will fix its own place?' Conyers Middleton, in the later editions of his 'Free Enquiry into the Miraculous Powers of the Christian Church,' remonstrated somewhat querulously with a clerical opponent who had called him an apostate priest. 'I do not at all admire this letter,' said Macaulay. 'Indeed Middleton should have counted the cost before he took his part. He never appears to so little advantage as when he complains in this way of the calumnies and invectives of the orthodox. The only language for a philosopher in his circumstances is that of the first great type of all reformers, Prometheus:[1] or, in Milton's words:

> To suffer, as to do,
> Our strength is equal, nor the law unjust
> That so ordains. This was at first resolved,
> If we were wise, against so great a foe
> Contending.

Macaulay invariably marked his books in pencil, except four plays of Shakspeare,—Romeo and Juliet,

[1] 'I knew beforehand the penalty which awaited me, for it is in nature that an enemy should suffer at an enemy's hands.' —*Prometheus Vinctus: lines* 1040–2.

King Lear, Midsummer Night's Dream, and Hamlet, where everything is written with ink, in a neat and most legible hand. He used the twelve volume edition of 1778, illustrated with copious notes by Doctor Johnson, Bishop Warburton, Steevens, and other commentators, whose emendations and criticisms are treated by Macaulay with discriminating, but uncompromising, vigour. On the first page of his Romeo and Juliet he writes: 'An admirable opening scene, whatever the French critics may say. It at once puts us thoroughly in possession of the state of the two families. We have an infinitely more vivid notion of their feud from the conduct of their servants than we should have obtained from a long story told by old Capulet to his confidant, *à la Française*. It is bad joking, but in character. The puns are not Shakspeare's, but Sampson's and Gregory's.' Opposite the passage about the biting of thumbs is written: 'This is not what would be commonly called fine; but I would give any six plays of Rowe for it.' Of the scene in the street which begins with Mercutio asking,

> Where the devil should this Romeo be?
> Came he not home to-night?—

Macaulay says, 'This the free conversation of lively, high-spirited young gentlemen;' and, with reference to the quarrel at the commencement of the Third Act, he writes: 'Mercutio, here, is beyond the reach of anybody but Shakspeare.'[1] When, on his way to the ballroom, Romeo tells Benvolio that his mind misgives

> Some consequence, yet hanging in the stars,
> Shall bitterly begin his fearful date
> With this night's revels,

[1] The poet, (wrote Steevens,) appeared to have taken the suggestion of Mercutio from a single sentence in the old story of the Painter's Palace of Pleasure. 'Another gentleman called Mercutio, which was a courtlike gentleman, very well beloved of all men, and, by reason of his pleasant and courteous behaviour, in all companies well entertained.' 'Shakspeare,' said Macaulay, 'was just the man to expand a hint like this. How much he has made of Thersites, who is nothing in Homer!'

Macaulay writes: 'This as fine an instance of presentiment as I remember in poetry. It throws a sadness over all the gaiety that follows, and prepares us for the catastrophe.' At the close of the Third Act he says: 'Very fine is the way in which Juliet at once withdraws her whole confidence from the nurse without disclosing her feelings;' and when, in the ensuing scene, the poor child commits her life to the hands of Friar Lawrence, Macaulay remarks on the wonderful genius with which the poet delineates a timid, delicate girl of fourteen excited and exalted to an act of desperate courage. The respect which he paid to Shakspeare, and to Shakspeare's creations, was very seldom extended to Shakspeare's commentators.

> Now, afore God, this reverend holy friar
> All our whole city is much bound to him.

'Warburton,' writes Macaulay, 'proposed to read "hymn" for "him";—the most ludicrous emendation ever suggested.'

Of the actor's favourite passage, about Queen Mab and her doings, Macaulay says: 'This speech,—full of matter, of thought, of fancy, as it is,—seems to me, like much of this play, to be not in Shakspeare's very best manner. It is stuck on like one of Horace's "purple patches." It does not seem to spring naturally out of the conversation. This is a fault which, in his finest works, Shakspeare never commits.' 'I think Romeo and Juliet,' (such was Macaulay's ultimate conclusion,) 'is the play in which Shakspeare's best and worst modes of writing are exhibited in the closest juxtaposition. If we knew the precise order in which his pieces followed each other, I am persuaded that we should find that this play was the turning point in the history of that most wonderful and sublime genius. The comic part is almost uniformly good. His comic manner attained perfection earlier than his tragic manner. There are passages in Romeo and Juliet equal to anything in Lear or Othello; but there are also very many passages as poor as anything in Love's Labour's Lost. Arimanes and Oromasdes were fighting for him. At last Oromasdes had him all to himself.' I well remember how my uncle, in one of his very few conversations which I can clearly recall, bade me observe the contrast between Juliet's reception of what she supposes to be Romeo's death, and Romeo's reception of the report of the death of Juliet. He quoted to me, in something of a disparaging and ironical tone, the lines:

> Hath Romeo slain himself? Say thou but 'I,'
> And that bare vowel 'I' shall poison more
> Than the death-darting eye of cockatrice.
> I am not I, if there be such an I;
> Or those eyes shut, that make thee answer 'I.'

Opposite these five lines I now find written: 'If this had been in Cibber, Cibber would never have heard the last of it.' And then he recited, with energy and solemn feeling, the First Scene of the Fifth Act. I can still hear his voice as he pronounced the words:

> Is it even so? Then I defy you, stars!—
> Thou know'st my lodging. Get me ink and paper,
> And hire post-horses. I will hence to-night.

At the point where Balthazar brings the evil tidings to Mantua, Macaulay has written: 'Here begins a noble series of scenes. I know nothing grander than the way in which Romeo hears the news. It moves me even more than Lear's agonies.' Of the closing passage in the vault of death he says: 'The desperate calmness of Romeo is sublime beyond expression; and the manner in which he is softened into tenderness when he sees the body of Juliet is perhaps the most affecting touch in all poetry.'[1]

> [1] O, my love! my wife!
> Death, that hath sucked the honey of thy breath,
> Hath had no power yet upon thy beauty.
> Thou art not conquered. Beauty's ensign yet
> Is crimson in thy lips, and in thy cheeks;
> And death's pale flag is not advanced there.

'His comic scenes,' (so Johnson wrote in his review of Romeo and Juliet,) 'are happily wrought; but his pathetic strains are always polluted by some unexpected depravation.' 'Surely not always!' said Macaulay. 'The first scenes of the fifth act are as near perfection as any ever written.'

'I believe,' said Macaulay, 'that Hamlet was the only play on which Shakspeare really bestowed much care and attention.' Macaulay himself devoted to the examination of that drama as much time and thought as if it had been his intention to edit it. It would be superfluous to re-produce the eloquent expressions of unreserved admiration with which the margin of almost every page is thickly studded. They were written for Macaulay's own satisfaction, and the world can appreciate Hamlet without their aid; but it may not be amiss to present a few specimens of his literary and ethical comments. He regarded the dramatic style of the opening dialogue as 'beyond praise;' and he applied the unwonted epithet of 'sweet writing' to the passage describing the peace and calm in which the natural world is steeped when

> that season comes
> Wherein our Saviour's birth is celebrated.

In the middle of the same scene came something which pleased him less. 'The long story,' he said, 'about Fortinbras, and all that follows from it, seems to me to be a clumsy addition to the plot.' Of the royal audience in the room of state, which immediately follows, Macaulay writes: 'The silence of Hamlet during the earlier part of this scene is very fine, but not equal to the silence of Prometheus and Cassandra in the Prometheus and Agamemnon of Æschylus.' In the Third Scene of the same Act, 'There is,' he says, 'perhaps a little too much extension given to the talk of Laertes and Ophelia, though many lines have great merit. But Shakspeare meant to exhibit them in the free intercourse of perfect confidence and affection, in order that the subsequent distress of Laertes might be more fully comprehended. This is a common practice with him, and explains many passages which seem, at first sight, incongruous additions to his best plays.' With regard to the strolling player's declamation about Pyrrhus, Macaulay holds that 'the only thing deserving of much admiration in the speech is the manner in which it is raised above the ordinary diction which surrounds it. It is poetry within poetry,—a play within a play. It was therefore proper to make its language bear the same relation to the language, in which Hamlet and Horatio talk, which the language of Hamlet and Horatio bears to the common style of conversation among gentlemen. This is a sufficient defence of the style, which is undoubtedly in itself far too turgid for dramatic, or even for lyric, composition.'

The opening of the Fourth Scene in the First Act, on the platform of the Castle at Elsinore, suggests these reflections to Macaulay. 'Nothing can be finer than this specimen of Hamlet's peculiar character. His intellect is out of all proportion to his will or his passions. Under the most exciting circumstances, while expecting every moment to see the ghost of his father rise before him, he goes on discussing questions of morals, manners, or politics, as if he were in the schools of Wittenberg.' Of the address to Horatio, in the Third Act,—

> Dost thou hear?
> Since my dear soul was mistress of her choice,
> And could of men distinguish, her election
> Hath sealed thee for herself,—

Macaulay writes: 'An exquisitely beautiful scene. It always moved me more than any other in the play. There is something very striking in the way in which Hamlet,—a man of a gentle nature, quick in speculation, morbidly sluggish in action, unfit to struggle with the real evils of life, and finding himself plunged into the midst of them,—delights to repose on the strong mind of a man who had been severely tried, and who had learned stoicism from experience. There is wonderful truth in this.' The marginal note about the conversation between Hamlet and the courtier, in the Fifth Act, runs as follows: 'This is a most admirable scene. The fooling of Osric is nothing; but it is most striking to see how completely Hamlet forgets his father, his mistress, the terrible duty imposed upon him, the imminent danger which he has to run, as soon as a subject of observation comes before him;—as soon as a good butt is offered to his wit. The ghost of his father finds him speculating on the causes of the decline of the fame of Denmark. Immediately before he puts his uncle's conscience to the decisive test, he reads a lecture on the principles of dramatic composition and representation. And now, just after Ophelia's burial, he is analysing and describing the fashionable follies of the age, with as much apparent ease of heart as if he had never known sorrow.'

Macaulay had much to say about the editors of Hamlet. Two lines of the most famous soliloquy in the world were printed thus in his copy of Shakspeare:

> Who would fardels bear,
> To groan and sweat under a weary life?

To this passage Doctor Johnson had appended the following note: 'All the old copies have to "grunt and sweat." It is undoubtedly the true reading, but can scarcely be borne by modern ears.' 'We want Shakspeare,' said Macaulay, 'not your fine modern English.' Warburton had amended the words of Hamlet, 'For if the sun breeds maggots in a dead dog, being a good kissing carrion,'—by substituting 'god' for 'good.' 'This,' said Doctor Johnson, 'is a noble emendation which almost sets the critic above the author.' 'It is,' wrote Macaulay, 'a noble emendation. Had Warburton often hit off such corrections, he would be entitled to the first place among critics.' When Hamlet declined to kill his uncle in the act of praying, on the ground that he would go straight to heaven, Doctor Johnson pronounced that the speech in which 'not content with taking blood for blood, he contrived damnation for his enemy, was too horrible to be read or uttered.' 'Johnson,' said Macaulay, 'does not understand the character. Hamlet is irresolute; and he makes the first excuse that suggests itself for not striking. If he had met the King drunk, he would have refrained from avenging himself lest he should kill both soul and body.'

Macaulay gave to King Lear as close a study as to Hamlet, and he was moved by it even more profoundly. Before the Third Scene of the First Act he writes: 'Here begins the finest of all human performances.' He judged Shakspeare's Lear by what to him was a very high standard of comparison,—the masterpieces of those Attic Tragedians whom, for several years together, he used to read through, from end to end, yearly. In the Second Scene of the Second Act, opposite Cornwall's description of the fellow who has been praised for bluntness, he writes: 'Excellent! It is worth while to compare these moral speeches of Shakspeare with those which are so much admired in Euripides. The superiority of Shakspeare's observations is immense. But the dramatic art with which they are introduced,—always in the right place,—always from the right person,—is still more admirable.' When Lear despatches Gloucester on a second message to Regan and her husband,—

> The King would speak with Cornwall. The dear father
> Would with his daughter speak; commands her service.
> Are they informed of this?—

Macaulay pronounces the passage superior to any speech of passion in the Greek Drama. He observes how the nonsense of the poor fool about the eels and the buttered hay, 'coming in between the bursts of the King's agony, heightens the effect beyond description.' And of the appeal to Goneril in the same scene,—

> Now I pr'ythee, daughter, do not make me mad!
> I will not trouble thee, my child; farewell!

he says, 'This last struggle between rage and tenderness is, I think, unequalled in poetry.' When the outraged father breaks forth into the terrible apostrophe commencing

> O, let not women's weapons, water-drops,
> Stain my man's cheeks!

Macaulay writes: 'Where is there anything like this in the world?'

If my uncle had been composing literary criticism for the Edinburgh Review, he would have been more frugal of his superlatives. But these spontaneous and unstudied expressions of admiration will have a value of their own for those who love great poetry, as indicating the awe and emotion produced upon an impressionable mind, of exceptional power, by the loftiest work of mankind's finest genius. There is ample proof in every act and scene of King Lear that Macaulay's judgment was not asleep, and that his praise was guided by discrimination. With regard to the opening of the play he writes: 'Idolising Shakspeare as I do, I cannot but feel that the whole scene is very unnatural. He took it, to be sure, from an old story. What miracles his genius has brought out from materials so unpromising!' Of the quarrel between Kent and Cornwall's steward he says: 'It is rather a fault in the play, to my thinking, that Kent should behave so very insolently in this scene. A man of his rank and sense should have had more self-command and dignity even in his anger. One can hardly blame Cornwall for putting him in the stocks.' 'Albany,' said Macaulay, 'is very slightly touched; yet, with an art peculiar to Shakspeare, quite enough to give us a very good idea of the man;—amiable, and not deficient in spirit, but borne down by the violent temper of a wife who has brought him an immense dowry. Cornwall is, like Albany, slightly touched, but with wonderful skill. No poet ever made such strong likenesses with so few strokes.' In the Fourth Scene of the Third Act, where Lear insists that his two followers should seek cover from the storm, Macaulay writes: 'The softening of Lear's nature and manners, under the discipline of severe sorrow, is most happily marked in several places;' and, where Edgar issues from the hovel, attention is called to the masterly contrast between the feigned madman and the King whose brain is beginning to turn in earnest. Doctor Johnson, at the end of the play, made a solemn protest against the unpleasing character of a story, 'in which the wicked prosper, and the virtuous miscarry.' Macaulay did not concur in the verdict. 'There is nothing,' he wrote, 'like this last scene in the world. Johnson talks nonsense. Torn to pieces as Lear's heart had been, was he to live happily ever after, as the story-books say? Wonderful as the whole play is, this last passage is the triumph of Shakspeare's genius. Every character is perfectly supported.'

Macaulay reckoned Othello the best play extant in any language; but it shows none of his pencil marks. It may well be that he had ceased reading it because he knew the whole of it by heart.[1] The specimens which have already been given of his annotations sufficiently illustrate the spirit in which he always read his poet. Everywhere may be found the same reverential delight in Shakspeare, and the same disrespectful attitude towards Shakspeare's commentators. When, in Antony and Cleopatra, a cloud is likened to a bear or a lion, a castle or a mountain, Steevens considered himself bound to make this observation; 'Perhaps Shakspeare received the thought from the Second Book of Holland's translation of Pliny's Natural History: "In one place there appeareth the resemblance of a waine or a chariot; in another of a beare."' 'Solemn nonsense!' said Macaulay. 'Had Shakspeare no eyes to see the

[1] Macaulay did not affect to underrate the extraordinary strength of his memory. Bishop Monk wrote of Dr. Bentley: 'In the faculty of memory he has himself candidly declared that he was not particularly gifted.' 'I do not think much of this declaration,' said Macaulay. 'It shows no candour, for people are rather vain than ashamed of the badness of their memories. I have known people, who had excellent memories, use the same sort of language. They reason thus, The less memory the more invention. Congreve makes Mirabell say something of this sort.' The passage which was in Macaulay's mind may be found in the Way of the World, Act I, Scene 6.

'*Witwoud*. No, but prithee excuse me. My memory is such a memory.

Mirabell. Have a care of such apologies, Witwoud; for I never knew a fool but he affected to complain, either of the spleen or his memory.'

sky with?' When the poet, in the Prologue to Henry the Fifth, asks:

> Can this cock-pit hold
> The vasty field of France? Or may we cram
> Within this wooden O the very casques
> That did affright the air at Agincourt?

Johnson remarks that to call a circle an O was a very mean metaphor. 'Surely,' wrote Macaulay, 'if O were really the usual name of a circle there would be nothing mean in it, any more than in the Delta of the Nile.' The talk at the Boar's Head Tavern between Prince Hal and Francis the drawer, according to Doctor Johnson, 'may entertain on the stage, but affords not much delight to the reader.' 'It is an excellent scene, by your leave, Doctor,' is Macaulay's rejoinder. Warburton pronounced the first line of the Fool's Prophecy, in the Third Act of King Lear, to be corrupt. 'Or ere I go,' he says, 'is not English.' 'Warburton,' (wrote Macaulay,) 'had forgotten his Psalter, "Or ever your pots be made hot with thorns." And in the Book of Daniel, "Or ever they came at the bottom of the den."' Where Lear prays that 'cadent tears' may fret his daughter's cheeks, Steevens appends the following note: '*Cadent tears*; that is, *falling tears*. Doctor Warburton would read *candent*.' 'More fool Warburton;' said Macaulay.

In the Second Act of Midsummer Night's Dream Oberon bids Puck remember—

> Since once I sat upon a promontory,
> And heard a mermaid, on a dolphin's back,
> Uttering such dulcet and harmonious breath
> That the rude sea grew civil at her song;
> And certain stars shot madly from their spheres
> To hear the sea-maid's musick.

Warburton maintained that Mary Queen of Scots was the mermaid, 'to denote her beauty, and intemperate lust;' that the dolphin was Mary's husband the Dauphin of France; that the rude sea was 'Scotland, encircled by the ocean;' and that the stars, which shot from their spheres, were those great English noblemen who had espoused Mary's quarrel. 'I do not,' wrote Macaulay, 'believe that Shakspeare meant any allusion to Mary Queen of Scots. If he did, he was a very bad courtier; for he has alluded only to her charms, and suppressed all allusion to her vices. Who ever heard of the licentiousness of mermaids? And, as to the dolphin, the Dauphin had been king of France, and had been dead, many years before any of the stars shot from their spheres in consequence of Mary's fascinations. I allow that Warburton's theory is ingenious.' Later on, in Midsummer Night's Dream, in an ironical mood, he directed the attention of the commentators to an historical blunder on the part of the poet. When Hippolyta relates how she had once been out hunting with Hercules and Cadmus, Macaulay says: 'Cadmus had been turned into a snake some generations before Hercules was born. This may be added to the list of Shakspeare's anachronisms.' In the Fifth Act of the play he made some amends to Warburton.

> Now the hungry lions roar,
> And the wolf beholds the moon.

'As 'tis the design of these lines,' wrote Warburton, 'to characterise the animals, as they present themselves at the hour of midnight; and as the wolf is not justly characterised by saying that he *beholds* the moon, which other beasts of prey, then awake, do; and as the sounds, which these animals make at that season, seem also intended to be represented, I make no question but the poet wrote:

> And the wolf *behowls* the moon.'

'In my opinion,' said Macaulay, 'this is one of Warburton's very best corrections.' The passage in the same play, where Theseus describes how even 'great clerks' sometimes break down over their orations in the presence of their sovereign, and how their confusion affords a more flattering proof of loyalty than

> the rattling tongue
> Of saucy and audacious eloquence,

pleased Macaulay as much as it pleases every true Shakspearean. 'This,' he wrote, 'is Shakspeare's manly sense, and knowledge of the world, introduced with perfect dramatic propriety. How different from Euripides's lectures on such subjects!' The verses in the Fourth Act,

> Be, as thou wast wont to be.
> See, as thou was wont to see.
> Dian's bud o'er Cupid's flower
> Hath such force and blessed power,

he calls 'beautiful and easy beyond expression.' And on the last page he writes: 'A glorious play. The love-scenes Fletcher might perhaps have written. The fairy scenes no man but one since the world began could have written.'

Shakspeare's Roman dramas had an especial attraction for Macaulay. Never was a great scholar so little of a pedant. He knew that what Shakspeare could teach him about human nature was worth more than anything which he himself could have taught Shakspeare about Roman history and Roman institutions. He was well aware how very scanty a stock of erudition will qualify a transcendent genius to produce admirable literary effects; and he infinitely preferred Shakspeare's Romans, and even his Greeks, to the classical heroes of Ben Jonson, and Addison, and Racine, and Corneille, and Voltaire. Of the conversation in the street between Brutus and Cassius, in the First Act of Julius Cæsar, Macaulay says: 'These two or three pages are worth the whole French drama ten times over;' and, in his little essay at the end of the play, he writes, 'The last scenes are huddled up, and affect me less than Plutarch's narrative. But the working up of Brutus by Cassius, the meeting of the conspirators, the stirring of the mob by Antony, and, (above all,) the dispute and reconciliation of the two generals, are things far beyond the reach of any other poet that ever lived.' He frequently notices the art with which the dramatist turned to account the most slender materials. When Julius Cæsar expressed his preference for having those about him

> That are fat;
> Sleek-headed men, and such as sleep o' nights;

'Plutarch's hint,' (said Macaulay,) 'is admirably expanded here.' When Steevens reminds the reader that Cleopatra's story of the salt fish on Antony's hook was taken from North's Plutarch, 'Yes,' says Macaulay; 'but how happily introduced, and with what skill and spirit worked up by Shakspeare!' He keenly appreciated the unerring literary instinct which detected, and exhibited in enduring colours, the true character of young Octavius Cæsar. 'It is most remarkable,' he writes, 'that Shakspeare's portrait of Augustus should be so correct. Through all the flattery of his eulogists, it is easy to see that he was exactly the crafty, timid, cold-blooded man that he is represented here.'

Coriolanus was a favourite play with Macaulay; and all the more because it related to a period of history about which, in his view, Shakspeare knew just as much, and as little, as his learned commentators. With reference to the passage where the Tribune Sicinius spoke of the Senate as 'our assembly,' Warburton wrote: 'He should have said *your* assembly. For till the Lex Attinia,—the author of which is supposed by Sigonius, (De Vetere Italiæ Jure,) to have been contemporary with Quintus Metellus Macedonicus,—the Tribunes had not the privilege of entering the Senate, but had seats placed near the door on the outside of the house.' 'Absurd!' said Macaulay. 'Who knows anything about the usages of the Senate, and the privileges of the Tribunes, in Coriolanus's time?' Warburton took still greater exception to the speech of Coriolanus as reported by the Third Citizen.

> 'I would be consul,' (says he.) 'Aged custom,
> But by your voices, will not so permit me.
> Your voices therefore!'

'This,' observed the Bishop, 'was a strange inattention.

The Romans at this time had but lately changed the Regal for the Consular Government; for Coriolanus was banished the eighteenth year after the expulsion of the kings.' 'Well!' wrote Macaulay; 'but there had certainly been elective magistracies in Rome before the expulsion of the kings, and there might have been canvassing. Shakspeare cared so little about historical accuracy that an editor who notices expressions, which really are not grossly inaccurate, is unpardonable.' In the same scene Brutus says of Coriolanus

> Censorinus, darling of the people,
> And nobly named so, twice being Censor,
> Was his great ancestor.

Warburton justly remarks that the first Censor was created half a century after the days of Coriolanus. Shakspeare, (he explains,) had misread his authorities, and had confounded the ancestors of Coriolanus with his posterity. 'This undoubtedly was a mistake,' said Macaulay; 'and what *does* it matter?' On the last page he writes: 'A noble play. As usual, Shakspeare had thumbed his translation of Plutarch to rags.'

'With regard to Cicero as an author,' (so Niebuhr wrote,) 'I cannot say anything better than was said by Quintilian,—that the pleasure which a man takes in the works of Cicero is the standard by which we may estimate his own intellectual culture.' It was a test which Macaulay was qualified to pass; for he read Cicero's works twice during those three years at Calcutta when he was reading Plautus and Terence [1] four times, and Demosthenes thrice. It was all a labour of

[1] Macaulay, all his life through, was very fond of Terence. When the poet maintains in a prologue that the diction of his comedy is 'pura oratio,' Macaulay exclaims: 'Pura oratio, indeed! I doubt whether the mere art of style was ever carried higher than by Terence.' He says of the conversation between Micio and his son Æschinus, in the Fourth Act of the Adelphi: 'I hardly know whether the moral of the play, and of this scene in particular, be quite sound. But I am sure that nothing can be more sweetly written.'

love. Macaulay read Greek and Latin for their own sake, and not in order to use them for purposes of literary copy. He has left us eight pages, as fascinating as any that he ever penned, about the Phalaris controversy in the Essay on Sir William Temple; and six pages, on the same topic, in the short article on Bishop Atterbury. Those twelve or fifteen paragraphs, and the prefaces to the Lays of Ancient Rome, are the sole visible fruit of the thousands of hours which he spent over the classical writers during the last thirty years of his life. His manuscript notes extend through the long range of Greek authors from Hesiod to Athenæus, and of Latin authors from Cato the Censor,—through Livy, and Sallust, and Tacitus, and Aulus Gellius, and Suetonius,—down to the very latest Augustan histories. They testify to his vivid and comprehensive knowledge of the facts, dates, and personages of the ancient world. That knowledge was acquired, not at second hand from the dissertations of other scholars, but by strenuous and enraptured study of the original books themselves. Macaulay had always in his head the materials, and the thoughts, for an Essay on Greek and Roman history which might have ranked with the Essay on Clive, and with the article in the Encyclopædia Britannica on William Pitt. But it was not so to be; and a Life of Pericles, or a Life of Cicero, are among the unwritten biographies which were buried with him under the pavement of Poet's Corner in the transept of the Abbey.

Cicero's philosophical writings were among the productions of their own class which Macaulay read with the greatest profit to himself. He was favourably disposed towards Cicero's views on the crucial problem of the foundations of morality; for he was an Academician so far as he was anything. Those two parallel lines in pencil, which were his highest form of compliment, are scored down page after page of the De Finibus, the Academic Questions, and the Tusculan Disputations. 'Exquisitely written, graceful, calm, luminous, and full of interest; but the Epicurean theory of morals is hardly deserving of refutation.' That sentence relates to the first book of the De Finibus; and for Cicero's exposition of the Stoic theory, as apart from the theory itself, he has nothing but commendation. It is 'Trashy sophistry, admirably explained;' or 'Beautifully lucid, though the system is excessively absurd.' 'Fine anointing for broken bones!' he writes, when we are told that the sage, whose child has died, grieves for the possibilities of happiness which his child has missed, and not for his own loss. 'Does not a man feel grief,' (Macaulay asked,) 'when he sends his favourite son to India?' He placed Cicero's treatises on oratory altogether above anything that ever had been written in that department of literature. He greatly admired the theological disputations, and the discussions on omens, prodigies, and oracles. He pronounced the first book of the De Natura Deorum 'Equal to anything that Cicero ever did;' and he esteemed the De Divinatione, (and how could he do otherwise?) as among the most curiously interesting of human compositions. Cicero's argument against the credibility of visions and prophecies, in the Second Book of the De Divinatione, is double-lined in Macaulay's copy. That eloquent display of scepticism, on the part of the most famous and keen-witted professional soothsayer that ever lived, was in his mind when he read Ben Jonson's Catiline.

> *Lentulus*. The Augurs all are constant *I* am meant.
> *Catiline*. They had lost their science else.

'The dialogue here,' wrote Macaulay, 'is good and natural. But it is strange that so excellent a scholar as Jonson should represent the Augurs as giving any encouragement to Lentulus's dreams. The Augurs were the first nobles of Rome. In this generation Pompey, Hortensius, Cicero, and other men of the same class, belonged to the College.'

Macaulay had a special liking for the De Officiis, and was in general agreement with Cicero's doctrine of duty; although he protested vehemently whenever the author thought fit to draw his examples of the just man made perfect from Scipio Nasica and Lucius Opimius,—the pair of worthies who murdered the brothers Gracchi.[1] My uncle regarded the De Officiis as a young man's model for Latin prose composition. When I first went to Cambridge he solemnly enjoined me to read it during mathematical lecture, and thereby involved me in a scrape which I long had reason to remember. Even for Cicero's poetry Macaulay had enough respect to distinguish carefully between the bad, and the less bad. Whatever that praise may be worth, he characterises the translations from Æschylus and Sophocles in the Second Book of the Tusculan Disputations as 'Cicero's best.' He enjoyed and valued Cicero's Letters to a degree that he found difficult to express. The document that he most admired, in the whole collection of the correspondence, was Cæsar's answer to Cicero's message of gratitude for the humanity which the conqueror had displayed towards those political adversaries who had fallen into his power at the surrender of Corfinium. It contained, (so Macaulay used to say,) the finest sentence ever written, 'Meum factum probari abs te, triumpho, gaudeo. *Neque illud me movet quod ii, qui a me dimissi sunt, discessisse dicuntur ut mihi rursus bellum inferrent; nihil enim malo quam et me mei similem esse, et illos sui.*'[2]

[1] That was after Cicero had become a partisan of the aristocracy. As late in the day as his oration on the Agrarian Law he spoke of Tiberius and Caius Gracchus as 'two most illustrious men of genius, who were among the very best friends of the Roman people.' 'I believe,' wrote Macaulay, 'that, when Cicero was adopted into the class of nobles, his tastes and opinions underwent a change, like those of many other politicians.' The highest rank among Roman citizens is adjudged, in the Eighth Philippic, to 'Publius Nasica, who killed Tiberius Gracchus;' and who, (said Macaulay,) by so doing, gave the first example to Marius, Cinna, Cæsar, and Antony of settling civil disputes by arms.

[2] 'I triumph and rejoice that my action should have obtained your approval. *Nor am I disturbed when I hear it said that those, whom I have sent off alive and free, will again bear arms against me; for there is nothing which I so much covet as that I should be like myself, and they like themselves.*'

Opposite that sentence appear the words: 'Noble fellow!'

Macaulay's pencilled observations upon each successive speech of Cicero form a continuous history of the great orator's public career, and a far from unsympathetic analysis of his mobile, and singularly interesting, character. The early efforts of the young advocate were mainly directed to the defence and rescue of quiet citizens from the rapacity and cruelty of Sulla's partisans. Of the oration on behalf of Quintius, delivered when Cicero was only six-and-twenty, Macaulay writes: 'I like this speech better than any of the Greek speeches in mere private cases. It would in any age produce a prodigious effect on any tribunal. It would seem that the confusion of the times, and the speedy ways of getting rich which the proscriptions had opened to cupidity, had destroyed all feeling of honour and honesty in many minds.' He considered the oration for Roscius of Ameria, with its exposure of the villanies perpetrated by Sulla's freedman, the infamous Chrysogonus, as more creditable to Cicero's heart than any that he ever made. 'I cannot,' he said, 'help thinking that he strengthened the language after Sulla's resignation. But, after making full allowance for re-touching, it is impossible to deny that he performed a bold service to humanity and to his country. Si sic omnia!' With regard to the first, and shorter, oration against Verres, Macaulay remarks: 'There is great force about this speech. Cicero had not attained that perfect mastery of the whole art of rhetoric which he possessed at a later period. But on the other hand there is a freedom, a boldness, a zeal for popular rights, a scorn of the vicious and insolent gang whom he afterwards called the *boni*, which makes these early speeches more pleasing than the later. Flattery,—and, after his exile, cowardice,—destroyed all that was generous and elevated in his mind.' Of the Third Section of the Second Oration he says: 'A very powerful speech indeed. It makes my blood boil, less against Verres than against the detestable system of government which Cicero was so desirous to uphold, though he himself was not an accomplice in the crimes which were inseparable from it.'

It was Macaulay's fixed belief that the debate on the punishment of the Catilinarian conspirators was a fateful crisis in Cicero's history. Cæsar had almost persuaded the Senate to refrain from sending Roman citizens to a violent and illegal death, when Cicero the Consul,—in an evil hour for his fame, and still more for his happiness,—raised his voice against the policy of clemency and self-control. 'Fine declamation:' said Macaulay. 'But it is no answer to Cæsar's admirable speech. This was the turning point of Cicero's life. He was a new man, and a popular man. Till his Consulship he had always leaned against the Optimates. He had defended Sulla's victims. He had brought Verres to justice in spite of strong aristocratical protection. He had always spoken handsomely of the Gracchi and other heroes of the democratic party. He appears, when he became Consul, to have been very much liked by the multitude, and much distrusted by the nobles. But the peculiar circumstances in which he now was placed rendered it his duty to take the side of the aristocracy on some important questions. He supported them on the Agrarian Law. He also took vigorous measures against Catiline. They began to coax and flatter him. He went further. He was hurried by adulation, vanity, and vindictive feeling into a highly unconstitutional act in favour of the nobles. He followed, with more excuse indeed, the odious example set by Scipio Nasica and by Opimius. From that time he was an instrument in the hands of the grandees, whom he hated and despised: and who fully returned his hatred, and despised, not his talents indeed, but his character.' Cicero, and his new political allies, had very little in common. At a serious crisis in Roman history he told Atticus that the leaders of the aristocratic party cared nothing about the ruin of the Republic as long as their fishponds were safe, and believed themselves to have attained celestial honours if they had great mullets which came up to be fed by hand. 'These,' said Macaulay, 'are your *boni!*' and on a later occasion my uncle remarks, in caustic language, on the circumstance that the most creditable act of Cicero's official career was his effort to protect the miserable provincials of Cyprus from the cruelty and rapacity of no less a Senator than Marcus Brutus. Cicero's opinion of the nobles went steadily down as his experience of them grew more intimate. The time came when he confided to Atticus that they were altogether insupportable. 'I cannot endure,' he said, 'to be the object of their sneering talk. They certainly do not merit their name of *boni*.' 'You have found it out at last!' wrote Macaulay.[1]

That was the precise point at which Cicero's usefulness as a statesman and a patriot declined, and his misfortunes began. His nerve and courage were impaired, and he surrendered his political independence to bolder and stronger men. 'Cæsar and Pompey,' said Macaulay, 'liked Cicero personally, it should seem; but they saw that he was inclined to disturb their coalition. Accordingly they let Clodius loose upon him; connived at his being banished; fairly frightened him; and, when they now saw that he had been rendered thoroughly tractable, they recalled him home. The struggle in poor Cicero's mind between fear and self-importance is one which all his great powers are quite unable to disguise.' Under cruel pressure, from both Pompey and Cæsar, Cicero was reluctantly induced to appear in court on behalf of Gabinius,—a man (so he complained to Atticus,) whose presence in the Roman Senate was a personal disgrace to all his colleagues.[2] 'After having stooped to defend Gabinius,' wrote Macaulay, 'he might well bear to sit with him.' 'My motive,' (Cicero once said in public,) 'for defending Gabinius was the desire to make up the quarrel between us; for I never repent of behaving as if my enmities were transient, and my

[1] Cicero to Atticus; Book II, Letter 1; VI, 1; IX, 2.
[2] Cicero to Atticus, X, 8.

friendships eternal.' 'A fine sentence,' (said Macaulay,) 'quoted very happily by Fox. But poor Cicero was ready to sink into the earth with shame, though he tried to put a good face on the matter.'

'Meanwhile,' said Macaulay, 'the vice of egotism was now rapidly growing on Cicero. He had attained the highest point of power which he ever reached, and his head was undoubtedly a little turned by his elevation. Afterwards this vile habit tainted his speaking and writing, so as to make much of his finest rhetoric almost disgusting. He gave himself airs, on all occasions, which, as Plutarch tells us, made him generally odious, and were the real cause of his exile.' My uncle describes the speech for the poet Archias, with its exquisitely worded encomium on the delights of literature, as a magnificent composition, blemished as usual by insufferable egotism. 'What unhappy madness,' he says, 'led Cicero always to talk of himself?' And of the attack on Piso in the Senate he writes: 'A splendid invective certainly, but he was really mad with vanity.' 'The defence of Sextius is very interesting. Indeed those parts of the speech, which seem most out of place in a forensic address, are historically the most valuable. Cicero doubtless knew that his client was safe, and that the judges were all Optimates; and so he ventured to luxuriate in narratives and disquisitions not very closely connected with the subject.' The tribute of adulation which, in the course of that speech, the orator paid to the degenerate aristocracy of the later Republic angered his reader as he seldom had been angered by any passage in literature. When Cicero asked what sort of men were these *Optimates*, who so well deserved their honourable title, Macaulay replied that they were 'the murderers of the Gracchi, the hirelings of Jugurtha, the butchers of Sulla, the plunderers of the provinces, the buyers and sellers of magistracies,—such men as Opimius and Scaurus, Domitius Ahenobarbus and Caius Verres.'[1]

[1] Macaulay, while he was severe upon these ancient Romans, did not spare himself whenever he had been betrayed into an

In his comments on the Epistles to Atticus Macaulay's sympathy with their author is more conspicuous than in his comments on the Speeches. When Cicero confesses, at the end of a letter the contents of which otherwise do him little credit, that the loss of his reader Sositheus, whom he calls a charming lad, had distressed him more than the death of a slave might be thought to justify, Macaulay writes: 'A kind-hearted man, with all his faults.' When the unhappy ex-Consul complained that he had been rudely expelled from on board the ship of state, and relegated against his will, and before his time, to the haven of literary leisure; 'Poor fellow!' said Macaulay. 'He had not the firmness to do what he felt to be necessary for his peace.' And when the darkness gathered round Cicero, and a sense of impending danger filled the air;—when Atticus was absent from Rome, and amidst a crowd of flatterers and clients he had not a single friend with whom he could exchange a word of confidence; and when he found comfort nowhere except in the privacy of family life, with his darling Tulliola, and his 'sweet little Cicero';—the narrative of his sorrows and anxieties seemed to Macaulay 'As exquisitely beautiful a passage as ever was written.' The melancholy letters sent home to Atticus from Illyria and Macedonia during the period of Cicero's banishment suggested the following reflections to the English statesman at Calcutta. 'Poor fellow! He makes a pitiful figure. But it is impossible not to feel for him. Since I left England I have not despised Cicero and Ovid for their lamentations in exile as much as I did.' That was a remarkable and characteristic confession for a brilliant and successful man of five-and-thirty, who had gone to India for a very few years in order

error of literary judgment. He makes these two successive entries with reference to the oration for Marcus Marcellus.

'A splendid and highly finished declamation; but, taken in connection with Cicero's letter written at the time, it does little honour to his character. September 27, 1835.'

'It does him neither honor nor dishonor. For it is not his. March 17, 1856.'

to secure a competence, and fill a most important and dignified office. When Cicero tells his friend how, on his return from exile, he was welcomed home by the entire population of the city, 'That day,' said Macaulay, 'was indeed worth a life to a man so sensitive, and so passionately fond of glory.' In the Twelfth Letter of the Ninth Book is the passage commencing, 'Cneius Pompeius is blockaded by a Roman army. He is enclosed, and held captive, within a wall of circumvallation built by Roman hands. And I live, and the city stands! And the Prætors deliver their judgments, and the Ædiles prepare to hold the public games, and wealthy men calmly reckon up the value of their investments!' 'Very fine writing, certainly;' Macaulay says. 'I like some of the letters in this book as much as any of Cicero's compositions.'[1]

After Cæsar's death Cicero emerged from a period of retirement and irksome silence; and the third and last phase of his oratory commenced. Macaulay styles the Second Philippic 'a most wonderful display of rhetorical talent, worthy of all its fame.' With regard to the Third Philippic, he writes: 'The close of this speech is very fine. His later and earlier speeches have a freedom and an air of sincerity about them which, in the interval between his Consulship and Cæsar's death, I do not find. During that interval he was mixed up with the aristocratical party, and yet afraid of the Triumvirate. When all the great party-leaders were dead, he found himself at the head of the state, and spoke with a boldness and energy which he had not shown since his youthful days.' Macaulay did full justice to Cicero's vigour and eloquence at this grave political conjuncture; but he condemned his course of action, and deeply disapproved his motives. 'His whole conduct,' he writes, 'was as bad as possible. His love of peace, the best part of his public character, was overcome by personal animosity and wounded vanity.' At the end of the last Philippic Macaulay compares him with Demosthenes, whom he ranks

[1] Cicero to Atticus, I, 12; II, 7; I, 18; III, 13; IV, 1.

above him as an orator. 'As a man,' he writes, 'I think of Cicero much as I always did, except that I am more disgusted with his conduct after Cæsar's death. I really think that he met with little more than his deserts from the Triumvirs. It is quite certain, as Livy says, that he suffered nothing more than he would have inflicted. There is an impatience of peaceful counsels, a shrinking from all plans of conciliation, a thirst for blood, in all the Philippics, which, (whatever he may say,) can be attributed only to personal hatred, and is particularly odious in a timid man.'

That the great orator met with his deserts at the hands of the Triumvirs is a hard saying; but his actions and his utterances, during the last years of his life, were repugnant, and sometimes even shocking, to Macaulay. Cæsar had shown himself a kind and considerate friend to Cicero, and Cicero had professed gratitude and esteem for Cæsar; but, after Cæsar's murder in the Senate-house, Cicero exulted over his fate in words as sharp and cruel as the dagger of Cassius. Antony, again, had urged Cicero to lay aside ancient enmities, and secure for himself a tranquil and honourable old age as the crown of his splendid career. 'I only wish,' answered Cicero, 'that you had addressed me face to face, instead of by writing; for you might then have perceived not by my words alone, but by my countenance, my eyes, and my forehead, the affection that I bear to you. For,—as I always loved you for the attentions you have shown me, and the services you have done me,—so, in these later days, your public conduct has been such that I hold no one dearer than you.' That was how Cicero wrote *to* Antony; but, before a year was over, he thus wrote *about* Antony to one of Cæsar's assassins: 'Would to heaven you had invited me to that noble feast which you made on the Ides of March! No remnants, most assuredly, would have been left behind. * * * I have a grudge even against so good a man as yourself when I reflect that it was through *your* intervention that this pest of humanity is still among the living.' 'Infamous!'

wrote Macaulay. 'Compare this with his language about Antony before their quarrel.'

None the less did Macaulay regard Cicero as among the foremost men of all the ages. I remember paying him a visit in his rose-garden at Campden Hill,—as pleasant a corner of the earth as any that Marcus Tullius himself possessed at Tusculum, or Antium, or Arpinum. I was in a hurry to communicate to him my discovery of the magnificent verses in which Juvenal bids observe how the world's two mightiest orators were brought by their genius and eloquence to a violent and tragic death. I can almost repeat the exact words of Macaulay's reply. 'It is,' he said, 'very fine satire; but there is another aspect of the question. A man cannot expect to win great fame without running great risks and perils. In spite of all that Juvenal says, Cicero and Demosthenes would never have consented to renounce their place in history in order to be sure of dying quietly in their beds.'[1]

My uncle read Plato in a ponderous folio, sixteen inches long by ten broad, and weighing within half an ounce of twelve pounds;—which was very near the weight of a regulation musket at the period when he himself was Secretary at War. Published at Frankfort in the year 1602, it contained nearly fourteen hundred closely-printed pages of antique Greek type, bristling with those contractions which are a terror to the luxurious modern scholar. The Latin translation by Marsilius Ficinus, arranged in parallel columns by the side of the original text, presents an aspect of positively revolting dullness. The blank spaces of this grim volume are lit up by Macaulay's comments, sparkling with vitality and fire, but sometimes softened

[1] Macaulay read Latin authors in the Bipontine edition of 1781, and Greek authors in Dindorf's collection. His books contained nothing except the text; for, on whatever language he was engaged, whether ancient or modern, he had a profound aversion to explanatory notes. I cannot tell how much use he had made of a Lexicon. At that period of his life when he read with me the Plutus of Aristophanes, the Midias of Demosthenes, and the Gorgias of Plato, he knew the meaning of every word.

and awed into a strain of touching beauty. The Timæus, the Parmenides, and others of the more abstruse dialogues, appear to have interested him little; for, greatly as he loved Plato, it was not chiefly for the sake of Plato's metaphysics. But at any pitched battle between Socrates and a tough opponent, Macaulay assisted in a spirit of joyous exhilaration which people seldom bring to the perusal of a philosophical treatise. The Euthydemus, in particular, is enlivened throughout by his exclamations of amusement and delight. 'It seems incredible that these absurdities of Dionysodorus and Euthydemus should have been mistaken for wisdom, even by the weakest of mankind. I can hardly help thinking that Plato has overcharged the portrait. But the humour of the dialogue is admirable.' 'Glorious irony!' 'Incomparably ludicrous!' 'No writer, not even Cervantes, was so great a master of this solemn ridicule as Plato.' 'There is hardly any comedy, in any language, more diverting than this dialogue. It is not only richly humorous. The characters are most happily sustained and discriminated. The contrast between the youthful petulance of Ctesippus and the sly, sarcastic mock humility of Socrates is admirable.' There are personal touches among the annotations on the Euthydemus. To Plato's rather grudging description of the man of the world, who is likewise a man of the study, and who divides his time between philosophy and politics, Macaulay appends the remark: 'Dulcissima hercle, eademque nobilissima vita.' And, below the last line of the dialogue, there occurs the following entry: 'Calcutta, May 1835. Yesterday the London News of the 2nd of March arrived by steamer from Bombay. Peel beaten in two divisions. Suave mari magno——'

Macaulay viewed the Republic with the eyes of a Whig and an Englishman; but, whatever he might think of Plato's political and social ideals, he had a deep and abiding admiration for Plato himself. 'Plato,' Macaulay wrote, 'has been censured with great justice for his doctrine about the community of women and the exposure of children. But nobody, as far as I remember, has done justice to him on one important point. No ancient politician appears to have thought so highly of the capacity of women, and to have been inclined to make them so important. He was to blame for wishing to divest them of all their characteristic attractions; but, in return, he proposed to admit them to a full participation in the power and honour enjoyed by men.' When the philosopher enjoins the inhabitants of his Utopia to treat a great poet with profound reverence, but to get him outside their community at all hazards,—to anoint his head with precious unguents, and crown him with garlands, and then pass him on as soon as possible to some neighbouring city,—Macaulay remarks: 'You may see that Plato was passionately fond of poetry, even when arguing against it.' Where Plato recommends a broader patriotism as a corrective to the fierce and narrow municipal sentiment of the small Greek states, 'this passage,' he writes, 'does Plato great honour. Philhellenism is a step towards philanthropy. There is an enlargement of mind in this work which I do not remember to have found in any earlier composition, and in very few ancient works, either earlier or later.' There was, (said Macaulay,) something far beyond the ordinary political philosophy of Greece in that fine definition of the object for which civil government should exist,—'the relief and respite of mankind from misfortune.' Of the striking conception of abstract justice, in the Second Book of the Republic, he writes: 'This is indeed a noble dream. Pity that it should come through the gate of ivory!' The Eighth Book, in the judgment of the great critic, was above and beyond all detailed criticism. 'I remember,' he says, 'nothing in Greek philosophy superior to this in profundity, ingenuity, and eloquence.'

Macaulay rated the Protagoras exceedingly high as a work of literary art. 'A very lively picture,' he wrote, 'of Athenian manners. There is scarcely anywhere so interesting a view of the interior of a Greek house in the most interesting age of Greece.'[1] 'Callias seems to have been a munificent and courteous patron of learning. What with sophists, what with pretty women, and what with sycophants, he came to the end of a noble fortune.' 'Alcibiades is very well represented here. It is plain that he wants only to get up a row among the sophists.' 'Protagoras seems to deserve the character he gives himself. Nothing can be more courteous and generous than his language. Socrates shows abundance of talent and acuteness in this dialogue; but the more I read of his conversation, the less I wonder at the fierce hatred he provoked. He evidently had an ill-natured pleasure in making men,—particularly men famed for wisdom and eloquence,—look like fools; and it would not be difficult, even for a person of far inferior powers to his, to draw the ablest speculator into contradictions upon questions as subtle as those which he loved to investigate. Protagoras seems to have been a man of great eloquence and accomplishments, though no match for Socrates at Socrates's own weapons. It is plain from many passages that this dialogue, if it be not altogether a fiction, took place about thirty years before the death of Socrates. Pericles seems to have been still living. Alcibiades was hardly arrived at manhood. I should think, from one or two expressions, that the Peloponnesian war had not yet begun. I can hardly suppose this, and the other dialogues in which Socrates is introduced, to be purely fictitious. Some such conversation took place, I imagine. Socrates had often related in Plato's hearing what had passed; and this most beautiful drama, for such it is, was formed out of those materials.'

At the commencement of the Gorgias is written: 'This was my favourite dialogue at College. I do not know whether I shall like it as well now. May 1, 1837.'

[1] When the porter slammed the door in the face of Socrates, with the observation that his master was busy. 'A more sincere, and a less civil, answer,' said Macaulay, 'than our "Not at home."'

Macaulay followed the cut-and-thrust of the controversy with brisk attention. 'Polus is much in the right. Socrates abused scandalously the advantages which his wonderful talents, and his command of temper, gave him.' 'You have made a blunder, and Socrates will have you in an instant.' 'Hem! Retiarium astutum!' 'There you are in the Sophist's net. I think that, if I had been in the place of Polus, Socrates would hardly have had so easy a job of it.' When Callicles, the unscrupulous and dexterous votary of politics and pleasure, took up the foil, the exchanges came quick and sharp. 'What a command of his temper the old fellow had, and what terrible, though delicate, ridicule! A bitter fellow, too, with all his suavity.' 'This is not pure morality; but there is a good deal of weight in what Callicles says. He is wrong in not perceiving that the real happiness, not only of the weak many, but of the able few, is promoted by virtue. The character of Callicles throws great light on that fine disquisition of Thucydides on the state of political morality in Greece during the contest between the oligarchical and democratic principles. When I read this dialogue as a lad at college, I thought Callicles the most wicked wretch that ever lived; and when, about the time of my leaving college, I wrote a trifling piece for Knight's Magazine, in which some Athenian characters were introduced, I made this Callicles the villain of the drama.[1] I now see that he was merely a fair specimen of the public men of Athens in that age. Although his principles were those of aspiring and voluptuous men in unquiet times, his feelings seem to have been friendly and kind.' His warning to Socrates, (added Macaulay,) about the perils which, in a city like Athens, beset a man who neglected politics, and devoted himself exclusively to philosophical speculation, was well meant, and, as the event proved, only too well founded.

[1] Scenes from 'The Athenian Revels,' January 1824. The little drama, together with its sister piece, 'The Fragments of a Roman Tale,' may be found in the Miscellaneous Writings.

Macaulay unreservedly admired the glorious rhapsody which ends the dialogue. 'This,' he wrote, 'is one of the finest passages in Greek literature. Plato is a real poet.' 'Those doctrines of yours,' (said Socrates to Gorgias and Callicles), 'have now been examined and found wanting; and this doctrine alone has stood the test,—that we ought to be more afraid of wronging than of being wronged, and that the prime business of every man is, not to seem good, but to be good, in all his private and public dealings.' That sentence was marked by Macaulay with three pencil-lines of assent and admiration. 'This just and noble conclusion,' he writes, 'atones for much fallacy in the reasoning by which Socrates arrived at it. The Gorgias is certainly a very fine work. It is deformed by a prodigious quantity of sophistry. But the characters are so happily supported, the conversations so animated and natural, the close so eloquent, and the doctrines inculcated, though over-strained, are so lofty and pure, that it is impossible not to consider it as one of the greatest performances which have descended to us from that wonderful generation.'

When Socrates was put upon his trial, he reminded the Court, in the course of his celebrated defence, how he had braved the popular fury by refusing to concur in the judicial murder of the Generals who had conquered at Arginusæ; and how, at the peril of his life, he had silently disobeyed the unjust behests of the Thirty Tyrants. Macaulay pronounced that portion of the speech to be as interesting and striking a passage as he ever heard or read. When Socrates expressed a serene conviction that to die was gain, even if death were nothing more than an untroubled and dreamless sleep, 'Milton,' said Macaulay, 'thought otherwise.

> Sad cure! For who would lose,
> Though full of pain, this intellectual being;
> Those thoughts that wander through eternity?

I once thought with Milton; but every day brings me nearer and nearer to the doctrine here laid down by

Socrates.' 'And now,' said the condemned criminal to his judges, 'the time has come when we must part, and go our respective ways,—I to die, you to live; and which of us has the happier fortune in store for him is known to none, except to God.' 'A most solemn and noble close!' said Macaulay. 'Nothing was ever written, or spoken, approaching in sober sublimity to the latter part of the Apology. It is impossible to read it without feeling one's mind elevated and strengthened.'

Phædo relates how Socrates, on the last morning of his life, amused himself by recalling his own youthful interest in the problems of natural science. 'This,' said Macaulay, 'is what Aristophanes charged Socrates with, and what Xenophon most stoutly denied. The truth seems to be that the mind of that wonderful man, as he grew older, gradually turned itself away from physical speculations, and addicted itself more and more to moral philosophy. Aristophanes knew this probably before Xenophon was born.' Macaulay thus remarks on the beautiful legend about the purification of souls in Acheron and Cocytus, with which Socrates concluded his final talk on earth: 'All this is merely a fine poem, like Dante's. Milton has borrowed largely from it; and, considered as an effort of the imagination, it is one from which no poet need be ashamed to borrow.' When the master drank the poison, and when Apollodorus burst into a passion of weeping, and broke down in a moment the composure of the whole company of disciples, Macaulay says, 'This is the passage, I dare say, which Cicero could never read without tears. I never could. Phædo tells a noble and most touching story. Addison meant to have written a tragedy on it. He would infallibly have spoiled it. The reasonings of Socrates, on his last day, convey no satisfaction to my mind; but the example of benevolence, patience, and self-possession, which he exhibited, is incomparable and inestimable.' And again, on the last page of the Crito, he writes: 'There is much that may be questioned in the reasoning of Socrates; but it is imposssible not to admire the wisdom and virtue which it indicates. When we consider the moral state of Greece in his time, and the revolution which he produced in men's notions of good and evil, we must pronounce him one of the greatest men that ever lived.'

APPENDICES

APPENDIX I

(See vol. i, page 105.)

Macaulay's Speech to the Anti-Slavery Society.

THE following letter was written to Mrs. Hannah More by a young lady belonging to a very well-known Clapham family. She was Macaulay's contemporary, and his friend through life. 'Mr. Macaulay,' throughout the letter, is Zachary Macaulay, the young man's father.

June 26th, 1824.

'Mrs. Hannah More must be written to, for they will never tell her about it. Oh! how I wish she had been there!' was repeatedly said to me by Henry as we left the Freemasons' Hall to-day, where, to use Mr. Wilberforce's expression, as used to him, "Tom Macaulay has most nobly won his spurs on that hard-fought field,—the anti-slavery," when he made a speech of which I really feel it is perfectly impossible to say too much. I was so completely delighted with it, that I should hardly have trusted my own feelings about it; but when I saw the grave old steady Senators all so carried away by the eloquence of the youthful orator that even the decorums of the platform were forgotten, and the dignity of the Royal Duke compromised, by Mr. Wilberforce and Mr. Stephen catching hold of him as he was going back to his place, and keeping him there, each shaking a hand, while the very walls seemed to be coming down with the thunders of applause! The argumentative parts reminded me of Brougham, and the eloquence of Charles Grant; but really in sober earnest he exceeded anything I have heard of either; but perhaps his marvellous composure and statesmanlike manner of speaking was more imposing than anything else. They say it is to be published, so I won't try to give you any idea of what he said; and of the effects of it only the hearers can judge; and really it was delightful to watch Mr. Wilberforce's looks and exclamations of delight,—"Capital!" "Wonderful!"—while he was speaking, and his high congratulations to Mr. Macaulay when it was over. He spoke very shortly himself, but so beautifully we were all melted almost away. He said Mr. Macaulay's long life of labour was almost at a close; his own sun was nearly setting, as well as that of most of the veterans in the cause; but he could feel it would rise again most gloriously in the extraordinary hopes and prospects that day had afforded. He then turned so affectionately to Mr. Macaulay and said, 'Much as Mr. Macaulay had suffered, much as he had laboured, all the obloquy, all the calumny he had endured,—would he not suffer it tenfold to enjoy such feelings as that marvellous speech had called forth?" It really did me good to look at Mr. Macaulay's expression of calm delight while this was going on, and while Mr. Stephen was loud in his exclamations; and even Lord Calthorpe's composure was overset. Mr. Macaulay was quite overcome at the thunders of applause, which were far louder than I ever heard to any other speaker. Mr. Macaulay's only observation to Henry was so like himself; 'Was he not too long?"—the only person in the room who could have asked the question. Mrs. Smith, the wife of the poor missionary, was there; and, if anything could console her under afflictions such as her's, I think this would have done it. I am writing in haste, hoping this may go to-day, for you have always felt so much interest in Tom Macaulay that I was sure you would be delighted to hear he had succeeded so splendidly. And yet you see all his own family will take it so quietly. So I must now conclude, ever dearest Mrs. Hannah More.

Your affectionate,

——

The family to which the writer of the foregoing letter belonged preserved several anecdotes illustrating my uncle's lifelong habit, (a characteristic indication of his Clapham breeding,) of employing Biblical phrases which were always apt, and not essentially irreverent. They told me how the Macaulay children, on reaching London after a summer visit to Rothley Temple, were transferring themselves, under the directions of their eldest brother, from the Leicester mail into a hackney-coach. The driver of that vehicle expressed his astonishment at the size of the party, and Tom Macaulay explained the matter by saying: 'We be all one man's sons.'

Another story, derived from the same source, refers to a much later period. 'We were sitting in the Trevelyans' drawing-room at Clapham, and the conversation happened to turn on the approaching departure of a local curate. George Trevelyan, then a very little fellow, who was lying ill on the sofa, listening to our talk, asked whether the Reverend gentleman was to have a testimonial. "My boy," (said Macaulay,) "I am glad to know that you are not one of those who would muzzle the ox that treadeth out the corn." '

APPENDIX II

(See vol. i, page 411.)

Macaulay's Studies at Calcutta.

A FEW extracts from the notes pencilled in Macaulay's Greek and Latin books may interest any one who is wise enough to have kept up his classics, or young enough for it to be still his happy duty to read them. The number of the dates scribbled at the conclusion of each volume, and their proximity in point of time, are astonishing when we reflect that every such memorandum implies a separate perusal.

'This day I finished Thucydides, after reading him with inexpressible interest and admiration. He is the greatest historian that ever lived.—*February* 27, 1835.'

'I am still of the same mind.—*May* 30, 1836.'

At the end of Xenophon's Anabasis, may be read the words:

'Decidedly his best work.—*December* 17, 1835.'

'Most certainly.—*February* 24, 1837.'

'One of the very first works that antiquity has left us. Perfect in its kind.—*October* 9, 1837.'

'I read Plautus four times at Calcutta.

The first in November and December 1834.

The second in January and the beginning of February 1835.

The third on the Sundays from the 24th of May to the 23rd of August 1835.

The fourth on the Sundays beginning from the 1st of January 1837.

I have since read him in the Isle of Wight (1850), and in the South of France (1858).'

'Finished the second reading of Lucretius this day,

March 24, 1835. It is a great pity that the poem is in an unfinished state. The philosophy is for the most part utterly worthless; but in energy, perspicuity, variety of illustration, knowledge of life and manners, talent for description, sense of the beauty of the external world, and elevation and dignity of moral feeling, he had hardly ever an equal.'

'Finished Catullus August 3, 1835. An admirable poet. No Latin writer is so Greek. The simplicity, the pathos, the perfect grace, which I find in the great Athenian models, are all in Catullus, and in him alone of the Romans.'

To the Thebaïs of Statius are simply appended the dates 'October 26, 1835.' 'October 31, 1836.' The expressions 'Stuff!' and 'Trash!' occur frequently enough throughout the dreary pages of the poem; while evidence of the attention with which those pages were studied is afforded by such observations as 'Gray has translated this passage;' 'Racine took a hint here;' and 'Nobly imitated, indeed far surpassed, by Chaucer.'

'Finished Silius Italicus; for which heaven be praised! December 24, 1835. Pope must have read him before me. In the Temple of Fame, and the Essay on Criticism, are some touches plainly suggested by Silius.'

In the last page of Velleius Paterculus come the following comments: 'Vile flatterer! Yet, after all, he could hardly help it. But how the strong, acute, cynical mind of Tiberius must have been revolted by adulation, the absence of which he would probably have punished! Velleius Paterculus seems to me a remarkable good epitomist. I hardly know any historical work of which the scale is so small, and the subject so extensive. The Bishop of London admires his style. I do not. There are sentences worthy of Tacitus; but there is an immense quantity of rant, and far too much ejaculation and interrogation for oratory, let alone history. June 6, 1835. Again, May 14, 1836.'

'I think Sallust inferior to both Livy and Tacitus in the talents of an historian. There is a lecturing, declaiming tone about him which would suit a teacher of rhetoric better than a statesman engaged in recording great events. Still, he is a good writer; and the view which he here gives of the state of parties at Rome, and the frightful demoralization of the aristocracy, is full of interest. June 10, 1835. May 6, 1837.'

'I do not think that there is better evidence of the genuineness of any book in the world than of the first seven books of Cæsar's Commentaries. To doubt on that subject is the mere rage of scepticism.'

After Cæsar's De Bello Civili: 'He is an admirable writer, worth ten of Sallust. His manner is the perfection of good sense and good taste. He rises on me, also, as a man. He was on the right side, as far as in such a miserable government there could be a right side. He used his victory with glorious humanity. Pompey, whether he inclined to it or not, must have established a reign of terror to gratify the execrable aristocracy whose tool he had stooped to be.'

To the De Bello Alexandrino: 'This is not a bad history. Hirtius is a very respectable writer. The Alexandrian affair is a curious episode in Cæsar's life. No doubt the influence of Cleopatra was the real cause of his strange conduct. He was not a man to play Charles XII at Bender, except when under the tyranny of some strong passion. The ability with which he got out of scrapes is some set-off against the rashness with which he got into them.'

To the De Bello Hispaniensi: 'This book must have been written by some sturdy old centurion, who fought better than he composed.'

The odds and ends of Cæsar's conversation, gathered far and wide from classical literature into what is perhaps the most tantalising biographical fragment in the world, are characterised by Macaulay as 'Disjecta membra gigantis.'

The three volumes of Macaulay's Ovid are enlivened, throughout, with pencil-notes charming in their vivacity and versatility. At the end of the last book of the Metamorphoses he writes: 'There are some very fine things in this poem; and in ingenuity, and the art of doing difficult things in expression and versification as if they were the easiest in the world, Ovid is incomparable. But, on the whole, I am much disappointed. I like the romantic poets of Italy far better;—not only Ariosto; but Boiardo, and even Forteguerri. The second book of the Metamorphoses is by far the best. Next to that comes the first half of the thirteenth.

Finished at Calcutta April 28, 1835.'

'I like it better this second time of reading.—*January* 14, 1837.'

He was evidently surfeited by the Heroides, and pleased by the Amores; though he read them both twice through with the strictest impartiality. Of the Ars Amatoria he says: 'Ovid's best. The subject did not require the power, which he did not possess, of moving the passions. The love, which he has reduced to a system, was little more than mere sexual appetite, heightened by the art of dress, manner, and conversation. This was an excellent subject for a man so witty and so heartless.'

The Fasti were almost too much for him. 'June 30, 1835. It is odd that I should finish the Fasti on the very day with which the Fasti terminate. I am cloyed with Ovid. Yet I cannot but admire him.'

'Finished the Fasti again.—*February* 26, 1837.'

After the Tristia: 'A very melancholy set of poems. They make me very sad, and the more so because I am myself an exile, though in far happier circumstances, externally, than those of Ovid. It is impossible not to feel contempt, mingled with a sort of pitying kindness, for a man so clever, so accomplished, so weak-spirited and timid, placed, unjustly as it should seem, in so painful a situation. It is curious that the three most celebrated Roman writers who were banished, and whose compositions written in exile have come down to us, Cicero, Seneca, and Ovid, have all shown an impatience and pusillanimity which lower their characters;' and which, he might have added, are strangely at variance with the proverbial manliness and constancy of the Roman nature.

At the end of the last volume: 'I have now gone through the whole of Ovid's works, and heartily tired I am of him and them. Yet he is a wonderfully clever man. But he has two insupportable faults. The one is that he will always be clever; and the other that he never knows when to have done. He is rather a rhetorician than a poet. There is little feeling in his poems; even in those which were written during his exile. The pathetic effect of his supplications and lamentations is injured by the ingenious turns of expression, and by the learned allusions with which he sets off his sorrow.

'He seems to have been a very good fellow: rather too fond of women; a flatterer and a coward; but kind and generous: and free from envy, though a man of letters, and though sufficiently vain of his literary performances. The Art of Love, which ruined poor Ovid, is, in my opinion, decidedly his best work.'

'I finished Livy, after reading him with the greatest delight, interest, and admiration, May 31, 1835. Again, April 29, 1837.'

At the end of Livy's twenty-seventh book there appear the following remarks; which, in a letter to Mr. Ellis, Macaulay entitles 'Historic Doubts touching the Battle of the Metaurus': 'I suspect that the whole narrative is too highly coloured, and that far too large a share of the praise is allotted to Nero. Who was Nero? What did he ever do before or after this great achievement? His conduct in Spain had been that of an incapable driveller, and we hear of nothing to set off against that conduct till he was made Consul. And, after his first Consulship, why was he not re-elected? All ordinary rules about succession to offices were suspended while Hannibal was in Italy. Fabius, Fulvius, Marcellus, were elected Consuls over and over. The youth of Scipio did not keep him from holding the highest commands. Why was Nero, who, if Livy can be trusted, was a far abler man than any general whom Rome employed in that war,—who out-generalled Hasdrubal,—who saved the Republic from the most imminent danger, —never re-employed against the Carthaginians?

'And then, how strange is the silence of the Latin writers anterior to the Augustan age! There does not exist, as far as I recollect, a single allusion to Nero in all Cicero's works. But, when we come to the time at which Tiberius was rising to the first importance in the State, we find Nero represented as the most illustrious captain of his age. The earliest panegyric on him that I know is in Horace's fine ode, Qualem Ministrum. That ode was written to the praise and glory of Tiberius and Drusus,—both Neros. Livy wrote when Tiberius was partner with Augustus in the Empire; Velleius Paterculus when Tiberius was sovereign. They seem to me to have looked back into history for the purpose of finding some topic flattering to the house of Nero; and they found a victory,—certainly a considerable victory,—gained in the Consulship of a Nero, and by an army, part of which he commanded. Accordingly, they ascribed to him all the glory of the success. They represented him as having contrived the whole plan; as having executed it on his own responsibility; as having completely outwitted both the Carthaginian generals. Yet, after all, the Senate would not let him enter Rome in triumph, but gave all the honour of the victory to his colleague Livius; and I cannot find in Polybius any compliment whatsoever to Nero's generalship on this occasion.

'I dare say that, if the truth were known, it would be something of this sort. The senate ordered Nero to march, and to effect a junction with Livius. The direction of the operations subsequent to that junction probably lay with Livius, as the province was especially his, and as he was general of by far the larger force. In the action, Livy himself tells us that Livius was opposed to Hasdrubal, which was doubtless the most important post. The universal impression at the time was that the glory of the day belonged to Livius. He alone triumphed for the victory: and no Roman writer, for many generations, ranked Nero with Fabius or Marcellus. But, when the house of Nero acquired supreme power, men of letters employed all their talents in extolling the only Nero of whom it was possible to make a great man; and they have described his conduct in such a way that ne appears to have been a greater man than Scipio, and fully a match for Hannibal.'

At the end of each drama of the Greek Tragedians Macaulay wrote with a pencil, (and, unfortunately, not a very good pencil,) a little critical essay, from three to twenty lines in length.

'The first part of the Ajax is prodigiously fine. I do not know that the agonies of wounded honour have ever been so sublimely represented. Basil, in one of Miss Baillie's best plays, is a faint shadow of this grand creation of Sophocles. But the interest of the piece dies with Ajax. In the debates which follow, Sophocles does not succeed as well as Euripides would have done. The odes, too, are not very good.'

'I have been less pleased with this perusal of the Œdipus Tyrannus than I was when I read it in January; perhaps because I then read it all at one sitting. The construction seems to me less perfect than I formerly thought it. But nothing can exceed the skill with which the discovery is managed. The agony of Œdipus is so unutterably grand; and the tender sorrow, in which his mind at last reposes after his daughters have been brought to him, is as moving as anything in the Greek Drama.'

'The Philoctetes is a most noble play; conspicuous even among the works of Sophocles for the grace and majesty of effect produced by the most simple means. There is more character in it than in any play in the Greek language: two or three of Euripides's best excepted.'

'The first half of the Eumenides is equal to anything in poetry. The close is also very fine.'

'The Seven against Thebes is a noble poem; full of dramatic improprieties: but all on fire with the finest poetical spirit. *October* 25, 1835.—My birthday.

μὴ φῦναι τὸν ἅπαντα νικᾷ λόγον·
τὸ δ', ἐπεὶ φανῇ,
βῆναι κεῖθεν, ὅθενπερ ἥκει,
πολὺ δεύτερον, ὡς τάχιστα.'[1]

'The Agamemnon is indeed very fine. From the king's entrance into the house, to the appearance on the stage of Ægistheus, it is beyond all praise. I shall turn it over again next week.'

To the Prometheus are appended the words, 'One of the greatest of human compositions.'

'The Orestes is one of the very finest plays in the Greek language. Among those of Euripides, I should place it next to the Medea and the Bacchæ.[2] It has some very real faults; but it possesses that strong human interest which neither Æschylus nor Sophocles,—poets in many respects far superior to Euripides,—ever gave to their dramas. Orestes and Electra keep a very strong hold on our sympathy. The friendship of Pylades is more amiably represented here than anywhere else. Menelaus keeps the character which the Athenian dramatists have agreed to give him. The sick-chamber scene, and the scene after the trial, are two of the finest things in ancient poetry. When Milton designated Euripides "sad Electra's poet," he was thinking of the Orestes, I suppose; and not of the Electra. Schlegel says, (and he is perfectly right,) that the Electra is Euripides's worst play. It is quite detestable.'

'I can hardly account for the contempt which, at school

[1] 'The happiest destiny is never to have been born; and the next best, by far, is to return, as swiftly as may be, to the bourn whence we came.' The wound caused by his sister Margaret's death was then ten months old.

[2] Macaulay ranked the plays of Euripides thus: The Medea; the Bacchæ; the Orestes; the Iphigenia in Aulis; the Alcestis; the Phœnissæ; the Troades; the Hippolytus.

and college, I felt for Euripides. I own that I like him now better than Sophocles. The Alcestis has faults enough; but there are scenes in it of surpassing beauty and tenderness. The Choruses, too, are very fine. Fox thought it the best of Euripides's plays. I cannot like it so well as the Medea. The odious baseness of Admetus, in accepting the sacrifice of his wife, is a greater drawback than even the absurd machinery. Thomson avoided this very happily in his imitation, by making Eleanora suck the poison while Edward is sleeping.'

'The Bacchæ is a most glorious play. I doubt whether it be not superior to the Medea. It is often very obscure; and I am not sure that I fully understand its general scope. But, as a piece of language, it is hardly equalled in the world. And, whether it was intended to encourage or to discourage fanaticism, the picture of fanatical excitement which it exhibits has never been rivalled.'

APPENDIX III

(See vol. ii, page 44.)

Macaulay and the Book-stalls.

An account of Macaulay as a frequenter of book-stalls has been given by Mr. Salkeld, an enterprising Northumbrian who had migrated southwards, with whom the historian often did business.

'The first shop I opened in London,' (so the record runs,) 'was in the Featherstone Buildings, a little thoroughfare off Holborn. I was unpacking some cases of books one morning, and, because there was no other place available, I was unpacking them in the roadway. Up came a grave and pleasant gentleman, very well set up and neatly dressed, who stopped, and looked on, as if he were fully at home in that kind of neighbourhood, and also with the job I was engaged on. It was a long time afterwards that I heard he was Lord Macaulay; and the customer who told me became Lord Justice Fry. "May I look at these books?" the stranger asked. I said, "Certainly," and went and got a chair for him; but I was in so small a way then that I had to borrow it. He sat down and went through the lot, quickly but thoroughly, and made a big selection of historical tracts of the period just after the Civil War. He asked what he was to pay, and I said a shilling a piece. He seemed astonished, and I was prepared to hear him grumble, when he said, "I am very pleased to have come across them, and to find you are so reasonable in your terms." He came again and again, and each time took several pounds' worth away with him, carrying them himself, and never allowing me to make a parcel except so far as to string them up. He was always eager to learn when I had new consignments coming, and once when I told him I had bought a fresh lot of Civil War tracts and stuff relating to the time of William and Mary, he showed some mild impatience at learning it was too late to unpack them that day. He begged me to go through them soon, and I said I would sit up that night and sort them out by the morning. He asked me what time I opened shop, and I said eight o'clock. He was there on the step next morning to the minute, and commenced on his task, one pile after another. I soon found he had had no breakfast, but all I could persuade him to take was a cup of coffee. After a couple of hours' hard sorting, he chose two or three hundred pieces, and paid for them, and engaged for me to deliver them at the Albany that night. I took them myself, and I should say the year was 1855, or 1856. * * * I remember his repeating his pleasure, the last time I saw him, that I had dealt with him so fairly; which I thought very fair of him, considering how slow buyers are, as a rule, to see any side but their own.'

Macaulay was at some pains to inculcate upon me the duty of never beating a seller down below a fair price and never keeping a tradesman waiting for his money. I recollect his telling us how he had received his annual bill from a very well-known London shop, and had sent a cheque by return of post. Next morning the head of the firm brought the receipt himself, and burst out crying in Macaulay's room. Every morning, (the poor man said,) two people walked past his office window, one of whom owed him thirteen hundred, and the other fifteen hundred, pounds; and the last of the two was among the most distinguished and powerful statesmen in the country. Whether as a customer, an employer, or a tourist, Macaulay never underpaid a service rendered. Wherever he went, (to use his own words,) he loved 'to make his mother's son welcome.' His unfailing consideration for others made him liked by all, high and low, with whom he came into relation over the current affairs of life. An eminent practitioner told me that Macaulay on more than one occasion, when he was shown in by appointment for a medical consultation, said that he had noticed in the waiting-room a lady who appeared to be suffering, and that her case had better be taken first, since his own time was of no great value.

APPENDIX IV [1]

(See vol. ii, page 390.)

Macaulay and Miss Seward's Letters.

MACAULAY'S library contained many books, of no great intrinsic value in themselves, which are readable, from the first page to the last, for the sake of his manuscript notes, inscribed in immense profusion down their margins. He was contented, when the humour took him, to amuse his solitary hours with such productions as Percival Stockdale's memoirs, and the six volumes of Miss Anna Seward's Letters. His running commentary on those trivial and pretentious authors was as the breaking of a butterfly beneath the impact of a cheerful steam-hammer. 'Ingenious,' (so Miss Seward wrote to a correspondent,) 'is your parallel between the elder and the modern Erasmus.' 'The modern Erasmus,' said Macaulay, 'is Darwin. That nobody should have thought of making a parallel between him and the elder Erasmus is odd indeed. They had nothing but the name in common. One might as well make a parallel between Cæsar and Sir Cæsar Hawkins.' 'The chief amusement,' wrote Miss Seward, 'that the Inferno gives me is from the tracing the plagiarisms which have been made from it by more interesting and pleasing bards than Dante; since there is little for the heart, or even for the curiosity as to story, in this poem. Then the plan is most clumsily arranged:—Virgil, and the three talking quadrupeds, as guides! An odd association!' 'What can she mean?' said Macaulay. 'She must allude to the panther, the lion, and the she-wolf in the First Canto. But they are not guides; and they do not talk.'

The lady, who claimed rank as a Lyric poet, had published what she called a paraphrase of Horace's Odes without knowing a word of Horace's native language. Her version, which is inconceivably bad, was based upon an English translation by the Reverend Philip Francis; and from that time forward she always considered herself entitled to lay down the law on classical questions. 'Pleasant Mrs. Piozzi,' she said, 'is somewhat ignorant upon poetic subjects. She speaks of ode-writing as an inferior species of composition, which can place no man on a level with the epic, the dramatic, or the didactic bard. Now the rank of the lyric poet, as settled by the ancients, succeeds immediately to that of the epic. She ought to know that the Latins place their lyric Horace next to their epic Virgil, much more on account of his odes than of his satires.' 'What Latins?' asked Macaulay. 'There is not a word of the sort in any Latin writer.' Macaulay, who was a purist in spelling, took exception to Miss Seward calling a speech a 'Phillipic,' and seldom speaking of a pretty girl except as a 'Syren;' and he was always greatly puzzled by the references in her letters to her collection of 'centennial' sonnets. At length he caught her meaning. 'Now I understand. She calls her sonnets "centennial" because there were a hundred of them. Was ever such pedantry found in company with such ignorance?'

It was worse with French than with Greek and Latin; and worst of all with English. 'My conviction was perfect,' (Miss Seward wrote to a lady friend,) 'that you would all four be delightful acquisitions to each other. I might travel far ere I should find so interesting a *parté quarré*.' 'What language is that?' said Macaulay. He was soon to know. A year later Miss Seward received from her friend what she praises as a graceful and sparkling epistle. 'It speaks of a plan in agitation to visit me, accompanied by Helen Williams, the poetic; Albinia Mathias, the musical; and Miss Maylin, the beauteous.' 'So this,' exclaimed Macaulay, 'is the *parté quarré*. She did not know that a *partie carrée* means a party of two gentlemen and two ladies.' Macaulay was at some pains to correct Miss Seward's grammar. 'Come, my dear Lady, let you and I attend these gentlemen in the study!' That was Miss Seward's report of Doctor Johnson's words. 'Nay:' observed Macaulay; 'Johnson said *me*, I will be sworn.' Miss Seward characterised some sonnets, in the style of Petrarch, as 'Avignon little gems.' 'Little Avignon gems, if you please, Miss Seward!' is the comment in the margin. 'So the brilliant Sophia,' remarked the lady, 'has commenced Babylonian!' 'That is to say,' explained Macaulay, 'she has taken a house in town.' 'Taste,' said Miss Seward on one occasion, 'is extremely various. Where good sense, metaphoric consistency, or the rules of grammar are accused of having suffered violation, the cause may not be tried at her arbitrary tribunal.' 'A most striking instance,' wrote Macaulay, 'of metaphoric inconsistency. You may accuse a bad writer of violating good sense and grammar; but who can accuse good sense and grammar of having suffered violation?'

Macaulay was never implacable when a woman was concerned,—even a woman who could describe a country-house as an 'Edenic villa in a bloomy garden.' Miss Seward, after her father's death, gave a friend an account of his long illness. 'The pleasure he took in my attendance and caresses survived until within the last three months. His reply to my inquiries after his health was always "Pretty well, my darling;" and,—when I gave him his food and his wine,—"That's my darling!"—with a smile of comfort and delight inexpressibly dear to my heart. I often used to ask him if he loved me. His almost constant answer was, "Do I love my own eyes?"' 'Why, (asked Macaulay,) 'could she not always write thus?'

INDEX